Optimizing Building Performance,
Tenant Satisfaction,
and Financial Return

retrofitting
OFFICE BUILDINGS
to Be GREEN and Energy-Efficient

Urban Land Institute
1025 Thomas Jefferson Street, N.W.
Washington, D.C. 20007-5201

Tobias, Leanne, and George Vavaroutsos, et al. *Retrofitting Office Buildings to Be Green and Energy-
Efficient: Optimizing Building Performance, Tenant Satisfaction, and Financial Return*. Washington, D.C.:
Urban Land Institute, 2009.

ULI Catalog Number: R48
ISBN: 978-0-87420-133-8

10 9 8 7 6 5 4 3 2 1
Printed in the United States of America.

This book was made possible in part through the generous sponsorship of BASF.
    As The Chemical Company, BASF is a leader in the construction industry. With more than
600 products serving 75 construction product categories, BASF offers the broadest portfolio of
products used directly on construction sites, or integrated into other products, to improve the
performance of construction projects.
    Our offer extends throughout the building envelope from roof to foundation. In wall systems
and insulation. Sealants and adhesives. Concrete and asphalt. In bridges and pavement. In
windows and doors. HVAC and plumbing. Interior. Exterior. Cladding. Landscaping. Electronics.
Whether new construction, retrofit, or historical restoration, BASF chemistry makes a significant
contribution to improved performance.

ABOUT THE URBAN LAND INSTITUTE

The mission of the Urban Land Institute is to provide leadership in the responsible use of land and in creating and sustaining thriving communities worldwide. ULI is committed to

▸▸ **BRINGING TOGETHER** leaders from across the fields of real estate and land use policy to exchange best practices and serve community needs;

▸▸ **FOSTERING** collaboration within and beyond ULI's membership through mentoring, dialogue, and problem solving;

▸▸ **EXPLORING** issues of urbanization, conservation, regeneration, land use, capital formation, and sustainable development;

▸▸ **ADVANCING** land use policies and design practices that respect the uniqueness of both built and natural environments;

▸▸ **SHARING** knowledge through education, applied research, publishing, and electronic media; and

▸▸ **SUSTAINING** a diverse global network of local practice and advisory efforts that address current and future challenges.

Established in 1936, the Institute today has more than 32,000 members worldwide, representing the entire spectrum of the land use and development disciplines. ULI relies heavily on the experience of its members. It is through member involvement and information resources that ULI has been able to set standards of excellence in development practice. The Institute has long been recognized as one of the world's most respected and widely quoted sources of objective information on urban planning, growth, and development.

PROJECT STAFF

DEAN SCHWANKE
Senior Vice President, Publications

ANITA KRAMER
Senior Director,
Commercial Development

JAMES MULLIGAN
Managing Editor

LISE LINGO
Manuscript Editor
Publications Professionals LLC

BETSY VANBUSKIRK
Creative Director

CRAIG CHAPMAN
Director, Publishing Operations

JOHN HALL DESIGN GROUP
Book Design and Layout
www.johnhalldesign.com

Preface

This book was written with a simple intent: to offer a broad audience a clear and authoritative guide to the retrofitting of office buildings to be green and energy-efficient. To this end, office retrofits have been discussed from numerous perspectives, including architecture, engineering, interior design, feasibility and facilities planning, construction, finance, leasing, and operation. As well, this volume includes chapters on the policy implications of green and energy-efficient office retrofits, and their pivotal role in shaping international strategies on economic stimulus and climate change.

As a long-time commercial real estate investment manager, sustainable real estate adviser, and asset manager, I am keenly aware of the breadth and depth of experience needed to bring a green retrofit or renovation project to market. Thus, this book was written to be useful not only to the owners and developers of office space but also to diverse members of the commercial real estate community, including architects, engineers, contractors, interior designers, investment and finance professionals, attorneys, and those engaged in property operations, leasing, acquisitions, and sales. Equally important, this volume is intended as an accessible guide for policy makers and members of the public who want to know how an ordinary office building can be made energy-efficient and green. My co-authors and I will have fulfilled our hopes for the book if readers come away with a clear understanding of the features that can be incorporated into a green office building and how a successful energy-efficient retrofit can be accomplished.

This project drew on the talents of many accomplished professionals in the commercial real estate and energy efficiency sectors, who gave generously of their time and experience to develop material for this book. Readers will meet them in these pages. Equally important are the peer reviewers, who offered unstintingly of their insight and expertise to improve earlier versions of the manuscript and who are acknowledged on page viii. My profound thanks to all of these colleagues, without whom this book would not have been possible.

Others in the commercial real estate and energy efficiency sectors who made important contributions to the finished product are Jack Armstrong and Kent Stumpe of BASF; Christopher Arnaoutelis, Susan MacLaurin, Pascale Roy, and Ian Stewart of GWL Realty Advisors; Phil Bernstein of Autodesk; John Christmas of Hannon Armstrong; LaRee DeFreece of HOK; Benjamin J.M. Dutton of Faithful+Gould; Shannon Eckhart, Michael Deane, and Christopher McFadden of Turner Construction; Stacey Eddington of Transwestern; Patrice Frey of the National Trust for Historic Preservation; Sarah Friedman and Peter Miscovich of Jones Lang LaSalle; Frederick Fucci of Arnold & Porter; Steve Gossett, Jr., of Transcend Equity; Holger Hagge and Robert Schaeublin of Deutsche Bank; Meyer Harrell of Weber Thompson; Bill LaPatra of Mithun; Ron King of the National Insulation Association; Terry McCormick of EHDD Architects; Hal Myers and Sally Wilson of CB Richard Ellis; Judi Palmer of A&R Edelman; Dick Pearson of Pearson Engineering; Allan Ross of the Christman Companies; Andrea Simpson of Boston Properties; and Bob Spreat of Tremco Roofing.

This project originated at the Urban Land Institute and was brought to completion by its extraordinary staff. Rachelle Levitt conceived of, initiated, and championed the book, including its international dimensions. Dean Schwanke was an adept steward of the project. Uwe Brandes offered helpful perspectives on the case studies. The manuscript was shaped and edited under the expert guidance of Anita Kramer, who is always thoughtful, insightful, and judicious in her comments. Copyediting was performed by Lise Lingo of Publications Professionals LLC, under the direction of James Mulligan. The design and graphics, by John Hall of John Hall Design Group, took shape under the artful guidance of Betsy VanBuskirk. Karrie Underwood offered organizational support.

My gifted colleagues at Malachite LLC provided ongoing insights across the numerous dimensions of green and energy efficient real estate. Thanks to Martha Paschal for her important and timely observations on the real estate capital markets and related governmental programs and to Nick Katz for his expertise on emerging energy efficiency initiatives and their implications for real estate owners and developers. From inception to completion, Malachite's George Vavaroutsos has been a key partner and a valued contributing author on this project. George's acumen in the areas of green and energy-efficient design, engineering, and project management has been indispensable in researching and writing this book.

On a personal note, my mother, Janet Aronson, and my father-in-law, Leon Tobias, have been sources of unflagging interest and enthusiasm during the development and completion of this book, as has Goldie Wiesner. I would especially like to thank my husband, Jeff Tobias, for his steadfast encouragement and support.

LEANNE TOBIAS

Authors and Contributors

PRINCIPAL AUTHORS

LEANNE TOBIAS, a LEED accredited professional, is the founder and managing principal of Malachite LLC, a green real estate advisory firm that specializes in green building development, retrofit, investment, finance, and management for properties, portfolios, real estate funds, and policymakers. Tobias has over 20 years of experience in advising pension funds, developers, property owners, governments, and others on real estate investment and management. She serves on the U.S. Environmental Protection Agency's Environmental Finance Advisory Board and is a member of the advisory board of the Green Building Finance Consortium.

GEORGE VAVAROUTSOS, a LEED accredited professional, is a sustainable real estate consultant for Malachite LLC on a wide range of green building advisory matters. In his work for Malachite and others, Vavaroutsos has specialized in sustainable real estate, building energy efficiency, financial analysis, development management, and the preparation of market and feasibility studies for commercial and residential development, including senior living, retail, and mixed-use properties. He holds a professional development certificate from New York University in real estate finance and investment, has studied at the London School of Economics, and is an honors graduate of the University of Michigan with a concentration in economics.

CONTRIBUTING AUTHORS

MARK J. BENNETT is senior counsel and leads the climate change practice at Miller Canfield. He focuses his practice on carbon finance, renewable energy capital formation, and green building and sustainable development. With more than 20 years of experience in environmental due diligence, Bennett is widely recognized as an expert in incorporating sustainability risk and opportunity due diligence into real estate and commercial transactions.

ERIC A. GRASBERGER is an attorney in the Portland, Oregon, office of Stoel Rives LLP, where he is cochair of the Sustainable Real Estate Development Team and chair of the Construction and Design Section. His practice focuses on development and construction law, including green real estate matters.

TOM PALADINO is president of Paladino and Company, a leading green building consulting company. He was a contributor to development of the LEED rating system and has consulted on more than 250 green and LEED building projects.

ROD WILLE, a LEED accredited professional, is a senior consultant to Turner Construction Company, a professional engineer, and an expert on sustainable construction.

MICHAEL ZIMMER is of counsel with Thompson Hine LLP and focuses his legal practice on energy regulation, climate change, and energy finance transactions. He has been involved in construction and project financing assignments in the nonutility generation, renewables, gas and electric, emissions credits, green buildings, energy and emissions trading, and manufacturing industries. Zimmer is national cochair of the American Bar Association (ABA) Renewable Energy Resources Committee for 2008–2009, and vice chair of the ABA Committee on Energy and Environmental Finance. He has been a member of the U.S. Green Building Council's Energy and Atmosphere Technical Advisory Group since 2005 and was a member of the American Council on Renewable Energy Strategy Committee.

CASE STUDY AUTHORS

RICHARD A. BARTHOLOMEW
Principal
Wallace Roberts & Todd LLC (WRT)
Philadelphia, Pennsylvania

PHILIP BOCCALATTE
General Manager
CB Richard Ellis
Boston, Massachusetts

JAMES M. CASH
President and Chief Operating Officer
Christman Capital Development Company
Lansing, Michigan

VINCENT CHENG
Associate Director
Ove Arup & Partners HK Ltd. (Arup)
Hong Kong, China

LARA CONAWAY
Sustainability Manager
Morgan Lovell
London, U.K.

GEORGE DENISE
General Manager of Facilities for Adobe Systems
Cushman & Wakefield
San Jose, California

GAVIN L. GARDI
Sustainable Programs Manager
The Christman Company
Lansing, Michigan

HELEE HILLMAN
Project Manager, Project Development
    Services Division
Jones Lang LaSalle
Chicago, Illinois

SUSAN LOGAN
Founder
Ecoteric Ltd.
West Sussex, U.K.

BONNEY MAYERS
Writer
Haslett, Michigan

KEVIN MILLER
Director
Collard Clarke Jackson Canberra Pty Ltd.
Canberra, Australia

DONNA PARA
Senior Director, McDonald's Workplace
    Solutions Team
McDonald's Corporation
Oak Brook, Illinois

HOWARD PENDER
Director
Australian Ethical Investment Ltd. and Australian
    Ethical Super
Canberra, Australia.

DAVE PETERSEN
Vice President
Jones Lang LaSalle
Oak Brook, Illinois

DAVID A. SIGMAN
Senior Vice President
LCOR
New York, New York

RONALD D. STALEY
Senior Vice President and Director, National
    Preservation
The Christman Company
Lansing, Michigan

NATHAN TAFT
Director of Acquisitions
Rose Smart Investment Growth Investment
    Fund I, L.P
Jonathan Rose Companies
New York, New York

STEVE VITOFF
Senior Vice President
Marino Organization
New York, New York

SIDEBAR AUTHORS

PIOTR BEREBECKI
Sustainability and Energy Consultant
Faithful+Gould
London, U.K.

NEIL CHAMBERS
Architect
New York, New York

CHRIS FLINT CHATTO
Sustainability Specialist
Zimmer Gunsul Frasca Architects LLP
Portland, Oregon

ANDREW I. DAVIS
Partner
Stoel Rives LLP
Portland, Oregon

RALPH DINOLA
Principal
Green Building Services
Portland, Oregon

AMY FABRY
Senior Interior Designer
HOK
Washington, D.C.

JAMES F. FINLAY
Vice President/Commercial Appraisal Manager
Wells Fargo Bank
Los Angeles, California

MARGARITA FOSTER
Vice President, Office Markets
Fulton Research and Consulting
Fairfax, Virginia

PHILIP K. GLICK
Senior Vice President
ECBM Insurance
West Conshohocken, Pennsylvania

GABE HANSON
Weber Thompson
Seattle, Washington

ADAM HINGE
Managing Director
Sustainable Energy Partnerships
Tarrytown, New York

ERIN RAE HOFFER
Industry Manager
Autodesk
Waltham, Massachusetts

RYAN R. HOGER
Product Manager, Commercial Systems
HVAC Solutions
Chicago, Illinois

CAPPY KIDD
Director of Energy Services
AKT Peerless Environmental and Energy Services
Chicago, Illinois

ANICA LANDRENEAU
Sustainable Design Practice Leader
HOK
Washington, D.C.

SEAN LOCKIE
Director of Sustainability
Faithful+Gould
London, U.K.

BRIAN J. MCCARTER
CEO
Sustainable Real Estate Solutions
Monroe, Connecticut

ROBERT E. MIDDLEBROOKS
Industry Manager
Autodesk
Chesapeake, Virginia

SCOTT MULDAVIN
President, The Muldavin Company, Inc.
Founder and Executive Director, Green Building
    Finance Consortium
San Rafael, California

TOM NELSON
Principal
Mithun
Seattle, Washington

MICHAEL B. SCHNEIDER
Vice President and Regional Manager
Northwest Division of Marx|Okubo Associates Inc.
Seattle, Washington

ELLEN SINREICH
President
Green Edge LLC
New York, New York

EVA STERNER
Managing Director
Watts International
Stockholm, Sweden

LEIGH STRINGER
Vice President, Senior Workplace Specialist
HOK
Washington, D.C.

COLBY SWANSON
Manager, Green Strategy Development
The BASF Group
Florham, New Jersey

NITA TUVESSON
Interiors Specialist
HOK
Washington, D.C.

RALPH VELASQUEZ
Director of the Sustainable Technology Group
Tremco Roofing and Building Maintenance
Beachwood, Ohio

MARY VOGEL
Principal
PlanGreen
Portland, Oregon

JODI WILLIAMS
Workplace Specialist
HOK
Washington, D.C.

MARC WINTERS
Senior Partner
McNaul Ebel Nawrot & Helgren PLLC
Seattle, Washington

PEER REVIEWERS

Chapter 1

PAUL R. EPSTEIN
Associate Director
Center for Health and the Global Environment
Harvard Medical School
Boston, Massachusetts

Chapter 2

KENNETH A. HAWKINS, JR.
Principal
Realty Service Advisors, LLC
Fairfax, Virginia

MICHAEL B. SCHNEIDER
Vice President
Marx|Okubo Associates, Inc.
Seattle, Washington

Chapter 3

PEGGY CHU
Associate
HOK
Hong Kong, China

BARRY GILES
CEO
BuildingWise LLC
Watsonville, California

SANDY MENDLER
Principal
Mithun
San Francisco, California

JOSEPH A. ORLANDO
Director, Mid-Atlantic CHP Application Center
University of Maryland
College Park, Maryland

Principal, Platinum Energy
Annandale, Virginia

MICHAEL J. ZIMMER
Attorney
Thompson Hine LLP
Washington, D.C.

Chapter 4

ANJA S. CALDWELL
Principal
ecoipso, LLC
Bethesda, Maryland

SERENA SAYANI
Attorney
McNaul Ebel Nawrot & Helgren PLLC
Seattle, Washington

DIANE M. STEELE
Project Engineer
The Pike Company
Rochester, New York

DOUGLAS L. WHITE
Attorney
Greenberg Traurig
Los Angeles, California

Chapter 5

DEBRA A. ITALIANO
Managing Principal
Merintra Co., LLC
Jersey City, New Jersey

Chapter 6

KENNETH A. HAWKINS, JR.
Principal
Realty Service Advisors, LLC
Fairfax, Virginia

Chapter 7

KATE Q. KNIGHT
AIG Global Real Estate Investment Corp.
New York, New York

DAVID WOOD
Director, Institute for Responsible Investment
Boston College Center for Corporate Citizenship
Carroll School of Management
Boston College
Chestnut Hill, Massachusetts

Chapter 8

CHRIS FLINT CHATTO
Associate
Zimmer Gunsul Frasca Architects LLP
Portland, Oregon

AMANDA KEATING
Associate
Weber Thompson
Seattle, Washington

JANIKA MCFEELY
EHDD Architecture
San Francisco, California

Contents

retrofitting

OFFICE BUILDINGS
to Be GREEN and Energy-Efficient

The Importance of Green Building and Green Office Retrofits

GEORGE VAVAROUTSOS AND LEANNE TOBIAS

Why does sustainability matter? What is the connection among building energy usage, the introduction of sustainable technologies into the built environment, and climate change concerns? What do office building owners and tenants gain by incorporating energy efficiency and sustainable building practices into their operations? This chapter addresses these overarching issues and provides the practical rationale for pursuing the retrofitting of office space to be green.

THE GLOBAL GROWTH OF GREEN BUILDING

In the past decade, green building has gained significant global momentum. Although Germany has enforced aspects of sustainable and energy-efficient practices as part of its building codes for more than 30 years and Thailand began to take similar steps in the early 1990s, the broader push for sustainable building is a more recent phenomenon.

Current global awareness of green building among real estate, design, and construction industry professionals is high. A 2007 survey by the World Business Council for Sustainable Development (WBCSD) reports that more than 80 percent of building professionals in France, Germany, Spain, and the United States are aware of green building. The survey also indicates that in Brazil, China, and India—three fast-growing countries that account for 40 percent of global population—more than 60 percent of building professionals are aware of green building.[1]

This growing level of familiarity has been encouraged by the establishment of widely recognized voluntary rating systems, such as the Building Research Establishment's (BRE's) Environmental Assessment Method (BREEAM) in the United Kingdom, Green Star in Australia and New Zealand, the Comprehensive Assessment System for Building Environmental Efficiency (CASBEE) in Japan, Haute Qualité Environnementale (HQE) in France, Green Mark in Singapore,

Green Globe in Canada, and Leadership in Energy and Environmental Design (LEED) in the United States. Most developed countries have their own rating systems or have adopted versions of systems made popular in other countries (examples include LEED Brazil, LEED India, and BREEAM Netherlands). The rapid growth in certifications through these rating systems, especially through LEED and BREEAM, is testimony to growing public awareness of green buildings and their positive attributes. The widespread adoption of these systems is important because it creates an opportunity to benchmark sustainability and introduce transparency in the marketplace for green buildings.

THE IMPORTANCE OF GREEN BUILDING RETROFITS

Although progress toward the adoption of sustainable building practices across the globe is encouraging, the green movement initially focused on transforming building practices for new construction. This is especially meaningful for large, emerging economies such as China and India, which together are building and expanding cities to accommodate a rural-to-urban migration of more than 30 million people per year. To date, however, green building practices have underemphasized the importance of sustainable retrofits of existing building stock across the globe.[2]

In most developed countries, more than 98 percent of the building stock consists of existing buildings, and new construction accounts for 1 to 1.5 percent of total building stock at any time.[3] For dense urban areas, the percentage of buildings represented by new construction may be less. New York City's Office of Sustainability estimates that of the 950,000 buildings in the city today, 85 percent will still be standing in 2030.[4] Sustainable new construction, no matter how environmentally sensitive and energy-efficient, cannot by itself significantly change the environmental impact of the built environment.

In addition, many existing structures were built before the establishment of energy efficiency codes. In the United Kingdom, more than 77 percent of the commercial building stock was constructed before the establishment of building regulations that enforced energy conservation.[5] The buildings that we currently occupy, and their respective energy and water use profiles, will be with us for the long term. Thus, green property retrofits are critical to global energy conservation, and green design and construction technologies will fully realize their promise only when applied to the existing building stock.

THE BUILT ENVIRONMENT AND ENERGY USE

In most developed countries, buildings are one of the largest users of energy, accounting for roughly 40 percent of primary energy consumption. The International Energy Agency estimates that by 2030, building energy demand will account for about half of the total investment in energy supply.[6]

Given the significance of the property sector in determining worldwide energy demand, improvements in the energy efficiency of both new and existing buildings are likely to have a major effect on global energy usage. Recent U.S. data, for example, indicate that newly constructed LEED commercial buildings use approximately 28 percent less energy, on average, than conventional structures. Energy savings rise to 33 percent for newly constructed, green-certified office buildings and close to 50 percent for newly built LEED Gold and Platinum office buildings.[7] U.S. data on properties that have earned the Energy Star certification suggest that significant improvements in energy efficiency can be made for both renovated buildings and new construction.[8] Buildings that have achieved Energy Star certification use an average of 40 percent less energy than conventional buildings and emit 35 percent less carbon.[9]

The Built Environment and Greenhouse Gas Emissions

The energy efficiency of the existing building stock is critically important because conditioning and powering buildings is one of the biggest contributors to global emissions of greenhouse gases (GHGs). The GHG effect stems from the combustion of high-carbon fossil fuels for heating, cooling, and generating the electricity used in the operation of buildings.

Buildings are second only to the manufacturing and production sector in annual carbon dioxide (CO_2) output, exceeding emissions from both agriculture and transport combined. In 2004 direct emissions from buildings totaled about 3 gigatons of CO_2—and 8.6 gigatons when upstream emissions from electrical generation were included. That 8.6 gigatons of CO_2 per year represents roughly a third of the total global output.[10]

CO_2 emissions from commercial buildings, including office properties, are exerting a growing influence on GHG production. The ratio of emissions from residential and commercial structures is changing. From 1970 to 2004, overall CO_2 emissions from buildings increased roughly 2 percent per year,

THE IPCC AND THE BUILT ENVIRONMENT

Overview

Established in 1988 by the World Meteorological Organization and the United Nations Environment Programme (UNEP), the Intergovernmental Panel on Climate Change (IPCC) was established to provide an objective source of information on climate change.

The IPCC does not conduct research. Instead, the panel analyzes the latest scientific and economic research on climate change, determines the validity of the data, and then provides an objective evaluation of the risk and potential impact of anthropogenic (manmade) climate change.

Report Structure

Since 1990, the IPCC has released four assessment reports that have analyzed the newest publications and drawn conclusions from the data, advancing our knowledge of the human role in global warming.

Each report features the assessments of three working groups, each of which covers specific topics related to climate change:

▸▸ **Working Group I:** Assesses scientific aspects of the climate system and climate change.

▸▸ **Working Group II:** Assesses the vulnerability of socioeconomic and natural systems to climate change, its consequences, and adaptation options.

▸▸ **Working Group III:** Assesses options for limiting GHG emissions and otherwise mitigating climate change

Assessment Report 4

Assessment Report 4 (AR4) was released in 2007; in producing it, more than 2,500 experts reviewed the available research. AR4 represented a major step forward from Assessment Report 3, which had been published in 2001, before the publication of some significant studies regarding climate change.

Although previous reports from the IPCC indicated that anthropogenic emissions of GHGs could be responsible for global warming, AR4 was more forceful in its assertion that such emissions are responsible for global warming. Key findings of AR4 include the following:

▸▸ There is unquestionable evidence (99 percent certainty) of global warming, as indicated by higher global average temperatures. It is also very likely (90 percent certainty) that global warming has contributed to rising sea levels.

▸▸ Most of the observed increase in global average temperatures since 1950 is very likely due to the observed increase in concentrations of anthropogenic GHG emissions.

▸▸ There is "high agreement" and "much evidence" that such emissions of GHGs will continue to grow over the next few decades.

▸▸ Continued anthropogenic emissions of GHGs at or above the current rate will cause further warming and exacerbate changes in the global climate system.

▸▸ Many of the global climate effects can be reduced, delayed, or avoided through mitigation efforts.

mirroring the overall growth rate in total emissions. Although the overall growth rate has stayed the same, the growth rate in emissions from residential buildings has decreased while the growth rate in emissions from commercial buildings has accelerated to 2.5 percent per year. During this period, emissions associated with commercial buildings in both North America and developing Asia (defined as the 44 developing member countries of the Asian Development Bank) grew by 30 percent.[11]

The global growth rate for CO_2 emissions from commercial buildings has continued to accelerate. Since 2001, CO_2 emissions associated with commercial buildings have grown at an average annual rate of 3 percent, 0.8 percent faster than the 30-year long-term average for CO_2 emissions growth.[12] Global demand for commercial buildings and the GHG emissions associated with the construction and operation of these structures should be a key consideration in any strategies to reduce the risk of adverse environmental impact from climate change.

Buildings and Global Warming Mitigation

Working Group III evaluated cost-effective methods for reducing GHG emissions and mitigating their potential effects on climate systems. In AR4, Working Group III concluded that existing buildings represent a significant opportunity for reducing anthropogenic emissions of GHGs, potentially reducing building emissions by 30 percent and total emissions by 10 percent of estimated 2020 emission levels. The majority of these reductions would be cost-negative, meaning that they would be both environmentally and economically beneficial.

The working group assessed building system and policy-based methods for reducing GHG emissions from buildings and found that the potential reductions could be significant and readily achieved with the following:

BUILDING SYSTEM METHODS:

▸▸ Use of solar shading and advanced daylighting
▸▸ Renewable energy systems
▸▸ Improved thermal envelope (improved insulation and windows)
▸▸ Natural ventilation systems (as opposed to forced-air heating and cooling)
▸▸ Reflective exterior surfaces
▸▸ Advanced heating and cooling technologies
▸▸ Building energy management systems
▸▸ Efficient lighting systems
▸▸ Integrated design process

POLICY-BASED METHODS:

▸▸ Improved appliance standards
▸▸ Demand-side management programs
▸▸ Energy-efficient building codes (performance-based versus prescriptive)
▸▸ Mandatory building certification or energy performance labeling systems
▸▸ Tax deductions and investment subsidies
▸▸ Promotion of energy service companies
▸▸ Increased government research and development (R&D) budgets for improved technologies

According to the IPCC, emission reductions from existing buildings represent the low-hanging fruit in the effort to reduce GHG emissions and mitigate climate change. Property owners will encounter these building systems and policies as they undertake the retrofit of existing buildings. These measures not only reduce carbon emissions but also can improve net cash flow and long-term asset value.

SOURCES

Intergovernmental Panel on Climate Change (IPCC). "About IPCC." June 11, 2008. www.ipcc.ch/about/index.htm.

Bernstein, L., et al. *Climate Change 2007: Synthesis Report. An Assessment of the Intergovernmental Panel on Climate Change*. Cambridge, U.K.: Cambridge University Press, 2007.

Levine, M., et al. "2007: Residential and Commercial Buildings." In *Climate Change 2007: Mitigation. Contribution of Working Group III to the Fourth Assessment Report of the Intergovernmental Panel on Climate Change*. Cambridge, U.K.: Cambridge University Press, 2007.

Levermore, G.J. "A Review of the IPCC Assessment Report Four, Part 1: The IPCC Process and Greenhouse Gas Emission Trends from Buildings Worldwide." *Building Services Engineering Research and Technology*, vol. 29, no. 4, pp. 349–361.

Greenhouse Gases and Climate Change

Climate change and anthropogenic (man-made) global warming have frequently been deemed controversial topics. The most complete and objective review of the scientific evidence on the subject is the Fourth Assessment Report from the Intergovernmental Panel on Climate Change (IPCC). Released in 2007, this report provides a comprehensive overview of evidence for climate change and the role of anthropogenic GHG emissions in global warming. The report offers predictive models for future changes in GHG emissions, global temperature change, and the resulting environmental impacts. (See the sidebar on the previous page for more information about the findings and implications of the IPCC process.)

There is consensus in the scientific community that global warming is observable. From 1906 to 2005, global average temperature increased by 1.2°F (0.74°C). Scientists predict that temperatures will increase by 0.4°F (0.2°C) over each of the next two decades.[13] While an increase of 2.0°F (1.14°C) in average global temperature over the course of 120 years does not seem dramatic, continued growth in average global temperature may lead to catastrophic results. According to the IPCC, an increase of 1.8 to 5.4°F (1 to 3°C) over 1990 temperature levels would significantly harm low-latitude and polar regions. With an increase in net temperature greater than 3.6 to 5.4°F (2 to 3°C), the IPCC predicts that all regions would be adversely affected and face net costs from climate change.[14]

The economic consequences of unchecked global warming are likely to be devastating. A Tufts University report estimates that a 7°F (4°C) net increase in temperature could reduce annual global gross domestic product (GDP) by 6 to 8 percent, conservatively.[15] Economic models developed for the *Stern Review on the Economics of Climate Change*, issued by the U.K. Treasury in 2006, project that the immediate costs and risks of climate change caused by a 9 to 11°F (5 to 6°C) net increase in temperature will be equivalent to "an average reduction in global per capita consumption of at least 5 percent, now and forever" and if "a wider range of risks and impacts is taken into account, the estimates of damage could rise to a 20 percent reduction in per capita consumption or more."[16]

To better understand the specific risks of unchecked global warming, following are some of the potential human health and environmental effects:[17]

▸▸ **AGRICULTURE AND FOOD SUPPLY**. Yields of cereal grains, which are staple crops, will be reduced—as will livestock counts. Prolonged heat exposure, drought, and flooding may exert a significant, adverse effect on subsistence farming near the equator.

▸▸ **ECOSYSTEMS AND BIODIVERSITY**. Certain species of plants and animals will face extinction. Regional climate effects may alter natural growing environments, shifting animal and plant habitats into previously colder climates or higher elevations. The changes can bring earlier spring events, extend the growing season for vegetation, lead to longer life spans for mosquitoes and other insects, and alter long-established migration patterns for animals.

▸▸ **FRESHWATER RESOURCES**. Hundreds of millions of people could be exposed to reduced availability of water and deterioration in water quality. Current high-precipitation regions may face greater precipitation variability, leading to prolonged flooding and water quality issues.

▸▸ **COASTAL ZONES AND SEA LEVEL RISE**. Coastal regions face the potential loss of land and greater risk of storm flooding. Changes in water composition and ocean circulation may lead to massive climate alterations, potential extinction of regional coral reefs, and risks to fish and marine mammal populations.

All these environmental changes would have direct and far-reaching consequences for humans and their habitat.

POTENTIAL REDUCTIONS IN GHG EMISSIONS FROM RETROFITTING BUILDINGS

In its 2007 report, the IPCC concluded that an anthropogenic role in climate change was "likely," meaning that scientists and researchers were more than 90 percent certain that anthropogenic GHG emissions were contributing to global warming.[18] The panel also determined which sectors held the most promise for achieving large-scale and cost-effective reductions in those emissions.

After reviewing more than 80 studies on buildings and energy use, the panel determined that cost-effective energy efficiency measures in buildings could reduce emissions by 30 percent from the estimated 2020 baseline. Thus, building energy efficiency measures have the potential to eliminate roughly 3.2 gigatons of CO_2, which represents a 7 to 10 percent reduction in estimated total annual GHG emissions in 2020.[19]

These reductions would come from reduced demand for electricity in buildings and from reduced fuel use. Fundamental improvements would derive from the use of

- ▸▸ **IMPROVED BUILDING INSULATION**,
- ▸▸ **HIGHER HEATING AND COOLING** efficiencies,
- ▸▸ **ENERGY-EFFICIENT LIGHTING**, and
- ▸▸ **REDUCED PLUG LOADS** from energy-efficient appliances and business machines.

The panel determined that the potential reduction in GHG emissions from improvements in the energy efficiency of buildings relied on existing, proven technologies and would not require the use of experimental technologies or strategies not commonly applied to existing structures.

Utilizing discount rates between 3 and 10 percent, the panel also determined that these GHG emission reductions could be cost-negative, meaning that the cost of implementation would be less than the value of the energy saved.[20] For commercial building owners, "cost negative" would represent measures that have a positive return on investment (ROI) by reducing operating costs.

545 Madison Avenue in New York City, built in 1955, underwent a gut rehabilitation in 2007–2008 that incorporated energy efficiency and indoor environmental quality features into its design and subsequent operations.

KEVIN CHU/KCJP

One Beacon Street (tallest building pictured), a multitenant office building in Boston, was built in the 1970s and retrofitted as a green building in 2006–2008.

These results were also predicted by McKinsey & Company, which analyzed the potential size and cost of GHG emission abatement measures across all economic sectors, including power generation, manufacturing, transportation, residential and commercial buildings, forestry, agriculture, and waste disposal. Improvements in energy efficiency for both new construction and existing residential and commercial buildings were the lowest-cost source of GHG emission reductions, producing net savings (expressed by McKinsey as negative costs) by reducing energy costs. Improving building insulation for new construction produced net energy savings of $225 (€160) per ton of CO_2 equivalent, while improving insulation in existing structures produced energy savings of $175 (€125) per ton of CO_2 equivalent. Reductions in GHG emissions through investments in efficient lighting, air-conditioning, and water heating systems also had net benefits as a consequence of reductions in energy costs.[21]

BARRIERS TO RETROFITTING EXISTING BUILDINGS

If the reduction in GHG emissions through measures that increase building energy efficiency is both financially and environmentally beneficial, why has there not been more activity in the building sector to renovate property so as to reduce GHG emissions? At the aggregate level, the potential for reductions in emissions and energy costs is compelling, but action at the property level has been impeded by a number of barriers, including the following:

▸▸ **FINANCIAL CONSIDERATIONS**. Building owners tend to focus on initial capital costs, without appropriately considering medium- and long-term costs and benefits. If owners utilize a very short investment time frame or do not accurately determine the overall rate of return on GHG emission abatement measures, the higher upfront costs of more energy-efficient equipment discourages their purchase and use.

▸▸ **DISCONNECT BETWEEN COSTS AND BEN-EFITS**. If building owners bear the costs of GHG-reducing measures and the benefits, expressed as lower energy costs, accrue only to building tenants, there may be a disincentive to investment. If the benefit cannot be recouped by the cost-bearer, the investment will not occur.

▸▸ **LACK OF KNOWLEDGE AND EXPERIENCED WORKFORCE**. A lack of practical understanding among building owners about energy efficiency and green building, including overestimates of the green first-cost premium, hinders reductions in GHG emissions. While the WBCSD study indicated a high awareness of green building among real estate professionals and building owners, it also indicated that less than 13 percent of those surveyed had been involved with green building.[22] The lack of experienced service providers ultimately raises the cost of GHG emission reductions.

▸▸ **INCREASE IN RISK AND UNCERTAINTY**. The lack of practical green knowledge among real estate professionals compounds the problem of assessing green building and energy-efficient practices. Because some GHG emission reductions rely on building practices that are perceived as new to a marketplace that is traditionally slow to adapt, there is uncertainty about both physical and financial performance. In addition, green or energy-efficient building practices may require the use of new suppliers and contractors, which could increase the risk profile for the application and lower the risk-adjusted financial returns from the retrofit.

▸▸ **IGNORING SMALL OPPORTUNITIES FOR ENERGY CONSERVATION**. Many small energy-saving measures are overlooked by building owners, especially in residential structures. At the aggregate level, the reductions in GHG emissions from such measures are substantial, but if the ROI for these measures does not satisfy owners' minimum return thresholds, the reductions will not be undertaken.

Although some of these impediments have limited the large-scale application of green retrofits in the past, there is growing consensus that many of these barriers are diminishing. As property owners, tenants, contractors, and bankers begin to appreciate the value proposition of a green strategy, there is lessened resistance and greater comfort with the green retrofit process. Heightened understanding of the business case for green commercial property retrofits, in general, and green office retrofits, in particular, may be expected to motivate property developers, owners, and investors to direct capital into green and energy-efficient renovations.

THE BUSINESS CASE FOR GREEN RETROFITS OF OFFICE BUILDINGS

The business case for the greening of existing commercial buildings, and in particular office buildings, is strong: greening existing office buildings is about preserving asset value and competitiveness, and there is significant value risk in inaction. The business case for green retrofits has three significant components: the risk of environmental regulation, mitigating energy and water price risk, and growing tenant demand for green office space.

The Risk of Environmental Regulation

The serious risks from climate change and the role of anthropogenic GHG emissions in global warming are not being ignored by governments at the national, state or territory, or local level. Since 2005, more than 900 mayors of U.S. cities and towns have signed the U.S. Conference of Mayors Climate Protection Agreement, committing to do their part to reduce GHG emissions from their community to 7 percent below 1990 levels by 2012. These mayors have agreed to the loose framework of the Kyoto Protocol, including the potential use of market-based tradable allowances and green tags. More than 1,000 cities, towns, and counties in more than 30 countries are members of the International Council for Local Environmental Initiatives' (ICLEI) Cities for Climate Protection campaign. The campaign assists local governments in integrating climate change mitigation into their decision-making processes, adopting policies and implementing quantifiable measures to reduce local GHG emissions, improve air quality, and enhance local urban livability and sustainability. Jurisdictions that participate in the ICLEI campaign are also beginning to adopt green building and energy efficiency requirements.

National governments and multinational entities are also focusing on green building practices as a significant component of energy policy and, with growing frequency, economic stimulus programs:

▶▶ **IN CHINA**, the creation of energy-efficient buildings has been targeted as one of the ten key energy efficiency initiatives in the 11th Five-Year Plan, which lasts through 2010. Under the plan, 40 percent of China's energy savings are expected to come from the built environment, and the plan envisions an ambitious program of energy-efficient new construction and retrofits.[23]

▶▶ **IN THE EUROPEAN UNION**, energy-efficient buildings, lighting, and heating and cooling systems are key components of an economic stimulus effort that was announced in November 2008.[24]

▶▶ **IN THE UNITED STATES**, climate change legislation—including mechanisms that regulate emissions of GHGs, such as cap and trade—is part of President Barack Obama's legislative agenda. As of mid-2009, the U.S. Congress was considering targets for building energy efficiency as part of climate change legislation. The Obama administration has also made the creation of green jobs, the energy-efficient retrofitting of federal office buildings, and home weatherization key planks of its economic stimulus program.

▶▶ **IN JAPAN**, ten cities require CASBEE registration for all new construction projects. By making registration mandatory, local governments will encourage the development and retrofitting of more green buildings.[25]

▶▶ **IN CANADA**, the province of British Columbia has adopted stringent green building codes for smaller new structures and is requiring larger buildings to conform to the American Society of Heating, Refrigerating, and Air-Conditioning Engineers (ASHRAE) 90.1-2004 standard.[26]

▶▶ **IN THE UNITED KINGDOM**, climate change legislation affecting commercial buildings is in effect. As of October 1, 2008, all commercial buildings for sale or lease are required to have energy performance certificates (EPCs). The EPC is a graded measurement of building energy efficiency and carbon emissions, conducted by an approved assessor, that allows potential buyers and tenants to compare and contrast the energy performance of buildings that they are considering purchasing or renting.

Although the U.K. legislation is new and issues with the certification process still need to be smoothed out, initial results indicate that EPCs are having the desired outcome. A recent survey of members in the British Council for Offices, which has over 1,500 members, indicates that more than 55 percent of those surveyed believe that buildings that score poorly will face a decrease in value. Additionally, more than 68 percent indicate that they will improve the energy performance of their existing and planned retrofits in order to improve the EPC score of their assets, so as to maintain value and remain competitive in the marketplace.[27]

Environmental regulations affecting the property sector are still in their infancy, but their potential effect on the value of existing buildings is expected to grow. Taking steps now to "green" existing office buildings, improving energy efficiency and lowering associated GHG emissions, can mitigate risk from emerging regulatory regimes. As well, property owners may find that it is more cost-effective to undertake energy efficiency retrofits preemptively: after regulations are passed, the costs of compliance will increase as building owners rush to meet the requirements of new regulations.

Mitigating Energy and Water Price Risk

The second component in the business case for retrofitting existing office buildings to be green is the reduction in exposure to energy and water price risk that results from such retrofitting. Focusing on energy efficiency and water conservation strategies, green building retrofits reduce the amount of energy and water necessary for normal operations of the structure. Most of these conservation measures in office buildings have a positive ROI, meaning that the discounted benefit in energy and water savings is greater than the cost of implementing these measures.

In green office buildings with gross leases, the owner has less exposure to the effects of changes in pricing for electricity, gas, or water, preserving the net cash flow. For office buildings with net leases, the reduction in energy and water use will lower the total costs of occupancy for tenants of the structure, leading to improved tenant retention, shorter lease-up periods, and higher occupancy and asset value for the owner.

Growing Tenant Demand for Green Office Space

The third component in the business case for retrofitting is growing tenant demand for green office space. Tenants see value in occupying green office space: It is a selling point for their employees and a tangible indicator of company concern for the environment. Green offices are recognized for being occupant friendly, featuring abundant daylight, superior indoor air quality, and more comfortable interior temperatures. These indoor environmental amenities are coveted by employees, and employers have taken notice.

Several studies link green office space with heightened occupant comfort, lowered absenteeism, and enhanced productivity. These gains can have a positive effect on an organization's financial performance and help to enhance the attractiveness of green space.[28] As detailed in numerous case studies in this volume, companies across the globe view green premises as marketing, recruitment, and employee retention tools, citing positive reactions to green space from both customers and workers.

Additionally, leasing green space fits the environmental sustainability objectives that many firms have adopted pursuant to their corporate social responsibility initiatives. Leading global companies, including Cisco, IBM, and Citigroup, have begun to implement green leasing strategies, when appropriate space is available in a given market.

In the United States, strong tenant demand for green space means that new Class A office space is increasingly being developed as certified green space. In order to stay competitive in a marketplace with new demands, owners of existing buildings will need to consider green retrofits as part of their strategy to maintain asset value. In the "war for tenants," buildings that are not retrofitted to accommodate the changes in tenant demand are likely to lose their competitive position and be discounted in the marketplace.

Investors, particularly the institutional investors who dominate the Class A property market, have begun to take note of these trends. A 2007 report prepared by RREEF, the real estate asset management arm of Deutsche Bank, concludes that institutional-grade real estate is being increasingly defined as green:

> Green building is fundamentally altering real estate market dynamics—the nature of product demanded by tenants, constructed by developers, required by governments, and favored by capital providers. The upshot will be a redefinition of what constitutes Class A properties and even institutional-quality real estate. Unlike other recent technological innovations in building materials and systems, the greater tangibility of today's sustainable design features are driving tenant expectations for greener buildings.[29]

RETROFITTING AN ICON: THE EMPIRE STATE BUILDING GOES GREEN

New York City's 102-story Empire State Building, completed in 1931, is one of the world's most renowned skyscrapers. In April 2009, the building's management announced a four-year green retrofit, illustrating the growing importance of sustainable features in office building renovation, as well as many of the themes discussed throughout this volume.

The $20 million green retrofit initiative is intended to reduce energy consumption by 38 percent, save an estimated $4.4 million in energy costs annually, and reduce GHG emissions by some 105,000 metric tons over 15 years. Upgrades to base building systems are expected to be completed by the close of 2010, and the retrofit of tenant spaces concluded by the end of 2013.

The retrofit, which will seek Energy Star status from the U.S. Environmental Protection Agency (EPA) and certification at the Gold Level under LEED, will incorporate eight initiatives:

▸▸ **WINDOW RETROFIT PROGRAM**. The retrofit will refurbish 6,514 windows with suspended coated films (efficient films inserted within the glass panes) and insulating gas fills to minimize heat loss and gain, thereby reducing interior energy use.

▸▸ **RADIATOR INSULATION RETROFIT**. The renovation will install insulation behind the building's radiators to reduce heat loss and more efficiently heat the building perimeter.

▸▸ **LIGHTING AND PLUG LOAD IMPROVEMENTS**. Daylight sensors will be integrated with dimmable lighting controls to reduce energy consumption for interior lighting. Tenant workstations will be equipped with plug load occupancy sensors to reduce power usage.

▸▸ **AIR HANDLER REPLACEMENT**. Air handling units will be replaced with temperature-regulated variable-frequency drive (VFD) fans. The use of VFD fans will reduce energy use, improve indoor temperature comfort, and reduce interior noise. In addition, only two floor-mounted VFD fans are required on each floor, instead of the four ceiling-mounted air handling units previously required.

▸▸ **CHILLER PLANT RETROFIT**. Chillers will be fitted with VFD motors and upgraded to incorporate new mechanical elements and control systems. VFD motors allow equipment to operate at reduced speeds during off-peak hours. Together, these improvements will enhance energy efficiency.

▸▸ **CONTROL SYSTEM UPGRADE**. Building controls will be upgraded to optimize operation of the heating, ventilating, and air-conditioning (HVAC) system and to provide additional energy usage detail from submeters.

▸▸ **VENTILATION CONTROLS**. CO_2 sensors will be linked to the building management system to optimize fresh air levels based on building occupancy and interior conditions. The sensors save energy by more precisely regulating required air intake and release.

▸▸ TENANT ENERGY MANAGEMENT SYSTEMS.
Interior spaces will be fully submetered, and
tenants will be given access to individualized,
Web-based systems that will enable them to
monitor and adjust their energy usage. Such
"smart metering" systems help office occupants
control their energy use and expenditures.

Additional sustainability measures to be
incorporated in the retrofit include the recycling of waste and construction debris, the
use of recycled materials, and the establishment of green cleaning and pest management
programs. Green design guidelines are also
being drafted to guide the construction of
tenant improvements.

The green upgrades to the Empire State
Building are part of a $500 million refurbish-
ment now underway. The timing of the retrofit
takes advantage of scheduled lease expirations: some 40 percent of tenant leases are
scheduled to expire during the retrofit.
Sustainable features added $13.2 million to the
cost of the retrofit, or about 2.6 percent. These
incremental costs are expected to be recouped
through energy savings in less than four years

These green retrofit plans illustrate the
themes captured in this book:

▸▸ CAREFUL, INTERDISCIPLINARY PLANNING
is needed to prepare for a green office retrofit.
The project team spent eight months reviewing 60 retrofit options before choosing the
eight capital improvement initiatives. The
planning team included the building owners,
the property management firm, and architectural, engineering, glazing, and energy management professionals. See chapter 2 for
advice on planning a green office retrofit.

▸▸ GREEN OFFICE RETROFITS TYPICALLY
AFFECT all major building elements. The sustainable retrofit of the Empire State Building
affected the building envelope, mechanical
elements, lighting systems, and the choice of
building materials. Design features of green
office retrofits are discussed in chapter 3.

▸▸ GREEN OFFICE RETROFITS ARE TYPICALLY
BEST CONDUCTED through an integrated
design and construction process, especially if
green certification is sought. The Empire
State Building retrofit addressed green
design, certification, and installation concerns from project inception onward. Chapter
4 discusses the use of integrated design and
construction, and related contractual issues
associated with green office retrofits.

The Empire State
Building in New York
City, completed in
1931, is undergoing a
four-year green retrofit
intended to reduce
energy consumption
by 38 percent, as well
as significantly reduce
GHG emissions.

▸ FINANCIAL PERFORMANCE ASSESSMENT and the evaluation of financing alternatives are important aspects of executing a green office retrofit. The green retrofit of the Empire State Building was planned in accordance with business objectives for the building, including lease-up plans and cost reduction objectives. The eight retrofit initiatives were selected on the basis of both financial and environmental impact, and each option was scrutinized for economic viability. The final project utilized an ESCO (energy services company) program to finance energy improvements. The financial analysis and outcomes of green office retrofits are discussed in chapter 5, as are ESCO and other financing alternatives.

▸ THE GREENING OF ONGOING BUILDING OPERATIONS is a key element of a green office retrofit. The Empire State Building owners intend to introduce green design protocols for tenant improvements, offer submetering and smart metering to encourage tenants to minimize energy use, and implement green requirements for construction waste recycling, cleaning, and pest management. These approaches and other aspects of green office building operation and management are discussed in chapter 6.

▸ THE PUBLIC POLICY IMPLICATIONS of green office retrofits are significant. National, provincial, state, and local governments around the globe have begun to encourage green building renovation and development as a way of combating climate change. New York City Mayor Michael Bloomberg views the green retrofit of the Empire State Building as a way of "showing the rest of the city that existing buildings, no matter how tall they are, no matter how old they are, can take steps to significantly reduce their energy consumption." New York City requires that municipal buildings be built green and has enacted a stringent energy code. Bloomberg is also developing an energy audit bill that would apply to all buildings larger than 50,000 square feet and plans to use funds released under the U.S. government's 2009 economic stimulus for green building retrofits. Public policy trends that affect the retrofit of green office buildings are discussed in chapter 7.

▸ THE INCREASING USE OF BUILDING INFORMATION MODELING and other advances in building science will no doubt influence the green office retrofits of the future. The Empire State Building retrofit relied heavily on modeling to determine optimal green retrofit initiatives. New developments in building science, technology, and design that have significant implications for green office retrofits are discussed in chapter 8.

The Empire State Building is a living case study that encourages others to learn from its example, with the hope of inspiring additional green building retrofits. This volume does the same through the presentation of case studies from around the world, including green office retrofits from North America, Europe, Asia, and Australia. The authors and the Urban Land Institute hope that readers will draw on the lessons of these case studies to undertake or participate in new green office retrofit projects.

NOTES

1 World Business Council for Sustainable Development (WBCSD), "Energy Efficiency in Buildings Facts & Trends," September 8, 2008, www.wbcsd.org/includes/getTarget.asp?type=d&id=MzE0Njk.

2 Tobias Just, Deutsche Bank Research, "Real Estate Investments in China and India: Big Returns in Big Countries?" presentation at ULI Germany (Berlin), June 5, 2008, www.dbresearch.com/PROD/DBR_INTERNET_EN-PROD/PROD0000000000226887.pdf.

3 I. McAllister and C. Sweett, "Transforming Existing Buildings: The Green Challenge," March 2007, www.rics.org/NR/rdonlyres/381CCB81-EF08-45B9-B42C-54735E0ABF20/0/TransformingExistingBuildingsTheGreenChallenge.pdf.

4 Interview with Rohit Aggarwala, New York City Office of Long Term Planning and Sustainability, www.sustainlane.com/us-city-rankings/articles/new-york-speaks-q-a-with-city-officials/CSYRSFR8ISMO3A2I2SXPS2FKRNY2.

5 "Surveyors Lead Plan To Transform Existing Commercial Buildings," *Energy in Buildings and Industry,* 2007, vol. 4, p. 8.

6 WBCSD, September 8, 2008.

7 New Buildings Institute, *Energy Performance of LEED® for New Construction Buildings,* March 4, 2008, pp. 1–5.

8 Energy Star is a joint energy efficiency program of the U.S. Environmental Protection Agency and the Department of Energy.

9 Andrew C. Burr, "CoStar Study Finds Energy Star, LEED Bldgs. Outperform Peers," CoStar Group press release, March 26, 2008, www.costar.com/News/Article.aspx?id=D968F1E0DC F73712B03A099E0E99C679.

10 IPCC, "Summary for Policy Makers: Fourth Assessment Report, Working Group 3," 2007, pg. 4, www.ipcc.ch/pdf/ assessment-report/ar4/wg3/ar4-wg3-spm.pdf.

11 M. Levine et al., "Residential and Commercial Buildings," in *Climate Change 2007: Mitigation. Contribution of Working Group III to the Fourth Assessment Report of the Intergovernmental Panel on Climate Change* (Cambridge, U.K.: Cambridge University Press, 2007).

12 *Ibid.*

13 S. Solomon et al., "Summary for Policymakers," in *Climate Change 2007: The Physical Science Basis. Contribution of Working Group I to the Fourth Assessment Report of the Intergovernmental Panel on Climate Change* (Cambridge, U.K.: Cambridge University Press, 2007).

14 M.L. Parry et al., "Summary for Policymakers," in *Climate Change 2007: Impacts, Adaptation and Vulnerability. Contribution of Working Group II to the Fourth Assessment Report of the Intergovernmental Panel on Climate Change* (Cambridge, U.K.: Cambridge University Press, 2007).

15 F. Ackerman and E. Stanton, *Climate Change – the Costs of Inaction*, Global Development and Environment Institute, Tufts University, October 2006, http://ase.tufts.edu/gdae/Pubs/rp/ Climate-Costsofinaction.pdf.

16 Sir Nicholas Stern et al., U.K. Treasury, *Stern Review on the Economics of Climate Change*, October 2006, p. i.

17 Parry et al., 2007.

18 Solomon et al., 2007.

19 B.S. Fisher et al., "Issues Related to Mitigation in the Long-Term Context," in *Climate Change 2007: Mitigation. Contribution of Working Group III to the Fourth Assessment Report of the Intergovernmental Panel on Climate Change* (Cambridge, U.K.: Cambridge University Press, 2007).

20 G.J. Levermore, "A Review of the IPCC Assessment Report Four, Part 1: The IPCC Process and Greenhouse Gas Emission Trends from Buildings Worldwide," *Building Services Engineering Research and Technology*, vol. 29, no. 4, pp. 349–361.

21 P. Enkvist, T. Naucler, and J. Rosander, "A Cost Curve for Greenhouse Gas Reductions," *The McKinsey Quarterly*, February 2007, www.mckinseyquarterly.com/A_cost_curve_for_ greenhouse_gas_reduction_1911.

22 WBCSD, September 8, 2008.

23 United Nations Environment Programme (UNEP), "Sustainable Building and Construction Initiative," *Briefing: Policies for Energy Efficient Buildings in China,* March 26, 2008.

24 EurActiv, "EU Eyes Tax Breaks to Green Economic Recovery," November 27, 2008, www.euractiv.com/en/sustainability/ eu-eyes-tax-breaks-green-economic-recovery/article-177490.

25 Institute for Building Environment and Energy Conservation, "Dissemination of CASBEE in Japan," December 2008, www.ibec.or.jp/CASBEE/english/statistics.htm.

26 British Columbia Ministry of Housing and Social Development, "Greening the BC Building Code: First Steps," December 2008, www.housing.gov.bc.ca/building/green.

27 Thomas Lane, "Energy Performance Certificates: Don't Kid Yourself," *Building*, 2008, issue 17, www.building.co.uk/story.asp ?sectioncode=662&storycode=3112437.

28 William Fisk, "Review of Health and Productivity Gains from Better IEQ," *Proceedings of Healthy Buildings*, 2000, vol. 4, pp. 23–34. Greg Kats et al., "The Costs and Financial Benefits of Green Building: A Report to California's Sustainable Building Task Force," 2003.

29 Andrew J. Nelson, "The Greening of U.S. Investment Real Estate," RREEF Research, Report Number 57, November 2007, p. i.

Planning a Green Office Retrofit

LEANNE TOBIAS AND GEORGE VAVAROUTSOS

Planning is a key element in a successful green retrofit. This chapter educates readers about the most important elements of planning a green retrofit, including the use of codes and voluntary certification systems, and of conducting preliminary evaluations to guide the retrofit, including market feasibility studies, tenant surveys, energy audits, condition assessments, and gap analysis. This chapter also details the decision criteria that optimize the timing and duration of a successful green retrofit; discusses the need for integrated planning, design, and documentation methods; and suggests budgeting and financial modeling techniques for evaluating and selecting among retrofit alternatives.

CODE STANDARDS AND VOLUNTARY CERTIFICATION SYSTEMS

As of 2009, a growing number of building code standards and voluntary certification systems have been established across the world to guide the planning of green office retrofits. Typically, model codes and certification schemes provide standards for construction, renovation, and operation in five areas:

▸▸ **ENERGY EFFICIENCY;**

▸▸ **WATER CONSERVATION;**

▸▸ **USE OF ENVIRONMENTALLY SENSITIVE,** recycled, or regional products and materials in construction, furnishing, and operation;

▸▸ **SITING** to facilitate mass transit use, encourage infill development, and preserve open space; and

▸▸ **OCCUPANT COMFORT** with respect to natural light, temperature controls, and healthful building operation and maintenance.

To date, the boundary between the voluntary certification schemes and codes has been fluid. In Asia, certification schemes have been frequently developed and administered by government entities. In Singapore, the government was instrumental in creating the Green Mark certification system, which has been made mandatory for all new buildings and for substantial renovations with gross floor area of at least 2,000 square meters (21,528 square feet). The new German Certificate for Sustainable Buildings was launched by the Federal Ministry of Transport, Building, and Urban Affairs and the German Sustainable Building Council (DGNB). In the United States, where voluntary certification schemes have preceded the development of green building code standards, local governments have begun to mandate the use of such certification schemes to regulate the construction and refurbishment of public and, in a growing number of cases, private offices. (See chapter 7 for additional material on government programs relating to green real estate.)

Code Standards

Green building code standards are typically developed through standard-setting processes in which government officials, research organizations, and building and green building experts participate. Codes typically set minimum standards for construction of green buildings. Such standards have been prescribed for the European Union (EU) nations, and a standard-setting process has been convened in the United States to develop a model green building code for adoption by municipalities:

▸▸ **EUROPEAN ENERGY PERFORMANCE OF BUILDINGS DIRECTIVE (EPBD).** Developed by the European Commission, this directive establishes minimum requirements for the energy performance of new buildings and substantially renovated buildings with useful floor areas in excess of 1,000 square meters (10,764 square feet). The directive also provides for the energy certification of new and existing buildings and the ongoing inspection of boilers and of heating and air-conditioning systems, to ensure energy efficiency. EU member nations have discretion in how they implement the directive, as long as they satisfy its requirements. As of 2009, the EPBD is being implemented throughout the European

Union through the creation of national energy efficiency standards, and initial requirements are being refined.

▸▸ **STANDARD 189.1.** This standard is a U.S. initiative to establish national green building criteria for incorporation into municipal building codes. The standard is being developed through the consensus protocol of the American National Standards Institute (ANSI). Standard 189.1 would apply to new and substantially renovated buildings, with the exception of low-rise, residential construction. The drafting process is being led by the American Society of Heating, Refrigerating, and Air-Conditioning Engineers (ASHRAE), the Illuminating Engineering Society of North America (IESNA), and the U.S. Green Building Council, with additional representation from business, government, utility, and university organizations. The goal is to achieve a minimum reduction of 30 percent over the energy usage specified in ASHRAE 90.1-2004. The standard is also expected to establish minimum standards for water use reduction, on-site generation capacity, indoor air quality, and project siting. As of early 2009, the standard was being developed by a 34-member committee.

Certification Systems

Where code standards attempt to establish a minimum threshold for green building development, green certification schemes are intended to guide developers and owners to adopt best practices related to green building renovation. Green building certification schemes are typically developed by private, nonprofit organizations.

The typical certification scheme is based on a system of prerequisites and a checklist of possible points linked to specific building features or operational practices. The achievement of all prerequisites and a minimum level of points is needed to obtain green building certification. Most voluntary green certification schemes differentiate between certified properties on the basis of the number of points earned, allowing property owners to certify buildings at varying levels of compliance.

The dominant global model for voluntary certification systems stresses third-party verification of property compliance, with points determined on the basis of standard documentation submitted by the project owner or developer. Since their inception, certification schemes have grown more refined; specialized certification systems are available for substantial rehabilitation projects, interior tenant buildouts, and maintenance and operations upgrades for existing projects. Hence, developers and building owners are increasingly able to select a tailored green compliance pathway, one that is best suited for a specific office renovation project.

As detailed in figure 2-1, standardized certification schemes have been introduced around the globe. To date, the Building Research Establishment's Environmental Assessment Method (BREEAM) and the U.S. Green Building Council's Leadership in Energy and Environmental Design (LEED) have been adapted most frequently for international use. Under both schemes, accredited experts (BREEAM assessors and LEED Accredited Professionals) can guide property developers and owners through the certification process.

BREEAM

The BREEAM building certification system has developed schemes for a wide array of building types, ranging from offices, retail developments, and multifamily structures to courts, prisons, industrial facilities, educational facilities, health care facilities, and eco-homes. BREEAM Bespoke is specifically designed to be used in the certification of projects that do not fit into an existing BREEAM scheme.

The BREEAM office certification system offers two compliance pathways, one for newly designed projects and the other for operations and maintenance in existing buildings. The BREEAM operations and maintenance protocol is appropriate for many office retrofits. Extensive building renovations can be rated under the BREEAM scheme for new project design. Prerequisites and certification points encompass the management, health, and well-being of occupants as well as energy, transport, water, land use ecology, and materials and pollution. Five ratings can

Figure 2-1

Voluntary Certification Protocols for Green Buildings Around the World

FEBRUARY 2009

Region/Country	Certification Protocol
NORTH AMERICA	
United States	LEED, Energy Star
Canada	BOMA Green Globes, LEED
Mexico	LEED
EUROPE	
France	HQE
Germany	DGNB
Netherlands	BREEAM Netherlands
United Kingdom	BREEAM UK
Other Europe	BREEAM International
Turkey	BREEAM International
AFRICA	
South Africa	Green Star
MIDDLE EAST	
Iran	BREEAM Gulf
Iraq	BREEAM Gulf
Israel	Standard 5282, LEED
Qatar	BREEAM Gulf, LEED
Saudi Arabia	BREEAM Gulf
UAE	BREEAM Gulf, LEED
ASIA	
China	LEED, MoC Evaluation Std.
Hong Kong	HK-BEAM
India	LEED India, GRIHA
Japan	CASBEE
Singapore	Green Mark
Taiwan	EEWH
PACIFIC	
Australia	Green Star
New Zealand	Green Star

Note: LEED = Leadership in Energy and Environmental Design. BOMA = Building Owners and Managers Association International. HQE = Haute Qualité Environnementale. DGNB = German Sustainable Building Council. BREEAM = Building Research Establishment's Environmental Assessment Method. MoC = Ministry of Construction. HK-BEAM = Hong Kong Building Environmental Assessment Method. GRIHA = Green Rating for Integrated Habitat Assessment (Ministry of New and Renewable Energy and the Energy Resource Institute). CASBEE = Comprehensive Assessment System for Building Environmental Efficiency. EEWH = Ecology, Energy Saving, Waste Reduction, and Health.

be earned under the BREEAM system: Pass, Good, Very Good, Excellent, and Outstanding.

Established initially in the United Kingdom, BREEAM has been adapted and adopted throughout the world. BREEAM UK is used in the United Kingdom and Ireland. The Netherlands has adopted a customized BREEAM system, and BREEAM International is available throughout the EU nations; in Iceland, Norway, and Switzerland; and in Eastern Europe, the Balkan states, and Turkey. BREEAM Gulf is in use in emirates in the Persian Gulf, as well as in Iran, Iraq, and Saudi Arabia. BREEAM has also been used selectively for projects in Asia.

LEED

The LEED certification system has adopted compliance pathways for new construction and substantial renovation projects (LEED-New Construction or LEED-NC); base building construction or substantial renovation for speculative projects (LEED-Core and Shell or LEED CS); tenant interiors (LEED-Commercial Interiors or LEED-CI); and existing buildings operation and maintenance (LEED-Existing Buildings Operation and Maintenance or LEED-EBOM). An earlier version of LEED for existing buildings, LEED-EB, is being phased out. In addition to these certification pathways, all of which can be used for office projects, another pathway (LEED-Neighborhood Development or LEED-ND) addresses neighborhoods and planned communities that desire LEED certification. Additional certification systems are available for schools and homes. Four ratings can be attained under the LEED system: Certified, Silver, Gold, and Platinum.

LEED prerequisites and points are awarded in five categories: sustainable sites, water efficiency, energy and atmosphere, materials and resources, and indoor environmental quality. In 2009, all U.S. LEED certification schemes were adjusted to a 100-point scale, and additional weight was given to sustainable siting decisions, energy conservation, and the miti-

gation of carbon emissions. Materials credits have been redesigned to introduce life-cycle assessment—the measurement of a product's environmental impact from manufacture through use and disposal—into product selection. Regionally determined bonus credits have been added to the system to tailor building certification more closely to local conditions. Developed in the United States, LEED has been introduced worldwide, with country-specific certification systems in use in Canada, Mexico, India, China, and some emirates in the Persian Gulf.

OTHER SYSTEMS

Other well-known green certification systems that have been applied to office construction and renovation projects include Green Globes, widely used in Canada; Green Star, used throughout Australia and New Zealand and available in South Africa; Haute Qualité Environnementale (HQE), used in France; Comprehensive Assessment

Financing for the rehabilitation of the Christman Building involved a public/private partnership between the Christman Company and the city of Lansing, Michigan, through its Brownfield Authority. Pictured here is an atrium created between the two rear extensions of the building.

System for Building Environmental Efficiency (CASBEE), used in Japan; and Green Mark, used in Singapore. In January 2009, Germany announced the first awards under its pilot Deutsche Gesellschaft für Nachhaltiges Bauen (DGNB, or German Sustainable Building Council) certification system. The DGNB expands the definition of sustainability to include credits for economic value, as measured by the quality of construction and the ease of maintaining and repairing building materials.

Using a Voluntary Certification System

Property owners and developers who wish to use a voluntary certification system are advised to select the system that best fits the scope of their renovation project. Gut rehabilitation projects in the United Kingdom, for example, would be best advised to use BREEAM's compliance pathway for newly designed office buildings, while their U.S. counterparts would be best advised to use LEED-NC or LEED-CS (see the case studies of the Christman Building and 545 Madison Avenue in chapter 9). For existing buildings, BREEAM's office operations and maintenance certification system is preferable, as is LEED's EBOM scheme (see the case studies of the Adobe, One Beacon Street, and Transwestern retrofits, all certified under LEED-EB). The LEED-CI certification system is designed specifically for the renovation of tenant spaces (see the Wallace Roberts & Todd case study). The use of Australia's Green Star system is detailed in the case study of the renovation of the Australian Ethical Institute's headquarters.

It is possible to certify projects under BREEAM and LEED outside their countries of origin. BREEAM International can tailor certification schemes to fit local circumstances throughout the world. The U.S. LEED standards have been used to certify projects in China (see the Shui On Land case study) and Israel.

It is also advisable to design, construct, and certify the renovation with the assistance of pro-

fessionals who are accredited in that certification method and who have participated in the construction of certified improvements (see chapter 4). The use of an experienced project team typically accelerates the project certification process.

ANALYZING THE GREEN RETROFIT OPPORTUNITY

The first step in planning a green office retrofit is to evaluate the green opportunity for the asset through an analysis of property conditions, market feasibility, regulation risk, and asset obsolescence. The decision to execute a green office retrofit is not just about efficient building systems and the potential for energy savings; it is a comprehensive asset strategy that incorporates tenant demand, regulatory risk, and competitiveness.

Criteria

A number of market- and property-specific assessment criteria should be evaluated in planning a green office retrofit. The most critical are the following:

▸▸ **MARKET-SPECIFIC CRITERIA**

- Market and submarket conditions,
- Tenant demand for green space,
- Regulations (current and pending), and
- Tenant lease structure.

▸▸ **PROPERTY-SPECIFIC CRITERIA**

- Indoor environmental quality and occupant comfort,
- Building energy consumption,
- Building water consumption and wastewater discharge,
- Facility maintenance and operations, and
- Site and environmental impacts.

Figures 2-2 and 2-3 provides a detailed breakdown of the assessment criteria and tools that can be used to measure and assess those criteria during the planning phase. Although not all the assessment criteria apply to every office property, the more insight and information that a property owner has on the forces that affect the need for building sustainability, the more likely the owner is to develop a successful retrofit strategy.

Methods

Most green retrofit criteria can be measured and analyzed through building and market analysis methods that are in common use in the commercial real estate industry. Several kinds of reports provide the most useful information and therefore should be completed before the retrofit process begins. First among them are marketing and market feasibility studies, and tenant and occupant surveys. Building owners can also choose among energy audits, property conditions assessments, and gap analyses as tools for

Figure 2-2

Market-Specific Criteria for Assessing a Green Retrofit Opportunity

Property Assessment Criteria	Assessment Objective	Potential Assessment Tools
Market and submarket conditions	Identify market conditions (rents, occupancy rates, rental concessions, etc.)	Market feasibility study, appraisal
	Identify pipeline of new office space in market (planned or under construction)	
Tenant demand for green space	Measure tenant interest and acceptable cost premium for green space	Market feasibility study, appraisal, tenant survey, interviews with leasing brokers
	Identify tenants' specific interest in green building	
Regulations, current and pending	Identify regulatory policies that may affectc building use, value, and competitiveness	Regulatory review, market feasibility study, appraisal
Tenant lease structure	Identify lease types (gross, net, etc.) for building tenants	Lease documents and abstracts, market feasibility study, appraisal, interviews with leasing brokers
	Identify options for passing cost of building improvements through to tenants	

Figure 2-3

Property-Specific Criteria for Assessing a Green Retrofit Opportunity

Property Assessment Criteria	Assessment Objective	Potential Assessment Tools
Indoor environmental quality and occupant comfort	Measure indoor air quality	Indoor air quality report, tenant/occupancy survey
	Identify thermal comfort, ventilation, and lighting conditions issues for building occupants	
Building energy consumption	Identify the energy profile and energy use intensity (EUI) for the building	Energy audit, building energy modeling
	Compare EUI and energy profiles with those of similar office buildings	
	Identify opportunities to reduce performance gap and energy use	
Building water consumption and waste-water discharge	Identify water consumption and discharge profile for the property	Facility water use assessment (water audit), water efficiency management plan
	Identify options to maximize water use efficiency and reduce water use	
Facilities maintenance and operations	Identify building systems in need of repair or approaching the end of their useful life	Property conditions assessment
Site environmental impact	Evaluate site features for potential landscaping and hardscaping improvement	Various land planning, civil, and water engineering studies (depending on site location)

selecting the most appropriate green retrofit program. Energy audits create actionable recommendations for reducing energy usage, while property conditions assessments offer repair and replacement recommendations for optimizing performance across all building elements. Gap analyses relate building conditions to the feasibility and cost of attaining certification under a specific green building rating system.

MARKETING AND MARKET FEASIBILITY STUDIES

The decision to undertake a green office renovation should be considered in the context of general market and submarket economic conditions, the competitive position of the property, tenant demand for green space, and the contemplated holding period for the asset. Owners should consider whether the provision of green features will affect rental levels, the pace of leasing and tenant retention, or the operating costs passed through to tenants. As detailed in chapter 5 and in the case studies, green office renovation projects frequently deliver rapid and robust paybacks and are often characterized by subsequent higher occupancies, faster lease-up, and higher rents and sale prices than their conventional equivalents. In order to evaluate the probable success of a specific green project, however, a market feasibility study should be conducted (for details, see the sidebar by Margarita Foster).

GREENING AN OFFICE BUILDING: STRATEGIC CONSIDERATIONS

MARGARITA FOSTER

The decision to green an office structure is made in the context of larger asset management issues such as optimal building positioning, available lease terms and concessions, intended hold period, and the highest and best use for a structure. Greening an asset is not an additive concept but an integral one.

All the typical elements that are considered when redeveloping an asset must be taken into account when considering a green retrofit. The following list identifies questions to consider:

▸▸ **Owner's goals.** What are the owner's goals? Is there a short-term focus on lease-up, and might a green label provide a competitive marketing advantage? Is the focus on the long term, with emphasis on building value and attractiveness to investors? The former strategy might make it advisable to concentrate on green tenant buildouts, while the latter might require a more extensive renovation of the base building.

▸▸ **Asset positioning strategy.** What is the building's optimal position in the submarket? Is it located in a Class A submarket, thus requiring the building to be upgraded, or is the submarket considered Class B, where the finest building design and materials may not be necessary in order to maximize rents?

▸▸ **Project location.** Does the building's location support a green strategy? Where are the majority of stabilized green buildings that have recently been delivered or are under development in the subject market? Are they concentrated in one submarket such as the central business district, or are they scattered around the region? Are most multistory buildings in dense transit- and pedestrian-oriented environments, or are they suburban buildings surrounded by surface parking?

Understanding the preferred location of green tenants and where they are clustering is critical. For example, if the asset under consideration is in the suburbs and most of the occupied green buildings are in the core markets, lease-up of the suburban asset may not be facilitated by a green retrofit.

▸▸ **Tenant demand.** Which tenants have occupied green space? Is there demand among certain industries? Is demand segmented by building class? Is there deep and wide demand for green features among all tenants in the market?

For high-end users such as law firms that compete for the best and the brightest graduates and professionals, a green label may confer an advantage for recruitment and retention purposes. Occupying green-certified space enables companies to project to employees and competitors that their space is environmentally friendly, conveying that employee comfort and productivity are a priority. In the future, a green office environment may be offered as a benefit, much like health insurance and retirement plans.

TENANT AND OCCUPANT SURVEYS

A survey of current tenants can be helpful in developing a green retrofit strategy for a property. The tenant survey can be performed as an adjunct to the market feasibility study or as a component of that study. The tenant survey should consider current occupant comfort and building performance issues. Are there cold spots on certain floors, or does the sun intensity through the windows create an uncomfortably hot work environment in the afternoon? These are both occupant comfort and energy efficiency issues: the cold areas may indicate issues with the building's heating, ventilating, and air conditioning (HVAC) or thermal boundary, and the heat gain from the afternoon sun means that the owner should consider shading on the sun-facing

sides of the building. These tenant observations help building management and owners identify green retrofit priorities and provide useful guidance for conducting energy audits and conditions assessments.

▸ **Office metrics: absorption, leasing velocity, and rents.** How does leasing velocity in green buildings compare with that in truly comparable conventional buildings? Is there more leasing activity in green-certified buildings? At this early stage in the analysis of green-certified versus conventional buildings, comparable properties may be difficult to find in many submarkets. As a result, market analysis needs to be qualitative, drawn from interviews with tenants and leasing brokers, rather than quantitative.

Understanding the story of why a tenant selected a certain building is critical. Was the user drawn by the healthy and productive work environment, or was the space chosen because it was optimally located in the tenant's target market, or were both factors significant? Understanding tenant priorities is crucial to determining the desirability of a green retrofit.

Most tenants are location conscious. They generally focus on one or two submarkets based on client location and employee housing. It is unlikely that a tenant will make a green building a priority over the submarket location and agree to go anywhere in the region just to occupy a green-certified building. However, if a tenant search boils down to two buildings, comparably located and priced, with green certification being the only significant difference, the green-certified building will likely win out, because it offers the healthiest and most productive work environment, is attractive for employee recruitment, projects the company as socially responsible, and

has the potential to reduce operating expenses for the tenant.

Because each lease negotiation is unique, there are always additional nuances to consider. The LEED-CI designation is achievable, for example, in buildings that are not LEED certified, but it is more costly to implement than in a LEED-certified building. Thus, one can envision a scenario in which a tenant compares costs in two buildings and finds that although rents in the LEED-certified building are slightly higher, the cost of building out to LEED-CI will be lower. Developers and owners, by contrast, face a different decision: whether to implement a LEED-EB renovation with lower LEED-CI tenant improvement allowances, or whether to provide higher buildout allowances for tenants who want LEED-CI space. In exceptionally tight markets, of course, a market-standard allowance might satisfy both tenant and owner.

As developers and owners wrestle with the notion of greening assets, keeping tenant and market perspectives in mind is critical. Looking ahead, it seems unimaginable that tenants will do an about-face and suddenly request less natural light, worse air quality, and toxic materials in their work space. Instead, it will be necessary for developers and owners to consider appropriate greening strategies in the context of owners' strategic goals, market fundamentals, and tenant requirements.

Margarita Foster is vice president, Office Markets, at Fulton Research and Consulting in Fairfax, Virginia.

A primary goal of the retrofit of the HOK offices in Hong Kong was to adhere to a firm construction budget— without a special allowance for sustainable design aspects.

The tenant survey should also consider the attitudes of building tenants with respect to utility costs and amenities. If a recent utility cost increase significantly affected the bottom line of tenants who rent space under triple net or modified gross leases, those tenants will likely pay particular attention to relative energy and water efficiency. Tenant interest in conventional versus sustainable amenities can also help to determine the degree of interest in potential green retrofit features.

ENERGY AUDIT

Also referred to as an energy analysis, an energy audit creates an energy use profile for the building and identifies energy inefficiencies within the building systems and envelope. The objective is to create actionable recommendations that can be implemented to reduce energy usage (and associated carbon emissions) and building operating costs. An energy audit is an extraordinarily valuable assessment tool for planning a green retrofit. (For an example of how the energy audit process was recently utilized as a value-add for an office building that was aiming for LEED-EBOM certification, see the sidebar by Adam Hinge.)

An energy audit has four stages:

▸▸ **PRELIMINARY ENERGY USE** analysis,

▸▸ **WALK-THROUGH ANALYSIS** (ASHRAE Level 1 analysis),

▸▸ **ENERGY SURVEY AND ENGINEERING ANALYSIS** (ASHRAE Level 2 analysis), and

▸▸ **CAPITAL-INTENSIVE MODIFICATIONS**, detailed analysis (ASHRAE Level 3 analysis).

The preliminary energy use analysis reviews property utility bills to assess the likelihood of potential savings; the walk-through analysis combines a site inspection and interviews with building owners and managers to evaluate

HOW AN ENERGY AUDIT CAN IMPROVE BUILDING PERFORMANCE

ADAM HINGE

An energy audit is usually the first step toward identifying energy cost-saving measures, which can often subsidize additional costs for other greening initiatives in existing buildings. Energy audits (sometimes called energy analyses or appraisals to avoid the negative connotation of financial audits) can be very simple or extremely detailed. In the United States, the Environmental Protection Agency's (EPA's) free Energy Star Buildings Portfolio Manager tool often can be used for an initial screen of a group of buildings to determine which have the greatest savings potential from a green retrofit and where further energy auditing dollars are best spent. At the other end of the cost spectrum, building owners can conduct detailed "investment grade" energy audits, generally on a specific system or potential improvement, before major capital investments are made.

In the case of a 600,000-square-foot, 15-floor office building built in New York City during the 1990s and pursuing LEED-EBOM certification, the first step was benchmarking using the Energy Star tool. The results informed the owner that the building was close to meeting the prerequisites but still had opportunities for saving energy costs. An energy audit was commissioned for the building, with the cost partially funded by the New York State Energy Research & Development Authority, which offers a variety of energy savings incentive programs. The study identified several projects that could reduce energy costs, all of which the owner considered.

A number of lighting improvement projects were identified, some of which had already been considered by the building engineering staff. These had rapid paybacks. The biggest challenge was finding appropriate energy-saving lamps that would enable the building to attain LEED-EBOM credits for low-mercury lighting.

The biggest-ticket items identified in the energy audit related to the mechanical system. The facility has a dual-fuel chiller system. Although the audit recommended changing chiller operating strategies to track fuel costs more closely, the engineering staff thought that the strategies suggested would risk higher peak demand charges and would not produce the savings estimated by the auditing firm. Therefore, this measure was not implemented.

Because the building houses a major financial services firm, maintaining occupants' comfort was a critical consideration in any potential changes. The biggest potential savings identified in the energy audit came from utilization of "demand-controlled ventilation," which enables outside air ventilation levels to be reduced on the basis of the number of people occupying the space. Demand-control ventilation brings in additional fresh-air ventilation when needed but cuts back on the amount of fresh, unconditioned, outdoor air brought into empty or unoccupied spaces. The building owner sought proposals from its controls vendor to confirm the costs of implementing the strategy and to verify the level of savings that could be expected. Implementing this strategy required adding more CO_2 sensors in a number of spaces throughout the building and adding control algorithms to the building's automation system to allow for automatic throttling of fans and dampers. At an implementation cost of $55,000, demand-control ventilation resulted in energy savings at the property of more than $150,000 annually.

The audit identified additional energy cost savings that could be obtained from optimizing the scheduling of HVAC and lighting systems, to minimize use of the system when occupants do not need it. This measure resulted in an additional $50,000 in annual energy savings.

In total, energy savings measures introduced in this New York building created estimated savings of more than $250,000 each year. The first year of savings more than paid for all the costs of the audit and the implementation of measures in the first year. Those savings gave the building owner spare cash to purchase off-site renewable energy credits (RECs) and a wide range of environmentally preferable products, including recycled paper.

The biggest culture change that resulted from the LEED-EBOM process at this building was the recognition of continuous improvement opportunities in an already sophisticated operation. Facilities management staff better understood the need for and savings opportunities derived from continued monitoring of all systems, the need for vigilant review of energy and water costs, and the effects of changes in operating strategy on resource consumption.

A good source of information for building owners and managers who are interested in learning more about energy audits is "Procedures for Commercial Building Energy Audits," published by ASHRAE. This publication has specific information about energy audit requirements and forms the basis for LEED-EBOM energy performance prerequisites and credits. The publication provides definitions of Level 1, 2, and 3 energy audits, enabling building owners or managers to specify the services they wish to procure.

Adam Hinge, PE, is the managing director of Sustainable Energy Partnerships in Tarrytown, New York.

SUSTAINABILITY AND TRANSACTION DUE DILIGENCE

MICHAEL B. SCHNEIDER

With the growing focus in the real estate industry on sustainability, traditional due diligence services have needed to adapt to new considerations that affect risk. Financial stakeholders in both the equity and debt markets have become increasingly aware of the potential investment implications of environmental performance. The increasing emphasis on reducing environmental risk comes in response to more stringent credit requirements, as well as such considerations as corporate governance issues, ability to attract foreign investment capital, the need to reduce operating costs in order to enhance financial performance, concerns about greenhouse gas (GHG) emissions and organizational carbon footprints, the implications of emerging carbon tax and cap-and-trade strategies, and clear indicators of popular attraction to sustainable environments across all building categories.

As these trends suggest, traditional due diligence services for real estate transactions are being modified to address sustainability concerns. New due diligence tools for commercial real estate are emerging in the context of new sustainability requirements.

The Traditional Property Condition Assessment

One of the typical services provided for the evaluation of existing buildings is the property condition assessment (PCA). The Standard Guide for the PCA was developed in 2001 as ASTM Standard E2018-01. The current edition of the standard is essentially the same protocol with some modifications for terminology and qualifying language, to clarify the obligations and expectations of consultants and clients. Despite the growing interest in sustainability, there is no specific requirement in the standard for the assessment of the sustainable features of a building.

To respond to the demand for sustainability evaluations, several tools provide useful results related to PCAs. They are intended to be used in conjunction with basic services, as an overlay or as a subsequent phased service, and they have proved useful in evaluating real property for sustainability.

New Reviews to Address Sustainability Requirements

A standard PCA focuses on the condition of an existing building, including site, structure, exterior, interior, mechanical and electrical systems, vertical transportation (elevators and escalators), and building code compliance. Opinions of probable costs associated with immediate issues, deferred maintenance, and capital improvements are indicated over a specified term. Supplemental sustainability reviews can include many other items: sustainability profiles, a value analysis, and energy and water audits.

SUSTAINABILITY PROFILE (PHASE I)

A profile for sustainable features includes a list of positive and negative features of a building generally related to the sustainability categories of relevant certification systems. In the United States, the sustainability profile might consist of the five categories established by the U.S. Green Building Council for its LEED certification program (sustainable sites, water efficiency, energy and atmosphere, materials and resources, and indoor environmental quality).

SUSTAINABILITY PROFILE (PHASE II)

A certification system gap assessment is used to determine whether the project meets or could reasonably meet any prerequisites for a targeted certification system. If it can, a more detailed review is undertaken to evaluate certification credits, gathering information during the PCA site evaluation and through an interview with the property manager or owner. Specific questions are asked to determine whether a credit has already been achieved; is reasonably achievable; can be achieved with a modification to operations and maintenance policies; can be achieved with capital expenses to modify the building or site; is not achievable; or will require additional investigation to determine the credit status. (For more information and an example of this evaluation in the context of the LEED-EBOM rating system, see the sidebar on gap assessment by Helee Hillman.)

VALUE ANALYSIS OR ECO-CHARRETTE

If green certification is deemed feasible, alternative strategies for achieving certification credits are developed, and both first-cost and life-cycle cost savings are calculated to determine the simple payback over time for the initial capital outlay by way of operating cost reductions. Criteria are established and prioritized to ensure that the achievement of prerequisites and credits is not detrimental to other important investment objectives. Recommendations are compared with existing conditions and measured for improvements to first costs, life-cycle cost, function, and quality. Long-term objectives of the owners are taken into consideration:

▸▸ **Durability:** Is the choice to attain a credit appropriate? (To cite a simple example, wood components made of rapidly renewable resources but used in an exterior environment may be subject to deterioration.)

▸▸ **Dependability:** Does the product or system have a performance track record?

- **Serviceability:** Is there access for maintenance, and is there a local labor pool with appropriate skills to service the product or system?

- **Measurability:** Can the system's operational performance be quantified to determine whether it meets project objectives?

Value analysis can be discussed and the results evaluated in an eco-charrette attended by the project owner; key design, engineering, and construction personnel; the commissioning agent; and other key team members.

Additional reviews, including the energy and water audits discussed below, can be undertaken in support of the value analysis or conducted separately. The focus is on identifying sustainable building improvements that may have both low first costs and low life-cycle costs. The identification of public incentives, including local utility rebates or grants, should be included in the value analysis. (See chapter 7 for a discussion of public incentives that support sustainable development and retrofit projects.)

ENERGY AUDIT

Following on-site profiling, an energy audit can be conducted. Such audits focus on reducing operating expenses while minimizing undesirable environmental effects associated with the project. Guided by the client's energy efficiency goals, a group of architects, engineers, and LEED Accredited Professionals provide several levels of review to determine how modifications to existing operations and systems can better serve occupants and reduce energy usage. Energy audit services can include the following:

- **Preliminary analysis.** The building's current energy usage is assessed from utility bill information for a minimum of 12 months. Actual usage is compared with that of similar buildings using existing standards and scored against performance databases, such as the EPA's Portfolio Manager in the United States. The preliminary analysis is used primarily to determine the potential benefit of further analysis.

- **Walk-through analysis (ASHRAE Level 1 analysis).** This review is done subsequent to, or in conjunction with, the preliminary analysis. It includes a site survey and interviews with owners and operators to determine the efficiency of systems and operating procedures. The assessment focuses on low-cost and no-cost upgrades that will generate energy savings and identifies potential capital improvements that may require further study. For buildings aiming for LEED certification, this review satisfies the LEED-EBOM Energy and Atmosphere Prerequisite 1 requirements.

- **Energy survey and engineering analysis (ASHRAE Level 2 analysis).** This review is done subsequent to, or in conjunction with, the walk-through analysis. It includes a thorough review of the mechanical and electrical system design, installation, maintenance, and operation. Measurements of the system's operation will be analyzed to determine its actual operating condition. A comprehensive list of possible modifications is then developed and assessed to determine the feasibility of the various modifications based on preliminary cost data and savings estimates. This review qualifies for two LEED-EBOM points under Energy and Atmosphere Credit 2.1.

- **Capital-intensive modifications**, detailed analysis (ASHRAE Level 3 analysis). This review is performed after the energy survey and engineering analysis and is guided by the client's request for further analysis of specific measures that are being considered for implementation. The analysis includes additional system measurements, systems modeling to verify energy savings, and proposed system schematics and equipment lists.

- **Architectural building efficiency analysis**. This review can be performed in conjunction with any of the above reviews, with the exception of the preliminary analysis. The assessment includes a comprehensive review of building components that are accessible without destructive actions and a review of construction drawings, if available, to determine whether the current building components, including insulation, windows, doors, roofing, and exterior penetrations, are negatively affecting energy efficiency. The assessment will result in recommended modifications, including projected costs and estimated savings.

WATER AUDIT

A concurrent or separate water audit can be conducted. Guided by the client's water efficiency goals, several levels of reviews can be provided to determine how modifications to the existing operations and systems can better serve occupants and reduce water usage. Services can include the following:

- **Preliminary analysis.** The current water consumption of the project is calculated and compared with efficient baseline water usage. Calculations are based on information provided by the owner or operator, because this review does not include a site visit. Data include water and sewer bills for a minimum of 12 months, along with data from any sub-meters that may be present for special usage, a list of existing types of plumbing fixtures and the consumption of each, and information related to the number of residents, employees, and visitors. From this information, the water efficiency of the project is assessed and the achievability of prerequisites for certification systems determined. This analysis is primarily used to determine the potential benefit of further analysis.

▸▸ **Water usage site analysis.** This review builds on the preliminary analysis, which must be completed as part of this review if it has not previously been performed, and includes a site survey and interviews with owners and operators to determine the efficiency of the systems and operating procedures. Information provided for the preliminary analysis is verified, measurements of the systems water usage performed, and a breakdown of the water usage determined. The assessment report focuses on upgrades that do not require system redesign. Projected costs and estimated savings of the recommended modifications are provided. Potential capital improvements that require redesign of the systems are identified to be considered for further study.

▸▸ **Capital-intensive modifications, detailed analysis.** This review is done subsequent to the water usage site analysis and is guided by the client's request for further analysis of specific capital improvements that are being considered for implementation. Improvements that require additional investigation may include modifying the irrigation system to provide drip irrigation to conserve water and providing rainwater harvesting systems to offset potable water usage. The analysis may include additional systems measurements, modeling of the systems to verify water savings, and proposed systems schematics and equipment lists. At the client's request, this level of review can also include an assessment of the landscape planting and a proposed redesign integrating native plants or xeriscaping to minimize or eliminate water used to irrigate the site.

Emerging Standards for Transaction Due Diligence

It is expected that sustainable development will continue to capture a greater market share for both new construction and existing buildings. Credit and investment markets will focus on sustainable assets to reduce financial risk, provide higher-valued collateral, and increase investor confidence.

In consideration of this growing industry, it is anticipated that additional transaction due diligence standards will be introduced. One is the National Consensus Green Building Underwriting Standards developed and supported by the Capital Markets Partnership (CMP), a collaboration of financial institutions, investment banks, real estate investors, governmental entities, nongovernmental organizations, nonprofits, and other interested parties. The standard was developed and approved in September 2008 following ANSI protocols. It offers a CMP Green Value Score, derived from combined scores in four areas: Energy Star rating, climate neutrality certification, LEED rating, and the CMP's Green Building Underwriting Standards, which highlight sustainable attributes believed by CMP to have the highest impact on financial risk.

Michael R. Schneider, AIA, NCARB, LEED AP, is vice president and regional manager for the Northwest Division of Marx|Okubo Associates, Inc., in Seattle, Washington.

current energy performance and identify low- and no-cost improvements. The last two analyses provide in-depth reviews and modeling of system performance and proposed alternatives.

Although the preliminary analysis and the walk-through analysis are general in scope and adequate for low-cost or no-cost energy improvements, the next two analyses offer significantly more detailed reviews and specific recommendations for more intensive energy-saving measures.[1] Those analyses also evaluate payback for the energy-saving recommendations provided. (For a detailed assessment of the stages of an energy audit, see the sidebar on sustainability and transaction due diligence by Michael Schneider.)

For each audit stage, the project team should receive an easy-to-use report that summarizes the results and offers recommendations for the next step. There is no requirement to complete all four stages; in fact, the results of the walk-through may indicate that energy-reducing and cost-saving opportunities are limited. Analyses of engineering and capital-intensive modifications are more expensive and should be undertaken only if there are significant opportunities for energy and cost savings.

Energy audits of office buildings should be conducted by a qualified engineering analyst. Some owners may use a qualified member of their facilities staff to perform the audit, while others will hire a qualified engineering firm to complete the analysis. In either case, the most important consideration in picking an engineering analyst is substantial experience in commercial building energy audits, and preferably, in structures with relevant building systems.

PROPERTY CONDITIONS ASSESSMENT

A property conditions assessment (PCA) is an evaluation of the current state of the building, providing an examination of existing conditions and serviceability and recommendations concerning repair and replacement. The PCA is a key component of transaction due diligence. In the context of planning a green retrofit, the PCA will identify which building systems are either obsolete or near the end of their functional life and can therefore be replaced with green alternatives as part of the retrofit. These actions enhance the resource efficiency and potentially the carbon-reduction potential of the green retrofit.

The PCA evaluates all building components:

▸▸ **BUILDING STRUCTURE** (visual inspection of the building's structural elements),

▸▸ **BUILDING ENVELOPE** (roof, walls, windows),

▸▸ **MECHANICAL SYSTEMS,**

▸▸ **ELECTRICAL SYSTEMS,**

▸▸ **INTERIOR FINISHES,**

▸▸ **FIRE AND LIFE SAFETY,**

▸▸ **ELEVATORS,** and

▸▸ **SITE FEATURES** (walkways, roadways, landscaping, etc.).

Generally, qualified engineering staff will inspect all building systems, review documentation of maintenance and repairs, and discuss maintenance and repair issues with facilities staff. Each building system will have specific audit protocols and report deliverables.

The final PCA report is an evaluation that shows which building systems need repair or replacement, and their probable costs. (To learn more about how sustainability concerns are modifying transaction due diligence, see the sidebar by Michael Schneider.)

GREEN CERTIFICATION GAP ASSESSMENT

If building owners are considering green certification, an early step in the process should be a certification gap assessment. This assessment determines the potential for certification under a specific system, ranking the points that can be achieved by their estimated cost and feasibility. Often, the gap assessment overlaps with other analysis tools, such as an energy audit and analysis, and the processes can be combined and streamlined.

The gap assessment should predict what level of certification the property is likely to achieve and estimate the cost of securing higher levels, if feasible. The property owner should determine the target certification level on the basis of the objectives of the retrofit.

The gap assessment process can be conducted in house with the assistance of experienced third-party professionals or outsourced to a vendor that specializes in the relevant certification systems. (For a detailed overview of how an outside vendor conducts a gap assessment, see the sidebar by Hclee Hillman.)

DEFINING THE RETROFIT STRATEGY

Much as there is no one-size-fits-all office building, there is no one-size-fits-all retrofit strategy. The strategy depends on the owner's objectives, and, for investment real estate leased to third-party tenants, is typically driven by the owner's desire for asset competitiveness and asset value.

Owner-occupied office buildings may warrant a slightly different calculus, incorporating a broader view of financial performance. To the owner-occupier, a high-performance, green office building may be a strategic tool to maximize the productivity of employees or to enhance the company's corporate social responsibility profile. Therefore, such an owner may be willing to consider a range of retrofit options, including those with lower financial returns, if it is believed that those options will benefit organizational performance. For example, Adobe Systems (see the case study in chapter 9) has undertaken a wide range of green retrofit initiatives over time, ranging from the long-term development of a sophisticated, integrated, building interface system to monitor energy use to

GREEN CERTIFICATION GAP ASSESSMENT FOR AN EXISTING BUILDING

HELEE HILLMAN

A gap assessment is an early and cost-effective step to assist a property owner in undertaking the greening of an existing building. It is a relatively low-cost initial investment, and establishes a baseline for the building's current performance with regard to the following:

» Energy usage,
» Water usage,
» Green cleaning practices,
» Sustainable product purchasing,
» Green building materials, and
» Indoor air quality.

The gap assessment helps the owner and management team understand current building conditions, identify potential low- or no-cost improvements, and recognize larger capital projects that might be necessary in the short to medium term in order to certify a green building retrofit under a voluntary system such as LEED, Energy Star, or similar rating protocols.

Complete the Gap Assessment Before Starting a Retrofit

It is important to conduct a feasibility assessment of an existing building before beginning a retrofit. The assessment provides the project team with valuable information about the building's current condition and system functions, and establishes a starting point for the retrofit project. This gap assessment can create a roadmap to guide the project team through the certification or retrofit efforts. It also helps the project team and owners to prioritize building improvement efforts by cost and rating system credit, to answer three questions:

» What points or credits should be pursued?
» Which should wait until the next fiscal year?
» Which may not be beneficial to pursue at all?

If owners or managers choose to pursue certification under one of the existing systems for rating green buildings, the system should be specified before the feasibility assessment begins. Though all rating systems address similar building performance parameters for energy use, water use, and green building practices, the systems differ significantly when it comes to the certification process. To be effective, a gap assessment should be structured to evaluate the costs and benefits and feasibility of achieving credits under a particular rating system.

Gap Assessment: LEED-EBOM

The U.S. Green Building Council's LEED-EBOM rating system focuses on the achievement of points within six categories:

» Sustainable Sites,
» Water Efficiency,
» Energy and Atmosphere,
» Materials and Resources,
» Indoor Environmental Quality, and
» Innovations in Operations.

Jones Lang LaSalle provides LEED-EBOM gap analysis by preparing a feasibility assessment study for the property owner. The study report is a tool to determine whether the building can meet or be retrofitted to meet all certification prerequisites, what range of certification levels the building can realistically pursue, and what cost is associated with achieving each credit. The certification roadmap includes actionable recommendations and estimates of the time frame for and cost of achieving certification most efficiently and economically. The final report documents both the assessment and the roadmap.

The LEED-EBOM assessment provides valuable information on current building practices and protocols and suggestions for operational improvements. These operating changes can be implemented immediately by the management team and chief

simpler projects with more immediate and dramatic payoffs. (For a review of how an owner-occupier evaluated its energy retrofit options, see the sidebar by Sean Lockie and Piotr Beribecki.)

For any office property, building and market analyses will identify property performance deficiencies and specific retrofit opportunities. The project team should use this information to define the retrofit goals and objectives. The team should keep in mind that property-specific limiting factors, such as existing leases and capital constraints, may affect or inhibit the achievement of certain objectives.

---

engineer for measurable and tangible results, even if the building owner decides not to pursue formal certification.

The feasibility analysis begins with a questionnaire for the management team to fill out before an on-site assessment. The questionnaire enables the building's team to gather pertinent information such as utility bills, basic building information, floor plans, site plans, and vendor contract agreements. Once the questionnaire is complete, a LEED project manager will conduct an on-site interview and site investigation with the building's management team, owner, and engineering staff. The goal of the day-long meeting is to obtain the information necessary for the more detailed feasibility study. Information collected in the questionnaire and during the on-site visit includes the following:

‣ **Building population** (full-time and part-time occupants). This number is important when calculating energy and water usage.

‣ **Stormwater management.** The analysis addresses whether stormwater mitigation and graywater reuse are in effect and whether the installation of a new system is cost-effective.

‣ **Parking and public transportation.** Credits can be achieved for proximity to public transportation and employee incentives related to alternative work strategies.

‣ **Baseline water use.** Establishing a baseline and performing preliminary calculations can help the owner address the feasibility and benefits of a partial or complete fixture retrofit.

‣ **Energy Star and building systems.** Retroactive commissioning and energy efficiency are two of the most important aspects of green retrofits and LEED certification. The results of an Energy Star analysis are key components of evaluating the likelihood of achieving certification under both Energy Star and LEED-EBOM. Management teams and building engineers are frequently encouraged to apply for Energy Star certification before completing the more extensive LEED-EBOM assessment.

‣ **Operations and maintenance.** Standard operating practices are discussed with the management and engineering team with respect to hardscape and landscape management, pest control, indoor air quality guidelines, parameters for facility alterations and additions, waste stream recycling, janitorial procedures, lighting and energy use, and other relevant factors. The team is encouraged to document such practices in a building policy or plan.

‣ **Indoor air quality management.** The LEED-EBOM rating system suggests that buildings utilize Minimum Efficiency Reporting Value (MERV) 13 filters and have in place a documented program for indoor air quality. The gap analysis determines whether the property can comply with the MERV requirement and what will be needed to document an acceptable program.

‣ **Construction materials.** The ease of achieving credit for materials often depends on whether a building has a single owner-occupant or multiple tenants. In multitenant buildings, tenants' cost sensitivities might make it more difficult to dictate the use of green construction materials and diversion of construction waste from a landfill.

‣ **Furniture and lighting systems.** Current furniture standards as well as standards for future additions or improvements are addressed with regard to low-emitting and recycled materials. Lighting systems are analyzed to identify opportunities for upgrading to more efficient fixtures or bulbs, occupancy sensors, and daylighting solutions.

Certification studies are most readily used if they are user-friendly. Jones Lang LaSalle's Certification Feasibility Study is written to be accessible to those who do not have technical knowledge of building systems. The report scores each point on its feasibility (yes, already complies, easy, difficult, or no) and provides the estimated cost to achieve each credit, if applicable. The report also includes a schedule and indicates whether the project meets all prerequisite requirements for certification.

Helee Hillman, LEED AP, is a project manager in the Project Development Services Division at Jones Lang LaSalle in Chicago, Illinois.

A FEASIBILITY ASSESSMENT AND SUSTAINABLE RETROFIT EVALUATION IN LONDON

SEAN LOCKIE AND PIOTR BERIBECKI

Feasibility and cost-benefit analysis were utilized to determine a retrofit strategy for an existing office building.

Background and Objective

The building is a four-story, 81,000-square-foot (7,525-square-meter) office building on the outskirts of London, England. The owner-occupied building, which was built in the 1970s, required a feasibility assessment and an evaluation of sustainability retrofit options to address the following objectives:

▸ **Objective 1:** Improve the working environment and comfort levels.

▸ **Objective 2:** Reduce energy consumption and CO_2 emissions.

▸ **Objective 3:** Demonstrate the application of low-carbon strategies and renewable energy technologies.

The budget for the major refurbishment was roughly £6 million ($8.8 million), or approximately £800 per square meter ($110 per square foot).

A feasibility study was developed by a multidisciplinary design team assembled by Faithful+Gould. The team then used a multicriteria analysis to create a numerical score, ranking the retrofit options. The analysis considered affordability, maintenance, carbon reduction, and improved comfort. The performance for each potential solution was scored from low to high on a scale of 1 to 10. An equal weighting was applied to all categories, because they represented the same degree of importance to the client and the design team. The individual scores were then summed for the overall score, and the potential solutions for each objective were ranked accordingly.

The analysis allowed the design team to compare the proposed options in terms of both capital costs and carbon emission reduction potential, as well as improvements in comfort levels. The results indicated that the best options to pursue were the incorporation of five features:

▸▸ A high-performance building facade with external shading;

▸▸ A new lighting system with daylight and occupancy sensors;

▸▸ A new zoned heating system;

▸▸ An open plan working environment; and

▸▸ Renewable energy technologies.

Assessing the Options

Next, the Faithful+Gould team defined key performance objectives, in consultation with the owner-occupant, and reviewed each sustainability option against the performance criteria.

OBJECTIVE 1: IMPROVE THE WORKING ENVIRONMENT AND COMFORT LEVELS

The occupants complained that the building had a tendency to overheat during the summer months, and they also felt that the air quality inside could get stuffy. Analysis of the inside temperature over the summer months indicated that for approximately 250 working hours each year, the building temperature exceeded 28°C (82°F) (see figure 1).

After consulting with the client, the design team set a parameter to reduce the number of working hours during which the building exceeded 28°C (82°F) to 45 per year. This is a higher temperature threshold than normal: the high threshold was chosen because the client did not want to increase the building's

Figure 1

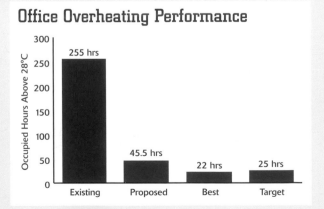

Office Overheating Performance

(Bar chart — Occupied Hours Above 28°C)

- Existing: 255 hrs
- Proposed: 45.5 hrs
- Best: 22 hrs
- Target: 25 hrs

Figure 2

Probable Overheating Sources

	Possible Causes of Overheating	Possible Contributing Share (%)
A	Excessive glazing with ineffective shading and solar control	High: 50+
B	High internal gains from computer equipment	Medium: 20
B	Internal heat gains from office inhabitants	Medium: 20
C	Cellular offices blocking the natural movement of air	Medium: 10

Figure 3

Possible Solutions for Objective 1

Problem	Solution	Capital Costs	Maintenance/ Running Costs	Comment	Rank (1 = Best 5 = Worst)	Overall Score (Minimum 0, Maximum 40)	
OPTIONS SELECTED							
A Ineffective shading and thermal performance	Replace windows with high-efficiency windows and adopt external shading.	High	Low		1	Total	29
						Low Cost	3
						Maintenance	8
						CO_2 Reduction	9
						Comfort	9
B Cellular offices affecting air movement across the floor plate	Demolish existing enclosed offices and move to open plan.	Low	Nil		1	Total	32
						Low Cost	7
						Maintenance	8
						CO_2 Reduction	9
						Comfort	8
OPTIONS REJECTED							
C Excessive overglazing causing overheating	Reduce glazed area.	High	Low	Would reduce daylight levels.	4	Total	19
						Low Cost	6
						Maintenance	7
						CO_2 Reduction	3
						Comfort	3
D Ineffective shading	Install internal blinds.	Low	Medium	Would increase lighting demand.	5	Total	14
						Low Cost	7
						Maintenance	3
						CO_2 Reduction	2
						Comfort	2
E Ineffective shading	Solar control film on the glass.	Low	Medium	Would increase lighting demand and not have desired effect on comfort levels.	5	Total	14
						Low Cost	7
						Maintenance	2
						CO_2 Reduction	3
						Comfort	2
F Ineffective shading	Replace windows with ones that have integral blinds.	High	Medium	Would increase lighting load.	4	Total	23
						Low Cost	5
						Maintenance	6
						CO_2 Reduction	5
						Comfort	7

carbon footprint by utilizing mechanical cooling (air conditioning). It was determined that the client could improve the building's comfort levels by using passive rather than active means.

The origins of overheating were researched and presented to the project team and owner-occupant. Probable overheating sources are presented in figure 2.

The feasibility and cost of each potential solution were studied and scored based on the multicriteria analysis. The results of this exercise are shown in figure 3.

In order to achieve the objective of improving comfort within the budget without increasing the carbon emissions, the following options were selected:

▸▸ **Option A,** Replace windows with high-performance glazing and adopt external shading. Capital cost estimate: £2.4 million ($3.5 million).

Figure 4

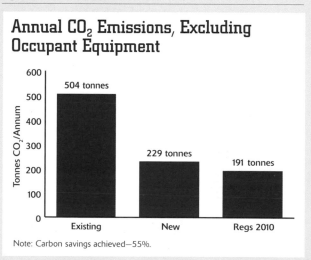

Annual CO_2 Emissions, Excluding Occupant Equipment

Note: Carbon savings achieved—55%.

Option B, Remove the cellular office partitions (permanent walls that divide the floor space into individual offices), and adopt an open office plan for cross-ventilation purposes. Capital cost estimate: £700,000 ($1.02 million).

OBJECTIVE 2: REDUCE ENERGY CONSUMPTION AND CO_2 EMISSIONS

The building had relatively high energy intensity, because of several characteristics:

» An inefficient central plant,

» Uncontrolled heating,

» Poor insulation,

» Single-glazed windows,

» Lighting that did not respond to daylight or occupancy controls, and

» Lack of external shading, resulting in blinds being closed most of the time, thereby causing excessive lighting use.

These factors had a major implication on the electricity load and overall building carbon footprint. Figure 4 shows the current carbon emissions from the building (excluding office equipment) and the proposed target.

The feasibility and cost of each potential solution were studied and scored based on the multicriteria analysis. The results of this exercise are shown in figure 5.

The following option was selected as the solution for objective 2:

Figure 5

Possible Solutions for Objective 2

	Problem	Solution	Capital Costs	Maintenance/ Running Costs	Comment	Rank (1= Best 5 = Worst)	Overall Score (Minimum 0, Maximum 40)	
OPTIONS SELECTED								
A	Poor user control on heating plant	Replace boilers and improve efficiency of zoning.	Medium	Low	Boilers are 55% efficient and have reached the end of economic life.	1	Total Low Cost Maintenance CO_2 Reduction Comfort	32 7 8 9 8
OPTIONS REJECTED								
B	Office equipment generating high amounts of internal heat gain	Move to "thin client" server solution to reduce the cooling load.	High	Low	To pursue later. Would require entire refresh of company's IT system.	4	Total Low Cost Maintenance CO_2 Reduction Comfort	21 3 6 6 6

a. A "thin client" computer network uses the central server for processing activities, reducing the energy requirements for each individual computer and leading to system efficiencies. It may bring significant reductions in the cooling load and in electricity consumption.

Figure 7

Implemented and Rejected Systems

Technology	Displaced Fuel	System Size (kW)	Cost Rate (£)	Capital Cost (£)	Energy Savings (kWh/yr)	Energy Cost Savings (£/yr)	Simple Payback (years)	CO_2 Emissions Savings (kg/yr)
IMPLEMENTED SYSTEMS								
Biomass	Gas	100	500/kW	50,000	185,000	9,250	5	35,890
Free Cooling	Electricity	28	1,250/kW	35,000	12,000	1,560	22	5,064
Photovoltaics	Electricity	45	800/m²	260,064	36,180	4,703	55	15,268
Solar Hot Water System	Gas	13	900/m²	16,200	10,450	523	31	2,027
Totals				361,264	243,630	16,036	23	58,249
REJECTED SYSTEMS								
GSHP	Gas	50	1,600/kW	80,000	85,000	4,250	19	16,490
Micro CHP	Gas	5.5	610/kW	3,355	−49,544	−2,477	—	−9,612
	Electricity	12.5	610/kW	7,625	35,100	4,703	5.5	14,812
Wind	Electricity	6	3,750/kW	22,500	15,596	523	11	2,582
Totals				113,480	85,152	8,363	14	28,272

Note: GSHP = ground-source heat pump. CHP = combined heat and power. — = not available.

Option A, Upgrade the heating system central plant, user controls, and zoning. Capital cost estimate: £1.8 million ($2.65 million).

OBJECTIVE 3: DEMONSTRATE THE APPLICATION OF LOW-CARBON STRATEGIES AND RENEWABLE ENERGY TECHNOLOGIES

The applicability of low-carbon space conditioning and on-site renewable energy systems was considered. The client was interested in testing several of these systems and had established a £500,000 ($745,000) budget. The systems considered are shown in figure 6; figure 7 shows an evaluation of their specific financial parameters and their estimated carbon reduction.

After establishing the feasibility of each system, multicriteria analysis was used to determine the best systems. The following options were selected as the solutions for objective 3:

Figure 6

Possible Solutions for Objective 3

Demonstration Renewables	Solution	Capital Costs	Maintenance/ Running Costs	Comment	Rank (1 = Best, 5 = Worst)	Overall Score (Minimum 0, Maximum 40)	
OPTIONS SELECTED							
A Heating	Biomass boilers	Low	Low	Adopted because it demonstrated good value for money.	1	Total	34
						Low Cost	8
						Maintenance	7
						CO_2 Reduction	10
						Comfort	9
B Free cooling	Free cooling system	High	Low	Overall payback was 22 years, longer than client's acceptable payback period. However, client wanted to demonstrate the technology, and improved comfort levels for building occupants, which was not considered in the payback calculation, was seen as worth the investment.	4	Total	21
						Low Cost	4
						Maintenance	8
						CO_2 Reduction	4
						Comfort	5
C Electricity productions	Photovoltaic array	High	Low	Overall payback was 55 years, based on current energy pricing. Had a double positive by acting as a shading device. Client wanted to monitor electricity generation from the system to advise its clients on future projects. Client expects electricity rates to increase, reducing the payback period.	3	Total	24
						Low Cost	5
						Maintenance	9
						CO_2 Reduction	8
						Comfort	2
D Hot water	Solar thermal hot water	High	Low	Overall payback was 31 years, and hot-water demand is small. Client wanted to demonstrate the technology.	4	Total	21
						Low Cost	5
						Maintenance	9
						CO_2 Reduction	3
						Comfort	4
OPTIONS REJECTED							
E Cooling/ heating	Ground-source heat pumps	High	Low	Ground conditions were inappropriate. Also, by improving window U-values, installing a biomass boiler, and adopting free cooling, option would be unnecessary.	5	Total	14
						Low Cost	2
						Maintenance	2
						CO_2 Reduction	5
						Comfort	5
F Heat and power	Combined heat and power	Low	Medium	Summer heat demand is insufficient (a precondition for viability). Also not compatible with the technologies adopted.	5	Total	23
						Low Cost	7
						Maintenance	4
						CO_2 Reduction	4
						Comfort	8
G Electricity	Wind turbines	High	Low	Wind speeds were insufficient. Also, there is no appropriate site for a medium-scale wind turbine.	5	Total	13
						Low Cost	2
						Maintenance	7
						CO_2 Reduction	2
						Comfort	2

- ▶▶ **Option A, Biomass boilers,** which switches boilers from gas-fired to biomass burning. Capital cost estimate: £50,000 ($75,000).

- ▶▶ **Option B, Free cooling,** which uses low external air temperatures to chill water for cooling high-temperature computer rooms and office buildings. Capital cost estimate: £35,000 ($52,000).

- ▶▶ **Option C, Photovoltaic array,** which will both provide renewable energy to the building and act as a building shading system. Capital cost estimate: £260,000 ($388,000).

- ▶▶ **Option D, Solar thermal** hot-water system. Capital cost estimate: £16,200 ($24,000).

Although options B and D entail long payback periods, the client wanted to utilize the systems in order to test and measure their performance for future installations. Option C also entails a long payback period, but the client felt that the system's dual usage as both an energy-producing and a solar-shading device, along with the risk of higher electricity rates in the future, justified the investment.

Sean Lockie is a director of Sustainability at Faithful+Gould's London office. Piotr Berebecki is a London-based sustainability and energy consultant at Faithful+Gould.

Retrofit Timing and Duration

The timing and duration of the retrofit will depend on the owner's objectives. A number of factors can influence timing, including pending regulations of energy efficiency, asset repositioning needs, and the competitive environment.

An opportune timing decision is illustrated by the retrofit of 1801 McGill College in Montreal, Canada, profiled in a case study in chapter 9. The building owners and management completed an energy efficiency retrofit as part of an overall repositioning of the asset, timed to take advantage of an anchor tenant's departure and market concerns about rising utility prices. The retrofit and the ensuing leasing campaign, which emphasized the building's new energy efficiency features, brought occupancy up from approximately a third of building square footage to stabilized levels and resulted in substantial rental rate increases.

The expense of a building retrofit may create a need to implement and complete the renovation in a relatively short time. An efficient project schedule was a key objective for LCOR in the green retrofit of 545 Madison Avenue in New York City. LCOR was performing a gut rehabilitation of an office building at one of the most expensive addresses in midtown Manhattan. The project, which has attained LEED Gold certification, was implemented in a highly efficient time frame for a gut retrofit (21 months)

in order to optimize project economies. (See the detailed case study in chapter 9.)

Alternatively, the owners of owner-occupied properties and stabilized office buildings tenanted under long-term leases frequently take a longer-term view of greening their assets, implementing a more gradual sustainability plan. Adobe Systems views green retrofit efforts at its headquarters complex as ongoing and continues to add green initiatives to its operating and long-term capital budgets years after winning LEED Platinum certification. Similarly, the One Beacon Street property in Boston, Massachusetts, continues to implement new green operating protocols after achieving LEED certification.

For all green retrofit initiatives, whatever the timing or duration, the project's objectives, scope, and timeline should be communicated clearly to building tenants, and tenants should receive frequent updates regarding progress and target dates that may affect them.

Integrated Planning, Design, and Documentation

Integrated planning and design processes are crucial to the success of a green retrofit initiative, as is the maintenance of detailed project documentation. The detailed case studies in chapter 9 demonstrate that project planning should engage multifunctional project teams representing owners as well as all disciplines involved in design, construction, and

operation. It also is helpful to include leasing and finance personnel in the planning process, to ensure that the retrofit program appeals to current and prospective tenants and that the strategy is a cost-effective one. The use of integrated planning and design protocols in the context of green retrofits is discussed in greater depth in chapter 4.

For office properties that are aiming for voluntary green certification, a checklist is invaluable. After determining the rating system and target certification level (if applicable), the project team should use the rating system's points and prerequisites as a basis for developing the checklist. By doing so the project team will minimize the risk of overlooking any required points, which would jeopardize the certification and lead to expensive alterations and improvements to correct the omission.

Maintaining detailed project checklists and supporting records is critical to achieving project certification. Project documentation needs are discussed by Tom Paladino and Rod Wille in chapter 4, as well as in many of the case studies, including those detailing the retrofits of the Christman Building, 1801 McGill College, and 545 Madison Avenue.

Setting a Retrofit Budget

The budget for a green retrofit should reflect the owner's objectives, the requirements of the chosen retrofit strategy, and the extent to which the retrofit is expected to produce enhanced leasing, tenant retention, and reduced operating costs over an appropriate holding period. The time frame of the retrofit will have a significant effect on the size of the budget. If substantial building system upgrades are contemplated within a limited period, significant capital outlays are likely to be required. In such instances, financing for retrofit outlays will need to be obtained from owner equity, capital reserves, debt refinancing, or alternative vehicles.

Chapter 5 discusses the financing of green retrofits, including innovative new mechanisms that limit the need for upfront capital (such as financing obtained through a contract with an energy services company) or that provide extended repayment periods (such as on-bill financing). Chapter 5 also discusses government and utility company incentives that may offset retrofit costs. Most of the retrofits profiled in this volume were paid for with owner equity, but a number made use of government and utility subsidies to offset costs. The use of incentives is illustrated in the Christman Building, 545 Madison Avenue, and 1801 McGill College case studies.

A strategy for minimizing the initial size of a green retrofit budget is to integrate the retrofit strategy into ongoing building operations and capital budgeting protocols. This is best accomplished by extending the retrofit program over multiple budget cycles, allowing for green-related

Among improvements to the Campus Office Building at the McDonald's Corporation world headquarters in Oakbrook, Illinois, was the installation of additional meters to closely monitor building systems efficiency.

spending under the appropriate line items in the operating and capital budget. An office property can begin a green retrofit with a minimal capital outlay, focusing on no-cost or low-cost energy efficiency measures, such as training facility staff on the proper operation of building equipment and upgrading lighting. Green procurement and building maintenance protocols for janitorial, landscaping, and pest management services, and the procurement of green paper products and cleaning supplies can also be initiated for no or minimal upfront costs. (See chapter 6 for a detailed discussion of green building operations.)

Two basic strategies minimize the costs of a green building retrofit over time:

▸▸ **INCORPORATING SUSTAINABILITY** into the ongoing repair and maintenance budget. Sustainability should be an integral part of building operations. The operating budget should include a line item for preventive maintenance and building system optimization. The repair and maintenance budget should be used to ensure that building systems continue to operate as efficiently as possible, minimizing energy use and extending the useful life of equipment.

▸▸ **REPLACING EXISTING BUILDING SYSTEMS** on the basis of economic viability. Although an energy audit might reveal inefficiencies in a building system, it may not always be economically viable to replace an existing system until the end of its useful life. Therefore, the replacement of a building system or systems might optimally be addressed in the context of the property's long-term capital budget. This strategy is best for a building with a long-term approach to the green retrofit process. Note, however, that substantial utility usage and cost savings may warrant the replacement of a building system before the end of its useful

UTILIZING LIFE-CYCLE COST ANALYSIS FOR GREEN OFFICE RETROFITTING

EVA STERNER

Even though there are obvious advantages to the use of life-cycle cost analysis (LCCA) for evaluating investments, first-cost considerations have remained the primary litmus test for many building owners in evaluating the economic acceptability of competing design alternatives. In the European Union, the use of LCCA has been given a push with the passage of the EPBD, which requires that the application documents for the mandatory EPCs include LCCA for energy conservation measures.

Important considerations for the use of LCCA:

▸▸ **USE LCCA PRIMARILY** with energy and water conservation measures. LCCA is best utilized when evaluating potential investments that have an ongoing cost component, such as regular utility payments. For each potential investment, the energy savings potential can lead to substantially different calculations of financial return, thus identifying the superior investment.

▸▸ **ESTABLISH THE CURRENT PERFORMANCE BASELINE.** The first step in calculating the energy- or water-saving potential of retrofit components is to establish the comparative property baseline before the retrofit. Estimated energy or water savings from retrofit components can be compared with the baseline, making it possible to measure the energy and water savings.

▸▸ **SUPPORT LCCA WITH MODELING** of energy and water performance. When evaluating potential retrofit investments and their proposed energy and water savings, building performance modeling programs can support LCCA results.

▸▸ **CONSIDER COMBINING LCCA** with life-cycle analysis. LCCA can also be combined with environmental impact assessments such as life-cycle analysis, to identify which components have the greatest potential for reducing environmental impacts at a competitive cost level. Life-cycle analysis evaluates the environmental costs and outcomes associated with developing, using, and disposing of a product or a system.

Eva Sterner, Ph.D., is a managing director with Watts International in Stockholm, Sweden.

life, especially in periods of rising utility costs. In general, the decision to replace building systems should be validated by financial analysis that demonstrates that the replacement will produce an economically appropriate outcome.

COST AND BENEFIT ASSESSMENT OF GREEN RETROFITS

When a project team is considering the costs and benefits of implementing retrofit options, the primary financial analysis metric should be the project's return over its holding period or useful life. A key tenet of green real estate is maximizing the resource efficiency of the built environment. To do so, property owners and developers will wish to consider the value of building systems that may have higher upfront costs but offer an increase in long-term value through operating savings and revenue enhancements.

In order to measure and value green retrofit options, appropriate financial analysis tools should be utilized:

▸▸ **SIMPLE PAYBACK ANALYSIS**. Simple payback is a tool that measures how long it will take the cumulative value gained from an investment (for example, energy savings) to equal the initial investment. Expressed as a time period, simple payback is a good tool for small investments with quick paybacks and as an initial screen for larger investments. Simple payback is not suitable for complex investments with irregular costs and savings, and it does not account for the time value of money.

▸▸ **DISCOUNTED CASH FLOW METHODS**. Discounted cash flow methods, including discounted cash flow (DCF) analysis and life-cycle cost analysis (LCCA), are more robust methods of quantifying the costs and benefits of green office retrofits over time. DCF and LCCA methods are similar in that both rely on projecting the capital and operating costs for a retrofit project over time and calculating the project's net present value and internal rate of return. LCCA analyses are frequently restricted to the costs and energy savings associated with the retrofit initiative over a desired holding period; they are especially useful for owner-occupied or government buildings. LCCA has come into wider use in the European Union in response to the European Commission's EPBD, which requires the presentation of LCCA for energy conservation measures in the application documents for mandatory building energy performance certificates (EPCs). (For additional guidance on using LCCA for an office retrofit, see the sidebar by Eva Sterner.)

DCF analysis frequently uses a broader framework than does LCCA. In a DCF model, the costs and benefits of a retrofit project are related to a building's leasing performance, cash flow, and sale potential over an anticipated holding period. DCF analysis, a widely used financial assessment tool, is more frequently used by the owners of investment real estate. Such analyses consider not only the costs and energy savings of green retrofits but also the probable effect of the retrofits on project lease-up, tenant retention, long-term capital replacement and maintenance costs, and holding risk.

If the owner desires, both DCF and LCCA methods can be modified to incorporate equipment disposal costs (an approach recommended by the U.S. Department of Energy in its LCCA guidelines) and to quantify long-term environmental costs or occupant productivity gains.

Unlike simple payback, DCF and LCCA analyses account for the time value of money and are suitable for comparing complex investments with irregular costs and savings. For more information on financial calculations associated with green office retrofits, see chapter 5.

NOTE

1 The levels of an energy audit do not have precise boundaries. They are general categories that outline the type of analysis that is completed in each stage of the audit.

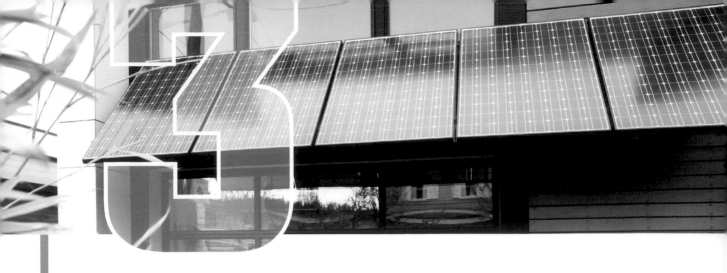

Elements of Green Office Retrofits

GEORGE VAVAROUTSOS AND LEANNE TOBIAS

The elements of a green office retrofit encompass all aspects of a renovation project, including the site and grounds, the building envelope, the mechanical and electrical systems, and the interiors. Because implementation of green retrofitting strategies requires the involvement of multiple members of the renovation team, project owners and developers are advised to plan for green features from the earliest stages and to rely on the integrated design and construction principles detailed in chapter 4.

EVALUATING SITE AND CLIMATE CONDITIONS

A green office retrofit plan should be specific to the site, structure, and climate zone of the proposed project. To maximize the energy reduction potential of a green retrofit, it is necessary to evaluate the structure's siting and climate conditions. A number of passive strategies (lighting, heating, cooling, and ventilation) can be used in a retrofit, but climate analysis is needed in order to evaluate which strategies are most applicable. Evaluation criteria should include the following:

▸▸ **SOLAR ORIENTATION**. A sun path diagram can be used to evaluate the building's sun exposure. Information from the diagram can be used to measure the potential impact of solar radiation on the building; indicate

opportunities for solar shading, passive heating and cooling, and daylighting; and assess the increased cooling requirements that the exposure may place on the structure.

▸▸ **TOPOGRAPHICAL AND OTHER OBSTRUCTIONS**. Sun exposure hours, shadowing from obstructions or buildings, wind access for ventilation, wind protection, and other local factors will affect the structure's energy efficiency and the comfort of occupants.

▸▸ **CLIMATE REGION**. Climate conditions (temperature and humidity) are a dynamic force affecting the building. Identifying and evaluating the local climate region classification aids in determining the expected heating and cooling loads, and the potential for savings from passive solar, ventilation, and cooling strategies.

The project team should work with qualified architecture and engineering firms that can develop this information and use it to evaluate the potential effectiveness of specific options. The results of this evaluation should help determine some of the specific green retrofit strategies that can be employed at the site.

GREEN LANDSCAPING STRATEGIES

Green sites incorporate landscaping that minimizes stormwater runoff, conserves water usage, and is compatible with local climatic conditions. Green site creation strategies to capture stormwater and reduce runoff include the installation of retention ponds and bioswales (vegetated channels that capture, store, and slowly filter stormwater, allowing it to be reabsorbed into the water table); the installation of pervious pavements or permeable surface treatment, including vegetation; and the harvesting and reuse of rainwater.

The extensive use of native or adapted plantings, especially those that minimize the need for supplemental irrigation, can help both to reduce runoff and to conserve water. Xeriscaping, the use of drought-tolerant plantings, is particularly useful for dry climates and is being employed extensively throughout the southwestern United States and in similar climatic zones. Similarly, hydrophilic plantings can be considered for wet-humid zones that are prone to frequent rains or face typhoon seasons. Because green landscaping incorporates plants that are climatically specific (species that will naturally thrive in the climate), it frequently requires less maintenance than conventional landscaping and therefore may prove more cost-effective over time. Sustainable plantings can also be designed to provide cost-effective seasonal color to maximize a property's aesthetic appeal. (For key approaches to developing a sustainable site, see the sidebar by Mary Vogel).

Landscaping can also shield the building from wind penetration and shade it from

A new tenant buildout on the top floor of the historic 14-story Joseph Vance Building in Seattle.

solar heat gain in the summer. In areas with variable seasons, native or adaptive deciduous trees that lose their leaves in the winter are ideal for reducing summer sun and maximizing winter daylighting. The concept of "vertical landscaping"—the use of plantings on the building exterior—is used frequently in southeast Asia and in Mexico to shade building exteriors and provide visual appeal. Both conventional and vertical landscaping can also serve as a tenant or public amenity.

As discussed in the sidebar by Mary Vogel, a voluntary certification system for sustainable sites is being developed in the United States. Initial guidelines and performance benchmarks are scheduled be released in 2009; the voluntary certification system is expected to be introduced in 2011 and eventually incorporated into the U.S. Green Building Council's Leadership in Energy and Environmental Design (LEED) certification system.

CREATING A GREEN SITE FOR A GREEN OFFICE RENOVATION

MARY VOGEL

Not all green is "green." Ironically, a building may now be greener than the site it sits on—especially if that site is conventionally landscaped. Even if a building incorporates green plants, it could probably do more to protect, restore, and regenerate the ecosystem, in turn enhancing natural air and water filtration and cleaning, microclimate regulation, and human health and well-being.

A voluntary certification system for sites, the Sustainable Sites Initiative (SSI) is being created through an interdisciplinary effort of the American Society of Landscape Architects, the Lady Bird Johnson Wildflower Center, and the United States Botanic Garden. SSI has the potential to be a major catalyst for change in landscape architecture and do for landscapes what the LEED rating system is doing for buildings. SSI addresses soils, hydrology, vegetation, materials, and human health and well-being. "SSI Guidelines and Performance Benchmarks" was released in 2009. The rating system is due out in 2011 and will be incorporated into future versions of LEED.

While it may not be possible to achieve all of the goals in the SSI on an existing developed site, project teams on retrofits of office buildings should consider such environmentally sound approaches as native plant palettes, rain gardens or xeriscapes, green streets, and the use of local materials and pervious surfaces. Planting and landscapes can balance the natural and built worlds and help people to feel more connected to the environment.

MARY VOGEL, PLANGREEN, PORTLAND, OREGON

A bioswale installed at the River East Technology Center as part of the building retrofit in Portland, Oregon.

moisture because of its extensive root systems that extend three to ten feet or more into the ground. In contrast, the root zone of turf grass typically extends only about three to four inches. Deep-rooted native plants effectively stabilize soils and prevent erosion along steep slopes. Reduced maintenance needs of such landscapes not only save money but also reduce air, water, and noise pollution. Native plant landscapes also provide habitat for native and migrating birds, butterflies, and insects.

Native Plant Landscapes

A site that is sustainably landscaped will produce substantially less stormwater runoff than a conventional landscape. Native vegetation enhances both absorption of rainfall and evaporation of soil

Rain Gardens

Rain gardens help to protect water quality and provide direct environmental benefits by intercepting rain, acting as a natural

BUILDING ENVELOPE

Also referred to as the building shell, the building envelope consists of all building components that separate a building's interior from the external environment. By controlling the effects of moisture, heat (or lack thereof), light, and sound on building interiors, the envelope is crucial in maintaining desired interior comfort conditions for occupants. It is also crucial in determining the maximum potential for overall building performance.

Components of the building envelope include foundations, exterior walls, windows, roof, exterior doors, and floors. In most developed societies, office buildings were traditionally constructed with load-bearing exterior walls of masonry that featured openings for windows and doors.[1] Starting in the mid-20th century, the curtain wall—a non-load-bearing facade that creates a continuous exterior barrier (a curtain)—became very popular in office building construction. The

---

filter, and preventing flooding by capturing rainwater before it reaches impervious sidewalk surfaces. They typically incorporate native plants that are adaptable to varied drainage conditions. Rain gardens reduce the effects of drought and filter pollutants such as sediment, phosphorous, nitrogen, heavy metals, bacteria, greases, and oils.

Rain gardens can soften and enhance paved areas, unifying a group of buildings and providing pedestrians protection from the sun in a shaded, planted, sidewalk amenity. In addition, rain gardens increase biodiversity by providing habitats for birds, butterflies, and other pollinators. For ease of maintenance they should include native trees, grasses, rushes, ferns, and shrubs. Native wildflowers can be added for both their beauty and their value to pollinators. For wet or hurricane-prone climates, rain gardens can be used strategically with hydrophilic perennial plants that will thrive during the rainy season and tolerate the dry season with minimal drip irrigation or no irrigation.

Bioswales

Rain gardens installed in long, linear spaces such as a parking lot median or a planting strip between the sidewalk and curb are often called bioswales. Bioswales are designed as drainage courses, with gently sloped sides along a wide and shallow ditch. The water's flow path is designed to maximize the time water spends in the swale, thereby maximizing water infiltration and the trapping of pollutants. The drainage components and plant selection will affect the breakdown of pollutants. Runoff from parking lots and streets is usually more polluted than that from an office building, so designing landscaping bioswales along sidewalks, streets, and parking lots will have the most impact.

Xeriscapes

Although rain gardens and bioswales are useful for areas with rainfall, xeriscapes are appropriate for areas with dry or desert conditions. A xeriscape is a landscaped area that is specifically designed to withstand drought conditions and reduce water consumption. It should not be confused with zeroscaping, which uses rocks in lieu of plants to create a landscape that requires little water. Xeriscapes use native, water-efficient plants that can be grouped based on water needs to facilitate efficient maintenance.

Green Streets

The project team should consider partnering with a local jurisdiction to create a "green street" in front of a retrofitted building or development. Green streets often include features such as street trees, bioswales, native plantings, and special paving materials that allow surface water infiltration and limit runoff. Portland, Oregon, has been a leader in encouraging the creation of green streets. The city's Bureau of Environmental Services has a public-private agreement form that might be useful in crafting green street agreements with other local jurisdictions.

Some cities now consider rain gardens, native plant landscapes, and green streets to be part of the "green infrastructure" that will be critical in addressing climate change. Green infrastructure can include natural areas, parks and trees, and engineered components, like green streets and other landscapes that manage stormwater and add many other benefits to the environment.

Mary Vogel is the principal of PlanGreen in Portland, Oregon.

curtain wall merges exterior walls, windows, and doors into one building element and allows for greater use of glass in the facade.

Whether an office building features a load-bearing or a curtain wall design, the envelope plays a significant role in the building's energy performance, dictating how the building functions in the local climate region as well as what operation and maintenance protocols are needed. Envelope components work together to control and regulate the impact of the outside environment on the building's lighting, heating, cooling, and ventilation needs, and play a key role in determining the structure's energy efficiency.

Evaluating the overall performance of the building envelope is therefore one of the first steps in undertaking a green retrofit. If the objective is to improve energy efficiency, lower building operating costs, and reduce greenhouse gas (GHG) emissions, the greatest energy weaknesses of the envelope should be identified and prioritized for improvement.

The renovated office building of Adobe Systems in San Francisco, originally constructed in 1904, achieved a LEED-EB Platinum rating.

Roofing and Walls

The roof and walls of the structure are the primary components responsible for keeping out moisture and reducing heat transfer between building interiors and the outdoor environment. If either of these systems fails to perform as designed, the effectiveness of other measures to improve building energy efficiency will be diminished. Uncontrolled air and moisture infiltration through wall and roof seams and penetrations should be minimized or eliminated. A building energy audit and a property conditions assessment together should evaluate the performance of roofs and walls, and identify any deficiencies. (See chapter 2 for a detailed discussion of the role of energy audits and property conditions assessments in green office retrofits.) The project team should focus on addressing these deficiencies before undertaking any other improvements or upgrades.

IMPROVING BUILDING INSULATION IN ROOFING AND WALLS

Insulation slows heat transfer between conditioned and unconditioned spaces, including building exteriors. Generally, improving the insulation of the roof and walls reduces the energy required to heat and cool a building.[2]

Heat transfer through the building's roof and walls can be substantial, but it may be difficult to add insulation during a retrofit. Insulation is typically installed within wall, roof, and ceiling cavities during construction. During the planning process, the project team should evaluate opportunities to improve building insulation and determine the relative value of undertaking insulation upgrades versus other options. The building's use, design, and local climate conditions will influence the type and location of insulating materials that should be installed, if any.

In choosing insulation, the project team should utilize sustainable insulating materials wherever possible. Materials such as cellulose, made from recycled paper products coated with a nontoxic fire- and mold-resistant compound, or batt insulation made from recycled cotton are environmentally and thermally sound insulation products. For rigid board insulation, the project team should try to identify products that are not manufactured with chlorofluorocarbons (CFCs) or hydrochlorofluorocarbons (HCFCs), which are damaging to the ozone layer.[3] (For more information on sustainable building materials, see the sidebar by Anica Landreneau, Amy Fabry, Nita Tuvesson, Leigh Stringer, and Jodi Williams.)

Depending on the unique needs of the structure, opportunities to improve building insulation abound:

▸▸ **IMPROVING ROOF INSULATION**. Conventional office buildings typically feature a flat or low-slope roof. If the roof will be improved as part of the retrofit, additional insulation can be installed beneath the exterior surface layers. Additionally, friction-fit (batt) and foam insulations can be installed on the underside of the building roof or at the surface of the thermal envelope. It may also be possible to install a radiant barrier—a single reflective layer above the insulation that deflects unwanted heat radiated from the roof to the building interiors.

▸▸ **ADDING INSULATION TO EXTERIOR WALLS**. For buildings with masonry walls, insulation layers can be added on the building exterior. Rigid board insulation, made with polyisocyanurate or extruded polystyrene, can be attached to exterior walls and then covered with a protective barrier, such as metal siding panels or stucco. This option is best for projects in which the aesthetic qualities of the building's exterior walls are to be updated while the energy performance of the structure is improved.

▸▸ **ADDING INSULATION TO INTERIOR WALLS**. Insulation can be added to building wall cavities. Materials such as cellulose, mineral fiber, spray foams, or insulating granules can be added to increase the walls' insulating qualities. This is particularly important for older

STRATEGIES FOR SUSTAINABLE INTERIORS

ANICA LANDRENEAU, AMY FABRY, NITA TUVESSON, LEIGH STRINGER, AND JODI WILLIAMS

Green interiors are created by using an appropriate mix of design, technology, and operational "best practice" strategies that help maximize the building's energy performance, enable worker productivity, and reduce the building's carbon footprint. Flexible and intelligent space planning, coupled with responsible decisions on workplace materials and renovation practices, are key components of interior sustainability.

Sustainable Space Planning

Each space planning solution must be unique to the constraints and opportunities of the existing facility, and customized to the requirements of the occupants. The key components of a successful space plan include the following:

» Good programming;
» Flexible spaces;
» A focus on occupant productivity; and
» Leveraging technology to improve efficiency.

GOOD PROGRAMMING

When planning to remodel, the first step is to set goals that meet anticipated organizational needs. This step will provide the basis for design and ensure that the space is used efficiently and effectively. During the programming process, users should be engaged to determine the future number of occupants, to understand the work process, and to highlight critical space adjacencies for staff and facilities. The programming process provides an opportunity for the planning team to lay out the floor area more efficiently and to develop flexible planning strategies that may reduce the total square footage required, while still allowing for organizational growth and changing requirements over time.

FLEXIBLE SPACES

A simple way to achieve flexibility is to maximize the use of open space with minimal hard-walled areas like private offices and conference rooms. By defining a space with systems furniture, plants, or soft seating, the cost of reconfiguring space is greatly reduced as is the amount of demolition waste in the future. Open-space plans work well for organizations without significant need for private space and for organizations that reconfigure their space regularly.

Open offices are generally considered more green in that they require less artificial light, material use, and ventilation; however, in the absence of good space planning and design,

open offices are prone to visual and acoustical distractions. Balancing the need to reduce hard-wall construction and to minimize distraction is possible but requires thoughtful space planning, such as arranging enclosed spaces around the building core (rather than at the perimeter, which blocks natural light in open areas) and grouping open work areas into small clusters, reducing density and noise. Acoustical challenges can be mitigated through such design strategies as the isolation of noisy spaces, careful design of ductwork to minimize noise associated with open ceiling spaces, the use of acoustically absorptive materials, and the use of white-noise generators.

Providing a variety of spaces where workers can move throughout the workspace to support different tasks can also improve productivity. The most common way to provide flexibility in a space plan is to develop modular space standards, a defined set of space footprints for frequently used configurations. For example, an organization may offer two sizes of open workstation and two sizes of enclosed office, rather than many different sizes based on seniority. Ideally, space types should be dimensions that are factors of one another. For example, an organization might select workstations that are half the size of offices so that the space for two workstations could be converted easily into an enclosed office. Modularity not only provides more efficient space use but also minimizes waste when changes to the space plan are required.

Another way to achieve flexibility but still provide enclosed space is to use demountable walls—prefinished, prefitted, movable wall systems. Although the upfront costs of demountable walls can be greater than those of traditional interior partition assemblies, organizations that regularly change their space layout see a quick payback. The use of demountable walls eliminates the environmental cost of deconstructing, reconstructing, and disposing of hard-constructed walls.

Additionally, organizations should consider using raised floor systems to enhance office space flexibility. Raised floors allow for rapid floor-plan modifications, delivering information technology and power infrastructure where necessary. Using displacement ventilation in conjunction with raised floor systems allows heating and cooling to be controlled individually by building occupants. Displacement ventilation systems, which introduce fresh air supply at or near the floor area, require less energy than traditional systems, which both supply cool air and exhaust air at the ceiling level. Displacement ventilation allows for temperature stratification; cool air is supplied from below, creating comfortable temperatures in occupied zones. Warmer air rises to the ceiling, allowing unwanted heat and contaminants to be exhausted through ceiling air returns. These systems cool less air volume than traditional systems and therefore use less energy to maintain a comfortable indoor temperature.

A FOCUS ON OCCUPANT PRODUCTIVITY

In addition to providing flexibility, a critical factor for greening the workplace is designing space to support human health and productivity. Good design can help increase worker productivity by providing visual connections to daylight and nature; opportunities for regular movement, exercise, and interaction with others; and sensory change and variation—all qualities that are sought in a green workspace. Good space planning can also help reduce or eliminate productivity inhibitors such as audio and visual distractions and other interruptions. Enabling occupants to control light and temperature can also enhance productivity, as can other interior design strategies:

▶▶ **Establishing connections** to daylight and nature. Direct and indirect connections to nature have been shown to increase both individual well-being and productivity. Elements that help connect users to nature include access to daylight and clear views of outdoor natural space from within the workspace. Water features, gardens, and interior plants also create natural connections for workers, as well as providing the sensory changes and variability that enhance productivity and morale.

▶▶ **Encouraging exercise,** movement, and collaboration. In addition to providing exercise opportunities such as walking trails or fitness centers, offices can promote worker health through space planning. For example, centrally located and attractive staircases encourage employees to use the stairs, which reduces the energy needed to run elevators and encourages collaboration and exercise—stimulating creativity and improving health.

▶▶ **Allowing occupants to control** lighting and temperature. Numerous studies indicate that building occupants are more satisfied and productive when they can control their immediate lighting and temperature. Individually controlled task lighting is one strategy to increase individual comfort. In interiors without under-floor air supply, it is not typically possible to provide individual air control. In these situations, it is recommended that temperature controls be provided to smaller zones, to maximize occupants' control of interior temperatures.

LEVERAGING TECHNOLOGY TO IMPROVE EFFICIENCY

Modern space planning relies heavily on technologies that help people use space and equipment more effectively and efficiently. Technologies are now available that link room scheduling software into the building's automation system, so that lighting, heating, or cooling can be moderated on the basis of occupancy. Occupancy sensors are used frequently in green retrofits to reduce electricity use. Plug-load occupancy sensors can turn off electricity to workstations and shared office equipment overnight. Low-flow fixtures and motion sensors are used commonly to conserve water. The use of technologies that enable telecommuting and virtual collaboration, such as videoconferencing, can help companies reduce their environmental footprint by reducing travel requirements, while simultaneously enhancing worker productivity and employee satisfaction.

The configuration and placement of computer servers and business equipment can reduce energy consumption and increase productivity. The project team should consider providing a central server room, which can be cooled more efficiently than distributed servers. By consolidating printers, copiers, and scanners, or using multifunction devices, companies can reduce energy usage, cool and vent spaces more efficiently, and improve indoor air quality. An additional advantage of centrally located multifunction devices is that they encourage employees to move around the floor—good for productivity and increased interaction and collaboration.

Where spaces have been appropriately designed to provide individual occupant control, some companies are fully integrating building systems down to the occupants' desktops, allowing individual occupants to automatically adjust temperature and lighting controls based on their unique work patterns and preferences. Allowing such control is another way to increase worker productivity and satisfaction. Such strategies can also reduce energy use, especially if occupants are educated about the environmental impact of individual work habits.

Sustainable Indoor Construction Practices

Construction practices during renovations also have a significant effect on indoor environmental quality. It is important to keep materials protected from moisture and debris during construction, so that porous materials do not become vulnerable to mold, mildew, and the particulates that can be released into the airstream during renovation or when the space is occupied.

To ensure appropriate indoor air quality, the sequencing of materials installation is extremely important. Wet materials should always be applied and allowed to cure before dry materials are installed. In this way, when paint outgases as it dries, there is no sink—such as carpet, insulation, or fabrics—to absorb the volatile organic compounds (VOCs) and release them later. Even low-VOC paints off-gas when they are applied. Carpet adhesive should also be low- or no-VOC to minimize or eliminate indoor air quality problems associated with carpet installation. Alternatively, nonadhesive carpet installation alternatives can be sought.

One of the most important construction practices is to maintain a clean job site. Smoking and eating should not be permitted in the space during construction. Debris should be removed daily. Ductwork should be protected by sealing diffusers and return air grilles, or an appropriate filter should be used in the heating, ventilating, and air-conditioning (HVAC) equipment during construction. Filters used during construction should be removed and replaced before the building is occupied. Wet materials that may off-gas, such as carpet adhesive or paint, should be kept in closed containers when not in use. Any final cleaning should be completed with low-emitting and low-toxicity or green cleaning products, to avoid introducing new chemicals into the green workspace.

For more extensive green renovations, a "flush-out" period is recommended before the building is re-occupied to ensure that most emissions from building materials are removed. The flush-out process is conducted by forcing the maximum amount of outdoor air possible through the renovated space, with adequate ventilation, for a recommended duration. (Certification systems typically set flush-out requirements. LEED, for example, requires a minimum of 14,000 cubic feet of outdoor air per square foot.)

The flush-out procedure is important to ensure indoor air quality, because even low-VOC materials can off-gas. Additionally, if building supplies such as carpets or furniture that contain VOCs or formaldehydes cannot be avoided, these materials should be aired out before installation in a well-ventilated, third-party site. If the renovation occurs while the building is occupied, the area to be renovated should be sealed off and construction activities scheduled during periods when occupants are not present. The newly renovated space should be ventilated separately before occupants return.

Sustainable Building Materials

Sustainable building materials are low-impact, durable materials that are sourced, fabricated, or transported with minimal damage to the environment and that minimize or eliminate harmful effects on human health. There are a variety of strategies for using sustainable building materials in a green retrofit, including deconstructing and reusing existing materials, using materials with recycled content, and using rapidly renewable materials, certified wood products, and locally sourced products.

SPECIFYING GREEN MATERIALS

A due diligence review should be conducted by the project team before specifying green materials. Research should be conducted early on to ensure that product documentation is available and supports marketing claims, that materials are appropriate for the intended use, and that installation, fabrication, and maintenance information is readily available. A dynamic spreadsheet will be helpful in tracking this documentation, especially if green building certification will be sought.

Note that not all manufacturers have the necessary documentation to support sustainability product claims. In some markets, especially in international ones, it might be difficult to source products with documentation of sustainability. Given these challenges, it is up to the project team to make smart decisions regarding the environmental and human health effects of the products they select. When specifying materials, the team should consider the following:

▸▸ Is the material necessary or functional for the space?
▸▸ Where does it come from?
▸▸ How it is made?
▸▸ From how far is it transported to the project site?
▸▸ How long will it last?
▸▸ Is it easy to maintain?
▸▸ Can it be recycled or reused?
▸▸ How does it contribute to or detract from indoor air quality?

The performance and aesthetic qualities of many green materials equals—or surpasses—that of traditional materials. In the United States, environmentally friendly materials can be easily sourced as long as the performance criteria are included in the specifications. Some U.S. contractors even automatically use green materials, because there is typically no discernible price difference and it may be easier to maintain stock of only one type of each material. Third-party certifications, such as Green Seal, Green Spec, Green Label Plus, and Floor Score, can assist project teams in specifying appropriate materials. In locations outside the United States where third-party-certified products cannot be found locally, environmentally sensitive materials may still be procured through the global supply chain, although such products may command a premium.

DECONSTRUCTION AS A VALUE PROPOSITION

When possible, the project team should consider deconstruction as an alternative to demolition. Although deconstruction is typically time- and labor-intensive, the practice allows materials to be diverted from landfills. The salvaged materials are sorted and sent to the proper resale or recycling market. The costs associated with deconstruction can be offset at least in part by the minimization of traditional demolition costs and by the value of the materials reclaimed. Salvaged materials may include exterior cladding (glass, bricks), steel, doors, door hardware, millwork, wood paneling, tile or stone, bathroom fixtures, and light fixtures. Some projects are even able to salvage carpet, ceiling grid, or ceiling tiles. Many light fixtures can be removed before deconstruction, cleaned, relamped, and reinstalled in existing and newly constructed office spaces. Some materials can be recycled readily if they are sorted properly during deconstruction and demolition. For example, metal wiring, metal studs, drywall, carpet, and ceiling tiles are all highly recyclable.

REUSING EXISTING MATERIALS

The greenest materials are the ones that do not have to be extracted, manufactured, transported, and reinstalled. Furniture is relatively easy to reuse, but many projects are also able to make use of reused hardware, light fixtures, wood flooring or paneling, and stone.

Furniture is a significant investment that should also be considered for creative reuse when renovating an office. Many furniture lines can be reconfigured to fit today's workplace standards by introducing a minimal number of new parts and pieces. System furniture walls are easily "re-skinned" or reupholstered to create a clean, fresh new look. Wood case goods such as conference tables, desks, and credenzas can be refinished to look like new. If new furnishings are chosen, systems should be selected that are made so that their components can easily be upgraded, reskinned, or replaced in the future, thereby allowing for cost-effective refurbishment.

SPECIFYING RECYCLED MATERIALS

As a result of increasing demand and rising prices for raw materials, many building products contain high levels of recycled content. An additional reason to choose recycled materials is to reduce the negative effects on the environment that result from resource extraction, resource depletion, and unneeded manufacturing.

Recycled content comes in two forms:

▶▶ **Preconsumer materials.** Preconsumer materials contain the byproducts of an industrial or manufactured process and do not reach the hands of the consumer until after they have been reused in a recycled product. For example, an insulation company may take cotton scraps from an apparel factory and turn the material into batt insulation.

▶▶ **Postconsumer materials.** Postconsumer materials are made from products that have already passed through the hands of the consumer. Many carpet and ceiling tile manufacturers are now reclaiming their products at the end

of their initial use to be remanufactured and recycled. This practice saves the manufacturer money and diverts substantial demolition debris from landfill.

SPECIFYING RAPIDLY RENEWABLE MATERIALS

Materials are considered rapidly renewable if they have a growing cycle of ten years or less. Rapidly renewable materials are bio-based; most are derived from plants, but wool and other animal hair products are also considered rapidly renewable. Bamboo, linoleum, and cork are three well-known bio-based, rapidly renewable materials used in building interiors. Newer bio-based, rapidly renewable interior materials include agrifiber (produced from wheat chaff), Kirei (made from agricultural byproducts), and Dakota Burl (produced from sunflower seed hulls). Bio-based materials are being utilized increasingly in fabricating many building products; examples include corn-based carpet backing, plant-based carpet fibers, and soy foam insulation. While bio-based, rapidly renewable materials are beautiful and durable, many are harvested or manufactured only in certain parts of the world. When selecting bio-based products, the project team should consider the proximity of their harvesting and manufacture to the job site.

PURCHASING CERTIFIED WOOD PRODUCTS

Many hardwoods used in building construction come from old-growth trees and forests. These resources are typically hundreds of years old, and their conventional harvesting can harm ecosystems and precipitate other problems, including soil degradation and erosion, and adverse microclimate changes. Deforestation is one of the leading causes of GHG emissions worldwide. Living trees absorb CO_2; when they are cut down they release all the CO_2 they have been storing into the atmosphere.

Despite the foregoing challenges, wood products can be sustainable. Some wood product manufacturers practice sustainable harvesting techniques, such as hewing only one in ten trees each year and replanting new trees immediately thereafter. The Forest Stewardship Council (FSC) is an international organization active in 47 countries that tracks the sustainable harvesting practices of wood product producers. The FSC allows the wood products that come from sustainable harvests to be specified and tracked from the forest to the mill, and ultimately to the job site. FSC wood is accompanied by a chain-of-custody certificate and is certified by a third party. In a workspace retrofit, opportunities to use certified wood may include blocking, veneers, paneling, and trim.

SPECIFYING LOCALLY SOURCED MATERIALS

When selecting a product, the project team should consider the proximity of its harvesting and manufacture to the job site. Transporting building materials great distances uses fuel and

structures that lack wall insulation or in which the insulating materials have degraded. Insulating wall cavities requires cutting small openings into the finished walls at close intervals and filling, repairing, and repainting them after the installation. This process can be disruptive to building tenants and is best for extensive building retrofits.

Insulation within the building interior can also be useful for sound attenuation, especially in open-plan environments. Specialized products that simultaneously provide acoustical and thermal insulation and meet green standards are available in the marketplace.

COOL ROOFS

Cool roofs, or roof coatings that reflect the sun's energy instead of absorbing it, have become the new roofing standard. By reducing the amount of solar energy absorbed, office buildings reduce their summer cooling load and improve building energy efficiency. In hot summer sun, dark, flat roofs can reach temperatures 100°F (38°C) above the ambient air temperature.[4] This high temperature can break down roofing materials and shorten the effective lifespan of roofing systems. For this reason, cool roofs are usually more efficient roofing alternatives for the long term. Although there is some controversy about the

contributes to air pollution. It is preferable to look for regionally manufactured materials. Several green building certification systems, including LEED, recognize locally sourced materials as those that have traveled less than 500 miles from their place of origin through manufacturing and to the job site. Additionally, purchasing regionally sourced materials contributes to the local economy and demonstrates pride of place.

SPECIFYING HEALTHY MATERIALS

Workplace materials have a significant effect on the quality of the indoor environment, as well as on the health and well-being of building occupants. Many traditional building materials contain toxic materials that off-gas when they are first installed. Typical toxic culprits include

▶▶ **VOCs**—organic, carbon-containing compounds that evaporate readily at room temperature and are found in common interior building materials;

▶▶ **Urea formaldehyde**—used as a binding agent in composite wood products; and

▶▶ **Particulate matter**—generated during renovation activities and common in poorly ventilated or filtered spaces.

Following renovation, VOCs, urea formaldehyde, and particulates can create unpleasant odors, in addition to causing physical discomfort, with symptoms such as eye, nose, and throat irritation; headaches, loss of coordination, and nausea; and damage to the liver, kidney, and central nervous system. According to the EPA, urea formaldehyde and some VOCs are known or suspected to cause cancer.

Some of the most common products containing VOCs and other toxins are described here, along with their environmentally friendly alternatives:

▶▶ **Paints and adhesives.** Historically, commercial paints, coatings, adhesives, and sealants have been high emitters of VOCs. Components that have strong binding properties or that are intended to prevent degradation of materials through oxidation, mold, mildew, and corrosion have been determined to have some negative health effects. When new materials are installed wet, they are particularly conducive to off-gassing during the drying or curing process. In newly renovated spaces, many newly applied products may be off-gassing all at once, creating a toxic soup in the indoor environment. To prevent this, design professionals can specify low-emitting versions of any of these products. Owing to increasing demand in the U.S. marketplace, low-emitting or no-emitting paints, coatings, adhesives, and sealants are now readily available at little to no cost premium compared with their high-emitting counterparts. In other regions of the world, these products may be challenging to source locally but should still be readily available through U.S. manufacturers of commercial building products.

▶▶ **Carpets and textiles.** Carpets and textiles are a common source of VOCs introduced into the workplace. Substances that are targeted at preventing material degradation during shipping and storage (such as color fading, mildew, and dry rot) can present indoor air quality issues, particularly when large quantities of new materials are installed all at once. Design professionals can prevent air quality issues from arising upon installation by

merit of using cool roofs in cold climates where the dominant need is to heat buildings, the favorable effects of cool roofs on roofing lifespan may produce a net economic benefit.

Additionally, cool roofs can reduce the urban heat island effect, which occurs when the use of dark, flat roofs and pavements combine with a lack of vegetation to raise the temperatures of urban areas significantly higher than those in surrounding semirural or rural regions. This negative environmental impact is especially relevant for office buildings located in central business districts. According to the U.S. Environmental Protection Agency (EPA), "heat islands can affect communities by increasing summertime peak energy demand, air-conditioning costs, air pollution and greenhouse gas emissions, heat-related illness and mortality, and water quality."[5]

The effectiveness of cool roof coatings is determined by their high reflectivity (the ability to reflect a large percentage of the sun's energy) and high emissivity (the ability to release solar energy that has been absorbed). While a roof's thermal performance is primarily determined by its reflectivity, emissivity also plays a role by releasing the energy that is absorbed from the sun. Emissivity is especially important in warm and sunny climates. A new method for measuring the cool

specifying low-emitting carpet. Such carpet is widely available in the United States at the same price points as traditional carpet. Similarly, there are many low-emitting solid flooring options such as wood, cork, linoleum, terrazzo, stone, concrete, tile, and rubber. Low-VOC carpets and textiles are available internationally, although these products may carry a premium.

▶▶ **Millwork and composite wood.** Urea formaldehyde resins are commonly used as binding agents in composite wood products such as plywood, particle board, oriented-strand board, and medium-density fiberboard. These wood products are usually introduced into the workplace as millwork, casework, countertop substrates, door cores, and paneling. Composite wood products with no added urea formaldehyde may carry a cost premium, but this premium should also decrease in the future as demand increases. Most rapidly renewable composite wood products (such as agrifiber) are also made with no added urea formaldehyde, which makes them doubly appropriate for use in a green office retrofit.

▶▶ **Furniture and upholstery:** Many textiles are treated with preservative chemicals to prevent material degradation, such as color fading, mildew, and dry rot, during shipping and storage. These chemicals can present indoor air quality issues, particularly when large quantities of new furniture are installed at once. If new upholstered furniture is to be introduced into the workplace, it is important to either allow it to "breathe" outside the workplace interior or to consider flushing out the space before it is reoccupied. Design professionals can minimize air quality issues associated with furniture installation by specifying low-emitting furniture. Fortunately, most major manufacturers of systems furniture have already introduced green lines that meet stringent air quality testing and are certified by third-party organizations. These materials are becoming more readily available globally but may carry a premium in some countries. Another alternative is to refurbish existing furniture locally with low-emitting paints and textiles.

CONSIDERING THE PRODUCT'S LIFE CYCLE

One of the most important aspects of material selection is its efficiency over its life cycle, from extraction and fabrication through use and ultimate disposition. A key question for a product is, What will happen at its end of initial use? Is the product reusable or recyclable? If not, the material will likely end up in a landfill. If the product or material cannot be readily disassembled, it probably will not be recycled or reused. Many designers like to work with demountable partition walls instead of installing stud walls for this reason: it is easier to reconfigure and reuse the same materials numerous times. Another alternative to extend product life cycles is to reskin or replace certain components while retaining the primary structure of the item. As well, a new generation of products is designed to be remanufactured repeatedly, without having to recycle the component materials. Some of these products have a third-party Cradle to Cradle certification.

Anica Landreneau, AIA, LEED AP, is a sustainable design practice leader. Amy Fabry, NCIDQ, LEED AP, is a senior interior designer. Nita Tuvesson, LEED AP, is an interiors specialist. Leigh Stringer, LEED AP, is a vice president and senior workplace specialist. Jodi Williams, LEED AP, is a workplace specialist. All are based in HOK's Washington, D.C. office.

roof potential of a roofing system is the Solar Reflectivity Index (SRI), created at Lawrence Berkeley National Laboratory at the University of California. The SRI measures a roof's cooling performance on a scale of 1 to 100, with 100 representing near-optimal performance.

OTHER ROOFING OPTIONS

In addition to cool roofs, other sustainable roofing options can both contribute to building energy performance and provide other useful benefits. Vegetated roofs insulate roof surfaces, can control stormwater runoff, and can serve as tenant amenities. Solar roofing

SUSTAINABLE ROOF OPTIONS AND GUIDELINES FOR EXISTING BUILDINGS

RALPH VELASQUEZ

Building owners have many sustainable roofing options to choose from for re-roofing applications and major renovations. Following are some basic guidelines for making the best decisions for both owner and building. Keep in mind that every roofing decision is unique and must be addressed on a case-by-case basis.

▸▸ **Replace the existing roof** only when necessary. The most sustainable option is to maintain the existing roof and make it last longer. A roofing professional should determine whether the existing roof can be repaired, restored, renovated, or upgraded. Maintaining the roof limits the use of new materials, eliminates waste, and reduces carbon emissions because no new product is manufactured or transported.

▸▸ **Cool roof coatings** can positively affect the building and the local environment. Whether improving an existing roof or installing a new one, evaluate whether adding a cool roof coating will be beneficial to building energy consumption and the local environment. Cool roofs, often referred to as reflective roofs, tend to last longer and significantly reduce rooftop temperatures when compared with conventional bituminous roofs. In most climates, especially where the summer is hot and sunny, cool roofs can reduce the amount of heat absorbed into the building interior, ease the cooling load on the building's HVAC system, and improve thermal comfort for building occupants. In the context of the local environment, cool roofs lessen the urban heat island effect and reduce carbon emissions. In the United States, reflective roofs are typically Energy Star–compliant and can qualify for rebates and other financial incentives.

▸▸ **Improve the roof insulation.** Adding insulation below an existing roof may save money if the building is under-insulated or the cost of energy escalates. If the existing roof membrane has not deteriorated and the underlying insulation is dry, consider a roof retrofit in which insulation is retained and more is added to increase the R-value (a measure of insulation effectiveness). If the retrofit insulation is not properly installed, it may not adequately extend the life of the roof and may actually reduce it, so care must be taken during installation.

▸▸ **Use high-quality, sustainable materials** to extend the roof lifespan. If the roof must be replaced, high-quality materials will reduce maintenance costs and the need for ongoing capital improvements. Where appropriate, specify new roofing made from durable, recycled materials, such as glass felts that contain recycled glass, and ply or sheet goods that use reground rubber or other recaptured polymers. Bio-based (plant-based resin) roofing and insulation materials are making their way into the market. In addition, if the roof will have a walkway, consider using sustainably harvested wood products certified by the FSC, such as ipe, a very durable hardwood.

▸▸ **Reuse or recycle old roofing.** Materials removed during roof replacement can be handled sustainably. Can the construction waste be reground and reused? Is any ballast (anchoring materials, such as large rocks or pavers, which hold unattached roofing membranes in place) reusable? How about the pavers or the metal from the fascia (the waterproof border around the roof perimeter)? If the existing insulation material is dry and meets building code requirements for fire resistance ratings, consider adding supplemental high R-value insulation. It makes economic and environmental sense to look at everything associated with the existing roof in the context of reuse or recycling.

(building-integrated photovoltaic roofing) can provide renewable energy for use throughout the office building. Alternatively, solar roofing can be introduced through the installation of photovoltaic panels on top of the existing roofing structure, if loads are acceptable. (See the sidebar by Ralph Velasquez for an evaluation of the application of various sustainable roofing systems and suggestions of roofing best practices for green retrofits.)

▸▸ **Maintain the investment.** Proper installation of a quality roof does not guarantee that it will remain an efficient barrier forever. Weather and aging can affect roof performance, leading to water infiltration and energy loss. To maximize performance, it is imperative to establish a maintenance program with regularly scheduled inspections and housekeeping, such as cleaning drains and making necessary repairs. Small problems that are not rectified can quickly become disasters.

Vegetated and Photovoltaic Roofing Options

Reflective roofs can help lower energy costs, but two other kinds of sustainable roofing systems—vegetated and photovoltaic—provide additional benefits.

VEGETATED ROOFS

Vegetated roofs can make economic sense if the roofing needs to address issues beyond energy reduction. In addition to their insulating qualities, vegetated roofs are beneficial for managing stormwater runoff, for sound attenuation, and for increasing the roof's useful life. Plants reduce the rooftop temperatures of a building through evapotranspiration (the release of moisture from the surfaces of plants and soil into the atmosphere). Vegetated roofs can improve building aesthetics, reduce the urban heat island effect, and be an attractive feature for potential tenants.

There are three basic types of vegetated roof:

▸▸ **Extensive:** Low-profile plantings with thinner, engineered soils. They require minimal maintenance, so the roof need only be accessed for maintenance and repairs.

▸▸ **Intensive:** All types of vegetation, including trees in deeper soil. Such roofs are labor intensive, requiring irrigation and other maintenance. Intensive vegetated roofs are designed to be easily accessible and can simulate a park environment. They can be valuable amenities for office buildings and residential properties.

▸▸ **Semi-intensive:** A roof system somewhere between the minimal planting and maintenance of an extensive roof and the public garden environment of an intensive roof. Like an intensive vegetated roof, a semi-intensive vegetated roof system can be an amenity for occupants.

Compared with conventional roof options, vegetated roofs can have significantly higher first costs. They also offer benefits over conventional options. An experienced vegetated roof supplier or designer can provide an accurate projection of return on investment (ROI) and simple payback analysis for a specific installation.

PHOTOVOLTAIC ROOFS

Building-integrated photovoltaics (BIPV) are materials that replace conventional material in the building envelope. BIPV can be used for flat or sloped roof installations, creating renewable energy in the form of electricity while also performing the role of a conventional roof.

Like vegetated roofs, BIPVs have substantially higher first costs than conventional roof options. The ROI is highly dependent on a number of factors, including retail electricity rates (especially peak demand rates) from the local provider, government incentives, the site's solar potential, the availability of net metering, technological improvements, and the building's energy use profile. In most scenarios, solar roofing systems are economically feasible in locations with moderate and higher solar potential, high retail electricity rates, and generous incentives. With the exception of the site's solar potential, these factors are highly variable; incentive packages can be altered, and retail electricity costs can change quickly. Additionally, the potential role of renewable energy credits, discussed in chapter 5, may motivate building owners to consider solar roofing installations. Given that the first costs of solar roofing options continue to drop and that the efficiency of solar systems continues to improve, building owners should monitor the economic feasibility of utilizing BIPV before making final retrofit decisions.

Ralph Velasquez is director of the Sustainable Technology Group at Tremco Roofing and Building Maintenance in Beachwood, Ohio.

WALL COLOR AND SHADING

Wall color can affect building energy efficiency. In hot climates, project teams should consider painting or staining the exterior walls with light colors. Light colors usually have a high albedo, reflecting the sun's energy, limiting solar heat gain, and reducing the energy required to cool the building. When considering high-albedo colors or other reflective materials, such as the installation of metal panels on the building exterior, project teams should carefully consider the impact of potential glare from the building on the surrounding environment.

An alternative to wall staining is to shield the building envelope with landscaping, as discussed earlier. Care should be taken when installing shading near the building to ensure that root systems will not interfere with the foundation as the tree matures.

Windows and Doors

Typically, windows and doors are the weakest points in the thermal envelope (the parts of the building that resist heat transfer between the outside environment and the building's interiors), increasing the heating or cooling load.[6] Windows and doors can also contribute positively to a building's energy efficiency by providing daylight for building interiors, which reduces the need for electrical lighting.

Envelope openings also provide outdoor views for occupants—a positive contribution that must be balanced against excessive heat gain or loss, particularly in extreme climates. During a retrofit, the goal should be to choose cost-effective window and door materials that have the best thermal properties for the climatic region, allow appropriate levels of visible light and air into building interiors, and offer views to occupants.

WINDOWS

The importance and role of windows in office buildings has come full circle. The traditional role of windows, which is to provide light, air, and views to interior spaces, was diminished with the advent in the 1950s (particularly in the United States) of hermetically sealed office buildings conditioned by central air systems and lit by artificial lighting. These sealed enclosures allowed for mechanical control of temperature and humidity but often had negative repercussions for indoor air quality, adversely affecting the health and productivity of occupants. Fortunately, a renewed focus on creating more occupant-friendly spaces, along with a better understanding of how windows can contribute to energy-efficient buildings, has brought the traditional role of windows back to the forefront in building construction and design.

For green office retrofits, window performance improvements can range from resealing existing windows to installing new reflective coatings, installing window shading devices, replacing the entire window unit, or, in a curtain wall building, upgrading the entire facade. An example of how a facade replacement can benefit the overall performance of an office building is the Greentowers project in Frankfurt, where Deutsche Bank is installing new operable glazing in the curtain wall to improve the thermal performance of the facade and allow for natural ventilation within the high-rise towers. (For more detail, see the sidebar by George Vavaroutsos.)

Light shelves increase the penetration of natural daylight into the building interior at the Wallace Roberts & Todd main offices on the 28th floor of 1700 Market Street in Philadelphia.

DEUTSCHE BANK'S TWIN TOWERS: THE NEW "GREENTOWERS"

GEORGE VAVAROUTSOS

In 2007, Deutsche Bank began a €200 million ($260 million) effort to transform its 155-meter (508-feet) tall, 103,600-square-meter (1,115,000-square-foot) Frankfurt headquarters into an energy-efficient, green complex. The renovation, one of the largest and most environmentally sensitive in the world, is intended to maintain the exterior character of the landmark twin towers, affectionately known in Frankfurt as Debit and Credit (*Soll und Haben*). The refurbished "Greentowers" promises to be a compelling example of how existing structures can be improved to meet new standards for resource-efficient operations and enhanced tenant comfort.

Management Objectives

Initially, the refurbishment was planned to improve fire protection levels in the now nearly 25-year-old towers. In light of the scope of the necessary improvements, the project team undertook a fundamental analysis of the entire building and determined that the best course of action was to dramatically improve the buildings' energy performance and occupant comfort. In addition, the building interiors underwent a design transformation intended to open the bank to the public and optimize space utilization.

Interior demolition began in December 2007 and the retrofit started in March 2008. Construction is scheduled for completion in the early summer of 2010, to be followed by extensive testing and commissioning before the start of operations.

In pursuing the project, Deutsche Bank's Management Board set the following objectives:

▸ **An active contribution** to climate protection;

▸ **A reduction of at least 50 percent** in energy consumption and CO_2 emissions from the building; and

▸ **A more attractive and comfortable environment** for staff and visitors.

Performance monitoring and work performed to date indicate that the following objectives have been achieved or are expected to be achieved:

▸ **CO_2 output** from operations is expected to be reduced by 55 percent, the equivalent of 44.4 million automobile miles.

▸ **Some 26,600 tons** of demolition material will be removed from the towers, and 98 percent of that material will be recycled or reused.

▸ **Models predict a 67 percent reduction** in heating energy utilization, which is equivalent to 10 gigawatt-hours (GWh) per year, enough to heat 750 households.

▸ **Models predict that electricity usage** will be reduced by 55 percent, the equivalent of 9 GWh per year, or enough energy to power 1,900 households.

▸ **Models predict a reduction in water use** of 43 percent, saving 26,000 cubic meters of water (close to 6.87 million gallons) per year.

Building Envelope

To achieve these performance objectives, the project team started with the building envelope. The existing mirrored curtain wall was still functional, but the use of recent advances in glazing and insulation technology could lead to dramatic improvements in the towers' energy performance.

The decision was made to replace the existing double-glazed facades with triple-glazed, argon-gas-filled, "breathing facades" that feature operable windows in every second grid. The operable windows, which are specially designed to open parallel to the facade and remain impervious to high winds, will allow for a natural air flow system that will significantly lower the need for mechanical ventilation—reducing the energy required for ventilation by an estimated 60 percent.

There were multiple reasons for choosing this particular facade. Decision factors used by Deutsche Bank included the following:

▸ **A conditions assessment** of the facade indicated that the current metal film on the glazing would dissolve in the next 12 to 15 years, resulting in discolored glass. The decision was made to upgrade the facade as part of the current building refurbishment, instead of waiting and interrupting building operations again in the future.

▸ **It was determined** that other operable window technologies, including tilted windows, box-type windows, and motor-controlled, parallel, hinged windows, would alter the appearance of the building and did not allow for the same flexibility in controlling the natural ventilation.

▸ **An operable window system** was required, to maximize the energy savings from the new heating and cooling system by allowing natural ventilation to significantly reduce the energy needed for mechanical ventilation.

▸▸

Operable windows that allow for natural ventilation are now standard for high-rise Class A office buildings in Germany. Deutsche Bank wanted the towers to have Class A status after the retrofit. A cost-benefit analysis conducted by two independent real estate consultants indicated that the investment in the facade would lead to an equivalent increase in asset value.

There were some challenges in replacing the towers' 55,500 square meters (592,015 square feet) of exterior glazing. The key challenge was that of fitting operable, tripled-glazed units into the spaces formerly occupied by double-glazed, inoperable units without reducing light intake or adversely affecting external appearance. To achieve this, the curtain wall manufacturer, who had built the previous curtain wall, created a new mounting system and energy-efficient coating for the glazing. By using triple-insulated glass and heat insulation of 140 millimeters (5.51 inches), superior energy efficiency has been attained. The new glazing is expected to reduce heat loss by 65 percent and reduce heat ingress in summer by 35 percent. The new curtain wall features

- **A U-factor** (a measure of how well the glass prevents heat loss) of 0.6 W/m²K;

- **A solar heat gain coefficient** (SGHC, a measure of how well a window resists heat from sunlight) of 0.25; and

- **A visual transmittance** (VT, a measure of how much visible light passes through a window) of 0.4.

Interior Ceilings and Slabs

Capitalizing on the existing structure of the twin towers, the project team decided to install ceilings that would help to heat and cool the building and to use existing concrete slabs to facilitate additional heating and cooling. These decisions improve thermal comfort for occupants and save energy. In the summer, cold water circulating in the ceilings cools the interior, and the concrete structure absorbs heat during the daytime. At night, the heat stored in the slabs is dissipated by the cold water circulation, chilling the interior for the next day. The advantage of the new concept: the volume of mechanically ventilated air required for the building is reduced by 80 percent, leading to a 50 percent reduction in energy used for ventilation. In the winter,

the minor heat loss is compensated for by radiant heating, also installed in the ceilings.

Additionally, the narrower configuration of the heating/cooling ceilings makes possible a reduction in the vertical dimensions of the ceiling plenum (the space between the structural ceiling and the dropped ceiling), raising the office ceiling height from 2.65 meters (8.7 feet) to 3.0 meters (9.5 feet). Raising the ceiling height will allow daylight to penetrate more deeply into the office interiors and provides more headroom.

Additional Green Improvements

The retrofit will also improve both the quality and the energy efficiency of interior lighting. Using high-efficiency light fixtures, along with daylight sensors (which automatically dim mechanical lighting when interior daylighting levels are adequate) and occupancy sensors (which turn off lights when workstations are unoccupied) will reduce the electricity required for lighting by 55 percent. Dedicated task lighting will ensure that all workstations have high-quality lighting.

The Greentowers will incorporate a number of water conservation and reuse strategies. By installing high-efficiency fixtures and incorporating rainwater harvesting and graywater recycling, potable water consumption should be reduced by more than 40 percent, even though postrenovation building occupancy could increase by 20 percent. A solar hot-water system installed on the angled glass at the towers' base will provide 50 percent of the buildings' hot water. A heat recovery system will capture waste heat from nonpotable water.

The project team expects that the improvements to the structure's systems—in addition to the new interiors, which will set new standards for user-friendliness—will increase building occupancy by 20 percent. Through optimized space planning, smaller space requirements for technical facilities, and the addition of approximately 850 square meters (9,150 square feet) of usable floor space, the renovated Greentowers will provide room for up to 600 additional employees.

George Vavaroutsos, LEED AP, is a sustainable real estate consultant with Malachite LLC.

If the window system will be replaced as part of the retrofit, the project team should select an insulated glazing unit, commonly referred to as an IGU. An IGU is designed with two or more layers of glass that are spaced apart and sealed to create a single unit. IGUs are typically fabricated with double or triple glazing, but quadruple-glazed units are available—each additional layer further insulates the window.

If it is not possible to install more than double glazing because of weight or cost issues, an alternative is to install double-glazed windows with suspended films that feature solar reflective coatings. These lightweight films, which are installed between glass panes, improve the thermal performance of IGUs by creating multiple air spaces that can be filled with a low-conductivity gas, improving the U-value, while also reducing solar heat gain for building interiors. If there is enough space, multiple suspended films can be installed. These films can also be installed in existing windows, making them ideal for any retrofit in which improving window performance is a primary objective.

IGUs are commonly filled with a low-conductivity gas like argon and feature one or more low-emissivity, or low-E, coatings (which reflect infrared radiated energy, reducing heat transmission through the window). Enhanced glazing, the use of low-conductivity gas between panes, and the use of low-E coatings further reduce heat loss.

Assessing and improving the energy performance of windows is especially important to building energy efficiency. This process must be balanced with the other multiple roles that windows fulfill in the building envelope:

▸▸ **DAYLIGHTING**. By utilizing natural light to illuminate interiors, buildings can benefit from a reduction in energy use and provide higher-quality light to occupants. The location of windows, coupled with decisions about the interior layout, will dictate the potential for good daylighting quality in building interiors.

▸▸ **VENTILATION**. Operable windows can be incorporated into a building ventilation system, allowing for fresh air intake. When coordinated with compatible interior layout decisions, the use of operable windows can create the potential for cross-ventilation.

▸▸ **CONNECTION TO OUTDOOR ENVIRON-MENTS**. Windows provide building occupants with views of the surrounding environment, which, together with daylighting, has been shown to improve employee productivity.[7]

Each role sets unique performance constraints on the window system, which are not necessarily complementary. It is necessary to balance these factors to maximize energy efficiency and occupant comfort. Standardized metrics can be used to profile window performance (see the sidebar on glazing metrics by George Vavaroutsos). During the planning phase, the project team should use energy models to determine which window improvements will deliver the most value in terms of energy use reductions, occupant comfort improvements, and ROI.

The energy performance of window frame components should not be overlooked, because they can account for 10 percent to 30 percent of the window area of a manufactured window unit.[8] While commonly used for curtain wall components and commercial windows, highly conductive aluminum frames without thermal breaks (materials with low thermal conductivity, which prevent the transfer of heat from interior to exterior) can lead to heat loss. If window units or parts of the curtain wall frame will be replaced as part of a retrofit, the project team should ensure that retrofit materials have adequate thermal breaking. Additionally, the team should ensure that any replacement units are installed properly, because poorly installed windows and frames can lead to condensation problems. For some window applications, frames fabricated from materials that have lower conductivity (such as fiberglass) may be suitable.

DOORS

Building entrances should be retrofitted to avoid the loss of conditioned air to the exterior. If possible, entrances should be located away from the direction of prevailing winds. Revolving doors or double-door pairings help limit air movement into and out of

MEASURING THE PERFORMANCE OF WINDOWS, SKYLIGHTS, AND CURTAIN WALLS

GEORGE VAVAROUTSOS

Several standardized metrics can be used to profile the performance of windows, skylights, and curtain-wall glass infills (large glass panels inserted into a curtain wall):

▸▸ **U-factor.** U-factor is the measurement of how well windows or glass panels prevent heat loss or, in hot climates, reduce heat gain. Also known as U-value, U-factor ratings for windows and skylights commonly range from 0.20 to 1.20. A lower U-factor indicates superior insulating qualities and thus limited thermal conductivity between warmer and cooler air in both hot and cold climates.

▸▸ **Solar heat gain coefficient (SHGC) or G-value.** SHGC is a measurement on a scale of 0 to 1 of how well a window resists heat from sunlight. A lower SHGC means that the glass transmits less solar heat. The term SHGC is used primarily in Australia and North America; G-value is used in Europe and is identical in meaning. The measurement of shading coefficient (SC), which is similar to SHGC, is being phased out in favor of SHGC.

Office buildings are typically warmed by heat generated by equipment and occupants inside the structure. Thus, solar heat gain is not generally desired, especially in warm climates. To limit solar heat gain, reflective coatings and films can be used to reduce solar transmission through the glazing. Spectrally selective coatings (also referred to as low-emissivity or low-E) reduce the transmission of infrared and ultraviolet rays through glass. These coatings reduce the SHGC of the glazing while allowing the transmission of visible light. Spectrally selective coatings and films can be installed on both the outside and inside surfaces of new or existing windows and glass infills. For double- and triple-glazed IGUs, they can be installed between glass panes, hermetically sealed inside the window.

▸▸ **Visible transmittance (VT).** Visible transmittance is a measurement of how much visible light passes through a window, which dictates the potential for interior daylighting. The scale for VT is 0 to 1, with higher values correlating with greater light transmittance. Although a higher VT measure is desirable for daylighting, direct sunlight can create an uncomfortable thermal environment, a lack of privacy, and glare for workers situated near the windows. Solar shading and glazing tints can be used to reduce the amount of problematic direct sunlight that reaches building interiors. Blue- or green-tinted glazing reduces glare but allows visible light to penetrate. More highly reflective tints, such as bronze or silver, reduce both the SHGC and VT.

These metrics can be applied individually to the glazing unit or to the entire window unit, frame included. Before comparing the relative performance of window systems, the project team should verify that the values to be compared represent the same window component.

A number of organizations test and measure window performance, including the National Fenestration Rating Council (NFRC) in the United States and Australia, and the British Fenestration Rating Council (BFRC) in the United Kingdom. These organizations rate the performance metrics of both manufactured windows units and curtain wall components, in order to identify window systems that have the best energy performance potential. Additionally, rating programs such as Energy Star in the United States and the Window Energy Rating Scheme (WERS) in Australia use these data to rate the appropriateness of a window system for a specific climate zone. Although climate-zone ratings are performed primarily for manufactured window units for residential buildings, the performance qualities that make a window unit appropriate for a specific climate zone are valid for other building types.

George Vavaroutsos, LEED AP, is a sustainable real estate consultant with Malachite LLC.

---

the building in heavily trafficked entrances. For both energy efficiency and security reasons, building operations staff should ensure that doors are not left open for extended time periods. This includes garage doors on loading docks and other utility doors. Exceptions can be made if security is not an issue and if opening doors facilitates passive cooling.

Doors should be insulated, and those that feature glass should follow the same performance recommendations prescribed for windows.[9] Particular attention should be paid to door frames; like windows, door frames can act as thermal bridges, transferring heat and leading to energy loss. Door frames that have thermal breaks can improve the energy efficiency of doors. Additionally, the project team should ensure that the door assemblies are properly installed and airtight. Improperly installed door assemblies or inadequate weather stripping can lead to significant air leakage and energy loss.

Sun Shading

The thermal envelope of a building is profoundly affected by solar radiation. During the summer months, excess heating from solar radiation should be reduced to diminish cooling requirements and minimize glare. In the Northern Hemisphere, unwanted solar heat gain can be prevented by using coatings and films with a low solar-heat-gain coefficient (SHGC) on the glazing of the building's southern and western exposures. In the Southern Hemisphere, the focus is the northern and eastern exposures. Such coatings and films can be installed on both the outside and inside surfaces of building glazing; many can also be installed between glass panes of IGUs.

In summer months, western exposures often benefit from shading as well as window coatings and films. The afternoon sun is frequently the most problematic for solar heat gain, casting its light at the hottest time of day—the hours of peak energy demand. In some latitudes, particularly near the equator, northern exposures also may benefit from shading. From a sun path diagram of the building, a shading system can be devised to minimize summer heat gain. There are a number of methods to shade an existing building facade:

▶▶ **EXTERIOR WINDOW OVERHANGS AND SCREENS**. Window overhangs and screens can be installed in the facade in any number of materials, designs, and orientations. These shading devices should be optimized for the building's solar orientation and climatic conditions.

▶▶ **LANDSCAPING**. For one- or two-story buildings, trees, shrubs, and climbing plants can act as sun shades. Deciduous trees can be very effective solar shades in certain latitudes but may limit daylighting opportunities during the summer. Another consideration is that because they lose their foliage in the winter, deciduous trees permit solar heat gain during colder periods. Landscaping may not be as effective as other shading methods on southern exposures but can be effective on eastern and western exposures. Landscaping can also reduce heating and cooling loads by shielding the building from the wind.

▶▶ **INTERNAL SHADES AND BLINDS**. While shades and blinds can limit the penetration of direct sunlight and reduce or eliminate visual discomfort from glare, their use may trap solar radiation inside the building, raising ambient internal air temperature. Shades that are hermetically sealed in the window glass may eliminate some of this heat gain but are not as effective as exterior shading systems.

BUILDING MECHANICAL SYSTEMS

Optimally, green buildings use the energy and capacity of the environment to light, heat and cool, and ventilate the structure naturally as much as possible, reducing energy demands on the building's mechanical and electrical systems. When these passive strategies (discussed later) have been fully utilized, building systems in a sustainable building are responsible for the same functions they perform in a conventional building: they heat, cool, ventilate, light, power, and provide water and waste removal to the building interiors. A key difference between a green and a conventional building is how the building functions are delivered. Conventional buildings traditionally deliver heating, cooling, and other energy-intensive services throughout the structure at all times. A green building utilizes advanced controls to provide energy in the right place, at the right time, and in the proper intensity and form to address the demand—and nothing more. Such optimization is a key strategy for improving energy efficiency, reducing operating costs, and reducing the emissions of GHGs from the built environment.

Heating, Ventilating, and Air Conditioning

Heating, cooling, and ventilating an office building requires a substantial amount of energy, accounting for roughly 50 percent of total energy use for buildings in the United States.[10] The retrofit process is an opportunity to both improve comfort for occupants and reduce the energy required for HVAC operations.

REDUCING HVAC ENERGY USE

The key strategies for reducing HVAC energy use in a green office retrofit are the following:

▸▸ **DURING THE PLANNING PHASE**, conduct an energy audit of the existing facility, including the HVAC systems, and a cost-benefit analysis of existing and potential HVAC systems to determine the best retrofit strategy.

▸▸ **IF PASSIVE STRATEGIES** are cost-effective, introduce such strategies to heat, cool, and ventilate the building without using the building's mechanical systems.

▸▸ **REPLACE MAJOR COMPONENTS** of the building's heating and cooling system with technologically advanced, energy-efficient systems. As well, consider alternative systems such as ground-source heat pumps (also known as geothermal systems), hybrid cooling, or off-peak cooling, as discussed in greater detail below.

▸▸ **INSTALL ADVANCED MODULATING EQUIPMENT** and controls to optimize the HVAC system. Use these tools to automatically control and limit the operation of the equipment to match real-time building heating and cooling demand.

▸▸ **ENSURE THAT BUILDING MECHANICAL SYSTEMS** are well insulated, preventing energy loss. Hot-water pipes, chilled-water pipes, and supply air ducts (for heating and cooling) should be appropriately insulated. If appropriate, pipes can be insulated with rigid foam insulation or flexible jackets, and care should be taken to cover the entire pipe length, if possible. When appropriate, air supply ducts should be insulated with rigid or flexible insulating wraps, and systems such as boilers and chillers should be insulated as specified by the manufacturer. A mechanical insulation audit will identify where insulating materials should be replaced and where additional materials are needed.

▸▸ **INSTALL EQUIPMENT FOR RETRIEVING** waste thermal energy. A heat recovery ventilator, for example, reclaims energy from exhaust airflows; a drain-water heat recovery system uses heat from drain water for preheating hot water. Elevator systems can also incorporate an energy recovery system.

(See the sidebar by Cappy Kidd for information about upgrades and replacements for HVAC systems and operating processes.)

Depending on a building's size, use, local climate zone, and energy intensity profile, a number of additional HVAC systems and strategies should be considered for energy reduction as part of a green retrofit:

▸▸ **EVAPORATIVE COOLERS**. Evaporative coolers are a very simple system that provides space cooling by evaporating water to chill the air. These systems are best for hot, dry climates and use significantly less energy than forced-air cooling systems. They force air through a water-saturated medium, dropping the air temperature and adding humidity to the air directly. Indirect systems add a heat exchanger to reduce the humidity gained by the cooled air.

SEVEN STRATEGIES FOR MECHANICAL SYSTEM RETROFITS

CAPPY KIDD

Older buildings are contradictory. On one hand, they contain considerable amounts of embodied energy, the energy consumed in their original construction. On the other hand, operating older buildings often requires much more energy than necessary. If money were no object, the decisions on retrofits would be easy: rip out all the old, inefficient mechanical systems and replace them with new, state-of-the-art technologies. In the real world, decisions on retrofitting must be based on a thorough analysis that begins with an investment-grade energy audit. The energy audit examines the building's specific energy characteristics—the condition of its operating systems and lighting, the integrity of its building envelope, the changing cost of fuel, and the potential cost of retrofits. The analysis must also include a use profile that evaluates the building's present and future use, its occupancy levels, even whether the building will remain open during renovations.

The completed analysis provides a sustainability team with the elements needed to create an energy efficiency road map. Detailed economic projections provide guidance on priorities— what to preserve and upgrade, what to replace—affording a level of confidence sufficient for major capital investment decisions.

When retrofitting older buildings, there are no one-size-fits-all solutions, no magic bullets, no single technology or combination of technologies that are appropriate in every situation. Fortunately, there are a number of strategies proven to extend the useful life of older structures.

Let's consider seven strategies for mechanical systems, along with some examples of the breakthrough technologies and energy cost reduction measures (ECRMs) that make them feasible. These strategies are intended to work in conjunction with other measures that lower overall energy requirements (loads), take advantage of available daylighting, improve indoor air quality, and recycle.

1. **Reduce the operating time** of mechanical equipment. Operating time reduction strategies include using time clock and occupancy sensors, and scheduling usage reductions (setbacks), especially when the building is unoccupied.

2. **Replace inefficient and outdated equipment** and lighting with versions that can adjust power draw or fuel consumption to various load conditions. Sometimes replacing large boilers and chillers with multiple, unevenly sized, smaller units or adding a small "jockey" boiler can make it easier to match output to changing load conditions. Technologies that improve the efficiency of building mechanical systems include the following:

- Modulating and condensing boilers and furnaces. Modulating equipment varies its firing rate in response to changing load conditions. Condensing equipment extracts more heat from hot combustion gases than conventional equipment does—a more efficient way to trap and use heat energy. If feasible, lowering the design temperature of all heat emitters in the building will increase the opportunity to utilize modulating and condensing equipment.

- Variable-frequency drives (VFDs), also known as variable-speed drives (VSDs), for fan motors and pumps. (See text box on VFDs.)

- Lighting that adjusts its intensity in response to the available daylight.

3. **Place an equals sign between energy and water.** Every innovation that conserves water also conserves substantial amounts of energy. Over 25 percent of the cost of water is the energy required to pump, filter, purify, treat, and dispose of it. There are two major categories of water use in office buildings: Domestic water is used for drinking, cooking, washing, and flushing. HVAC system water is used for the HVAC systems. Where water is used to move heat it is called a hydronic system. (See the text box on thermal storage

Thermal Storage Capacity of Water and Air

Water and air are the two mediums most commonly used to move heating and cooling in buildings. If air is the medium of choice, the system is called a forced-air system and the air is forced by fans to move through ducts. If water is the medium of choice, the system is referred to as a hydronic system and the water is moved through pipes, driven by pumps. Other components of hydronic systems include boilers, chillers, and cooling towers. Many systems are combinations, using water to deliver heating or cooling while using air to condition the spaces. The terminal units where the energy from the water is transferred to the air are either fan coils or air-handling units. It is a lot easier to move heat with water than with air. In fact, the thermal storage capacity of a given volume of water is nearly 3,500 times greater than the thermal storage capacity of the same volume of air.

▶▶

▶▶ **HYBRID COOLING**. Hybrid cooling systems combine a conventional, electrically driven chiller (which produces cold water for use in building cooling) with one that operates on an alternative fuel source, such as natural gas or waste heat. These systems are classified as traditional or nontraditional. In a traditional system, the two chillers are the same size; during peak demand hours when rates are highest, the alternative fuel chiller handles the building's cooling needs, while the electrically driven chiller covers any remaining demand. In a nontraditional system, the alternative fuel source chiller is larger and operates most of the time, while the smaller, electrically driven chiller operates only when

▶▶

capacity of water and air.) The following ECRMs address both domestic water and HVAC system water:

- Installing dual-flush toilets and waterless or low-flush urinals.

- Supplying lavatories with cold water only or using point-of-use water heaters.

- Using nonpotable water (such as rainwater, graywater, and condenser water) for functions that do not require potable water.

- Improving chemical treatment protocols for boiler and chiller water. Reducing scaling on the inside of pipes and coils improves heat transfer through the surfaces.

- Using filters on hydronic systems to remove particles that can clog up the system and reduce water flow and heat transfer.

- Developing alternative systems to supply water to conventional cooling towers, such as hybrid cooling tower technology or geothermal systems. Conventional cooling towers lose considerable water through evaporation. Hybrid cooling towers recapture most of the water; geothermal pipe fields are closed loops.

4. **Use the same energy and water multiple times** in the same building. Energy consumed to heat or cool the air or to heat water can be recovered from exhaust air and drainpipes and reused in the building. ECRMs include the following:

- Installing heat recovery ventilators and energy recovery ventilators. These devices work by using the moisture and energy contained in exhaust air to precondition incoming air. Heat recovery ventilators exchange heat only; energy recovery ventilators recover water vapor as well. The two airstreams do not mix; they flow through separate pathways.

- Recovering heat from drain water. Most of the energy used for domestic hot water goes down the drain. A substantial portion can be recovered.

- Using rainwater and graywater to flush toilets and for other applications where potable water is not required (as suggested in strategy #3).

5. **Improve command and control of HVAC systems** to give greater precision to the application of energy. By using advanced control systems, energy can be used at the time, place, and duration that it is actually needed. Control ECRMs include

- Direct digital control for all heating equipment,
- Programmable-logic thermostats capable of "learning,"
- Building automation systems,
- Variable air volume systems,
- Thermal process control,
- Occupancy sensors for lighting and HVAC controls, and
- Smart pumps that feature built-in control systems.

VFDs—What They Are and How They Work

VFDs are devices that can modulate the speed of electric motors. HVAC systems are typically designed to meet a building's loads at peak conditions. However, most buildings operate at full load conditions for only short periods. Effectively they operate with oversized equipment the rest of the time. The fans and pumps that drive the HVAC systems are some of the largest consumers of electric power in the building. These include chilled-water and hot-water distribution pumps, cooling tower fans, air-handling unit fans, and ventilation fans.

VFDs work by changing the frequency of the alternating current, which in turn changes the rotational speed of the electric motor. Substantial energy savings can be achieved when the speed of these electric motors is reduced in response to changing load conditions; the larger the motor, the greater the savings potential. Very large reductions in power consumption can be achieved through relatively small reductions in speed. For example, if the rotational speed of an electric motor is reduced by one-half, the corresponding electricity use will be only one-eighth of the initial power draw. VFDs are now available and economical options for all sizes of motors, from the largest triple-phase induction motors down to fractional horsepower applications.

electricity is the lower-cost option. These systems are well-suited for high-cost electricity markets, especially if peak rates are high relative to off-peak rates.

▶▶ **OFF-PEAK COOLING.** Off-peak cooling systems produce and store ice during nighttime hours, when temperatures are cooler and electricity rates are lower. The ice is stored in large insulated containers, on the roof or on the ground, and used to chill a refrigerant (an enclosed liquid or gas that is circulated to absorb or remove heat, in both heating and cooling systems). The chilled refrigerant is used to cool the building during the day, when

Thermal Process Control (TPC)

Maximizing the efficiency of hydronic heating systems has very little to do with boiler efficiency and far more to do with being in control of the boiler operation cycles. One of the most promising advances in hydronic heating control is known as thermal process control (TPC).

The greatest cause of energy waste in hydronic heating systems is the mismatch between the amount of heat that the building loses and the amount of heat that the boilers deliver. Traditional boiler control devices, including outdoor temperature resets with or without programmed learning logic, at best make educated guesses about the loads of the building at any given time. Boiler short cycling, overshooting, and standby losses can account for a significant portion of the total energy consumed.

The TPC controller works by constantly monitoring the flows and temperature differential of the supply and return water systems. It determines the real-time heating requirements for the building and modulates boiler output to make up only the amount of heat that is being lost. These controllers can control more than just boilers. They can also control pumps, dampers, and flow control valves. In a system that has a variety of boilers, the controller selects the best combination of boilers to run under any given load condition. This capability optimizes energy consumption.

(For more detailed information about building control systems, see the sidebar by Ryan Hoger.)

6. **Get better control of outside air intake.** In most cases, outdoor air is far cleaner than indoor air. It contains a higher percentage of oxygen and a lower percentage of contaminants. The importance of bringing a certain percentage of outdoor air into office buildings is codified in numerous international standards. Many buildings have either lost or never had control of their outdoor air intake. Problems occur when too little or too much is brought into the building. All outside air adds to a building's energy load. Outdoor air must be filtered, heated, cooled, and humidified or dehumidified. This process accounts for one of the largest expenditures of energy in a building. Therefore, the need for outdoor air intake should be balanced against the energy required to condition it. Less outside or "makeup" air is required when the building or portions of it are vacant. One technology that shows promise is a dedicated outside air system that precisely meters the right amount of makeup air to the occupied spaces and decouples the HVAC system from the requirement to supply fresh outside air.

7. **Reevaluate the human interface** with the building. Ultimately, the most important strategy for energy conservation is to change the way that humans interact with the building. Buildings are a complex interrelated series of systems that should not be operated on automatic pilot. Often the measures that give the best return on investments are the simplest and most basic, like addressing years of deferred maintenance, retro-commissioning the building by testing and adjusting the performance of all mechanical systems so that they perform as designed, and upgrading operator training. Obtaining higher efficiency in buildings requires the input and cooperation of many different practitioners with a wide range of skill sets. A sustainability team can include the building owners, fiscal managers, physical operators, employee-based sustainability committees, professional energy managers, and building energy professionals. Achieving sustainability is an ongoing effort, not a one-time pass through. It requires testing, verification, monitoring, and periodic reviews of performance.

Cappy Kidd is director of Energy Services for AKT Peerless Environmental and Energy Services.

SOURCE

The Alliance for Water Efficiency provides more information at www.allianceforwaterefficiency.org.

building energy demand is highest. Though storage capacity requirements may limit the application of these systems, off-peak cooling is cost-effective for buildings that are subject to both a substantial cost differential between peak and off-peak rates, and high demand charges (which are based on maximum electricity demand). Ice storage cooling is a load-shifting technology, shifting building energy demand from peak to off-peak hours, reducing energy demand peaks for the building.

▸▸ **ABSORPTION CHILLERS**. Absorption chillers use heat energy to create cold water for building usage. In contrast to conventional chillers, which use a condenser to chill a gas to a liquid, an absorption chiller uses evaporation to do so. Absorption chillers are quiet, are predominantly gas fired, and are an effective method of reducing the electricity required to cool a building in high-cost markets or during peak rate and use hours. They can be incorporated into hybrid cooling systems.

▸▸ **ECONOMIZERS**. When the outdoor temperature is mild (typically 5°F [roughly 3°C] lower than indoor temperatures) and humidity is low, buildings can circulate 100 percent outside air through the building without using mechanical heating or cooling. This "air-side economizer" cycle, while appropriate for temperate climates, is not recommended for environments where reducing the humidity of building interiors through air conditioning is necessary. Water-side economizers save energy by using water from the cooling tower to chill water when the outside temperature is sufficiently cool. Using a plate-heat (water to water) heat exchanger, the chilled water can be used to cool chiller water, which is circulated to parts of the building that require cooling.

▸▸ **DISPLACEMENT VENTILATION**. Usually coupled with a raised floor plenum (a separate space provided for air circulation for HVAC, typically in the space between the structural floor and the raised floor), low-velocity supply air is introduced to the office space at floor level at a temperature only slightly below the desired room temperature. Displacement ventilation takes advantage of the "stack effect," cooling air only to the level needed to assure occupant comfort and allowing hotter air to rise to ceiling level, where it is exhausted. By contrast, conventional ventilation systems force cooler air into interiors at ceiling levels, requiring larger volumes of cool air—and additional energy use—to maintain comfortable temperatures.

▸▸ **SUSTAINABLE HVAC OPTIONS**. Ground-source heat pumps, commonly referred to as geothermal systems, and combined heat and power (CHP) systems are especially sustainable options for heating and cooling (see the discussion in Sustainable Energy Options).

HVAC CONTROL AND MODULATING EQUIPMENT

Advanced control and modulating equipment can help to assure the high-efficiency operation of HVAC systems. VFDs, also referred to as variable-speed drives, are used to adjust or modulate fan speed in air-handling units, reducing the energy used by the fan motors. A 20 percent reduction in fan speed reduces the energy used by the motor by 50 percent.[11] (For more information on VFDs, see the sidebar by Cappy Kidd.) VFDs allow the HVAC system to control both the volume of delivered air and the air temperature, enabling the system to meet heating and cooling needs in the most efficient method possible. This can have dramatic implications for energy efficiency.

In tandem with VFDs, direct digital controls (DDCs), which automate HVAC operations, give facility managers unprecedented levels of control, improving systems' operating and energy efficiencies. DDCs use sensors in all building zones to measure conditions that can affect space conditioning, including supply air temperature, return air temperature, static pressure in the ducts, outside air temperature and humidity, internal humidity, and feedback from the VFDs. Using these data and programmable software, the automation system makes real-time adjustments in operations to deliver the amount of heating and or cooling needed by the building and eliminate excess capacity from the system. (For additional applications of advanced HVAC controls and building automation systems, see the sidebar by Ryan Hoger.)

Building Automation Systems

A building automation system (BAS), also known as a building control system, integrates the direct digital controls from all building systems, connecting HVAC, lighting, security and access, fire detection, and advanced communication system controls into a single control point. Relying on remote sensors and monitors, a BAS platform can be programmed to make automatic operating adjustments to systems and collect and measure performance data, providing managers with real-time information about building

The East Tower at Adobe Towers, the Adobe Systems headquarters in San Jose, California, was completed in 1998 and, along with headquarters' two other towers, was retrofitted from 2001 to 2006.

WILLIAM A. PORTER

THE REVOLUTION IN HVAC CONTROLS

RYAN R. HOGER

The revolution in HVAC control systems has really been more of an evolution. Developments have come slowly, in small increments, and without significant notice, but the benefits of applying 20 years of cumulative technology evolution to an existing building can be great. This sidebar highlights some of the most effective and widely implemented concepts.

Programmable Thermostats

Many existing buildings run heating and cooling systems 24 hours a day, seven days a week, even though the building may be occupied only 12 hours a day, five days a week. Using a programmed schedule to turn systems off or to operate them less intensively when a facility is unoccupied can save substantial amounts of energy for a very low cost, reducing heating and cooling expenses by as much as 25 percent. Programmable thermostats also adjust heating and cooling based on interior temperature. Because the installed cost of a programmable thermostat is low, an energy savings payback period of less than six months is common. Some tweaking will be necessary on each installation of a programmed thermostat to find the ideal number of degrees to set back and the optimal time to start the system each day.

Intelligent-Recovery Programmable Thermostats

This concept takes the programmable thermostat one step further by using recent history to determine the best time to start a system each morning to achieve the desired setpoint at the desired time. Instead of programming a system to start at 5 a.m. to have the space comfortable by 8 a.m., the thermostat can be programmed for 8 a.m. and it will adjust the system as needed to make the space comfortable by that time. On some days that may mean starting at 5 a.m. and on others it may mean starting at 7:30 a.m. Each minute that the thermostat is able to delay the startup past 5 a.m., it saves additional energy beyond what a standard programmable thermostat could save. The incremental cost for an intelligent-recovery programmable thermostat versus a standard programmable thermostat is very low and a payback period of less than one month is common.

Outdoor Economizers

Economizers are outdoor-air intake dampers that can be opened on mild days to use outdoor air to cool a building instead of running mechanical compressors to do so. There are numerous ways to control these devices, each offering incremental improvements in potential energy savings:

▸▸ **Dry bulb temperature method.** Open the outdoor air damper for free cooling when the outside temperature is below 55°F (13°C).

▸▸ **Enthalpy.** Open the outdoor air damper when the outdoor enthalpy (temperature and humidity) is below a certain level. This method often correlates to the same 55°F (13°C) setting on a humid day but permits a higher setting, say 65°F (18°C), on a dry day, thereby allowing free cooling over a wider range of outdoor temperatures.

▸▸ **Differential enthalpy.** This method compares the temperature and humidity of the outdoor air to that of the indoor or return air. If the outdoor air can be cooled more efficiently than the indoor air, energy can be saved by using the economizer damper and turning off the compressors.

▸▸ **Integrated economizer.** This method can be used in conjunction with any of the other three approaches. In certain temperature and humidity conditions, it allows the economizer to be used in conjunction with mechanical cooling. The economizer is used as the first system to cool the interior, and the compressor becomes the second, should the economizer alone not be able to achieve the desired level of comfort.

Zoning and VAV Systems

Organizing and grouping building areas with similar usage patterns and temperature conditions into zones can reduce energy use. Zoning can come in many forms, but one of the most popular is variable air volume (VAV). VAV systems use dampers to reduce airflow to areas that are comfortable (that is, the setpoint is achieved) or unoccupied, while directing larger airflows to the zones that need it. As some of these dampers close down, the main fan system can reduce its speed, and hence overall airflow and energy consumption, without reducing the airflow to the zones that need it.

VAV Reset

In a VAV system, cooling capacity as well as fan speed can be reduced to save energy. Why continue to deliver constant 55°F (13°C) supply air to cool a space on a day when 58 to 60°F (14 to 15°C) air will do the job? A VAV reset strategy looks at the needs of the various zones and calculates the degrees by which the system can reset the primary cooling discharge temperature. This saves energy at the cooling compressor and can reduce the need for reheating in zones that may have been overcooled with 55°F (13°C) air.

Occupancy Sensors

There are various ways to determine whether a room or space is occupied. Motion sensors are used frequently but can be problematic. They may operate with too-short time spans or may not register that a person is at a given desk. Because of these issues, motion sensors should be used only to control energy use in transient spaces, such as hallways, lavatories, or conference rooms, and for storage closets and mechanical rooms that are infrequently occupied.

CO_2 sensors provide occupancy measures for ventilation systems. People exhale CO_2 at very predictable rates; measuring CO_2 will show whether more or less fresh air needs to be brought in. Nearly all building codes permit CO_2 sensors to be used to reduce outdoor air ventilation rates below the code minimums. It is very expensive to heat, cool, and filter outdoor air for ventilation, especially on peak temperature days. Typical payback periods associated with the energy savings obtained from CO_2 sensors range from six to 24 months, depending on occupancy and usage patterns.

Operable Window Interlock

Operable windows are an amenity for any green building. However, it does not make much sense to open a window while the HVAC system tries to use mechanical energy to ventilate (and even heat or cool) the room with open windows. Window switches (similar to home-security window alarms) can be wired to the zone's VAV damper to disable that zone whenever the window is open and to re-enable the VAV damper when the window shuts. Freeze protection must be taken into account in cold climates, to avoid problems if occupants open a window and forget to shut it before they leave.

Building Automation Systems

The installation of a building automation system (BAS) seems like a daunting and costly task. However, like other electronic innovations (processor chips, DVD players, flat-panel televisions), the typical BAS has come down in price as popularity and volume have increased. No longer the domain of specialty control contractors, installing and maintaining a BAS can be done by most mechanical and electrical contractors. Most systems will include programmable thermostat features including adaptive intelligent recovery. They also permit the other concepts (zoning, VAV reset, CO_2 sensors, etc.) to become simple configuration choices at startup, instead of costly and elaborate electrical wiring projects.

The modern BAS, available since 2004, has taken the control power out of the mechanical room and brought it to the facility manager or even the occupants. The typical interface is now a Web browser, accessible from any computer in the building or even the world. Various access levels can be configured, allowing manager A to change schedules for department A but not be able to adjust anything in department B. Such configuration abilities allow occupants, in the person of the manager responsible for a zone, to make schedule adjustments as events dictate. A BAS also can be integrated with systems other than the HVAC, such as security card access. This allows yet another level of scheduling control. When an employee swipes out of a secured building, the system can automatically shut off ventilation air to his or her office, reduce the heating or cooling setpoints, and even turn off the lights if the employee forgot to do so.

Alarms, Notifications, and Diagnostics

A BAS and other control systems can benefit from built-in alarm, notification, and diagnostic devices. These systems can range from very simple to fairly sophisticated. An example of a sophisticated application is an "alarming" system—one that can

---

A Word on Occupant Comfort Controls

Obviously, it is the goal of every control system to make occupants comfortable. In the ideal world, every occupant would have his or her own HVAC equipment and associated controls. There is, however, a balance that must be realized between comfort control, first cost, and energy conservation. In regard to energy conservation, it is not advisable to lock thermostats and controls. Although this strategy can conserve energy in theory, it seldom will in actuality. People will do what they have to do to become comfortable. They will bring in electric desk heaters to stay warm and electric fans to stay cool. They will tamper with the thermostat and sensors. They will prop open doors and windows. These efforts to be comfortable may actually increase utility costs and will certainly decrease employee productivity. Therefore, it is recommended that HVAC control be given to as many individual occupants as is possible. At a minimum, every conference room and private office with enclosed partition walls should have its own VAV box and associated controls. For open office areas, thermostats will likely have to be shared for cost and sizing reasons, but the goal should be to have one thermostat for every two people.

What to Avoid in Designing and Installing HVAC Controls

⏩ **Large temperature setback.** In some cases, allowing the thermostat to be set back too far may use more energy to recover from setback than if nothing was done. Make sure to have at least six hours of unoccupied time and try to set back about 5°F (3°C)—to 65°F (18°C) for heating and to 80°F (27°C) for cooling.

⏩ **Too-early start times.** When using a thermostat with intelligent recovery, it is important to not schedule the start time too early. Set the controls for the actual time people will start arriving at the building and be patient: it can take seven days or more for the thermostat to start building a history in order to make accurate predictions about the startup time required each day.

⏩ **Motion sensors in nontransient spaces.** Motion sensors in private offices or cubicles are usually ineffective because most are not sensitive enough to register the typical office worker's only movements (typing and mouse use, phoning, and eye blinking). Reserve the use of motion sensors for transient areas and areas of the building that are occupied infrequently.

⏩ **VFDs on three-way piping systems.** VFDs can save a lot of pumping energy by throttling back the speed of a pump when the zones do not need full flow (similarly to the air control on a VAV system). However, this strategy only works with two-way control valves. As the valves throttle back, the pressure in the pipe increases and the VFD slows down. But in a three-way piping system, when a valve closes, it closes the path to the coil but allows the water to flow through a bypass line. As a result, pressure does not build and the VFD does not slow down, hence little to no energy savings result. Most two-way valve systems should be retrofitted with VFDs on the chilled and hot-water pumps, but it is not worth the expense if the system has all three-way control valves.

⏩ **Oversized equipment.** No matter how advanced the controls system, it will not improve the efficiency or comfort of an improperly sized heating and cooling unit.

diagnose itself and notify service personnel. A similar, low-cost alternative may be a thermostat that can send a text message notification to a building operator that the building temperature has dropped to 55°F (13°C) on a weekend even though the setback temperature was 65°F (18°C), indicating a system failure. This notification enables the operator to take action before pipes freeze and burst. Other items that are easy and useful to set alarm notification for are dirty filters, fan failure, and pump failure.

More complex diagnostics and alarming usually are available from equipment manufacturers for chillers, boilers, condensing units, VFDs, and VAV rooftop units. These components can report to the BAS if a compressor has failed, if refrigerant is low, if there is a power quality issue, if the burner did not ignite, and much more. This information enables the building operator to take action when the equipment fails instead of waiting until the failure affects occupant comfort. Diagnostics and alarming also enable the building operator to identify the problem quickly and notify the appropriate service company.

Ryan R. Hoger is the product manager of Commercial Systems at HVAC Solutions, a subsidiary of Temperature Equipment Corporation.

operations, including energy use, equipment usage, and system failures. Engineers can design systems that integrate all building operations into a user-friendly interface. Many of these systems can incorporate personal controls for building occupants, allowing occupants to adjust lighting and room or zone temperatures to their liking.

CO_2 monitors integrated into the BAS can be used to control fresh air ventilation, adjusting the intake of fresh air to meet the real-time demand of occupants. In tandem, CO_2 monitors and a BAS ensure adequate indoor air quality for building occupants while minimizing unnecessary heating and cooling of outside air, thereby reducing energy usage.

For life safety, carbon monoxide monitors in the building interiors, and if needed, in car park areas, should be integrated into the BAS.

They notify building managers or emergency response centers if carbon monoxide levels surpass critical safety thresholds.

Advanced applications of a BAS enable tenants and owners to track in real time occupant safety, energy use, environmental impact, and economic performance, while providing unprecedented ability to adjust building operations.[12] A BAS thereby results in building energy savings, reduced operating costs, and improved occupant comfort and safety.

Reintroducing Passive Heating and Cooling

One of the best ways to reduce the energy required for heating and cooling within a building is to let nature do it. Passive heating and cooling strategies utilize the sun, wind, and outside temperature to help regulate temperature and humidity in a building. These strategies frequently improve indoor air quality also, because outdoor air is typically cleaner than indoor air. Note, however, that passive cooling and ventilation that relies on the movement of unfiltered air into the building space should not be utilized in locations that have poor outdoor air quality.

Although the greatest opportunities for implementing passive heating and cooling are found in new construction, the project team should evaluate this approach for a retrofit. In most climates and locations, retrofits that encompass alterations to the building envelope should be designed with passive heating and cooling in mind. An energy model can help to identify the most efficient and effective passive cooling opportunities.

The use of passive heating and cooling can decrease the building's reliance on mechanical systems, lowering operating costs and possibly reducing the size and cost of any new HVAC equipment required in the retrofit. For example, exposing the thermal mass of the building (concrete and masonry walls and floors) so that it can be used as a heat sink (a material that absorbs and dissipates heat gradually), will moderate building temperature fluctuations. The moderation reduces peak heating and cooling needs, downsizing the mechanical system capacity required to condition the space.

PASSIVE COOLING

One of the simplest passive strategies is to use operable windows for ventilation in combination with an integrated ventilation strategy, such as cross-ventilation, stack-induced airflow (described earlier, in the discussion of displacement ventilation), to move air through the building. (Buildings that employ operable windows without undertaking an integrated ventilation strategy may incur a slight energy penalty.) Operable windows can be installed successfully into the curtain walls of high-rise structures, such as at Deutsche Bank's Greentowers in Frankfurt, Germany, where the use of operable windows is expected to reduce substantially the energy required for ventilation.

Depending on the building configuration, a number of passive cooling strategies can be used in office buildings. (See the sidebar by Tom Nelson for an analysis of several of these strategies and their implementation methods.)

PASSIVE HEATING

Passive solar heating utilizes the sun's energy to heat the interior space of an office building. Not all buildings will benefit from passive heating. Large office buildings are typically internal-load-driven structures, which means that they generate heat internally from equipment and people. Overheating of internal building spaces, especially in areas where there is sensitive computer equipment, can be a major concern. For this reason, office interiors should typically be controlled carefully to limit solar heat gain.

At the same time, passive heating may be useful for certain office buildings, such as smaller buildings in colder climates. The use of energy modeling is important in determining the need for passive heating, identifying passive solar heating options, and optimizing solutions.

PASSIVE COOLING IN EXISTING BUILDINGS

TOM NELSON

Before the advent of air-conditioning technology, all buildings were naturally ventilated and passively cooled to some extent. In many existing buildings, passive cooling features are still in place and just need to be rediscovered and returned to working order. In the others, passive cooling strategies can be introduced.

Passive cooling takes place when outside air that is cooler than body temperature comes in contact with occupants and they experience a cooling sensation through the evaporation of the moisture on their skin. A number of strategies stimulate and maintain conditions conducive to passive cooling in buildings:

▸ **Natural ventilation,** including operable windows, chimneys, and atriums;

▸ **Evaporative cooling systems,** which work with chimneys to cool and release hot air and to draw in cool air;

▸ **Exposure of high thermal mass,** which uncovers concrete frames, shear walls, interior slabs, or thick concrete floors, to store and gradually release energy received from the air, thereby regulating interior temperatures; and

▸ **Nighttime flushing,** which brings cooler, nighttime air into the interior to cool spaces for the following day.

The key steps in selecting and carrying out a passive cooling strategy are detailed in this sidebar.

Analyze and Inventory Existing Conditions

The selection of the appropriate passive cooling approach is dependent on climate, site, and building conditions. The first step in choosing a passive cooling strategy is therefore to analyze and inventory existing project conditions:

▸ **Climate.** Passive cooling strategies rely primarily on local climate conditions. An analysis of the surrounding climate is essential to maximizing passive cooling. It is all about microclimate. The weather data for most places is taken from the local airport or university and can be used only as a broad basis for analysis. For a small cost, a portable weather station can be located on site in advance of design and construction to log climate data for each season. Temperature, humidity, wind speed, wind direction, wind pressure, solar gain, and other factors can be cataloged. These data are fed into the analysis and performance software to inform, test, and verify design approaches.

▸ **Airborne contaminants.** Allowing unfiltered air into the building is usually required for passive cooling. An analysis of potential hazards from nearby uses is therefore also required. These hazards cannot always be mitigated at their sources. The position of air intakes can be informed by the existing condition analysis, and intakes can be placed out of the path of upwind contaminants. Through-wall filtered-air intakes can be integrated into the exterior wall and used in conditions where mild contaminants cannot be avoided. Filtration will slow down airflow and must be compensated for downstream.

▸ **Boundary conditions.** Buildings and open areas around a site have a significant effect on the microclimate. Data collected from the local weather station can help construct a picture of the wind patterns and hot and cold zones created by adjacent buildings. In the Northern Hemisphere, taller buildings to the south of the site will shade it for most of the day, creating cooler zones to the south that can be utilized for passive cooling. Conversely, low or no buildings to the south may create a hot zone there that must be dealt with by other means, such as landscape zones, solar shading, placement of high mass elements, or more sophisticated double-skin construction. By reducing solar heat gain or redirecting it from the building interiors, these solar protection measures reduce the amount of heat entering the building.

▸ **Landscaping.** Plantings that provide shade can produce temperatures that are significantly lower than the surrounding area. Judicious placement of air intake openings on the leeward side of the landscaped area, so that the openings are sheltered from the wind, can take advantage of those lower temperatures. Landscape plantings have the added effects of cleaning the supply air of particulate pollutants, elevating the oxygen content, and providing a linkage to nature for occupants. Plantings can be coupled with a mechanically cooled building by placing the landscaped area on the roof directly in the path of the intake of the air handling system. This will lower the temperature of the intake air, allowing the economizer cycle to run for longer periods. These concepts go back thousands of years to ancient societies whose houses were designed around garden courts that featured a pool of water. The combination of evaporative cooling from the pool and evapotranspiration—the return of moisture and oxygen to the air—from the garden plants allowed those societies to exist in hot, arid regions in relative comfort.

▸▸ **Building geometry and interior conditions.** A building's shape and interior conditions determine to a great extent how air will move through and around it, where high- and low-pressure zones are located, and how they change over time. A building's height and floor-to-skin ratio (the ratio of floor area to exterior cladding area) also affect the dynamics of air movement. A single-story building's surface area is dominated by its roof, so strategies that take advantage of the roof's solar exposure and mitigate solar heat gain should be considered. In taller buildings, the wall area dominates. In any size of building, the distance from the outside walls to the core is directly related to how easily air will move through the building. Air typically flows more easily through a shallow building and from high- to low-pressure zones. Conditions must be created inside the building to facilitate this type of air movement. A high internal heat load created by people and machinery can also be incorporated in a passive cooling approach, by taking advantage of the fact that heated air rises. The upward movement of heated air can be harnessed to stimulate the air currents that are essential to passive cooling.

Develop and Implement Passive Cooling Concepts

Once conditions in and around the building are understood, the next effort involves the development and implementation of appropriate passive cooling concepts.

▸▸ **Modeling and analysis.** In the case of an existing building, modeling and analysis can take place earlier than with new construction because the conditions can be modeled with known climate data and building geometry. Early modeling and analysis will help identify viable passive solutions that can be strengthened by suitable planning. Building information modeling (BIM) software can be used to create a three-dimensional model that contains information about the materials and systems within the building. The climate data are fed into analysis software that can give a very close approximation of the performance of the building under different circumstances and throughout the year. Different design scenarios can be created and analyzed to maximize the effectiveness of the strategies selected. (See chapter 8 for a more detailed discussion of BIM.)

▸▸ **Planning.** Once existing conditions are modeled and the building's climatic response is understood, planning can commence to create an indoor environment that supports passive cooling. Planning begins with the interior layout. Obstructions within the occupied space should be minimized in the area that is within 30 feet of the exterior wall. The most effective layouts use open-office planning with low walls and no private offices on the perimeter. Offices on the interior edges of the open-planned zone can also benefit from passive cooling strategies by having transoms, louvers, or operable lights that face the open areas. The size of the passively cooled zones should be determined by airflow analysis.

▸▸ **Implementation.** The key factor in a passively cooled environment is the creation of convection currents—the currents created from air circulation—from the exterior through the interior to an exhaust, cooling occupants along the way. There are numerous passive cooling strategies to choose from:

• Operable windows. The simplest way to provide passive cooling is through operable windows on both sides of a narrow floor plate, with air entering on the windward side and leaving through operable windows on the leeward or sheltered side. The outside air should enter low and exit high to take advantage of the natural stack effect, in which hot air rises. Stack ventilation allows cooler air to enter interior spaces at lower levels, to provide cooling to occupants. As cooler air reaches the interior and gains heat from occupants and equipment, it naturally rises. Stack ventilation releases the hottest air from higher windows, skylights, and other exhaust mechanisms to maintain comfortable temperatures and sufficient ventilation.

• Chimneys, cool towers, and evaporative cooling. In a building with a bigger footprint, a chimney or series of chimneys (also referred to as vertical shafts) can be introduced in the core area to provide exhaust. This technique can also be used in reverse in the form of a "cool tower." A cool tower is a chimney with an evaporative cooler on top. This technique works well in hot, dry climates to provide cool, humid air to the interior. Hot, dry air passes through wet media in the evaporative cooler and loses its heat through evaporation. Cool, humid air drops into the space through the chimney and displaces air that is already there. This system can be supplemented with a solar chimney located at the opposite end of the space. The solar chimney exhausts air as previously described but has an exposed projection that is heated by solar radiation and stimulates air currents to exhaust the indoor air. The area required for chimneys is a relatively small percentage of the floor area. If the building is entirely passively conditioned, the savings realized by the use of

Maximizing the sun's heating energy, or direct solar gain, uses the greenhouse effect to trap heat from solar radiation which enters the building through glass surfaces on sun-facing exposures (in the Northern Hemisphere, predominantly on the southern exposure, as well as on the western and eastern exposures).[13] Using glass with a high SHGC for these windows can help maximize solar heat gain. (Glass with a high SHGC transmits the sun's heat from the building exterior to the interior.)

In addition, indirect and isolated solar gain strategies, such as transpired solar walls and sunspaces, can be used to heat interiors. Transpired solar walls are perforated panels located on southern-facing outdoor walls. These walls allow outside air to pass the perforated solar collector wall, where it is heated by solar radiation and rises between the two chimneys in lieu of expensive mechanical equipment far outweigh the loss of floor area.

- Atriums. Atriums function similarly to chimneys but perform on a larger scale. Atriums harness convection currents to draw air through the building and out through openings in the atrium roof. Space inside an existing building frequently can be converted into an atrium. This process also narrows the floors, making internal air movement more effective. Additional benefits of an atrium are the creation of a pleasant environment at the bottom floor, views out of the internal portions of the building, and access to additional solar radiation. Careful attention must be paid to building codes that regulate atrium size and configuration to avoid the need for costly smoke evacuation equipment and rated walls.

- Exposure of thermal mass. The exposure of thermal mass to the building interior, including concrete slabs and framing or massive shear walls, can be used to regulate internal temperatures. Uncovered thermal mass stores energy from the air. Thus, heat introduced into the interior during the day is stored and helps to heat the interior overnight. Conversely, colder air introduced at night can be used to cool the interior for the following day. Nighttime flushing is used frequently in conjunction with thermal mass exposure.

- **Nighttime flushing.** Well suited to existing buildings, nighttime flushing has the greatest effect in buildings that have a high amount of mass exposed to the interior whether through a concrete frame, massive shear walls, or thick concrete floors. In climates with large diurnal temperature swings, air is brought in at night. This can be done passively with proper design or with assistance from a powered fan. The cooler night air lowers the temperature of the mass; those lower temperatures are radiated back into the interior overnight, cooling the environment for the next day's use. The small amount of fan energy required to flush the building could be generated on site with photovoltaic panels and battery storage.

- **Building operations.** Automated controls can be used to open and close windows and exhaust devices in a passively cooled building. This provides a higher degree of reliability of system performance. Windows and ventilation devices must be fitted with powered actuators and wired into the system. In a purely passive system, the opening and closing of windows is done by the occupants. Simple software systems such as email messaging can also be employed to alert occupants when windows in their zone should be opened or closed.

- **Occupant education.** Interior temperature ranges and comfort conditions should be clearly understood by the owner and users of the building. Occupants adapt to the passively cooled and naturally ventilated environments by wearing clothing appropriate to the season. This is a necessary element of a passively cooled building. Passively cooled buildings frequently have been called participatory buildings because they require the participation of the occupants in order to function properly.

Conclusion

Passively cooled buildings are frequently healthier and more pleasant places in which to live and work. Occupants have more control of their environment, more access to daylight and views, and a closer connection to the outdoors. Most existing buildings are candidates for passive cooling and natural ventilation strategies. Passive cooling strategies use less material resources, lower energy use, and provide healthier and more humane indoor environments.

Tom Nelson, AIA, LEED AP, is a principal with Mithun in Seattle, Washington.

walls to enter the building's ventilation system. This method can preheat air to 30 to 55°F (–1 to 10°C) on sunny winter days.[14] Sunspaces are comparatively small glass enclosures attached to the southern side of a building. Sunlight passes through the glazing, warming the sunspace, and the heated air can then be circulated into the building. During warm weather or when additional heating is not desired, the sunspace can be shaded or closed off from the rest of the structure, preventing circulation of the heated air.

Sustainable Energy Options

To further reduce a building's carbon footprint, building owners can specify power from renewable energy sources, such as wind, solar, biomass, and hydroelectric. Commonly referred to as green power, this electricity may entail a per kWh premium over unspecified conventional sources of electricity provided by the local utility. In many countries, public utility providers are being mandated to purchase a certain percentage of their power portfolio from renewable energy providers.

(For additional detail on green power purchase options through the use of renewable energy credits, see chapter 5.)

Geothermal heating and cooling is another source of renewable energy. Ground-source heat pump systems utilize the near constant temperature of the ground to heat, cool, and provide hot water to a building or a complex of buildings.

Office buildings can generate electrical power on site, reducing their carbon footprint and improving their power security through a distributed energy resources (DER) system, often known as a distributed generation (DG) system. Combined heat and power (CHP), is often added to a DER/DG system to capture the waste heat generated during electricity production and use it for heating or cooling. CHP can be combined with district energy systems, which allow buildings to access heating and cooling capacity from a central source, commonly serving building campuses or complexes. (For more information about sustainable energy choices for buildings, developments, and campuses, see the sidebar on sustainable energy options.)

The central ventilation unit at 545 Madison Avenue in New York City is located on the roof in order to avoid intake of street-level exhaust and pollutants. High-efficiency MERV 13 filters remove particulate contaminants.

KEVIN CHU/KCJP

SUSTAINABLE ENERGY OPTIONS FOR OFFICE BUILDINGS

GEORGE VAVAROUTSOS

While conventional office buildings will generally be on the grid, building owners can use a number of alternatives to traditional energy sources to reduce the GHG emissions associated with their buildings. In addition to reducing environmental impact, these technologies can improve energy reliability for the building and provide greater control over energy costs.

Distributed Energy Resources (DER) or Distributed Generation (DG)

DER or DG systems, often referred to as distributed generation, are small, decentralized energy systems located at or near the point where energy will be used. The systems can be on or off the grid, and are either dispatchable (can be turned on or off) or intermittent (energy source is uncontrollably variable). These systems can provide users with a number of energy-related benefits:

▸▸ **Controlled energy costs.** DER/DG technologies can produce some or all of the energy needed for building operations. For office buildings in high-cost fuel and electricity markets, DER/DG allows users to choose technologies and systems that operate at a lower overall cost. Renewable technologies, such as photovoltaics and wind, produce electricity with no variable cost for fuel sources. DER/DG systems can provide an operating hedge against rising electricity costs. In locations that have net metering and expedited interconnection policies for smaller DER/DG systems, these systems enable customers to sell or bank excess electric energy with the local electric supplier. In service areas that do not offer net metering and expedited interconnection policies, energy storage technologies can sometimes be used cost-effectively to store excess electricity for future use.

▸▸ **Peak demand reduction or peak shaving.** For office buildings where electricity costs are based on both energy used (measured in kilowatt-hours, or kWh) and peak demand (a measurement of capacity, or the maximum rate at which a building requires the electricity to be delivered, measured in kilowatts, or kW), peak shaving may substantially reduce electricity costs by reducing the amount or rate of electric use during more costly on-peak hours. When building energy demand rises above a predetermined level or becomes very costly, a small, auxiliary DER/DG system is used to meet some or all of the demand for electricity, thereby reducing the amount of peak demand charges imposed by electric utility rate design.

▸▸ **Emissions reductions.** Certain DER/DG technologies, such as photovoltaics, wind, and fuel cells, are no- or low-emission systems. Most other DER/DG systems, which are powered by light diesel fuel or natural gas, have carbon or nitrous oxide emissions that are less than half those of burning coal (measured in lbs/kWh) in a traditional central power plant.

▸▸ **Improved power reliability.** For facilities with greater power continuity or power quality requirements, DER/DG systems can be used to provide power or backup generation, thus improving overall system reliability as compared with grid-supplied electricity. In some cases, emergency generators can be employed for peak shaving purposes, as is being promoted in some states. DER/DG technologies can significantly reduce the risk of system downtime, a critically important feature for high-technology, computer server, laboratory, or medical tenants.

▸▸ **Improved efficiencies** from combined heat and power (CHP) applications. Also referred to as cogeneration, CHP systems can be added to a DER/DG system to capture the waste heat generated during electricity production and use it for heating or cooling applications, reducing or removing the need to use another energy source. The waste heat is used to generate hot water or steam for heating or run through an absorption chiller for cooling (see the discussion in this chapter for more information about absorption chillers). A CHP system creates substantially greater efficiencies for a DER/DG system, lowering facility energy costs and leading to emission reductions.

A number of DER/DG technologies can be used on site, but not all are considered sustainable energy sources. The best DER/DG options for sustainable energy include the following:

▸▸ **Photovoltaic (PV).** PV systems are an intermittent renewable energy source, converting the sun's energy to electricity. System size is constrained by the space available for installing the PV array on or near the building. The typical PV system installed on an office building has less than 150 kW capacity, at a cost of $6,000 to $10,000 per kW installed.[2] PV systems are generally suitable for retrofit applications. These systems are gaining market share as DER/DG units; government incentives for purchase and installation, coupled with technological improvements and lower costs, are increasing the size of the solar market.

Wind. These systems, which are composed of fan blades and a generator located on the top of a tall tower, building, or pole to create electricity from wind energy, are considered an intermittent renewable source. Only small wind systems are considered to be a DER/DG system. They have a typical capacity of 10 kW per turbine.[3] These systems are typically not suitable for urban or suburban settings because of zoning restrictions; the rule of thumb for efficient operation of a horizontal-axis wind turbine is that the blades must be 30 feet higher than any other object within a 300-foot radius. This is difficult to accomplish in a dense urban setting, although new approaches are being developed to incorporate wind power more extensively into commercial properties.

Fuel cells. A fuel cell combines oxygen with hydrogen derived from a fuel source such as natural gas, propane, or landfill methane to create electricity and heat without the need for combustion. These dispatchable systems have near zero emissions and can be powered by a number of fuel sources, allowing them to be run on the lowest-cost source available. Fuel cells for office buildings typically produce 40 kW to 250 kW of power and can be used as part of a cogeneration (CHP) system. Fuel cells are still considered an emerging DER/DG system; researchers expect that technological advances in the next five to ten years should improve system performance, while expanded production should lower system costs.[4] Current installed system costs are $4,000 to $10,000 per kW.

Microturbines. Small combustion turbines can produce between 25 kW and 500 kW of power, and, in smaller sizes, are a newer, cleaner alternative to reciprocating engines. These systems can be run on multiple fuels (including natural gas, hydrogen, propane, and diesel) and can be used for cogeneration applications. They are one of the more economical DER/DG systems, with an equipment cost of $1,000 to $1,200 per kW installed.[5]

Biomass systems. By converting organic materials to fuel, biomass systems can be used to heat and cool buildings, and provide electricity.[6] These systems use agricultural waste, such as plant husks or animal waste, or wood-based biomass, as a low-carbon, organic fuel source. In addition, paper and other on-site waste materials can be used as fuel sources for biomass systems. Biomass technologies are well suited for CHP applications and for use as a district energy system (discussed later). Buildings located near a biomass fuel source or on an established biomass delivery route are the best candidates for biomass systems.

The costs and application of each DER/DG technology will depend on the size and the use of the system, building and site limitations, and local energy costs, including standby and backup service rates from the utility. A careful feasibility study and cost-benefit analysis should be conducted before installation to determine which, if any, of the technologies is suitable.

Ground-Source Heat Pumps or Geothermal Systems

Ground-source heat pumps or geothermal systems are another highly sustainable way to deliver heating, cooling, and hot water to a building or to a complex of buildings. The technology utilizes the near-constant temperature of the ground for space heating and cooling, and to provide hot water.

Generally, geothermal systems do not produce electricity. They are a clean source of energy developed by circulating a refrigerant (water or an antifreeze-water solution) through pipes (loops) installed in the ground, in a closed-loop system. For heating, geothermal systems absorb heat from the ground and then carry it through the system and into the building. For cooling, the process is reversed: the building cools itself by pulling heat out of the structure through the refrigerant and re-injecting it into the ground. In an open-loop geothermal system, water from an outdoor source (such as a well, lake, or stream) is pumped into the structure to provide heating or cooling and is then discharged back to the source.

Depending on the availability of open land, underground pipes for geothermal systems can be installed vertically or horizontally in the ground. Most office buildings, because of internal heat gain, have higher cooling than heating requirements, especially in warmer climates. A hybrid system, which couples a ground-source heat pump with a cooling tower or fluid cooler to provide auxiliary cooling, can effectively manage heightened cooling requirements.[7] In a hybrid system, the piping is sized appropriately for the smaller heating load, maximizing the cost-effectiveness of the overall heating and cooling system.

System and installation costs and value for geothermal systems range significantly with geography, site conditions, and building type, but installation costs are typically more expensive than for gas-fired heating and electric-driven mechanical cooling systems. Although first costs may be higher, buildings with geothermal systems benefit from the the reduction in energy required to heat and cool the structure, and reduced maintenance costs for the system. A site-specific feasibility study can measure the opportunity for replacing gas-fired equipment with a geothermal-based heating and cooling system.

District Energy

District energy systems allow buildings to access heating and cooling capacity from a central source outside the structure, eliminating the use of or need for separate systems in each building. A central heating/chilled-water plant can also use CHP to create steam or warm and chilled water, to pass through a piping network to the buildings on the district energy loop.

A district energy system can support a university or office campus, a medical facility, an airport, a military complex, a shopping mall, or a large city (the largest commercial system in the world is located in New York City, covering a significant portion of Manhattan). A number of energy sources, both renewable and fossil fuel based, can fuel the central plant system. District heating and cooling based on CHP or renewable fuels is a sustainable source of energy because it uses waste heat from another application. A number of retrofitted buildings in certain markets have the infrastructure necessary to connect to a district energy system for improved efficiencies and lower energy costs, which would enable the decommissioning of their existing boilers and chillers.

George Vavaroutsos, LEED AP, is a sustainable real estate consultant with Malachite LLC.

NOTES

1 Joseph Iannucci, Distributed Utility Associates, "Planning a Federal DER Project: Steps in the Process," presented May 14, 2003, www1.eere.energy.gov/femp/pdfs/derchp_jiannucci.pdf.

2 California Energy Commission, www.energy.ca.gov/distgen/equipment/photovoltaic/photovoltaic.html.

3 American Wind Energy Association, www.awea.org/smallwind/toolbox/TOOLS/fs_smallwind.asp.

4 California Energy Commission, www.energy.ca.gov/distgen/equipment/fuel_cells/future.html.

5 Distributed Generation: Reciprocating Engines, Microturbines, Fuel Cells, Stirling Engines, and Photovoltaics" www.wisconsinpublicservice.com/business/PDF/P_PA_44.pdf.

6 Biomass cooling is accomplished with an absorption chiller system.

7 U.S. Department of Energy, Federal Energy Management Program, "Assessment of Hybrid Geothermal Heat Pump Systems," www1.eere.energy.gov/femp/pdfs/hyhgp_tir.pdf. This report provides case studies identifying both the financial value and the effectiveness of hybrid GSHP systems for office buildings in warm climates.

Lighting

Effective lighting is a crucial component of occupant comfort and productivity. A key objective in the development of a green lighting system is to reduce the use of electric lighting, which can account for roughly 20 percent of the energy consumed in office buildings.[15] The use of electric lighting also contributes to internal heat gain within the building, raising cooling requirements and forcing the building's HVAC system to work harder. There are two primary strategies for improving the energy efficiency of lighting: reducing the overall demand for electric lighting, and redesigning and reconfiguring the existing electric lighting system to be more efficient.

REDUCING DEMAND FOR ELECTRIC LIGHTING

A key strategy in reducing demand for electric lighting is to maximize the use of daylighting within the building interiors. The effectiveness of daylighting will be affected by the building's exterior shading, window locations, glazing type, and interior space planning. Because many of the envelope decisions that affect daylighting potential may also lead to heat loss or gain through the building envelope, it is best to consider daylighting within the context of an integrated design strategy.

In addition to the improvement in lighting energy performance, preliminary studies show that daylighting and outdoor views can reduce employee absenteeism in the workplace, an important side benefit for employers.[16] (For a detailed discussion of daylighting in existing office buildings, see the sidebar by Neil Chambers.)

Another strategy for reducing lighting demand is to reduce levels of ambient light (general lighting from all directions) within interiors. Properly designed task lighting can ensure adequate light levels and quality in specific locations where it is needed. While a workstation may require task lights to ensure adequate work surface illuminance of 50 foot-candles (or 538 lux), a hallway requires half that light intensity (25 foot-candles, or 269 lux, average illumination) and can therefore rely on reduced ambient lighting.[17]

Lighting controls are an important component of a strategy to reduce lighting demand. No energy benefits will be realized from daylighting unless electric lighting is turned off or dimmed. Building teams can use a number of lighting control systems, including photosensors for daylighting, advanced room-occupancy sensors where appropriate, and scheduled controls. Daylight photosensors should be incorporated into the lighting system so that electric lighting can work in tandem with existing daylighting. The sensors control the electric lighting, adjusting the levels based upon the required illuminance for particular spaces. Some photosensors can turn on electric lights gradually to complement decreased daylight, while other simply turn on lights when daylighting alone does not achieve predetermined illuminance levels. The sensors selected should be appropriate for the area, and building staff and occupants should be trained in their use.

Passive infrared sensors and ultrasonic sensors are the latest potential alternatives to motion sensors in offices. Passive infrared sensors detect temperature changes in a room and work well if the entire room is within the sensor's field of view. Ultrasonic sensors use high frequency sound to detect motion and can work even around corners. Dual-technology sensors use both methods, increasing accuracy and flexibility, but at a higher price. Alternatively, office lighting can be programmed to turn off at closing time, should occupants forget to do so when they leave.

IMPROVING LIGHTING ENERGY EFFICIENCY

Where appropriate, existing electric lighting should be upgraded to improve energy efficiency. Some of the more common lighting enhancements for green office building retrofits include the following:

▸▸ **INSTALLING T5 AND T8 LAMPS.**[18] T5 lamps (bulbs) are the new standard for fluorescent lamps. These lamps are thinner, available in shorter lengths, and can have a higher light output than either T8 lamps or obsolete T12 lamps. The smaller size of T5 lamps provides lighting designers with more flexible lighting options, and their higher light output may reduce the number of light fixtures needed to light building interiors effectively. If lighting will be redesigned during a retrofit, T5 lamps offer high levels of lighting efficiency and greater flexibility in lighting design.

If the existing fluorescent fixtures will not be replaced and have T12 lamps, the lamps should be replaced with more efficient T8 lamps or with T5 lamps (using an adapter). To minimize the impact of toxic metals on the environment, the design team should specify low-mercury lights for the retrofit and for the ongoing lamp replacement program.

▸▸ **LED LIGHTS.** The use of light-emitting diodes (LEDs) for building lighting has grown significantly in the last few years. Commonly used for exit signs and task lighting, these solid-state lights are beginning to be incorporated into more general lighting applications, although costs are still high. LEDs have an extremely long lifespan (they can last 40,000 to 100,000 hours, depending on their color) and burn cool. The widespread application of LEDs should significantly reduce heat gain from lighting. (For more information about the future of LED lighting, see chapter 8.)

▸▸ **DIMMING ELECTRONIC BALLASTS.** Ballasts regulate the flow of electricity to lights. A dimming ballast allows for greater control over lighting, based on user needs. Electronic ballasts are lighter and more efficient then magnetic or hybrid ballasts.

▸▸ **PHOTOLUMINESCENT (PL) EXIT SIGNS.** PL exit signs are glow-in-the dark, nonelectric emergency exit signs that can replace powered systems. PL systems must be charged by

EVALUATING AND OPTIMIZING DAYLIGHTING IN EXISTING OFFICE BUILDINGS

NEIL CHAMBERS

Daylighting is a highly beneficial design strategy for retrofitting buildings; in addition to saving energy required for electric lighting, daylighting can reduce the energy required to cool an existing building by 10 to 20 percent. Daylighting optimization in existing buildings can increase the amount of natural light in interior spaces, reduce the need for artificial lighting, and minimize undesirable side effects such as glare and solar heat gain. Optimizing daylight is a complex challenge for the project team, requiring a careful assessment of daylight opportunities and coordination of design strategies. Working with a daylighting consultant can help maximize both energy cost reductions and lighting quality improvements for building occupants.

Evaluating Daylighting Potential

The first step in assessing daylighting potential for a building retrofit is to evaluate the surrounding conditions. The building's latitude, which determines both the amount of sunlight and the location of the sun in reference to the building, will influence the daylighting strategy. Additionally, the presence of surrounding buildings, trees, plants, and local topography will affect the potential for using daylighting. If taller buildings are in the direct line of the sun, those buildings will cast shadows at certain hours.

The use of daylighting simulation software can help the team identify which areas of the building receive the most daylight. If the team is not using simulation software, daylight penetration can be determined through the use of a sunpath diagram or sunpath calculator. The sunpath diagram or calculator graphically shows the position of the sun by latitude and gives the sun's altitude (the angle of the sun above the horizon) and azimuth (the angular distance along the horizon to the location of the sun, typically measured from due north to the east) for every hour of the year.[1]

When evaluating daylighting potential for an existing structure, there are two types of daylighting to consider:

» **Perimeter daylighting.** Natural light within 15 feet of the building envelope, where the light is easiest to utilize.

» **Extensive daylighting.** Natural light that penetrates deeper into the built space. This penetration is usually accomplished by using strategies to maximize natural light infiltration.

For daylit areas the project team should target an average daylight factor (ADF) that is suitable for the designated use. The ADF is the ratio of the illumination indoors to that outdoors on an overcast day.[2] Hallways typically call for a minimum of 0.5 ADF, while offices require 2 ADF. A general rule of thumb is that an ADF of 3 or better is a good-quality light for spaces that may not need to be supplemented by artificial lighting. There are also recommended minimums for internal light levels for common office tasks and building areas. The recommended minimum light levels, measured in foot-candles or lumens per square meter (lm/m^2, or lux), will determine the need for artificial lighting in specified areas and on work surfaces in the building. If the structure is not designed so that natural light penetrates deep into building interiors, extensive daylighting strategies will be needed to ensure that these areas receive natural light.

How to Optimize Daylighting

Optimizing daylighting is about controlling how daylight enters a building rather than maximizing measurable daylight. Uncontrolled daylighting can have negative repercussions, such as undesirable solar heat gain, visual glare, and the fading of interior materials.

CONTROL LIGHT QUALITY

For maximum benefit, daylight should be distributed evenly, not concentrated in direct beams of intense light. High-contrast, intense light creates visual discomfort for building occupants and may lead occupants near windows to block sunlight completely with window blinds, thus canceling any benefit from daylighting.

External shading on each exposure (with solar shades, landscaping, exterior light shelves, etc.) prevents direct penetration of sunlight to the building interiors and improves interior light balance. Each exposure has different shading needs: horizontal shading on the building's southern glazing, vertical shading for windows on the eastern and western exposures, and no shading on the northern exposure, except at latitudes near the equator.[3] External shading devices can be mounted on an existing building as part of a retrofit.

Additionally, if glazing (glass) can be replaced or visual film or tinting can be installed, the project team should select glass or film with high VT. Optimally, if the glazing area is split into two horizontal sections (as separate panes or windows), different VT levels can be specified: for the lower section, a medium VT that provides occupants with enhanced views; for the upper section, a higher VT that maximizes the daylight penetration deeper into the building interiors.

PLAN SPACE EFFECTIVELY

Interior partition walls and materials selection can influence the effectiveness of efforts to harvest daylight deep inside the floor plate. Open-floor plans allow the greatest amount of light to flow into the space; where private offices are necessary, they should be situated away from the windows in the building interiors. Wherever possible, translucent or transparent materials should be used in walls to allow daylight penetration. Locating corridors at the building's edge can help bring daylight into larger portions of the floor plate.

If the building is undergoing substantial renovation, window height can be increased to the bottom of the ceiling or ceiling height can be increased, in areas that have both northern and southern exposures.[4] These strategies increase interior daylight levels. Additionally, the project team should consider "cutting" an atrium into the building, which can extend daylight deeper into the interiors. (See the case study on the historic preservation of the Christman Building in Lansing, Michigan, which highlights the benefits of adding an atrium to an existing building.)

USE EXTENSIVE DAYLIGHTING TECHNIQUES

Most retrofits use a number of techniques to introduce daylight deep into the building floor plate:

▸ **Light-colored interiors.** One of the simplest strategies is to specify light colors for interior paints, materials, and furniture. Light-colored walls and ceilings diffuse daylight, spreading it evenly throughout an office area, improving the quality of the light. (See the Wallace Roberts & Todd case study for a discussion of how a light-colored interior can facilitate daylight transmission.)

▸ **Light shelves.** Typically, daylight from a window can extend 1.2 to 1.5 times the distance between the top of the window and the floor; light shelves can increase this distance up to 2.5 times.[5] The shelves feature a full or partial glass partition aligned at the correct angle to send reflected and refracted light deeper into the interior spaces. Light shelves can be attached to the outside or inside of windows, though the exterior ones typically perform better overall. Light shelves work best when installed on the southern exposure of buildings in the Northern Hemisphere and the northern exposure in the Southern Hemisphere.

▸ **Skylights, roof monitors, and solar tubes.** Skylights and roof monitors (popped-up extensions of the roof, with vertical glass areas) can also provide extensive daylighting, although their application is limited because they primarily function for one-story office buildings or the top floor of multistory buildings. Solar tubes, which capture light through a dome at the exterior of the building and channel it throughout the interior, can be used more extensively than skylights or roof monitors in multistory buildings. Solar tubes resemble a recessed light fixture; they do not provide the same level of illumination as a skylight or roof monitor.

▸ **Daylight sensors and dimmers.** The amount of daylight changes throughout the day, with both the time of day and the cloudiness of the sky. The best way to optimize energy savings with daylighting strategies is to install daylight sensors (or dimmers). When natural light levels change, the sensors increase electrical lighting to maintain adequate illumination levels. For best energy-use results, lighting fixtures in daylit areas should be arranged in parallel to the windows. These lights should be zoned so that each section can be dimmed or turned off, depending on the availability of adequate daylight. Because the lighting provides supplementary illumination only when required, energy savings from daylighting are maximized. According to research conducted by the Heschong Mahone Group, energy savings from daylighting control can range from 50 to 75 cents per square foot.[6]

Neil Chambers, LEED AP, is an architect whose work includes ecological restoration, green building, and LEED consulting.

NOTES

1 G.Z. Brown and Mark DeKay, *Sun, Wind, and Light, Architectural Design Strategies* (New York: John Wiley and Sons, Inc., 2001).

2 Norbert Lechner, *Heating, Cooling, Lighting: Design Methods for Architects* (New York: John Wiley and Sons, Inc., 2001).

3 For buildings in the Southern Hemisphere, the northern exposure should feature horizontal shading, and the southern exposure does not require shading. Eastern and western exposures should still be treated with vertical shading elements.

4 For smaller office buildings in cold climates, care should be take when expanding the size of windows on the northern exposure, because of concerns about heating loss.

5 U.S. Department of Energy, "Laboratories For the 21st Century: Daylighting Laboratories," www.nrel.gov/docs/fy04osti/33938.pdf.

6 Kozlowski, David, "Using Daylighting to Save on Energy Costs," *Building Operations Management*, April 2006, www.facilitiesnet.com/energyefficiency/article/Harnessing-Daylight-For-Energy-Savings--4267.

another light source, such as daylight or adequate electric lighting. Given this constraint, not all exit signs can be switched to PL; LED exit signs are an environmentally friendly and cost-effective alternative.

The most appropriate combination of lamps, ballasts, and light fixtures will depend on the specific lighting application. For large office buildings, the project team should consider the relative costs of establishing a relamping operations and maintenance (O&M) program with a number of lamps and lighting systems, versus a simplified O&M program with one or two lamps and ballasts. The team should work with a lighting engineer to evaluate the best options for the building.

Project teams should also evaluate outdoor lighting to optimize energy efficiency and reduce potential contribution to light pollution, while ensuring occupant safety and complying with local regulations. Light pollution is caused by excessive artificial lighting of a building's surroundings and is considered a threat to local ecosystems. Using full cut-off fixtures for outdoor lighting, which focus light directly down to the horizontal surface below, can help to eliminate light pollution concerns. Additionally, turning off interior lights at night, when they are not required for occupant safety, can also reduce the building's light pollution and carbon footprint.

Water: Conservation Measures and Plumbing Retrofit

In commercial office buildings, water is used for both domestic purposes (irrigation, sanitation, cooking) and mechanical purposes (heating and cooling). The key sustainability objectives with respect to water use are to lower overall use and to reduce the building's usage of potable water. Water use is inherently energy intensive; over 25 percent of the cost of water is created by the energy needed to pump, filter, treat, and dispose of it.

The production of potable water is especially resource intensive because it requires purification. In some locations, water that is suitable for human consumption is also scarce; using water resources efficiently is imperative for maintaining an adequate water supply. In some municipalities, water use reduction may be mandated during times of drought or a low water table. Buildings that use water more efficiently will minimize the operational impact of any such regulation. Given that potable water can also be expensive, reducing its use can have a beneficial effect on operating costs.

The most cost-effective water conservation programs focus on both demand-side and supply-side measures. Demand-side initiatives reduce building demand for water. Supply-side programs expand the building's water sources through water reuse and recycling. In many jurisdictions in the United States and elsewhere, municipal water sources charge for supplied water and for wastewater discharge; therefore, using water more than once is an effective way to reduce water costs. Key elements of reducing water consumption in the context of a green retrofit are described in the following sections.

WATER AUDIT
To identify the most cost-effective methods of reducing the building's water consumption, one option is to complete a facility water use assessment or water audit, as discussed in chapter 2. The assessment determines how and where water is being used, and how much it costs the facility. It also highlights areas of potential improvement. A water audit should indicate whether there are any major water leaks which, if left unrepaired, could lead to substantial wasted water or building damage.

WATER REUSE AND RECYCLING
The reuse and recycling of nonpotable water on site is a key supply-side strategy for water-use efficiency in office buildings. Both graywater (domestic wastewater from showers,

sinks, and laundry facilities) and harvested rainwater can be reused on site for irrigation, toilet flushing, and other applications that do not require potable water, such as site cleaning. Condensate, water extracted from the air during dehumidification, can be collected and reused for nonpotable uses or fed into a cooling tower. In hot and moist climates, a large office building can create 1 gallon of condensate per minute (1,440 gallons of water per day). This is a substantial source of water for reuse and recycling.

Although some municipalities may offer a nonpotable water supply, collecting and storing rainwater in storage tanks often offers a low-cost water source for nonpotable uses and reduces wastewater discharge. In India, rainwater harvesting policies have been mandated in many circumstances. Rainwater harvesting may not be feasible, however, in some densely settled areas where space is at a premium. Outside urban areas, stormwater retention ponds can be used for water storage.

There are a number of challenges in developing systems for on-site water reuse at existing office buildings. Potable water and graywater must be passed through separate piping systems. Graywater systems might not be allowed in certain local jurisdictions, so potential users of these systems should examine local regulations ahead of time.

WATER-EFFICIENT IRRIGATION

Reducing the water required for landscape irrigation, particularly the use of potable water, is a key water conservation strategy. Proper plant selection is critical to reducing the irrigation associated with landscaping (see the earlier discussion of green landscaping). When irrigation is necessary, a number of advanced irrigation systems can deliver water to the required location more effectively than conventional overhead systems. Property owners can upgrade existing overhead irrigation systems with low-flow sprinkler heads or switch to drip irrigation systems, which water plants directly at their roots or with a

microspray. Irrigation systems can also be equipped with rain sensors and in-ground moisture sensors to disable irrigation systems when additional water is not needed.

METERING AND SUBMETERING

During a retrofit, the project team should consider the installation of additional water metering or submetering devices to track water consumption and discharge for specific uses or building areas. The installation of metering or submetering devices will help identify building performance issues in the future and permit improved data tracking to help determine the efficiency and efficacy of any future behavioral policies implemented.

WATER-EFFICIENT FIXTURES

Sanitary water usage can represent 30 to 40 percent of a building's total water usage; that number can be reduced significantly through the installation of water-efficient plumbing fixtures.[19] Existing toilets, urinals, showerheads, and faucets can be replaced with low-flow versions, often referred to as ultra-low-flow (ULF) fixtures.

▸▸ **TOILETS**. Currently, high-efficiency toilet models on the market in the United States use 1.1 to 1.28 gallons of water per flush, or roughly 2 to 4 liters per flush. This performance represents a major reduction from standard flush values in the early 1990s. In parts of Europe, low-flow toilets with these reduced flush rates are considered standard. Dual-flush toilets, which have different flush volumes for liquid and solid waste, are readily available in most countries. ULF or waterless urinals can replace existing models, although some cities and municipalities have not yet updated their building codes to allow for waterless systems. Note that cultural norms may preclude the use of waterless urinals in some areas. As well, waterless urinals are not recommended for use in public areas with dense populations because of the maintenance frequency they require.

> ▸ **FAUCETS AND SHOWERHEADS**. Faucets that feature low-flow mechanisms, sensor controls, or automatic shutoff features are also effective in reducing occupant water use, as are low-flow showerheads. An even more important economy resulting from low-flow showerheads and faucets is a reduction in the energy used to heat water.

MINIMIZING HOT-WATER USE

Particular attention should be paid to the use of hot water within the building, because it is more energy intensive than cold water. For domestic water purposes, using cold water only, wherever possible, and switching to point-of-use water heaters can sometimes eliminate the need for less efficient, conventional hot-water systems. Point-of-use water heaters operate without the standby heat loss of a typical central hot-water system, which has long piping runs and recirculation loops. The efficiency of point-of-use systems, however, should be evaluated on a case-by-case basis; In larger buildings with very regular water use, recirculating hot-water systems may prove to be more efficient.

Additional methods to reduce the energy required to heat water may also be useful in the context of office retrofits:

> ▸ **INSTALLING HOT-WATER HEAT PUMPS**, which can be two to three times more efficient than conventional hot-water heater systems for small-scale needs;

> ▸ **INSTALLING A SOLAR HOT-WATER SYSTEM**, which uses solar radiation to heat water for building usage and can be used year-round; and

> ▸ **USING A DRAINWATER HEAT EXCHANGER**, which recovers the energy from discarded water and uses it to preheat cold water. (This method may require significant replumbing and is most readily incorporated as part of a major plumbing retrofit.)

OTHER APPROACHES

The use of water can also be reduced in the operation of building heating and cooling systems. Single-pass cooling equipment, which can include ice machines, some refrigerators, and air conditioners, is highly inefficient. Single-pass systems use water to remove heat and then discharge the water into the wastewater system. If the single-pass equipment cannot be replaced with closed-loop systems (which are significantly more resource-efficient and can reduce building operating costs), the discharge water should be passed through a heat exchanger to recover energy. The water can then be reused for other heating and cooling uses, such as for a cooling tower, or used for irrigation.

SUSTAINABLE INTERIORS

The creation of sustainable, renovated interiors relies on the use of sustainable space planning and construction practices and the use of sustainable building materials:

> ▸ **SUSTAINABLE SPACE PLANNING** emphasizes the design of flexible, open, and modular spaces to minimize the use of materials and the potential for generating construction waste. Occupant productivity and health and the use of technologies that permit occupants to use space more efficiently and effectively are also key tenets of sustainable space planning.

> ▸ **SUSTAINABLE CONSTRUCTION PRACTICES** focus on the recycling of construction waste, the maintenance of a clean and healthy job site, and the flush-out of newly renovated space after the completion of construction and before the building is occupied, to ensure healthful indoor air quality.

> ▸ **SUSTAINABLE BUILDING MATERIALS** are extracted and manufactured so as to minimize or eliminate harm to the environment and to occupant health. Numerous strategies can be employed to enhance the sustainability of building materials, including the use of salvaged, locally sourced, reused, recycled,

and rapidly renewable materials. The use of materials with no or low levels of VOCs, which can be harmful to human health, is also an important practice in the renovation of green office buildings.

(For details on the use of sustainable space planning and construction practices and the characteristics of sustainable building materials see the earlier sidebar by Anica Landreneau, Amy Fabry, Nita Tuvesson, Leigh Stringer, and Jodi Williams.)

HISTORIC PRESERVATION AND GREEN RETROFIT

In the context of green office retrofits, historic properties present challenges and opportunities. Given their embodied energy (the energy previously expended in their construction), reusing existing buildings is inherently more sustainable than building new ones. Preserving and operating historic structures to their full potential is a smart investment in sustainability. (For an evaluation of the case for sustainable preservation see the sidebar by Ralph DiNola, which provides several strategies to help ensure that existing historic structures are put to their best use.)

Most historic properties were designed and built before the advent of mechanical heating and cooling; therefore, these structures were designed for passive heating, cooling, and ventilation. Often, particularly in the Northern Hemisphere, historic buildings feature thick masonry walls with substantial thermal mass (the capacity of an object in a building to absorb heat) that can help regulate interior temperatures throughout the day. Large windows and high ceilings maximize daylighting for the building interiors. During the retrofit of historic structures, it is frequently energy-efficient to remove individual offices on the building perimeter and switch to an open-floor plan to help bring natural light deeper into the interior. This strategy was used in the sustainable preservation retrofit of the Christman Building in Lansing, Michigan, which is profiled in the full-length case studies.

Historic elements were retained at the offices of Autodesk at One Market Street in San Francisco. Solar impact, shading, daylighting, view availability, ventilation, and airflow modeling affected layout and organization.

Many historic structures have building layouts that promote cross-ventilation. The use of original operating windows in these structures can naturally ventilate the space. A common problem encountered in green preservation is the window glazings typically found in historic buildings. Historic windows typically feature a single pane with no special coating; they are energy-inefficient in comparison to window technologies commonly in use today. If these windows cannot be replaced because of their historic character, the project team should make sure they are repaired for airtightness. Restoring any historic canopies or window shading devices to limit summertime heat gain should be an element of a sustainable historic retrofit.

NOTES

1 A load-bearing wall supports the weight of the building above it. A curtain wall is supported by interior framing and does not support the building weight.

2 The thermal envelope of a buildings consists of the walls, roofs, ceilings, and floors that separate conditioned space from unconditioned spaces, such as an unheated parking garage and building exteriors. Depending on building design, the building envelope can make up all or just part of the thermal envelope; if unconditioned spaces are enclosed within the building envelope, the thermal envelope will be the wall or ceiling that seperates conditioned spaces from unconditioned.

3 CFCs have a higher potential for depleting ozone than HCFCs and should be avoided. LEED bans the use of CFCs in new construction. In existing buildings, LEED requires the

FIVE PRINCIPLES OF SUSTAINABLE PRESERVATION

RALPH DINOLA

Sustainable preservation brings together two important values-based movements that, for many, may appear to be in conflict but are actually quite complementary. Over the past several years a dialogue has begun between adherents and practitioners of green building and their counterparts in historic preservation. They seek common ground: a mutual philosophy and approach to preserving our built environment as a means of satisfying the tenets of both movements.

The perceived conflict between the sustainable real estate and historic preservation movements is typically presented as follows: Green builders believe that historic buildings are not sustainable because they consume excessive amounts of energy, discourage increases in urban density, and require significant resources to maintain. Historic preservationists believe that green and energy efficiency requirements mandate the destruction of a property's historic elements and lead property owners to neglect or dismiss the substantial cultural contributions of historic structures. Many in both groups presume that that LEED certification is not possible if historic identity is to be maintained.

Sustainable preservation bridges this seeming conflict to produce a win-win result, uniting the green building and historic preservation movements under a single philosophy: The built environment should be conserved and sustained for future generations, while preserving a society's cultural heritage. Density should be encouraged in ways that enhance communities and curtail sprawl into natural areas.

Five principles of sustainable preservation can support efforts to sustain the built environment.

1. Repair Rather than Replace—at Every Scale

New materials, products, and buildings require tremendous investments in resources and energy to extract, transport, manufacture, install, and dispose. A culture of reuse, by contrast, seeks to repair rather than replace. Repair and reuse minimize adverse consequences to the environment and historic elements. If we think of this approach at every scale, we can envision repairing a door lockset as well as an underutilized industrial district or deserted factory town. In embracing repair and reuse, embodied energy—the energy expended in initial manufacture, fabrication, or construction—is retained and the environmental and historic risks of new construction are reduced significantly. The potential for reuse should be considered before demolishing a building in whole or in part. Often, demolishing an old building instead of renovating or expanding it may be expedient, but it results in tremendous resource and energy expenditure as well as the loss of historic fabric.

2. Rediscover and Redeploy Original Green Features of Historic Structures

Most historic buildings, developed before the advent of such technologies as electric lighting and air conditioning, were designed and built with what we would today consider green features. Unfortunately, in some of these buildings, some

replacement, conversion, or phaseout of equipment that uses CFCs, unless precluded by economic infeasibility.

4 Lawrence Berkeley National Laboratory, Heat Island Projects, http://eetd.lbl.gov/HeatIsland/PROJECTS.

5 www.epa.gov/hiri.

6 Heating load refers to the amount of heat per unit of time that is required to keep a building at a predetermined temperature; cooling load refers to the amount of cooling per unit of time that is required to keep a building at a predetermined temperature.

7 www1.eere.energy.gov/femp/pdfs/buscase_appendixf.pdf.

8 This figure is significantly smaller for curtain walls, but curtain walls are almost exclusively built with aluminum, a highly conductive metal with poor thermal qualities.

9 In temperate climate zones, insulated doors with high thermal resistance may not be cost-effective.

10 E Source: Commercial Energy Advisor, www.esource.com/BEA/demo/PDF/CEA_offices.pdf

11 U.S. Department of Energy, www1.eere.energy.gov/femp/pdfs/29267-5.7.2.pdf.

12 Ken Sinclair, "Reinventing Building Automation," May 2009, www.automatedbuildings.com/news/may09/reviews/09428031230reinventionksin.htm

13 In the Southern Hemisphere, solar gain is highest on northern exposures and, to some extent, eastern and western exposures.

14 "Transpired Solar Heating for your Commercial Building," www.nrel.gov/docs/fy01osti/30176.pdf.

15 E Source: Commercial Energy Advisor, www.esource.com/BEA/demo/PDF/CEA_offices.pdf.

16 www1.eere.energy.gov/femp/pdfs/buscase_appendixf.pdf.

17 Foot-candles and lux are measurements of light intensity on a surface: 1 foot-candle equals roughly 10.76 lux.

18 For fluorescent lighting, the T-value represents the diameter of the lamp in 1/8-inch intervals. Therefore, a T8 lamp is 1 inch in diameter, and a T12 is 1.5 inches in diameter.

19 Singapore Environmental Council (www.tenpercent.sec.org.sg/commercial.html), U.S. EPA (www.epa.gov/oaintrnt/water/background.htm), Sydney Water (Australia) (www.sydneywater.com.au/savingwater/inyourbusiness/Howtosavewater/OfficeAndShoppingComplexes.cfm).

sustainable features were dismantled in subsequent renovations. Tall, operable classroom windows that brought in daylight and natural ventilation were closed off or sealed shut to reduce drafts after air conditioning was installed. Awnings that managed solar exposure were removed because of disrepair. These features can be redeployed as a means to green existing buildings and restore their original sustainable features.

3. Communicate with Regulatory Authorities Early and Often

When retrofitting historic buildings to be green, it is important to comply with the appropriate regulations and public policies that affect the project. Both green and historic preservation projects can be affected by local, state, or federal requirements, especially if financial incentives are sought. It is therefore important to identify the regulators who have authority over the project and then to engage these authorities throughout the design and construction process. It is important to ensure that regulators understand the goals and approach, and that the project team can find a workable solution that will satisfy authorities' concerns and meet the project intent. As with any good relationship, communication is essential to understanding and common ground.

For an example of strong collaboration between a property owner and government authorities in the green renovation of an historic structure, see the case study of the Christman Building. The Christman Building historic renovation attracted significant governmental financing and achieved a rare Double Platinum LEED rating under the guidelines for Core and Shell and for Commercial Interiors. Early and ongoing communication between the Christman Company, historic preservation officials, and other policy makers was central to successful project completion.

4. Use Incentives and Grants to Reinvest and Improve Returns

Sustainable preservation projects require a substantially greater level of effort than typical new construction. The good news is that there are many opportunities to leverage grants, tax credits, and development bonuses that will enhance the bottom line dramatically. Sustainable preservation projects can maximize public financial support by applying both green building and historic preservation incentives. Project teams should conduct research early to determine what incentives are available. For example, in the United States, Historic Tax Credits can be coupled with New Markets Tax Credits and incentives for energy-efficient investment.

5. Look for Opportunities at a District Scale

Project teams should consider expanding the boundary of a project to include adjacent sites or even entire districts. This helps take advantage of economies of scale and capitalize on the potential for locating systems and technologies off site. Examples include tying into a district central utility plant for heating, cooling, or power or placing renewable energy systems on an adjacent, non-historic building in order to protect a building's historic character. Rehabilitation of a single building in a historic district can also catalyze numerous other projects and transform a community.

Ralph DiNola is a principal of Green Building Services, based in Portland, Oregon.

Managing the Green Retrofit Process

TOM PALADINO, ROD WILLE, AND ERIC A. GRASBERGER

The management sequencing of a green office retrofit differs materially from that of a conventional office project. The design and construction of a green office renovation relies on integrated management procedures that draw simultaneously on a variety of disciplines, rather than on the sequential processes typically employed in commercial redevelopment. If green certification is desired, the project team should also include a green certification professional who is an expert in the certification system chosen. In this chapter, Tom Paladino of Paladino and Company discusses the process of selecting and working with a green certification professional through an integrated design protocol, while Rod Wille, special consultant to Turner Construction Company, advises on the organization and management of the construction process for green renovation projects.

The use of green standards and integrated design and construction protocols also impose new legal requirements on sustainable renovation and development projects. These requirements are reviewed in this chapter by Eric A. Grasberger of Stoel, Rives, who discusses recommendations on minimizing the legal risks associated with green design and construction.

COLLABORATING WITH A GREEN BUILDING CONSULTANT TO CREATE AN EXEMPLARY GREEN OFFICE RENOVATION

TOM PALADINO

With green building maturing rapidly in early adopter markets, developers are faced with increased tenant demand for green space and competition from new Leadership in Energy and Environmental Design (LEED)-rated products entering the market. Green office renovations offer an opportunity to retain current tenants and better compete for new ones. A qualified green building consultant can ease the process and help to ensure that the project meets both tenant and owner expectations for a quality green office space that aligns with owner budget and occupant corporate values.

Paladino and Company helped to develop the LEED green building rating system, has taken more than 70 projects successfully through certification as a LEED consultant, and had approximately 50 additional projects in progress as of 2009. This section offers the company's perspective on how to collaborate with a green building consultant to deliver an exemplary green office renovation focused on the business outcomes that owners and tenants care about.

RATING SYSTEM INTEGRATION PROCESS— THE CONSULTANT'S ROLE

The role of the green building consultant is to facilitate a restructuring of the conventional design and construction process in a way that allows the owner and design team members to work together toward an integrated sustainable design solution. This improves the flow of information and communication on a project, a crucial factor in achieving a well-integrated and efficient design. Paladino and Company has forged an effective approach that integrates the use of green building rating systems—primarily LEED—into design and construction. This process applies regardless of the rating system used, because its defining distinction is the integrated design process, which is predicated by very

early goal setting and consistent monitoring of green strategy integration throughout all phases of development. Early setting of goals for sustainability is key to delivering an outcome aligned with the owner's goals.

The process includes four major phases (figure 4-1):

▸▸ **PHASE ONE, PROJECT VISIONING.** The key objective during visioning is to identify high-level goals for the renovation that map to the owner's business objective, and that will provide a compelling value proposition to tenants. Early goal setting is then aligned with the chosen rating system, and rating system credits or points that support the objectives are given greater emphasis. The green building consultant's role is to drive the visioning process with the owner, design team, and tenant (if known) toward viable green design strategies.

▸▸ **PHASE TWO, DESIGN IMPLEMENTATION.** The key objective during this phase is to carry the sustainable design strategy through the design process and to validate selected strategies with technical and financial feasibility analysis. The green building consultant's role during design implementation is to provide guidance and coaching to the design team and owner; perform regular assessments of the design against the agreed strategy, rating system, and budget; and to perform necessary technical and financial analysis to validate the strategy.

▸▸ **PHASE THREE, CONSTRUCTION AND COMMISSIONING**. The focus during construction is on ensuring that design strategies are manifested in the project as it is built and validating that they perform as intended through commissioning, the performance testing of building systems that takes place at the end of construction. The green building consultant's role is to train and coach the contractor and its subcontractors, monitor their progress, and manage the commissioning process by either performing commissioning or engaging an agent on behalf of the owner.

▸▸ **PHASE FOUR, OCCUPANCY AND CERTIFICATION**. This phase includes project handover, submittal of the rating system application for review by the governing body, and ultimate award of the green building rating. The green building consultant should prepare and submit the final application to the governing body of the rating system for review and monitor its progress through the review process.

PHASE ONE: PROJECT VISIONING

During the project visioning process, it is necessary for the owners to select the project team and decide whether to engage a green building consultant. After the team is assembled, the visioning phase is used to set project goals, including the value proposition that the project will offer eventual occupants; select the appropriate green rating system; and determine which rating system points and credits will be emphasized in the project design.

Selecting a Qualified Green Building Consultant

Before initiating any design work, the owner should consider whether to engage a qualified consultant to help guide it in determining project sustainability goals, and to manage the design team to achieve the outcomes the owner has identified as important. The key to working successfully with a green building consultant is to engage a qualified firm or independent consultant during very early planning and then involve the consultant completely throughout the project.

Figure 4-1

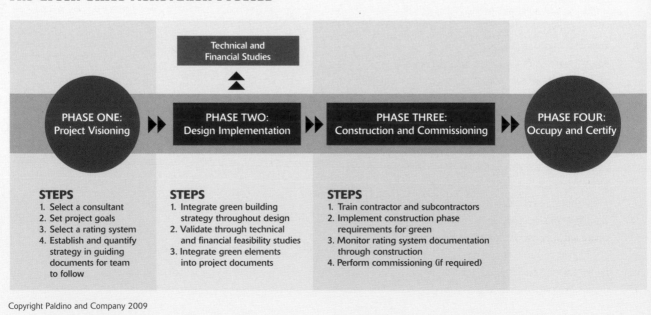

The Green Office Renovation Process

Technical and Financial Studies

PHASE ONE: Project Visioning ▸▸ PHASE TWO: Design Implementation ▸▸ PHASE THREE: Construction and Commissioning ▸▸ PHASE FOUR: Occupy and Certify

STEPS
1. Select a consultant
2. Set project goals
3. Select a rating system
4. Establish and quantify strategy in guiding documents for team to follow

STEPS
1. Integrate green building strategy throughout design
2. Validate through technical and financial feasibility studies
3. Integrate green elements into project documents

STEPS
1. Train contractor and subcontractors
2. Implement construction phase requirements for green
3. Monitor rating system documentation through construction
4. Perform commissioning (if required)

Copyright Paldino and Company 2009

Working with a qualified and experienced consultant can offer several advantages to owners and project teams. An experienced consultant can protect the owner's interest and investment by providing valuable perspective and insight on the most economical and expedient paths to achieve a rating and can save the owner from costly mistakes. Paladino recommends that an owner contract directly with the consultant to enable the consultant to better monitor design team performance without conflict of interest. The consultant should collaborate fully with the design team and have visibility into critical project decisions as they are being made, to positively affect the project's ability to receive a rating and maximize opportunities to achieve a sustainable outcome within cost parameters.

Among the most frequently cited drawbacks to hiring a consultant is cost. A good consultant will command a fair fee, but a strong one can demonstrate value by guiding the team toward economical decisions based on knowledge of the rating system being used, and by coaching the design and construction team toward integrated design solutions that reduce overall project cost—in the long run saving the owner much more than the consultant's fee.

For the best and most economical outcome, the selected consultant should have the following qualifications:

▸▸ **DEMONSTRATED EXPERIENCE** taking several similar projects through the selected rating system to certification. Currently, there are approximately 80,000 LEED Accredited Professionals, but only 2,000 LEED-rated buildings, which means many consultants do not have direct experience with LEED yet.

The design process for the retrofit of Autodesk at One Market Street in San Francisco combined building information modeling (BIM) and integrated project delivery in a design-build process. Pictured here is an enclosed meeting space (at left in photo) and open perimeter office space.

▸ **AN ARCHITECTURAL**, engineering, building science, or development background. It is important to know how buildings are designed and constructed in order to seamlessly integrate actions related to the rating system into the design and construction process when and how they need to be integrated, and to understand the various disciplines' effects on sustainable outcomes.

▸ **PROFICIENCY** in technical concepts of green building and the ability to perform (or at least provide input to and interpret) detailed technical and financial analysis to inform decisions by the owner and design team. These concepts might include climate analysis, energy modeling, daylighting analysis, and sizing studies for systems such as rainwater harvest or renewable energy.

▸ **DEMONSTRATED KNOWLEDGE** of business and financial concepts related to building ownership, including knowing how to read and build a pro forma or develop a total cost of ownership study.

▸ **EXPERIENCE** working with similar owners and with the specific rating system being applied to the project. Green office renovations primarily fall under two LEED rating systems: LEED for Commercial Interiors (LEED-CI) and, in the case of substantial or gut renovations, LEED for New Construction (LEED-NC).Other retrofits typically fall under LEED for Existing Buildings Operations and Maintenance (LEED-EBOM). The consultant should be conversant in the rating system being used and able to guide the owner in the selection of the most economical option.

▸ **UP-TO-DATE KNOWLEDGE** of the latest version and training for the rating system the project is aiming for. LEED, for example, has frequent updates, so the consultant's professional development and continuous education is critical.

Often, referrals are the best source of qualified consultants.

Early Project Visioning— the Key to Success

The key to successfully achieving a green office rating is to define project goals early in the process and select a rating system aligned with those goals. A strong green building consultant should be able to lead the team (and tenants) in a discovery process and generate measurable goals for the owner and design team to follow, without using the scorecard as a proxy to drive the design.

Because green building rating systems focus primarily on environmental outcomes, Paladino bridges the gap between the goals of the rating system and the goals of the property owner by developing custom scorecards that help owners and designers focus on sustainable design strategies productively. Paladino uses a "triple top line" rating system that ranks social and environmental value along with economics to drive project results. The scoring system is called triple top line because the goal is to improve the overall project outcome by increasing top line opportunities (more good), rather than working toward reducing negative impacts (less bad). The resultant framework can then be used to select an aligned rating system and inform the structure and direction of the eco-charrette.

The green building consultant should quantify the outcome of the visioning process in a guiding document for the owner and team to follow. Appropriate documents commonly used by Paladino include "Owner's Project Requirements for Sustainable Design," "The Green Basis of Design," and the "Eco Charrette Report."

Regardless of whether the project encompasses an entire building or the area leased by a single tenant, it is always advisable to align the renovation and value proposition with the green features that a tenant or prospective tenant may want or for which they may be willing to pay a premium. In the process of advising a large Washington, D.C.–based real estate investment trust in the development of a joint venture project with a major tenant, Paladino and Company was able to help validate additional investment in a high-performance facade and window glazing by showing that prospective tenants, largely consisting of knowledge enterprises, would be willing to pay a premium for floor-to-ceiling windows and increased access to daylight and views for its most productive and highly compensated professionals. Figure 4-2 shows the sustainability framework developed for this project, highlighting its focus on features of importance to prospective tenants.

Selecting a Rating System

Once high-level project goals are established, the next task is to select an appropriate rating system. This step can overlap the visioning process when project goals are clear early on. The role of the green building consultant is to guide the owner and project team in the selection of the appropriate rating system version, taking into account parameters such as project scope, whether the building will remain occupied during the retrofit, how extensive the renovation will be, and which rating system version offers the most cost-effective result. Although several rating systems may apply to office renovations, the major challenge often is confusion over which LEED system is most appropriate. Typically, renovations fall under either LEED-CI or LEED-NC. In some cases, LEED Core and Shell (LEED-CS) or LEED-EBOM may be used. Figure 4-3 provides simple guidance on selecting the appropriate LEED version on the basis of the project parameters.

At either the close of Phase One or very early in Phase Two, a comparison is made between project goals and selected sustainable design strategies and the chosen rating system. This exercise is called a rating system assessment, or gap analysis. The objective is to identify how well the preferred design concept aligns with the rating system. An initial

Figure 4-2

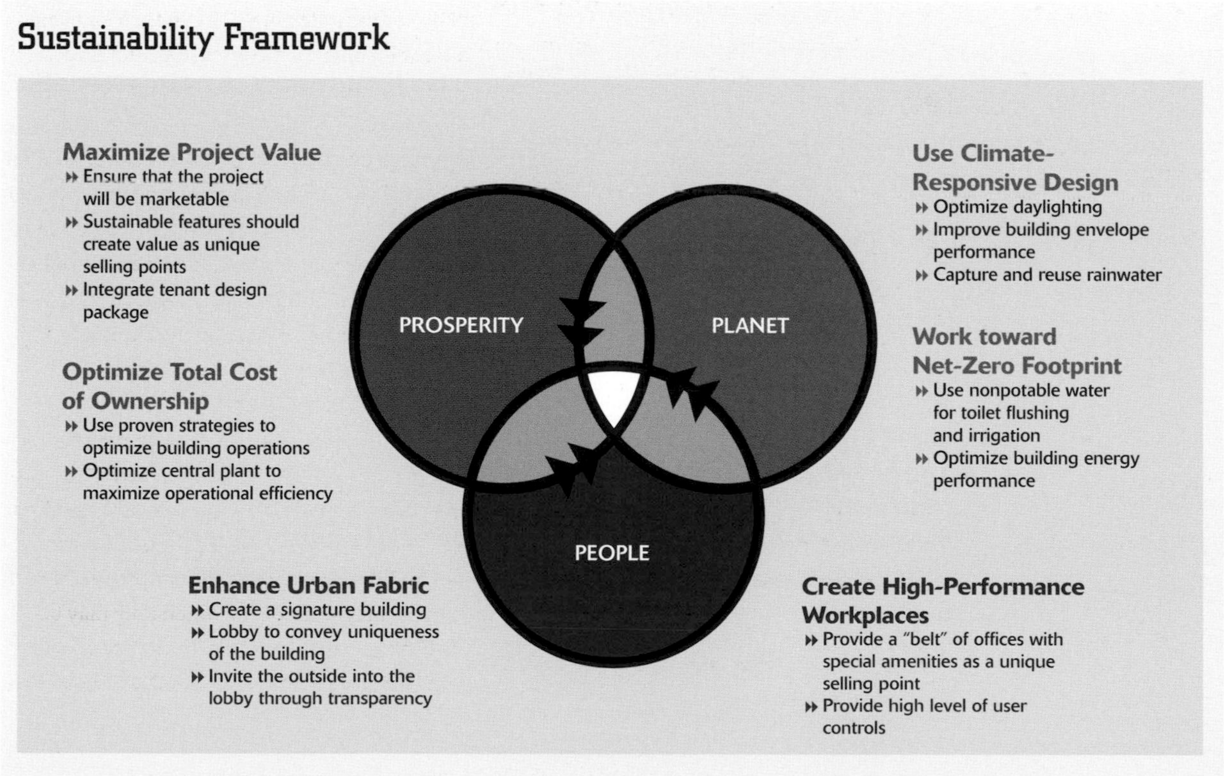

Sustainability Framework

Maximize Project Value
▸▸ Ensure that the project will be marketable
▸▸ Sustainable features should create value as unique selling points
▸▸ Integrate tenant design package

Optimize Total Cost of Ownership
▸▸ Use proven strategies to optimize building operations
▸▸ Optimize central plant to maximize operational efficiency

Enhance Urban Fabric
▸▸ Create a signature building
▸▸ Lobby to convey uniqueness of the building
▸▸ Invite the outside into the lobby through transparency

PROSPERITY   PLANET   PEOPLE

Use Climate-Responsive Design
▸▸ Optimize daylighting
▸▸ Improve building envelope performance
▸▸ Capture and reuse rainwater

Work toward Net-Zero Footprint
▸▸ Use nonpotable water for toilet flushing and irrigation
▸▸ Optimize building energy performance

Create High-Performance Workplaces
▸▸ Provide a "belt" of offices with special amenities as a unique selling point
▸▸ Provide high level of user controls

Figure 4-3

LEED Selection Criteria for Office Renovation Projects

	LEED-CI Select When	LEED-NC Select When	LEED-CS Select When	LEED-EBOM Select When
Building and Interior Rating Goals	A LEED rated building is not desired, or use in conjunction with LEED-CS.	A LEED rated building is desired.	A LEED rated building is desired.	A LEED rated building is desired.
Owner and Tenant Goals	LEED is a tenant goal more than an owner goal.	LEED is an owner goal more than a tenant goal.	LEED is an owner goal more than a tenant goal, but can use in conjunction with LEED-CI for tenant spaces.	LEED is an owner goal and tenants are willing to implement certain operational policies required by LEED-EBOM.
Occupancy during Renovation	The space will remain mostly unoccupied during renovation.	The interior space may remain occupied, but is mostly unoccupied.	The interior space will remain unoccupied during renovation.	At least 75 percent of the floor area will remain physically occupied at normal capacity for at least a year postrenovation.
Scope of Renovation	Only the interior space will be renovated.	Renovations will be extensive and include significant HVAC, envelope, or major interior rehabilitation, including common spaces.	Renovation to the core (and possibly envelope) but tenant spaces are not built out at the same time.	Renovation is major or minor, depending on outcome of building performance assessment.

rating system scorecard is generated from this exercise. The main output is the performance assessment report, which defines how the project performs against the rating system, what actions are needed to further align the design with the selected rating system goal, and which team member owns that alignment process. The consultant should perform this assessment.

PHASE TWO: DESIGN IMPLEMENTATION

The LEED consultant supports all phases of design implementation.

Driving the Team toward Success

During Phase Two, the role of the consultant is to support the team in implementing the strategies set in Phase One. The expectation is that the consultant works on the owner's behalf to deliver agreed outcomes related to sustainability and the rating system, simultaneously considering the tenant's needs, the owner's budget parameters, the project schedule, and design team skills. The consultant should drive team interaction on sustainable design aspects by providing strong

coaching and guidance, performing technical and financial analysis as needed, and ensuring the sustainable design goals are met, through regular assessment of progress against the selected rating system.

An integrated design process is preferred and particularly critical to successful green office retrofits, for two primary reasons: it allows related strategies that span several performance categories to be optimized simultaneously, thus improving performance and reducing overall cost, and optimizing the selection of green strategies when options are constricted at the outset due to limitations inherent in the base building. For example, a comprehensive energy strategy includes not only the use of high-efficiency heating, ventilating, and air-conditioning (HVAC) systems but also an integrated strategy for daylighting and electric lighting supported by proper building orientation and massing as well as use of light shelves, exterior sun shades, and even more advanced technologies like under-floor air distribution or chilled beams. In contrast, an unintegrated process is one in which the sustainable and green strategies are added after the design has significantly progressed, typically creating incremental costs to the project for each strategy. As design progresses, opportunities to incorporate various efficiency measures by making tradeoffs within the pro forma are lost.

Validating the Strategy through Feasibility Analysis

During Phase Two, specific design decisions need to be validated through further technical or financial analysis either to determine whether they are feasible within the project budget or to inform design or technical decisions related to the strategy. The green building consultant should either perform this analysis or engage a qualified provider to do so on the owner's behalf.

These studies are typically performed during schematic design (the design phase in which high-level design objectives are determined) and design development (the design phase in which detailed design elements are determined). Such studies might include energy modeling, daylighting analysis, water balance, cost and payback studies, or analysis of specific high-performance systems—such as radiant cooling terminal units, natural ventilation, or direct and indirect lighting—to inform sizing and cost of ownership. Rating systems typically require the demonstration of design performance, and the output of this analysis is provided as evidence.

For green office retrofits, the need to study major systems is somewhat limited because the base building systems may already be selected. The focus is then limited to those strategies touched by interior renovations such as optimization of combined daylighting and electric lighting strategies, specification of low-flow lavatory fixtures, and use of interior materials, finishes, and furniture that are sustainable and emit low levels of volatile organic compounds (VOCs).

PHASE THREE: CONSTRUCTION AND COMMISSIONING

Once the design is complete, the consultant's task is to ensure that sustainable design strategies are carried out through construction. The green building consultant should support the owner in selecting a qualified contractor early during design and engaging the contractor during the visioning process to gain input for construction-related issues and opportunities. It is crucial to select a contractor who is familiar with the rating system being used and to embed the requirement into the RFQ/RFP process. Adding rating system compliance requirements after selecting a contractor will generate additional costs through change orders. In Paladino's experience, contractors who are not familiar with LEED typically anticipate a steeper learning curve for LEED and may put in a larger number for it than an experienced contractor will.

The contractor's role is an important one, because most rating systems incorporate a number of construction phase requirements that the contractor is responsible for performing, monitoring, or documenting. The role of the sustainable design consultant is to provide additional training, if needed, for the contractor and subcontractors—before the start of construction—in how to comply with rating system requirements. This activity involves an initial contractor training session delivered to the prime contractor and its subcontractors, as well as monitoring and coaching, and review of submittals and documentation throughout the construction process. LEED contractor training should cover the construction waste management plan, tracking of recycled and local or regional materials, use of low-VOC adhesives, paints, and sealants, and all related submittals.

Fundamental systems commissioning is also required for LEED and occurs at the completion of construction. For office renovation projects using the LEED-CI rating system, commissioning is limited to systems within spaces controlled by the tenant, such as electric lighting systems or HVAC terminal systems. A full-service green building consulting firm typically offers this service or should be able to engage a commissioning agent on the owner's behalf.

PHASE FOUR: OCCUPY AND CERTIFY

The final step in the process of seeking a green building rating is to compile and submit the final application to the rating system's governing body for review. The consultant adds value to this process by bringing knowledge of the rating system and, in the case of LEED, knowledge of credit interpretation rulings that may affect the application review. LEED submittals can occur in two stages, at the design phase and the construction phase, but green office renovations are frequently faster-moving projects that necessitate a single application submitted at the end of construction. Rating system submittals for LEED are reviewed by an independent third party engaged by the rating system's governing body to confirm that the building design and construction process demonstrated compliance with the rating system requirements. Any deficiencies in documentation are returned to the submitting party for confirmation and correction before final review and certification.

The consultant should be familiar with navigating this process and liaising with the rating system body to ensure that all documentation meets system requirements for delivering the expected rating. Once the application is reviewed by the verifying party and the project is confirmed as meeting performance requirements, the project is awarded a rating.

Appropriately selected, a qualified and experienced green building consultant can greatly ease the green office renovation project by helping generate and deliver a green value proposition that resonates with tenants. Given that the majority of buildings expected to be in service in 2020 are in service today, green office renovations represent significant opportunities for owners who are looking to refresh existing inventory and improve operational performance in the interest of both reducing expenses and achieving sustainability goals. The ongoing relationship between the building owner and the green building consultant can bring significant value to the overall performance of an owner's portfolio through long-term management of sustainability goals that repeat on every project.

COMMON RATING SYSTEM PITFALLS

TOM PALADINO

▸▸ **Integrating a system late in design.** Opportunities to optimize performance using integrated design principles are lost when the rating system requirement is overlaid on a completed design.

▸▸ **Aligning the design with the incorrect system.** Sometimes project teams select and align the design with the wrong version of a rating system. With respect to renovation projects, teams often select LEED-EB (now LEED-EBOM) when LEED-NC was more appropriate and easier to achieve, given project parameters.

▸▸ **Failing to validate a costly strategy** with financial analysis: Selection of advanced systems such as green roofs, rainwater harvest and reuse, and renewable energy options, should be validated with cost and payback studies to understand not only first costs but the terms of payback.

Tom Paladino is president of Paladino and Company.

CONSTRUCTION CONSIDERATIONS FOR GREEN RENOVATION AND DEVELOPMENT PROJECTS

ROD WILLE

The construction or renovation of a green office building frequently requires significant modifications in the construction process. This section delineates these modifications and provides guidance on selecting appropriate contractors and subcontractors for green building projects and incorporating green certification objectives into the construction process.

In the United States, general contractors historically have competed for building construction projects by submitting lump-sum bids based on completed drawings and specifications. More recently, construction management has become a popular delivery methodology. It involves a qualifications-based selection process that brings the contractor onto the project team early in the design phase to provide preconstruction services to the owner. Preconstruction services generally include cost estimating, value engineering, and scheduling; the details of each item are updated as the design evolves. At or near the completion of contract documents, the contractor consolidates all estimated construction costs into a final estimate and proceeds on a cost-plus basis or provides a guaranteed maximum price and proceeds into construction on an at-risk basis. Both the lump-sum and construction management approaches are sequential processes in which the construction professional provides services that parallel the designer's and owner's activities.

Under both the lump-sum and construction management approaches, the design team and the owner's team all feed information into the design in sequence. Then, as the first shovel of dirt is overturned, all parties hope for a coordinated, buildable design that meets the owner's needs and budget requirements.

In today's world of sustainable development, it is no longer acceptable to allow the efforts of these talented players to progress independently on separate, parallel paths. If an owner has done due diligence and deter-mined to create a sustainable project through renovation or new development, he must consider bringing the appropriate professionals together in an integrated team. The team's mission will be to create a project with systems and materials that meet the owner's present needs without compromising future options for sustainability.

Each team member should be selected on the basis of anticipated strategic and tactical contributions, should be retained early, and should be expected to remain an active part of the team from the concept stage through project completion and functional testing. One must be mindful that this process does not end until the building functions in full accordance with the owner's program and the designer's intent.

KEY SERVICES PROVIDED BY THE CONTRACTOR

Assuming that an owner retains a general contractor from early project concept through the commissioning of a functional building, many key services must be procured for a green retrofit project. During the preconstruction design phase, these services might include comprehensive cost estimating, system value analysis, green product and regional material identification, master scheduling, constructability reviews, and an overall analysis of the project's green functionality in the context of market requirements. Moving into construction, the contractor must set in place a proactive green procurement plan, site logistics studies, manpower analyses, lead-time verification, detailed scheduling, a green quality assurance/quality control program, and supporting administrative and documentation procedures. A general contractor with previous green experience should have the in-house capability to provide these services; at worst, the general contractor may be obliged to retain a qualified subconsultant to provide any services that the contractor is not capable of providing.

Preconstruction

The contractor should participate in the major aspects of preconstruction for green renovation or new development to ensure that the project proceeds smoothly from start to finish.

THE CHARRETTE

The first activity in which a contactor should actively participate is the design charrette. If the owner has decided to develop or renovate a green project but is unsure just how green to make it, a charrette allows all stakeholders in the project to brainstorm ideas for sustainable features. Typically, charrettes are organized by a third party, frequently the green consultant, who also becomes the facilitator for this one- or two-day session. Invitees typically include representatives from the owner's facility, financial, maintenance, and user groups, all architectural and engineering consultants, and the contractor. In addition, city officials, lenders, neighboring property owners, and other interested parties might be invited for all or portions of the event.

The ultimate goal of the charrette is to assess and establish the project's sustainability criteria. These criteria typically include environmental impact, energy consumption, the health and productivity of occupants, available technology, and project costs, including initial and life-cycle costs. Sometimes, a mission statement is created for the project, to serve as a litmus test for choosing green features. Assignments are delegated and follow-up

meetings scheduled to fine-tune the information that eventually becomes the basis for green design and construction. Minutes are kept of all discussions, follow-up responsibilities assigned, and time frames established to guide the design process.

The contractor is a key participant in the charrette, not only as a contributor of ideas for sustainability but also as the resource for developing information on costs, availability of materials, local market analysis, lead time for delivery, evaluation of tradeoffs (value engineering), analysis of constructability, and overall scheduling for the project.

On a recent green office renovation project for which Turner Construction Company served as construction manager, the charrette not only identified more than 50 sustainable ideas that the client accepted as cost-effective but also yielded a mutually agreed-upon, phased construction schedule that minimized disruptions to both the tenant's and building owner's activities throughout a four-month construction period.

COMPREHENSIVE COST ESTIMATING

Although excellent cost estimating is a prerequisite for any good contractor who provides preconstruction services, it is even more critical for the evaluation of green buildings. The owner wants to know upfront what the project will cost to construct or renovate, including the value of its green components. The contractor estimates this first cost for construction using historical data (particularly in the conceptual stage of design) as well as local unit pricing that considers labor productivity, material prices and availability, and other market conditions. Green products, materials, equipment, and systems must be carefully evaluated and priced using multiple factors: Is the green product or material locally available? Is local labor familiar with the installation of the green product or material? Is the product or material proprietary with no competition? For example, substituting recycled fly ash for cement in ready-mix

Green features incorporated in the retrofit of the SCA Americas headquarters in the Circa Centre in Philadelphia included recycling of 81 percent of construction-related waste and use of recycled materials (more than 32 percent) in construction.

concrete should result in no cost premium, if fly ash is readily available from local fossil fuel power plants and if local labor knows how to work with fly ash mix.

As green design, construction, and renovation become mainstream, the availability of accurate first-cost and life-cycle cost data will increase. Moreover, increasing competition among suppliers and qualified subcontractors—the result of the recent flood of green projects—has the potential to continue to reduce green construction costs. Nevertheless, ongoing and diligent research by the contractor is required to identify the costs for manufactured goods and installation costs for those goods. Many subcontrac-

tors are willing to invest effort into gaining a better understanding of green technology and to educate their workers. A good general contractor can help to minimize the impact of any learning curve by clearly delineating the green requirements in supplementary specifications.

Sound estimation of construction costs increasingly relies on life-cycle cost analysis (LCCA). The LCCA for a product or system encompasses the first cost as well as cost factors for energy savings, maintenance, replacement, and operating efficiency. The analysis is based on assumptions about interest rates, energy costs, and operations and management costs for a fixed term.

Although the initial costs of some green technologies may be relatively expensive, their benefits frequently become abundantly clear when LCCA is used. The contractor must be able to provide relevant, high-quality cost data and work with the team (usually the engineering consultant) to prepare the appropriate analyses. The provision of life-cycle cost data equips the owner to make more informed decisions about how green the facility should be.

When New York City's flagship public radio station, WNYC, relocated its offices and broadcast studios, the station moved into a former printing house in Manhattan. Turner Construction Company is serving as the construction manager for the development of this 56,000-square-foot space into offices, control rooms, production facilities, and equipment rooms. Turner used LCCA to help the owners select the appropriate green features. The project is on track for LEED Gold certification. The open-floor plan, a signature of old printing houses, was maintained to allow for perimeter daylight in most of the work spaces. The newly installed lighting is energy-efficient and controlled by timers to reduce energy usage.

SYSTEM VALUE ANALYSIS

Another specific area where green cost estimating is important is in the analysis of tradeoffs. Tradeoffs come into play in two ways. First, tradeoffs might simply involve the substitution of one product or material for another. A case in point might be the substitution of a rapidly renewable bamboo floor for a cherry wood floor. In this case, the initial cost, durability, and maintenance of each material are factors, as is the effect of material selection on the likelihood of obtaining green project certification; additional environmental issues related to the foresting of these woods are also important, but they are more subjective and difficult to quantify.

The second, and perhaps more important, aspect of tradeoffs in green building construction is the analysis of competing building systems with respect to cost and efficiency. For example, a developer or owner might consider the savings from use of insulation with a higher R value versus the savings generated by a reduction in chiller capacity. If this simplistic example is extrapolated to an evaluation of every building component affected by a potential revision to one material or piece of equipment, the complexity and importance of the comprehensive analyses of tradeoffs become obvious.

If the architects and engineers are creating an integrated design for the project, the contractor must work in parallel with them, providing accurate cost estimates that become the basis for the owner's essential decisions. Only by following this integrated process can an owner be assured that the project envisioned is high performance, cost-effective, energy efficient, and environmentally friendly.

GREEN PRODUCTS AND REGIONAL MATERIALS

For traditional projects, the architect has intimate knowledge of products and materials and writes specifications to incorporate them into the design. For green projects, the architect retains overall design responsibility, but it is incumbent on the contractor to assist with this task. Team members need to collaborate on the identification of suppliers of green products before they specify products. Factors such as regional availability, local subcontractors' familiarity with installation, lead times for manufacturing and delivery, the supplier's track record, and agency test requirements must all be considered—and the contractor must play a key role in this analysis.

The project team must also decide during preconstruction whether the design will feature leading-edge or "bleeding"-edge technology. The contractor's review of systems will help to educate the team on any risk factors that must be considered with very new technologies. Risk may be associated with a product or system that is not suitable for a given application. Alternatively, risk may derive from the choice of a project goal (for example, an extremely high level of energy savings) that may not be achievable with well-tested products or systems. Because many green products, equipment, and materials are so new, credible track records may not yet be available. It is the contractor's role to educate the project team and ownership about the risks of using innovative products or materials.

SCHEDULING

For a green building, scheduling takes on added significance early in the design phase. The road map from the initial charrette to ground breaking must be drawn in detail to avoid costly redesign, unnecessary studies, budget overruns, and a lack of timely decision making. If these delays can be eliminated through the development of a comprehensive preconstruction schedule, then fees and reimbursable costs can be reduced and the projected completion date achieved.

The contractor should be charged with creating and monitoring the master development schedule that is updated at every team meeting. As concepts envisioned during the charrette start to take form, each team member will be accountable for the on-time completion of assigned activities to bring these plans to reality. For example, when an underfloor air distribution system is being considered for a project, numerous activities must be undertaken, including energy modeling; LCCA; and evaluation of equipment tradeoffs, noise, air quality, health and productivity factors, building controls, aesthetic considerations, and even the effect of the building's height for planning and zoning approvals. These activities must be coordinated, scheduled, and accomplished on schedule to enable a fully integrated (and cost-effective) design.

Further, the master development schedule must take into consideration the construction phase. Issues such as lead times for manufacturing, shop drawings (the detailed plans, elevations, and sections used to direct construction), and delivery must be carefully researched for specialty green products or equipment. Also to be considered is whether items such as building-integrated photovoltaic modules require certification by Underwriters Laboratories or whether the local building department requires extra time to approve the use of a fuel cell on the project. The contractor must anticipate the special scheduling requirements of a green building and its special features.

Construction

Many green certification requirements relate to construction activities, and it is the contractor's role to ensure that these requirements are fulfilled.

SITE LOGISTICS

Two important green activities occur during the transition from the preconstruction phase to the construction phase. The first entails the preparation and implementation of an environmentally friendly site logistics plan, and the second entails a reused or recycled material analysis. On renovation projects, the logistics plan would also consider the deconstruction (or possible reuse) of existing materials and how to remove them from the building without undue disruption to ongoing activities. The amount of existing material or equipment that can be reused or recycled is an important consideration for green renovation projects.

SUBCONTRACTORS AND PROJECT DOCUMENTATION

Procuring trade subcontracts is another of the contractor's very important activities that in essence kicks off the construction phase of the project. This activity effectively leads to the implementation and documentation of green activities on the site.

As shop drawings and material samples are submitted for approval, the contractor must ensure that the standards for all specified green products, materials, equipment, and systems are maintained. Frequently, subcontractors and vendors offer substitutions that do not meet the rigid guidelines for energy efficiency, recycled content, low emissions of VOCs, and other criteria. The contractor must monitor the sources of locally manufactured materials to ensure that standards for embodied energy are maintained. As well, the on-site installation process requires careful field inspection to ensure the provision of an energy-efficient and environmentally friendly building. These activities require that a contractor assign personnel to the project who are knowledgeable of and familiar with the intent and implementation of a sustainable design, so that costly rework or delays are avoided whenever possible.

Depending on the owner's intentions for verification of all green features on a project (through either LEED or another formal certification system or an informal self-certification), the level of documentation varies. Formal green certification systems have very well-defined processes for documentation to which all team members contribute. This documentation begins early in design, extends through construction, and continues through turnover and building operation. The contractor relies on subcontractors and vendors for much of the information, which ideally should be collected during construction so that at completion, a well-maintained binder of information is available for review and analysis. The documentation process should be established during the design phase so that a clear definition of documentation requirements is established before procurement of trade subcontracts.

Another area under a contractor's control during construction is usually referred to as "general conditions." A contractor assesses countless items while planning how to manage a project, many of which affect sustain-

ability objectives. Keeping a building clean during construction optimizes indoor air quality after occupancy. Temporary protection of the work and stored materials minimizes damage from moisture, which also affects air quality. Flushing out the completed building, including replacing filters for all air-handling units and wrapping the ends of all ductwork before use, also affects air quality. A well-thought-out program of temporary lighting (including trailers) saves energy and money. Two other general conditions for the contractor to address are recycling waste paper and using vehicles that use alternative fuels or are hybrid designs.

Postconstruction

Certainly, commissioning is one of the most important activities in the overall development of a green construction or renovation project. Commissioning is a process that assures the owner that the completed building and its systems function as designed. The contractor is a key player in commissioning, from design through occupancy. He must ensure that systems are buildable and cost-effective, procure technical assistance from subcontractors and vendors, carefully monitor submittals to ensure they strictly meet specifications, and inspect the installation for quality control. As the project nears completion, the contractor assists the commissioning agent and designers with starting, calibrating, and testing systems, and with training the owner's operations staff. Once all systems are performing as designed, a performance manual is prepared, comparing as-built results with the original intent (for example, whether the chiller is producing the desired flow of water at the design temperature while consuming a predetermined amount of energy). Warranties, as-built drawings, and operations and maintenance manuals are incorporated in this process.

One last activity to consider is a walk-through 11 months after completion—just before the one-year warranty period expires. The walk-through identifies items that may need to be repaired or replaced and allows analysis of how the building's systems have been performing over the course of four seasons.

SELECTING A GREEN CONTRACTOR

Perhaps the first factor to consider when selecting a contractor to renovate or construct a green building is the timing. The list of services suggested during the preconstruction phase indicates the need to bring a contractor on board very early in the process—no later than the schematic design phase, when project scope and concepts are being developed—to provide input that will allow the project team to make informed decisions. Although many preconstruction services could be provided by third parties (quantity surveyors or scheduling consultants, for example), an integrated approach to sustainable development is best achieved by a project team that is seamless from concept through occupancy.

With a program and potential conceptual design concept in hand, the owner must decide how to contract for the construction of the project. Several methodologies might be considered: a lump-sum bid, construction management (at risk or not at risk), and design-build.

A lump-sum bid process does not lend itself to green building construction and substantial renovation for three reasons. First, by its nature, a lump-sum bid does not include preconstruction services, because the contractor submits a fixed-price bid based on completed design documents. Second, it does not allow for the important continuity from design to construction, thus losing the concept of an integrated approach. Third, a lump-sum bid does not promote an atmosphere of teamwork, which is so essential in a successful green project.

Construction management offers the owner comprehensive preconstruction services at a reasonable cost. It enables the owner to control the design and receive meaningful input from the eventual builder so he can make informed decisions. Contractors typically provide preconstruction services at cost, looking to earn their profit from a fee for the actual construction.

Upon the completion of design, the owner may elect to have the contractor provide a fixed price for the construction (construction management at risk) or proceed to construction based on a firm cost estimate on a cost-plus basis. Most owners need a firm price before beginning construction and therefore prefer construction management at risk, usually with a guaranteed maximum price.

The benefits of construction management at risk include a guaranteed maximum price developed on the basis of competitively bid trade subcontracts, using a list of prequalified bidders. This process provides the owner with a team of financially stable subcontractors with experience in building green projects. Quality control and adherence to the strict intent of sustainable design are issues that many subcontractors are not familiar with. A successful green building project depends on the experience and commitment of every subcontractor and worker on site.

Other benefits of a guaranteed maximum price contract include an open-book approach to costs (that is, there are no secrets about the cost of any item), a return of any savings to the owner, and a complete price that fills any gaps in the documents required to meet the intent of a sustainable design. On renovation projects, it is important for the contractor to consider issues involving existing conditions that cannot always be detailed on the plans, a requirement compatible with guaranteed maximum pricing. This methodology should be considered the most compatible with achieving a successful green project.

Another construction option to consider is design-build. Under this option, the owner needs a program, a conceptual design, and preferably an idea of the level of greenness that he hopes to achieve (for example, LEED

The SCA Americas headquarters building in Philadelphia was certified LEED-CI Gold. Pictured here is an internal staircase in the 81,000-square-foot office space.

Silver certification). The designer-builder then develops the design within a predetermined budget and delivers the project under a sole source of responsibility. Another option with design-build is to base the selection of a design-builder on a preliminary design and price proposal that also commits to achieve a certain LEED rating. In this way (with all other factors being equal), the owner could choose a team that could produce a LEED Gold rating versus one, say, that targets only LEED Silver. The benefits of design-build include full design and preconstruction services, a fixed price before construction begins, and a single point of overall accountability. A disadvantage might be the owner's perceived loss of control over design.

If lump-sum bidding is excluded as an option, the selection process for a green contractor usually proceeds on the following path: prequalification of firms; request for proposals; presentation of staff; services, and experience; evaluation based on selection criteria; and award.

National surveys have confirmed that the first costs of building green tend to decrease in proportion to the experience of the project team members, including the contractor and designer, with this building type. Therefore, from the perspective of the bottom line, an owner should select a contractor more on the basis of his experience with green building than on the basis of a low fee. This factor also applies to LEED or other green certification documentation required from the contractor, which is not difficult to supply if the contractor has been through the process a few times.

Another selection criterion to consider is the contractor's procurement process. A key factor is having a centralized purchasing group that is familiar with the green market-place, including product vendors and subcontractors familiar with green construction and with the lead times and availability of green specialty materials. It is a very dynamic market, and the person responsible for procurement needs to understand the market's pulse.

The contractor's staff—both on-site staff and the depth of green expertise available in house—is a major factor. On-site supervision by those with green building experience is important for many reasons: scheduling (what is the lead time to fabricate a fuel cell?), constructability (why does a bamboo floor need room for movement?), trade jurisdiction (who installs building-integrated photovoltaic modules?), and quality control (does the label on the paint can really say it contains no VOCs?).

A final factor to consider is whether the contractor has truly embraced a green culture. Is there a companywide commitment to sustainability demonstrated by internal training, participation in organizations like the U.S. Green Building Council, the World Green Building Council, Energy Star, or the United Kingdom's Building Research Establishment; dedicated green resources; and other signs that the commitment goes beyond a few staffers who may have a personal interest in sustainability? An owner deserves a commitment that all the contractor's resources will be pointed in the same direction to create a cost-effective, energy-efficient, and environmentally friendly project.

GREEN PROCUREMENT PLANS

In any type of construction, a contractor's performance is directly proportional to the performance of subcontractors and material vendors. Therefore, it is critical that the contractor have in place a procurement plan or process that identifies and awards work to firms that are the most qualified and financially stable and have experience with green buildings. The list of experienced firms, however, may be rather limited (although the supply continues to grow), and no owner or con-

tractor wants to risk failure by retaining someone who is not committed to or familiar with the design intent of sustainability.

Like the selection process for the contractor, the first issue to consider with subcontractors and vendors is timing. On many green projects, the subcontractors or vendors for high-technology or integrated systems need to be on board during design to lend their expertise to the design team. Examples might include providers of underfloor air distribution systems, modular partitions, or lighting controls. A contractor could retain these providers on a design-build or design-assist basis: the difference is that with design-build, the provider becomes the designer of record, and with design-assist, the provider collaborates with the architect and engineer of record and offers technical advice so that the documents are ultimately complete and functional for their systems.

The trick is obtaining competitive bids from subcontractors or vendors when the design is based on one specific provider's system or technology. The contractor must solicit proposals early in the design process, on the basis of schematic layouts and a performance specification. The prequalified subcontractors or vendors then submit their not-to-exceed proposals either to design or assist with the design of the system, obtain any necessary governmental or agency approvals, and then when the design is complete, convert their not-to-exceed price into a fixed price (at or below their original proposal). This process allows the contractor to creatively maintain competition early in the design phase and yet be protected by a fixed-price commitment before entering into a formal subcontract agreement or purchase order at the time construction begins. A similar process can be followed for proprietary items of work, even if design assistance is not required. Competition must be maintained in some form for the contractor to obtain the best pricing on behalf of the owner.

The timing of trade buyouts—the procurement of building materials and products—is also related to the lead times required for bid, award, shop drawings, fabrication, and delivery. With green construction, the contractor needs a special understanding of these time frames as they relate to specialty products or equipment. How long will it take to obtain finished wood paneling from a sustainable forest and document its travels from forest to building site? In many cases, green products are manufactured in small facilities, and their availability is a function of the order backlog. So the contractor must have the resources to investigate such issues, so that procurement is scheduled accurately to allow for delivery to the site when required.

On traditional projects, a contractor can usually rely on the designer's specifications to ensure that he is buying materials that conform to the intent of the design. On green projects, however, the contractor must reinforce the scope of work being procured, because even minor deviations (or substitutions) can cause a well-designed, integrated system to miss the mark. Subcontractors are very adept at using the "or equal" provision in the general requirements of most specifications to their advantage. The contractor, to prevent any misunderstandings, must therefore develop project-specific special conditions and individual trade requisitions that clearly spell out the scope of work. In fact, it is sometimes necessary to have the subcontractor list the manufacturers and products on which it is basing its bid so their acceptability can be evaluated. More than one green project has been seriously delayed when a product that arrives on site for installation does not conform to specifications. Sometimes getting the correct product delivered at this point is a major issue.

Many designers have third-party testing agencies verify in the field that the contents of products (recycled content or chemical composition, for example) are in fact the same as the contents the manufacturer claims. It is surprising how often misleading information (intentional and unintentional) causes products to fall short of expectations. Several trade associations claim to monitor the quality and greenness of their members' products, but investigative research by the designers and the contractor is the only way to ensure that standards are being maintained. The lack of universal green product standards continues to create industry confusion and is a shortcoming that warrants correction in the near future.

Performance is clearly the bottom line of green products and systems. The contractor must be aligned with the owner and designers to demand that subcontractors and vendors stand behind their products. The responsibility for design normally rests with the architect and engineer, but they must be able to rely on the integrity of suppliers and the contractor must support this reliance. If a product fails to perform as the manufacturer claims, then there must be recourse for replacement or repair. Warranties must be written carefully to ensure longer-term performance. Performance bonds are a wise investment: they can help alleviate the financial pain when a subcontractor or vendor becomes insolvent, an all too frequent occurrence with many newer green subcontractors.

The procurement process takes on a special meaning for green buildings. Time and money can be wasted or saved as a direct result of the contractor's ability to create a practical plan early in the design phase. Owners should be satisfied that the green contractor has met this obligation.

INTEGRATING CERTIFICATION IN THE CONSTRUCTION PROCESS

The contractor plays a significant role in the process of certifying a building's greenness, and a building owner should be aware of this role when selecting a contractor for a project that is seeking to be certified. (A variety of certification programs are used around the world, and the process of integrating them into the construction process is similar. See chapters 1 and 2 for details about the most-used programs.)

The first consideration should be the contractor's experience with the relevant certification process. It is widely acknowledged that the cost and time required to design and build a green-certified project can be significantly reduced when the contractor and other team members have experience with the certification system. Contractor experience is an even greater issue for projects that seek high levels of certification. The learning curve associated with conforming to green certification requirements can be accelerated or eliminated with experience.

It is important to retain the contractor early in the design phase to strategize about green certification criteria. A certification credit matrix should be created at the charrette and monitored by the contractor through design and construction. Input to this matrix includes first-cost and life-cycle cost data that allow the project team to evaluate which credits are worth pursuing and whether tradeoffs should be considered to gain the highest possible certification. As the design evolves, the targeted credits may change as they are continuously evaluated in comparison with the whole building design in terms of cost, schedule, availability, and constructability. As the design is finalized, the project team tabulates the total credits available that, if validated, will result in appropriate green certification at completion. It is a good idea to create a cushion when tabulating these credits in the event that certain criteria are not met in the final submittal.

Documentation of criteria needed for LEED or other green certification is another important activity undertaken by the contractor. It is preferable to have an early understanding of the documentation required, because it is very difficult to retrieve this type of information after the project is completed. Even though the designer may spell out the documentation requirements in the specifications, it is also necessary for the contractor to reinforce them in the solicitation of bids from subcontractors and vendors. Green certification systems typically stipulate that technical data and certifications on products and materials be incorporated with shop drawings. As these materials arrive on the job site, the contractor must verify that they are the same as those previously approved. At the project's closeout, the party responsible for gathering and submitting project documentation for green certification will expect the contractor to have an orderly and complete package of information.

For projects in which the LEED rating system is used, the contractor can directly influence several credits associated with the construction or renovation process, and similar requirements are found under alternative green certification protocols. In both renovation and new construction projects, the contractor controls the recycling of construction and any demolition waste, the reuse of existing materials, building commissioning, and the monitoring of indoor environmental quality as a result of construction activities. Although LEED and other green certification systems prescribe strict criteria to be achieved in these areas, they all entail good common sense and should be a part of every experienced contractor's tool kit. That said, documentation is again required to meet green certification criteria. Like most other construction activities, these credits to be documented need to be identified and planned for early in the design phase.

The contractor is a key player in the development or renovation of any green building. By engaging the contractor early in project development, a truly integrated approach to design and construction can be achieved, leading to a cost-effective project that meets the sustainability needs of the present and sets a firm foundation for continued efforts by future generations.

MINIMIZING LEGAL RISKS IN THE GREEN DESIGN AND CONSTRUCTION PROCESS

ERIC A. GRASBERGER

It is well known that green buildings and office spaces require special design and construction considerations. These considerations include identification of the appropriate materials, systems, construction sequences, and even occupant habits. All these factors affect the contractual terms associated with green development and retrofit projects. This section outlines the developing legal considerations for any green construction project: alternate project delivery methods best suited to green construction; key contract clauses that deserve special consideration; unique and developing insurance issues; and dispute and litigation risks.

ALTERNATE PROJECT DELIVERY METHODS TO REDUCE RISKS

A project delivery method is the process by which the owner retains design professionals and construction professionals to build a project. The three most common methods are as follows:

▸▸ **DESIGN-BID-BUILD**. In this traditional method, the owner first contracts with the architect or engineer to design the project. The owner then takes the design documents to a contractor or contractors to bid on the work. The owner then selects a contractor and executes a separate contract with it. Under this model, there is no contractual relationship between the designer and the contractor and there is little or no collaboration between the two during the design process.

▸▸ **DESIGN-BUILD**. This is another popular method, especially for large or complex projects. Under this method, the owner contracts with a single entity that will provide both design and construction under one contract. This method encourages significant partnering between design and construction professionals (often a joint venture is formed between a design firm and a construction firm for this purpose) and provides the owner with a single point of responsibility for managing the construction process and resolving any disputes.

▸▸ **CONSTRUCTION MANAGER/GENERAL CONTRACTOR**. This method is popular for large or complex projects. It is a hybrid of the traditional method and the design-build method. In this method, the owner maintains a separate contract with the designer and the contractor, but the contractor becomes involved early in the design process to collaborate with the architect regarding constructability issues, feasibility, scheduling, etc. During this phase of the work, the contractor is performing services as a construction manager rather than a true general contractor. Once the design is complete, the contractor then provides a bid and, if accepted, performs the traditional role of general contractor. This delivery method provides some of the collaborative benefits of design-build without forcing a partnership between the design entity and the construction entity.

Selecting the right delivery method is particularly important in green construction projects because of the developing nature of the systems, sequences, and technologies involved. Although not every green project is necessarily complex, owners and developers should consider the benefits of early collaboration between the designer and contractor and also the possible benefits of having a single point of responsibility. Indeed, the Leadership in Energy and Environmental Design (LEED) process encourages early collaboration between the design and construction teams and assigns points for incorporating commissioning professionals early in the design process and for employing a LEED Accredited Professional. The LEED system, therefore, acknowledges that for a green project to be successful, a heightened degree of collaboration and communication is essential. The design-build and construction manager/general contractor processes seem particularly well-suited for green projects.

KEY CONTRACTING ISSUES AND CLAUSES

LEED is the most well-established and popular certification system in the United States. The most common competing alternatives are Green Globes and, for energy efficiency certification, the Environmental Protection Agency's Energy Star. Other nations also have established green rating schemes, as detailed in chapter 2. Design and construction contracts should be drafted to specify the type and level of certification sought by the owner. For simplicity, this discussion will focus on LEED certification, but its principles are applicable to other rating systems.

The following are key concepts for owners and developers to understand and apply in contracting for projects that they want certified under LEED.

▸▸ **INVOLVEMENT OF A LEED ACCREDITED PROFESSIONAL** is critical. It is critical for the project team to include an architect, engineers, a prime contractor, and key subcontractors and consultants that are experienced with and knowledgeable about green and sustainable development generally and LEED certification specifically. The team should include a LEED Accredited Professional, who is typically designated as the LEED representative for the project. In the United States,

many LEED Accredited Professionals also work with alternative certification systems. The LEED representative serves as the interface with the U.S. Green Building Council for filing the certification application or any appeal thereof. He or she should be involved in the project from the drafting of the design documents through to any tenant improvements and alterations at the project. Alternatively, owners are advised to require in tenant leases that tenants hire a LEED Accredited Professional to perform tenant improvements and alterations.

▸▸ **OWNER-ARCHITECT AGREEMENT** is the key. The most important contract in which to address LEED is the owner-architect agreement. The owner-contractor contract should also address LEED requirements. But the prime contractor's obligations should be included in the construction specifications, and those specifications are prepared by the architect and its engineering consultants. As such, the key is to obligate the architect to address LEED issues, not only in the specifications but also in the drawings and basic design of the building.

▸▸ **AIA AND OTHER STANDARD CONTRACT FORMS** lack LEED language. Typical owner-architect and owner-contractor contracts, including standardized contracts such as those of the American Institute of Architects ("AIA forms"), have little or no language dealing with LEED. The standard 2007 AIA B101 owner-architect agreement merely requires the architect to "consider environmentally responsible design alternatives." AIA forms are geared to the needs of the architect; therefore, it may be necessary to modify the forms considerably to afford greater protection to owners and developers. Of course, owners and developers may choose to use alternative forms and contracts. Whichever forms are used, owners and developers should add specialized text to the agreement with specific LEED-related requirements or use a specialized AIA form.

▶▶ **THE AIA B214 DOCUMENT** is useful. The specialized AIA form that focuses on LEED, the 2004 or 2007 AIA B214 document, is useful. It should be used by most owners and developers, with such modifications to the form as are necessary to reallocate the risks between the parties. Still, the AIA B214 document is a process-oriented form that fails to specify a LEED goal. The owner's LEED goal thus must be added to the AIA B101 owner-architect agreement or the AIA B214 document.

▶▶ **THE ARCHITECT'S LEED OBLIGATION** should be carefully phrased. When specifying the owner's LEED goal in owner-architect agreement forms, care should be taken in phrasing the architect's LEED obligation. If the architect has a flat obligation to achieve the owner's LEED certification goal, that obligation likely would be viewed as a warranty by the architect's insurance company, resulting in a denial of professional liability insurance coverage should the architect fail to achieve the goal. The owner could assert that the architect also committed negligence by not performing pursuant to the applicable standard of care in failing to achieve the LEED goal, and that there should be insurance coverage on that basis. The owner also could assert a breach of warranty or negligence claim against the architect, irrespective of insurance coverage. These issues suggest that legal advice be sought regarding how to phrase the architect's obligation with respect to achieving the LEED goal. More importantly, the owner-architect agreement should address issues related to the growing requirements for LEED certification so that owners and developers have the proper remedies and indemnities should the architect fail to meet the LEED requirements in the design or should the project fail to receive tax and other governmental incentives because LEED requirements are not met.

▶▶ **GREEN GOALS OTHER THAN LEED CERTIFICATION** also should be addressed. The LEED text in the agreement forms should address the architect's obligations regarding the owner's building-type certification goals, desired certification level, and expected performance objectives, if any, as well as the owner's interest in qualifying for tax and other governmental incentives for green projects. Such incentives are growing increasingly significant in financing green building projects. Various states, cities, and counties have passed new regulations that require new construction to be LEED certified. In such jurisdictions, it is important that owners and developers have recourse against the architect for the architect's failure to comply with these codes and regulations.

▶▶ **THE LEED PROCESS IN B214** should be squared with process of design team. Even though the AIA B214 form provides substantial text regarding LEED, the process described will likely not be the same as the LEED process that the owner's project team—including the project's LEED representative—will want to follow. This difference must be reconciled. The process should also include early and direct involvement of the owner in LEED decision making. Such involvement is very important, both so that significant tradeoffs inherent in LEED decisions are made by the owner and so that LEED-generated decisions do not inappropriately skew the remainder of the project's design.

▶▶ **SYNERGY BETWEEN THE ARCHITECT AND THE PROJECT TEAM** is important. In order to achieve the owner's LEED certification goals, the architect should work with various members of the project team early in the design process. Collaboration should include all disciplines, including the mechanical, electrical, and plumbing (MEP) engineer, the interior design consultant, the contractor, and the LEED representative. The architect should have each engineer and consultant who works for the project prepare a discipline-specific

checklist of LEED certification requirements that should be incorporated in the plans and specifications for each level of the project. Together, these discipline-specific checklists should form a master LEED checklist for project design.

For additional protection against potential design shortcomings related to LEED certification, owners might consider nontraditional methods of design team assembly and contracting. Engineers and consultants hired for project design might be hired as consultants of the architect (rather than the owner) to enable the owner to recover against the architect for any failure of the overall design of the project to achieve LEED certification. At the very least, however, owners should consider requiring the architect agreement to impose a higher level of monitoring and supervision by the architect over the engineers and consultants who contribute elements to the design related to LEED certification.

▸▸ **RELATED CONTRACT PROVISIONS SHOULD NOT BE IGNORED**. When focusing on LEED-related concerns in contracts, an owner or developer should be mindful of other standard contract provisions that could be important should there be LEED-related issues—such as provisions relating to the standard of care and waiver of consequential damages. Owners or developers may wish to ensure that the appropriate standards of care address the satisfaction of LEED objectives or that loss of operating revenues or profits related to the failure to meet green objectives be considered when drafting contractual terms related to consequential damages.

The main conference room is the only one with outside windows at the Wallace Roberts & Todd main offices on the 28th floor of 1700 Market Street, a multi-tenant office building in Philadelphia.

RABER PHOTOGRAPHY

▸ **PARTICULAR LEED-RELATED CONTRACT PROVISIONS** should be considered. To address certain LEED-related concerns, the addition of these LEED-specific contract provisions should be considered:

- Additional compensation ("bonus") to be paid upon receipt of the desired LEED certification;

- Part of agreed compensation to be retained pending receipt of the desired LEED certification;

- Liquidated damages to be paid upon the desired LEED certification not being received;

- A statement that the architect's certification of the LEED submittal for the project is not a warranty regarding receipt of the desired LEED certification;

- A special damages provision and separate cure rights for any delays related to conforming the project to the LEED design requirements;

- Early notification of the owner about any problems related to the LEED certification process or efforts, in order to reduce the number of change orders in connection with conforming the plans and specifications to the LEED requirements.

▸ **AN ADVERSE LEED DECISION** can be appealed. The LEED system has an administrative appeal process. If a project is not issued a LEED certification or is issued certification at a lower level than sought (Silver rather than Gold, for example), the right of appeal should at least be considered before legal penalties or remedies become operative.

SPECIAL INSURANCE CONSIDERATIONS

For the past 15 years, construction and design defects and related litigation have plagued the construction industry. Recent data indicate that little has been done to curb the defect trend and that related litigation continues to rise. The advent of green construction holds the promise, on the one hand, that architects and contractors will more carefully consider environmental factors and the livability of built space. The increasing use of green building principles also promises more thoughtful design from beginning to end, which perhaps, may lead to fewer defects. On the other hand, the use of new products and technologies may, at least for a while, lead to a higher incidence of defects as the industry tries to adjust to the new world order. This section discusses four special considerations regarding insurance and bonding to protect against the risk of design and construction defects. (For additional discussion of green insurance options, see chapter 6.)

Bolster Design Coverage

Most defect cases are settled with money coming primarily from contractors' insurance policies. While every case is different, a (very close) general rule of thumb is that for every $10 contributed to a construction defect settlement by a contractor, only $1 is contributed by a design professional. Green design and construction may change this dynamic, however, because much attention must be given to the design itself in order to achieve LEED goals or other green objectives.

Especially in the case of larger structures or loftier green objectives, the owner or developer should consider increasing the amount of professional liability coverage carried by the project architect, civil engineer, landscape architect, envelope consultant, or LEED consultant. The failure of a green project to meet energy efficiency objectives or qualify for LEED Platinum certification, as examples, will result in real economic harm to the project owner but will not result in property damage or personal injury in most cases. Contractors' general liability insurance generally covers only property damage or personal injury, whereas designers' professional liability insurance will cover economic losses as well as personal injury or property damage. Given the emphasis on design and the lack of applicable coverage for contractors, buying extra design insurance is advisable in many cases.

Avoid Certain Insurance Exclusions

As litigation risks grow, insurance companies evaluate those risks and often draft new exclusions to the coverage afforded under their policies. Owners should carefully review the insurance policies of both design professionals and contractors, particularly the endorsements to those policies, looking for exclusions for green building-related damages. These might include exclusions for coverage for lost tax benefits, lost revenues, or redesign or rebuilding expense associated with green shortcomings, or even broad exclusions preventing coverage for increased replacement cost of damaged green building components.

Consider Green Replacement Endorsements

Conversely, some insurance companies have seen an opportunity to sell special endorsements (frequently for an extra premium) aimed at assuring the green building owner that any covered loss would be insured to the full replacement value of either the preexisting green goals achieved or even to the next higher green objective under one or more of the green rating systems, such as LEED. At the time of this writing, such green endorsements are being offered by only a limited number of insurance companies, but that number is likely to grow. At least one company, Lexington Insurance Company, is currently referring to its program as the "upgrade to green commercial" endorsement. It covers rebuilding costs as well as recycling during reconstruction, indoor air testing, and increased outdoor air ventilation of the reconstructed space. The Lexington program also allows for the retention of a LEED-accredited architect or engineer and the payment of registration and certification fees

with the U.S. Green Building Council. However, because green building and construction is relatively new to the industry, current insurance industry coverage is limited and should be negotiated, if possible, to afford owners and developers greater protection for their projects.

Consider Performance Bonds

Insurance generally protects against damages caused by improper performance. As mentioned above, for design professionals, the types of damage covered are broader than they are for construction companies, which generally have coverage only for property damage or personal injury resulting from construction errors. Performance bonds, by contrast, can be purchased by the contractor from a surety company (and usually can be reimbursed by the owner) to guarantee the full performance of the contractor under the agreement with the owner. Rather than covering only personal injury or property damage, performance bonds guarantee all obligations of the contractor, including but not limited to the obligation to finish the project or correct the project under warranty obligations consistent with the architect's design documents. If a contractor fails to build according to the design documents and green objectives are not reached, an insurance policy typically would not provide coverage for the loss, but a performance bond, assuming the claim is brought timely, would likely provide such coverage.

Bonds typically cost between 1 and, at most, 2 percent of the prime construction contract value. While bonds are not common in private development or retrofit projects, they should be given new consideration in light of the unique risks posed by green design and construction. Although performance bonds will not guarantee that a project will be LEED certified or guarantee the economic incentives associated with green construction will be obtained, they will guarantee construction of the project in accordance with the plans and specifications, including the elements of the design related to the LEED certification requirements. To this extent, the performance bond obligates the bonding company (on behalf of the contractor) to correct the components of the project which fail to conform to the LEED requirements.

UNDERSTAND THE INCREASED LITIGATION RISKS

Green building creates a new litigation arena. Changes in products, materials, systems, goals, expectations, strategies, and sequences will undoubtedly lead to confusion, mistakes, misunderstandings, and eventually disputes. The increased risk for litigation certainly should not dissuade anyone from investment or involvement in a green building project. Nonetheless, it is important to understand the risks and to involve an attorney who is familiar with the LEED process and other sustainability issues to add provisions to the agreements that appropriately allocate the risks between the parties.

Special Risks to Each Project Participant

The growing use of green building technologies and construction methods introduces new elements of risk for all participants in green building projects, including design and engineering professionals, contractors, product manufacturers and distributors, and owners and tenants.

A common area at Adobe Systems' San Francisco office, a renovated historic office building.

WILLIAM A. PORTER

DESIGNERS

Architects, engineers, and consultants have essentially been given a new playbook. Product and material innovations are occurring at a rapid pace and owner expectations require familiarity with the latest, greatest advances. Design professionals need to worry about the end result, including whether the LEED standard is achieved and whether energy savings will actually be realized, among other things. Designers need to worry about the compatibility of the many new materials, products, and systems, as well as the ability of contractors and subcontractors to understand the design and implement it correctly. Finally, as mentioned earlier, designers need to understand that contractors' insurance is less likely to be applicable to many failures in a green building project. Some believe that this will make designers and their broader professional liability policies a greater target. Regardless of insurance, the role of the design professional in a green building project is simply more advanced and more involved, with greater expectations for measureable success.

CONTRACTORS

Contractors and subcontractors also have a new playbook, much of which will be dictated by the project designers. The playbook will look different and require the construction team to navigate a steep learning curve successfully. Similarly, many points in the green rating systems are achieved through contractor efficiencies (and the ability to document these efficiencies) in the use of materials, the recycling of containers and leftovers, site containment for runoff, smart landscaping and water usage, and other systems and processes that will largely be left for the contractor to implement. Like designers, contractors will be expected to deliver an end product that meets the owner's green objectives, delivers energy savings, and, in many cases, adds revenue and money to the bottom line through increased sales or leases of the built space.

The contractor will be liable for the performance of its work in conformity with the plans and specifications; however, because the LEED requirements involve quantifiable savings and revenues to the project, the owner should include specific cure rights and special damages in the construction contract for the contractor's failure to carry out the LEED requirements in the design. In addition to constructing the project to meet the LEED requirements in the design, the owner should encourage contractors to use green construction practices such as minimizing dust and other pollutants; appropriately disposing of construction waste; and sequencing and scheduling construction so as to conserve energy, increase efficiency in the use of materials, and minimize noise and adverse effects on occupants. LEED awards credits for following green construction practices.

MANUFACTURERS AND DISTRIBUTORS

Manufacturers and distributors will have product liability for all green products they market, sell, and distribute. If these products fail prematurely, fail to deliver savings as promised, or simply fail to be as green as they were marketed to be, manufacturers face unique and distinct liability. In many cases, manufacturers limit their liability with onerous terms on the backs of invoices and purchase orders. These terms limit or disclaim liability to either zero dollars or the cost of the item itself, or they may specify shorter periods in which claims must be brought, or they may limit the recovery of incidental and consequential damages. Owners should realize that the products going into the project are very important to the project's green objectives and, thus, the terms under which those products are purchased must be analyzed and negotiated either directly by the owner or through the contractor or subcontractor middleman.

OWNERS AND TENANTS

Arguably, the greatest risk posed to the owner comes from those who lease or purchase the built space from the owner. When systems or materials fail or energy efficiencies are not realized, the first pocketbook hit belongs typically to the tenant or purchaser of that space. In some cases, the tenants or purchasers will be many in number and may align their interests in a concerted effort to put pressure on the owner or developer to correct or pay for the damages. Although the green litigation arena is still being formed, it would appear that managing the expectations of tenants, purchasers, and other consumers of green built spaces is paramount. This means that marketing literature, verbal sales pitches, and discussions need to be worded carefully to avoid any performance guarantees or overstatement of the benefits to be realized by occupying a green building. In addition, owners should include LEED certification requirements for tenant improvements and alterations and green building rules and regulations in their leases with their tenants.

Types of Claims That Will Be Asserted

While available legal theories vary from state to state, the following claims are generally found in most states and are likely to be asserted in the green building context:

▸▸ **NEGLIGENT OR INTENTIONAL MISREPRESENTATION**. Misrepresentation claims will likely be founded on products or systems that fail to deliver as stated or as reasonably expected. Such claims will be asserted by owners and developers against product manufacturers and others. Building occupants might also bring claims for fraudulent or negligent misrepresentation based on sales literature, sales pitches, or even casual discussions that contain promises or statements about the economic, energy, or even social benefits of occupying a green building.

▸▸ **BREACH OF CONTRACT**. This is the most common theory of liability in the construction arena generally, and the green arena will be no different. In particular, the failure to meet stated objectives found in the agreement will certainly be the basis for claims of breach.

▸▸ **BREACH OF WARRANTY**. Contracts often contain express warranties; in other cases warranties may be implied by law. Any express or implied warranty relating to the performance or characteristics of a green product, system, or building will be the basis for breach of warranty claims.

▸▸ **NEGLIGENCE**. Perhaps the second most common claim in the construction arena is a claim for negligence. Negligence claims will be founded on the failure of any involved party to perform as a reasonable person similarly situated would perform under the circumstances. Negligence claims often trigger insurance policies, but the trend among many states allows for breach and misrepresentation claims to also trigger insurance policies.

▸▸ **CONSUMER PROTECTION STATUTES**. Most states have consumer protection statues that provide for special remedies to consumers who have in some way been wronged by businesses or companies. These statutes may provide a different limitations period for bringing claims, different or typically higher dollar remedies, and, in some cases, the ability to recover attorneys' fees by the prevailing party. It is possible that such claims will be asserted against green buildings that fail to perform as anticipated or as required by statute.

▶ **PATENT INFRINGEMENT**. The rush to develop green products will undoubtedly give rise to disputes over who was the original creator or owner of a certain design, copyright, or patent that is protected intellectual property. Although most of these claims will be fought between manufacturers and inventors of competing green products, in some cases the claims may be brought against owners or developers who are using a particular product, design, or process without first obtaining the intellectual property rights or license to do so.

Types of Damages

The types of damages that will be incurred when green building projects meet with failure are not difficult to imagine. Loss of energy savings; loss of tax credits or government incentives; the inability to sell or lease the end product; green investment dollars wasted; the cost of repair, replacement, or supplementation of systems; the diminished value of the product; and increased maintenance expense are all likely to be seen in the near future. In jurisdictions with mandatory green building requirements, owners and developers may be assessed fines and penalties for failure of the project to comply with such regulations.

As a legal matter, some damages may be difficult to prove. For example, when asserting a claim for loss of energy savings, the influence of numerous variables on energy consumption will muddy the waters and make strict proof difficult. Tenant or occupant habits, average outdoor temperature variations, fluctuating energy prices, and a host of other factors will all come into play.

Similarly, isolating the role each party played in the failure to achieve a certain green rating level or other performance objective will be difficult. Calculating and allocating damages among a team with multiple members when one point was lost for design failure and another point was lost for contractor failure will lead to finger-pointing and cross-claims. Also, whether performance is adequate in many cases will be left to the subjective determination of the parties involved and the final decision maker in any dispute. Most contracts will likely not contain objective, quantifiable, and measurable standards by which failure can be determined as a black or white matter. Proving when the standard of care has not been met may also be difficult considering the relative youth of green building in general. Indeed, for some period of time the standard may involve more failure than success. Ascertaining and allocating the damages pose one set of problems; collecting damages poses an additional set. Participants will undoubtedly pay close attention to their contracts. They will limit or disclaim liability wherever possible. Product warranties will likely be very limited and strict. Insurance coverage, at least for contractors, will continue to cover only property damage or personal injury and not pure economic losses, and performance bonds will likely continue to be an uncommon occurrence in private development.

CONCLUSION

Green building and green retrofit projects certainly pose some new and challenging issues at both the contracting stage and the dispute resolution stage. These challenges should not dissuade any owner from embarking on a green building project, with all of its environmental and hopefully, economic benefits. Neither should owners be so blinded by the spirit and positive energy of a green building project that they fail to recognize that errors, perhaps more than usual, can and will be made by all those involved—with monetary consequences to the unwary.

The Business of
Green Office Renovations

LEANNE TOBIAS AND MICHAEL J. ZIMMER

Green real estate has become a substantial global business, growing significantly more rapidly than the construction industry and the underlying economy. According to McGraw-Hill Construction, green building construction starts in the United States increased from $10 billion in 2005 to an estimated $36 to $49 billion in 2008 and could triple by 2013, to levels reaching $96 to $140 billion.[1] In China, the creation of energy-efficient buildings has been targeted as one of the ten key energy efficiency initiatives included in the 11th Five-Year Plan, which extends through 2010. Under the plan, which envisions an ambitious program of energy-efficient new construction and retrofits, 40 percent of China's energy savings are expected to come from the built environment.[2] Energy-efficient buildings are also key components in a number of newly created economic stimulus efforts launched by national governments around the globe (see discussion in chapter 7).

As these developments suggest, green real estate construction and renovation have entered the mainstream of business practice and will be a growing and permanent global market factor in the future. The latest international data also suggest that investment in green buildings is good business, offering strong payback and market returns for limited additional cost.

GREEN BUILDING COSTS AND PAYBACKS

The economics of green building development and renovation have improved as green building practices and technologies have been adopted in the commercial real estate industry. These changes have reduced cost premiums for retrofitting or constructing sustainable properties and have enhanced green payback metrics.

Diminishing Global Cost Premium
The cost premium to build green has diminished significantly as green technologies have penetrated the design and construction

markets. A 2008 international study of 150 green buildings in ten nations conducted by Good Energies, a global investor in renewable energy and energy efficiency technologies, found that green buildings cost, on average, only 2 percent more to construct than conventional properties, with the largest concentration of green cost premiums between 0 and 1 percent.[3]

Strong Paybacks and Returns

The paybacks and returns associated with green building development and renovation are frequently robust. Good Energies found that roughly 50 percent of green buildings in the study's data set saw the initial "green premium" paid back by energy and water savings in five years or less.[4] Additional data compiled by Craig Sheehy of Envision Realty Services, a green real estate consulting firm, on 25 building retrofits certified under the U.S. Green Building Council's Leadership in Energy and Environmental Design (LEED) program as of September 2008 indicate an average payback of 1.4 years and a simple return on investment (ROI) of 73 percent. All projects demonstrated positive returns, with a minimum return of 21 percent and a maximum payback period of 4.7 years (see the sidebar on LEED for Existing Buildings [LEED-EB] retrofits).

Case study data on green retrofits also suggest that returns can be significant and payback periods comparatively short. Sixty-four energy efficiency renovation projects undertaken by Adobe Systems and Cushman & Wakefield at Adobe's San Jose, California headquarters produced an average ROI of 121 percent, and a number of initiatives paid off immediately (see the case study in chapter 9). The renovation of One Beacon Street in Boston, Massachusetts, by Beacon Capital Partners and CB Richard Ellis achieved a payback period of less than nine months and a first-year ROI of 39 percent (see the case study in chapter 9).

LEASING, RENTAL RATE, AND SALES PRICE BENEFITS

Over the past several years, case study reports have suggested that green office properties may produce superior rental rates, occupancies, and sales prices. The first wave of aggregate data on this subject, published in 2008 and 2009, provides additional evidence that a green value premium is emerging in the marketplace. The initial studies, conducted by researchers from the United States, the United Kingdom, and the Netherlands, are based on the U.S. data set of CoStar Group, one of the leading providers of property performance data. This database tracks financial performance metrics, including rental rates, occupancy, and sale prices, for conventional office properties, for energy-efficient properties certified under the U.S. government's Energy Star program, and for green buildings certified under LEED. The CoStar information is the first large-scale database that permits economic comparisons between conventional, energy-efficient, and green properties throughout the United States. As of early 2008, the database contained 44 billion square feet of conventional space and 351 million square feet of LEED- and Energy Star–certified property. As of April 2009, the CoStar database contained 66 billion square feet of commercial space, including 402 LEED-certified properties and 1,925 Energy Star–certified properties.

The initial studies of the CoStar data have been prepared by a CoStar-led team, by a team from the University of California at Berkeley and the Netherlands' Maastricht University and by a team from the United Kingdom's University of Reading. Results, summarized in figure 5-1, indicate that green-certified properties generally produce higher rental rates and sale prices.

CoStar

CoStar's July 2008 report provided matched comparisons of office properties, controlled for location, class, age, and size, among Energy

Figure 5-1

Comparison Studies of Green Premiums in Office Buildings: Rents, Occupancies, and Sales Prices, 2008 to 2009

CoStar, Large, Multitenanted Office Buildings, March 2008[a]	All Green-Certified	LEED	Energy Star
Occupancy Percentage Points		+4.2	+3.7
Rental Rate Premium ($ per Square Foot)		14.15	2.50
University of California, Berkeley, Office Buildings, Quarter-Mile Radius, October 2008			
Direct Rental Rate Premium (Percent)[b]	3.0	—[c]	3.3
Effective Rental Rate Premium (Percent)[b]	6.4	—[c]	10.0
Sale Price Premium (Percent)[b]	16.0	—[c]	19.1
University of Reading, Office Properties, CoStar-defined Submarket, April 2009			
Direct Rental Rate Premium (Percent)[b]	6.0	5.0	6.0
Sale Price Premium (Percent)[b]	36.0	35.0	31.0

Note: — = not available.
a. Sample of multitenant office buildings of 200,000 or more square feet and five stories or more, built since 1970.
b. Statistically significant at the 1 percent level of confidence.
c. Not statistically significant at the 5 percent level of confidence or better.

Star–certified, LEED-certified, and conventional buildings.[5] Results indicated that, on average, LEED and Energy Star properties attained higher occupancies (an additional 4.1 occupancy percentage points for LEED buildings and 3.7 points for Energy Star properties) and rental rates (an additional $14.15 per square foot for LEED properties and $2.50 per square foot for Energy Star properties).

University of California at Berkeley and Maastricht University

An analysis of CoStar's 2008 U.S. database, published by the Royal Institution of Chartered Surveyors in March 2009, was performed by a team from Maastricht University and the University of California at Berkeley. The study matched conventional, Energy Star–certified, and LEED-certified office buildings situated within a quarter-mile radius. Rents for green office buildings located within 694 quarter-mile clusters were approximately 3 percent higher than rents for comparable buildings, and effective rents adjusted for occupancy were approximately 6 percent higher. The study also examined sales prices for 199 green-certified buildings and a matched sample of conventional properties sold between 2004 and 2007. It estimated that the selling prices of the green office buildings were about 16 percent higher than selling prices for comparable conventional properties.[6] Results were statistically significant at the 1 percent level of confidence for the green-certified properties as a group and for the Energy Star–certified properties; results for the comparatively small number of LEED-certified properties were not statistically significant.[7]

The research suggested that energy efficiency was a key driver for green premiums: the research team concluded that "a $1 saving in energy costs from increased thermal efficiency yields a return of roughly $18 in the increased valuation of an Energy Star–certified building."[8] An examination of 27 green buildings operating under net leases for which energy utilization data were available suggested that tenants who pay their own utilities may be willing to pay additional rent—in excess of the green premium—for energy-efficient features: "a 10 percent increase in the site energy utilization efficiency of a green building is associated with a 0.2 percent increase in effective rent, and this is over and above the 6 percent premium for a labeled building."[9] The net lease findings, while preliminary, suggest that "when tenants in office buildings pay their own utilities and when they have chosen to pay a premium for tenancy in green buildings, they are nevertheless still willing to pay higher rents for more energy-efficient buildings."[10]

University of Reading

An April 2009 regression analysis prepared by investigators from Henley Business School at the University of Reading and employing two methodologies found that properties with green certifications demonstrated sale price premiums of 19.6 percent to 36 percent. Under a standard modeling method, eco-certified properties as a group displayed a 36 percent premium, Energy Star–certified properties showed a 31 percent premium, and LEED-certified properties

LEED-EB RETROFITS: STRONG PAYBACK RESULTS

SCOTT MULDAVIN

LEED for Existing Buildings (LEED-EB) retrofits can be performed cost-effectively, as demonstrated by the results from 25 LEED-EB retrofits reported by Craig Sheehy of Envision Realty Services in September 2008 (figure 1). The Envision Realty analysis focuses on the investment return created by savings in operating costs created by each retrofit.

As the 25 properties in the data set show, returns were robust, with an average payback of 1.4 years and a simple ROI of 73 percent the first year. Perhaps more important, all 25 projects demonstrated positive returns, with a minimum return of 21 percent and maximum payback period of 4.7 years. Returns were strong across geographies and across levels of LEED certification.

Figure 1

Savings and ROI Associated with 25 LEED-Certified Retrofits

City, State	Energy Star Rating	LEED Level	Size (Sq. Ft.)	Cost ($)	Cost Per Sq. Ft. ($)	First-Year Savings ($)	Payback Period	First-Year ROI (Percent)
Charlotte, NC	75	Silver	324,305	53,777	0.17	60,000	9 months	112
Charlotte, NC	75	Certified	298,371	52,910	0.18	58,000	8.8 months	110
Walnut Creek, CA	89	Gold	249,391	88,808	0.36	96,100	11 months	108
Sacramento, CA	78	Gold	336,104	88,853	0.26	90,000	10 months	101
Minneapolis, MN	91	Gold	621,193	191,130	0.31	186,238	1.01 years	97
Denver, CO	79	Certified	263,716	108,097	0.41	102,750	1.05 years	95
Dallas, TX	89	Silver	1,113,575	291,136	0.26	237,400	1.4 years	82
Dallas, TX	78	Certified	515,388	64,460	0.13	50,000	1.2 years	78
Los Angeles, CA	90	Silver	587,022	71,700	0.12	55,000	1.3 years	77
Atlanta, GA	87	Gold	410,357	116,812	0.28	89,000	1.3 years	76
Fort Lauderdale, FL	92	Gold	261,676	108,641	0.42	77,000	1.5 years	71
Atlanta, GA	73	Certified	670,000	57,950	0.09	40,000	1.4 years	69
Chicago, IL	85	Gold	800,000	114,950	0.14	75,000	1.5 years	65
Billerica, MA	74	Certified	353,242	54,281	0.15	35,000	1.5 years	64
Vienna, VA	83	Silver	346,618	53,700	0.15	32,000	1.6 years	60
Denver, CO	87	Silver	435,672	67,821	0.16	40,000	1.6 years	59
Los Angeles, CA	98	Gold	317,058	58,437	0.18	33,000	1.7 years	56
Atlanta, GA	82	Silver	625,071	91,520	0.15	50,000	1.8 years	55
Atlanta, GA	73	Certified	670,000	78,110	0.12	40,000	1.9 years	51
Greenwood Village, CO	78	Silver	317,218	68,530	0.22	30,000	2.2 years	44
Atlanta, GA	73	Certified	312,000	72,990	0.23	31,000	2.3 years	42
Oakland, CA	80	Silver	273,355	59,033	0.22	25,000	2.3 years	42
Denver, CO	78	Certified	150,673	48,766	0.32	15,000	3.2 years	31
Los Angeles, CA	84	Silver	137,369	51,084	0.37	13,000	3.9 years	25
Greenwood Village, CO	82	Silver	115,408	47,885	0.41	10,000	4.7 years	21
Average			420,191	86,455	0.21	62,820	1.38 years	73

Note: ROI is defined as simple return on investment, calculated as first-year savings divided by investment amount. Simple ROI is typically calculated to track investment performance over short periods.

The Envision Realty analysis, while important, focuses on only one measure of financial performance—net financial benefits of operating cost savings. Accordingly, while the results were impressive, they fail to take into consideration potential increases in revenue due to increased tenant demand, government incentives, reduced risk, and increased investor demand. Although these benefits do not accrue to every project, strong interest by investors, owners, tenants, and policy makes a comprehensive analysis of potential benefits important.

Detailed analysis of financial benefits beyond simple cost savings and payback calculations is not typically necessary in making the relatively small (average of $86,500) investments in existing buildings shown in Envision Realty's analysis. More detailed analysis will become critical, however, as the focus changes from making the minimum investments necessary to achieve a LEED rating to achieving more substantial energy and water savings through more significant capital investments and building retrofits. Capital-intensive projects require greater investment but also experience more uncertainty in performance outcomes, requiring greater understanding of financial

benefits and the ability to articulate such benefits to sources of capital.

When interpreting data like those presented here, it is important to understand that the implementation results are likely to be more robust then the average results for a portfolio of buildings, because of selection bias. Selection bias arises because real estate consultants like Envision Realty and other service providers and owners are implementing increasingly sophisticated screening tools in order to select which buildings to retrofit first. Logically, money should be spent on those buildings that will have the highest ROI; thus any analysis in the early years of LEED-EB implementation needs to be examined carefully for its general applicability to future decisions. At the same time, the Envision Realty results suggest that green building retrofits can offer attractive returns to property owners and, if selected prudently, can represent attractive financing options for lenders.

Scott Muldavin is president of the Muldavin Company, Inc., and founder and executive director of the Green Building Finance Consortium.

demonstrated a 35 percent premium. All results were statistically significant at the 1 percent level of confidence. A second modeling method that introduced additional statistical controls and that tested LEED properties only showed a 19.6 percent sales price premium.

Properties with green certifications demonstrated rental rate premiums ranging from 3.7 percent to 6 percent. Under a standard modeling method, rental rate premiums for all green-certified properties, LEED-certified properties, and Energy Star–certified proper-

ties measured 6 percent. Results were statistically significant at the 5 percent level of confidence or better. A second modeling method that introduced additional statistical controls and tested LEED properties found only a 3.7 percent rental rate premium.[11]

Together, these three studies corroborate that green certification is associated with enhanced occupancy levels, rental rates, and sale prices for commercial real estate. Additional research is needed to determine whether these results are valid outside the

Figure 5-2

Factors Influencing Attitudes toward Sustainability, Worldwide Survey of Corporate Space Executives

Factor	Share Citing Factor (%)
Significant Increases in Energy Costs	79.9
Increased Regulation of Energy and Carbon Emissions	72.7
Increased Demand from Customers and Clients for Sustainability	65.5
Availability of Technology to Support Improved Sustainability	59.6
Increased Focus of CEO on Sustainability	58.8
New or Increased Energy and Carbon Taxes	56.3
Increased Importance of Sustainability for Current and Potential Employees	54.4
Meaningful Government Incentives to Encourage Sustainability	46.4
Shareholder Action Targeting Company's Sustainability Record	36.3

Source: Jones Lang LaSalle, CoreNet Global, "Global Trends in Sustainable Real Estate: An Occupier's Perspective," February 2008, p. 7.

United States, whether green rental rate and sale price premiums remain stable or fluctuate, and whether pricing differs significantly across green certification systems.

STRONG GLOBAL DEMAND

Recent survey evidence suggests that premium values for energy-efficient real estate are undergirded by strong occupant demand in the face of still-limited, albeit growing, supply. Findings of a 2007 worldwide study of more than 400 corporate real estate occupiers and their advisers completed by Jones Lang LaSalle and CoreNet Global and published in early 2008, indicate that corporate tenants are highly motivated to lease space in energy-efficient and green properties, and are willing to pay a price premium in the face of supply constraints. Corporate occupiers were most frequently motivated by concerns about increases in energy costs and trends toward increased regulation of energy and carbon emissions. Other factors perceived to influence corporate attitudes about occupancy of sustainable space are detailed in figure 5-2.

RESTRICTED GLOBAL SUPPLY AND PREMIUM GREEN RENTS

In addition, corporate building occupants perceive the supply of green buildings to be suboptimal relative to demand. Worldwide, 83 percent of those surveyed characterized the supply of environmentally friendly real estate as patchy, limited, or minimal. Seventy percent of those surveyed stated that they would pay a rental premium for green com-

mercial real estate, with most respondents agreeing that a 1 to 10 percent rental premium was appropriate.[12] As detailed in figure 5-3, there is broad international support for the payment of a rental premium for green corporate space.

UNDERWRITING GREEN OFFICE RETROFITS AND RENOVATIONS

The underwriting of green office retrofits and renovations is typically tailored to the scope and capital source of a proposed project.

When Limited Analysis Is Appropriate

Many green office renovations are financed by the occupant's retained earnings or through a tenant improvement allowance provided by the property owner. As detailed in many of the case studies in this volume—including those of Transwestern's Atlanta offices; the Wallace Roberts & Todd headquarters in Philadelphia; and Australian Ethical Investment's offices in Canberra—green retrofits can frequently be produced for the same costs as conventional renovations. Projects that are financed through the occupant's retained earnings or through a tenant improvement allowance frequently can be documented on the basis of a detailed budget, qualified contractor bids, and an analysis of expected payback from energy and water savings.

Figure 5-3

Premium Rents for Green Space: Views of Global Commercial Occupiers

	All	EMEA	North America	Asia Pacific	Australasia
Willing to Pay Premium	70	66	77	64	68
Size of Premium					
1–10 percent	62	64	74	48	61
>10 percent	8	2	3	16	7

Note: EMEA = Europe, Middle East, Africa.
Source: Jones Lang LaSalle, CoreNet Global, "Global Trends in Sustainable Real Estate: An Occupier's Perspective," February 2008, p. 5.

Using Discounted Cash Flow Methodology

More extensive renovations that rely on capital from outside financing sources demand more detailed analysis. Permanent lenders, construction lenders, and equity investors assess real estate projects on the basis of their ability to deliver a market rate of return relative to elements of project risk. The standard methodology is a discounted cash flow (DCF) model, which evaluates diverse sources of risk and return over an appropriate holding period of up to ten years.

The view of most real estate finance professionals is that the DCF methodology provides an appropriate framework for evaluating more extensive green building projects, including office renovations. The Green Building Finance Consortium (GBFC), an alliance of real estate industry professionals, has developed recommendations to guide the commercial real estate industry, including equity investors, lenders, and developers, in valuing sustainable real estate. As detailed in the sidebar by Scott Muldavin, GBFC's executive director, the outcomes of sustainable property renovations must be modeled carefully with respect to their effect on financial performance. For example, a commonly cited sustainable property benefit—increased worker productivity—is just one of the many sustainable factors that influence space user demand, which in combination with other nonsustainable factors—such as market and

At One Market Street in San Francisco, Autodesk uses multiple water-saving techniques in the building operations, resulting in water efficiency that exceeds U.S. Environmental Protection Agency guidelines by more than 30 percent.

submarket economic conditions, property location, and project functionality—will enable a determination of financial implications (among them, probable rents, pace of leasing, and rate of tenant retention) and performance (rate of return and value). As Muldavin notes, the DCF model, if carefully composed, provides the means to translate "intermediate" sustainable property outcomes like health or productivity benefits, expedited permitting, or lower operating costs into the rate of return or net present value metrics traditionally used by real estate capital providers.

HOW DO GREEN PROJECTS AFFECT RISK PERCEPTIONS?

The business case data indicate that green buildings can typically be delivered for costs that are similar to conventional construction and that green features can favorably affect operating costs, building occupancies, rental rates, and sale prices. At the same time, green buildings share many of the same risk characteristics as conventional development projects. Area economic analysis and market and submarket supply and demand parameters will be identical for green and conventional projects. Although green buildings may outperform many of their conventional peers, they are not immune from larger real estate market forces.

As well, the desire to build or renovate with green technologies may heighten perceived risk in the eyes of a capital provider who is unfamiliar with green building techniques. The use of innovative design elements and construction methods can elicit concern, particularly if those elements are perceived to heighten construction costs or increase the length of the project's development schedule.

Developer, lender, or investor concerns relating to project costs or construction schedules can be reduced or mitigated by careful project planning, and the use of experienced architectural, construction management, and contracting teams that have suc-

cessfully designed and built green projects on time and on budget. Cost savings associated with green building practices, including the recycling of construction site waste and the use of commissioning, should be clearly articulated and included in the project budget and project documentation.

If the project team has been associated with comparable projects in the same market or submarket that achieved replicable savings, these "comps" are an important piece of evidence for the lender and can help to allay concerns about the threat of cost overruns. Similarly, comps that document the energy savings achieved by green projects will be helpful to the lender in order to document that green projects lead to savings and enhanced value over the loan period. If comparable data specific to the project's submarket or metropolitan area indicate that green projects can deliver other economic benefits, such as faster lease-up, higher rents, or improved tenant retention, those factors should also be documented to enable lenders to take these factors into account when considering project financing.

GREEN REAL ESTATE FINANCE VEHICLES

As the business case for green properties has moved into the mainstream, specialized vehicles to finance green development projects, including office renovations, have been brought to market. This section provides an overview of available and emerging financing options.

Public Loan, Grant, and Tax Incentive Programs

In the wake of the 2008 credit crisis, public financial support has become an increasingly important aspect of financing energy-efficient real estate and can be combined with private financing to offset development and retrofit costs. In the United States, one or more public programs to support energy efficiency are found in a majority of states;

UNDERWRITING SUSTAINABLE PROPERTY INVESTMENT

SCOTT MULDAVIN

Historically unprecedented changes in regulatory interest and demand by space users and investors for sustainable property necessitate the refinement of real estate underwriting and valuation methodologies. These rapid changes in demand have moved the practice of sustainable property investment well past energy or water cost savings. That shift reinforces the need to supplement traditional simple payback and simple ROI decision-making practices with analytical approaches that capture critical revenue and risk considerations.

Within this context, the Green Building Finance Consortium (GBFC) was founded to develop underwriting and valuation methods and practices that will enable investors in private sector commercial and multifamily property to evaluate green buildings from a financial and fiduciary perspective.[1] This sidebar outlines some of the findings arising from the Consortium's research and its preparation of two books released in the summer of 2009: *Underwriting Sustainable Property Investment* and *Sustainable Property Performance*.

Key Challenge: Moving from General to Specific

The general case supporting enhanced value for sustainable properties is compelling. While operating cost savings achieved through reduced energy, water, maintenance, waste, insurance, and other costs get the most attention, it is the significantly increased regulatory concern and demand by space users and investors since 2007 that drives the value.[2]

Increased demand positively influences revenues (rents, occupancies, tenant retention, regulatory incentives, etc.) and risks (capitalization and discount rates). These positive benefits, in combination with operating cost savings, outweigh heightened risks and costs, many of which can be mitigated through improved contracts, integrated design, commissioning, and other processes and practices.

The underwriter's key challenge is to assess the applicability of the general value argument for a specific property. Fortunately, the most widely recognized financial model for evaluating real estate investments—DCF analysis—is well suited to address the financial implications of sustainability. DCF analysis provides a conceptual framework and model that enables the user to integrate quantitative and qualitative analysis so as to measure the financial performance of sustainable property. It can be readily implemented with commercially available software, such as Argus. Most importantly, DCF analysis provides the means to translate the "intermediate" cost and benefit outcomes (health or productivity benefits, expedited permitting, reduced cash flow risk, or enhanced space user demand), into financial measures (rate of return and net present value) that are used by the providers of real estate capital.

Figure 1

GBFC Sustainable Property Performance Framework

PROCESS PERFORMANCE ▸▸	FEATURE/SYSTEM PERFORMANCE ▸▸	BUILDING PERFORMANCE ▸▸	MARKET PERFORMANCE ▸▸	FINANCIAL PERFORMANCE
Integrated Design	Energy/Water	Development Costs	Operating Costs	Return on Investment
Contracts	Indoor Environmental Quality	Resource Use	Regulator/Utility Demand	Risk
Services Capacity	Materials and Resources	Location and Access	Space User Demand	Value
Energy Modeling	Sustainable Sites	Occupant Performance	Investor Demand	
Commissioning	Energy/Water	Sustainability Compliance	Broker Recognition	
Sustainable Certifications	Indoor Environmental Quality	Flexibility/Adaptability	Appraiser Recognition	
Measurement and Verification	Materials and Resources	Public Benefits		
Training Occupants and Staff	Sustainable Sites			

Figure 2

Six Steps to Sustainable Property Financial Analysis

Step One	Select Financial Model
Step Two	Evaluate Property Sustainability
Step Three	Access Costs and Benefits of Sustainability
Step Four	Evaluate Financial Implications of Costs and Benefits
Step Five	Determine Financial Model Inputs
Step Six	Risk Analysis and Presentation

Simple payback, simple ROI, and related cost-focused models can still provide useful information for making decisions between different strategies or features (types of lighting systems or bulbs, material or product selection, etc.). Many decisions for existing buildings can be made utilizing these techniques. However, if the industry and society is going to move toward higher levels of energy efficiency and sustainability, methods such as DCF analysis will be needed in order to move beyond cost to incorporate revenue and risk considerations into sustainable investment decisions.

New Framework for Sustainable Property Performance

To better support financial analysis and valuation of sustainable property investments, property performance must be measured and evaluated on multiple levels. Five types of performance are most important: process performance, feature performance, building performance, market performance, and financial performance (figure 1).

Process performance is critical to successful performance of both the feature or system and the building. Soundly executed and integrated design, commissioning, and contracts can significantly reduce risks and improve the performance of specific features like green roofs, underfloor air systems, and daylighting strategies. Importantly, because most sustainable property investment decisions are based on forecasts of building performance, a thorough review of process and the performance of features and systems is critical for underwriters assessing the accuracy and reliability of estimates. Risk mitigation, through understanding the specific risks of different features and avoiding untested features or strategies with unclear track records, is a key foundation to underwriting.

The most important point of the GBFC Performance Framework is the recognition that even if the analyst knows how a building is performing, including its resource use,

health and productivity, and level of sustainability, financial performance cannot be assessed without evaluating the market's response to the building performance (Market Performance). This analysis will be unique to the property being analyzed and influenced by market conditions, the types of space users contemplated for the property, the types of most likely buyers, and the recognition of the value of sustainable properties by commercial brokers and appraisers in the market, among other factors.

GBFC Process for Sustainable Property Financial Analysis

Six distinct steps are necessary to implement sustainable property financial analysis properly, as shown in figure 2. Failure to implement each step can result in neglecting key costs and benefits, attributing incorrect influence to any particular sustainable cost or benefit, and ignoring the influence of sustainable property investment on important financial model inputs.

STEP 1: SELECT FINANCIAL MODEL

The first step is to select the financial models and analytic methods appropriate to the particular decision. To do this, the underwriter must clearly understand the decision being addressed and the context in which the decision is being made, as shown in figure 3. While the need for clear specification of the investment context seems obvious, the lack of attention to understanding what decision makers need and employing appropriate analytic techniques and data has been a significant barrier to good decision making about sustainable property investments.

To aid the selection process, the Consortium has identified approximately 40 types of financial analyses that can logically be separated into four categories:

▶▶ **Traditional Sustainability Financial Analyses:** Compare relative merits of sustainable features.

▶▶ **Sustainability Sub-Financial Analyses:** Evaluate health and productivity benefits.

▶▶ **Public Sustainable Benefits Analysis:** Evaluate societal benefits that may be monetized.

▶▶ **Traditional Real Estate Financial Analysis:** Evaluate real estate project returns.

Results from analyses in the first three categories can be incorporated into the traditional real estate financial analysis, which typically is based on a DCF model.

Figure 3

Investment Context Drives Underwriting Methodology

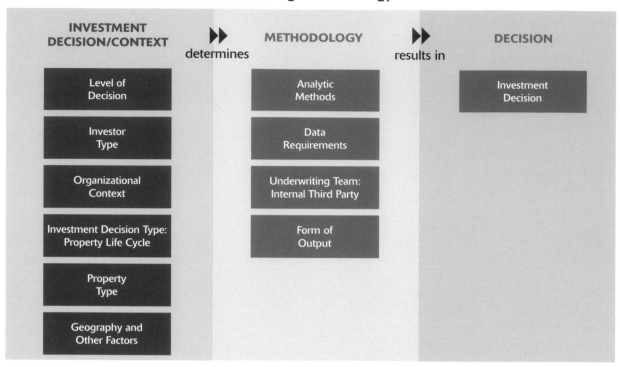

STEP 2: EVALUATE PROPERTY SUSTAINABILITY

Definitions and certifications play an important role in the financial assessment of sustainable properties. They provide a basis for investors to measure and compare properties, a critical foundation for financial analysis. Financial professionals should note, however, that green building certifications like LEED, BREEAM, GreenStar, and Green Globes measure environmental outcomes, not financial outcomes, and thus cannot be the sole basis for underwriting from a financial perspective. Practically, investors will also be confronted with underwriting properties that have varying sustainable features, performance, and green certifications.

Accordingly, financial analysis of a specific property requires a more sophisticated understanding of the linkage between how a property is defined as sustainable and its related value. More focus must be put on specific sustainable features and processes. No single certification or rating will suffice. At a minimum, the specific threshold sustainability requirements necessary to obtain benefits from regulators, users, and investors must be identified and evaluated for each property

STEP 3: ASSESS COSTS AND BENEFITS OF SUSTAINABILITY

After the most appropriate financial analyses have been selected and a property's sustainability has been assessed, the valuer needs to evaluate the property's specific sustainable costs and benefits. It is this detailed, property-specific analysis that separates independent valuation and underwriting of a sustainable property from the more prevalent "general business case" analysis. It is critical to start this analysis with a well-organized and complete checklist of potential costs and benefits from which to assess their applicability for the property being underwritten. The Consortium's GBFC Sustainable Property Cost-Benefit Checklist provides a detailed list of costs and benefits, with description and commentary on how to assess their applicability for specific properties.

STEP 4: EVALUATE FINANCIAL IMPLICATIONS OF SUSTAINABILITY

Now that sustainable property costs and benefits have been identified and evaluated, the next step is to determine how the property's sustainable costs and benefits will influence its financial performance. The Sustainable Property Cost-Benefit Checklist is designed to aid financial performance assessment. First, all sustainable costs and benefits should be organized under key categories that are closely tied to developing the inputs to financial models that enable an assessment of financial performance:

▶ Development costs,
▶ Development risks,
▶ Space user demand,
▶ Resource use and operating costs,
▶ Building operations,
▶ Cash flow and building ownership risk,
▶ Public benefits, and
▶ Increased investor demand.

By organizing the results of the cost-benefit checklist in this manner, specific sustainable attributes are grouped so as to enable assessment of their probable financial impact on the property. This assessment constitutes a net impact analysis that aids in the determination of financial model inputs in step 5. While specific costs or benefits sometimes exist outside the eight categories identified, it is difficult to assess their potential implications for financial performance unless they can be appropriately categorized under one of these categories.

STEP 5: DETERMINE FINANCIAL MODEL INPUTS

The fifth step is to apply the information assembled in the net impact analysis to develop the financial model assumptions that will be input into a DCF model to estimate financial performance. Step 5 is distinct from step 4 in that step 4 only tries to assess or measure and describe how a property's sustainability "could affect key financial model inputs." In step 5, the key goal is to specify specific financial model inputs—rents, occupancies, tenant retention, etc.—taking into consideration all factors, both sustainable and nonsustainable, that affect the financial model inputs. The financial model specifications developed in step 5 can and should be designed in accordance with the input requirements of supporting modeling software, such as Argus.

STEP 6: RISK ANALYSIS AND PRESENTATION

One of the most important issues in underwriting the financial performance of sustainable properties is a full understanding of the risks associated with the pro forma cash flows in the DCF model. For the purposes of improving sustainable investment decision making, the Consortium recommends more detailed documentation of the risks of such investment, both positive and negative, to provide decision makers with the proper context for evaluating pro forma financial performance.[3]

Risk analysis is particularly critical to sustainable property underwriting and valuation because of the substantial negative development and cash flow risks (costs). Negative risks arise from the pioneering nature of sustainable property investment and the required changes in organizations, processes, systems, and materials that are necessary for successful sustainable projects. Sustainable property investment often involves a major retrofit or new construction and related projected changes in operating costs and revenues. By definition, such projects are more risky than investment in an existing, seasoned property.

The priority of risk analysis for sustainable property investment is further underscored by the many positive risk attributes (benefits). Given the rapid and dramatic increase in demand for sustainable properties by regulators, space users, and investors, properties that are not at an appropriate level of sustainability for their market, as well as those for which the cost to cure potential functional economic obsolescence is too high, will suffer financially. A clear, well-supported discussion of potential benefits and their financial implications, specific to the property, is critical to support appropriate changes in DCF model assumptions.

Conclusion

Underwriting and valuation of a specific sustainable property requires a disciplined approach in order to assess the applicability of the compelling general arguments supporting enhanced value from sustainable property investment. While it is enticing to rely on the "killer study" to get the answer to the value of sustainable investment, the reality is that the industry must do what it has always done: roll up its sleeves and get to work to better understand and analyze the nuances of sustainable property investment. Happily, the DCF analysis on which the real estate industry has traditionally relied offers an appropriate framework for valuing sustainable buildings.

Scott Muldavin is president of the Muldavin Company, Inc., and founder and executive director of the Green Building Finance Consortium.

NOTES

1   The Green Building Finance Consortium is a research project founded and led by the Muldavin Company, Inc. The Consortium's work is funded by the real estate industry and select governmental and nongovernmental organizations. More detail on the Consortium can be found at www.greenbuildingfc.com.

2   "Space user" is a term to describe the occupants or users of real estate. It includes corporate and noncorporate owner-occupants, tenants, retail customers, and other nonowner or tenant users of space.

3   Given the declines in the financial and capital markets that accelerated in the fourth quarter of 2008 and the resulting significant increase in risk and uncertainty in the market overall, the ideas presented in this sidebar are well suited to real estate investment generally.

Project financing for the retrofit of the Wallace Roberts & Todd (WRT) main offices on the 28th floor of 1700 Market Street in Philadelphia was obtained through a tenant-improvement allowance negotiated by WRT with its landlord, initial rent concessions, and a bank loan.

available programs include grants, loans, business income tax credits and deductions, and property tax exemptions, as well as utility company rebates for energy-efficient improvements. A comprehensive listing of U.S. state and local energy efficiency programs can be found at the Database of State Incentives for Renewable Energy (DSIRE, at www.dsireusa.org). The 2009 U.S. economic stimulus and similar programs in China, Australia, South Korea, and several European Union (EU) member states also have begun to focus on the provision of financing and tax incentives for energy efficiency in buildings. (See chapter 7 for a more detailed discussion of public programs and financial incentives related to green and energy-efficient building projects.)

EQUITY INVESTMENT VEHICLES

The first wave of green real estate funds and investment vehicles, many of which incorporate office renovations, has begun to appear:

▸▸ The first U.S. green real estate funds were launched in 2006. The Rose Smart Growth Investment Fund I focuses on sustainable principles in renovations of commercial properties in transit-oriented locations (see the case study of the Joseph Vance Building). The Hines-CalPERS Green Development Fund, a closed-end fund with $277 million in equity, focuses on new office development.

▸▸ A key early entrant in the green property fund market was Australia's Investa, now a privately held subsidiary of Morgan Stanley, with A$2 billion in fund assets under management. Properties in Investa's office portfolio, inclusive of assets held outside its pooled funds, are managed according to sustainable principles. As of 2007, emissions had been reduced by 23 percent and water use by 37 percent below 2003–2004 benchmarks.[13]

▸▸ Wereldhave, a publicly traded real estate investment company headquartered in the Netherlands, has made sustainability a core operating principle for its international portfolio, valued at €2.8 billion ($4 billion) at the start of 2008. Wereldhave, which invests in a diversified portfolio that includes office space, has equity holdings in Belgium, Finland, France, the Netherlands, Spain, the United Kingdom, and the United States. Wereldhave's contracting requirements highlight the use of sustainable products and materials; the company also emphasizes energy and water savings in the management of its portfolio.[14]

Other green property funds are being introduced to the market. Green retrofits are the focus of the Green Realty Trust, a new venture reportedly being developed by U.S. commercial real estate investor Rob Hannah. Retrofits are also the exclusive focus of a $200 million Morgan Stanley fund that invests in solar power retrofits installed by Recurrent Energy for institutional real estate projects through-

out the United States. Additional green property funds introduced to the U.S. market in 2008 include JP Morgan's $500 million Green Urban Renaissance Fund and a vehicle launched by Principal Real Estate Investors that seeks to invest approximately $300 million. Both funds focus on urban infill and transit-oriented properties and will invest in new construction and retrofits.

In the United Kingdom, Prince Charles has hired an experienced executive team and the Credit Suisse investment bank to launch the £1 billion ($2 billion) Tellesma sustainable property fund. A third of Tellesma, which is expected to combine sustainable principles with traditional planning and design, is expected to be owned by the Prince's Charities, a group of 19 charities sponsored by the Prince of Wales, and the Prince's Foundation for the Built Environment.[15]

DEBT CAPITAL

While the commercial real estate credit markets contracted sharply in 2008, green real estate lending began to emerge as a focus area for a growing number of financial institutions. Bank of America is launching a program to fully educate its North American lenders about the financing opportunities associated with green real estate, and Bank of America, Citigroup, and JP Morgan have

Figure 5-4

Selected Regional Green Construction Programs

Bank	Locations Served	Incentives	Green Criteria
Banner Bank	Oregon, Washington, Idaho; Arizona considered	¼ point discount	LEED
Community Bank of Arizona	Arizona, Southern California	½ point discount	LEED, Energy Star
Howard Bank	Howard County, Maryland	¼ point discount	LEED, Energy Star
New Resource Bank	San Francisco, California area; other California	¼ point discount	Third-party certification, LEED, Energy Star
Second Angel Bancorp	California, Oregon, Washington, Nevada	Preferred review	LEED elements, flexible
Shorebank Pacific	Oregon, Washington	Potentially higher LTV, performance pricing, Oregon tax credit pass-through	Third-party certification, LEED, Energy Star
Umpqua Bank	Oregon, Washington, California, Idaho	Preferred review, Oregon tax credit pass-through	LEED, Energy Star
United Community Bank	Chatham, Georgia; contiguous counties	¼ point discount	Pilot program, LEED

Note: LTV = loan to value. Source: *Green Real Estate News*, February 2008, www.greenrealestatenews.com.

indicated their interest in significant, long-term commitments to lending for energy-efficient projects. As well, a number of regional lenders in the United States have developed construction finance programs that offer borrower incentives such as interest rate reductions, longer loan payback periods, higher loan-to-value ratios and preferred review terms for green real estate projects, with most of the projects geared to real estate projects seeking LEED or Energy Star certification (see figure 5-4).

The use of public bonding or other financing authority to support loans for energy-efficient property renovation aroused growing interest in 2008 and in 2009. The state of California; Boulder County, Colorado; Annapolis, Maryland; and Babylon, New York, have approved the creation of public programs in which loans for retrofits are paid back as part of a property's utility or property tax bill. Such "on-bill" financing programs can be capitalized through a public bonding authority (Berkeley, California, and Boulder County, Colorado), through other locally controlled funds (Babylon, New York), or with private capital supplied by local lenders (Annapolis, Maryland). (For greater detail on the practice, see the sidebar by James F. Finlay.)

Internationally, the United Nations Environment Programme Finance Initiative (UNEP FI) works with over 170 financial institutions, including banks and insurers, to encourage the development of sustainable finance practices. UNEP FI's Property Working Group seeks to demonstrate how responsible property investment can protect or enhance financial returns while simultaneously reducing negative environmental or social outcomes.[16] As of 2009, a dozen financial institutions or advisers were members of the group: AXA Real Estate Investment Managers France; Caisse des Dépôts; Calvert Group; F&C Property Asset Management PLC; Hermes Investment Management Limited; Infrastructure Leasing & Financial Services; Innovest Strategic Value Advisors

Inc.; Mitsubishi UFJ Trust and Banking Corporation; Morley Fund Management; PRUPIM; Sumitomo Trust & Banking Co., Ltd.; and WestLB AG. (For details on sustainable property initiatives undertaken by Sumitomo Trust and Banking Co. in conjunction with its UNEP FI activities, see the sidebar by Leanne Tobias.)

LONGER-TERM INITIATIVES

Looking toward the longer term, the European Parliament in April 2009 approved recommendations to develop additional financing guidelines for energy-efficient buildings by 2010, and to consider value-added tax reductions for goods and services related to renewable energy and building energy efficiency. The European Parliament has also endorsed a recommendation to establish an Energy Efficiency Fund for EU member nations by 2014, with funding to be supplied by member states, the European Community budget, and the European Investment Bank.[17] Final approval of these recommendations is expected in the second half of 2009. (See chapters 7 and 8 for a discussion of the European Parliament's endorsement of related recommendations to enhance the European Performance of Buildings Directive.)

ESCOs AND PERFORMANCE-BASED CONTRACTING

Financing supplied through an energy service company (ESCO) is becoming increasingly important for green and energy-efficient retrofits. An ESCO is a business that plans, selects, installs, and arranges financing for systems and technologies designed to improve the energy efficiency and maintenance costs for commercial, governmental, and other facilities.[18] ESCOs provide heating, cooling, and ventilation systems; building control systems; insulation; and other energy-efficient technologies. An ESCO typically acts as a project developer and assumes the technical and performance risk associated with the project. The ESCO's services also may

FINANCING OFFICE BUILDING AND OTHER ENERGY-EFFICIENT RETROFITS THROUGH "ON-BILL" FINANCING

JAMES F. FINLAY

"On-bill" financing provides low- or no-downpayment, long-term loans for energy retrofits, which are repaid through property tax or utility bills. This powerful financing option has been used on a limited basis for decades but is now starting to be implemented more widely. It is expected to become a major resource for financing energy efficiency improvements for existing office buildings, other commercial properties, and residential real estate.

Under on-bill financing, a city, county, state, or utility provider designs and administers a program to provide up to 100 percent financing for approved, long-term energy conservation and on-site generation upgrades to existing property. The loan is secured directly by the existing real property so the debt runs with the land, not with the property owner. Because the loan is property-secured, it is not tied to the credit rating of the current or future owner, and there is no due on sale clause. If the property sells, the debt can be assumed by the new owner with no qualification and become a condition of the transaction.

Repayment of loan principal and interest appears as a line item on the property tax or electricity or gas bill. Amortization periods can be as long as 20 years. The long repayment period typically

Figure 1

The Positives and Negatives of On-Bill Financing

POSITIVES

- ▸▸ Zero downpayment financing has long-term payback at attractive interest rates.

- ▸▸ There is no unrecoverable cost or direct risk to government funds. The "contractual assessment" obligations are between individuals and the municipality and are highly secured.

- ▸▸ Loan security is through property value, at the top level of recoverable debt.

- ▸▸ Funds are for energy conservation, on-site energy creation, or cogeneration.

- ▸▸ The application process can be simple and low cost, with much of the management structure in place

- ▸▸ The debt is property-secured and runs with the land, is not due on sale, and is fully assumable by new owners.

- ▸▸ The debt is superior to bank mortgage debt and survives foreclosure.

- ▸▸ In the event of default, any payments due are repaid at the tax sale as part of the purchase.

- ▸▸ Eventual payment is reasonably assured based on the offset of energy cost savings.

NEGATIVES/RISKS

- ▸▸ Fully executed loan programs are just being created.

- ▸▸ Tax and investment credit issues are unresolved.

- ▸▸ The municipal bond market is in turmoil; questions exist about how the bonds will be underwritten.

- ▸▸ Energy conservation investments, on-site distributed power generation investment, and combined heat and power (CHP) system investment have different payback risk profiles. This complicates accurate projections of project return. Complications in projecting project returns include the following:

  - Investment returns are typically affected by use profile and will vary according to real estate property type, project scale, and location.
  - Maintenance and monitoring are needed to ensure that pro forma returns are realized, but many property owners have limited experience in project oversight, especially in the residential sector.
  - CHP systems—including projects that utilize fuel cells, geothermal heat pumps, solar thermal applications, and turbines—blend conservation and power generation, making return calculations more complex.

- ▸▸ Some upgrades have untested operating performance over long periods.

- ▸▸ Energy price spikes and crashes in 2007–08 show energy payback rates to be vulnerable to fluctuation.

ensures that the loan repayment amount will be lower than the utility cost savings associated with the retrofit. Loan principal amounts would be determined by the program administrator.

The on-bill structure is a well-secured form of financing because the loans are superior to bank mortgages and survive foreclosure and bankruptcy if a forced property sale occurs. In the event of default, payments might be postponed, but they would not be wiped out and eventually would be paid in full by a new title holder as a condition of title transfer.

Interest in on-bill financing picked up substantially in July 2008, when California Assembly Bill (AB) 811 was enacted as an emergency measure in response to escalating fuel prices. The bill extended on-bill financing authority for localities throughout California and streamlined the process to permit loans to individual property owners. The new law grants local governments the authority to finance the installation of power-generating renewable energy sources and energy efficiency improvements that are permanently fixed to residential, commercial, industrial, or other real property. At the close of 2008, programs were being readied in Palm Desert and Berkeley, the first two communities with approved AB 811 implementation plans. The Berkeley plan will finance solar photovoltaic installations Palm Desert's Energy Improvement Program has begun to finance a variety of energy improvements, including high-efficiency air conditioners, dual-pane windows, and solar panels.

In November 2008, voters in Boulder County, Colorado, adopted Bond Issue 1A, a measure similar to AB 811—by a 66 percent majority. It authorized a bond issuance of $40 million to finance an on-bill financing program. Other on-bill energy retrofit financings are being considered at dozens of locations throughout the United States and around the world. The impact of this shift on the pace of energy upgrades for office and commercial property could be huge.

There is also considerable political interest in on-bill financing, as many mayors, utility operators, and state governments see this as a way to help meet their greenhouse gas (GHG) reduction targets. Interest in creating green jobs also generates support for on-bill financing.

There are many devils in the details. Numerous implementation questions remain, and new on-bill financing programs are still being developed and tested. Nonetheless, on-bill financing is tracking for much wider adoption and can offer significant advantages that are not available through traditional, borrower-secured financing.

James F. Finlay is a vice president and commercial appraisal manager at Wells Fargo Bank and an expert on the appraisal and financing of high-performance green property.

include handling equipment operation and maintenance and verifying energy savings.

The energy service performance contract (ESPC) is the vehicle most frequently employed to finance energy retrofits in the United States and Australia. Performance-based contracting means that the compensation and project financing for a company that undertakes a project is directly linked to the amount of energy that is actually saved by the facility when the project is complete.[19] This is what differentiates ESCOs from consultants that provide energy efficiency consulting and from equipment contractors. Some ESCO services are linked with equipment vendors, and some are provided through engineering, construction, or independent third-party companies.

Under an ESPC, the property owner leases from the ESCO on a long-term basis the energy-saving equipment needed for project retrofit. Leases are frequently structured as lease-purchase agreements, also known as capital leases; under such an agreement, the ESCO retains title to the equipment until the lease expires, at which time title transfers to the property owner. Lease payments to the ESCO are offset by the dollar savings generated by reduced energy usage. If contracted energy usage reductions are not realized, the ESCO is typically obligated to make payment to the customer for the shortfall. Note, however, that ESPCs are negotiated on the basis of the quantity of energy consumed before and after the retrofit; ESPCs do not shield users from upward movements in underlying fuel or electricity prices. In the United States, the ESCO/ESPC model was developed initially for the U.S. government.

The public sector (federal, state, and local governments and nongovernmental organizations) continues to account for almost 80 percent of the U.S. market, but the model is being adapted for private owners who wish to undertake green retrofits. Private equity and hedge funds are likely new sources of capital to support expansion and new products to be offered by ESCOs for the green building market.

The predominant ESCO/ESPC contract framework in the United States and Australia is the guaranteed savings model, in which the ESCO guarantees a specified amount of energy savings and compensates the property owner if that amount is not attained. ESCO/ESPC practices are also being utilized throughout Europe, most markedly in France, Germany, Austria, and Hungary, and to a more limited degree in Italy, Spain, and the Czech Republic.[20] As detailed in the sidebar, ESCO/ESPC contracts have diverse structures, including guaranteed and shared savings contracts, first-out contracts, and chauffage and energy supply contracts.

Public buildings dominate the ESCO market in Europe and contractual practices vary by country:[21]

▸▸ FRANCE is the oldest ESCO market and one of the largest in Europe. The dominant form of contract is the chauffage contract (see the sidebar by Leanne Tobias), and French companies supply ESCO services to Spain, Italy, Belgium, and central Europe.

▸▸ GERMANY is the premier European ESCO market, with more than 500 ESCO firms, about 50 of which provide ESPCs. Estimated annual volume is €2 billion ($2.87 billion). The market is dominated by municipal government facilities, although the sector has expanded to private buildings. The dominant form of contract is the shared savings contract.

▸▸ AUSTRIA, like Germany, has a well-developed ESCO market. As of 2005, some 1,000 ESCO building renovation projects had been completed and 300 were in development.

While ESCOs have been most frequently used for public sector buildings, the model is being extended to the private sector.

▸▸ HUNGARY's ESCO market, established in the early 1990s, encompasses conventional and alternative energy lighting, heating, cooling, and hot-water projects. The sector includes an estimated 30 ESCOS, with five or six firms supplying some 80 percent of the market. As has been the case elsewhere, public buildings have dominated the market.

A global ESCO/ESPC program also has been launched by the Clinton Climate Initiative (CCI) in partnership with ABN AMRO, Citigroup, Deutsche Bank, JPMorgan Chase, and UBS. The $5 billion effort will renovate existing buildings in major cities to energy-efficient

McDonald's Corporation has enrolled the Campus Office Building at its world headquarters in Oakbrook, Illinois, in the Illinois Clear Air Counts Program, committing to track and report reductions of greenhouse gas emissions.

EVAN THOMAS

RESPONSIBLE PROPERTY INVESTING AT SUMITOMO TRUST & BANKING COMPANY, LTD.

LEANNE TOBIAS

The Sumitomo Trust and Banking Company, Ltd., one of Japan's leading banking trusts, joined the Property Working Group of the UNEP FI in June 2007. Since that time, Sumitomo Trust has worked diligently to evaluate the property investment impact of sustainable design and construction and to expand its environmentally friendly lending and investment practices.

Responsible property investment activities undertaken by Sumitomo Trust include the following:

▸▸ Participation in research evaluating how green and environmentally favorable features affect property values. Research initiatives in which Sumitomo is engaged include studies being conducted by Japan's Ministry of Land, Infrastructure, Transportation, and Tourism and by the Japanese Association of Real Estate Appraisal.

▸▸ Provision of consulting support services to developers who wish to attain property certification under CASBEE, Japan's dominant voluntary rating system for sustainable buildings. Consulting services, which include advice on energy conservation, landscaping, recycling systems, and lengthening building life, are offered through Sumitomo's Architecture Consulting Department, which was established in June 2006.

▸▸ Development of a proposed ESCO financing program that would lend funds for energy conservation to limited-liability partnerships formed by landlords and tenants. Shared energy savings in excess of loan repayments would be shared by members of the partnerships.

▸▸ Investment in the EcoLand Fund, a fund that brings contaminated plots of land back into use by buying them for resale after cleanup.

▸▸ Research to support the possible launch of a sustainable real estate fund. Each property in the fund would be required to meet environmental efficiency standards and to highlight sustainability initiatives.

Leanne Tobias is the founder and managing principal at Malachite LLC.

---

standards.[22] The program anticipates that borrowers, including cities and building owners, will pay back the loans, plus interest, with the energy savings generated by the reduced energy costs created by the building retrofits. CCI has brought together many of the world's largest energy service companies, banks, and building owners to cut energy consumption in buildings in more than 20 cities across the globe. Cities including London, Houston, Johannesburg, Melbourne, and Seoul are already working on projects to retrofit more than 250 municipal buildings. Private building owners and investors, including GE Capital Real Estate and the owners of the Merchandise Mart in Chicago and the Empire State Building in New York, have begun commercial retrofit projects. More than 500 million square feet of project work is underway.[23]

RENEWABLE ENERGY CREDITS

Renewable energy credits (RECs, also known as renewable energy certificates, tradable renewable certificates, or "green tags") were originally developed to support the purchase of green power from utilities. The sale of RECs also can be used to monetize green or energy-efficient construction or renovation, especially for projects that generate surplus energy. The use of RECs as a source of real estate project financing is in its infancy but offers potential as technology advances, making it possible for individual projects to generate more power than they consume. The trading of RECs also is expected to grow in importance in the United States if a national, mandatory cap-and-trade program is enacted.

RECs are issued to the providers of electricity generated through alternative energy sources, including solar, wind, geothermal, biomass, biofuel, and low-impact hydropower, depending on the requirements of state law. RECs are measured in terms of electricity production, and one REC generally represents the environmental attributes associated with one megawatt-hour of electricity from renewable resources.[24]

In the United States, RECs are most frequently issued and traded under statutes known as renewable portfolio standards (RPS). These statutes, which have been adopted by a majority of states and the District of Columbia, require that certain percentages of renewable energy be delivered by public utilities, and in some cases a broader group of energy suppliers, to their customers.[25] RPS efforts also have expanded to allow, in some cases, the customers who use renewable energy processes to generate electricity, heat, or steam, to return the excess of the electricity created to the distribution grid. By purchasing RECs, utilities can meet their RPS requirements to purchase power from renewable sources. REC trading in the context of RPS requirements is known as the compliance or mandatory market; it represents the bulk of REC purchases.

The voluntary REC market is driven by consumers interested in supporting renewable energy or in reducing their environmental footprint. Electricity end users can meet their environmental goals and support the development of renewable power by purchasing RECs. In a highly publicized example, the Oscars, the annual American cinema awards program, purchased RECs in 2007 and 2008 to offset the program's use of conventional power.

The historic Joseph Vance Building in Seattle invests in renewable energy credits in order to meet 100 percent of its energy demands.

©LARA SWIMMER

Developers and owners of properties applying for LEED certification who are unable to purchase green power directly are permitted to purchase RECs to satisfy the LEED credit requirement for green power purchase.

RECs that have been certified by a third party are considered the most credible. The most common certification standard is Green-e, which is administered by the Center for Resource Solutions.[26] Green-e or a similar standard certifies that the REC meets the standard's environmental and consumer protection requirements, which ensures that the electricity generated and its associated RECs are produced from the purported renewable generation facility and delivered in the amount claimed, and that the environmental attributes have not been double-sold.

The long-term pricing of RECs can vary significantly, is opaque, and can fluctuate. As the use of renewable power increases, market liquidity will be enhanced. Factors influencing the price of RECs include the technology used to produce the power and associated RECs, local supply and demand, technology stability, and the regulations in compliance markets.[27] REC buyers will often have preferences for RECs produced by specific technologies (like wind versus landfill gas), and these preferences will affect the RECs' price. Buyers also may prefer to purchase RECs produced locally to show community support, which can increase prices in areas where production capacity is limited and local demand is high. Local purchases can also avoid transmission compliance complications. Finally, RECs in compliance markets are generally more expensive than those in voluntary markets because of regulations that mandate renewables volume, specific technologies, and noncompliance penalties.

In addition to procuring RECs to fulfill their sustainability requirements, companies that install and own on-site renewable power–generating facilities can choose to sell the RECs the facilities produce. The sale of RECs can improve building economics; however, the owner will lose the right to claim it is using green power because the environmental attributes will be transferred with the RECs, even if the building uses the power generated at its facilities and operations.[28] For nonmanufacturing companies, the opportunity to install on-site generation will likely be limited to solar photovoltaic panels, solar water heaters, or geothermal heat pumps.[29] In states that have approved net metering, where the company generates more electricity on-site than it purchases from its utility in a given month, the company may be able to sell the excess power back to the utility.[30] A company interested in installing on-site generation may find that working with an ESCO may help to lower the upfront cost, as discussed earlier.

Building developers and owners may wish to maximize the future economic benefit of their green certification strategies by utilizing project design and operational elements that will produce renewable energy to meet the RPS needs of utilities, supply the voluntary "green tag" or REC needs of other corporations, or generate emissions savings that can be monetized in the pollution trading markets. Emissions savings that often can be traded include those related to greenhouse gases (GHGs) including carbon, sulfur oxides, and nitrous oxides. Building developers and operators also may want to explore these voluntary alternatives as a source of monetized value that can be calculated in the overall return on capital.

CARBON TRADING AND THE KYOTO PROTOCOL

Carbon credits can be used to monetize the energy savings produced by green or energy-efficient construction or renovation. At the close of 2007, the value of the global carbon emissions trading market (the carbon market) stood at more than $58 billion. The carbon market is segmented into two areas:

▸▸ **THE TRADING OF DESIGNATED ALLOWANCES,** such as those awarded by the European Union under its Emissions Trading Scheme (ETS); and

TYPES OF ENERGY SAVINGS PERFORMANCE CONTRACTS

LEANNE TOBIAS

Energy savings performance contracts are offered globally and can be drawn up under a variety of savings structures.

▸▸ **Guaranteed savings.** This is the most common type of contract offered in the United States and Australia. The contractor guarantees the amount of energy savings that can be achieved under the contract and compensates the property owner if these levels of savings are not attained.

▸▸ **Shared savings.** Energy savings achieved under this type of contract are shared between the property owner and the contractor over a set period of time. The shared savings contract is the most common type of contract offered in Germany and was originally used in the U.S. real estate sector in the 1980s. Under this arrangement, the contractor is usually responsible for financing the project; capital invested by the contractor is repaid from any savings realized from energy efficiency and operating improvements.

▸▸ **First-out.** All savings achieved under this type of contract belong to the contractor. Once the contractor recoups the expenses incurred during the project, the contract ends. Once the contract ends, any future savings belong solely to the property owner.

▸▸ **Chauffage.** Under a chauffage contract, the contractor charges a fixed fee; in return, the property owner receives a guaranteed level of service. The contractor covers all aspects of the property's energy usage including utility bill payment, operations, and maintenance. The equipment supplied by the contractor is wholly owned by the owner at the close of the contract term.

▸▸ **Energy supply.** Contractors receive a fee in return for creating energy as a byproduct from existing business processes. For example, the contractor may receive a fee for using cogeneration to produce electricity in addition to the heat a building might normally produce or for running a property's waste heat through chillers to provide additional power for cooling.

Leanne Tobias is the founder and managing principal at Malachite LLC.

SOURCE

Adapted from Australian Government, Department of Environment, Water, Heritage, and the Arts, "Energy Performance Contracting: Ways to Reduce Greenhouse Gas Emissions for Small and Medium Enterprises," www.environment.gov.au/settlements/challenge/publications/factsheets/fs-energy-performance.html.

▸▸ **THE TRADING OF PROJECT-BASED CREDITS**, wherein a buyer purchases credits from a project that achieves verifiable reductions of GHG emissions relative to standard practice.

The Clean Development Mechanism (CDM) and Joint Implementation (JI) programs established under the Kyoto Protocol are the most extensive project-based schemes. The ETS, the CDM, and the JI are the most robust governmental and quasi-governmental programs. Other governmental carbon trading frameworks include the regional efforts being developed by a number of state-level alliances in the United States, including the Regional Greenhouse Gas Initiative—an alliance of northeastern and mid-Atlantic states; the Midwest Greenhouse Gas Reduction Accord; and the Western Climate Initiative, in which Manitoba also participates. Privately established carbon trading exchanges include Japan's Keidanren Voluntary Action Plan, Canada's Montreal Climate Exchange, and the United States' Chicago Climate Exchange and, for futures trading, New York Mercantile Exchange.

Real estate companies can participate in the carbon markets in two ways. First, they can buy and sell carbon credits as members of voluntary carbon exchanges. ProLogis, a U.S.-headquartered real estate investment trust with an international industrial portfolio, has become the first real estate member of the Chicago Climate Exchange.[31] Second, the real estate sector is a potential source of credits under project-based trading mechanisms,

CHAUFFAGE AND A U.S. VARIANT, THE MANAGED ENERGY SERVICE AGREEMENT

LEANNE TOBIAS

Chauffage contracts were introduced in Europe to provide heating and related energy or utility services. (*Chauffage* is French for "heating" or "heat.") Under a chauffage contract, a third-party contractor takes full responsibility for providing energy efficiency services to a business or property owner in exchange for a series of payments. In Europe, chauffage contracts are frequently used to provide municipal services and usually run from seven to 10 years.[1] France is a leading supplier of ESCO services under the chauffage contract business model and exports these services to Spain, Italy, Belgium, and central Europe.[2]

Transcend Equity Development Corporation, an energy retrofit provider in Dallas, Texas, has adopted the chauffage model for U.S. use as the managed energy service agreement (MESA). Unlike most U.S. ESCO contracts, in which the energy retrofit company retains title to the energy efficiency equipment and leases the improvements to the property owner under a long-term lease, the MESA transfers title to the energy efficiency and equipment improvements to the property owner. In exchange, the property owner makes a five- to ten-year series of payments—calculated on the basis of its historical energy costs—to Transcend, the MESA provider.

During the contract term, Transcend assumes complete responsibility for the property's utility bills. The contracted payments to Transcend are typically adjusted for changes in energy prices in accordance with the methods established in the underlying contract executed between Transcend and the property owner. Contracts between Transcend and the property owner are negotiated on a case-by-case basis, with terms dictated by property conditions, baseline energy usage, and the required improvements.

The MESA business model, unlike the typical ESCO agreement, provides the property owner with clear title to the energy efficiency improvements, an arrangement preferred by mortgage lenders. Although the property owner does not realize energy savings above historical costs until the conclusion of the primary term of the contract, the MESA allows the property owner to own the energy-saving equipment outright without additional capital expenditure or the assumption of additional debt, and exchanges the uncertainties of planning for and managing long-term energy needs for payments due under the MESA. At the expiration of the MESA, the building owner reclaims responsibility for paying substantially lowered utility bills because of the continued access to the energy efficiency and equipment improvements which are now fully paid for. Upon conclusion of the MESA, the property owner also assumes responsibility for managing equipment obsolescence, operations, and maintenance, and controlling systems operations.

Leanne Tobias is the founder and managing principal at Malachite LLC.

NOTES

1 Energy Resources Canada, "Energy Performance Contracting Primer." http://oee.nrcan.gc.ca/ppublications/infosource/pub/ici/eii/m27-109-1993E.cfm.

2 Wilhemus de Wilt, "Developments of Energy Services Companies across Europe: A European ESCO Overview," European Commission, DG TREN. www.rusrec.ru/files/11_De_Wilt_ESCO_ENG.ppt#435.

for projects that meet appropriate GHG reduction standards. Typically, project-based trading mechanisms require that GHG reduction projects embody "additionality"—the production of GHG reductions in excess of those that would occur under a business-as-usual scenario. Eligible projects also typically must provide independently verifiable and permanent results and offer controls that exclude the sale of a set of credits to more than one buyer at the same time.[32] Offset providers vetted by the Chicago Climate Exchange are sources of project-based credits, as are projects verified under the Kyoto Protocol's CDM and JI programs.

Many carbon market observers anticipate that green real estate is likely to serve as a growing source of salable carbon trading credits. At present, the CDM and JI project-based programs, in which buyers from industrialized nations typically procure credits from green projects in developing nations, are the most extensive project-based exchanges. To date, however, few real estate projects have been undertaken under the Kyoto framework. As of October 2008, only ten projects to reduce building energy use were in the CDM pipeline of more than 4,000 projects. The United Nations' Sustainable Buildings and Climate Initiative has recommended revising the CDM framework to encourage additional participation by the property sector. Recommended reforms for enhanced property sector involvement include developing national regulations and standards for building energy efficiency or sustainable building; developing common baselines and building benchmarks for the CDM; and instituting the use of performance-based indicators, such as energy use per square meter for project validation, monitoring, and verification.[33]

NOTES

1 McGraw-Hill Construction, News Release, "Green Building Could Triple by 2013, Says McGraw-Hill," November 18, 2008.

2 UNEP, Sustainable Buildings and Climate Initiative, *Briefing: Policies for Energy Efficient Buildings in China,* March 26, 2008. www.unepsbci.org/SBCINews/latestNews/showNews.asp?what=Briefing__Policies_for_Energy_Efficient_Buildings_in_China.

3 Good Energies, "Landmark International Green Building Study Finds Benefits of Building Green Outweigh Cost Premium," November 19, 2008, www.goodenergies.com/news/-pdfs/Green%20Buildings%20Study%20Press%20Release%20FINAL_5.pdf.

4 Good Energies, November 19, 2008.

5 Norm Miller, Jay Spivey, and Andy Florance, "Does Green Pay Off? Final Draft," July 12, 2008, www.usgbc.org/ShowFile.aspx?DocumentID=5537. Locational controls were established at the submarket level when possible and within a five-mile radius if a submarket comparison was not possible. Leasing comparisons, reported herein, had more robust locational controls. Sales data, especially for LEED properties, were more sparse and reflected less robust locational controls.

6 Piet Eichholtz, Nils Kok, and John M. Quigley, "Doing Well by Doing Good? An Analysis of the Financial Performance of Green Office Buildings in the USA," RICS Research, Royal Institution of Chartered Surveyors, March 2009, pp. 8, 9, 28.

7 *Ibid.,* pp. 8, 9, 28.

8 *Ibid.,* p. 9.

9 *Ibid.,* p. 9. Site energy utilization efficiency measures building energy efficiency at the site. See chapter 8 for a review of different ways of measuring energy efficiency.

10 *Ibid.,* p. 26.

11 Franz Fuerst and Patrick McAllister, "New Evidence on the Green Building Rent and Price Premium," paper presented at the annual meeting of the American Real Estate Society, Monterey, Calif., April 3, 2009, published by Henley Business School, University of Reading, in *Working Papers in Real Estate and Planning,* July 2009, www.henley.reading.ac.uk/rep/fulltxt/0709.pdf.

12 Jones Lang LaSalle, CoreNet Global, February 2008.

13 Investa, "2008 Sustainability Report," www.investa.com.au/Reports/2008/sustainability.

14 See www.wereldhave.nl.

15 "Prince Charles to Launch £1bn Property Fund," July 3, 2008, www.telegraph.co.uk/finance/newsbysector/constructionandproperty/2792416/Prince-Charles-to-launch-andpound1bn-property-fund.html; "Prince Charles Launches £1 Billion Fund for Urban Regeneration," San Francisco Sentinel.com, July 11, 2008, www.sanfranciscosentinel.com/?p=14601.

16 UNEP, Finance Initiative, "Working Groups: Property," www.unepfi.org/work_streams/property/working_group.

17 European Parliament, "All New Buildings to be Zero Energy from 2019 Say MEPs," Press Release, April 23, 2009, www.europarl.europa.eu/news/expert/infopress_page/051-54164-111-04-17-909-20090422IPR54163-21-04-2009-2009-false/default_en.htm.

18 National Association of Energy Service Companies (NAESCO), "What Is an ESCO?," www.naesco.org/resources/esco.htm.

19 NAESCO.

20 Paolo Bertoldi, "Energy Service Companies (ESCOs) in Europe," European Commission, Directorate General, Joint Research Commission, December 16, 2005, www.fire-italia.it/convegni/milanostelline2005/stel_05_conti.pdf.

21 Wilhemus de Wilt, "Developments of Energy Services Companies across Europe: A European ESCO Overview," European Commission, DG TREN, www.rusrec.ru/files/11_De_Wilt_ESCO_ENG.ppt#435.

22 William J. Clinton Foundation, "President Clinton Announces Landmark Program to Reduce Energy Use in Buildings Worldwide," May 16, 2007, www.clintonfoundation.org/news/news-media/051607-nr-cf-pr-cci-president-clinton-announces-landmark-program-to-reduce-energy-use-in-buildings-world-wide.

23 William J. Clinton Foundation, "Making Buildings Energy-Efficient," www.clintonfoundation.org/what-we-do/clinton-climate-initiative/our-approach/cities/building-retrofit.

24 World Resources Institute, "The Bottom Line on Renewable Energy Certificates," Issue 11, November 2008.

25 As of January 2009, mandatory RPS statutes had been adopted by 29 states and the District of Columbia, while five states had adopted nonbinding renewable energy purchase targets, according to the Pew Center for Climate Research (www.pewclimate.org/what_s_being_done/in_the_states/rps.cfm).

26 Green-e, "Energy," www.green-e.org/getcert_re.shtml.

27 World Resources Institute, November 2008.

28 *Ibid.*

29 Samantha Putt Del Pino, "Switching to Green: A Renewable Energy Guide for Office and Retail Companies," World Resources Institute, October 2006, p. 9.

30 As of September 2009, 42 U.S. states, the District of Columbia, and several U.S. protectorates, including American Samoa, Guam, and Puerto Rico, had adopted net metering programs. Three additional states (Idaho, Texas, and South Carolina) permit utilities to adopt net metering on a voluntary basis. Five states (Alabama, Alaska, Mississippi, Tennessee, and Wyoming) had not established net metering programs. Summaries of the programs can be found using the Database of State Incentives for Renewables & Efficiency (DSIRE) at www.dsireusa.org.

31 See "About CCX" and "Offsets" at the Chicago Climate Exchange, www.chicagoclimatex.com.

32 World Bank Institute and International Emissions Trading Association, "State and Trends of the Carbon Market," May 2007, p. 37.

33 UNEP, "Boosting the 'Green House' Effect—CDM Reform Key to Climate-Friendly Building and Construction Sector," December 6, 2008, www.unep.org/Documents.Multilingual/Default.asp?DocumentID=553&ArticleID=6012&l=en.

Green Property Operations

LEANNE TOBIAS

After the completion and, if desired, certification of green office renovations, property operations become key in ensuring that the project continues to be managed sustainably. This chapter summarizes key strategies for managing a green building on an ongoing basis.

PROPERTY MANAGEMENT AGREEMENTS, LEASES, AND RISK MANAGEMENT

Property management and leasing agreements, the foundation documents for real estate operations, should be revised to establish the sustainability requirements that must be met by building owners, operators, and tenants. The procurement of appropriate property insurance to cover green building improvements is also an important foundation requirement that building owners are well advised to address. Guidance on these subjects is provided in this chapter.

Writing a Green Property Management Agreement

A green property management agreement is a foundation document for managing a green property. Key elements in the drafting of such an agreement or in the development of

a related RFP (request for proposals) include the following:

▸▸ **DEFINITION OF OWNERSHIP'S SUSTAINABILITY GOALS;**

▸▸ **DELINEATION OF THE GREEN CERTIFICATION** or other standards that the property will be expected to meet; and

▸▸ **IDENTIFICATION OF NEEDED ENVIRONMENTAL AND PURCHASING PROGRAMS** and required standards relating thereto.

Owners might also wish to require that the property management staff engage in ongoing training related to the fulfillment of green property management objectives. (See the sidebar by Marc O. Winters for the central considerations in the drafting of a green property management agreement.)

Writing a Green Lease

A green standard lease form is a second foundation document for operating a green property. Such documents are in their infancy. Many experts, including REALpac, Canada's leading national industry association for owners and managers of investment real estate, advocate that owners and tenants work in partnership to create an appropriate document (see the sidebar by Ellen Sinreich).

Green building renovations frequently pose challenges that are not present in the case of a newly constructed green building (see the sidebar by Andrew I. Davis). As Davis notes, to cite a commonly encountered circumstance, the rights of current tenants under existing leases may not provide the landlord with sufficient flexibility to access the leased premises, disturb or relocate tenants, and recover the costs of the retrofit. If a retrofit project is contemplated, Davis recommends that landlords try to include provisions in all new leases for tenant relocation, termination rights, broad rights of entry, and cost recovery. This advice becomes increasingly relevant as owners of existing buildings undertake sustainable retrofits in order to refresh and reposition their properties.

As discussed in the sidebars by Davis and Sinreich, key elements in a green lease include the following:

▸▸ **THE ESTABLISHMENT OF GREEN BUILDING PERFORMANCE OBJECTIVES** or requirements that will govern the conduct of landlord and tenant. These objectives or requirements can include energy, water conservation, and perhaps other environmental targets such as indoor air quality or carbon emissions objectives, and milestone dates at which progress is measured or compliance mandated. Green performance objectives also can encompass achievement and maintenance of certification under a green building rating system or systems. These objectives can be drafted with the assistance of green technical experts.

▸▸ **PROVISION FOR METERING OR SUBMETERING** to measure water, sewer, and energy usage, and data collection or measurement protocols to track progress on other green objectives.

DRAFTING A GREEN PROPERTY MANAGEMENT CONTRACT
MARC O. WINTERS

Property owners have long suspected that the marketplace would reward green construction, retrofits, and operations. Now, various studies are confirming that third-party-certified buildings outperform their conventional counterparts in areas such as rental rates, occupancy rates, and sale price, as well as achieving significant energy savings. A study conducted by the New Buildings Institute indicates that Leadership in Energy and Environmental Design (LEED)-certified buildings perform an average of 25 to 30 percent better than non-LEED-certified buildings in terms of energy use. The study also indicates that LEED Gold and Platinum buildings have an average energy savings approaching 50 percent. As discussed in chapter 5, a 2008 study conducted by CoStar found that LEED and Energy Star buildings command rent and occupancy premiums relative to their conventional peers.

Concepts for Property Management Contracts
The property management contract (PMC) is the central tool for the owner to implement green renovation and operation strategies. The owner's first step is to undertake a complete review of the existing PMCs for all of its properties. This step usually reveals significant shortcomings that should be remedied by amending the PMC to include various green provisions which both obligate and motivate the property manager to achieve the owner's goals for green renovations and operations. These amendments should arise from a collaborative process with the property manager.

MANAGING FOR OWNER'S RESPONSIBLE PROPERTY INVESTING GOALS
The first step is to include a general provision which requires the property manager to acknowledge and pursue the owner's

goals of responsible investing and obligates the property manager to evaluate and recommend energy efficiency and conservation strategies. The following is an example of such a provision:

Property Manager shall diligently pursue Owner's goals pertaining to conservation, energy efficiency, and green technologies at the Property. When requested by Owner, Property Manager shall provide detailed updates as specified by Owner on Property-related conservation, energy efficiency, and other green initiatives and activities. In addition to duties specified elsewhere in this Agreement, Property Manager shall improve the Property's energy efficiency through the use of energy management tools such as Energy Star benchmarking, utilize operations and maintenance best practices, conduct ongoing strategic evaluations and recommendations of possible lighting retrofit and other systems upgrades, and provide tenant education and outreach on energy conservation.

MANAGING FOR OWNER'S LEED CERTIFICATION GOALS

The next step is to make sure the PMC obligates the property manager to understand and manage toward achievement of the owner's LEED certification goals. The following is an example of such a provision:

Owner expects Property Manager to understand the relevant Leadership in Energy and Environmental Design (LEED) Standard(s) and actively participate in all tasks required to achieve possible LEED for Existing Buildings (LEED-EB) or similar certification as designated by Owner, as well as engage in ongoing education pertaining to sustainable property operations, including completing the BOMA Energy Efficiency Program (BEEP).

WASTE MANAGEMENT, AIR QUALITY, AND WATER CONSERVATION

The owner should consider adding provisions to the PMC obligating the property manager to make improvements in the areas of waste management, air quality, and water conservation. The following is an example of such a provision:

Property Manager shall improve waste management at the Property by ensuring the Property has both an ongoing recycling program and a program or policy to divert demolition waste from local landfill or incineration disposal created by construction, demolition, or renovation activities at the Property. To sustain the comfort and well-being of construction workers and building occupants, Property Manager will use a construction indoor air quality (IAQ) management plan as described by

accepted professional standards such as the Sheet Metal and Air Conditioning National Contractors Association (SMACNA) IAQ Guideline for Occupied Building Under Construction (1995) for the construction and occupancy phases of the property. To improve water conservation, Property Manager shall evaluate the use of low-flow fixtures and irrigation systems and native landscaping, where feasible, in common area and tenant improvement projects and changes to existing landscaping.

SUSTAINABLE PRODUCTS AND MATERIALS

The owner should consider adding provisions to the PMC obligating the property manager to use sustainable products and materials. The following is an example of such a provision:

Property Manager shall be responsible for ensuring the purchase and use of sustainable cleaning products and materials that meet applicable environmental standards set by Green Seal and the implementation of green cleaning practices through the negotiation of applicable activities described within this Agreement. Property Manager shall specify, where possible, the use of building materials such as paints and coating, carpets, adhesives, and sealants with low volatile organic compound (VOC) content that meets or exceeds professionally accepted indoor air quality (IAQ) standards required by LEED, such as Green Seal and CRI Green Label.

Conclusion

The PMC should be one of the focal points for any owner who is considering undertaking a green building retrofit or renovation program. The evaluation, implementation, and measurement of the program will depend in large part on the cooperation of the property manager. Owners may even consider adding financial incentives in the PMC to motivate the property manager to cause the building to achieve certain benchmarks for conservation and energy efficiency. For example, the property manager could receive bonus compensation for the achievement of specified benchmarks within certain time frames, or could even receive a share of demonstrated operating cost savings achieved for the property. The concept is to find an incentive program that motivates the property manager not just to cooperate with initiatives mandated by the owner but also to become proactive in suggesting green technologies and operating protocols for the property.

Marc O. Winters is a senior partner with McNaul Ebel Nawrot & Helgren PLLC in Seattle, Washington.

▸ **ALLOCATION OF ECONOMIC COSTS AND BENEFITS** surrounding the achievement of green building objectives and resulting energy savings. Under a net lease, owners may wish to define building operating expenses payable by tenants to include all costs of complying with green building goals and standards and with green certification. Owners may also find it appropriate to pass through to tenants the costs of green capital improvements over the useful life of the improvements. Tenants will likely propose that any tax benefits or other subsidies received by the landlord for sustainable improvements first be deducted from such capital costs.

▸ **SUSTAINABILITY REQUIREMENTS** related to pertinent aspects of building operation, including recycling; the construction of tenant improvements, building upgrades and repairs, and casualty restorations; the recycling versus the disposal of construction waste; the provi-sion of utility and janitorial services; hours of operation; the use of green materials and cleaning products; transportation services to be made available to tenants; and insurance.

▸ **REVISION OF BOILERPLATE LEASE CLAUSES**, including changes of laws that affect energy usage, environmental compliance, and other sustainability matters; building access requirements; relocation rights; compliance with laws; and defaults, remedies, and consents to ensure ongoing compliance with sustainability goals, green and energy certification standards, and related laws and building codes. In addition, lease clauses might be written to relate building hours of operation to energy consumption, with additional operating costs assessed against tenants who have operating hours in excess of building standards or what is otherwise agreed to in the lease.

The ventilation strategy at Trevor Pearcey House, head office of Australian Ethical Investment, in Bruce, Australia, includes the use of high and low window openings, cross-ventilation, and stack ventilation, with fans that help draw out hot air when necessary.

A COLLABORATIVE FRAMEWORK FOR GREENING THE OFFICE LEASE

ELLEN SINREICH

In order for a commercial office building to achieve the most in terms of sustainability, the landlord and tenants must partner in working toward that goal. The document governing this partnership between landlord and tenant would be a "green" lease. The following are suggestions for preparing a green lease, one that contemplates the landlord and tenant working together as partners to facilitate the sustainable construction, operation, and renovation of an office building. A collaborative approach to the drafting of green leases has been advocated in Canada and elsewhere as the most beneficial approach to achieving sustainable outcomes for both occupants and building owners.

Set Goals for Reduced Consumption of Energy and Water

Clear goals related to the establishment, measurement, and monitoring of energy and water consumption are key elements of a green lease, as is the allocation of economic benefits and costs between landlord and tenant:

▸ **State energy and water consumption goals.** Ideally, a green lease should incorporate goals for reduced energy and water consumption that are arrived at jointly by landlord and tenant. Failure to achieve prospective goals should not constitute a default under the lease or give rise to remedies on either party's part. Rather, in the spirit of partnership, the parties should agree in the lease document that failure to achieve the stated goals will trigger communication and a good faith effort by both parties to identify and remedy whatever stands in the way. This position is being advocated by REALpac, Canada's long-standing national industry association for owners and managers of investment real estate. At the same time, it is wise to provide in the lease for accurate tracking of actual energy, water, and sewer consumption costs and payment of these costs by the user, especially to mitigate against a tenant's usage being in excess of building norms.

▸ **Make metering and submetering transparent and shared.** A green lease should provide for metering or submetering the tenant's consumption of energy and water in its premises and should address the cost and responsibility of installing and periodically reading the meters. The party responsible for reading the meters should also be respon-

sible for promptly communicating the information gleaned from the meter readings to the other party to the lease. If a tenant in a multitenant building keeps utilities operating substantially longer than the building standard, the lease should provide for the installation of a submeter and the tenant's payment for such usage, or for an additional assessment of energy, water, and sewer fees when common area charges are assessed.

▸ **Allocate economic costs and benefits.** The economic costs and benefits of reduced resource consumption should be allocated between landlord and tenant in a manner that both facilitates the goal of reduced consumption and compensates the appropriate party for the costs incurred to reach that goal. Thus the traditional office lease arrangement—in which the cost of the energy and water consumed by the tenant in its premises is included in the base rent, with the tenant often paying its share of building-wide cost increases over base year costs—needs to be examined and modified. New financial lease structures are needed in order to appropriately motivate the landlord and tenant to incorporate energy- and water-saving features into the building and observe energy- and water-saving practices. As well, leases might be drafted to discourage the excessive use of energy. For example, tenants might be billed for energy, water, and sewer consumption associated with operating hours in excess of building standards or what is agreed to in the lease.

▸ **Set milestone dates.** The green office lease should set forth milestone dates on which the parties agree to discuss how actual consumption compares with the sustainability goals set forth in the lease and to use reasonable efforts to correct any discrepancies.

Divert Waste from Landfills

The introduction and management of recycling initiatives are important aspects of green building operations and should be addressed in the lease document:

▸ **Implement mandatory recycling.** It is hard to imagine a green office building that does not have a recycling program, including a reasonably convenient space for the collection and separation of materials to be recycled and arrangements with third parties to pick up the materials to be recycled. Thus, a green lease should obligate the landlord to institute and maintain a recycling program for the building and obligate the tenant to participate in that program and recycle both construction and operational waste.

▸▸ **Provide for data collection.** The green lease should also require both parties to keep track of and share with one another the percentage of waste that is recycled and the percentage that goes to landfills. Over time that information, along with the other data collection and sharing recommended in this sidebar, will help both parties understand, measure, and track their carbon footprint and see how the green lease is helping them reduce it.

Address Indoor Environmental Quality

A green lease should address the use of sustainable and renewable materials and set guidelines for tenant buildouts and acceptable cleaning products and protocols:

▸▸ **Use sustainable materials.** Both landlord and tenants should be obligated in a green lease to use materials with low or no VOCs in the construction of the interior of the building. They should also be obligated to use materials that are rapidly renewable, are regionally extracted and manufactured, contain recycled content, and are themselves recyclable at the end of their useful life to the extent commercially reasonable.

▸▸ **Incorporate tenant guidelines.** In order to facilitate the use of green materials and make "going green" easy—especially if the tenant is doing any construction or buildout work on the premises—a green lease should include an exhibit or be accompanied by guidelines that will educate the tenant about the green options for materials, mechanical and utility systems, and local contractors. These guidelines should indentify specific local vendors who have experience with green products and systems and, if possible, with whom the landlord or its other tenants has had personal experience.

▸▸ **Incorporate green cleaning.** The green lease should require both landlord and tenant to use nontoxic cleaning and janitorial products and sustainable cleaning procedures and protocols in the building and on the premises. The guidelines described above should identify specific cleaning products that the tenants can use. Furthermore, the landlord and tenant should consider whether cleaning services may be performed during the work day, which would cut down on energy consumption during the building's off hours.

Plan for Renovations and Upgrades

Buildings are renovated and upgraded over time. A green lease should define acceptable products and procedures for capital improvements and address the sharing of capital expenses by the landlord and tenant:

▸▸ **Require consideration of the most sustainable alternatives.** Because the green lease ideally will be a long-lived document, it should provide that when upgrades or renovations are being contemplated by either landlord or tenant, sustainable products and systems will be incorporated to the extent commercially reasonable, given specific building characteristics.

▸▸ **Revise the definition of operating expenses to facilitate sustainability.** If the green lease provides for the tenant to share in the operating expenses of the building, which is often the case in traditional commercial office leases, the definition of operating expenses that can be passed through to the tenant should include (on an amortized basis) the cost of building upgrades that result in increased energy and water efficiencies and ultimate tenant savings, provided that the pass-through does not exceed the utility savings realized. The ability to pass through capital costs for sustainable upgrades and renovations could be enough of an incentive for a landlord to make changes that will significantly reduce the building's carbon footprint or improve the quality of life for its tenants.

Conclusion

There is not much precedent for creating a green office lease. Therefore it is an opportunity to be creative and respond to the goals and realities of the situation at hand, rather than an opportunity to follow a formula. In other words, green leases offer a chance for landlords and tenants and their real estate attorneys to break new ground and really make a difference for the environment.

Ellen Sinreich, LEED AP, is president of Green Edge LLC in New York City.

A GREEN LEASE FOR SUSTAINABLE BUILDING RETROFITS

ANDREW I. DAVIS

A green lease is a lease agreement in which the landlord and tenant make a contractual commitment to ecologically sustainable goals, standards, and practices aimed at reducing the adverse environmental effects of the building's occupancy and operations. This sidebar provides an overview of the key elements of a green lease for sustainable building retrofits. Sustainable considerations affect numerous clauses of a lease, and drafting a green lease requires careful consideration by legal counsel and building owners.

Converting an existing occupied building to a green building entails a number of significant lease-related challenges—challenges that are not present when constructing a new green building. The rights of current tenants under existing leases may or may not provide the landlord with sufficient flexibility to access the leased premises, disturb or relocate tenants, and recover the costs of the retrofit. If they do not, the landlord must renegotiate the terms of the leases, negotiate lease terminations, or wait for leases to expire. Consequently, many green retrofit projects occur in phases so as to allow for lease turnover and minimize tenant disruption. If a retrofit project is contemplated (and perhaps even if it is not), landlords should try to include provisions in all new leases for tenant relocation, termination rights, broad rights of entry, and cost recovery, among others, with the express intent of implementing a green building retrofit.

Green Building Goals and Standards

The heart of a green lease is the detailed and largely technical environmental goals, standards, and practices that are developed for the building and its occupants. Such provisions are referred to in this sidebar collectively as "green standards." These requirements will likely be developed by a landlord with engineering, architectural, and other expert technical advice, taking into consideration the building's specific features and technologies and the sustainability goals that the landlord sets for the building (and to which tenants must either agree or otherwise negotiate). These green standards may also set targets or benchmarks for environmental performance that the parties may be held to achieve, whether individually or collectively.

The green standards established in the lease will cover requirements for building operations and maintenance applicable to both landlord and tenant, such as energy use targets and monitoring, carbon reduction measures, water reduction, waste management and recycling, material purchases, chemical use, construction material requirements, building equipment main-

tenance, and, if applicable, compliance with the requirements of a recognized rating or certification that has been or may be obtained for the building (collectively, the "rating").

The green standards are implicated in provisions throughout a green lease and may be set forth in the body of the lease, in exhibits or schedules to the lease, or in a separate tenant manual. To the extent that implementation of a particular green standard is unclear or applies future or evolving sustainability goals and practices (whether under an applicable rating or otherwise), the parties will need to work together to seek a mutually acceptable interpretation of the requirement. In the absence of such agreement, the green lease should provide a means of alternative dispute resolution to resolve the matter, such as mediation or arbitration by a qualified expert.

Green Lease Provisions

Each green lease will be tailored to reflect the specific building and its environmental features, the business understandings of the parties, and their respective commitments to sustainability. Nonetheless, there will be many common themes. Although the following list is not intended to be comprehensive, it identifies central issues and provisions that should be considered in creating a green lease:

- **Relocation right.** The landlord should reserve the right to relocate the tenant, especially if the building may undergo a green retrofit during the lease term.

- **Compliance with laws.** The parties' respective obligations to comply with applicable laws should include current and future green building requirements.

- **Building operating hours.** The landlord should reserve the right to modify standard hours of operation for the building to reflect the tenant's actual average operating hours, including possibly eliminating weekend building hours, except on an as-needed basis.

- **Access.** The landlord should reserve broad rights of access to the leased premises for installing, inspecting, monitoring, repairing, replacing, and maintaining green building technologies and equipment, especially if a retrofit is contemplated.

- **Operating expenses.** In the case of a net lease, landlords are advised that the definition of building operating expenses payable by tenants should include all costs to comply with the green standards and rating requirements. This may include the following costs:

- Alterations, additions, replacements, and upgrades to the building and building systems to reduce operating costs, utility consumption, or greenhouse gas (GHG) emissions;

- Repair and maintenance of green building technologies;

- Environmental auditing and monitoring (including energy usage, air quality, and waste streams) and resulting corrective actions;

- Implementing or achieving the green standards and certification, including specified targets for reducing energy use and GHG emissions;

- Periodic building commissioning;

- Green building insurance; or

- Incentives, rebates, credits, or other benefits sought to support green building improvements or practices.

  To the extent that any such operating costs are considered capital expenditures, the landlord should amortize them on a straight-line basis over the useful life of the capital item. The tenant may argue that any tax benefits or other subsidies received by the landlord for such improvements must first be deducted from such capital costs.

- **Sustainable building operations.** Both parties should agree to comply with the green standards and the rating requirements, as they apply to their respective responsibilities, operations, and activities. This obligation may include maintaining or seeking appropriate ratings or certifications, or other specific targets or benchmarks for reducing resource consumption, GHG emissions, or other adverse environmental effects. This provision should also include an agreement for information sharing regarding the parties' operations and activities affecting environmental matters and an agreement of mutual cooperation in the effort to reduce environmental impacts. The landlord and tenant may also agree to work together to pursue sustainability targets, incentives, rebates, credits, and other policies or benefits that one or both of them may elect to pursue.

- **Recycling and waste management.** The parties should comply with the green standards and all laws regarding the collection, sorting, separation, composting, and recycling of garbage, trash, rubbish, and other refuse. If applicable, the parties should designate a recycling area for the building, provide for recycling receptacles, and arrange for pickup of recycled materials, as well as agree to the periodic monitoring, reporting, and assessment of wastes. The parties should be obligated to modify the recycling and waste management programs on the basis of such periodic assessments. All construction debris and any other items to be removed from the premises by a party (including at lease termination) should likewise be sorted, recycled, redirected, or otherwise diverted from landfills or incineration.

- **Maintenance and repairs.** The green standards and rating requirements include matters related to the maintenance, repair, and replacement obligations under the lease, such as the use of specified chemicals, supplies, materials, and equipment. The lease should provide for periodic commissioning of the building and building systems and all recommended maintenance and repairs for maximum efficiency.

- **Alterations and improvements.** All improvements, alterations, and additions to the building should be designed and constructed in accordance with the green standards and rating requirements. The party performing such work should engage a qualified green building professional to review all designs, material purchases, demolition, construction, and waste management procedures during all design and construction phases to ensure such conformance. The use of air quality–compliant materials inside the building should be required in order to reduce emissions from materials used in the building, including without limitation, the use of low- or no-VOC paints, solvents, adhesives, furniture, and fabrics and other construction materials, and the use of low-flow water fixtures and high-efficiency equipment. In the case of tenant improvements, the parties may be required to seek and maintain an appropriate certification such as LEED for Commercial Interiors (LEED-CI).

- **Utilities.** The landlord should reserve the right to select or change building utility providers and to purchase green or renewable energy for the building. In addition, the landlord may wish to reserve the right to approve all utility providers serving tenant directly. The landlord should have the right to install renewable energy technologies on site, such as solar or wind systems. The landlord should have the right to install, monitor, and maintain smart meters or submeters for electricity, water, and natural gas, if they do not already exist. The parties should agree to a range of acceptable climate and temperature settings for hot-water and heating, ventilating and air-conditioning) (HVAC) systems.

- **Electrical usage.** The parties may set targets for maximum energy use. In addition to paying excess energy costs, the party that exceeds such targets may be responsible for purchasing carbon credits to offset the excess usage.

- **Transportation.** The landlord will typically maintain the transportation services, facilities, and amenities for the building, such as shuttles, a preferred parking program, bike storage, and locker or shower facilities. The tenant should cooperate in reporting transportation matters related to its occupancy, including the use of mass transit, parking ratios, and the use of alternative fuel vehicles or other green transportation modes (such as biking or walking).

- **Janitorial services.** The parties may agree that janitorial services may be performed during normal business hours, in accordance with the green standards (including green cleaning products and practices), and in a manner so as to minimize disruption to the tenant's business.

- **Insurance.** The landlord's property insurance should include such coverage as is necessary and available to repair, replace, and commission the building and associated improvements and fixtures to comply with the green standards and to obtain the rating according to then-current requirements, which may include the installation of improved green building technologies.

- **Restoration due to casualty damage or condemnation.** All restoration should likewise be performed to comply with the green standards and maintain the rating that existed before such casualty damage or condemnation occurred.

- **Default and remedies.** The parties should agree to provide adequate documentation and evidence of their compliance with the green standards and rating requirements. In the event of a dispute regarding compliance, the lease may require the parties to submit to alternative dispute resolution, such as mediation or binding arbitration. In some cases, the use of a qualified green building expert is appropriate. For a default in compliance, the parties may agree to specific remedies such as the purchase of carbon credits, recovery of damages for estimated lost energy savings, rent adjustments, the right to take specified corrective actions, reimbursement for penalties or taxes caused by such default, or perhaps even termination.

- **Consent.** For any matter that requires the consent of a party under the lease, it may be reasonable for that party to withhold consent if it reasonably determines or demonstrates that the requested action would be inconsistent or incompatible with the green standards or rating requirements or would otherwise place excessive demands on energy or water use or result in adverse environmental effects.

Andrew I. Davis is a partner with the law firm of Stoel Rives LLP.

Procuring Green Property Insurance

A third foundational consideration related to the operation of a green office building is the procurement of green property insurance. Since 2006, a number of green insurance products have been introduced to the market. In the United States, most programs have been written for buildings certified under the Leadership in Energy and Environmental Design (LEED) system (see the sidebar by Philip K. Glick). Among recent advances:

- **EXISTING LEED-CERTIFIED BUILDINGS** can procure property insurance that will cover the additional LEED-related costs to complete repairs following an insured casualty loss. A number of programs cover the extra costs incurred to rebuild a previously LEED-certified building to the next highest level of LEED certification.

- **PROPERTY INSURANCE IS AVAILABLE** to explicitly cover additional LEED-related certification expenses for new buildings under construction, and such coverage is expected to be extended to LEED retrofits as insurance product offerings evolve. Specialized "soft costs" coverage can added to a builder's risk policy to cover costs incurred from the additional time and expense needed to build to LEED standards, including additional construction period interest, financing fees, legal and accounting fees, and engineering fees arising from the extended time needed to complete LEED modifications.

▶▶ **SEVERAL INSURANCE COMPANIES OFFER COVERAGE** for the increased cost to repair or rebuild a conventional, non-LEED-certified building as a LEED-certified project after a casualty loss. Such coverages are typically offered in circumstances where conventional buildings must comply with LEED standards under local government requirements. Policies in this category cover the additional costs, including professional fees, to rebuild a damaged building to comply with current LEED certification standards under local code. Such policies are helpful for property owners who wish to renovate a conventional building as a LEED-certified building after a casualty loss, especially as increasing numbers of local governments adopt green building requirements (see chapter 7).

GREEN OPERATING METRICS

A central aspect of green property operations is the continuous measurement of actual performance against green operating objectives and the assurance that building systems are performing as designed. Baseline performance measures (before the retrofit) for energy consumption, water usage, and waste recycling are the initial metrics for assessing property performance. Energy and water usage guidelines for existing buildings, as established under the Building Research Establishment's Environmental Assessment Method (BREEAM), LEED, Energy Star, and other certification systems, are useful in establishing performance standards for reductions in energy and water usage. Where governmental entities have established target requirements for the reduction of energy and water use, these are also appropriate performance standards.

A variety of techniques are available to obtain these metrics:

▶▶ **BENCHMARKING.** Benchmarking is accomplished by the ongoing review of energy and water consumption data through metering or submetering and by the tracking of progress on other sustainable performance objectives (see the overview of energy benchmarking in the sidebar by Chris Flint Chatto). Smart metering, the linkage of metering to computerized output that can be viewed by the owner or occupant, is a new metering possibility.

It is highly recommended that property-level goals on energy and water consumption, waste recycling, and other key sustainability objectives be incorporated in the monthly, quarterly, and annual budgeting and reporting process, and that property performance be tracked both in appropriate output measures

NEW INSURANCE OPTIONS FOR GREEN BUILDINGS

PHILIP K. GLICK

The U.S. Green Building Council introduced its original LEED building standards in 2000. Over the next several years, the Council certified hundreds of buildings under its new standards. In contrast, the U.S. property and liability insurance industry did not develop any specialized insurance coverages for LEED-certified buildings until 2006 when the Fireman's Fund Insurance Company introduced its Green-Gard coverages. Since that time a number of major insurance companies—including Chubb, Lexington, Zürich, Liberty Mutual, Ace, FM Global, XL, and Travelers—have developed specialized property insurance coverage to meet the unique needs of LEED certification and construction. This sidebar provides a summary of the insurance coverages available and discusses likely trends and risk management issues that commercial building owners and tenants should address.

Property Insurance Coverages

Property insurance coverages for sustainable improvements are available for existing LEED-certified buildings, new buildings under construction, and existing buildings that have not obtained LEED certification.

▶▶

EXISTING LEED-CERTIFIED BUILDINGS

The basic LEED property insurance enhancements are intended to cover the additional costs that will be incurred by the owner of a LEED-certified building to complete repairs following a fire, explosion, windstorm, water damage, or other insured casualty loss. The intent is to cover the extra costs that will be incurred to bring the damaged building back up to its prior level of LEED certification. Several of the property insurance coverages now available will also cover the extra costs incurred to rebuild a previously LEED-certified building to the next highest level of LEED certification. For example, if a building was certified LEED Silver, the insurance coverage would cover the rebuilding costs incurred to repair it and bring it up to LEED Gold certification.

Although insurers differ somewhat in specific coverages, most policies will include a variety of costs:

» Costs in excess of those associated with conventional construction to repair or replace damaged buildings using "green" products, materials, or construction methods. Products and materials covered in such clauses include Energy Star appliances; electrical, and heating and air-conditioning systems; low-flow plumbing fixtures and sensors; and sustainable materials, such as cabinets, molding, and flooring that use bamboo, eucalyptus, or recycled content. The increased cost of using Green Seal or GREENGUARD products such as paints, primers, adhesives, and carpet and floor coverings, as well as certified furniture, wood cabinets, and seating will also be covered.

» Cost of replacing or repairing vegetated roofs.

» Additional LEED-related repair or reconstruction costs, including the additional cost of debris removal or demolition, such as the extra cost of recycling debris using environmentally responsible disposal standards and methods.

» Other LEED-related certification expenses including the cost to hire a LEED Accredited Professional architect, engineer, or other consultant to oversee building repairs.

» Building commissioning expenses, including the cost to monitor heating and air-conditioning systems to make sure that airflow is properly balanced and that systems are working in an efficient manner.

» Building flush-out expenses, to ensure that any contaminants in heating and air-conditioning systems have been cleaned before the building is reoccupied.

» Additional loss of rents or business income due to the extra time needed to rebuild using green products or construction methods.

NEW BUILDINGS UNDER CONSTRUCTION

Property insurance is available to explicitly cover all additional LEED-related certification expenses for new buildings under construction. Although some builders' risk policies may automatically cover some of these expenses if the policy is properly written, many policy forms do not automatically cover all of these additional costs. In addition, specialized "soft costs" coverage can added to a builder's risk policy to cover any delay costs such as additional construction period interest, financing fees, legal and accounting fees, and engineering fees incurred from the extended time needed to complete repairs subject to LEED standards.

EXISTING, UNCERTIFIED, TRADITIONAL BUILDINGS

As a creative extension of this new green insurance, several insurance companies offer coverage for the increased cost to repair or rebuild a traditional, non-LEED-certified building as LEED-certified. This is a new type of building code coverage. Standard building code coverage or upgrade protection covers the additional costs incurred to rebuild a fire-damaged building to bring it up to current building code requirements—such as compliance with the Americans with Disabilities Act or with new life safety code requirements. LEED building code coverage takes such insurance a step forward to cover the additional rebuilding costs, including professional fees, to rebuild a damaged building to comply with current LEED certification standards.

PREMIUMS

Most insurers offering LEED property coverage have indicated that they charge an additional premium corresponding to the additional limits of coverage being provided. However, at least one insurer has indicated that it will offer a 5 percent reduction in premiums for qualified buildings whose owners procure LEED-related coverage enhancements. As these diverse pricing policies suggest, property owners should canvass the market for the most cost-effective LEED property coverage.

Liability Insurance Coverages

Insurance liability coverages also are being developed to address specialized LEED requirements:

» **Commercial general liability insurance.** The commercial insurance industry is just beginning to consider new extensions of general liability insurance coverage. One insurer has just begun to offer policy enhancements that will provide coverage for bodily injury liability claims caused by heating, air-conditioning, and water control equipment used in a LEED-certified building. It is also likely that a number of insurance companies will begin to offer a combined general liability and pollution liability policy to property owners and tenants in LEED-certified buildings that pass their underwriting requirements. This would eliminate the need to purchase a separate pollution liability policy at additional cost, as is now the case.

In the future, it is possible that insurance companies will begin to offer general liability premium savings to building owners and tenants in LEED-certified buildings, provided that strict underwriting standards are met. Premium savings, if any, would have to be supported by favorable safety and operating records of LEED-certified equipment. Policies that combine pollution and general liability coverages for LEED buildings may be able to offer premium reductions on the basis of superior indoor environmental quality and lower environmental risk. At present, insurers have diverse views about the cost-effectiveness of LEED construction, and compilation of the necessary loss experience data is still in its infancy.

▶▶ **Pollution liability insurance.** In contrast to commercial general liability insurers, who have yet to offer explicit premium savings for LEED-certified buildings, several major environmental insurers have indicated they will provide premium savings of between 8 and 10 percent on the pollution policies they write for building owners who have met LEED certification standards. It is likely that this trend will continue in the future in acknowledgment of the stronger indoor environmental quality of LEED properties.

▶▶ **Professional liability coverage for architects and engineers.** Architects and other design professionals are taking on new responsibilities as part of their engagement letters and other contracts for LEED-certified work. Recent revisions in the Code of Professional Standards published by the American Institute of Architects (AIA) codify these additional obligations for LEED-certified projects. At least two professional liability insurers have developed coverage endorsements to address the new requirements. However, almost all architects' professional liability policies exclude claims arising from cost overruns, project delays, and express guarantees of performance, such as guarantees of LEED certification or achievement of a specific level of certification.

▶▶ **Surety bonds.** In contrast to professional liability insurance, surety bonds—including contract payment and performance bonds—may cover a portion of the guarantees of project costs, completion dates, and performance warranties from contractors, equipment suppliers, and architects. The cost and availability of such bonds may differ significantly depending on the experience and financial strength of the vendor or contractor and on surety market conditions. One insurance company is currently developing a policy to guarantee the projected cost savings of energy-efficient heating and air-conditioning systems installed in LEED-certified buildings.

Future Trends and Other Considerations

Based on the insurance industry's response to LEED-certified building construction and renovation, it is very likely that innovative insurance products will continue to be developed as the sustainable building market grows. At present, there is a great diversity of opinion as to whether LEED-certified buildings will actually decrease or increase the insurance industry's risks and likely losses, particularly if projects are undertaken with contractors and architects who do not offer substantial experience in LEED construction and design. Building owners will also need to work closely with major tenants to oversee the initial sustainable construction and buildout performed by these tenants, as well as for any interior renovations or repairs made following a fire or other loss to the leased space, because tenant failure to comply with LEED standards can jeopardize not only the owner's LEED certification but also the related insurance coverage.

The evaluation of the potential risks and advantages of LEED certification and construction appears to differ significantly among European insurers, compared with U.S. insurers. Several property insurers in the United Kingdom have stated that they will not insure homes or other buildings that have vegetated roofs. They are very concerned with the potential fire risks if the vegetation is not property irrigated and maintained. In contrast, most property insurers in Germany have stated that they will offer premium discounts for homes that have vegetative roofs.

Clearly, the insurance industry needs to go a long way in developing claims experience and underwriting standards to consistently address the unique risks and potential advantages of LEED-certified construction. In addition to ensuring that construction is undertaken by designers, engineers, and contractors who are experienced with sustainable property development, insurers would be well-advised to institute underwriting requirements to ensure that LEED-certified buildings are operated and maintained by firms or personnel that are qualified to operate sustainable building systems.

Philip K. Glick is senior vice president of ECBM Insurance.

(power and water usage statistics, amount of waste recycled) and in financial metrics. Both output and financial outcomes should be tracked in aggregate and on a per square foot or per square meter basis. Incorporation of green goals and performance into operating budgets and regular property reporting will highlight sustainability objectives, link them to property performance, and track progress on an ongoing basis for ownership and management.

▶▶ **BENCHMARKING SOFTWARE**. Growing demand in the commercial real estate sector for green benchmarking and performance measurement has led to the development of commercial energy and sustainability tracking, performance assessment, and management software platforms, many of which integrate Energy Star, LEED, and other rating systems with their proprietary information technology applications (for details, see the sidebar by Brian J. McCarter).

▶▶ **BUILDING AUTOMATION SYSTEMS AND SENSORS**. Building automation systems (BASs), which monitor, regulate, and generate reports on building energy consumption, offer performance benchmarking in real time. The sidebar in this chapter by Boston Properties and the case study on Adobe Systems discuss the use of BASs. Continuous commissioning (discussed later) can help to optimize the performance of BASs and their benchmarking capabilities. As well, the installation of sensors to turn off unneeded devices works with a BAS to control the use of energy and water. See chapter 3 and the green lighting discussion in this chapter for a review of the use of sensors to reduce the use of water and artificial lighting. Property owners, managers, and tenants should also be aware of plug load occupancy sensors, which switch off computers and other office equipment when not in use; plug load occupancy sensors can result in additional energy economies.

The building management system at the Christman Building in Lansing, Michigan, is programmed to trigger automatic alarms when energy systems are operating outside their programmed parameters.

BENCHMARKING BUILDING ENERGY USE

CHRIS FLINT CHATTO

Benchmarking a building's energy use is simply the act of measuring and comparing a building's energy use. Such comparisons are helpful to evaluate energy use against the following:

▸ The same building's historical performance, to confirm that performance remains within expected parameters;

▸ Predicated use by energy models, to ensure that systems are operating efficiently as designed; and

▸ Established metrics based on other buildings' performance, to put the energy use in context.

The Commercial Buildings Energy Consumption Survey (CBECS) in the United States is one of the best examples of established metrics. CBECS comprises more than 5,000 building types representing more than 80 percent of the commercial building energy use in the country. Other countries and private entities have or are developing databases as well, like the National Australian Built Environment Rating System and, in the United Kingdom, the Carbon Trust's benchmarking tools for schools, offices, and government buildings. The availability of accurate metrics varies from country to country and by building type, but the quantity of available data is growing quickly worldwide.

Typically, building energy consumption is measured and expressed as annual energy use intensity (EUI) per unit of conditioned gross area. Conditioned gross area includes all spaces that are heated or cooled for building occupants. In the United States, it is measured as thousands of Btu per square foot per year (kBtu/SF/yr); elsewhere kilowatt-hours per square meter per year (kWh/m^2/yr) are typically used. Benchmarking by EUI enables quick comparisons with similar buildings, although this method does not capture many related aspects (for example, how densely occupied an office building is or the number of hours it is used).

Other related metrics can be illuminating as well, such as energy use as a function of product or building process efficiency. Hospitals, for example, might be more interested in energy use per "patient-adjusted day" (a standardized measure of hospital facility usage) as a measure of performance. Tools also exist to convert EUI into a measurement of annual carbon emissions, which of course is a function of the local utility grid. The U.S. Environmental Protection Agency's (EPA's) Target Finder and CarbonBuzz in the United Kingdom are two such examples. It can also be worthwhile to convert energy use metrics to measures of cost. An understanding of local utility rate structures or the use of utility bills enables quick and effective conversion of energy consumption statistics to measures of energy cost per square foot or square meter. The use of cost data underscores to building owners and portfolio managers the importance of energy-efficient buildings. Performance data for property or portfolio cross-comparisons should be adjusted for differences in property type, occupancy, and utility rate structures.

Getting the raw data for such analysis is simply a matter of reading utility meters or, more simply, looking at utility bills. On-line calculators, like CarbonBuzz or the EPA's Portfolio Manager, can compile, convert, and analyze this information, although manually entering the information in a standalone spreadsheet is not difficult. As well, numerous new software applications are being developed to track and analyze building energy use (see the sidebar by Brian McCarter). Some care must be taken when converting energy use to common units and, for more complex building types, ensuring that all energy use is measured.

Summing and converting all monthly metered use for an entire year and dividing by the relevant conditioned square footage is a quick way to calculate annual EUI. This method is often sufficient for annual tracking of a building or portfolio of holdings. However, if the intention is to compare a building's energy use to expected predictions through an energy model, more work must be done to modify the model to reflect actual use patterns, climate, and other differences from the model's initial assumptions.

Given new requirements for public disclosure of building energy use in Europe and some American states, it is very likely that at some point such information will populate larger, more representative databases of energy use. This information has tremendous potential to assist building owners and designers in better understanding, and thus reducing, overall building energy use.

Chris Flint Chatto, LEED AP, is a sustainability specialist at Zimmer Gunsul Frasca Architects LLP.

▸▸ OCCUPANT SURVEYS. Occupant satisfaction surveys, already a staple in institutional property management, can also be utilized to track the effectiveness of green programs. Surveys can be used to assess tenant views on thermal and acoustic comfort and indoor air quality and their satisfaction with recycling programs and property-level initiatives to encourage the use of alternative transportation options. As documented in the case studies from Australia, China, the United States, and the United Kingdom, occupant surveys are used widely to track satisfaction with green renovations. The LEED certification system gives credit for conducting occupant comfort surveys. Standard occupant satisfaction surveys can readily be expanded to include feedback on green renovations and operating programs.

MAINTAINING ENERGY-EFFICIENT OPERATIONS THROUGH CONTINUOUS COMMISSIONING

A key objective in green property operations is to maintain property energy efficiency over time, often a challenging goal, as noted in a November 2008 article in *HPAC Engineering*:

In a study of 60 new buildings conducted by Lawrence Berkeley National Laboratory, 50 percent of the build-

ENERGY AND SUSTAINABILITY PERFORMANCE ASSESSMENT SOFTWARE

BRIAN J. MCCARTER

For many building portfolio owners and operators, aggregating and maintaining ongoing energy consumption and cost data and integrating this information with the property metrics necessary to benchmark performance can be time-intensive, difficult to manage, and fraught with error potential. This challenge has given rise to commercial software platforms for energy and sustainability tracking, performance assessment, and performance management. Many of these platforms have integrated Energy Star, LEED, and other rating systems with their proprietary information technology applications. Key software platforms designed to evaluate and manage building energy and sustainability performance for commercial buildings include the following new products:

▸▸ **Green Compass.** Johnson Controls, whose core competency is in high-efficiency building automation technology and consulting, developed Green Compass as an online application for comparing a project's green building features with the LEED for New Construction (LEED-NC) and LEED-EB requirements (www.johnsoncontrols.com). Green Compass enables users to generate a scorecard that indicates how green a building or project plan is. The software estimates first costs, ranks potential green strategies according to financial viability, and estimates potential savings streams on the basis of building size. For users interested in pursuing LEED certification, a scope-of-work report can be generated that contains credit-level details.

▸▸ **Green Globes.** Green Globes assessment software is available in the United Kingdom, Canada, and the United States for both new and existing buildings (www.greenglobes.com). The software can be used in conjunction with the Green Globes rating system or independently. Especially useful for owners and managers of existing buildings is Green Globes' Continual Improvement Tool for Existing Buildings (CIEB) on-line assessment. CIEB enables building owners and operators to assess the environmental and sustainability performance of their buildings through a question-and-answer protocol. In Canada, where Green Globes for Existing Buildings is owned and operated by the Building Owners and Managers Association of Canada (BOMA Canada), CIEB is widely used by leading portfolio managers to assess building energy efficiency and to position commercial properties for a Green Globes rating. In July 2008, Jones Lang LaSalle acquired ECD Energy, the environmental consulting firm that developed the underlying Green Globes technology platform. Jones Lang LaSalle is now positioning the ECD technology platform as a building portfolio assessment and benchmarking tool.

▸▸ **Sustainable Real Estate Solutions (SRS).** SRS, whose core competency is the development of energy and environmental assessment and performance management software for commercial real estate, offers Sustainable Real

ings suffered controls problems, 40 percent suffered HVAC problems, 15 percent had missing equipment, and 25 percent had energy-management systems, economizers, and VFDs [variable-frequency drives] that did not function properly. Remember, this was a study of new buildings. Existing buildings almost certainly would have fared far worse simply because of natural HVAC system degradation and changing building conditions.[1]

Continuous commissioning, the process of optimizing the performance of building mechanical and electrical systems for existing property conditions, can be a key element in monitoring and improving green property performance. It is a key element in the Energy Star and LEED certification systems. Commissioning includes the ongoing monitoring and adjustment of building systems to improve reliability, optimize operations, and ensure that equipment operates as designed. A federal government–financed study of 130 large buildings, including offices, found that the commissioning of existing buildings yielded average measured savings of approximately 20 percent, with simple paybacks in fewer than two years.[2]

Estate Manager, a Web-based energy and sustainability assessment and management platform designed to optimize portfolio performance (www.srmnetwork.com). The SRS technology was originally developed by the Department of Energy (DOE) in conjunction with Pacific Northwest National Laboratory to monitor real-time energy consumption in commercial buildings. In addition to automating the assessment of building utility consumption and cost, the platform provides enterprise-wide monitoring of costs, savings, and ROI associated with sustainability-related capital improvements. Through its partnership with the Energy Star program, SRS offers automated Energy Star rating updates to benchmark a building's energy efficiency performance relative to comparable buildings. The SRS platform also incorporates the LEED for Existing Building Operation and Maintenance (LEED-EBOM) assessment and management standards to facilitate LEED compliance tracking and certification. The SRS platform enables standard and custom reporting at the property and portfolio levels to track key sustainability performance indicators over time.

▸▸ **TeleBright Software Corporation.** TeleBright, whose origins lie in telecommunications expense management software, has expanded its flagship ManageRight product to include energy efficiency benchmarking and monitoring of utilities in commercial buildings (www.telebright.com). The software assists building owners and managers in organizing building energy data to provide analysis of peak energy consumption, utility rates, and total energy costs. It helps to identify energy consumption trends and expenses that can be reduced by applying energy efficiency strategies. The software generates detailed building utility reports, including Energy Star scoring, and enables building owners and operators to benchmark like buildings within a portfolio in order to compare consumption trends and identify expense reduction opportunities. TeleBright also offers utility expense management and equipment load monitoring services designed to increase the effectiveness of energy cost reduction strategies.

▸▸ **TRIRIGA.** TRIRIGA, whose core competency is corporate workplace performance management software, has launched an enterprise-level carbon footprint assessment and management software program called TREES— (TRIRIGA Real Estate Environmental Sustainability, www.tririga.com). TREES offers assessment and analysis tools to inventory and measure the environmental impact of buildings and identify the greatest opportunities to reduce energy consumption and emissions, generate energy savings, and increase stakeholder value. The software maps an organization's real estate carbon footprint, provides an energy value calculator that includes Energy Star ratings, and offers reporting capabilities to prioritize environmental opportunities across the real estate portfolio. TRIRIGA also offers a suite of applications to manage the real estate life cycle, including portfolio planning, transaction management, and contract administration.

Brian J. McCarter is CEO of Sustainable Real Estate Solutions in Monroe, Connecticut.

SUSTAINABLE OPERATIONS

We all share a responsibility to do our part for the environment. But what do we do in our professional lives to make a difference? As one of the nation's leading office REITs, Boston Properties is committed to improving its natural resource efficiency and demonstrating that the operation and development of commercial real estate can be conducted with a conscious regard for the environment. We have always built for the lasting health of our buildings and their occupants, creating value for our shareholders through our long-term view. As such, we will continue to identify, execute, and improve sustainable strategies to forever better our ongoing environmental footprint.

—Bryan Koop, SVP and Regional Manager,
Boston Properties – Boston Region

Boston Properties takes a sustainable look at the whole, not just the sum, of a building's parts. The Boston Properties business strategy is reinforced through a three-pronged approach:

- Sustainability in new construction,
- Sustainability in existing buildings, and
- Sustainability in corporate operations.

Efforts are benchmarked in four major areas:

- Energy efficiency,
- Waste reduction,
- Water conservation, and
- Total reduction of carbon emissions.

When making decisions, Boston Properties has always asked, Is it good for customers? Is it good for shareholders? Now, the company also asks, Is it good for the environment?

Decreasing Environmental Impact

On the operational side, the green building philosophy includes not just new developments but also the existing portfolio of properties. Through green cleaning, office waste recycling, and energy and water reduction measures, the properties in these portfolios are significantly decreasing their environmental impact. The Boston Region of the company began a benchmarking program in 2007, and the results of these programs—after only a few short years of operational modifications—are significant. By the end of 2008 the Boston Region had

- Recycled 150 more tons of solid waste or 9 percent more than the preceding year;

- Reduced water consumption by 5 percent;

- Improved energy efficiency, using 6 percent less energy (BTUs per square foot) than the preceding year. With the Energy Star program in place, the company estimates that its suburban office buildings will save nearly 15 million kWh through 2009;

- 2,061,660 rentable square feet of Energy Star–rated property;

- A food waste composting program being tested in the suburban properties, with the goal of expanding it across the portfolio;

- A green roof system for the Russia Wharf project being tested to determine the feasibility of expanding green roof applications throughout the region; and

- 8,346,477 rentable square feet of property where green cleaning is conducted, an increase of 90 percent in 2008.

Introducing and Implementing Sustainable Programs

Boston Properties has introduced a wide-ranging suite of sustainable programs to improve operating economies and reduce the environmental footprint of its Boston Region portfolio. These programs are benchmarked and evaluated regularly to assure economic and environmental effectiveness.

ENERGY SAVINGS PROGRAM

All the Boston Region properties are rated and benchmarked using the EPA's Energy Star program, which allows the property team to quantify upgrades and manage the property's energy efficiency. Buildings do not always run as they were designed to, and sometimes a simple retrofit approach can help achieve substantial savings by recalibrating equipment or replacing motors. In 2008, eight of the Boston Region properties earned the Energy Star Award, making Boston Properties the largest owner of Energy Star properties in Massachusetts, with more than 2.3 million square feet.

Simple and complex initiatives were rolled out across these eight buildings to achieve the ranking:

- Relamping fixtures with 25-watt fixtures (down from 32 watts);

- Installing optimal smart BASs, reducing the number of system operating hours, and saving energy by not maintaining the optimum occupied indoor temperature when the building is unoccupied;

- Retrofitting lighting by replacing fluorescents and electronic ballasts;

- Installing occupancy sensors to allow the lights to turn on only when a room is occupied;

- Installing VFDs on fans, allowing management to reduce the speed of fan motors at night and on weekends and holidays, thereby cutting energy consumption;

- Installing high-efficiency motors, bringing the motor efficiency level up from 85 percent to 94 percent;

- Placing solar film on windows, permitting buildings to maintain cooler temperatures without using the HVAC system;

- Installing light-emitting diode (LED) lights when applicable, including on exit signs;

- Turning off escalators during early-morning hours; and

- Implementing "Saturday" HVAC hours during low-occupancy hours.

BUILDING AND EQUIPMENT MAINTENANCE

Utilities can be a building's largest operational cost, but they can also be the easiest to control and lower if understood and maintained. To enhance the operations and maintenance program, Boston Properties took the following steps:

- A state-of-the-art building monitoring facility was built to monitor all system operations in the Boston, Cambridge, and Boston suburban region 24 hours a day. This enables engineers to respond to a system issue when it happens, not when it is stumbled upon or called in. The Boston Properties Command Center is the only one of its kind in New England.

- Several BASs were installed in the portfolio to manage the temperature within a building with energy-saving control strategies. Boston Properties is also taking the steps necessary to ensure that the teams working on these projects are on the cutting edge of sustainable program and practice movements.

- The director of engineering gained certification as a LEED Commissioning Authority and ensures that building requirements are met and that systems function as engineered. The Boston office also has six construction managers who are LEED Accredited Professionals and are charged with project reviews to ensure that sustainable features are incorporated into each project wherever and whenever possible. In 2008, they booked more than 100 hours of training in sustainable design.

- In 2005 the steam-driven chillers at 101 Huntington Avenue were replaced with three 750-ton, high-efficiency, electrically driven centrifugal chillers. The new chillers use HFC-134a, a nonchlorine-based refrigerant that is much friendlier to the environment than chlorine. The conversion from steam turbine–driven units to electric-drive units cut the cooling energy budget by 50 percent. The CO_2 emissions avoided by installing these chillers is almost 5.5 million pounds annually.

- Since 1998, Boston Properties has increased the use of electronic communication, reporting, and tracking through automated preventive maintenance and tenant request systems and automated testing reports from service vendors (elevator maintenance, fire alarm system testing and maintenance, etc.). Ninety percent of operations and maintenance communication is done electronically.

RECYCLING AND SOLID WASTE MANAGEMENT

Property managers for all 8.8 million square feet of office space in the company's Boston Region portfolio actively recycle—from office paper, cans, bottles, fluorescent fixtures, cardboard, and regular office-related waste to landscape composting. Boston Properties also works closely with its vendors and tenants to promote café and restaurant composting. A trial program with Legal Sea Foods at the Prudential Center is effectively reducing kitchen waste, and similar composting programs are being launched with building cafés across the portfolio.

WATER CONSERVATION

The Boston Properties corporate offices are LEED-CI registered and were to be certified in 2009. The offices are the site of the company's first trial of water-free urinals and dual-flush lavatories. This program contributes to a 30 percent reduction in water use in the corporate offices, with savings of 70,000 to 80,000 gallons per year in one men's bathroom alone. To further support water conservation, the John Deere Rain Master Eagle-I Central ET irrigation system is being rolled out to the suburban properties as the systems are scheduled for replacement. This irrigation program receives information daily and adjusts water levels depending on the needs of the landscaping. With this program in place each property can expect to use 50 percent less water to achieve the same results.

TRANSPORTATION AND PARKING PROGRAMS

Commercial building owners are increasingly looking beyond bike racks, showers, and local public transportation options:

▶▶ Boston Properties offers these amenities at 95 percent of its buildings in the Boston Region.

▶▶ Complexes such as the Prudential Center in Boston promote density of population with hotels, convention centers, public transportation, office, retail, and residential components all under "one" roof. Wherever and whenever possible, this model is replicated in one or more ways as buildings are developed, redeveloped, or retrofitted. Reservoir Place in Waltham, Massachusetts, has enhanced the base building amenities to include a barber shop, gym, convenience store, coffee shop, café, and post office. All reduce tenants' need to leave the complex, thus effectively reducing gas usage and carbon output by personal vehicles.

▶▶ Boston Properties office leases now contain a transportation clause that urges the tenant to promote the local transportation management authority and alternative methods of transportation to their employees. Boston Properties further promotes these programs through on-site events, newsletters, and one-on-one meetings with office tenant contacts.

▶▶ Supporting alternative transportation, Boston Properties continues to actively participate in local transportation management efforts, "guaranteed ride home" programs, and commuting incentive programs. Between 2008 and early 2009, the company hosted four transportation fairs and four bike week breakfasts, and attended more than 10 hours of transportation-related conferences and meetings. An "April is Green Month" campaign rolled out across the Boston Region portfolio with tenants at multiple properties participating in "Earth fairs," "green breakfasts," and awareness programs. In 2009 this program will roll out to additional regions.

GREEN CLEANING

Boston Properties formalized the "Green Cleaning Requirement" in 2006 for the Boston region. In 2007, 8,813,628 square feet of office space used Green Seal–approved cleaning products, HEPA (high-efficiency particulate air) vacuums, and restroom supply products made from 60 percent recycled materials. Effective April 2008, all restroom supply products in downtown properties were moved to 100 percent recycled content and those in suburban properties to a 60 percent minimum.

DEVELOPING CRITERIA TO ASSESS COST-EFFECTIVENESS AND GREEN PROGRAMS

The Boston Properties Regional Sustainability Committee was formed in 2008. Created to promote communication across

Continuous commissioning is performed by a team of engineers and technicians in cooperation with property operations and maintenance staffs on major building mechanical and electrical systems, including control systems; HVAC equipment; lighting and other electrical equipment; central chillers and heating plants; and water and steam distribution systems. Continuous commissioning has four key steps:

▶▶ **MEASURING ENERGY** and maintenance cost savings,

▶▶ **TRAINING OPERATING** and maintenance staff,

▶▶ **MEASURING ENERGY DATA** and continuously measuring energy performance, and

▶▶ **OBTAINING ONGOING ASSISTANCE** from continuous commissioning engineers.[3]

Commissioning is a key element of renovating existing buildings and its use is described in many of the case studies, including those for Adobe Systems, McDonald's Corporate Headquarters, and One Beacon Street.

ESTABLISHING GREEN OPERATING PROGRAMS

As detailed in the case studies, green property operations encompass all aspects of building management, including energy and water usage; landscaping; contracting for janitorial, waste management, and cleaning services; and sustainable purchasing. Green operating programs are becoming increasingly widespread and affordable. When the use of outside contractors is desirable, such programs can be initiated by property management staff through a competitive RFP process.

regions and sharing of best practices, the committee assesses the cost-effectiveness of green projects and programs. The committee meets bimonthly to discuss ROI, tenant feedback, existing green initiatives, and new programs and manages the company's Sustainable Best Practices collection. Selected programs other than those listed in this sidebar focus on the following:

- Indoor air quality,
- Acquisitions,
- Procurement, and
- Vendor compliance.

EDUCATION

Boston Properties uses both internal and external education programs and communications to help employees and clients move toward sustainability:

- The Boston Properties "Green Brochure" was created and rolled out in 2008 to educate staff and tenants on what it means to build and operate green and the benefits that come with it.

- Additional communications with tenants include newsletters with a special section dedicated to green news, event collateral materials, magnetic reminders to save energy and recycle, and daily postings of green content on elevator screens. Boston Properties has also hosted recycling challenges among building occupants and urged tenants to help with citywide energy-saving efforts such as Lights Out Boston.

- In 2008, more than 30 executives hosted or participated in more than 20 local and national green building forums to further sustainable education.

- Through Boston Properties University, employees attended over 150 "sustainability classroom hours" in 2007 and 192 in 2008. "Sustainable Operations" was taught in 2008, highlighting energy efficiency and the retrofitting process.

- Boston Properties employees involved in operations and maintenance are educated on the advantages of operating sustainability and on the action items they need to execute in order to support the mission. Property-level goals on energy, water consumption, and recycling make sustainability actionable.

BENCHMARKING AND MEASURING

Benchmarking and measuring sustainable programs is a cornerstone of the Boston Properties and Boston region sustainability program. Energy use, recycling, and water consumption are measured on a quarterly basis against previous years. These reports are distributed and displayed in regional management offices and incorporated into annual goals.

Boston Properties is a real estate investment trust that owns, manages, and develops first-class office properties in the United States.

Green Operating Programs

Boston Properties has initiated a comprehensive set of green operating programs throughout its Boston Region portfolio (see sidebar), as have many of the properties profiled in the case studies.

Green certification systems typically award credits for the following green operating initiatives:

- **GREEN POWER PURCHASE.** Green power purchase programs, which enable properties to buy electricity generated from renewable sources, including solar, wind, geothermal, biomass, wave, and small-impact hydropower, are becoming increasingly common in Europe, Australia, and the United States. Power purchased from alternative sources has typically been more expensive than conven-

tional power, but cost decreases are probable over time as the alternative energy sector gains additional public and private investment support. Properties in the case studies that have purchased green power include 545 Madison Avenue, Morgan Lovell, and Trevor Pearcey House. Green certification systems typically offer credit for green power purchased from a qualified source.

- **PURCHASE OF RENEWABLE ENERGY CREDITS (RECS).** When the direct purchase of green power is not feasible, it is possible to purchase RECs in amounts equivalent to historic electricity consumption to offset a property's use of conventional power. The purchase of RECs supports the generation of electricity from renewable sources. RECs are typically certified, to provide purchaser protection and substantiate their environmental performance, as discussed in chapter 5. The Christman and Joseph Vance Buildings are examples of properties that have purchased RECs in a green retrofit.

▸▸ **GREEN LIGHTING PROGRAMS**. Green lighting retrofit programs are typically a key feature in sustainable office renovations. Lighting efficiency improvements include relamping existing fixtures to support lower wattages, replacing ballasts in common area lighting, exit lights, and parking area lights, and using motion sensors, daylighting, and compact fluorescent lightbulbs to reduce electricity consumption. These subjects are discussed in greater detail in chapter 3.

▸▸ **WASTE AUDITING, RECYCLING, AND COMPOSTING**. Waste auditing and recycling is central to green building operations and is required under sustainable building certification protocols. Materials that are typically recycled include office paper, cans, bottles, fluorescent fixtures, cardboard, and landscape-related waste. Because research indicates that as much as 70 percent of office waste can be composted, office buildings are beginning to move beyond standard recycling programs to embrace composting. The Joseph Vance Building (see case study) has instituted a building-wide composting program. Boston Properties works closely with food vendors and tenants in the Boston region to promote composting at cafés and restaurants. A trial composting program with Legal Sea Foods at Boston's Prudential Center is reducing kitchen waste, and Boston Properties is launching similar programs across the region.

▸▸ **GREEN CONSTRUCTION MANAGEMENT PRACTICES**. The case studies demonstrate that green retrofit projects make widespread use of green construction management practices for base building retrofits, ongoing tenant improvements, and building repairs and upgrades. These practices include the recycling of construction waste; the containment and isolation of construction debris, including dust; and the imposition of sound reduction requirements. These practices can be incorporated into building regulations, tenant manuals, construction contracts, and RFPs.

▸▸ **GREEN JANITORIAL AND CLEANING PROGRAMS**. Green cleaning programs and janitorial contracts are another widely used aspect of green property operations, as illustrated by the case studies. These programs include the use of environmentally friendly cleaning supplies such as products certified by Green Seal; the use of recycled paper toweling; the use of equipment with HEPA filters that ensure that over 99 percent of particulate matter is collected; and the use of carpet cleaning equipment and processes that minimize the possibility of mildew and mold. Real estate management companies are beginning to report that green janitorial and cleaning programs are becoming financially competitive with conventional options. Green janitorial and cleaning requirements can be incorporated into building regulations, tenant manuals, construction contracts, and RFPs.

▸▸ **ENVIRONMENTALLY SOUND PEST MANAGEMENT**. Green pest management programs are also coming into wider use. Environmentally friendly pest management focuses on the removal of pest habitat, food sources, and breeding areas; prevention of access; and management of environmental factors. Pests are controlled primarily through traps, lures, and repellents; they are frequently excluded from a property by sealing holes and areas that permit ingress and by installing vinyl strips on the bottom of doors to eliminate small gaps through which they can enter. When additional treatment is required, low- or no-toxicity products are favored.

▸▸ **LANDSCAPING**. Environmentally friendly landscaping has come into broad use globally. Key principles include the use of native and drought-tolerant plantings compatible with

ONE BEACON

the local climate; the use of drip irrigation (which saves substantial water relative to spray irrigation); and the use of captured rainwater, recycled wastewater, or nonpotable water for irrigation. Xeriscaping—the use of plantings that do not require supplemental irrigation— is another environmentally friendly approach. Green landscaping is typically cost-effective over time in that it reduces maintenance costs and water usage.

▸▸ **SUSTAINABLE PURCHASING AND REUSE OF CONSUMABLE AND DURABLE GOODS**. Many green certification programs for existing buildings, including LEED, BREEAM, and Green Star, give credit for programs to purchase environmentally friendly products. Typically, qualifying products contain recycled materials or are sourced locally or regionally. Consumable products included in green certification programs include paper items, toner cartridges, binders, batteries, and desk accessories. Durable goods for which credit is typically available under green certification programs include

- Building components and structures (wall studs, insulation, doors, windows);
- Panels;
- Attached finishings (drywall, trim, ceiling panels);
- Carpet and other floorings;
- Adhesives, sealants, paints, and coatings;
- Furniture; and
- Energy-efficient electrical equipment, certified under a suitable program.

Operational initiatives to save energy without significant expense at One Beacon Street in Boston include reductions in garage steam use, draining of the cooling tower during the winter, adjusting HVAC fan use to reflect actual tenant occupancy schedules, and modification of the chilled-water temperature.

Green certification programs also encourage properties that offer food service programs to purchase certified organic or locally grown foodstuffs. As detailed in the case studies of Transwestern, the Christman Building, the Joseph Vance Building, Morgan Lovell, and the Trevor Pearcey House, the reuse of building fixtures and furniture and the use of repurposed objects in artwork and decorative items are also commonly used strategies in refurbishing and furnishing green buildings.

Timing Green Property Operating Programs

Green property operations programs are best incorporated into a property's ongoing management cycle. New operating and capital programs can be considered and launched in the context of annual and long-term budgeting. The greening of individual tenant suites can be linked to lease renewals and tenant turnover. Green contractors and suppliers can be obtained as part of the ongoing cycle of issuing RFPs and selecting new vendors.

Staff and Tenant Training

Ongoing staff and tenant training is integral to ongoing green operations, as documented in the case studies. Property management staff must be taught to operate central building systems correctly; tenants must be taught to operate equipment in their suites correctly. Green protocols governing tenant buildouts and other on-site construction, waste recycling, cleaning and janitorial services, and hours of HVAC operation must be understood and carried out both by building staff, tenant facilities coordinators, and contractors. The use of enhanced commissioning in green building retrofits includes the development of green system manuals and initial training for property staff. As well, building regulations and the tenant manual should be rewritten to include green practices and protocols and tenants should be educated on green requirements. Tenant visits by property management staff, green programming developed by management for tenants, Web sites created for tenant outreach, and electronic programming on computerized elevator displays are all means of educating tenants about property-level sustainability initiatives.

NOTES

1 Steve Harrell, "Continuous Commissioning," *HPAC Engineering*, November 4, 2008, http://hpac.com/fastrack/continuous-commissioning.

2 U.S. Department of Energy (DOE), Federal Energy Management Program, *Continuous Commissioning Guidebook for Federal Energy Managers*, October 2002, p. 1, www1.eere.energy.gov/femp/pdfs/ccg03_ch1.pdf.

3 DOE, Federal Energy Management Program, *Continuous Commissioning Guidebook for Federal Energy Managers*, October 2002, chapter 9, p. 1, www1.eere.energy.gov/femp/pdfs/ccg11_ch9.pdf.

Public Policy: Sustainability Comes to the Fore

MARK J. BENNETT AND LEANNE TOBIAS

Governments have had a profound effect on the international growth and mainstreaming of green building technologies and standards. Public policies on the green building front have arisen in response to multiple factors, including energy cost and building efficiency concerns, environmental and climate change concerns, concerns about economic growth, and concerns about transaction transparency:

▸▸ **ENERGY COST AND BUILDING EFFICIENCY CONCERNS**. The first public policies relating to building sustainability were born out of concerns over sharp increases in energy costs during the 1970s. Regulations and policies focused on energy efficiency, with the aim to operate both public and private properties more cost-effectively. Energy cost considerations continued as a focus area for building regulations in Europe and Asia into the first half of the 1990s and have again emerged as a core policy focus area around the globe since the early years of this century.

▸▸ **ENVIRONMENTAL AND CLIMATE CHANGE CONCERNS**. The work of the United Nations' Intergovernmental Panel on Climate Change (IPCC), especially Assessment Reports 3 and 4 in 2001 and 2007, respectively, established the threat of global warming and determined that most of the observed increase in global average temperatures since 1950 is very likely due to the observed increase in anthropogenic (manmade) greenhouse gas (GHG) concentrations. (See chapter 1 for a detailed review of the IPCC's work.) The IPCC also has determined that building retrofits to conserve energy and shift energy consumption to environmentally friendly sources could achieve meaningful GHG reductions and be both environmentally and economically beneficial. In the European Union, North America, South Africa, and Asia, recent policies and programs have been shaped to address climate change issues.

The retrofit of Shui On Land Ltd. headquarters on the 25th and 26th floors of Shui On Plaza in Shanghai achieved LEED-CI Silver certification. The aim of each project Shui On Land undertakes is the highest possible LEED rating or the China Ministry of Construction's Evaluation Standard for Green Building rating, whichever is deemed more appropriate for the project.

▸▸ **ECONOMIC GROWTH CONCERNS**. Concerns about economic growth have dominated the public policy front in response to the global economic downturn that began in 2007–2008. As global economies have faltered, the creation of green jobs has been identified as a mechanism for restoring prosperity. A key element of green job creation takes place in the construction, renovation and retrofit of energy-efficient and sustainable buildings.

▸▸ **ECONOMIC TRANSPARENCY**. Growing interest in economic transparency has spurred the global development of regulations to disclose publicly the energy performance of real property, and to make such disclosures a condition of leasing or sale.

As a result of these overarching concerns, national, provincial, and local governments around the world have begun to require or encourage the use of energy-efficient and green building practices in the construction of public and, increasingly, private buildings. Over time, European and Asian nations have typically relied more exclusively than have the United States and Canada on detailed regulations to ensure energy efficiency in the property sector. In the United States and Canada, policy responses have been more likely to include financial incentives to encourage building energy efficiency. This

distinction appears to be blurring, however, in the wake of the global economic emergency of 2008. In response to the sharp economic downturn, public financial incentives for green building retrofit and renovation have been adopted in economic stimulus programs launched in a number of nations, including Australia, France, Germany, the United Kingdom, China, Japan, and South Korea. (For details on green building and economic stimuli, see the sidebar by Mark Bennett and Leanne Tobias.)

The United States utilizes both regulation—frequently linked to voluntary certification standards—and the widespread use of financial incentives to encourage investment in energy-efficient and sustainable properties. Indeed, public incentives for the retrofitting and development of green buildings are on the increase in the United States. Energy-efficient and sustainable buildings are a centerpiece of the 2009 U.S. economic stimulus program, as a means to create economic revitalization and green employment. Additional federal programs proposed by the Obama administration are expected to bolster this effort.

This chapter reviews public policy approaches devised by a variety of nations to encourage building energy efficiency and the use of sustainable design, construction, renovation and retrofit practices. Such

GREEN BUILDINGS:
ADDRESSING THE GLOBAL ECONOMIC EMERGENCY

MARK J. BENNETT AND LEANNE TOBIAS

In the wake of the 2008 global financial emergency, policy makers worldwide have begun to associate green buildings and energy efficiency with economic stimulus and job creation. This trend puts sustainable building renovation on the front lines of economic recovery efforts. As detailed in a recent report written by Nick Robins and Robert Clover of HSBC Global Research, nations around the globe have incorporated green building initiatives into their latest economic stimulus agendas:[1]

▸▸ **European Union.** In addition to recommending heightened standards for building energy efficiency, the European Union has proposed that its member nations reduce property taxes for energy-efficient buildings and reduced value-added taxes for green products and materials. Programs are being adopted on the national level:

- **Germany** has allocated €3 billion ($4.3 billion) for residential renovations to heighten energy efficiency and reduce carbon reductions.

- **France** has awarded €760 million ($1.1 billion) for the energy-efficient renovation of public buildings and €200 million ($287 million) for energy-efficient housing renovation.

- **The United Kingdom** has allocated £350 million ($570 million) for a community energy-saving program, £100 million ($163 million) for building insulation and efficient heating programs, and £60 million ($98 million) for energy-efficient residential retrofits.

▸▸ **Australia.** Australia's A$28.8 billion ($24.2 billion) stimulus program includes funding to provide free ceiling insulation for 2.7 million Australian homes. The program is expected to cut annual energy bills, on average, by A$200 (approximately $170) per house.

▸▸ **China.** China's RMB 4 trillion ($586 billion) economic stimulus program is expected to allocate an estimated 10 percent to renewable energy, energy savings in buildings, and related areas. As well, RMB 9 billion ($1.3 billion) has been allocated to the production of low-income housing, much of which is expected to use energy-saving construction methods.

▸▸ **Japan.** Japan has launched a green economy and social reform plan that includes funding for photovoltaic equipment and energy-efficient appliances.

▸▸ **South Korea.** South Korea's Green New Job Creation Plan focuses heavily on construction-related efforts. Funding equivalent to $6 billion is directed to energy conservation in buildings, schools, and residences. The program is expected to create 2 million green homes and install LED lighting in public facilities. South Korea has also announced a target of producing 5 percent of its energy from renewable sources by 2011.

▸▸ **Canada.** Canada's C$40 billion ($36.7 billion) green stimulus program offers C$300 million (approximately $275 million) for energy-efficient home retrofits. The ecoENERGY Retrofit – Homes program will provide homeowners with grants of up to C$5,000 (approximately $4,600) to offset the cost of making energy efficiency improvements. Credits can be used to improve insulation, upgrade windows and doors, and install energy-efficient furnaces, among other uses. It is estimated that 200,000 homeowners will participate in the program over the next two years. Homeowners eligible for the program may also be able to qualify for home renovation tax credits enacted under Canada's 2009 economic stimulus program.[2]

▸▸ **United States.** The American Reinvestment and Recovery Act (ARRA) provides significant national support for the renovation and development of green buildings. The program allocates $4.5 billion for the green renovation of federal office buildings and supplies $3.2 billion for block grants to states and local governments to finance energy efficiency and green building renovations. The ARRA also provides $6.25 billion for the weatherization of housing occupied by lower-income Americans. Other ARRA monies that can be used for green building support include $3.1 billion for state energy programs and funds for the construction of military facilities as well as housing and schools.

NOTES

1 Nick Robins and Robert Clover, "A Climate for Recovery: The Colour of Stimulus Goes Green," HSBC Global Research, February 25, 2009.

2 Office of Lois Brown, Member of Parliament, "EcoEnergy – Home Retrofit Program Expanded," March 30, 2009, www.loisbrown.ca/EN/8285/85523.

Mark J. Bennett is senior counsel and leads the Climate Change Practice at Miller Canfield. Leanne Tobias, LEED AP, is the founder and managing principal of Malachite LLC.

Figure 7-1

Key Factors in Green Building Public Policy

Country	European Union	South Africa	ASIA — China	Singapore	Taiwan	Thailand
Key Regulatory Plan or Entity	European Performance of Buildings Directive (EPBD)	Various government programs	Five-Year Plan	Building Construction Authority regulations	Bureau of Energy, Construction & Planning Agency	Energy Conservation Promotion A[...]
Key Goals	Address rising energy costs and global warming; implement building energy-efficiency standards and practices	Increase building energy efficiency; reduce waste	Reduce building energy use in urban areas by 50% overall, by 65% in largest four cities; economic stimulus	Increase building energy and water efficiency; manage climate change emissions	Reduce energy consumption and fuel expense	Encourage energy efficiency; manag[...] energy demand
Areas of Focus	Commercial new construction and major renovations	Public buildings, utility companies	Urban buildings, public buildings, housing	Commercial buildings, hotels	Commercial: new construction, major renovations	Commercial buildings, factories
National	■	■	■	■	■	■
Provincial, State, Local	■		■			
Mandatory Components	■	■	■	■	■	■
Voluntary Components	■			■	■	■
New Construction	■		■	■	■	■
Renovation	■	■	■	■	■	■
Building Practices	■	■	■	■	■	
Energy Efficiency	■	■	■	■	■	■
Heat	■		■			
Water Heating	■					
Cooling	■		■			
Ventilation	■		■	■		
Lighting	■	■	■	■		
Appliances	■	■			■	■
Green Energy Sourcing					■	
Water Consumption				■	■	
Financial Incentives		■				■
Favorable Lending						■
Tax Incentives		■				■
Density Bonus						
Grant Programs		■				
Utility Partnerships		■				
Inspection Required	■					
Performance Information	Distributed to owners, tenants		Annual energy reports, energy use audits			
Required Disclosure of Building Energy Performance	EPBD: enforced upon sale; UK: enforced; Germany: phasing in		Enforced: Annual energy reports, energy audits for government organizations			Enforced: energy audits for government buildings
Future Focus (proposed)	Apply EPBD to all renovations, regardless of size	Local energy efficiency initiatives	Water conservation			

Figure 7-2

Summary of Core Policy Areas

Country	European Union	South Africa	ASIA — China	Singapore	Taiwan	Thailand
Green Building Practices	■	■	■	■	■	
Energy Efficiency	■	■	■	■	■	■
Water Efficiency				■	■	
Financial Incentives		■				■

Brazil	Mexico	Canada: National	Canada: British Columbia	Canada: Ontario	U.S.: National
National Building Energy labeling, PROCEL	National Housing Authority, Green Plan	Primarily provincial and local programs; national stimulus spending	Province of British Columbia Government, 2008 Energy Efficiency Act	Province of Ontario Green Energy & Green Economy Act	Energy Policy Act of 2005, EISA of 2007, Executive Order 13423, ARRA of 2009, national climate change proposal
Raise building efficiency; establish efficiency standards for electrical appliances	Increase housing affordability and quality through sustainable design	Energy efficiency and sustainability at the regional level	Increase energy efficiency, expand the use of building energy assessments	Create a smart power grid, provide low- or no-interest loans to encourage renewable power	Increase green building practices and energy efficiency in public and private buildings; economic stimulus
Nonindustrial commercial buildings, electrical appliances	Residential	Regional standards for green building, home retrofits	Commercial buildings, multifamily, single-family residential	Public sector buildings	Commercial: new construction, major renovations; residential: weatherization of lower-income housing
	■				■
		■	■	■	■
			■	■	■
■	■			■	■
■	■			■	■
			■	■	■
■	■		■	■	■
■	■		■	■	■
			■		
■			■	■	
			■	■	
			■		
■			■	■	■
				■	■
■			■		■
					■
			■		■
					■
				■	
				Five-year performance reviews, sales transactions	
building energy labeling being phased in			Phasing in: building energy assessments	Proposed: five-year performance reviews, disclosure upon sale	DC, WA, CA: phasing in; federal government: proposed, 2009 legislation
residential energy rating (2010)			GHG reduction targets and plans	Job creation	Job creation

Brazil	Mexico	Canada: National	Canada: British Columbia	Canada: Ontario	U.S.: National
■		■	■	■	
■		■	■	■	
		■			
■		■	■	■	

policies were frequently created to address new building construction but are rapidly being adapted to address the existing building segment. Although the review is not comprehensive—the field of green building policy is fluid and changing rapidly—it illustrates the growing importance of government initiatives in shaping green outcomes in the real estate sector. Policies are grouped by region, and attention is given to both regulatory requirements and the use of financial and other incentives. (For a summary of key policies by region and nation, see figures 7-1 and 7-2.) Voluntary green building certification systems, the use of which are sometimes mandated by governments for public and, increasingly, private construction, are discussed here with respect to their interaction with public policy. For a more complete discussion of voluntary certification systems, see chapter 2.

EUROPEAN UNION

The European Union has developed a shared regulatory framework, the Energy Performance of Buildings Directive (EPBD), to shape policy on building energy efficiency. This section details the key provisions of the directive, examines its implementation in Germany and the United Kingdom, and summarizes proposed revisions.

European Energy Performance of Buildings Directive Requirements

The EPBD was adopted by the European Parliament and the Council of the European Union in 2002 in response to concerns about rising energy costs and the emergence of global warming as an environmental threat. The EPBD has created a regulatory framework to implement building energy efficiency standards and practices for new construction and major renovations of buildings throughout the European Union. Intended to be enacted at the national or regional levels by member governments, the EPBD establishes minimum energy performance standards for

new buildings larger than 1,000 square meters (10,764 square feet) in area. Major renovations are defined as renovations affecting more than 25 percent of a building's area or costing more than 25 percent of the building's value, excluding the value of the underlying land.

▸▸ **ENERGY EFFICIENCY REQUIREMENTS.** The EPBD includes minimum standards for energy consumption in all major building systems, including heating, hot-water heating, cooling, ventilation, and lighting. Recommended energy efficiency standards have been set for new construction and renovation projects in accordance with building type, location, building age and function, and outdoor and indoor climate conditions.[1]

▸▸ **INSPECTION REQUIREMENTS.** The EPBD establishes minimum standards for regular inspection of air-conditioning systems with outputs in excess of 12 kW and boilers with outputs in excess of 20 kW. Boilers with outputs in excess of 100 kW are to be inspected at two- to four-year intervals. In addition, owners of boilers older than 15 years are to be given recommendations on the replacement or modification of the system, or on alternative energy-efficient heating solutions. All EPBD inspections and recommendations are to be carried out by independent qualified or accredited experts.[2] Germany has been a leader in the adoption of building energy performance standards and inspection requirements under the EPBD framework (for details, see the sidebar by Leanne Tobias).

▸▸ **ENERGY PERFORMANCE CERTIFICATES (EPCs).** The EPBD establishes a framework for the use of EPCs as a condition for the sale and rental of newly constructed or existing properties. The framework requires new owners or tenants to be supplied with a copy of the property's EPC, measuring the performance of the building relative to legal or benchmark reference values. Certificates are to be updated at least every ten years and are to be accompanied by recommendations for cost-

IMPLEMENTATION OF THE ENERGY PERFORMANCE OF BUILDINGS DIRECTIVE IN GERMANY

LEANNE TOBIAS

Germany has been a leader in the adoption of building energy performance standards and in the implementation of inspection protocols to ensure that standards are maintained. While many of these requirements predated the European Union's EPBD, Germany has used the EPBD to enhance its regulation of building energy performance.

Germany first introduced regulations on building energy efficiency in 1976, pursuant to the Energy Saving Act. The statute established standards on thermal insulation and the efficiency and energy usage of heating, ventilation, and water systems, and required that heating and hot water be billed on the basis of individual consumption. Boiler inspections have been required since 1978, with replacement typically mandated if the boiler does not meet statutory standards. Energy efficiency standards for existing buildings were introduced in 1984, requiring that energy usage could not exceed 140 percent of usage in similar, newly constructed buildings.

The 2002 adoption of the EPBD by the European Union led to the strengthening of Germany's building energy statutes:

▸ **The Energy Saving Act of 2002** extended energy efficiency standards to residential air-conditioning and built-in lighting systems, and required that new buildings and certain major refurbishments measure compliance by calculated demand methodologies that are consistent with the EPBD. Other buildings are required to measure energy consumption either by a calculated demand method or by measured consumption, calculated on the basis of the most recent three years of utility bills.

▸ **The Energy Saving Act of 2007** adopted building reference standards to measure the energy efficiency of nonresidential air-conditioning and built-in lighting systems. The 2007 Act also refined qualifications for energy efficiency inspectors for commercial and residential properties. Commercial inspections can be performed by architects and engineers and by other scientists with a building-related field of study who have completed special training. Residential inspections can be performed by craftsmen who have completed special training.

▸ **Buildings were required** to obtain and display EPCs by 2002 (although they were not required to be made available to renters or buyers). The provision of EPCs to building purchasers and renters and the display of certificates in public buildings has been subject to a phased introduction, with the oldest residential buildings required to comply by July 2008, remaining residential buildings required to comply by January 2009, and nonresidential buildings required to comply by July 2009.

▸ **Germany has committed** to ongoing improvements in building energy efficiency. As of this writing, standards for building energy efficiency are expected to be increased by 30 percent in 2009 and by an additional 30 percent in 2012.

SOURCE

Horst-P. Schettler-Köhler, Federal Office for Building and Regional Planning, Germany, "Implementation of the EPBD in Germany: Status and Future Planning, March 2008," European Union, Environmental Performance of Buildings Directive, Country Review P 73, April 18, 2008.

Leanne Tobias, LEED AP, is the founder and managing principal of Malachite LLC.

effective improvement of the building's energy performance. The EPC must be posted in buildings occupied by public authorities or by institutions providing public services to a large number of people. Regulated properties must post information on the range of recommended and current indoor temperatures and, when appropriate, other relevant climatic conditions. The United Kingdom has pioneered the adoption of EPCs in connection with purchase, sale, and rental transactions (see the sidebar by Mark Bennett and Leanne Tobias), and Germany is phasing in similar transaction requirements. Requirements for such certificates have begun to be adopted in the United States, as discussed later in this chapter.[3]

Proposed Revisions

Proposed revisions to the EPBD were endorsed in a vote of the European Parliament in April 2009, with final provisions expected to be approved by the end of 2009. The proposed revisions include the following:

ENERGY PERFORMANCE CERTIFICATES IN THE UNITED KINGDOM

MARK J. BENNETT AND LEANNE TOBIAS

The United Kingdom has led EU nations in the use of EPCs. Buildings account for close to half of the country's carbon emissions, and commercial buildings account for approximately 25 percent.[1] Since October 2008, all properties in the United Kingdom—residential, commercial, and public—have been required to produce an EPC when built, bought, sold, or rented. Larger government buildings must also display EPCs. The phase-in of the commercial building requirements began in 2007. Initially, the means of executing the EPC process were unclear to many building owners, and an insufficient number of independent assessment professionals were in place to carry out EPC inspections and evaluations. The owners of smaller properties were especially concerned that they had neither the technical expertise nor the financial means to comply with the requirements.[2] After many fits and starts which included delayed implementation of the requirement, the EPC disclosure obligation is now in place and is being replicated in other countries.

The United Kingdom's ultimately successful experience with the implementation of EPCs offers several lessons for other governments desiring to implement similar requirements:

▸▸ **Issue clear,** broadly agreed-to standards for measuring building energy performance.

▸▸ **Work with professional organizations** to ensure that sufficient qualified, independent energy auditors or other professionals are trained to implement the system. (The EU requirements mandate the use of independent inspectors.)

▸▸ **Alternatively,** work to ensure that public building inspectors are trained to implement the required energy efficiency inspections.

▸▸ **Allow for sufficient lead time** to provide for smooth implementation of the inspection process.

The United Kingdom is also implementing other aspects of the EPBD. Existing air-conditioning systems with output of more than 250 kW were required to comply with energy efficiency inspection requirements by January 4, 2009. Energy efficiency inspections of all remaining air-conditioning systems with output of more than 12 kW must be completed by January 4, 2011.[3]

NOTES

1 Communities and Local Government, "Energy Performance of Buildings," www.communities.gov.uk/planningandbuilding/theenvironment/energyperformance.

2 "Chaos Feared over Introduction of Energy-Efficiency Certificates," *The Scotsman,* April 14, 2008.

3 Communities and Local Government, "Energy Performance of Buildings," www.communities.gov.uk/planningandbuilding/theenvironment/energyperformance, www.communities.gov.uk/planningandbuilding/theenvironment/energyperformance/publiccommercialbuildings.

Mark J. Bennett is senior counsel and leads the Climate Change Practice at Miller Canfield. Leanne Tobias, LEED AP, is the founder and managing principal of Malachite LLC.

▸▸ **EXTENDING EPBD REQUIREMENTS** to additional building renovations, regardless of property size. Proposed revisions would require compliance of all buildings in which a renovation covered more than 25 percent of the building's area or renovations cost more than 20 percent of the building's value.

▸▸ **REQUIRING THAT ALL PUBLIC BUILDINGS** of more than 250 square meters (2,691 square feet) display EPCs.

▸▸ **ENCOURAGING THE CREATION** of low- or net-zero-energy buildings through development and retrofit standards and practices. (See chapter 8 for additional discussion of net-zero-energy requirements.)

▸▸ **EXPANDING THE DEFINITION** of independent energy efficiency experts to include energy savings companies and energy agencies, in order to expand the number of technically qualified experts and encourage competition.[4]

The EU forecasts anticipate that a revised directive would result in the following minimum impacts:

▸▸ **ENERGY SAVINGS** of 60 to 80 million tons of oil equivalent per year by 2020, for a 5 to 6 percent reduction in the European Union's energy use in 2020.

▸▸ **CO₂ SAVINGS** of 160 to 210 megatons per year, for a 4 to 5 percent reduction of the European Union's CO_2 emissions in 2020.

▸▸ **THE CREATION OF** 280,000 to 450,000 potential new jobs by 2020, principally in the construction sector and for energy certifiers and auditors and inspectors of heating and air-conditioning systems. Additional new jobs—not quantified in the EU impact assessment—are also expected to be created by the need for products, components, and materials used or installed in better-performing buildings.[5]

AFRICA

South Africa has led the African continent in the development of public and utility initiatives to promote energy efficiency and minimize adverse climate change. While coal reserves are plentiful in South Africa, economic and population growth have led to a shortage of power generation capacity, a problem that has intensified since 2006.

South Africa adopted national energy efficiency targets in 2005 which, if achieved, would reduce projected 2015 energy use by 12 percent. A national energy regulatory body was established in 2006.[6] While progress toward national goals has been uneven, numerous initiatives have begun to be implemented to support national energy reduction targets:

▸▸ **THE GOVERNMENT** has begun a program to perform energy-efficient retrofits of the nation's 106,000 public buildings. Some 4,000 buildings had reportedly been renovated by the close of 2008.[7]

▸▸ **DEMAND-SIDE MANAGEMENT PROGRAMS** have been implemented through Eskom, the dominant South African utility. The programs, introduced in 2007, included 50 percent capital subsidies for commercial energy efficiency retrofits, retailer exchange programs of incandescent for compact fluorescent bulbs, and consumer incentives to encourage the purchase of solar hot-water heaters. As of late 2008, subsidies for commercial energy efficiency programs had been suspended because of the economic downturn, but they may resume.[8]

▸▸ **NATIONAL TAX AND REGULATORY POLICIES** in South Africa have increasingly addressed building energy issues. In 2008, national tariffs were imposed on energy use on the basis of volume and time of use. The tariffs are intended to reduce electricity demand at peak times. Users with monthly consumption of 1,000 kWh or more will be required to install smart meters and abide by time-of-use restrictions by January 1, 2012.[9]

▸▸ **THE NATIONAL BUDGET** proposed in 2009 would increase public spending for energy efficiency and introduce tax incentives for the commercial purchase of energy-efficient equipment. The budget also proposes a new tax on incandescent lighting and a tax increase on plastic bags.[10]

Additional energy efficiency initiatives are being undertaken at the local level. The city of Cape Town has introduced a public-private energy efficiency initiative to encourage the retrofitting of commercial buildings. Results gathered from the first group of program participants indicated average building energy savings of 27 percent.[11].

ASIA

Several governments in Asia have taken an active role in the creation of regulations and green building rating systems for construction and renovation. These rating systems establish both mandatory minimum performance for regulated buildings and voluntary standards for unregulated properties and for benchmarking higher levels of green performance.

China

China, the world's most rapidly developing construction economy, has made energy-efficient building technologies a centerpiece of its 11th Five-Year Plan, which spans the period from 2006 to 2010. The plan seeks to reduce national energy consumption by approximately 20 percent, with some 40 percent of the savings expected to come from the building sector. The plan seeks to cut building energy use in urban areas by 50 percent by 2010, relative to a 1980 baseline. The plan also seeks to cut building energy use by 65 percent by 2010 in China's four largest cities: Beijing, Shanghai, Tianjin, and Chongqing.[12]

Work toward achieving China's goals for building energy efficiency began in 2005, with the issuance of mandatory energy efficiency standards for heating, cooling, ventilation, and lighting in public buildings. In 2006 a government-created voluntary green building rating system was issued. In 2008, the government issued a directive asking all government-funded organizations to supervise and audit energy use and file annual energy reports.[13]

By 2008, China's Ministry of Construction had developed estimates suggesting that, as of 2007, 97 percent of all new urban projects were complying with the energy efficiency standards at the project design phase and 71 percent were complying at the construction phase.[14] Additional progress to reduce building energy consumption is to be attained by retrofitting public buildings. In this sphere, much remains to be done: only 5 percent of public buildings had been retrofitted as of 2007, and the retrofitting process is not expected to be completed until 2020.[15]

China continues to build on its energy conservation goals. A comprehensive energy law is slated for adoption in 2010. The nation's 12th Five-Year Plan, for the period 2011 to 2015, is expected to establish water conservation goals and to extend building energy efficiency efforts to rural areas.[16] Challenges facing the nation in implementing building energy efficiency objectives include shortages of materials and of qualified engineering and construction professionals.[17] In response to these pressures, the Chinese government is considering the introduction of financial incentives to encourage energy-efficient construction and housing retrofits.[18]

Singapore

Singapore's sustainable building rating system, Green Mark, was established in 2005 by the Building and Construction Authority, the governmental entity that regulates property development and renovation. Green Mark was designed to enhance building energy efficiency, reduce energy costs, and manage climate change emissions. The rating system establishes sustainable construction criteria in the areas of energy and water efficiency, indoor environmental quality and environmental protection, and innovation. Development and substantial renovation projects must meet sustainable site and project development criteria, while existing buildings must meet criteria for green building management and operations. Voluntary sustainability ratings can be attained at the Certified, Gold, Gold Plus, and Platinum levels.[19]

Green Mark standards are used to define mandatory minimum requirements for energy efficiency and occupant comfort. All commercial buildings in Singapore with floor areas in excess of 500 square meters (5,382 square feet) must meet energy efficiency prerequisites for building envelope, roof, and lighting and air-conditioning systems, and must comply with air leakage and ventilation standards. Air-conditioning systems must be equipped with switches, timers, or automatic controls that permit shutoff when warranted. Submetering of differentiated building services and users is mandatory. All hotels must be equipped with devices that automatically turn off air conditioning and lighting in unoccupied rooms.[20]

Taiwan

As has been the case in China and Singapore, Taiwan's national government has been involved heavily in the development of building energy efficiency and green rating systems.

▸▸ BUILDING ENERGY EFFICIENCY STANDARDS.

Taiwan adopted energy efficiency requirements for nonresidential air-conditioned buildings in 1995 and for air-conditioned residential buildings in 2007. The national standards, initially developed to reduce energy consumption and fuel expense, stipulate maximum cooling levels for building envelopes based on property type and local climate zone. The regulations were drafted by Taiwan's Bureau of Energy and its Construction and Planning Agency. As of 2006, over 80 percent of new construction projects complied with the statutes. The Bureau of Energy has initiated an Energy Labeling Program for appliances and office equipment and has announced voluntary energy benchmarking for many types of buildings.[21] Taiwan has also been a pioneer in the use of net metering to encourage the adoption of solar energy technologies: the government-operated Taiwan Power Company is required to purchase surplus solar power from rooftop photovoltaic arrays.[22]

▸▸ EEWH GREEN BUILDING RATING SYSTEM.

Taiwan's Ecology, Energy Saving, Waste Reduction, and Health (EEWH) rating system—Asia's first green building certification protocol—was launched in 1999. The program was developed by the government's Architecture and Building Research Institute. EEWH was designed for subtropical and tropical climates and focuses on Taiwanese priorities, including the conservation of water. Green building design is mandatory for new and substantially remodeled government buildings. As well, government-backed projects worth NT$50 million ($1.5 million) or more and projects receiving government subsidies that account for 50 percent or more of their total

The green refurbishment of Trevor Pearcey House, head office for Australian Ethical Investment in Bruce, Australia, received a 6-Star Green Star rating from the Green Building Council of Australia, the highest rating under the Green Star protocol.

budget must attain satisfactory credit scores in four of the nine EEWH categories. A growing number of private buildings are seeking EEWH certification. As of April 2007 some 170 buildings had received EEWH certification and 1,170 properties were candidates.[23]

Thailand

Thailand, a net importer of the majority of its energy, moved early to adopt a comprehensive energy regulation framework. A comprehensive energy demand management program was instituted in 1991, and the 1992 Energy Conservation Promotion Act established a framework for setting minimum energy standards for buildings and facilities, and for energy labeling. Energy labeling for refrigerators and air-conditioning systems was introduced in 1995. Energy audits of government buildings were launched in 1997. Thailand also mandates energy efficiency standards for designated factories and commercial buildings. The standards were adopted to reduce energy usage and expense.

In contrast to most Asian nations, Thailand has also begun to provide public financial incentives to encourage energy efficiency. In 2003, the government introduced a public-private revolving loan fund for building improvements for key industrial and commercial facilities. Under the credit facility, which has been expanded since its inception, loans are provided by the national government in collaboration with 11 banking institutions; government support helps to reduce loan interest rates.[24]

Thailand also has established a tax incentive program for energy efficiency investments that achieve required savings and payback periods. In its initial form, the program provided a 25 percent corporate tax reduction for those improvements that saved at least B25,000 ($735) annually and achieved payback in seven years or less. In December 2007, the program was revised to include renewable energy investments, to increase allowable investment amounts under the program, and to permit investors to deduct achieved energy savings attributable to the improvements from corporate taxes owed.[25]

LATIN AMERICA

Latin American countries' policies on green buildings are being shaped by interest in conserving fossil fuels, achieving economic growth through the development of indigenous biofuel and alternative fuel industries, housing rapidly growing populations, and combating climate change. A January 2009 meeting organized by the United Nations Environment Programme and the Dominican Republic's State Secretariat for the Environment and Natural Resources convened environment ministers from Latin American and Caribbean countries to discuss the future of sustainable building in the region. The meeting concluded with a decision to promote sustainable building practices throughout Latin America and the Caribbean, with an emphasis on sustainable housing, awareness building, incentive implementation, and risk assessments for disaster-prone areas. Green building practices were recognized for their beneficial effects on environmental quality and climate change and for their potential to enhance the quality of life in the region.[26] The governments of Brazil and Mexico have been leaders within the region on green building and building energy efficiency matters.

Brazil

Brazil launched PROCEL, a program of national efficiency standards for electrical appliances, in 1993. The standards, initially voluntary, have since been made mandatory and apply to refrigerators, freezers, washing machines, and air conditioners as well as other consumer electric appliances. PROCEL extended mandatory efficiency requirements to computer monitors, DVDs, set-top boxes, and television sets in July 2008.[27]

Brazil completed a national initiative to develop standards for building energy performance in 2008. A national building energy labeling scheme for nonindustrial commercial buildings, linked to the standards, was proposed in early 2009. Brazil's proposed building energy label would rate a property's overall energy efficiency and would supply subsidiary efficiency ratings for the building envelope, the lighting system, and the air-conditioning system. Ratings would be based on the bioclimatic zone in which the property is located and would be determined on the basis of assessments conducted by auditors from government-accredited inspection laboratories. The labeling scheme would initially be voluntary. A proposed energy efficiency rating system for residential properties is expected to be released in 2010.[28]

Mexico

Mexico's green building policies have been shaped substantially by the nation's housing needs. Between 2000 and 2030, household formation is expected to increase by 800,000 per year. As a consequence of the burgeoning demand for housing combined with the need to replace substandard units, the Mexican government has committed to produce a million housing units annually from 2010 to 2030. Energy efficiency and sustainable design and construction are regarded as vehicles to increase housing affordability and improve environmental and housing quality.[29]

Since 2004, Mexico has implemented 16 official standards related to the efficiency of appliances and building components, including lightbulbs, electric home appliances, air-conditioning systems, pumping mechanisms, and insulation. Pursuant to a 2006 housing law, Conavi, Mexico's national housing authority, has created code standards on home energy efficiency and the management of graywater, sewage, rainwater, and solid waste disposal. The standards are intended to move Mexico toward a more sustainable home construction industry.[30] A coalition of government agencies and private industries signed a memorandum of understanding in early 2009 to develop a joint action plan to achieve building energy efficiency at the state and municipal levels throughout Mexico. Signatories to the memorandum included the National Commission for Energy Efficiency, a unit of the Energy Secretariat; the National Network of State Energy Commissions; and the Association for Energy Efficiency in Buildings, an association for private businesses from the building sector.[31]

Mexico City has been in the forefront of local government initiatives on sustainability. In late 2008, Mexico City announced plans for a $5.5 billion Green Plan. Under the plan, the city has begun to finance the sustainable renovation of multifamily housing with such enhancements as vertical gardens, solar panels, and rainwater filters. The Green Plan also calls for the installation of more than 500,000 green roofs by 2012 and the development of a local green certification standard for offices and residences. Initially, the certification standard (still under development as of early 2009) would be voluntary; buildings that achieve certification would be eligible for property tax discounts of up to 25 percent.[32]

CANADA

Canada regulates buildings primarily at the provincial and municipal levels, and combines building regulation with financial incentives to promote energy efficiency and associated environmental objectives. Numerous Canadian cities, including Alberta, Calgary, Edmonton, and Vancouver, require that municipal buildings meet Leadership in Energy and Environmental Design (LEED) requirements. In December 2008, Toronto adopted the Toronto Green Standard, which imposes minimum energy efficiency and sustainability standards on residential and commercial construction. Properties that meet more stringent "Tier 2" requirements receive performance incentives, including reductions in development fees.[33]

Canadian provinces have also adopted or proposed significant green building programs. Among them:

▸▸ **BRITISH COLUMBIA**. The province has enacted a comprehensive green building code for commercial buildings, homes, and multi-family buildings of fewer than five stories. The code encompasses energy efficiency and water conservation standards. British Columbia's 2006 and 2008 Energy Efficiency Acts also raised energy efficiency standards for furnaces, windows, fluorescent lighting ballasts, and other building components.[34] In 2008, the province introduced a $60 million, three-year Efficiency Incentive Program of grants and sales tax exemptions to expand the use of building energy assessments, promote the use of energy conservation equipment, retrofit provincial public sector buildings, and promote the use of solar energy and other renewable technologies.[35] By May 31, 2010, local governments in British Columbia are required to include GHG reduction targets and supporting policy proposals in official community plans. GHG emission reduction plans must be adopted at the regional level by May 31, 2011.[36] The planning requirements support an initiative to reduce GHG levels throughout the province by 33 percent by 2020 and by 80 percent by 2050, relative to a 2007 baseline.[37]

▸▸ **ONTARIO**. The province unveiled a proposed Green Energy and Green Economy Act (Bill 150) in February 2009. The plan would create a smart power grid and provide low- or no-interest loans to encourage the generation of

The energy-efficient retrofit of 1801 McGill College in downtown Montreal was awarded BOMA Go Green certification, since rebranded BOMA BESt—Building Environmental Standards.

renewable power. Reviews of building energy efficiency would be required at five-year intervals, and new public sector buildings would be required to meet the Silver standards of the U.S. Green Building Council's LEED certification. Incentives would be provided to upgrade the energy efficiency of property, and property owners would be required to provide energy labeling in connection with sales transactions.[38] All appliances sold in the province would be required to meet Energy Star standards.[39] The proposed legislation is estimated to create 50,000 jobs throughout Ontario in three years.[40]

UNITED STATES

Like Canada, the United States—in contrast to many EU and Asian nations—typically regulates buildings at the local and state levels, rather than at the national level.[41] As a result, the United States is typified by diversity in green building and energy efficiency regulation, although the federal government has been influential in the mainstreaming of green building practices and is becoming more so. While the U.S. government has not traditionally undertaken a direct role in building regulation, it has served as an advocate and leader in the use of green building design and construction methods, which has in turn accelerated the national dissemination of sustainable building practices.

Green building regulations in the United States have most frequently been linked to the mandated use of green building certification systems rather than to the revision of local codes to include green standards. Completion of Standard 189.1, a model U.S. green building code undergoing revision in 2009, would likely lead to the increased adoption of code-based green building regulations, thereby expanding and accelerating the application of green building practices for renovation, retrofit, and new construction throughout the country.

The United States also has made greater use of financial incentives to encourage green building development than have other nations. State, local, and utility program incentives have become increasingly available for the financing of green and energy-efficient construction. As well, the 2009 American Recovery and Reinvestment Act (ARRA), more commonly referred to as the federal stimulus program, offers heightened federal financial support for the renovation and construction of energy-efficient and green real estate.

Federal Regulations

The federal government was an early champion of green building practices. The U.S. General Services Administration (GSA), the agency that develops and manages most federal government real estate, requires that new construction and major renovations be built to a certified LEED standard and encourages the use of the Silver LEED standard for federal projects.[42]

Federal requirements enacted in 2005 and in 2007 mandated additional energy and sustainability improvements at the federal level. The Energy Policy Act of 2005 mandated that U.S. federal buildings, when it is cost-effective over their life cycle, be developed to meet energy efficiency standards at least 30 percent more stringent than the applicable International Energy Conservation Code (IECC) or American Society of Heating, Refrigerating, and Air-Conditioning Engineers (ASHRAE) standards, as well as water conservation standards. The Energy Policy Act requires that the federal government apply sustainable design principles to the siting, design, and construction of all new and replacement buildings.[43] The Act also requires federal agencies, when it is cost-effective, to procure equipment—including building appliances—that is certified under the Energy Star program or the Federal Energy Management Program, as well as to adopt specific energy use reduction goals, and, when practicable, to use advanced meters or metering devices to measure energy use.[44]

In January 2007, President George Bush signed Executive Order 13423, which requires that federal agencies improve energy efficiency and reduce GHG emissions by 3 percent annually through the end of 2015, or 30 percent by the end of 2015, relative to each agency's 2003 baseline. For major renovations, the energy cost budget should be 20 percent below the (pre-renovation) 2003 baseline.

The Energy Independence and Security Act (EISA), signed into law in December 2007, extended energy efficiency requirements to space leased by the federal government. By the close of 2010, most such premises in excess of 10,000 square feet will be required to meet energy efficiency standards under the Energy Star program or undergo an energy efficiency retrofit within a year of federal occupancy.[45] The new leasing requirement will serve as further impetus to private developers and commercial real estate owners to build and renovate green.

State Regulations

State governments have been following in the footsteps of the federal government. As of 2009, 41 states and the District of Columbia have established sustainability requirements in the management of their real estate portfolios with an emphasis on energy efficiency targets which escalate over time.[46] For example, Texas requires that state buildings reduce annual electricity consumption over a six-year period beginning September 1, 2007, by at least 5 percent per year.[47]

The LEED rating system has been used frequently by state governments as a standard for the construction of state government buildings. At the close of 2008, 23 states and the District of Columbia had adopted LEED to guide the design and construction of state facilities.[48] The most frequently mandated standard is LEED Silver or its equivalent. An executive order signed in Florida in 2007 requires that all state new construction projects strive for the LEED Platinum rating, the highest available. Florida also requires that all new state office leases be in Energy Star–compliant space.[49]

Increasingly, state regulations relating to energy efficiency and the use of sustainable practices have been extended to the private sector. Connecticut has enacted green building code requirements that will be applied in 2009 to new, private sector construction projects of $5 million or more and to private sector renovations of $2 million or more in 2010.[50] California's Green Building Standards Code, approved in July 2008, requires the reduction of water and energy use in buildings through landscaping, appliance efficiency, and the use of green building design principles and recycled materials. The code became mandatory throughout the state in 2009 and applies to new construction and major renovations.[51]

State governments also are beginning to mandate energy reporting requirements for private buildings, under statutes similar to the European Commission's EPBD. In California AB 1103, signed into law in 2007 and modeled largely after the EPBD, requires that electric utilities develop and maintain records of energy consumption data for all nonresidential buildings to which they provide service, starting in 2009. Effective January 1, 2010, the statute requires building owners or operators to provide benchmarking data to prospective buyers, lessees, or lenders.

Similar energy disclosure requirements are in various stages of legislative approval in several states. Disclosure obligations of this type are also being phased in between 2010 and 2013 for larger commercial buildings in the District of Columbia under the Clean and Affordable Energy Act of 2008.[52] The Senate in the state of Washington recently passed a bill with language virtually identical to California's bill, to take effect in January 2011.[53]

Local Regulations

As of 2009, at least 186 U.S. localities have adopted green building regulations.[54] The dominant regulatory construct has been to require green standards. Green requirements have been mandated most frequently for the construction of public buildings, but a growing trend has been to impose green or energy efficiency standards on new, private construction. Early adopters of such laws included Boston; Washington, D.C.; and Salt Lake City. More recently, green building laws that affect private construction have been enacted in Baltimore (summer 2007); Annapolis, Maryland (March 2008); and Dallas (April 2008), among others. These statutes typically require that new private construction, typically in excess of a minimum square footage standard, be constructed in accordance with LEED or equivalent standards.

In a statute enacted in August 2008, San Francisco amended its building code in order to conserve energy and water and to reduce GHG emissions. The revisions adopt LEED certification requirements for all new construction and renovated space in commercial buildings of 25,000 square feet or more. New commercial construction and renovation projects of 25,000 square feet or more must achieve LEED Silver certification from 2009 through 2011 and LEED Gold certification from 2012 onward. Buildings in this class must also comply with requirements for recycling and composting, water-efficient landscaping, water use reduction, construction debris management, and stormwater management. The ordinance also imposes sustainability requirements on mid-size commercial construction (construction of at least 5,000 gross square feet) and on certain residential construction.

Comprehensive building code reform to incorporate green and energy-efficient practices into municipal regulation is expected to be the next important trend in the green building arena. Like San Francisco,

Washington, D.C., has amended the city's building code for properties that must comply with the jurisdiction's Green Building Act. As of 2009, a model municipal green building code, Standard 189.1, is being developed by ASHRAE, the Illuminating Engineering Society of North America (IESNA), and the U.S. Green Building Council, with additional representation from business, government, utility, and university organizations. The completion and dissemination of Section 189.1 is expected to spur substantial local adoption of green building codes—as is the federal economic stimulus program enacted in February 2009 (discussed later).

State and Local Incentives for Green Construction

Increasing regulatory requirements have been accompanied by a growing number of state and local financial incentives for green and energy-efficient construction. Incentives at the state and local level to encourage green or energy efficient development include a variety of programs:

▸▸ **UTILITY AND OTHER REBATE PROGRAMS**, to offset the purchase costs of energy efficiency and renewable energy equipment. Such programs, provided most frequently through local utility systems, give property owners a valuable incentive to replace or upgrade existing systems or to install energy-efficient or renewable equipment in new construction. As of early 2009, utilities and governmental entities in 46 states offer rebate programs for energy efficiency expenditures for lighting, furnaces, boilers, heat pumps and programmable thermostats, HVAC systems, control systems, and weatherization, among other uses.[55] Programs in 43 states and the District of Columbia offer rebates for a variety of renewable technologies including solar water heating, solar photovoltaic systems, geothermal heat pumps, and wind technologies.[56]

▸ **GRANT AND LOAN PROGRAMS**. Utility or governmental grant programs to promote energy efficiency technologies are underway in 22 states, and loan programs are offered in 42 states. As of early 2009, grant programs to encourage the use of renewable technologies were underway in 27 states, and state governments, local governments, or utilities in 40 states provided loan programs. Among permitted uses for these programs are project design and planning, equipment purchase, and construction and installation costs.[57]

As discussed in chapter 5, on-bill financing is a new public policy tool that allows loans for energy efficiency upgrades to be repaid through charges on property tax or utility bills. Because repayment runs with the land, loan repayment schedules can be longer—and hence more affordable—than would be the case with a conventional loan. Loan assumption by a new buyer is automatic when the property changes hands. If a property owner defaults, the new buyer must make the loan current upon taking title to the property and is required to assume the loan. On-bill financing programs have been adopted in Berkeley, California; Boulder, Colorado; and other jurisdictions. (See chapter 5 for additional information.)

▸ **TAX INCENTIVES**. Tax incentives to encourage the use of sustainable construction are widespread.

• **PROPERTY TAX INCENTIVES**. According to the Database of State Incentives for Renewable Energy, 34 states have approved the enactment of property tax incentives, including exemptions or reductions in assessed values, to encourage sustainable development or the use of alternative energy technologies. Such incentives confer an operating cost advantage on properties that utilize sustainable construction or alternative energy systems. Of these, 32 states grant incentives to commercial properties or permit local governments to do so.[58]

• **CORPORATE TAX INCENTIVES**. Twenty-four states provide income tax credits or deductions to commercial property owners who install alternative energy systems or construct green buildings. These incentives offset the development costs of building sustainable projects. Programs enacted in Maryland, New York, and Oregon are geared specifically to green projects that meet standards established at the state level.[59]

▸ **DENSITY BONUSES**. As reported by the American Institute of Architects (AIA), a number of localities confer density bonuses for sustainable construction. Possible approaches include height bonuses, floor/area ratio bonuses, reductions in landscaping requirements, or the ability to count vegetated roofs as landscaping or open space. Density bonuses are typically granted for achieving mandated green building levels. Seattle confers density bonuses on buildings downtown that are certified at the LEED Silver level or better. Arlington, Virginia, links the density incentive to the level of LEED certification achieved; permitted density increases with the level of LEED certification.[60] The granting of a density bonus is valued by developers and investors because it permanently increases rentable area, cash flow, and sale price. Density bonuses can also be cost-effective for local governments because they do not entail financial outlays—and, indeed, may increase tax revenues by increasing the amount of rentable space subject to property taxation.

▸ **EXPEDITED PERMITTING AND FEE WAIVERS**. A number of jurisdictions have enacted ordinances to streamline permitting processes or to waive certain development fees for sustainable construction. An expedited permitting program has been enacted by the state of Hawaii, which requires county authorities to

streamline local approvals for green projects seeking certification at the LEED Silver level or higher. Chicago and Santa Monica, California, also have enacted expedited permitting programs for projects seeking LEED certification. Other jurisdictions, including Asheville, North Carolina, have waived or reduced permitting fees associated with LEED or Energy Star certification.[61]

State, local, and utility company incentives for energy-efficient and green construction have expanded rapidly in recent years. It behooves developers, investors, and property owners to combine such incentives with private capital to reduce the cost of financing sustainable renovations and new development. The importance of such incentives increased substantially in the capital-constrained environment associated with the economic downturn that began in 2007. The role of the public sector in green building finance is expected to expand even further in the wake of the federal economic stimulus enacted in February 2009.

The HOK Hong Kong office, which achieved a LEED-CI Gold rating, was the first project to pursue LEED certification in Hong Kong.

JOHN BUTLIN/HOK

The Public Sector, Green Buildings, and the Federal Stimulus

Public policy initiatives in the sustainability arena and resultant government regulation are expected to expand broadly in the near term because of a combination of political momentum at the federal level and the effect of the ARRA, commonly referred to as the as the federal stimulus.[62] This heavily funded initiative will have a significant impact on the commercial real estate industry, including due diligence practices.

Federal stimulus programs in the green building arena have been funded primarily through existing federal initiatives that had been passed over for appropriation before 2009.[63] Key vehicles include direct sustainability-related investment in federally owned and occupied properties, additional funding for state and local energy-efficiency initiatives, and "green strings" associated with energy-related funding to state governments.

DIRECT INVESTMENT IN GREEN RETROFITS OF FEDERAL PROPERTIES

Direct investment is illustrated in a dramatic way by funding under the ARRA of a $4.5 billion green retrofitting program for federal buildings, to be overseen by the GSA.[64] The GSA manages more than 8,500 federal properties, comprising more than 500 million square feet across a broad array of property types. The retrofitting program will be administered by the GSA's Office of Federal High-Performance Green Buildings, created under the EISA signed by President Bush in December 2007.[65] This entity is required to obligate 80 percent of the green retrofitting funding by September 2010. Funds that are not obligated by September 2010 will be subject to reappropriation.

The first green stimulus commitments of the Office of Federal High-Performance Green Buildings, announced in April 2009, included a list of more than 20 federal facilities. These buildings are to be retrofitted with a mix of traditional energy efficiency measures and innovative technologies. As with all ARRA funding, transparency is a hallmark of the initiative: the GSA will post each of its projects publicly and report on progress as the retrofits proceed. Says Kevin Kampshroer, director of the Office of Federal High-Performance Green Buildings,

> What we are doing with the funding is going to be very public and very transparent so people will have an unprecedented ease of access to all of this information.... We are working with the Department of Energy and are creating a benchmarking site so that we will put our buildings up so everybody can see them and we encourage the private sector to add their buildings. This [builds on] ... the broader program that Energy Star pioneered years ago.[66]

The GSA retrofit process will affect the commercial real estate industry in two primary areas. First, it will provide detailed information about the costs associated with green retrofits on a wide array of commercial property types. Second, it will be a signal to commercial real estate owners of the importance of green and energy-efficient features to remaining competitive in the marketplace.

The extensive green renovation of GSA facilities under the stimulus reinforces the importance of earlier federal initiatives to promote sustainability in the federal sector. As noted previously, effective December 2010 federal leasing policy will require, with limited exceptions, Energy Star labeling on all facilities greater than 10,000 square feet.[67] As well, the GSA gives preference to the use of LEED Silver certification in federal facilities. This combination of Energy Star and LEED is a harbinger of likely developments in the commercial real estate sector, presaging the wider adoption of LEED and Energy Star as tools in the due diligence process for green building.

FEDERAL FUNDING FOR STATE AND LOCAL ENERGY EFFICIENCY INITIATIVES

The development and expansion of state and local energy efficiency initiatives is a second focus area of the ARRA that will have significant impact on the development, renovation and retrofit of green and energy-efficient buildings. Some $3.1 billion in ARRA funding provides direct grants to state energy offices, through a program initially authorized under the EISA.[68] As well, the Energy Efficiency and Conservation Block Grant (EECBG) program of EISA received $3.2 billion in stimulus funding.[69] The broad permissible uses of EECBG funds allow funding of numerous initiatives to assist in the implementation of energy efficiency, green building, and conservation strategies.[70] As of the summer of 2009, EECBG funds are beginning to be disbursed to cities and states through population-based formulas. Enhanced funding of state energy offices and state and local green building, energy efficiency, and conservation programs will no doubt bolster the use of public incentives for the construction and renovation of green real estate.

"GREEN STRINGS": THE FEDERAL STIMULUS AND BUILDING CODES

The federal stimulus bill is likely to accelerate the revision of building codes by localities and states to include green and energy efficiency requirements. States and municipalities that have not yet "greened" their building codes may soon find themselves required to do so under the fine print of the ARRA statute, should they wish to avail themselves of federal stimulus dollars targeted for energy-related uses.[71] Most notable in this regard is the obligation of states receiving portions of the $16.8 billion in funding for energy efficiency and renewable energy to do the following, if the state or its units of local government have the ability (which exists broadly throughout the country):

▸▸ **REQUIRE THAT** building codes for residential property meet or exceed the most recently published IECC standards or achieves equivalent or greater efficiency;

▸▸ **REQUIRE THAT** building codes for commercial properties meet or exceed the ANSI/ASHRAE/IESNA Standard 90.1 2007 or achieve equivalent or greater energy savings; and

▸▸ **ENSURE ACHIEVEMENT** of these goals within eight years for at least 90 percent of new and renovated commercial building space.

Given the leverage exerted by the federal government over states and localities during this time of fiscal hardship, it is quite likely that states and local governments will comply with ARRA's "green strings," especially in light of the broad-based commitment to transparency and program compliance associated with the ARRA process.

BEYOND THE STIMULUS: EMERGING U.S. PRIORITIES

Following quickly on the heels of the February 2009 federal stimulus came the 2009 budget proposal of President Barack Obama, outlined in a white paper titled "A New Era of Responsibility."[72] The budget proposal offers ambitious plans for U.S. energy independence, including a $150 billion, ten-year cap-and-trade regimen to regulate carbon emissions. The budget proposed by President Obama also provides substantially expanded financial support for the Department of Energy (DOE).[73] In addition to the $38.7 billion appropriated for the DOE under the ARRA stimulus statute, appropriations for the department will rise from $24 billion in annual funding to nearly $34 billion in fiscal year 2009 and over $26 billion in fiscal year 2010. Many of the budget focus areas continue the emphasis of the federal stimulus statute: extensive research and development support for clean technology as well as a focus on energy efficiency, including smart-grid enhancements and clean fuel technologies.

The enactment of a cap-and-trade protocol also would place substantial additional emphasis—and considerable economic urgency—on the attainment of energy efficiency in the built environment. Indeed, climate change legislation passed by the U.S. House of Representatives in June 2009 includes provisions to create new, minimum federal standards for energy efficiency for new commercial and residential buildings and a model labeling system for building energy performance.[74]

NO PLACE TO HIDE: EMERGING TRANSACTIONAL ENERGY DISCLOSURE REQUIREMENTS

Energy usage disclosure requirements for commercial real estate—as recommended by the European Commission, being implemented in the United Kingdom, being introduced in Germany and in a handful of U.S. states, and proposed in Brazil and in the U.S. Congress—are also likely to become more prevalent in the wake of the federal stimulus. The creation and enforcement of such disclosure programs in the United States is an acceptable use of ARRA monies, especially funds targeted for state and local energy efficiency initiatives. This development will, at minimum, require commercial property owners to monitor energy usage—and very likely associated carbon emissions—more comprehensively. The development of appropriate measurement standards and technologies, including the management of data integrity issues, will likely gain importance over the next five years. (See chapter 6 for an overview of software programs that monitor and facilitate the reporting of building energy usage.)

Energy Star benchmarking will no doubt be part of the disclosure reporting mix, but data integrity and measurement refinements have been recommended by many. Additional standards will likely be needed in the area of water usage, which is not evaluated by Energy Star.[75] One vehicle developed recently to assist in the due diligence process is a consensus standard developed by the Capital Markets Partnership (CMP), a nonprofit coalition formed to accelerate the financing of sustainable real estate. The CMP's consensus standard acts as an overlay or "meta" rating system that evaluates a building on the basis of its Energy Star score, LEED rating, and other metrics to create a weighted score of a property's green attributes.

WHAT DOES IT ALL MEAN?

The global public policy initiatives outlined in this chapter promise to bring dramatic change to the process by which real estate is developed, financed, leased, insured, reconfigured, managed, and sold worldwide. The mutually reinforcing objectives of energy cost containment and building efficiency; environmental and climate change remediation; and economic stimulus and transaction transparency have led to the implementation of numerous regulatory reforms and financial incentives. While each nation has adopted diverse approaches to regulation and policy, some themes are visible:

▸▸ **WIDESPREAD ENACTMENT** of national, state, and local regulations related to building energy efficiency and sustainable practices, including requirements for base building systems and appliances.

▸▸ **THE ADOPTION OF INCENTIVES**, including rebates, property and corporate tax incentives, density bonuses, fee waivers, and expedited permitting, to encourage the use of green and energy-efficient design and construction approaches. As of 2009, fiscal stimulus programs around the globe are being drafted to incorporate energy efficiency objectives, including commercial and residential building renovations and retrofits, the purchase and installation of renewable energy equipment and systems, and the purchase of energy-efficient appliances.

▸▸ **AN EMERGING TREND** is the mandated disclosure of building energy performance, with results required to be shared upon rental and sale. Such requirements, fueled by concerns surrounding economic transparency, have been implemented in the United Kingdom and are undergoing implementation in Germany and in a number of American states. Similar requirements were proposed in 2009 in Brazil, in Ontario, Canada, and in climate change legislation approved by the U.S. House of Representatives.

Global policy initiatives will also no doubt give rise to a new generation of energy efficiency and retrofit technologies, building disclosure requirements, and associated monitoring and measurement standards and protocols to assess a property's green attributes and energy efficiency. Real estate professionals and the allied industries that support the real estate industry should heed these trends so as not to be caught at a competitive disadvantage as green and energy-efficient buildings become increasingly important in the marketplace.

Government policy initiatives are also likely to prove beneficial as catalysts for public information sharing on best practices and performance benchmarking for green construction and building retrofits. Public aggregation and dissemination of building performance data and the sharing of successful approaches to improve building energy usage and sustainability are potentially powerful mechanisms to accelerate the global use of sustainable design and construction technologies.

NOTES

1 European Parliament and the Council of the European Union, Directive 2002/91/EC on the Energy Performance of Buildings, December 16, 2002, Articles 1-6, http://eur-lex.europa.eu/LexUriServ/LexUriServ.do?uri=OJ:L:2003:001:0065:0071:EN:PDF.

2 Ibid.

3 Ibid.

4 Communication from the European Commission, "Proposal, Energy Performance of Buildings Directive, Recast," November 13, 2008, http://ec.europa.eu/energy/strategies/2008/doc/2008_11_ser2/buildings_directive_proposal.pdf.

5 Ibid.

6 Department of Minerals and Energy, "Energy Efficiency Strategy of the Republic of South Africa, March 2005"; Terri Hathaway, "South Africa's Elusive Negawatts," World Rivers Review, March 2009, http://internationalrivers.org/en/node/3928.

7 Roger McLeod, "Green Building and Energy Management," June 12, 2008, http://energymanagementinsa.blogspot.com/2008/08/green-building-energy-management.html; Terri Hathaway, March 2009.

8 Eskom, "Energy Efficiency and Demand Side Management Programme," 2008; Sarah De Villiers Leach, "Energy Efficiency in Existing Commercial Buildings," Cape Town Partnership, November 3, 2008.

9 Eskom, 2008.

10 "Green Buildings to Get More Tax Perks," RealEstateWeb, February 11, 2009, www.realestateweb.co.za/realestateweb/view/realestateweb/en/page228?oid=33136.

11 Sarah De Villiers Leach, November 3, 2008.

12 Rajesh Chhabara, "The Future of Green Building in China," March 17, 2009, Climate Change Corp., www.climatechangecorp.com/content.asp?ContentID=6023.

13 Ibid.

14 Ibid.

15 Ibid.

16 Ibid.

17 Ibid.

18 Ibid.

19 Government of Singapore, Building Construction Authority, BCA Green Mark Scheme, www.bca.gov.sg/GreenMark/green_mark_buildings.html.

20 Government of Singapore, Building Construction Authority, BCA Green Mark for Non-Residential Buildings, Version NRB/3.0, January 31, 2008.

21 Ya-fang Chen, Kuei-Peng Lee, and Chi-ming Lai, "Energy Efficiency Standards in Taiwan," undated monograph.

22 Steven Crook, "Taipei's Gre Libraries: Eco-friendly Architecture Making Headway," Taiwan Culture, August 28, 2007, www.culture.tw/index.php?option=com_content&task=view&id=242&Itemid=157en.

23 Steven Crook, "Green Buildings Paint Bright Future," Taiwan Journal, June 15, 2007, http://taiwanjournal.nat.gov.tw/site/Tj/ct.asp?xItem=24335&ctNode=122; Steven Crook, "Taipei's Gre Libraries," August 28, 2007.

24 Boonrod Sajjakulnukit, Thailand Ministry of Energy, Department of Alternative Energy Development and Efficiency, "Thailand's Experience with Its Energy Conservation Fund and EE Revolving Fund," June 2008.

25 Thailand Ministry of Energy, Department of Alternative Energy Development and Efficiency, "Energy Efficiency and Conservation Promotion in Thailand," December 17, 2007, www.aseanenergy.org/download/projects/promeec/2007-2008/industry/th/TH_Energy%20Efficiency%20and%20Conservation%20Promotion.pdf.

26 UNEP, Sustainable Buildings and Climate Initiative, "Latin American Ministers Resolve to Promote Sustainable Building," January 2009, www.unepsbci.org/SBCINews/LatestNews/showNews.asp?what=Latin_American_Ministers_Resolve_to_Promote_Sustainable_Building.

27 Lloyd Harrington and Melissa Damnics, Energy Labeling and Standards Programs Throughout the World, National Appliance and Equipment Energy Efficiency Committee Report 2004/04, Australia, July 2004, p. 5; Everson Pedro Burg, "Energy Efficiency Programs—Alive and Well in Brazil," July 15, 2008, http://wattwatt.com/pulses/299/energy-efficiency-programs-alive-and-well-in-brazil/.

28 Temas Actuales LLC, "Brazil Proposes Energy Labels for Build-ings," The Temas Blog, March 24, 2009, www.temasactuales.com/temasblog/environmental-protection/energy-the-environment/energy-efficiency/brazil-proposes-energy-labels-for-buildings.

29 Fernando Mayagoitia Witron, "Paper 4a: Green Residential Building in North America: Working Toward Affordable, Sus-tainable Housing in Mexico," Commission for Environmental Cooperation, March 2008, www.cec.org/greenbuilding.

30 Ibid.

31 Renewable Energy and Energy Efficiency Partner-ship, "Mexico EE Stakeholders Sign MOU to Develop Action Plan," March 10, 2009, www.reeep.org/index.php?assetType=news&assetId=237.

32 "Business and Government Tackle Pollution Together in Mexico," www.triplepundit.com/pages/sustainable-business-action-and-government; "Green Buildings in Mexico City Get Up to 25% Tax Credit," Green Momentum, March 9, 2009, www.greenmomentum.com/wb3/wb/gm/gm_content?id_content=1744.

33 Toronto Green Building Standard, www.toronto.ca/plan-ning/greendevelopment.htm.

34 Community Action on Energy and Emissions Initiative, Energy Efficiency and Buildings, 2009. www.bcclimateexchange.ca/pdfs/EnergyEfficiencyOnlineGuide2009.pdf

35 Ministry of Energy, Mines, and Petroleum Resources, "Making Energy Efficiency a Way of Life in BC," News Release, May 22, 2008, www.energyplan.gov.bc.ca/efficiency/PDF/EEBS-News-Release.pdf.

36 Community Action on Energy and Emissions Initiative, "En-ergy Efficiency and Buildings," 2009, www.bcclimateexchange.ca/pdfs/EnergyEfficiencyOnlineGuide2009.pdf.

37 "Greenhouse Gas Reduction Target Act Primer," www.walkingthetalk.bc.ca/bcclimateaction/ggrta_primer.

38 "BOMA Throws Support Behind Ontario's Green Energy Act," March 18, 2009.

39 Emily Seltzer, "Ontario Proposes Progressive Energy Policy," Smart Grid, February 25, 2009, www.matternetwork.com/2009/2/ontario-proposes-progressive-policy.cfm.

40 Jennifer Runyon, "Ontario Unveils Green Energy and Green Economy Act, 2009," Renewable Energy World.com, www.renewableenergyworld.com/rea/news/article/2009/02/ontario-unveils-green-energy-and-green-economy-act-2009.

41 In a marked departure from traditional practice, however, federal legislation to require building energy labels was intro-duced in the U.S. House of Representatives in early 2009; this development is discussed later in this section.

42 Leanne Tobias, "Paper 2b: Toward Sustainable Financing and Strong Markets for Green Building, U.S. Green Building Finance Review," Background paper, Green Building in North America, Commission for Environmental Cooperation, March 13, 2008, p. 2.

43 Energy Policy Act of 2005, Section 109.

44 Energy Policy Act of 2005, Sections 104, 102, 103.

45 Energy Independence and Security Act of 2007, Section 435, enacted into law as Public Law 110-140.

46 www.dsireusa.org/summarytables/regee.cfm?&CurrentPageID=7&EE=1&RE=1.

47 Texas Health & Safety Code § 388.005.

48 DOE, Office of Energy Efficiency and Renewable Energy, State Energy Program, "The Greening of State Facilities: State Policies to Encourage Green Building Principles in the Public Sector," Conservation Update, December 1, 2008.

49 U.S. Green Building Council, "LEED Initiatives in Government and Schools," www.usgbc.org/DisplayPage.aspx?CMSPageID=1852#state.

50 Ibid.

51 Ibid.

52 District of Columbia Clean and Affordable Energy Act of 2008, www.imt.org/Capital/DC_EnergyBill.pdf.

53 Senate Bill 5854 - 2009-10.

54 U.S. Green Building Council, "LEED Initiatives in Govern-ment and Schools."

55 Database of State Incentives for Renewable Energy, www.dsireusa.org.

56 Ibid.

57 Ibid.

58 Ibid.

59 Ibid.

60 AIA, "Local Leaders in Sustainability: Green Incentives," 2008, p. 8, www.aia.org/aiaucmp/groups/aia/documents/pdf/aias075288.pdf.

61 Ibid., pp. 9–10, p. 15.

62 H.R. 1—111th Congress (2009): American Recovery and Reinvestment Act of 2009 (ARRA).

63 "Green Package: The Stimulus Plan's Big Winners," The Wall Street Journal's "Environmental Capital" blog, March 20, 2009, http://blogs.wsj.com/environmentalcapital/2009/03/20/green-package-the-stimulus-plans-big-winners.

64 ARRA, Title IV, Section XX.

65 H.R. 6—110th Congress (2007): Energy Independence and Security Act of 2007.

66 Full interview can be found at www.srmnetwork.com/id59.html.

67 EISA Sections 435-436.

68 EISA Subtitle E.

69 ARRA Title IV, Section 410.

70 EISA Subtitle E, Section 544.

71 ARRA, Title IV, Section 410, subsection 2.

72 www.whitehouse.gov/omb/budget.

73 www.whitehouse.gov/omb/budget/fy2010/assets/summary.pdf.

74 Leanne Tobias, "How the Cap and Trade Bill Could Trans-form the Real Estate Sector," Greener Buildings, July 29, 2009, www.greenerbuildings.com/blog/2009/07/29/how-cap-and-trade-bill-could-transform-real-estate-sector.

75 Galley Eco Capital, "Energy Efficiency Scorecard: Compare Plaques to Real Emissions Reductions," March 16, 2009, www.galleyecocapital.com/?s=Energy+Efficiency+Scorecard%3A+Compare+Real+Plaques+to+Real+Emissions+Reduction.

Toward the Future:
New Directions in Green Building

LEANNE TOBIAS AND GEORGE VAVAROUTSOS

Innovations in building design software and the introduction of new building materials and technologies promise to deliver more cost-effective, energy-efficient, and environmentally sound retrofits of offices and other commercial properties. Recent industry advances are detailed in this chapter.

BUILDING INFORMATION MODELING

Building information modeling (BIM) is defined as "the process of creating and using digital models for design, construction, and/or operations of the building."[1] BIM permits the three-dimensional modeling of a project's architectural, structural, and mechanical elements, including physical dimensions and functional behavior. The models provide an unprecedented level of information about a potential building design, allowing the project team to evaluate structural integrity, constructability, and prospective operating performance. BIM also permits project teams to engage in "clash detection" to ensure the compatibility of layout, equipment, and materials choices. The entry of sequencing, scheduling, and cost data into a BIM model enables the project team to identify and avoid many of the scheduling and budget concerns that can emerge in the course of a project.

BIM models can evaluate the energy performance of certain building systems before construction, allowing designers to consider and recommend more effective design and energy efficiency strategies. Currently, the BIM revolution is focused on new construction, but BIM technology may be used cost-effectively for office retrofits. (For a discussion of the application of BIM to the green renovation of existing buildings, see the sidebar by Erin Rae Hoffer and Robert Middlebrooks.)

NEW BUILDING MATERIALS AND SYSTEMS

Advances in building science directly benefit retrofitting projects as newer technologies create more efficient products, including new energy-smart systems and materials, for installation in existing buildings. Rising

ACCELERATING SUSTAINABILITY WITH BUILDING INFORMATION MODELING

ERIN RAE HOFFER AND ROBERT E. MIDDLEBROOKS

A remarkable transformation is occurring in the design and construction of the built environment. Historical technologies such as manual and CAD (computer-aided design) drafting are giving way to the technology of building information modeling (BIM). BIM enables designers to create three-dimensional, computer-based models of projects and permits the modeling of building systems and components to produce predictions about how these elements will behave together in the real world.

A building information model captures building location, size, volume, occupancy, function, and other metrics, including performance, cost, and construction scheduling requirements. When a designer introduces a new building element into the model, the project team builds a database of information that can be used to analyze its impact on predicted energy consumption, along with many other factors including water usage, waste, construction sequencing, and cost. A basic building model therefore enables a project team to analyze, compare, or audit potential renovation projects based on financial or environmental criteria. BIM data can be developed and shared by all stakeholders in a project, including architects; engineers; the general contractor, subcontractors, and suppliers; and building owners, thereby facilitating consensus-based decision making (figure 1).

Modeling for Existing Buildings and Retrofits

BIM assists developers and building owners in predicting the energy performance of proposed renovations and retrofits by

- ▸▸ **Creating models** for existing buildings;
- ▸▸ **Proposing alternatives**;
- ▸▸ **Analyzing and comparing** building performance for these alternatives; and
- ▸▸ **Modeling improvements** aimed at energy efficiency and improved financial performance.

For existing buildings, BIM can supplement traditional due diligence tools. BIM is not a replacement for retro-commissioning and energy audits, which identify building deficiencies and opportunities to improve the energy performance of existing buildings. However, BIM can help to facilitate the wise planning of a green retrofit. BIM technology and analysis tools are best used to predict and assess comparative performance results, helping to answer questions such as, "What generates a better economic and energy-efficient return: installing high-performance wall insulation or modifying a heating system?"

To begin the BIM-enabled process of energy retrofitting, the existing building must be represented as a building information model. A basic model requires generalized information on quantities, as well as size, shape, location, and orientation of the building. This includes windows, exterior doors, and openings; roof area and geometry; interior core arrangement and zoning; floor-to-floor slabs; and other major functional spaces, such as parking garages, auditoriums, and atriums.

Existing buildings are likely to be documented in either paper or CAD construction plans or design files. Some older buildings have no documentation at all. Whatever the state of existing documentation, a model can be developed for an existing building in the following ways:

- ▸▸ **Use paper documents** as dimensional takeoffs. Do paper documents accurately reflect the as-built condition of the structure? Construction documents may not reflect modifications to the design that took place in the field. The modification of construction documents to reflect as-built conditions

Figure 1

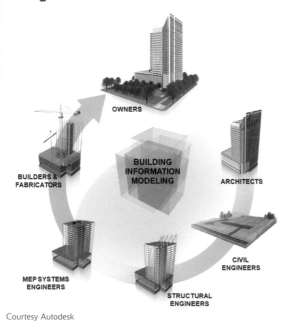

Using BIM Technology To Connect Design and Construction Stakeholders

OWNERS

BUILDING INFORMATION MODELING

ARCHITECTS

BUILDERS & FABRICATORS

CIVIL ENGINEERS

MEP SYSTEMS ENGINEERS

STRUCTURAL ENGINEERS

Courtesy Autodesk

is frequently a time-consuming process, but design firms can provide this service and can provide estimates for the cost.

▸▸ **Use CAD data** as a reference for model development. Are the CAD data accurate for as-built purposes? Often, CAD files represent only the original design—which may have undergone considerable modification during construction. CAD data should be confirmed if there are doubts as to accuracy. Two-dimensional or three-dimensional CAD files can be used as reference files in BIM software. Design firms that use both CAD and BIM systems can produce a building information model from CAD data.

▸▸ **Conduct a conventional survey,** with physical dimensioning and field verification. If no documents exist, a conventional survey can produce paper documents that can be used as dimensional takeoffs to start the development of a building information model.

▸▸ **Complete a three-dimensional laser scan** of the building and convert it to a model. When no documents exist or when drawings or CAD files do not show as-built conditions, three-dimensional laser scanning is becoming more common as a means of developing models for BIM projects. The process uses a laser device to precisely size and position roofs, exterior walls, windows, doors, and other openings into an accurate set of vertices in three dimensions, called a "point cloud." This point cloud can be imported into the BIM software. Additional interior volumetric verification completes the process of creating a basic model.

▸▸ **Use digital photography** to create a model. A series of digital photographs can be taken and entered into image-based modeling and photogrammetry software. The two-dimensional images are then converted into a three-dimensional model of the building or structure. This approach is useful for early-stage energy modeling investigations, where more costly and accurate dimensioned representations are not yet needed.

A building model produced only for the purposes of energy analysis, rather than for visualization or construction documentation, can be simplified to focus on the key elements—spaces, glazing, enclosures, and mechanical components. Once the building information model is completed, it must be converted to gbXML—the standard data format for green building assessment—and input into building performance analysis tools for quantitative or visual reports. During this process, the building information model and the resulting gbXML file must be evaluated and fine-tuned for accuracy.

Value of BIM for Energy Retrofits

BIM tools assist project teams in designing efficient systems to reduce the consumption of energy, water, and materials, and support a consensus-based decision-making process.

▸▸ **Energy.** Software tools for building performance analysis accept data from models to predict the comparative energy efficiency of proposed designs. These tools can be used to evaluate heating and cooling requirements, identify daylighting opportunities, and assess building equipment selections intended to reduce energy use. By predicting and evaluating the performance of comparative building systems, BIM helps project teams to choose building equipment with superior performance and value. Elements of BIM energy analysis are shown in figure 2.

▸▸ **Water.** BIM tools enable designers to assess and minimize water use. Analysis software considers potable and nonpotable water supply options for occupants and building processes, evaluates stormwater systems, and simulates options for collection systems, ponds, and culverts. Simulation tools assess the feasibility of using recycled water for landscaping irrigation and report on the effects of contaminants in wastewater.

▸▸ **Materials.** The use of recycled or renewable materials or finishes is a sustainable design practice recognized by LEED and other green building certifications. Building information models can calculate costs and quantities of these materials needed during building renovations to support the LEED documentation process.

▸▸ **Decision making.** Best practices in sustainable design call for the development of consensus among key stakeholders, including the owner, the design team, and the construction team. BIM analysis and visualization tools increase the clarity of proposed modifications presented to the project team, stakeholders, and decision makers, improving the process of consensus building (figure 1).

Sustainable Retrofit Examples

BIM has been used in a number of sustainable retrofits, including the following:

▸▸ **Independence Center.** The architectural and consulting firm of ARBA Studios recently used BIM to optimize energy retrofit strategies for the renovation of Independence Center, a historic brick industrial building built in 1924 in St. Louis, Missouri. Independence Center was renovated to provide office space for an adult services organization.

The ARBA Studios team built a model of the occupant spaces for energy analysis and conducted simulation and building performance analysis to reduce energy usage and minimize associated costs. Of the recommended energy reduction strategies, the team calculated that external shading devices would have a more rapid payback than glazing replacement. BIM tools helped the team compare the predicted outcomes of different orientations for shading devices. Comparing the savings predicted by building performance analysis with energy expenses actually incurred, as obtained from the utility company, showed that the analysis was accurate within a 5 percent margin of error. Modeling results also helped eliminate cost-ineffective alternatives: BIM indicated that a proposed modular green roof would produce estimated life-cycle savings of $6,000 for a projected cost of $150,000.

▶▶ **Autodesk Corporate Office Facility.** The recently completed buildout of the corporate office facility for Autodesk in Massachusetts illustrates how BIM and highly sustainable renovations will be linked in the future. The project targeted LEED-CI Platinum certification. To create an accurate as-built model, the project team used three-dimensional laser scanning of all four floors of the existing structure. The model revealed an important discovery—significant variations in the concrete floor levels, which would not have been apparent from existing CAD documents.

BIM was used throughout the design and construction process. Members of the cross-disciplinary project team built accurate design and construction models to facilitate fast-paced decision making and problem resolution. The combination of BIM and cross-functional collaboration resulted in a high-quality project that was completed within an aggressive schedule and budget.

BIM PROJECT SAVINGS AND SCHEDULING EFFICIENCIES

Scott Simpson, senior director of the KlingStubbins architectural firm, has studied the effect of BIM on project outcomes. Simpson evaluated outcomes for five sample projects and found construction cost savings ranging from 5.5 to 10.1 percent on projects ranging in cost from $25.4 million to $120 million. The projects also achieved schedule acceleration ranging from two months to 14 months. According to Simpson, average cost savings on these high-quality projects for signature clients were $5.38 million and average schedule acceleration was 8.4 months overall. As suggested by Simpson's data and the Independence Center and Autodesk experiences, BIM is likely to play a key role in designing and optimizing the performance of green and energy-efficient commercial buildings.

Erin Rae Hoffer, AIA, LEED AP, and Robert E. Middlebrooks, AIA are industry managers at Autodesk.

NOTE

1 See www.gbxml.org. Building performance analysis tools include Autodesk Ecotect and Autodesk GreenBuildingStudio.

Figure 2

Visualizing and Simulating Building Performance with Autodesk Ecotect Analysis

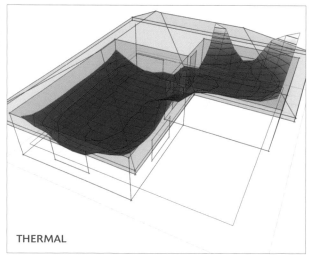

THERMAL

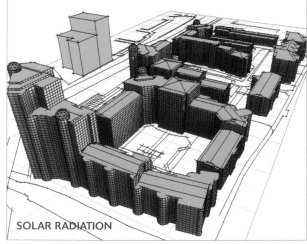

SOLAR RADIATION

energy costs, additional environmental regulation, and the need to reduce greenhouse gas (GHG) emissions from the built environment ensure the continued growth of building science research on products and methods.

Innovative Building Materials

A key method of reducing an existing building's energy use is to improve the insulating qualities of the building envelope. Innovative materials with higher insulating properties reduce energy loss through the envelope, thereby reducing heating and cooling requirements. (For an exploration of how advanced chemistry is improving the efficiency of building materials, see the sidebar by Colby Swanson.) New approaches include heat management pigments and advanced insulation materials.

Zero-Energy Windows and Switchable Glazing

Significant improvements also are being made in the energy efficiency of building window systems, which typically account for roughly 30 percent of building energy loss.[2] "Zero-energy windows," which feature technologies such as vacuum-insulated glass (VIG), may become commercially viable as manufacturing costs decline over time. They can decrease heat loss through the glazing and mimic the energy efficiency of a solid wall. Such windows can reduce heat loss while maximizing solar heat gain (for colder climates), enhancing daylighting, and producing a net reduction in energy use for the structure.

Switchable glazings, particularly electrochromic glass, are another window innovation that could lead to substantial energy savings in office buildings. By using a low-voltage electric charge to adjust the glass tint, electrochromic windows change color to control transmitted light, glare, and solar heat gain, while preserving outside views for building occupants. With built-in sensors, these window units can adjust automatically to outdoor light conditions, improving visual comfort for building occupants by reducing glare and minimizing solar heat gain when desired.

Glare, caused by excessive brightness from outside light, reduces the effectiveness of daylighting strategies because building occupants typically draw blinds and use indoor lighting, thus increasing energy use. Studies of buildings fitted with low-E glass and solar shading show that the addition of an electrochromic current that modulates glass color to reduce glare can reduce the building energy required for electric lighting by as much as 48 to 67 percent, and lead to a 10 percent reduction in total energy use in both hot and cold climates.[3] (Results may differ for properties that do not feature low-E glass or solar shading.) Electrochromic glass can cost two to three times as much as conventional glass, but the premium is expected to decline as production grows. For buildings with large expanses of unshaded glass on the southern, eastern, and western sides of the building, building owners should conduct a cost-benefit analysis to assess the potential for installing electrochromic glass on these exposures to reduce solar heat gain.

Next-Generation LEDs

In addition to reducing energy loss, newer technologies are reducing the energy needed within the structure. Continuous improvements in the performance of light-emitting diodes (LEDs) have widespread implications for office buildings (see chapter 3). Researchers expect that the luminous efficiency (which measures how effectively a light source converts power into visible light) of LEDs can eventually outpace that of fluorescent lighting by a factor of two or three.[4] While LEDs may not be suitable for all building lighting applications, their use has major implications for reducing the energy needed to illuminate office buildings; LEDs may single-handedly reduce U.S. building energy consumption by 5 percent by 2025.[5]

CHEMISTRY IS KEY TO HIGH-PERFORMANCE BUILDING MATERIALS

COLBY SWANSON

Advanced chemistry is a key to enabling technology for green building. Improved insulating values, reduced waste, increased durability, and improved air quality are just some of the benefits delivered by materials that have been optimized by chemists. Understanding some of the science behind the most promising construction products can help in wide-scale adoption of high-performance products for sustainable construction. This sidebar describes some of these products and the science behind them.

Improved Options for Insulation and Heat Management

Recent research advances have led to improvements in insulation products and heat management coatings for building exteriors and interiors.

GRAPHITE-ENHANCED INSULATION

One example of such products is a new graphite-enhanced, expandable polystyrene (EPS) insulation, called Neopor. Microscopic flakes of graphite act as small mirrors that reflect heat and increase insulation value up to 20 percent, reducing the thickness of insulation needed and providing greater design flexibility. Currently used for exterior walls and roofing insulation in Asia and Europe, Neopor has recently been introduced in the United States for similar commercial applications. For interior walls, Neopor is attached to gypsum board, providing a one-step process for both interior finishing and increased insulation. Improved insulation enhances the efficiency of the building shell and reduces the need for mechanical heating and cooling, thereby lowering energy costs.

PHASE-CHANGE MATERIAL

Perhaps an even more significant upgrade for gypsum board involves a revolutionary phase-change material called Micronal PCM. Using a new micro-encapsulation technology for interior building materials, such as plaster boards and wall boards, plastic capsules are filled with a special wax to absorb and release thermal energy by melting and solidifying in a controlled manner, reducing energy costs and increasing room comfort. The capsules increase the thermal capacity of building interiors and act to dampen temperature swings, reducing the heating and cooling load. Buildings constructed with Micronal PCM–modified plaster materials provide greater comfort for occupants. Energy modeling results indicate that the use of Micronal PCM can reduce air-conditioning energy needs by up

Rooftop installation of graphite-enhanced expandable polystyrene (EPS) insulation.

to one-third, depending on the climate and the overall design of the construction.

HEAT MANAGEMENT PIGMENTS

Heat management pigments, which are coatings that absorb less solar radiation than normal pigments, are of particular interest in warmer climates, including areas of Asia, the United States, and the Mediterranean. When applied extensively over large areas, heat management coatings can also counteract the urban heat island effect, which contributes to the overheating of entire metropolitan areas during the summer months. The cooler coatings reduce air-conditioning needs and therefore electrical demand and carbon emissions.

New breakthroughs in heat management pigments include near infrared (NIR) reflective pigments. Transparent NIR pigments can be formulated to reflect up to 45 percent of solar radiation, while NIR-reflecting black pigments reflect as much as 30 percent. By comparison, traditional carbon black pigments reflect less than 5 percent. (White material has a long-term solar reflectance of 80 percent.) In practical trials, the lower absorption of NIR-reflecting black pigment relative to other black pigments results in a temperature decrease of up to 68°F (20°C) on building surfaces.

VACUUM-INSULATED PANELS

Vacuum-insulated panels (VIPs) are an emerging technology that has drawn much attention internationally. The units consist of a core panel enclosed in a vacuum-sealed metallic or Mylarfoil envelope, providing an insulating value that is three to seven times that of an equivalent thickness of other insulation materials, such as rigid foam boards, foam beads, or fiber blankets. Currently, several types of core are being developed for this use, including polystyrene, polyurethane, and a combination of silica and carbon. Although VIPs represent a promising, continuously improving technology, they are currently very costly. In addition, the impressive insulating values could be greatly diminished if the vacuum seal protecting the panels is breached. In a retrofit scenario, however, VIPs could represent an important, easy-to-install solution for areas where the building envelope needs upgrading for energy efficiency, including interior walls and under the roofing deck.

NEW TWISTS ON FAMILIAR SYSTEMS

New applications of materials traditionally used in new construction can benefit retrofit projects in compelling ways. For example, in the United States, exterior insulation and finishing systems (EIFS)—originally developed for post–World War II reconstruction—have been used primarily for new construction. Throughout Europe, however, these systems are used as an insulating approach for green building retrofits

EIFS comprise EPS insulation, a fiberglass-reinforced base coat, and a textured acrylic finish coat. In addition to providing a cost-effective aesthetic upgrade, the systems have withstood Class 1 hurricanes and provide a blanket of insulation over the entire opaque wall surface. Most EIFS today also incorporate a liquid-applied, air- and water-resistant barrier over the sheathing, and many offer moisture drainage systems for substrate protection. This adds to building comfort and energy reductions by eliminating drafts and alleviating the intrusive moisture concerns that plagued earlier generations of residential EIFS products.

When it is not feasible to retrofit exterior walls with insulation from the inside—which is often the case because of interruptions to workspace use and timing issues—EIFS can be used to substantially improve the thermal performance of a wall with relative ease and minimal disruption to existing building occupants. Because they replace heavy brick and stone, EIFS also reduce the energy needed to transport materials to the job site. In addition, EIFS generates very little construction waste. Tests conducted by the U.S. Department of Energy near Charleston, South Carolina (a humid climatic zone), in 2006 and 2007 found that EIFS panels outperformed brick, stucco, and cement-fiber siding on energy efficiency, moisture control, and temperature control measures.

However, like every building product, EIFS must be correctly installed. For example, in single-family and in some multifamily wood frame construction, model building codes require water-drainage EIFS. Water-drainage EIFS systems were introduced in the mid 1990s to accommodate incidental moisture that can breach any wall system at penetrations such as windows, doors, and utilities.

No discussion of energy retrofits would be complete without the inclusion of closed-cell spray polyurethane foam (ccSPF) roofing systems. Developed approximately 40 years ago in Germany for aerospace and naval applications, the technology has been available for retrofit roofing for 35 years. The system is extremely durable, quick to install, water resistant, and able to be applied over existing roofing, thereby reducing construction waste. It is also extraordinarily cost-effective. In fact, according to a long-term energy study, ccSPF can pay for itself in energy savings alone in four and half years and requires little to no maintenance after 30 years. In addition, the use of newly available white acrylic coatings containing low to no volatile organic compounds (VOCs) further reduces the heat island effect and satisfies rigorous air quality codes in many regions and countries.

Improved Options for Windows and Skylights

Although improved daylighting may raise worker productivity and reduce lighting costs, fenestration has been viewed by some as the weak link in an energy-efficient building envelope. However, recent material advancements in window and skylights help make the case that increased daylighting can be a truly energy-efficient choice.

For instance, for a complete window replacement, high-performance windows are available that feature elastic, energy-efficient, warm-edge thermoplastic spacer (TPS) technology. This warm-edge system functions as a thermal break, which reduces the transfer of heat between conductive materials by sealing the edges of gas-filled insulated glazing units. Warm-edge TPS technology can improve the energy performance of a window unit by up to 10 percent. As an additional benefit, the TPS is flexible, so windows are better able to accommodate stresses from wind and impact, making the units less susceptible to shattering or losing their seal and insulating interior gasses.

For buildings with expansive glazing (glass), exterior shading and control devices—such as light shelves, overhangs, horizontal louvers, vertical louvers, and dynamic tracking or reflecting systems—can be designed to reduce undesirable solar heat gain while providing diffuse natural interior daylighting. Economical options for glazing retrofits also include a wide variety of tints, metallic and low-E coatings, and fritting that can be applied over existing glazing with little or no disruption of workplace activity.

On the Horizon: Nanotechnology and Organic Solar Cells

The combination of energy efficiency and renewable energy is a big leap forward for sustainable construction. Two game changers currently in development are nanotechnology insulating foams and organic solar cells.

NANOTECHNOLOGY INSULATING FOAMS

Nanotechnology insulating foams, also known as nanofoams, represent the next generation of insulating materials. The prefix "nano" describes an order of magnitude, one nanometer being one billionth of a meter. This is about the length of five to ten atoms arranged end to end. (For context, a nanometer is to a meter what a table tennis ball is to the Earth.) Nanotechnology, therefore, describes the targeted and controlled development, manufacture, and use of structures, materials, and systems in magnitudes smaller than a hundred nanometers.

One example of current nanofoam technology available in the market is in polycarbonate skylights and curtain walls. The nanofoam Aerogel is a silica-based insulation that improves the insulating value of these skylights and curtain walls by as much as five times, without the need for a vacuum seal.

Scientists are currently working on non-silica-based nanofoams that will deliver equivalent or greater insulating values while providing durability and wide-scale availability. For example, researchers are working on how to transform current, standard carbon-based insulations, such as EPS and polyurethane, into nanofoams—which promise to significantly reduce heat conduction to less than half of that observed with conventional materials. These early-stage nanofoams could be used to improve the overall performance of vacuum-insulated panels, because they retain greater insulating value than traditional materials if the fragile vacuum seal is breached.

ORGANIC SOLAR CELLS

Another emerging technology for green construction is the continued development of organic photovoltaics. Organic photovoltaic technology includes solar cells based on organic semiconductor materials, such as pentacene, polyfluorenes, and PCBM (phenyl-C61-butyric acid methyl ester), that replace the traditional silicon materials used today.

One of the biggest advantages of the emerging organic solar photovoltaics is that they are cheap and can be mass produced, unlike silicon-based solar cells. However, organic solar materials still need to achieve higher solar energy conversion efficiency and increased durability before they are mass produced. Every efficiency and durability enhancement increases the possible application of these products.

The advantages of organic solar cell technology include thinner, more flexible panels that can be incorporated into windows, exterior wall cladding, and roofing materials, transforming passive systems into active, energy-producing systems. Once this market is fully developed, organic photovoltaic systems may very well pave the way for sustainable and competitive energy production globally.

Colby Swanson is Building and Construction Markets manager for the BASF Group.

In addition to being energy-efficient, LEDs do not produce waste heat in the form of radiated energy. For a typical office building with fluorescent lighting, radiated energy can be a considerable source of internal heat gain, raising the building's cooling load. LEDs are also remarkably long lasting (with lifetimes more than three times those of fluorescent bulbs), which reduces the building maintenance costs associated with relamping.

Improved Solar Technologies

Researchers and manufacturers are also improving the technologies that produce on-site renewable energy, such as solar photovoltaic systems. Advances in solar technologies and production, and declining material costs will continue to lower the cost per watt of such systems, improving the economics of installation. Market analysts believe that the cost of producing crystalline silicon–based solar cells (considered the first generation of solar cells) should decline 40 percent by 2012, as additional manufacturing capacity abates the current silicon shortage.[6]

Additionally, efficiency and durability advances in "thin film" solar cells (considered the second generation of solar cells) should allow these systems to challenge the market supremacy of first-generation solar cells. Currently, manufacturers of thin-film solar products are projecting that manufacturing costs will drop to less than $1 per watt over the next several years, similar to those of first-generation solar panels.[7] Additionally, the potential for organic thin-film solar film—extremely low-cost solar cells that can be printed on flexible materials and installed virtually anywhere—has major implications for the built environment. (For more information on organic solar cells, see the sidebar by Colby Swanson.)

The growth in building-integrated photovoltaics (BIPV) also has substantial implications for office buildings. Solar cells can be embedded on almost any vertical, horizontal, or angled surface on a building's exterior, including glazing, walls, roofs, and solar shading devices. Some of these systems can be retrofitted onto existing structures. Researchers are also working on windows that can act as solar concentrators, reflecting visible light onto a solar cell embedded in the window frame.[8]

SMART BUILDINGS AND SMART GRIDS

Smart buildings enable building operators and managers to control building operations from a single user-friendly platform, known as a building automation system (BAS) or building control system. These systems can track in real time the energy use, environmental impact, and economic performance of a building, while providing unprecedented opportunities to manage, adjust, and optimize building operations.[9] (For more information about building controls, see chapter 3.)

Integrating all building controls makes it possible to monitor building systems and performance data remotely. An off-site facility manager, for example, can control lobby lighting from 2,000 miles away or can be notified of an operations failure in a heating system or an elevator anywhere around the globe.

Remote monitoring of building performance data has major implications for portfolio and corporate real estate managers. Operational and performance data can be pulled up in real time and tracked across the entire portfolio. Energy use and GHG emissions can be monitored, and the impact of portfolio energy efficiency measures can be reported easily.

Additionally, a BAS reduces the need for on-site visits to inspect building operations and ensure proper building management. The added security of remote monitoring can help to make portfolio owners more comfortable

As part of the retrofit of the Empire State Building, interior spaces will be fully submetered, and tenants will have access to individualized, Web-based systems for monitoring and adjusting their energy use.

with investing in distant markets, encouraging cross-border investment. Although these systems can be installed now, familiarity with the capacity of these systems by owners and building managers is not high. When the potential of these systems is fully realized, portfolio-wide installation will be accelerated, and perhaps required, for new construction.

What a BAS does for building operations, a smart grid does for energy infrastructure. Smart grid technology will incorporate digital communication systems with the electric grid, allowing for two-way communication between the utility provider and consumers. This communication system enables real-time monitoring of electrical performance, both at the consumer level and at the utility level, making it possible to manage electrical capacity more efficiently and to improve service reliability.[10] Smart grid infrastructure is already in use in test projects in the European Union and the United States. Both the United States and the European Union, along with China, Canada, and Australia, are currently in the planning and implementation phase of larger-scale smart grid technologies.

The implications for energy consumers and building owners are twofold: increased reliability of the electrical grid and dynamic pricing for energy use and production. Through net metering, which requires the installation of a wireless smart meter to track electricity consumption and production, a consumer or property owner can receive credit for renewable energy generated on site and sold back to the grid. In addition, real-time reporting of energy use, along with dynamic pricing that adjusts electricity costs to limit peak demand, can induce energy consumers to conserve energy.[11] Consumers can also use "load shifting," or switching energy use from peak to off-peak times, to reduce their consumption of high-cost energy. (For more information on net metering and load shifting in the United States and South Africa, see chapters 5 and 7.)

By integrating the dynamic pricing data from the utility provider into building control systems, smart buildings can automatically adjust operations to minimize energy use during high-cost periods. The dynamic pricing strategy can lead to significant reductions in energy costs for owners and occupants.

CREATING THE ZERO-ENERGY COMMERCIAL BUILDING

A zero-energy building (ZEB) represents a truly sustainable building, one that consumes no more energy than it produces on an annual basis. (Note that a ZEB is technically a net-zero-energy building, rather than a building that uses no energy at all.) Because the built environment is one of the largest users of energy, accounting for roughly 40 percent of primary energy consumption, the development of commercially viable zero-energy office buildings is a key component of the effort to reduce GHG emissions.[12] The United Kingdom has passed regulations requiring that by 2019 all new buildings be zero-energy buildings, and the European Parliament has endorsed similar recommendations which are expected to be finalized in the second half of 2009. (For more information, see the sidebar by Mark Bennett and Leanne Tobias.)

In the United States, the DOE has created the $1 billion Zero-Energy Commercial Building Initiative (CBI), with the goal of creating marketable zero-energy commercial buildings by 2030. The partnership includes large real estate firms, professional engineering and design organizations, and research institutions that work on innovations to improve building energy efficiency and renewable energy systems. CBI is supporting the development of ZEB technologies and the business case for ZEBs.

ZEBs achieve high levels of energy efficiency and utilize renewable energy systems to offset the remaining energy used for day-to-day operations. There are multiple ZEB classifications, which account for different definitions of building energy usage and whether the renewable energy is created on site. (For more detail on zero-energy classifications, see the sidebar on defining zero energy by George Vavaroutsos.)

To achieve net-zero-energy use, building energy demand should be reduced by 60 to 90 percent over current standards, with the balance of energy demand (10 to 40 percent) satisfied by on-site renewable generation, such as solar, wind, geothermal or biomass applications.[13] This represents a significant reduction in daily building energy consumption.

Common strategies used to reduce energy demand include passive strategies (daylight-ing, natural ventilation, evaporative cooling, and passive solar heating), energy-efficient building mechanical systems, and building control systems. Building envelope efficiency is also critical to ZEB performance. The building envelopes of ZEB structures significantly exceed the thermal performance of the building envelopes of conventional buildings.

A recent study by the U.S. National Renewable Energy Laboratory (NREL) indicates that, by 2025, the overall new commercial building market could be a net energy producer. Over time, this development could help reduce the current energy use intensity of the built environment.[14]

STRIVING FOR NET-ZERO

MARK J. BENNETT AND LEANNE TOBIAS

In the United Kingdom, legislation has passed requiring that existing and new construction buildings qualify as net-zero-energy buildings (ZEBs) by specified future dates. The European Union has approved a report making similar recommendations, In the United States, the federal government has developed net-zero-energy policy objectives and funding for net-zero-energy research, but national standards have not been set. The conditions and requirements differ for each country and may be subject to amendment as deadlines approach. Briefly, they are as follows:

▸▸ **United Kingdom.** In 2008, the United Kingdom passed regulations requiring that all new housing construction achieve net-zero emissions by 2016 and that new commercial construction achieve net-zero emissions by 2019. This is the shortest time frame of all the regulations, requiring prompt action to reach the legislative targets.

▸▸ **European Union.** In April 2009, the European Parliament approved a member report recommending that all new construction buildings use net-zero energy by 2019. The report calls on EU member states to establish interim targets, to be issued in 2016 and in 2020, for minimum percentages of existing buildings to be retrofitted to achieve net-zero-energy use. The recommendations are expected to be finalized by the close of 2009. The implementation recommendations

endorsed by the European Union in its April vote include the following milestones:

• March 2010: Development of EU-wide net-zero-energy calculation methods.

• June 2010: Submission of proposals for new sources of financing for improvements in building energy efficiency.

• December 2010: EU-wide definitions of net-zero-energy requirements.

• June 2011: National action plans issued by member states.

• 2014: Establishment of an EU Energy Efficiency Fund.

▸▸ **United States.** Although firm net-zero-energy requirements have not been adopted, the United States has set targets for long-term implementation. Pursuant to the Energy Independence and Security Act (EISA) of 2007, the government has set target objectives that by 2030 all new construction commercial buildings must be ZEBs. For existing commercial buildings, 50 percent of the total building stock must be ZEBs by 2040, and all existing commercial buildings must be ZEBs by 2050.

Mark J. Bennett is senior counsel and leads the Climate Change Practice at Miller Canfield. Leanne Tobias, LEED AP, is the founder and managing principal of Malachite LLC.

Several net-zero-energy (and near-net-zero-energy) office buildings currently in operation around the globe are being utilized as demonstration projects. Performance data, especially energy consumption information, are being monitored in these structures in order to improve building performance and establish best practices for zero-energy design. Retrofit ZEBs include the IDeAs Z-Squared design facility in San Jose, California, and the ZEB@BCA Academy in Singapore. (For further information on these pioneering buildings, see the sidebar by George Vavaroutsos on page 200.)

DEFINING NET-ZERO-ENERGY BUILDINGS: A PRIMER

GEORGE VAVAROUTSOS

What qualifies a building as a net-zero-energy building (ZEB)? The United States National Renewable Energy Laboratory (NREL) has developed the following definitions[1]:

» **Net-zero site energy building.** A net-zero site energy building produces at least as much energy as it uses, when measured at the site. This definition is useful because verification can be achieved through on-site metering. Measuring building energy usage and energy production from the site tends to encourage energy-efficient design; this measure, however, does not distinguish between fuel types or account for transmission inefficiencies in the utility grid. Because the site energy measure is easily calculated and understood, it is the most frequently used definition of a net ZEB.

» **Net-zero source energy building.** A net-zero source energy building produces at least as much energy as it uses, when accounted for at the source. Source energy refers to the primary energy used to generate and deliver energy to the site. To calculate a building's source energy, imported and exported energy is multiplied by the appropriate site-to-source conversion factors. The source energy measure encompasses the building, the energy transmission system, the power plant, and the energy consumed in transmitting fuel from the power plant to the end user and from the building to the energy grid. This definition is a more comprehensive definition of building energy usage than the site definition but is challenged by difficulties in acquiring reliable site-to-source conversion factors.

» **Net-zero energy cost building.** A net-zero energy cost building earns as much or more money by selling energy to the grid as it pays for energy consumption. Metrics are tracked on the basis of building revenues for energy sales to the grid and costs incurred for energy consumption, and are easy to verify with utility bills. Building owners are typically most interested in revenue and cost metrics because they influence a property's bottom line and can be related to annual and long-term financial plans. Cost metrics also implicitly account for fluctuations in fuel prices and availability, as well as transmission efficiencies.

Utility rate regulations, however, may make it difficult for property owners to realize revenue surpluses by selling to the grid more energy than they consume. Many utility rate structures will give credit for energy returned to the grid, but will not allow property consumption to go below zero on an annual basis. As a result, there may be no way for property owners to fully recover costs incurred by fixed and demand charges. The approval of additional net metering programs and rate reforms are needed to permit the comprehensive sale of excess energy to the utility grid.

» **Net-zero energy emissions building.** The net-zero energy emission building produces at least as much emissions-free renewable energy as it consumes from emissions-producing energy sources. Buildings in this category are truly net-zero carbon properties, and the net emissions metric is likely the best basis for calculating a property's impact on the environment. The emissions metric, however, can be difficult to calculate, which reduces its near-term utilization in the marketplace.

George Vavaroutsos, LEED AP, is a sustainable real estate consultant with Malachite LLC.

NOTE

1 Paul Torcellini et al., "Zero Energy Buildings: A Critical Look at the Definition," Conference Paper: ACEEE Summer Study, August 2006, www.nrel.gov/docs/fy06osti/39833.pdf.

BUILDINGS AS LIVING SYSTEMS: BIOMIMICRY, BIONICS, AND LIVING BUILDINGS

The newest development in the green building arena is the use of the natural world as a model for design innovations.

Biomimicry or Bionics

Biomimicry, known as bionics in the European Union, uses the example of the natural world to influence building and materials design.[15] Biomimicry endeavors to design building materials and systems to emulate biological systems, in order to enhance efficiency and environmental sensitivity. An easily understood application of biomimicry was the development of a nontoxic building adhesive derived from the naturally occurring chemical that permits mussels to attach themselves securely to rocks.[16]

A more complex example is found in Skidmore, Owings and Merrill's Pearl River Tower, a 2.3 million-square-foot, 71-story office complex in Guangzhou, China, scheduled for completion in 2009. Inspired by the sea sponge, Pearl River Tower utilizes a "porous" design intended to absorb wind and solar energy from the environment, rather than deflecting it. Wind energy will be harnessed through built-in wind turbines, while solar energy will be absorbed through photovoltaic cells. It is anticipated that the Pearl River Tower will realize energy savings of approximately 60 percent; the project is expected to be the world's most energy-efficient super tower.[17]

A celebrated example of biomimicry is the sustainable design of Eastgate Centre, the largest office and retail center in Harare, Zimbabwe, whose passive cooling system was inspired by African termite mounds (for details, see the sidebar by Leanne Tobias).

The IDeAs Z-Squared Design Facility is both a net-zero-energy and a net-zero emissions building; the 30-kW building-integrated photovoltaic system that forms part of the building's roof structure provides an estimated 55,000 kWh of electricity per year, meeting 100 percent of the structure's energy needs.

ACHIEVING NET-ZERO ENERGY IN RETROFITS: TWO PIONEERING EXAMPLES

GEORGE VAVAROUTSOS

While most new construction of net-zero-energy or near net-zero-energy structures has been for small public-use buildings, two retrofited structures highlight the opportunities and challenges of using net-zero strategies for existing offices and related uses.

IDeAs Z-Squared Design Facility (San Jose, California)

The IDeAs Z-Squared Design Facility serves as the San Jose, California headquarters for Integrated Design Associates, Inc. (IDeAs), an electrical engineering and lighting design firm specializing in sustainable systems. The original structure seemed an unlikely target for a ZEB: a one-story branch bank made of concrete and containing no windows, built in the 1960s. In 2007, the owner (and primary tenant) transformed this dilapidated structure into a 7,200-square-foot (670-square-meter), two-story office building that produces more power from rooftop photovoltaic panels than it consumes.

The Z-Squared building is both a net-zero-energy and a net-zero emissions building; the 30-kW BIPV system that forms part of the building's roof structure provides an estimated 55,000 kWh per year, meeting 100 percent of the structure's energy needs.[1]

To get to net zero, the project team had to reduce the building's energy consumption wherever possible. The project team used an integrated design strategy to eliminate every kilowatt-hour of energy use that was not vital to building operations or the occupants' job duties. As designed, the building requires an estimated 55,000 kWh of electricity every year, a 60 percent reduction from a typical office building of this size. The facility also features an energy monitoring and building control system, which provides detailed energy use information that can be used to track and improve building performance.[2]

Key strategies to achieving net zero energy at the Z-Squared design facility include the following:

▸▸ **Daylighting.** To reduce the need for mechanical lighting, windows and skylights were cut into the structure's walls and roof to deliver daylight deep into building interiors. To limit glare and solar heat gain from direct sunlight, the windows and skylights feature glass with a low solar heat gain coefficient (SHGC). Additionally, the southern exposure features a large overhang to limit direct sunlight, while windows on the

eastern exposure feature an electrochromic window shading system that darkens the glass with electric voltage to block heat transmission.

▸▸ **Reduced plug loads.** To further reduce building energy demand, all office equipment has an Energy Star rating, and occupancy sensors turn off equipment at workstations when they are not occupied. Select shared office equipment is automatically shut down at night when the building alarm system is activated.[3]

To limit glare and solar heat gain from direct sunlight at the Z-Squared Design Facility, the windows and skylights have glass with a low solar heat gain coefficient. This southern exposure also features a large overhang to limit direct sunlight.

- **Radiant heating and cooling.** In addition to solar photovoltaics, the structure uses a geothermal system to both heat and cool the structure. The underground piping for the ground-source heat pumps is buried horizontally beneath a 10,000-square-foot (929-square-meter) section of the parking lot. The warmed or chilled water is then run through pipes in the building slab to heat or cool the office space.[4]

- **Energy-efficient ventilation system.** The building ventilation system is separate from the heating and cooling system, allowing it to be reduced in scale and use roughly 25 percent of the energy typically required to ventilate the space. Warmed or chilled air is delivered from the ground-source heat pump to the air handler, allowing the outside air to be conditioned before it enters the building. The building also features operable windows; when outside temperature and humidity conditions are appropriate, 100 percent outside air can be used to ventilate the building.[5]

ZEB@BCA (Singapore)

ZEB@BCA, scheduled for completion in late 2009, is the renovation of a three-story campus building at Singapore's national Building and Construction Academy (BCA). The project will feature one of the largest solar photovoltaic systems in southeast Asia. The $6.8 million renovation of the facility, which will house offices, classrooms, and a library, is targeted to reduce building energy use by 60 percent from a conventionally built structure. The additional power necessary to achieve net-zero energy will be produced by a 13,000-square-foot (1,200-square-meter) photovoltaic array on the building's roof and vertical walls, which it is estimated will produce 185 MWh of electricity per year.[6]

In addition to standard energy efficiency practices, such as occupancy and daylight sensors with dimmers for lighting and a low-E coating on windows, unique energy reduction strategies will be utilized at the ZEB@BCA:

- **Extensive daylighting.** To deliver daylight deep into building interiors, the structure will use customized solar ductwork technology created by researchers at the school. This product looks similar to traditional heating, ventilating, and air-conditioning (HVAC) ductwork, but the interiors feature aluminum mirrors that can reflect and deliver daylight more than 50 feet into the structure. The solar duct system is useful for daylighting spaces that require electric lighting, reducing the amount of energy needed for adequate illumination.

- **Passive cooling for classrooms.** The classrooms in the structure will not be air conditioned. Instead, they will feature a solar chimney installation designed to accelerate natural stack ventilation, exhausting hot air through the roof of the building and drawing in fresh, cooler air from ventilation ducts close to the ground to create air flow and regulate classroom temperature.

- **Efficient air-conditioning system.** For the spaces that are air conditioned, a high-efficiency chiller system, combined with a unique personal ventilation system that gives building occupants control over their level of cooling, is expected to reduce the energy required to cool the space by more than 55 percent from that required in a conventional system.[7]

- **Vertical greening.** The structure will feature vertically landscaped exterior walls that will shade the building and reduce solar heat gain. Preliminary modeling indicates that vertical greening will save the building $60,000 in annual energy costs.[8]

Serving as both a teaching facility and a living laboratory, the BCA will showcase and integrate various green building technologies to demonstrate how a ZEB can be designed and built as a retrofit. The BCA hopes to influence the uptake of new technology by the building and construction industry in Singapore, and to encourage more building owners to retrofit existing buildings to significantly reduce energy consumption.

George Vavaroutsos, LEED AP, is a sustainable real estate consultant with Malachite LLC.

NOTES

1 Lewers, Christine, "From Zero to Net-Zero Squared," Architechweb.com, January 2008, www.architechweb.com/ArticleDetails/tabid/254/ArticleID/5605/Default.aspx.

2 Madsen, Jana, "Building a Zero Energy Commercial Office," Buildings.com, August 2007, www.buildings.com/ArticleDetails/tabid/3321/ArticleID/4988/Default.aspx.

3 Perry, Tekla, "The Zero-Zero Hero," IEEE Spectrum Online, September 2007, www.spectrum.ieee.org/sep07/5485.

4 Lewers, Christine, January 2008.

5 *Ibid.*

6 Stephen Wittkopf, et al., "735: BIPV Design for Singapore Zero-Energy Building" Presentation to Conference on Passive and Low Energy Architecture, October 22, 2008, http://architecture.ucd.ie/Paul/PLEA2008/content/papers/oral/PLEA_FinalPaper_ref_735.pdf.

7 Lee Siew Eang and Stephen Wittkopf, "Zero Energy Building @ BCA Academy," *Pillars* 05 (2007): 8–9.

8 Stephen Wittkopf, "Zero-Energy Building Singapore: Retrofit for Sustainable Construction," International Solid Waste Association, 2008 World Congress, Singapore, November 5, 2008.

Living Buildings

Living buildings, an emerging concept in green design, are intended to integrate seamlessly with the surrounding environment, to operate both for efficiency and for maximum beauty, to generate all their energy and water from renewable sources, and to maximize occupant comfort, health, and well-being. A new Living Building standard, developed and codified by Jason McLennan, now of the Cascadia chapter of the U.S. Green Building Council, significantly advances the living building model and the frontiers of green design. The standard imposes especially rigorous sustainability requirements, all of which must be met to attain certification:[17]

▸▸ **SUSTAINABLE SITE SELECTION**. As is the case for LEED-certified buildings, living buildings cannot be developed on prime

EASTGATE CENTRE: USING BIOMIMICRY TO BUILD GREEN IN ZIMBABWE

LEANNE TOBI

Eastgate Centre, the largest shopping and office complex in Harare, the capital of Zimbabwe, is a global model for the successful use of biomimicry or bionics in commercial real estate design. Designed by architect Michael Pearce and engineered by Arup, Eastgate is a nine-story, 340,000-square-foot (31,600-square-meter) development completed in 1996. The project's passive cooling system was inspired by the dwellings constructed by the mound-building termites of southern Africa, which can reach heights of several meters. The passive cooling strategies employed in the design of Eastgate can be incorporated in green building renovations.

The termite mounds are thought by many to maintain a constant interior temperature of 87°F (30°C)—the temperature said to be required to maintain the fungus that is the termites' chief food source. Temperature control is achieved inside a mound despite outdoor temperatures that fluctuate from 35°F to 104°F (0°C to 40°C). The internal temperature is generally believed to be maintained by a network of tunnels at and below ground level, which bring in cooler air, in combination with a porous surface or chimney-like opening at the top of the mound, which releases warm air. The ongoing mixture of cooler air with stored warmer air (which rises gradually and is released through the top of the mound), maintains appropriate internal temperatures.[1]

In designing Eastgate, Mick Pearce and Arup employed a mechanical version of the termite mound. Fans draw in fresh air from a shaded, breeze-cooled central atrium, which is then circulated through hollow floors and baseboard vents. As inside air warms and rises, it is drawn from the interiors by ceiling vents and ultimately exits through a system of 48 chimneys.

The development also uses exposed thermal mass to regulate interior temperature (see chapter 3 for a discussion of the use this strategy). Eastgate is constructed primarily of concrete, and its exposed concrete walls and floor slabs absorb heat energy during daytime; at night, the structure is flushed with naturally cooler air to cool the structure to withstand the heat of the coming day. When needed, supplemental heating is provided by small heaters located in the vents.

Eastgate is highly energy-efficient. The project is reported to consume less than 10 percent of the energy used by a conventional building of the same size. The $36 million project saved $3.5 million in initial construction costs because an air-conditioning system did not have to be imported from abroad. Operating savings over the project's first five years of operation have been estimated at an additional $3.5 million.

Leanne Tobias, LEED AP, is the founder and managing principal of Malachite LLC.

NOTES

1 This description details the typically reported functioning of such termite mounds the context of the Eastgate Centre. See, for example, Affan B: Learning Log, "Eastgate Centre in Zimbabwe: Modeled After Termite Mounds," January 19, 2009, http://affanblearninglog.blogspot.com/2009/01/eastgate-centre-in-zimbabwe-modeled.htm An alternative explanation proposes that the mounds maintain a range of comfortable temperatures instead of a constant set point and suggests that they operate more like the human lung, with porous walls and adaptive interfaces with the surrounding environment—an alternative biomimicry model. See J. Scott Turner and Rupert C. Soar, "Beyond Biomimicry: What Termites Can Tell Us About Realizing the Living Building," presented at the First International Conference on Industrialized, Intelligent Construction (I3CON), Loughborough University, May 14–16, 2008, www.esf.edu/efb/turner/publication%20pdfs/Beyond%20Biomimicry%20MS%20distribution.pd

2 Affan B:Learning Log, "Eastgate Centre in Zimbabwe: Modeled After Termite Mounds," January 19, 2009, http://affanblearninglog.blogspot.com/2009/01/eastgate-centre-in-zimbabwe-modeled.html.

3 *Ibid.*; Lisa Delgado, "Imitation of Life," The Architect's Newspaper, September 2007, www.archpaper.com/e-board_rev.asp?News_ID=401.

farmland, within the 100-year floodplain, or on or adjacent to ecologically sensitive land. In addition, living buildings can be built only on grayfield or brownfield sites developed before December 31, 2007, thus favoring infill development, major renovations, or reconstruction. For each acre developed, an equal amount of land must be set aside for at least 100 years through a habitat exchange program.

▸▸ **NET-ZERO ENERGY USE**. A living building must be 100 percent supplied by on-site renewable energy on a net annual basis. Permissible renewable energy sources include solar, wind, water, methane captured by composting, hydrogen fuel cells, and geothermal.

▸▸ **NET-ZERO WATER USE**. All water used in a living building project must be captured from precipitation or derived from closed loop systems.

▸▸ **CARBON OFFSET**. A living building must offset its carbon usage through a one-time carbon offset, calculated on the basis of its square footage, building usage, and general construction type.

▸▸ **CONSTRUCTION WASTE MANAGEMENT**. A living building project must divert 80 to 100 percent of its construction waste from landfill, with standards set according to the type of waste involved.

▸▸ **HEALTHY MATERIALS AND INDOOR QUALITY**. Living buildings may not contain materials that are prohibited because they are toxic or do not comply with mandated indoor air quality standards. Materials must be sourced from within a prescribed radius. All wood utilized in a living building project must be certified by the Forest Stewardship Council (FSC). Every space intended for occupancy must offer operable windows for fresh air and daylight and meet ventilation requirements.

▸▸ **BEAUTY AND INSPIRATION**. Living buildings must contain design elements intended "solely for human delight and the celebration of cul-

ture, spirit, and place appropriate to function."[18] Living buildings must also provide public education materials and open nonsensitive areas to the public at least annually.

The principles incorporated in the Living Building standard can also be applied to retrofit and renovation projects. According to the Cascadia Green Building Council, some 60 living building projects have been constructed or are underway as of this writing. A new office project that employs strategies that could prove beneficial in the design of living buildings is the Terry Thomas, the Seattle headquarters of the Weber Thompson architectural firm. Many of the features utilized in that building can be adapted for use in commercial office renovations. (For details, see the sidebar by Gabe Hanson.)

TOWARD THE FUTURE

As detailed above, numerous innovations in building science including BIM, the development of new materials and technologies, advances in nanotechnologies, and the enhanced use of information technology have much to offer sustainable building construction and renovation. The development of new design approaches, such as biomimicry, and more rigorous voluntary rating systems, such as the Living Building standard of the Cascadia chapter of the U.S. Green Building Council, can also be expected to produce innovations in the development and retrofit of green and energy-efficient buildings.

The public sector is also likely to play a key role in encouraging innovative approaches to the design and retrofit of green building systems. As discussed here and in chapter 7, governments around the globe are taking an increasingly active role in conducting and financing building science research, as well as in regulating building efficiency and sustainability. The growing global use of net metering, which allows owners of distributed generation systems and others to sell surplus energy back to the electrical grid, is also likely to encourage building owners to undertake energy-efficient retrofits, as are financing innovations (see chapter 5) that increase capital flows to the green building industry.

NOTES

1 McGraw-Hill Construction, "Building Information Modeling," SmartMarket Report, 2008.

2 Dariush Arasteh, Steve Selkowitz, and Josh Apte, "Zero Energy Windows," Lawrence Berkeley National Laboratory, August 2006, www.osti.gov/bridge/servlets/purl/898951YsG4Yt/898951.pdf.

3 Lawrence Berkeley National Laboratory, "Final Project Report: Advancement of Electrochromic Windows," April 2006, www.lbl.gov/Science-Articles/Archive/sabl/2007/Jan/Advance-EC-Windows.pdf.

4 Jeff Tsao, "Ultra-Efficient Solid-State Lighting: Performance Frontier, Progress, Challenges," Sandia National Laboratories, November 2008.

5 U.S. Department of Energy, Office of Energy Efficiency and Renewable Energy, "Energy Savings Potential of Solid State Lighting in General Illumination Applications," December 2006.

6 Jennifer Kho, "Charting a Path to Low-Cost Solar" Greentech Media, www.greentechmedia.com/articles/read/charting-a-path-to-low-cost-solar-1128.

7 Mark Osborne, "First Solar First to US$1 Per Watt Manufacturing Cost," PV Tech.org, February 2009, www.pv-tech.org/news/_a/first_solar_first_to_us1_per_watt_manufacturing_cost.

8 Elizabeth A. Thomson, "MIT opens new 'window' on solar energy," MIT News, http://web.mit.edu/newsoffice/2008/solar-cells-0710.html.

A STEP TOWARD LIVING BUILDINGS: THE TERRY THOMAS

GABE HANSON

The Terry Thomas, designed by the architectural firm of Weber Thompson, provides 64,600 square feet of space for office, retail, and structured parking uses. The project was completed in April 2008 and serves as the firm's new headquarters. The Terry Thomas has won numerous local and national environmental design awards, has been designated as a 2009 Top Ten Green Building by the AIA's National Committee on the Environment, and has earned LEED Gold Core and Shell certification and LEED Platinum Commercial Interior certification for the space occupied by Weber Thompson.

The Terry Thomas is the first Seattle office building in decades to be designed without a mechanical cooling system. Power usage from June 2008 through April 2009 was half that of a conventional office building. The Terry Thomas is at the forefront of advanced environmental design, offering a wealth of solutions that can be applied to green office building retrofits and to the creation of living buildings.

Multiple Benefit Solutions

The Terry Thomas design team used sustainable solutions with multiple benefits wherever possible. For example, distinctive castellated structural beams provide structural support, while hexagonal holes in the web of the beam permit cross-ventilation at perimeter vents. The use of castellated beams aids in material and weight reduction while admitting ample daylight.

Multiple-benefit solutions were also used in the building organization and programming. With the exception of an internal courtyard stair, all ancillary functions are located in a support bar along the southern portion of the building. This creates an open plan that maximizes layout flexibility and

future adaptability. In the courtyard, an external sculptural stair aids in energy reduction by replacing an elevator. The stair provides a surface for climbing vines, a landscaping feature that reinforces connections with nature. Fresh air and physical movement recharge workers as they move through the building.

Natural Ventilation Strategy

The mild Seattle climate favored eliminating a traditional HVAC system in favor of a passive cooling system, which produced cost savings in construction and operation. Thermal modeling demonstrated that interior temperatures will exceed the occupants' thermal comfort expectations for only a few hours each year. The central courtyard and narrow floor plates allow optimal distribution of natural light and air. The vents, controls, and window openings work together to create a stack effect, drawing warm air out and up through the courtyard. Thermostats and CO_2 sensors control exterior louvers distributed along the building perimeter, providing fresh air and maintaining optimum indoor air quality. Operable windows give occupants additional control over airflow into the space.

External Shading Strategy

The Terry Thomas makes use of extensive solar shading to reduce solar heat gain, regulate internal temperatures, and limit the use of artificial lighting:

▸▸ **Glass sunshades.** Glass sunshades act as "sunglasses" for the building by preventing the sun's heat from penetrating the interior while allowing visible light to enter the work space. Solar heat gain was reduced by 85 percent on the

9 Ken Sinclair, "Reinventing Building Automation," Automated Buildings.com, May 2009, www.automatedbuildings.com/news/may09/reviews/09428031230reinventionksin.htm.

10 Center for American Progress, "It's Easy Being Green: The Next Generation of Electricity?," June 2008, www.american-progress.org/issues/2008/06/smart_grids.html.

11 Wes Frye, "Smart Grid: Transforming the Electricity System to Meet Future Demand and Reduce Greenhouse Gas Emissions," Cisco Internet Business Solutions Group, November 2008, www.cisco.com/web/about/ac79/docs/Smart_Grid_WP_1124aFINAL.pdf.

12 WBCSD, "Energy Efficiency in Buildings: Business Realities and Opportunities," September 8, 2008, www.wbcsd.org/includes/getTarget.asp?type=d&id=MzE0Njk.

13 Paul Torcellini, Shanti Pless, Michael Deru, and Drury Crawley, "Zero Energy Buildings: A Critical Look at the Definition," National Renewable Energy Laboratory, Conference Paper NREL/CP-550-39833, June 2006, www.nrel.gov/docs/fy06osti/39833.pdf.

14 Jeremy Faludi, "Biomimicry 101," WorldChanging.com, October 13, 2005, www.worldchanging.com/archives/003625.html.

15 Dylan Rivera, "Nature's Success (Despite Us) Inspires Green-Building Mimics," OregonLive.com, April 30, 2009, www.oregonlive.com/environment/index.ssf/2009/04/natures_success_despite_us_ins.html.

16 Lisa Delgado, "Imitation of Life," The Architect's Newspaper, September 5, 2007, www.archpaper.com/e-board_rev.asp?News_ID=401.

17 Cascadia Region Green Building Council, The Living Building Challenge, Version 1.3, August 2008, www.cascadiagbc.org/lbc/lbc-v1.3.pdf.

18 Ibid.

east- and west-facing windows. Airflow behind the glass shades (produced by mechanical louvers installed to support the natural ventilation strategy) removes the heat energy before it enters the building.

- **Automated blinds.** Automated blinds help control morning and evening sunlight on the northeastern and northwestern sides of the building to reduce solar heat gain while admitting daylight. Automated blinds are also installed along the southern façade in the courtyard to minimize the negative effects of uncontrolled daylight such as increased heat gain from direct sunlight penetration and glare.

Building Skin
The exterior of the Terry Thomas was designed to maximize interior temperatures and energy efficiency:

- **Light surfaces.** The corrugated-metal exterior skin reflects light and reduces solar heat gain. A high-albedo roof helps to reduce the solar heat island effect and lowers energy demands significantly. Both of these features can be adapted to an existing building.

- **Modular systems.** The fenestration pattern is based on a one-, two-, four-, and eight-foot module to increase material efficiency. This standardization of building components helps to reduce construction waste and maximize window arrangements.

Interior
Building interiors at the Terry Thomas support sustainability and efficiency objectives:

- **Modular layout.** The floor plan is based on a regular four-foot module to accommodate the greatest number of workstation types. Renovations to an existing building could be conceived in a similar modular layout to reduce waste and maximize flexibility.

- **Workstations.** Workstations are lifted from the floor by four to five inches to allow cross-ventilation and keep occupants cool. Partitions are kept low to allow uninterrupted light and air flow, and to increase communication and a sense of community. These strategies could be utilized in the renovation of an existing office building.

- **Surfaces.** Interior surfaces are bright white to reflect light, thereby reducing the need for artificial lighting and minimizing solar heat gain. The use of white indoor surfaces can also be adapted to building retrofits. The use of low-VOC paints and environmentally friendly fixtures also help to reduce adverse environmental effects in both renovations and new construction.

Acoustics and Lighting
The acoustic and lighting features of the Terry Thomas were designed to enhance occupant comfort and cost-effectiveness. The acoustical panels incorporated in the design of the Weber Thompson interior office spaces provide multiple benefits. They mitigate interior noise, which can be a common problem in green offices with open plans. A simple, low-cost, energy-efficient fluorescent lighting fixture is directed at the panels to meet the office's indirect lighting needs. These combined strategies saved costs and materials, and improve the overall efficiency of the building. These strategies can be utilized readily in sustainable office renovations.

Gabe Hanson, Assoc. AIA, LEED AP, was Weber Thompson's senior project designer for the Terry Thomas (Core and Shell).

Case Studies

CASE STUDY • **DAVID A. SIGMAN AND STEVE VITOFF**

545 Madison Avenue

NEW YORK, NEW YORK

A newly renovated, 17-story, Class A, trophy office building that features a distinctive glass curtain wall, 545 Madison Avenue is situated in Manhattan's exclusive Plaza District. The Plaza District, long ranked as Manhattan's most lucrative commercial and retail venue, is a square zone running uptown from East 47th Street to East 65th Street. The Avenue of the Americas (Sixth Avenue) and Fifth Avenue share the district's western border, and the East River serves as its eastern boundary.

The combination of spectrally selective low-E windows and thermally broken window frames achieves a 30 percent improvement in energy efficiency over the insulating properties of the curtain wall.

Standing on the site of the former home of 1912 Nobel Peace Prize winner and U.S. Secretary of State Elihu Root, 545 Madison Avenue was constructed in 1955. It was acquired in November 2006 through a 75-year ground lease transaction by LCOR, a national real estate development and investment firm based in Berwyn, Pennsylvania. Exemplifying the company's corporate commitment to sus-

tainable development, LCOR completed a gut rehabilitation of the property under the guidelines of the Leadership in Energy and Environmental Design Core & Shell (LEED-CS) system. The project received Gold certification from the U.S. Green Building Council without resorting to expensive, untested, or exotic technologies.

Selected sustainable aspects of 545 Madison Avenue include the following:

▸▸ **SITE SELECTION**. The building is located on a dense, urban site with superior transportation access and connectivity. By facilitating walking and mass transit use, project siting is environmentally friendly.

▸▸ **ENERGY EFFICIENCY**. LCOR incorporated an array of energy-efficient features into the design, and the building will be commissioned and operated under strict, energy-related protocols.

▸▸ **INDOOR ENVIRONMENTAL QUALITY**. Elements include low-emitting finishes, high-efficiency filters, high rates of outside air, and ample daylight.

▸▸ **ENVIRONMENTALLY CONSIDERED MATERIALS**. LCOR made extensive use of recycled and locally manufactured materials, and recycled the waste generated during construction.

CONTEXT AND OWNERSHIP OBJECTIVES

LCOR's interest in renovating 545 Madison Avenue reflected its interest in optimizing floor layouts and usable tenant space and upgrading the property's market appeal. The building had been constructed in accordance with zoning laws in effect in 1955, which resulted in inefficient floor plates with oddly shaped setbacks that made office layouts difficult. The building was also underbuilt by approximately 2,400 zoning square feet.

Building Information

LCOR began gut rehabilitation of the building in March 2007 with Bovis Lend Lease serving as construction manager. The aging, half-century-old structure was stripped to its skeletal frame. Utilizing current zoning rules, the zoning floor area was redistributed from lower floors to higher floors where rental values are greater, and the setbacks were filled in to result in more rectilinear floor plates. A penthouse was added at the top of the building. The property's modern, floor-to-ceiling glass curtain wall—which replaced 1950s blonde brickwork and uninsulated aluminum-strip windows—was custom-made by a specialty glass manufacturer in Pennsylvania. The distinctive, nine-foot, clear glass windows are highly rare in commercial office buildings. The renovation was completed for occupancy in the late fall of 2008.

LCOR had budgeted hard costs equaling approximately $40 million. Adding lease-up and carrying costs, the overall project cost was about $90 million. The office tower's gross size of 141,583 square feet (13,153 square meters) includes net rentable area measuring 132,301 square feet (12,291 square meters). In addition to the office space above, 545 Madison's ground floor and cellar house 7,080 square feet (658 square meters) of retail space. The penthouse has 897 square feet (83 square meters). Floor plates range from 6,200 to 9,300 rentable square feet (576 to 864 square meters).

The building stands on the southeast corner of Madison Avenue at the corner of East 55th Street, along one of America's most lucrative commercial real estate venues. The property extends 50 feet (15.2 meters) along Madison Avenue and 125 feet (38.1 meters) along East 55th Street. Central Park is nearby and neighbors include Tiffany & Co., Louis Vuitton, Oceana, and the St. Regis Hotel, surroundings which add to the appeal of 545 Madison Avenue.

Richemont North America, a European holding company controlling many upscale brands, leases the building's 7,080 square feet (657.8 square meters) of retail space, which offers a total of 150 feet (13.9 meters) of total window frontage on Madison Avenue and 55th Street. CB Richard Ellis represented LCOR in closing a ten-year lease at $600 per square foot ($55.74 per square meter). The upscale British brand Alfred Dunhill relocated to the site from 711 Fifth Avenue, and Richemont established the first East Coast outlet for Officine Panerai, a leading Italian luxury watchmaker in a small portion of the retail space.

Ownership Objectives

LCOR's target tenants were elite, boutique financial services companies and law firms that desired prime, full-floor space in a contemporary, high-end office building located in a first-class Manhattan business district. LCOR characterized the transformation of the outdated building as a "Cinderella story" of renewal. The full-scale renovation represented a value-added strategy because the prior structure had been commanding some of the lowest rents in a highly upscale area.

The new building's lengthy list of amenities includes such elements as floor-to-ceiling windows, individually controlled heating and air-conditioning systems, full-floor identity, and premium concierge services, complemented by views of one of Manhattan's most esteemed streets and its stunning skyline. Common area interiors were designed to be compatible with a Class A tenant base. Finishes included a combination of Pietra Cardosa smooth stone, California maple burlwood veneer panels, and Moncervetto marble in the lobby, as well as five-star, hotel-like restrooms with porcelain enamel and marble. Underscoring the building's high-end character, the developer commissioned Willard Boepple, an internationally recognized artist and sculptor, to create a modernist sculpture series for the lobby.

Why LCOR Decided To Go Green

LCOR attributes its decision to seek LEED certification for 545 Madison Avenue to at least four factors:

» THE COMPANY'S CORPORATE CULTURE,

» BENEFITS RELATING TO FINANCING and prospective sale price,

» THE STEADY EXPANSION OF SUSTAINABILITY regulations in New York City and around the country, and

» THE MARKETING BENEFITS of a building with green features.

CORPORATE CULTURE

LCOR prides itself on a long-time corporate emphasis on industry practices that are sensitive to the environment. The firm supports its commitment to sustainability by acting as a responsible builder and a responsible consumer of energy and other natural resources, by guiding new development toward existing urban and suburban centers, and by serving as a strong advocate of mixed-use developments with greater density, particularly at transit hubs—which are able to support greater densities more efficiently. Before renovating 545 Madison Avenue, the company had undertaken several other sustainable projects, including the 1.3 million-square-foot (120,774-square-meter) Ted Weiss Federal Building in Manhattan; the 2.5 million-square-foot (203,000-square-meter) U.S. Patent and Trademark Office Headquarters in Alexandria, Virginia; and the mixed-use North Bethesda Center in North Bethesda, Maryland.

FINANCING RELATED-BENEFITS

Green design has rapidly emerged as a virtual requirement in real estate equity financing. The decision to seek a LEED Gold rating was an important benefit in the eyes of LCOR's joint venture partner, BlackRock Realty, and its pension fund client. The developer anticipated recovering some proportion of green-related costs through reduced operating expenses. Also, LCOR expected that a LEED-certified building would enjoy enhanced resale value.

REGULATORY ENVIRONMENT

LCOR is keenly aware that the city of New York and other jurisdictions around the country are increasingly adopting measures requiring green construction practices, attributes, and property management regimens. LCOR believes that a LEED building will be well positioned to comply with emerging codes relating to sustainability.

MARKETING BENEFITS

LCOR believed that LEED designation would make 545 Madison Avenue more desirable to commercial tenants in a marketplace and business environment that was becoming increasingly interested in sustainability. The company viewed LEED certification as a selling point and has highlighted the LEED message in its leasing, advertising, and public relations programming.

INTEGRATING THE LEED ADVISER INTO THE DESIGN TEAM

The developer selected key design team members in a conventional manner. LCOR first interviewed for an architecture firm, because the architect would be responsible for creating zoning diagrams and design projections. The developer chose New York-based Moed de Armas & Shannon. Then, in similar time frames, LCOR selected its general contractor (Bovis Lend Lease of New York) and its mechanical, electrical, and plumbing (MEP) engineering firm (Cosentini Associates, also of New York).

Once LCOR had made a corporate commitment to pursuing LEED certification at 545 Madison, the company recognized that a LEED consultant would immediately need to be added to the team. The developer ultimately selected Viridian Energy and Environmental, whose architects, engineers, and building scientists have provided LEED-related services for more than 100 projects.

Because Viridian's initial role was to devise a checklist of LEED performance targets, the company was brought into the process early. Instructed to build a design scenario capable of attaining a LEED Gold level, Viridian created its target list and presented it to architect Moed de Armas & Shannon and engineering firms Cosentini Associates and Ysrael A. Seinuk. Armed with the consultant's checklist of LEED performance criteria, the architect and engineer prepared their proposed designs. LCOR then instructed the construction manager to price out the various design elements.

Because of the small size of the building and the limited back-of-house space available, a number of LEED design options were not achievable. Systems such as stormwater retention tanks or on-site clean energy production were not feasible for this reason and were eliminated from the scoring process. When the proposed design emerged, the plan was modified to conform to budget and LEED targets.

During the initial phase of the development process, the LEED consultant regularly attended weekly design team meetings. LEED certification was a standing item on meeting agendas. As the design process entered more deeply into the details of construction documentation, however, there was less need for the LEED consultant to be present at weekly meetings, so Viridian did not attend. Once construction documents were completed, however, the LEED adviser again took part in the weekly sessions to vet the full plan for compliance with initial LEED targets. Throughout construction, the team would turn to Viridian to verify which targeted points were actually being achieved, which would require additional work to achieve, and which were simply out of reach.

GREEN DESIGN FEATURES

The location of 545 Madison Avenue itself qualified the project for certain LEED credits:

▸ **HIGH-DENSITY DEVELOPMENT AND COMMUNITY CONNECTIVITY.** A high-rise project, 545 Madison Avenue is in an area with more than 677,000 square feet (62,895 square meters) per acre of land. Developed at 724,750 square feet (67,331 square meters) per acre, the site is considered an exceptionally dense development under the LEED rating system. The project is close to a rich array of amenities recognized under LEED, including transit lines, restaurants, banks, beauty salons, places of worship, pharmacies, parks, recreational facilities, and museums.

▸ **PARKING AND TRANSIT ACCESS.** The building has no parking, thus earning credits by not expanding parking capacity. It is near a number of subway stations and bus stops, and close to two of America's busiest transit hubs, Penn Station and Grand Central Station.

▸ **BICYCLE RACKS AND CHANGING FACILITIES.** To encourage use of alternative transportation, 545 Madison pursued the LEED credit on bicycle racks and changing facilities by placing these features in the basement.

The decision to seek a LEED Gold rating for 545 Madison was an important benefit in the eyes of LCOR's joint venture partner, BlackRock Realty, and its pension fund client. The developer anticipated recovering some portion of green-related costs through reduced operating expenses. Also, LCOR expected a LEED-certified building to enjoy enhanced resale value.

KEVIN CHU/KCIP

CONSTRUCTION PROCESS

The project team adhered to LEED requirements for environmentally sensitive construction:

▸▸ **CONSTRUCTION WASTE RECYCLING**. Because the project involved the full-scale gut rehabilitation of a 17-story office building, construction and demolition activities generated large quantities of waste, a majority of which could be recycled. Recycled materials included metals, concrete, wood, carpet, and cardboard. Bovis Lend Lease implemented a construction waste management plan during renovation to ensure the maximum possible recycling of waste. The recycling initiative succeeded in directing more than 75 percent of the waste volume away from dump sites for reuse.

▸▸ **INDOOR AIR QUALITY DURING CONSTRUCTION**. During construction, Bovis Lend Lease created and implemented a regimen of procedures designed to foster good indoor air quality:

- Preventing construction dust, debris, and volatile gases from entering air-conditioning and ventilation systems;
- Preventing soft and absorptive materials from absorbing pollutants and odors given off by such wet-applied products as paint and adhesives; and
- Protecting materials from any moisture absorption that could support the growth of mold and fungus.

Bovis Lend Lease has since begun to use this pollution prevention checklist as a standard control measure on a growing number of its projects.

▸▸ **EROSION CONTROL**. During demolition and construction, the construction team paid careful attention to ensure that stormwater, wind, and vehicles did not carry sediment from the site to the surrounding air and sewer systems, which when overburdened release effluents into nearby waterways.

▸▸ **ASBESTOS REMEDIATION**. Before the renovation, the construction team took 102 samples from building materials. The inspection found asbestos-containing materials in 29 samples. These materials were safely removed before the renovation. Although the site is not classified as a brownfield, LEED recognizes the value of asbestos abatement and requires proper removal in order to qualify for certification.

BUILDING FEATURES

The project at 545 Madison Avenue was designed to conserve energy and water, use sustainable and low-emittance materials, promote indoor air quality, and operate in an environmentally friendly fashion.

Energy and Water Efficiency

LCOR incorporated energy efficiency features throughout all project elements, including mechanical systems, lighting, and the building envelope. The project was also designed to significantly reduce water use.

▸▸ **SETTING U-VALUE TARGETS**. Viridian gave the developer U-value targets for the curtain wall glass assembly and solar heat gain coefficient. U-values gauge how well a material allows heat to pass through. Products with low U-values are most resistant to heat flow. The U-value required by the LEED-CS reference standard is 0.57; anything below this figure represents an improvement over the standard. Cosentini and Moed de Armas & Shannon explored various curtain wall options and settled on a system with a highly efficient U-value of 0.4.

▸▸ **WELL-INSULATED CURTAIN WALL/WINDOW SYSTEM**. The building has well-insulated exterior walls that reduce both heat loss and heat gain when compared with a standard building. The property's curtain wall feels warmer in winter and admits less heat in summer than older generations of buildings. This improves the comfort of occupants in perimeter spaces. In general, a person who is close to a more efficient wall or window system will feel comfortable at a somewhat lower temperature in winter and a somewhat higher temperature in summer.

▸▸ **ROOFING, PAVEMENT, AND THE HEAT ISLAND EFFECT**. The property's roof terraces, as well as paved areas around the building, are light in color, which reduces the amount of heat that is absorbed and then reradiated by overheated pavement. This type of undesired heat generation, from both pavement and roofs, accounts for the creation of urban heat islands, where summer temperatures are significantly higher than areas outside the city.

▸▸ **OZONE PROTECTION AND GREENHOUSE GASES**. By using R-22 and R-407c refrigerants in the HVAC system, the building reduces its negative impact on the ozone layer and also diminishes the emission of greenhouse gas (GHG) emissions.

COOLING VERSUS VENTILATION. The fan coil system decouples the cooling capabilities of the HVAC system from the delivery of ventilation air to the spaces. This separation allows the cooling system to shut off during periods of temperate weather without negatively affecting indoor air quality.

MODULAR CENTRAL CHILLER PLANT. Cooling is provided by a central chilled-water system with modular chillers located in the cellar. This high-efficiency plant produces 42°F (6°C) chilled water which is supplied to fan coil units on the tenant floors. The fan coil system delivers cooling only to units that require it, allowing greater system efficiency and thereby reducing energy, an approach known as "right sizing." Additionally, the use of a central chiller plant locates all compressors in the cellar, away from tenant space. This design eliminates compressor noise on each occupied floor and also eliminates the need for maintenance personnel to access tenant floors for regular compressor maintenance.

WATERSIDE ECONOMIZER SYSTEMS. When the outside air temperature drops below 62°F (17°C), the building still requires cooling because of lighting and computer use. The core has the greatest need for cooling because there is no heat loss to the outside in that location. Waterside economizers provide cooling without running the compressors in the modular chillers. The economizers supply chilled water from the cooling tower through plate and frame heat exchangers. This operational strategy reduces the runtime for compressors, thus saving energy. To optimize energy savings, the waterside economizer system is initiated for simultaneous operation with the compressors when condenser water temperature is approximately 59°F (15°C).

PREMIUM-EFFICIENCY MOTORS. Energy consumption is reduced by using premium-efficiency motors and variable-speed drives (VSDs) for the central mechanical, electrical, and plumbing systems. The building's emergency generator is capable of handling computer loads from tenants, not just the usual emergency lighting.

CO_2-BASED MODULATION OF OUTSIDE AIR. A constant flow of outdoor air is necessary to maintain air quality within any occupied building. However, providing outdoor air at the correct temperature and humidity year-round can result in significant energy consumption. The provision of outside air is optimized by the use of CO_2

sensors, which reduce energy consumption while ensuring that excellent air quality is maintained indoors. Each floor is designed with the capacity to modulate the outside air supply through the use of sensors that monitor CO_2 content based on the number of people in the space. A minimum amount of outside air is supplied, regardless of CO_2 content, to disperse possible emissions from furniture and finishes. This demand-based system reduces energy use, while assuring suitable indoor air quality for occupants. Tenant guidelines advise occupants to place CO_2 sensors in critical spaces and larger assembly areas, and to install at least one CO_2 sensor per floor.

COOLING TOWER WITH VSDS. The cooling tower utilizes variable speed drives, allowing cooling equipment to operate at a range of speeds. Building management can adjust the cooling system to meet the building's specific cooling needs at particular times, instead of running at a constant capacity regardless of internal conditions.

INDIVIDUALIZED CONTROLS. The central building energy management system—that is, the heating and cooling systems—has the capacity to provide individual controls within each office, with the exception of the elevator core areas, at each floor. Such localized control is a rare feature in U.S. office buildings, which typically feature building-wide or, at best, floor-wide controls. This attribute saves energy by avoiding the over-heating or over-cooling of unoccupied spaces. The controls can be automated with the use of sensors to reduce energy consumption during unoccupied periods. The tenants' individualized controls also allow occupants to control lighting, blinds, and audiovisual devices from their desks.

ENERGY-EFFICIENT WINDOWS. The windows achieve a level of energy efficiency that delivers a 30 percent improvement over the insulating properties of the curtain wall. The windows are energy-efficient in two ways:

- Spectrally selective low-E windows. Windows feature glass fabricated with a special, spectrally selective low-E coating that retains more heat within the building during winter than that retained with conventional, double-pane glass. This coating blocks approximately one-third of incoming solar heat, while reducing incoming daylight by about 15 percent. This feature keeps tenant space cooler in the summer without affecting views. In addition, the space between the glass panes is filled with argon gas, which provides a higher level of insulation than air.

- Thermally broken window frames. Windows are encased in thermally broken aluminum frames and mullions. To create thermally broken window frames, each frame is split into an interior and exterior component and joined by a material less conductive than aluminum, thereby reducing heat loss. This feature is beneficial because aluminum is a high conductor of heat, which causes heat loss and condensation in the winter. The frames are light, strong, and durable, and require minimal maintenance.

▸▸ **LIGHTING**. Energy-efficient lighting is used throughout the building. Lighting power density is reduced in stairwells, in the mechanical rooms, and in the lobby.

▸▸ **MEASUREMENT AND VERIFICATION OF ENERGY USE**. Today, commercial tenants increasingly want to monitor the energy use of subsystems in their spaces so they can better control both usage and cost. The building management system at 545 Madison Avenue is sized to accommodate feeds from the tenant spaces. The information is available to tenants upon request.

▸▸ **PURCHASE OF GREEN POWER**. The building at 545 Madison Avenue receives a portion of its electrical energy in the form of renewable wind power provided by ConEdison Solutions, an energy services company based in White Plains, New York. The renewable wind power is produced in upstate New York and Pennsylvania by Community Energy, Inc. Pursuant to LEED guidelines, the ConEdison Solutions wind product is approved as a renewable energy source under the Center for Resource Solutions' Green-e certification program. Businesses tapping green power from ConEdison Solutions pay a slight premium above the cost of electricity supplied from conventional sources.

▸▸ **COMMISSIONING**. LEED certification requires owners to complete a fundamental commissioning—that is, testing—of energy-using systems. Commissioning is intended to ensure the proper functioning of a property's heating, cooling, and ventilation systems. The commissioning must be performed by a third-party reviewer that does not include anyone directly responsible for project design or construction management. LCOR tapped an independent team from within Cosentini to perform this commissioning prerequi-

site. Additionally, a project may complete enhanced commissioning tasks to earn an Energy & Atmosphere point. Since the enhanced commissioning agent may not be within the firms contracted for design, LCOR designated Viridian to perform the required tasks.

▸▸ **WATER CONSERVATION**. Men's lavatories are equipped with ultra-low-flow urinals. Low-flow urinals are similar to conventional urinals, but their flush systems clean the bowl with a smaller flush. In this case, the fixture uses one-eighth of a gallon (0.47 liters) per flush. Waterless urinals were considered but were deemed not to meet the required level of customer service. Women's lavatories feature dual-flush toilets, which have flush valves with two positions. The first is for solid waste, using the typical 1.6 gallons (6.05 liters) per flush. The second is for liquid waste, using approximately one gallon (3.8 liters) per flush. Users must be cognizant of the required flush option so that the intended water savings can be achieved. Lavatories also use low-flow faucets that run at a half-gallon (1.9 liters) per minute.

Glass railings preserve the views on the wraparound terraces; pictured here is the 12th-floor terrace before landscaping.

Environmentally Friendly Materials

The materials selected for 545 Madison Avenue were chosen for environmental sensitivity.

SUSTAINABLE MATERIALS

LCOR made extensive use of both recycled and locally produced materials in the exterior and interior of the building. Materials are defined as local if they are produced within 500 miles (805 kilometers) of the property. For geographical perspective, the 500-mile distance from New York City extends to Ohio and Toronto. Following is a list of environmentally friendly construction products used at 545 Madison Avenue:

▸▸ **CONCRETE AND MASONRY**. Concrete is composed of aggregate, water, and cement. Because cement is an energy-intensive material, it was partially replaced by fly ash or ground, granulated blast-furnace (GGBF) slag. Replacing cement with fly ash and slag reduces the energy needed to fabricate the concrete and diverts what would otherwise be considered waste from the waste stream. Fly ash is a byproduct of the coal burned at electric utility plants. When mixed at a certain ratio, fly ash may increase the strength of the material. GGBF slag is a byproduct of iron blast furnaces. All cement and masonry originated from sources located within 500 miles of the building site. It should be noted, however, that relatively little concrete was used because the project involved preservation of an existing structure.

▸▸ **STEEL AND METAL**. Virgin steel and metal are energy-intensive materials. The steel and metal materials used at 545 Madison Avenue—including the rebar steel in the concrete, the structural steel, and light-gauge framing—contain both postindustrial and postconsumer recycled content and were all sourced within 500 miles of the site. Additional recycled metal include the lobby wall panels, toilet partitions, stainless steel column covers, and metal doors and frames.

▸▸ **ALUMINUM**. The building's curtain wall and aluminum storefronts contain recycled content that originated within 500 miles of Manhattan.

▸▸ **GYPSUM BOARD**. The gypsum board is partially composed of recycled material, and the paper face is composed entirely of recycled material.

▸▸ **INSULATION**. The thermal insulation is composed of a combination of postindustrial and postconsumer recycled material.

▸▸ **CARPET**. Public areas are outfitted with carpet composed of postindustrial and postconsumer recycled products.

LOW-EMITTANCE MATERIALS

All adhesives, sealants, paints, and carpet installed in 545 Madison Avenue are low-VOC, minimizing the presence of pollutants and odors. To ensure continued use of low-emittance materials, the tenant design and construction guidelines specify maximum VOC levels for dozens of building materials, grouped into the following categories:

▸▸ Architectural applications,

▸▸ Aerosol adhesives,

▸▸ Sealants and sealers,

▸▸ Sealant primer,

▸▸ Paints and coatings, and

▸▸ Clear wood finishes.

Also, to ensure low emission levels from carpeting, all carpets installed in the building's core and shell meet the testing and product requirements of the Carpet and Rug Institute's Green Label Plus program. Similarly, all carpet cushion installed in the core and shell adheres to standards established in the institute's Green Label program.

In addition, to prevent exposure to toxic urea formaldehyde resins, the building uses a used-plywood product called Medex, which is produced by SierraPine. Medex is urea-formaldehyde-free composite wood. No urea-formaldehyde bonding agents are used in the manufacturing process for all composite wood inside public areas of the building—including the architectural work, rough carpentry, and finish carpentry.

Tenant Air Quality and Comfort

The building utilizes a variety of equipment and innovative design techniques to promote superior indoor air quality, including the following:

▸▸ **TOBACCO SMOKE CONTROL**. Smoking is prohibited in the building and within 25 feet (7.6 meters) of building entrances and outdoor air intakes.

AIR FILTERING. The building supplies outside air that is dehumidified, tempered, and filtered by a central ventilation air unit located at roof level (in order to avoid taking in street-level exhaust and pollutants) before being delivered to each floor. High-efficiency MERV 13 filters are used to remove particulate contaminants from the outdoor air.

INCREASED OUTDOOR AIR RATIOS. As of this writing, the standard for indoor air quality, American Society for Heating, Refrigerating, and Air-Conditioning Engineers Standard 62-2004, mandates a minimum amount of outside air deemed adequate for good indoor air quality. The building delivers 30 percent more fresh air than this standard requires.

CO_2 MONITORING. As noted above, the building is designed to accommodate the use of CO_2 monitoring systems by tenants. Such systems boost indoor air quality by consistently allowing appropriate levels of fresh air to enter the building in a way that promotes the energy efficiency of the overall HVAC system. The fresh air also disperses possible emissions from furniture and finishes.

THERMAL COMFORT. Tenants have the capability to install individual temperature controls for each office, providing comfort for each occupant. Individual remote controls allow occupants to control office temperature, lighting, blinds, and audiovisual devices from their desks.

DAYLIGHTING AND VIEWS. The building's glass facade offers generous daylight and views. Ninety-seven percent of the occupied spaces are provided with natural light and views to the exterior.

The tenant guidelines for 545 Madison Avenue recommend that occupants maximize daylighting and views by locating enclosed offices and conference rooms close to the core and locating open-office areas toward the building perimeter. The enclosed offices are recommended to have glass partitions toward the exteriors. Alternately, if enclosed offices are located on perimeter areas, the guidelines suggest that tenants consider providing them with glass partitions toward the interiors.

Planned Building Operations

Building operations at 545 Madison Avenue will be in keeping with the project's environmentally friendly design:

GREEN HOUSEKEEPING. The green housekeeping approach entails cleaning with materials that have low or no toxicity and odor. The use of walk-off mats and filters prevents dirt from entering the building. In addition, such cleaning materials as dust rags are recycled by using an on-site washing machine. Typically, these cleaning items would be used and discarded.

TENANT RECYCLING PROGRAM. The building employs a recycling program through which all clean paper, corrugated cardboard, glass, plastics, and metals are collected in separate, labeled bins located within the building. An outside service picks up the material free of charge and then sells it for a profit.

LOW-TOXICITY PEST MANAGEMENT. During construction, management implemented an integrated pest management plan focused on low-toxicity prevention and the targeted treatment of pests only as necessary. Bovis Lend Lease paid careful attention to caulking and sealing the exterior wall not only for energy performance but also to minimize the opportunity and likelihood of pests entering and migrating through the building. Should pesticides be required within the building, management will notify tenants well in advance of usage to reduce potential occupant exposure.

Tenant Buildouts

LCOR will assist tenants interested in applying for LEED-CI certification for their space. Upon project completion, LCOR built out the eighth floor to position the space for LEED-CI certification. Tenant guidelines encourage tenants to seek LEED-CI certification and provide extensive details on steps that tenants should take to do so.

GREEN DESIGN AND PROJECT FINANCING

The partnership that developed 545 Madison Avenue included LCOR and a major corporate pension fund client of BlackRock Realty. LCOR's acquisition of the property was structured under a 75-year ground lease put in place in November 2006. In addition to private equity, KeyBank provided LCOR with a $60.7 million construction loan, as well as an $11 million letter of credit that secured the ground lease during construction.

Figure 1

LEED-Related Soft Costs

Cost	Amount ($)
FEES TO U.S. GREEN BUILDING COUNCIL FOR LEED REVIEW	
Initial application fees	450
Design phase fee	3,125
Construction phase fee	1,250
Subtotal	**4,825**
FEES FOR LEED-RELATED CONSULTING	
Planning	51,908
LEED/Green	65,188
Commissioning	87,000
Subtotal, consultants	204,096
Total LEED-related soft costs	**208,921**
SOFT-COST REBATES[a]	
Planning	(28,454)
LEED/Green	(28,454)
Subtotal, rebates	(59,908)
Net LEED-related soft costs	**149,013**
SUMMARY	
Total LEED-related soft costs	208,921
NYSERDA soft-cost rebates	(59,908)
Net LEED-related soft costs (approx. $1.00/gross sq. ft.)	**149,013**

a. Rebates from the New York State Energy Research and Development Authority (NYSERDA).

Although green features did not affect the financing terms, the LEED Gold rating was an important benefit in the eyes of the joint venture partner, BlackRock Realty, and its pension fund client. Green elements accounted for some $150,000 in soft costs and are estimated to be less than 5 percent of hard costs. Figure1 presents a budget breakdown for LEED-associated soft costs. Additionally, LCOR plans to file for approximately $1 million in hard-cost grants from NYSERDA for building-related energy efficiency investments representing part of the incremental and installation cost beyond standard design practice.

LEASING AND MARKETING

Jones Lang LaSalle, the leasing agent for the building's office space, highlights the property's sustainable features in its marketing. The building's promotional brochure immediately notes the building's LEED Gold rating. The text later frames the building's sustainable features as a productivity booster:

> 545 Madison is a green building with ... LEED Gold Standard certification, further enhancing the quality of its interior environment while having minimal impact on the one outside. In addition to reduced energy usage, this eco-friendly design enhances productivity and reduces absenteeism.

LCOR's public relations agency, The Marino Organization, positioned the LEED element as a competitive differentiator. The firm has gained a number of LEED-related placements about 545 Madison in the New York City business press and in regional and national real estate trade publications.

As this chapter was written, 545 Madison Avenue was in the initial stages of leasing and was being short-listed by a number of prospects. The project has signed its first office lease on the building's eighth floor with financial services firm CS Tang, a company specializing in cross-border transactions. Many other financial services firms have been submitting proposals to lease space at 545 Madison, including full-floor requests from tenants who either require the space or anticipate growth.

EXPERIENCE GAINED

LCOR cites five lessons learned from its participation in the LEED process:

▸▸ **PURSUIT OF LEED CERTIFICATION** is a long-term process. For LCOR, the LEED experience at 545 Madison Avenue underscored the fact that certification requires a long-term commitment on the part of the developer. Owners need to involve themselves with sourcing materials at the outset, assembling and working with an expanded design team, learning about and evaluating sustainability-related options, and carrying the entire process forward through commissioning. If a developer is not prepared to exercise a proper management role throughout the LEED certification process, the process runs the risk of spinning out of control. Potential risks that might threaten a poorly managed LEED project include the potential hiring of too many consultants, failure to adequately coordinate the work of the LEED and design teams, and cost overruns.

▸▸ **DEVELOPERS CONSIDERING LEED CERTIFICATION** should register their projects as early as possible. The U.S. Green Building Council's requirements have tended to intensify with the passage of time and the increasingly strict standards typically carry higher price tags. Also, if developers begin the process but decide not to follow through, all they stand to lose is a relatively nominal filing fee and possibly some initial consulting costs.

LEED CERTIFICATION INTRODUCES NEW DYNAMICS and costs into the process of managing design teams and hiring subcontractors. The LEED process alters the conventional dynamics of design team management. It is necessary to involve the LEED consultant early in the design process. LCOR also utilized the LEED consultant in vetting construction documents for LEED compliance.

Another challenge that LCOR encountered in pursuing a LEED rating involved the hiring of subcontractors familiar with LEED obligations. While Bovis Lend Lease, the construction manager, itself had significant experience in LEED projects, even in the ostensibly sophisticated New York labor market Bovis had difficulty identifying subcontractors who had experience with LEED regulations and standards, and who were receptive to the prospect of undertaking a LEED-compliant project.

Fulfilling the LEED paperwork requirements required LCOR's subcontractors to take on additional staffing costs to deal with record keeping, and LCOR had to absorb the costs associated with this added staffing. All told, LCOR estimates that Gold LEED certification added less than 5 percent to project hard costs; this figure could be reduced substantially if a $1 million hard-cost grant is received from NYSERDA. Additional soft costs associated with LEED certification, after NYSERDA rebates, were $150,000—about $1.00 per square foot.

COMMISSIONING TIMETABLES VARY BY PROJECT. LCOR recommends that developers be cognizant that commissioning timetables can vary for multitenanted properties. For such buildings, all parties involved in the LEED process will have to come to consensus over the definition of full occupancy, which signals the starting point of energy model monitoring. The monitoring can run from 12 to 18 months. For large office buildings, pinpointing the moment of full occupancy will usually mean identifying a certain percentage of occupancy.

MAXIMIZING DAYLIGHT presents special challenges for buildings with low ceilings. One of 545 Madison's LEED-related design challenges involved generating maximum levels of reflectivity in the interiors to achieve the highest possible daylight quotients. But the building has short floors: top-of-slab-to-top-of-slab averages run 10 feet, 7 inches (2.92 meters).

LCOR needed to come up with an efficient way to introduce ducts, piping, and ceiling-hung mechanical and electrical equipment into such a short space. Installation would have to leave enough floor-to-ceiling dimension to allow for an open feeling and to allow daylight to reflect as deeply as possible into the space.

The team set ceiling height goals of 8 feet, 6 inches (2.59 meters) for the interior and 9 feet (2.74 meters) at the perimeter. This goal was set after deducting space for a 5-inch (12.7-centimeter) slab, the beam depth, and the ceiling assembly. Achieving this objective required close coordination among the architect, the MEP engineer, and the contractor. Strategies to leave sufficient floor-to-ceiling height included penetrating some beams by cutting holes into the middle of them to permit pipes and ducts to pass through the beams that normally would have hung below them. In addition, ducts were organized into the center of the floor and off the perimeter.

David A. Sigman is a senior vice president of LCOR in the company's New York City office. Steve Vitoff is senior vice president of the Marino Organization of New York.

Development Team

DEVELOPER:
LCOR Incorporated in joint venture with BlackRock Realty

ARCHITECT:
Moed de Armas & Shannon

GENERAL CONTRACTOR:
Bovis Lend Lease

MEP ENGINEERS:
Cosentini Associates

STRUCTURAL ENGINEERS:
Ysrael A. Seinuk, P.C.

SUSTAINABILITY CONSULTANT:
Viridian Energy and Environmental, LLC

LEASING AGENTS:
Jones Lang LaSalle
CB Richard Ellis

PROPERTY MANAGEMENT FIRM:
LCOR Asset Management LP

PUBLIC RELATIONS:
The Marino Organization

CASE STUDY · GWL REALTY ADVISORS

1801 McGill College

MONTREAL, CANADA

The 1801 McGill College building occupies a prominent business address in the heart of Montreal's downtown. This distinctive building with setback street elevations offers unsurpassed views of the downtown core: McGill College Avenue, Mount-Royal Park, and a private internal courtyard. The property offers a multitude of amenities to satisfy the highest standards and provides direct access to

more than 30 kilometers (18.6 miles) of Montreal's underground path network, which links numerous commercial retail centers, department stores, food courts, restaurants, hotels, movie theaters, sports venues, the arts district, convention centers, exposition halls, and numerous downtown office towers. The building has direct access to the Metro system, to the South Shore bus terminal, and to the Central Train Station, including the regional commuter rail network and national and international

The ten-story 1801 McGill College is a multitenant office building that sits above a multilevel retail center. Goals for the renovation and retrofit of the office space were to reduce energy costs, increase tenant comfort, optimize long-term financial performance, and promote environmental stewardship.

railways. It also benefits from north-south access to parking off McGill College Avenue.

This ten-story office tower with gross leasable area of 344,028 square feet (31,961 square meters) was built in 1976. It was the first office building in Montreal's downtown core to be built with nine-foot ceilings and full-height windows. Shortly after British Columbia Investment Management Corporation's (bcIMC) acquisition of the property in 2001, a full review was undertaken of the building's mechanical elements and their life cycles. The review established that some of the building's mechanical components (more specifically, the cooling towers and chillers) were in need of efficiency upgrades and modernization. With overall energy costs consistently on the rise, it also became evident that an energy consumption program should be developed and implemented.

An opportunity to accelerate the implementation of such a program presented itself in 2006, when a long-time anchor tenant that occupied close to 70 percent of the premises vacated its space. The move-out gave the building operations staff a rare opportunity to perform upgrades on a sizeable portion of the property and to reposition it to enhance functionality, tenant comfort, energy performance, and cash flow.

With the ultimate goals of reducing energy costs, increasing tenant comfort and environmental stewardship, and optimizing long-term financial performance, the owners of the building approved the commencement of a major renovation project. Base building renovation costs totaled C$3.7 million ($3.4 million). Of that amount, C$1.9 million ($1.75 million) was expended on new energy systems, while C$1.8 million ($1.65 million) was used to refurbish common areas, including lighting and lavatories, and to install a new security system. Upon completion of the renovation, the property was repositioned in the marketplace and successfully re-leased; power consumption ultimately declined 25 percent from prerenovation levels. In 2007, 1801 McGill College was named a Building of the Year by the Building Owners and Managers Association (BOMA) Canada and by BOMA Canada's Montreal chapter.

DEVELOPMENT PROCESS

Once bcIMC approved the project, the development team was assembled. This team consisted of three principal groups: GWL Realty Advisors (the management company), Pageau Morel and Associates (the engineering firm engaged to carry out the project), and Hydro Quebec, the public utility company that would eventually provide subsidies for the project. The grants provided by the public utility company were based on the reduction of energy consumption and the achievement of additional design parameters:

▸▸ **ALL NEW**, installed equipment had to meet energy efficiency requirements.

▸▸ **THE HEAT GENERATED** from new chillers had to be recaptured and sent back into the building to reduce heating costs during the winter season.

▸▸ **TO FURTHER REDUCE ENERGY USAGE**, equipment was required to be retrofitted with modulating drivers to reduce electrical usage during off hours or during hours when the building was closed.

Grant monies for the project were based on the achievement of design goals and the overall reduction in energy use.

The team took a very practical approach in developing the retrofit plan. The building's heating and cooling equipment had reached the end of its life cycle and needed to be replaced. Grants were available from the public utility company, and every effort was to be made to reduce escalating energy costs while taking a proactive approach toward containing or reducing the environmental impact of the property.

This simple framework was the road map to engineering a system that would place new, environmentally friendly equipment in 1801 McGill College, install a heat recovery system to reduce energy costs, and develop protocols to evaluate and manage the building's carbon footprint. The system also was designed to provide the highest possible efficiency without compromising tenant comfort, as well as to reduce occupancy costs over time. Additional green improvements installed at the property included water-saving fixtures and energy-efficient lighting. As well, comprehensive recycling, green restroom supply purchase, and green cleaning programs were instituted.

GREEN BUILDING DESIGN AND CONSTRUCTION

Taking care of the environment requires a commitment from all levels. Participation and cooperation is required from the owner, the management team, and the tenants, from anchor tenants to the smallest occupants. Both bcIMC and GWL Realty Advisors understood the importance of sound environmental management, as well as the need to ensure that all current environmental regulations were met or surpassed. The companies worked in concert to maintain their awareness and enhance their expertise. Even though the building was constructed in

The rooftop terrace serves as an amenity for tenants.

1976 and was considered relatively modern, the opportunity to take advantage of systems in place while optimizing the building's potential were recognized and acted upon. As enumerated below, the renovation encompassed numerous aspects of building construction and operation.

Energy Efficiency

Entering into an energy program offered many opportunities for the owners and building managers to demonstrate and even potentially excel in environmental stewardship. The program saw the conversion of the building's aging mechanical equipment, which was operating with R11 refrigerant, to a new system that operates with environmentally friendly refrigerant (R134a). Further, by redesigning the mechanical system, the renovation allowed for the introduction of a heat recovery system to further reduce energy costs. Together, these measures reduced the environmental emissions and carbon footprint of 1801 McGill College, while cutting energy expenditures.

A key feature of the energy retrofit was the introduction of a new building automation system (BAS). The BAS permitted building operations staff to reduce the operation of the heating, ventilating, and air-conditioning (HVAC) systems during off hours, as well as to efficiently limit the kilowatt-hours of operations during

peak consumption and cost periods. For example, the BAS permitted the building's HVAC systems to begin cooling or heating during the early morning hours, when energy costs are lower relative to peak daytime hours. By preheating or precooling the property, it was possible to reduce the capacity and energy required during peak hours, thereby reducing energy expenditures. The added flexibility of operation allowed for greater control of peak loads in the building. The ability to manage the building's peak load has shifted energy consumption more heavily to off-peak hours, reducing the billing rate charged by the utility supplier and overall energy costs.

Recycling Programs

The renovation incorporated new construction protocols to recycle materials on site, as well as to allow for partial recycling of materials that had not previously been recycled. In the first phase, a recycling program was implemented in which all data cabling was removed and sold to recyclers to offset the cost of labor for removing it. In the second phase, the recycling of all metals from demolition and all suspended ceiling systems, ceiling tiles, doors, frames, sidelights, hardware, lighting, ventilation diffusers, blinds, and acoustical insulation became part of the building recycling protocols. These materials were used in part for new tenant buildouts with two goals in mind: reducing the amount of material being sent to landfills and reducing construction costs for both the landlord and the tenant. A full recycling program also has been implemented for paper, cardboard, glass, metal, and plastic in order to reduce the quantity of waste going into landfills.

In addition, a program was implemented to encourage tenants to use carpet tiles made from recycled material for their new office finishes. This solution proves more cost-effective in the long run because only heavily trafficked areas need to be replaced. Suppliers were also encouraged to reclaim the used tiles and recycle them upon replacement. This also minimizes costs during subsequent leasing cycles, which would typically see the premises renovated for a new tenant or refreshed upon renewal. To date, approximately 85 percent of the tenants at 1801 McGill College have chosen the carpet recycling option.

The selling point of the programs listed above was simple: the use of recycled materials enables tenants to reduce their construction costs, as well as to reduce the quantity of materials that would be sent to landfills. For example, by using carpet tiles in lieu of broadloom, the replacement of carpeting over an entire tenant suite would be eliminated. Only sections of wear and tear would need to be replaced over the term of the lease. The associated costs of dismantling all the office furniture and reinstalling it once the carpeting was replaced would be reduced or no longer required. In fact, one tenant saved approximately $130,000 in renovation costs by reusing existing doors and hardware as well as reducing the construction time because of the availability of the materials on site.

Lighting and Solar Film

In connection with the new building standards, building management commenced a program to move from the use of high-energy-consuming lighting products to PL, T8, and light-emitting diode (LED)–type lighting in all common areas of the building. A program is also being implemented that will see the conversion of all tenant lighting from the current T12 lighting to energy-efficient T8 lighting over the next several years. Another feature that was implemented at the outset of the initiative was the installation of solar film on the full-height windows in order to reduce the heat load during the summer periods.

Washroom Fixtures and Supplies

All washroom fixtures have been replaced with new, automated fixtures in order to reduce water consumption. All hand and washroom tissue paper now used in the building is made from recycled paper, and all paper dispensers have been replaced with automatic feed dispensers for both hand and sanitary usage (paper towels and toilet paper). Overall, 1801 McGill College has reduced paper consumption by approximately 19 percent for sanitary paper and by approximately 21 percent for hand paper. This is due mainly to the installation of single-feed dispensers that deliver one sheet at a time for hand paper and the introduction of sanitary paper dispensers that do not allow paper rolls to be removed from the dispenser. Further, by reducing the amount of paper required on a daily basis, management has reduced the amount of labor needed to inspect and maintain the washrooms during the day.

Cleaning Contracts

The building's cleaning contractor was also asked to put a program in place in which it would only use environ-

mentally friendly, 100 percent biodegradable cleaning products produced from renewable resources.

FINANCING

Once the energy renovation project had been designed, approved, and accepted by the public utility company, the management team put forward a proposal to the building's ownership for approval. The C$1.9 million ($1.75 million) energy program benefited from grants from Hydro Quebec equivalent to approximately 25 percent of the total project cost. The C$1.8 million ($1.65 million) renovation of common areas and lavatories was financed by bcIMC. In the first year of operating with the new systems, the energy savings estimated by the professionals were surpassed, with a reduction of approximately 19 percent. Eventually, energy use at 1801 McGill College was reduced by approximately 25 percent relative to prerenovation levels.

MARKETING AND MANAGEMENT

At the conclusion of the retrofit program, 1801 McGill College offered to new and existing tenants a building with contiguous floor plates of up to 36,000 square feet, renovated common areas and building mechanical elements, and state-of-the-art building control and security access systems. The renovation of entrance and floor lobbies, corridors, washrooms, elevator cars, and the rooftop terrace, all encompassing energy-efficiency features, offered building occupants the highest standards in comfort. The newly refurbished building was complemented by its locational attributes (excellent views of Montreal's downtown core and Mount Royal Park, and direct links to the underground pedestrian network and the city's largest retail center).

The completion of the renovation led to the development of an aggressive leasing strategy devised to incorporate the innovative environmental stewardship initiative being promoted and practiced by the owners and managers. At the onset of the retenanting campaign, the leasing strategy focused on raising awareness. The building had been removed from most survey lists because it had historically been fully leased. With the departure of the anchor tenant and close to 70 percent of the gross leasable area coming back on the market, the retrofit programs and potential benefits to be derived from them were used to stimulate interest and generate activity. E-mail campaigns spotlighting specific vacancies, direct one-on-one tours, and a broker incentive program set the tone for a marketing event, attended by many members of the Montreal brokerage community, that reintroduced 1801 McGill College to the area office market.

A consistent theme of the ensuing leasing campaign was the willingness and commitment of the ownership and management teams to increasing the efficiency and cost-effectiveness of usable areas in the building, while creating a more comfortable working environment. Generous floor plates, which averaged 33,000 square feet, achievable HVAC efficiencies (owing to the flexibility offered by the new mechanical design), and the abundance of natural light from the full-height windows gave the leasing team tangible benefits to sell. These features, coupled with the commitment to reduce overall occupancy costs through energy savings and more environmentally friendly build-

ing processes and procedures, struck a chord with prospective and incoming tenants and differentiated 1801 McGill College from competing properties.

The marketing of green features at 1801 McGill College was linked most frequently to tangible tenant concerns about operating expenses and the working environment. The management team observed that although there is a movement toward environmental consciousness and social responsibility, overall occupancy cost and productivity remain predominant decision-making factors for most tenants. In a multitenant existing building such as 1801 McGill College, elements of greening such as reduced energy usage and expenses, increased levels of natural light, and better control of comfort levels highlight the more immediate potential benefits to tenants in the areas of cost savings, employee productivity, and job satisfaction.

The new emphasis on the recycling of building materials also proved to be a cost reduction incentive for incoming tenants. Prospective tenants were offered the potential to reuse an array of construction materials in order to reduce their tenant fit-up costs as much as possible. In one instance, a tenant benefited from reusing nine-foot-high, solid-core, cherry wood doors, frames, and hardware throughout its suite, resulting in a savings of well over $100,000 for the construction of approximately 60 offices in its premises. These savings were on top of other recycled materials that they received at no cost to them such as light fixtures, blinds, air-conditioning units for computer rooms, projection screens, millwork, and cabinetry. In short, the approach taken was one of, "If it is available and you can use it, you can have it at no cost." Protocols such as the recycling of materials have the obvious effect of reducing overall tenant improvement costs, which is of direct interest to both incoming and existing tenants.

All told, the green renovation of 1801 McGill College was a powerful marketing tool that highlighted an ongoing commitment to reinvesting in the property in order to increase its amenity cluster and service offering. The efficient configuration and size of the floor plates, the efficiency and cost-effectiveness of the new building systems, and the abundance of recyclable elements in the buildouts left by the departing anchor tenant

A typical floor lobby. As part of the retrofit program, building management began a program to move from use of high-energy-use lighting products to PL, T8, and LED lighting in all common areas of the building.

allowed the leasing team to focus on two strategies: leasing to numerous tenants that would occupy full floors and staggering lease expirations to minimize rollover risk going forward.

The re-leasing strategy, which highlighted the green and energy-efficient features of 1801 McGill College as tenant amenities, has proven successful and enabled the management company to lease the building to 95 percent occupancy within 22 months. The new rent roll also stages lease expirations over time, reducing turnover risk. The timing of the strategy was fortunate because the leasing team was able to take advantage of an upswing in market activity and an increase in market rents. The spaces that came back to the market and were re-leased generated rental rates 30 to 70 percent higher than those that had been provided for in the anchor lease.

The energy-efficient retrofit of 1801 McGill College has produced ongoing positive publicity for the property. The project was awarded BOMA Go Green—since rebranded as BOMA BESt (Building Environmental Standards)—certification in 2006 and was a 2007 BOMA Canada Office Building of the Year winner.

EXPERIENCE GAINED

The retrofit of 1801 McGill College yielded many valuable lessons:

‣ **THE MOST SIGNIFICANT PROCEDURAL LESSON** learned was the importance of maintaining and updating proper surveys of the existing site conditions as the project progressed, noting them on the project drawings and specifications, no matter how trivial the information might seem. Doing so enables all parties involved in the project to be up to date at all times and provides for a master reference for the project team.

‣ **CONTINGENCY BUDGETING** should be tailored to the scope and difficulty of work undertaken for various elements of the retrofit. Contingency amounts tailored to specific aspects of the scope of work, rather than as a flat-rate percentage of total project cost, proved more accurate and easier to track as the project progressed.

‣ **COOPERATION AND INPUT FROM ALL PARTIES** involved in the decision-making process and in the design and completion of the actual construction is needed from the conceptual design stage forward. In particular, the commitment of bcIMC, the project owner, to responsible property investment provided inspiration and support to the management company, consultants, engineers, contractors, and other participants in determining what a project of this importance and magnitude should involve.

‣ **GREEN AND ENERGY-EFFICIENT FEATURES** can be highlighted effectively in office leasing campaigns. The 1801 McGill College team found that green and energy-efficient features were well-accepted by prospective tenants and helped to differentiate the project from its competition with respect to occupant comfort, worker productivity, and energy savings.

‣ **RECYCLING** has proved a popular aspect of tenant buildouts. The recycling of building components has been well-accepted by tenants as a cost-saving opportunity, as has been the use of recycled carpet tiles in lieu of conventional carpeting. Eighty-five percent of the tenant base has chosen to participate in the carpet recycling program.

GWL Realty Advisors provides comprehensive asset management, property management, and specialized real estate services to pension funds and institutional clients in Canada.

Development Team

OWNER:
bcIMC (British Columbia Investment Management Corporation)

PROPERTY MANAGER:
GWL Realty Advisors

ARCHITECTS:
Esar Fry Architects

ENGINEERING CONSULTANTS:
Pageau Morel & Associates

GENERAL CONTRACTOR:
Jubinville Plumbing

PLUMBING CONTRACTOR:
Jubinville Plumbing

MECHANICAL CONTRACTOR:
Simpkin Mechanical

ELECTRICAL CONTRACTOR:
Britton Electric

BUILDING AUTOMATION CONTRACTOR:
Regulvar

MECHANICAL EQUIPMENT SUPPLIER:
McQuay Air Conditioning

LEASING AGENTS:
GWL Realty Advisors

CASE STUDY · GEORGE DENISE
Adobe Towers

SAN JOSE, CALIFORNIA

In 1999, Adobe Systems Incorporated hired Cushman & Wakefield, a global real estate services provider with a sustainable building operations track record, to provide facility management services for Adobe's San Jose headquarters buildings, the Adobe Towers. Since then, the two companies have worked together to achieve green

Adobe's East Tower Lobby is one of three lobbies at the headquarters.

building history, making Adobe the only company in the world to have achieved five Leadership in Energy and Environmental Design (LEED) certifications, four at the Platinum level.

Cushman & Wakefield has encouraged all of its U.S. managed properties to benchmark with Energy Star since 2001, shortly after the program was introduced. Thirteen of its managed properties are now certified as green buildings, including one in India and

WILLIAM A. PORTER

one in China. More recently, Cushman & Wakefield created a new position, director of Sustainable Strategies. Partnering with the U.S. Green Building Council in its pilot LEED for Portfolios program, Cushman & Wakefield now has more than 100 properties registered. Cushman & Wakefield has adopted sustainable best practices for its standard operating procedures globally, finding that they generally contribute to greater operating efficiency, reduced operating costs, and a healthier work environment.

Three years ago, only one building in California's Silicon Valley was certified as a green building. Six were registered and working on certification, and three of those were the Adobe Towers. Today 18 buildings in Silicon Valley are certified as green buildings and 118 are registered and working toward certification. Staff from virtually all these buildings have toured Adobe's buildings in the past three years to learn about Adobe's accomplishments.

CONTEXT AND OWNERSHIP OBJECTIVES

Adobe's corporate headquarters complex in San Jose, California, consists of three mid-rise office buildings. The Almaden, East, and West Towers are, respectively, 17, 16, and 18 stories high, and 3, 9, and 11 years old. Combined, they contain approximately 1 million square feet of office space, resting atop 938,473 square feet of enclosed parking.

On June 9, 2006, Adobe's West Tower was certified at the LEED Platinum level, the highest level attainable. The West Tower was the first building to be certified Platinum through the LEED for Existing Buildings (LEED-EB) program. A few months later, on December 1, Adobe's Almaden and East Towers in San Jose were also certified, completing certification for the company's headquarters and achieving another first: Adobe became the first organization in the world to have three LEED Platinum buildings. So began a journey that has since resulted in two more green building certifications for Adobe, more buildings in the process of being certified, and a new intensity in the collaborative sharing of sustainable practices between approximately 80 Adobe sites in some 30 countries.

Adobe has a long history of taking a proactive approach to resource conservation, waste reduction, environmental protection, and sustainability in its day-to-day practices. When its headquarters site was developed in 1996, state-of-the-art technologies and processes were incorporated into the building design. The second and third buildings also were designed and built to take advantage of the latest advancements in building operations and to operate more efficiently than the previous buildings. Since 2001, Adobe and Cushman & Wakefield have initiated programs to further enhance Adobe's operating efficiency and to reduce its environmental footprint. The decision to pursue LEED certification grew from these efforts; it was not an initial goal.

In 2001, California implemented "rolling blackouts" to protect the integrity of the statewide electric grid. In addition, the state called upon large electricity users like Adobe to reduce electricity use as much as possible during periods of critical peak demand. In response, Adobe initiated two energy conservation projects at its San Jose headquarters, working with Cushman & Wakefield: the delamping or the reduction in wattage of common area lamps throughout its facilities, and the installation of motion-activated power strips in every office to automatically turn off monitors, task lamps, and other electric accessories when not in use. These two initiatives alone resulted in a 10 percent saving in electricity over the previous year. The following year, the state requested all large users to reduce their electricity use 10 percent below that of 2000. Adobe took its corporate environmental performance to an entirely new level and reduced its electricity usage by an additional 10 percent, for a total reduction of 20 percent.

SAVINGS REALIZED

Over the next five and a half years, Adobe and Cushman & Wakefield initiated 64 energy and related conservation projects at a total cost of $1.4 million. Adobe received rebates or incentives totaling $389,000, mostly from PG&E, and realized total annual savings of approximately $1.2 million. These savings represent an average simple payback of 9.5 months and an a return on investment (ROI) of 121 percent.

As a part of its green initiative, Adobe also began benchmarking the energy efficiency of its buildings through the Environmental Protection Agency's (EPA's) Energy Star for Buildings program. A score of 75 or higher is required to earn the Energy Star label for superior energy performance, a designation Adobe has achieved for its headquarters buildings every year since 2003. The most recent

Energy Star scores achieved for the three buildings are 76, 78, and 85 including data centers, and 93, 94, and 100 when the data centers are excluded. These scores are all the more remarkable when one considers that the central plants run 24 hours a day, seven days a week, 365 days a year to provide cooling for the data centers and more than 40 software labs, whereas 11 to 12 hours per day is typical for most office buildings.

THE CERTIFICATION PROCESS

The steps to certify the buildings were straightforward:

▸▸ **ADOBE AND CUSHMAN & WAKEFIELD** benchmarked the buildings with the Energy Star for Commercial Buildings protocol, entering building data into the EPA's Web site to obtain an energy efficiency score for the buildings.

▸▸ **NEXT, PROJECT MANAGERS CONDUCTED AN ENERGY AUDIT.** Low-cost, high-return energy conservation projects were undertaken first. When building Energy Star scores passed 75, Adobe applied for the Energy Star label.

▸▸ **PROJECT MANAGERS THEN SELECTED A LEED ACCREDITED PROFESSIONAL** to guide Adobe through the certification process. After performing a gap analysis, a LEED self-audit to see where the buildings stood in relation to certification requirements, project managers discovered that the buildings were already at the Gold level. So Adobe decided to pursue Platinum certification.

▸▸ **THE NEXT STEP WAS TO SELECT THE LEED TEAM,** identifying key members of staff, and key contractors. Once the LEED team was selected, its members conducted three orientations—one with the entire staff, one for key members of staff together with key vendors, and one for janitorial staff. Each presentation explained what the company wanted to do and why it was important, and then had attendees vote on the changes, in order to obtain their buy-in.

▸▸ **THE VARIOUS LEED CREDITS WERE SORTED** according to logical areas of specialization, and champions were assigned for each area. At this point, the buildings were registered with the U.S. Green Building Council.

▸▸ **THE TEAM THEN BEGAN ADDRESSING THE CREDITS,** item by item. Staff met weekly with the team champions to review progress and resolve outstanding issues. Finally, Adobe applied for LEED certification.

SUMMARY OF PROJECTS UNDERTAKEN

The Adobe retrofit encompassed a diverse range of capital and operating projects affecting energy efficiency and environmental sensitivity.

Load Management

Of the 64 projects completed by Adobe through 2006, 26 were related to load management. These were some of the least expensive measures undertaken and some of the most effective. They included such simple measures as adjusting existing motion sensors to turn off more quickly when no movement is detected in the immediate area; reducing on-time for garage and exterior lighting; reducing run times for garage exhaust fans; reducing on-times for cooling towers and boilers; linking air supply dampers to motion sensors in Adobe's 200-plus conference rooms and storage rooms so the sensors close down automatically when these rooms are not in use; and adding motion sensors in stairwells to dim lighting when stairwells are not in use. Total cost for these 26 projects was $445,248, with an ROI of 304 percent.

The concept behind load management is a straightforward one; turn it off if it is not being used. One of the simplest projects had the greatest return—reducing the run time for the garage exhaust fans. When the buildings were completed, the mechanical contractor set the exhaust fans to run 24 hours a day, seven days a week. Cushman & Wakefield worked with an environmental firm to test various settings while the firm sampled and tested the air. In the final analysis, it was determined the fans needed to be on 15 minutes per hour, for three hours each in the morning and afternoon commute times to provide air that is between four and ten times cleaner than the minimum standards established by the EPA and the American Society of Heating, Refrigerating, and Air-Conditioning Engineers. From this change, Adobe reduced electricity costs by $98,000 per year.

▸▸ **LIGHTING.** The next largest returns came from lighting projects. These included replacing existing incandescent lamps with compact fluorescent bulbs; retrofitting high-pressure sodium lighting in garages to fluorescent lighting; upgrading existing fluorescent lamps to more efficient, latest-generation versions; and linking all lighting to the building's automated lighting controls system. Total costs for these projects was $300,701, with a 61 percent return on investment.

▸▸ **EQUIPMENT SYSTEMS.** Six projects involved retrofitting large equipment systems, including adding variable-frequency drives (VFDs) to main supply fans and chillers at a total cost of $298,439 and an ROI of 61 percent—similar to that of lighting retrofits.

▸▸ **REAL-TIME METERS.** Paying homage to the truism that "you can't manage what you can't measure," real-time, digital electric meters were added to the main electricity panels at a cost of $39,472, with an ROI of 42 percent. Being able to see a graph of building electricity demand in real time makes it easier for operating engineers to recognize variances from normal operating curves and correct them, improving efficiency and reducing operating costs in the process.

Water Management and Related Features

To reduce water use within the buildings, Adobe added automatic faucets and water-free urinals in the restrooms, and low-flow showerheads in the fitness center. These three measures reduced domestic water use by nearly 22 percent. It is also important to note that for every dollar Adobe saves in water costs, an additional $0.75 is saved in sewer treatment costs, because sewer costs are projected based on water use.

▸▸ **TOUCH-FREE RESTROOMS.** Both hygiene and aesthetics played into Adobe's decision to install automatic faucets, automatic flush toilets, automatic soap dispensers, and automatic paper towel dispensers—all contributing to a touch-free environment.

▸▸ **DYSON AIRBLADES.** While most of Adobe's retrofits involved the use of tested and accepted technologies, the effort also provided a rich beta test environment for a number of new products. Among these was the Dyson Airblade hand dryer. Airblades dry hands similarly to the way a car wash blows the water off a car near the end of the wash process. Energy costs associated with the use of Airblades is between 10 percent and 20 percent of the cost of paper towels. When Adobe first initiated testing of the Airblades, the product was so new that Adobe had to wait until its UL listing was approved before installation could occur. Adobe installed twelve Airblades on the floors with the highest traffic patterns. They worked well, tested successfully, and were well received by employees. Adobe is looking to install the Airblades in its new buildings going forward.

▸▸ **WATER-FREE URINALS.** Adobe initially installed four Falcon water-free urinals as a test at the end of 2003. It had just completed the construction of Almaden Tower, so it was able to test four such urinals alongside 26 traditional urinals in the new building. At the end of one year, Adobe was satisfied with the water-free urinals' performance, so Adobe applied to the city of San Jose for a permit to convert the remaining urinals in the Almaden Tower, plus an additional 48 in the other two headquarters buildings.

The three towers of the Adobe Systems headquarters in San Jose were built sequentially—in 1996, 1998, and 2003—and contain 1 million square feet of office space.

At the time, San Jose did not allow water-free urinals. Adobe presented the idea with the information that the Department of Defense and the Department of the Navy extensively tested water-free urinals in 1995 and approved them for all uses. City officials came to Adobe and inspected the urinals by running a fiber-optic lens down the drains to inspect the pipes. To the city's surprise, the pipes behind the water-free urinals were cleaner than those behind the traditional urinals. The conclusion: the uric acid residue in urinals needs water as a medium to distribute it throughout the pipes. Without water, only a small trickle of waste runs down the pipe, with a much smaller footprint, lessening the negative impact of the uric acid residue. Accordingly, the city changed its policy and now allows water-free urinals in buildings that have professional management.

▸ **LANDSCAPE IRRIGATION**. Water conservation projects related to landscaping included replacing non-native plants with varieties adapted to the local micro-climate, replacing spray irrigation with subsurface drip irrigation, and adding evapotranspiration controllers that adjust the irrigation automatically based on real-time climate conditions communicated through wireless technology from local weather stations. Plants that are adapted to local climate conditions have minimal irrigation requirements. Adobe has one small area of lawn planted with a dwarf tall fescue that is fairly drought-tolerant. All irrigation has been converted to drip irrigation. Drip irrigation is 90 percent efficient, compared with 50 percent to 70 percent efficiency for spray irrigation. Overall, Adobe has reduced water used for irrigation by 76 percent. The total cost for all water conservation projects implemented was $145,732, with an ROI of 22 percent.

Green Cleaning

Adobe implemented green cleaning practices to help improve indoor air quality and to eliminate the use of potentially hazardous chemicals. Changes include supplying the janitorial staff with Green Seal–certified cleaners, dust-free mops and wipes, and high-filtration, ergonomic vacuum cleaners. Adobe supplies restrooms with nonantimicrobial hand soap, which is hypoallergenic. Adobe also uses a floor scrubber with ionized water instead of detergents. Similarly, Adobe's carpet cleaning service now uses ionized water, rather than chemicals, with its extractors. These combined efforts result in a safer, healthier work environment.

Expanding the Recycling Program

San Jose allows mixed recycling, which has benefited Adobe's efforts to increase its recycling efforts. The company placed bins for mixed recycling and trash in each break room and in the cafeteria. In 2003, Adobe's waste hauler initiated a test composting program at the request of the city, for which Adobe volunteered to participate. Accordingly, Adobe placed bins in the kitchen to collect food waste. The company also added bins in the break rooms for battery recycling and toner cartridge recycling.

Recycling efforts extend outside the office buildings. The small lawn area on the second-floor patio is mowed with mulching mowers. Grass is cut extra-fine and allowed to fall back into the turf, adding nutrients to the soil as it decomposes. An area to the west of the property,

along the Guadalupe River Walk, is planted with a creeping red fescue, a native grass that does not need to be mowed, eliminating a potential source of waste clippings. Tree prunings are chipped and turned into mulch for the buildings' gardens. Even kitchen grease is picked up by a grease recycler and burned in a generator with other fuels to produce electricity. Total recycling through the certification period reached 85 percent, saving Adobe about $137,000 per year in avoided landfill fees.

In 2005, after Adobe began its green building certification process, the question of recycled content in copy paper arose. Adobe assumed that all paper had some recycled content, but discovered the paper it was using did not have any recycled content. It appeared that changing to paper with 30 percent recycled content was going to cost $1,800 more annually. Not a large amount, but nonetheless, an additional expense. Up to that point, Adobe had not implemented any projects that did not have a reasonable payback. Adobe's office supply representative reviewed all of the company's stationery purchases, found a number of recycled-content alternatives, and put together a package that saved Adobe $8,700 per year.

Adobe also reduces the amount of product packaging used for its own products. It uses packaging materials with greater recycled content and some of its product packaging is printed with vegetable-based inks.

Reaction to Change

Adobe has received an overwhelming amount of positive feedback from its employees about the greening of its buildings. Employees have said they see the changes as an improvement to their overall work environment and feel a sense of pride in the company for taking proactive efforts to reduce its overall environmental footprint. Staff members have offered many suggested changes and improvements to consider.

Previously Existing LEED-Compliant Practices

While many projects were undertaken and some practices were modified to align with LEED standards for certification, a number of procedures already in place were sustainable and met or exceeded LEED requirements:

» **SITE EROSION CONTROL PLAN**. Erosion Control Plans are required in most jurisdictions for projects that have the potential to result in erosion and runoff into local waterways. They are also a requirement for LEED. Cushman & Wakefield had already developed and completed such a plan for Adobe.

» **INDOOR AIR QUALITY MANAGEMENT PLAN**. Cushman & Wakefield policies require all their sites to develop and maintain a written plan to prevent, diagnose, and mitigate indoor air quality problems and complaints. The specifics of this program satisfy the requirements for LEED certification. Cushman & Wakefield developed such a plan for Adobe.

» **HAZARDOUS MATERIALS MINIMIZATION AND MANAGEMENT PLAN**. Cushman & Wakefield policies require all sites to provide a management plan for the safe handling and control of hazardous materials; to minimize risks to building occupants and to the client's interests; and to mandate management in accordance with federal and local guidelines. This policy also satisfies requirements for LEED certification. Cushman & Wakefield adheres to these policies on behalf of Adobe.

» **ALTERNATIVE TRANSPORTATION PROGRAM**. Adobe's alternative transportation program has been described as one of the best in Silicon Valley. The company's San Jose and San Francisco facilities are located within walking distance of public transit alternatives, including commuter trains, light rail, and bus lines. Adobe provides free passes for Caltrain and $100 a month per employee in commuter vouchers for all other transit systems. Adobe contributes to maintaining a shuttle service to nearby rail stations. Secure bicycle cages for approximately 160 bicycles are located within the semi-enclosed parking garages. Adobe employees lead by example—more than 24 percent of employees at the San Jose headquarters commute on public transit compared with a county-wide average of just 7.2 percent.

Summary of Sustainability Programs To Date

These projects and programs were completed between 2001 and the close of 2006, when the three Adobe Towers were LEED certified. Overall, these projects and programs resulted in electricity savings of 35 percent, natural gas savings of 41 percent, domestic water savings of 22 percent, landscape irrigation savings of 76 percent, and a reduction in CO_2 emissions of 16 percent—and,

with the purchase of renewable energy credits (RECs), 36 percent. RECs were purchased to gain one more point through the LEED certification program; 60 percent are for energy generated from methane landfill sites and 40 percent are from wind farms.

PROJECTS UNDERTAKEN SINCE CERTIFICATION

Achieving LEED certification did not end Adobe's commitment to finding and implementing better ways of managing energy more efficiently and operating sustainably. Building operations are ongoing. Technology advances. Processes and procedures evolve and are improved upon. Adobe intends to continue to investigate, test, and analyze new ideas that appear to have merit, and, where efficiencies can be achieved, to implement them.

Since 2006, Adobe has completed an additional 21 projects at a total cost of $572,531, received an additional $62,630 in rebates, and realized an additional $202,274 in annual operating cost savings for an overall ROI of 40 percent. These projects included the following:

» **RETROFITTING A MORE EFFICIENT DUCTING SYSTEM** in West Tower in conjunction with floor remodeling; heating, ventilating, and air-conditioning efficiency has improved more than 10 percent on those floors.

» **INSTALLING MORE EFFICIENT LIGHTING** in the main cafeteria as part of a remodel saves $147 per year, demonstrating Adobe's belief that no project is too small. It is the cumulative effect of all of Adobe's many projects, large and small, that have resulted in the company's substantial overall savings.

» **REPLACING 740 HALOGEN LAMPS** with light-emitting diodes (LEDs) cost $26,062, with an ROI of 36 percent.

» **APPLYING THERMAL FILM** on the southern- and western-facing windows to reduce heat buildup from the sun cost $258,699, with an ROI of 25 percent.

» **SWITCHING OF PAPER TOWELS**, paper food-service products, and plastic utensils to compostable versions, including potato-based "spudware," cost an additional $38,154 per year but allowed Adobe to increase the solid waste diversion rate from 85 percent to 96 percent, and increase savings from avoided landfill fees from approximately $137,000 per year to more than $200,000 per year. To facilitate this conversion, three bins were placed in every conference room, meeting room, and break room, as well as in the cafeteria: one each for compost, recycling, and trash. At each desk is a regular wastebasket for recycled materials, and a smaller "side-saddle" basket (that hangs on the side of the larger basket) for compostable items. Janitorial staff members are equipped with two bins on their carts, one for compostable items and one for recyclables. Trash is picked up separately—but other waste reduction efforts have decreased the amount of trash.

▸▸ **INSTALLING FILTERED WATER DISPENSERS** as an alternative to bottled water. The change has reduced bottled water use by 45 percent, saving $30,000 per year and providing an ROI of 20 percent.

▸▸ **REPROGRAMMING COPIERS** to default to dual-sided copying, which cost nothing to implement except the time it took to change the copier settings. The conversion saves Adobe $22,500 per year.

TECHNICAL INNOVATION

The use of new technologies continue to enhance Adobe's facilities:

▸▸ **ONE OF THE EARLY PROJECTS** undertaken was adding real-time electric meters to measure electricity use change as projects were implemented. These meters were a tremendous help in confirming the savings realized from each measure.

▸▸ **IN THE SUMMER OF 2003**, Adobe signed on to participate in PG&E's voluntary Demand Response Program. This program was developed to reduce electricity demand during periods of critical peak demand, thereby helping prevent rolling blackouts and keeping spot market energy prices down. When curtailment was called for, Adobe turned off decorative fountains and overhead lighting in perimeter offices, corridors, and garages (except for emergency lighting) and found it took two engineers 45 minutes to turn everything off manually. This led to the development of a Web-based interface that allows these systems to be modified with a single global command. It now takes one engineer less than a minute to perform this task.

▸▸ **THESE CHANGES POINTED THE WAY** toward a much more comprehensive innovation: a Web-based integrated building interface system, or IBIS. When completed, this system will enable building operating engineers to access any portion of the Adobe campus from anywhere with connectivity. Engineers will be able to monitor lighting, temperature, electricity use, natural gas use, and water use, not only by individual office, but by floor and building, as well as site.

▸▸ **ADOBE IS ALSO TESTING SEVERAL OFFSHOOTS OF IBIS**. One is a system that uses motion sensors to control overhead lighting, task lighting, computer monitors, and overhead air supply dampers in each office; the system records on-time to establish actual office utilization rates.

▸▸ **A SECOND OFFSHOOT OF THE IBIS** is a system that automatically puts Adobe's software lab servers into sleep mode when they are not in use. The reduction of power use is about 40 percent, incurring only minimal start-up spikes when the servers are turned back on and are ramping up.

LOOKING TO THE FUTURE

Adobe is researching 26 additional sustainability projects, including wind turbine generators; solar photovoltaic generation; a fuel-cell generator; virtualization of data centers; reconfiguration of chiller piping; retrofit of smaller motors with VFDs to improve efficiency; a program to retire older motors and replace them with newer motors with VFDs; retrofit of overhead fluorescent office lamps with LED lamps; retrofit of fluorescent task lamps with LED lamps; retrofit of overhead lamps along exterior windows with daylight-activated dimming ballasts; retrofit of cooling towers to use ground water rather than treated utility water; conversion of the cooling towers to ionized water, to eliminate still more hazardous chemicals from the site; and installation of low-flow toilets throughout the facilities. Adobe's green efforts have also affected the cafeteria menu; more organic and locally grown food selections are available.

In addition, Adobe has implemented metrics for measuring its carbon emissions globally. While the company is continuing to work to reduce carbon emissions through direct implementation of conservation measures, it has committed to purchase carbon offsets for those emissions that cannot be eliminated. Adobe's ultimate goal is to achieve complete carbon neutrality globally.

The Ripple Effect

Adobe now has five certified green buildings and is in the process of certifying two additional sites. Many of the sustainable practices developed at Adobe's San Jose headquarters are being carried out to its field offices. Conversely, a number of Adobe's field and satellite offices have developed sustainable projects on their own, which have been adopted at the corporate headquarters.

Awards and Recognition

Since the LEED certification of Adobe's headquarters buildings, Adobe and Cushman & Wakefield have received more than 40 awards for sustainability efforts, including awards from the Association of Energy Engineers, the Building Owners and Managers Association International, the state of California, and the International Facility Management Association.

EXPERIENCE GAINED

An important lesson learned through Adobe and Cushman & Wakefield's collaboration is that most cost savings were achieved by applying basic practices and principles of good property and facilities management. It is worthy of note that Adobe and Cushman & Wakefield were able to reduce Adobe's electricity load significantly simply by reevaluating the usage of energy-consuming devices. Adobe's 26 load management reduction projects delivered a combined ROI of 304 percent.

Another key principle was to pursue the low-cost, high-payback initiatives first. This strategy yielded strong initial program results and solidified enthusiasm for the energy retrofit program. In obtaining LEED-EB certification, Adobe and Cushman & Wakefield undertook 64 separate projects with a simple payback of 9.5 months and a combined ROI of 121 percent.

A third key principle to greening Adobe's operations has been working effectively with local building officials. Adobe and Cushman & Wakefield educated San Jose officials on the use of waterless urinals, resulting in new city regulations permitting the use of waterless urinals in professionally managed properties.

Impressive results also were achieved through complex and sophisticated projects such as IBIS, which has no parallel in the industry, as well as through far less complex projects. Adobe's ability to track data and its willingness to share the results of all its projects have helped pave the way for others in the industry.

George Denise of Cushman & Wakefield is general manager of facilities for Adobe Systems. He is based in San Jose, California.

Development Team

OWNER:
Adobe Systems Incorporated

ARCHITECT:
Hellmuth, Obata & Kassabaum, Inc. (HOK)

GENERAL CONTRACTOR:
Devcon Construction

STRUCTURAL ENGINEERS:
Nishkian & Associates

MECHANICAL & ELECTRICAL ENGINEERS:
Alpha Tech Bouillon

PROPERTY MANAGEMENT FIRM:
Cushman & Wakefield

SUSTAINABILITY CONSULTANT:
CTG Energetics

SUSTAINABLE CLEANING CONSULTANT:
The Ashkin Group, LLC

BUILDING SYSTEMS MONITORING:
Integrated Building Solutions, Inc.

JANITORIAL SUPPLIES SERVICE:
August Supply, Inc.

JANITORIAL CONTRACTOR:
GCA Cleaning

CARPET CLEANING CONTRACTOR:
McNevin Cleaning Specialists

LANDSCAPE MAINTENANCE CONTRACTOR:
Jensen Landscape Services

OFFICE SUPPLIES CONTRACTOR:
OfficeMax

LIGHTING SUPPLIES:
Grainger/GE Lighting

LIGHTING CONTRACTOR:
EnLight

CASE STUDY • BONNEY MAYERS, JAMES M. CASH, GAVIN L. GARDI, AND RONALD D. STALEY

The Christman Building

LANSING, MICHIGAN

The Christman Building, formerly known as the Mutual Building, is a six-story, 64,190-square-foot (5963-square-meter) Class A office building in downtown Lansing, Michigan. This 80-year-old building, which is listed on the National Register of Historic Places, had been poorly maintained for 20 years and had been vacant for the three years before its purchase by the Christman Company, a Lansing-based real estate company whose services include development, construction management, general contracting, and design.

Christman has been headquartered in Lansing since 1918 and operating out of the same building since 1927. Company leaders were eager for additional space to house their growing operations, to display their commitment to sustainable design and historic preservation, to demonstrate the effectiveness of integrated design and construction strategies, and to show that it was possible to deliver a financially competitive historic office renovation. Rather than building a new office building on a greenfield site in the suburbs, Christman chose to engage in a restoration project and contribute to emerging growth in Lansing's downtown.

Christman was also eager to contribute to the revitalization of the company's hometown. Lansing, a former automotive center, had been suffering for years as General Motors and other big corporations scaled back operations or closed down altogether. However, economic incentives and imaginative builders had begun to reshape the city's downtown area. The Mutual Building rehabilitation became part of a nearly $1 billion movement to revitalize Lansing.

The Christman Company provides development services through its real estate development division, Christman Capital Development Company (CCDC). CCDC owns the Christman Building, with the Christman Company leasing

An atrium was created between the two rear extensions of the U-shaped building on floors four and five and is accessible to all Christman staff.

GENE MEADOWS

the top three floors as its national headquarters. Additional tenants include the Michigan Municipal League, a state association for local governments, located on the first floor, and Kelley Cawthorne, a governmental relations and lobbying firm, on the third floor.

In rehabilitating the Mutual Building, the Christman Company wanted to create a living case study showcasing some of the firm's strengths: historical preservation, sustainable construction, and development of Class A office buildings. It took $12 million, two years of planning, and nearly a full year of actual physical construction to complete this project. The renovation made the Christman Building the world's first and only "Double Platinum" Leadership in Energy and Environmental Design (LEED) certification, for both Core and Shell (CS) and Commercial Interiors (CI).

DEVELOPMENT PROCESS

From project inception, it was Christman's goal to build a sustainable, high-quality, historic preservation project and to attain LEED-CS certification. Throughout the process, the company used LEED checklists to monitor progress, as opposed to designing to the LEED checklists. When it became apparent that the building could achieve Platinum certification for both CS and CI, Christman began to actively pursue some of the credits that were within reach and required minimal additional cost. LEED construction guidelines were tied to the contracts of all trade contractors.

Preplanning was a key aspect of the renovation. Christman has been a strong proponent of construction waste recycling for over a decade. The tight urban site limited the number of dumpster spaces available for on-site separation. Upfront planning with the trade contractors ensured that materials were separated on the floors and then deposited into appropriate dumpsters on given days. Nearby parking spaces were temporarily used for dumpster locations for a short period of time. The project was able to achieve a recycling rate of more than 77 percent.

The commissioning and LEED certification of the project was completed in house. LEED planning was facilitated by Christman's full-time sustainable programs manager, who was integrally involved in the design phase of the project. He was able to add a "sus-

tainable filter" to the design process to ensure that sustainable materials, energy efficiency, improved ventilation, and improved daylighting were key parts of the final design. The LEED certification process was managed internally by the sustainable programs manager with assistance from the architects and engineers. Commissioning was undertaken by Christman's technical staff; the commissioning team was also involved in the project from the earliest stages of design.

HISTORIC PRESERVATION CHALLENGES

For sustainable historic preservation, the biggest challenge is determining how to complete a sustainable, energy-efficient retrofit of the existing building using modern architectural designs, without compromising visual, historical, or structural integrity, a requirement of the Secretary of the Interior's criteria for new construction within historic structures. Working with historic preservation specialists on the design team, pains-

The Christman Building is on the National Register of Historic Places. Its original tall windows and open floor plan allow daylighting—an energy-saving feature.

taking precautions were taken to ensure the integrity of the building's historical aspects, dimensions, exterior enclosure, and monumental stairwells and hall spaces. All preservation work on the building was approved by Michigan's State Historic Preservation Office and the National Park Service to certify that standards protecting the National Register building were upheld and to permit receipt of federal and state historic preservation tax credits. The addition of the sixth floor and the enclosure of the new atrium were delicate design issues for the National Park Service and required extensive detailing adjustments to achieve consensus as to the amount of glass to be utilized and the setback at interface points to the historic building.

All historic surface refinishing was performed through a process common to good preservation, which included the use of the least aggressive, least amount of chemicals possible. Historic surfaces such as the original bluestone flooring and walnut millwork were uncovered from remodeling performed in the 1970s. With only minor repair and restoration, these materials were put back into service with the goal that they should last for another 50 years. Period ceramic tile in the main stairway, which had been damaged from previous work, was patched and hand painted to match original material, in lieu of total replacement.

Most of the exterior masonry was in reasonably good shape, but in the years the building was vacant, moisture had entered from multiple locations in the roof, and water, age, and corrosion had taken their collective toll on the upper levels. To correct the absence of expansion joints—a flaw in the original design—virtually all the stone from the top of the fifth floor windows to the parapet was removed, reinforced, and reset. The original exterior brick walls of the building were cleaned and tuckpointed to exacting historic preservation standards. Because of historic preservation requirements, the glass in the restored windows had to be completely clear; although insulated, windows could not have a low-E film coating. The need to maintain the "breathability" of exterior walls limited the opportunity to add wall insulation. This resulted in slightly higher usage of heating and cooling than would be found in a new building. Nonetheless, Christman was able to add six inches of insulation and a white roof to the building to reduce energy use and to offset urban heat island effects, allowing energy efficiency to be greatly improved.

GREEN BUILDING DESIGN AND CONSTRUCTION

The Mutual Building was constructed in 1928 with a solid concrete frame. The original design included several features which are now considered green-friendly, including tall windows and an open floor plate for substantial daylighting. The building features a U-shaped layout on floors two through five which, in essence, served as a light court to further facilitate daylighting. All these aspects of the original design were incorporated into the green features of the restored building. Reuse of the historic structure tapped the inherent embodied energy of the existing building, which is the most resource-efficient method of creating new space.

Project results demonstrate that sustainability is compatible with historic renovation. Energy modeling projections for the Christman Building show that it will exceed minimum energy efficiency requirements by 34 percent. Water savings are estimated at 40 percent. Ninety-two percent of the building's wall, roof, and floors were reused, and 77 percent of construction debris was recycled.

Sustainable Siting

The Christman Building is well-located for environmentally friendly commuting:

▸▸ **PROXIMITY TO MASS TRANSIT**. The Christman Building's location facilitates the use of existing parking facilities and public transportation. The downtown hub for the Capital Area Transportation Authority (CATA), which in 2007 was named the best transit system of its size in North America by the American Public Transportation Association, is less than five blocks away.

▸▸ **ENCOURAGEMENT OF GREEN COMMUTING**. The provision of bike racks, showers, and locker facilities encourage building occupants to walk, run, or bike to work.

Sustainable Design and Construction Practices

The Christman Building renovation incorporated the following green design and construction practices:

▸▸ **FLEXIBLE BUILDING INTERIORS** and collaborative space. One of the project's important design criteria was to plan for growth, change, and the accommodation of short-term, on-site project personnel. Glass-walled offices are placed along the perimeter of the building to meet the need for privacy without separating these offices physically from collaborative areas. The interior design kept fixed walls to a minimum, and demountable wall dividers in the new sixth floor allow the space to be adapted for use by function and number of people.

The building atrium was created between the two rear extensions of this U-shaped building on floors four and five, and is accessible to all Christman staff. This inner courtyard and large exterior windows provide daylight to the interior space. The inner courtyard also acts as an informal gathering and collaboration area. The space, called Christman Square, has become a popular place to work because of its natural light and unique architectural character.

▸▸ **RECYCLING DEMOLITION WASTE**. During the demolition phase of the project, all carpet squares in the building were saved and donated to Habit for Humanity. All ceiling tiles were sent to Armstrong Industries for recycling into new ceiling tiles. All wood used in the LEED-CS project was certified by the Forest Stewardship Council. Drywall was donated to be used as an additive for road construction projects. A comprehensive reclamation and recycling program during construction provided on-site recycling containers, and recycled materials were sent to specific recycling centers. These focused efforts diverted 77 percent of the project's interior construction waste from the local landfill.

▸▸ **MAINTENANCE OF INDOOR AIR QUALITY**. During construction, an indoor air quality plan was instituted to ensure the use of environmentally sensitive materials and construction practices, and to reduce any adverse air quality effects once the building was occupied. Measures undertaken during construction included dust control and covering all return air grilles with temporary MERV-8 filters. The air-handling systems use a MERV-13-rated air filtration system to create a healthier work environment. (MERV, or minimum efficiency report value, is measured from 1 to 16; the higher the rating, the more efficient the air filter is at removing particles.)

The heating, ventilating, and air-conditioning (HVAC) system installed was designed to substantially exceed the minimum indoor air quality requirements set by code. The under-floor air distribution system, installed on floors 2 through 6, provides 200 to 300 percent more ventilation to the breathing zone than conventional systems, as required by American Society of Heating, Refrigerating, and Air-Conditioning Engineers (ASHRAE) Standard 62.1–2004.

Installation and keeping under-floor air system space clean during construction proved to be a real challenge because of the debris generated by some of the historic preservation activities, such as plaster restoration. Even though all the joints of the access floor panels were duct-taped to keep out the dust, the space under the access floor had to be cleaned several additional times to ensure that the supply air space was clean.

Energy Efficiency

The Christman Building project was designed to enhance energy efficiency in a historic structure. The following "energy-smart" strategies were utilized:

▸▸ **EFFICIENT HVAC SYSTEMS**. Heating and cooling systems were designed and equipment selected to minimize energy use while providing individually controlled comfort conditions. The under-floor air distribution system is more energy efficient than conventional ducted systems. A computerized building management system (BMS) ensures that the HVAC system operates so as to maximize energy efficiency and occupant comfort. Commissioning of all HVAC, lighting, and domestic water systems was conducted upon building completion to ensure that all systems operated as designed and as efficiently as possible.

▸▸ **ENERGY-EFFICIENT LIGHTING**. Featuring large perimeter windows and the interior courtyard, the Christman Building provides daylighting to 92 percent of occupied spaces and outside views to 90 percent of the occupants. The building earned two LEED daylighting points for 75 and 95 percent of spaces having a daylighting factor of 2 percent or more. Even on the cloudiest day, the Christman Building does not get a daytime reading of less than 75 foot-candles. This extensive daylighting allowed designers to keep interior indirect light levels at the low end of the spectrum, at around 30 foot-candles.

Indirect lighting is provided by high-efficiency fixtures and T5 fluorescent lamps with a color rendering index (CRI) of 86. (The CRI of a lamp compares the color of the lamp with sunlight, which is given an index of 100—the closer the CRI is to sunlight, the more natural the artificial light is perceived by the eye.) The high CRI allows the effective foot-candles to be reduced (thereby reducing energy costs) in a way that is not noticeable to the eye.

Lighting levels are controlled by occupancy sensors in private offices and stairways, programmed timers in common spaces, and individually controlled task lighting. To reduce light pollution, exterior-cutoff light fixtures aim all light downward. The building was not rewarded a LEED point because the final foot-candle measurement for these fixtures came in one-tenth of one foot-candle higher than LEED requirements. The team chose not to spend the $500 appealing the denied point, as the intent of the credit had been met. Overall, the effect of extensive daylighting and efficient fixtures means that lighting energy savings are projected to be 27 percent less than a code building.

▸▸ USE OF ENERGY STAR–RATED EQUIPMENT AND APPLIANCES. All appliances and office equipment, including copiers, fax machines, and computers, are Energy Star rated. All cooling equipment uses refrigerants that cause minimal damage to the environment.

▸▸ SUSTAINABLE BUILDING CONTROL SYSTEM. The Christman Building features a digital BMS with several thousand control points. The system is used to continu-

ously fine-tune the operation of HVAC and lighting systems, with the current occupancy and climatic conditions. This system maximizes both energy efficiency and occupant comfort.

The BMS tracks and measures electricity and gas usage, as well as atmospheric conditions inside and outside the building, and is used to prompt maintenance activities. Energy use is metered at the building and tenant levels to encourage conservation. The BMS is also programmed to provide automatic alarms when any of the systems are operating outside of their programmed parameters. This results in prompt response from maintenance personnel, which in turn maintains a high level of energy conservation.

The BMS maintains temperatures and humidity in accordance with ASHRAE Standard 55-2004. Thermal, ventilation, and lighting systems can be controlled at every workstation and in every conference room by individual climate controls, floor registers, and task lighting. The HVAC systems were designed and equipment selected to minimize energy use while providing individually controlled comfort conditions.

▸▸ RENEWABLE ENERGY CREDITS (RECs). RECs were purchased for clean wind energy from Renewable Choice Energy, a Green-e–certified company. The RECs were purchased to offset conventional electricity use for two years for 70 percent of the building's common area and for all of the Christman Company's space. The RECs cost $3,624 for a two-year contract. The purchase of RECs to offset the use of 843,000 kWh of electricity reduces carbon emissions by 1.5 million pounds per year, sulfur emissions by more than 4,500 grams per year, and nitrogen emissions by more than 2,100 grams per year.

Water Efficiency

The following strategies were undertaken to cut water use at the Christman Building:

▸▸ REDUCED POTABLE WATER CONSUMPTION. A 40 percent reduction in potable water and sewage use was achieved by careful selection of water-efficient plumbing fixtures such as 0.5-gallon-per-flush automatic flush urinals, 0.5-gallon-per-flush ultra-low-flow automatic lavatory faucets with aerators, and dual-flush toilet valves throughout the building. In addition, the faucets at the coffee

As part of the historic rehabilitation design, 92 percent of existing structural walls, as well as roof and floor surfaces, were reused. Some original building components, such as the Pewabic wall tiles and the verdigris bronze handrail finish, were restored.

stations have low-flow aerators installed and the two showers are equipped with 1-gallon-per-flush showerheads.

▸▸ **LANDSCAPING**. Drought-resistant plants were chosen for the exterior landscaping, so that no potable irrigation would be required.

Sustainable, Reused, and Recycled Materials

The design and construction teams carried out an extensive and successful program to employ sustainable, reused, and recycled materials throughout the project:

▸▸ **REUSE OF BUILDING MATERIALS**. The design reused 92 percent of the structural walls, roof, and floors. Some original building components were also refurbished and reused. The project reused the following materials:

- Existing walnut trim moldings and office furniture were removed, rehabilitated, and reused in different locations.
- Antique millstones from the original owner—an insurer of the state's grain farmers—had been incorporated in the sidewalk in front of the building. These were carefully extracted when the sidewalk was replaced and are now featured in the landscaping along the facade.
- Door hardware was removed, polished, or replated and reinstalled.
- Metal components of the light fixtures were cleaned, new mica shades were installed, and the fixtures were converted electrically to be energy efficient.
- The main entrance doors and plaques, the Pewabic wall tiles—a vintage Arts and Crafts School tile much in demand in the Detroit area—and bronze handrails in the main hall and stairwell were restored.
- Bluestone and linoleum floors were restored to meet historic preservation standards.
- Wood windows were restored with the addition of insulated glazing.
- Bricks salvaged from the removal of the penthouse were used to patch exterior walls.
- Plaster walls were restored, using several restoration techniques, preventing their complete demolition and replacement.

▸▸ **USE OF RECYCLED, REGIONAL, AND ENVIRONMENTALLY FRIENDLY MATERIALS**. Recycled and regionally manufactured materials were used extensively, as were low-emission sealants, paints, carpets, and furniture.

The Christman Building has a digital building management system with several thousand control points, maximizing both energy efficiency and occupant comfort.

Benign products, such as citrus strippers, wet grinding and coatings with low emissions of volatile organic compounds (VOCs), were used to restore historic finishes such as the walnut paneling in the executive offices on the first floor. Carpet tiles were installed so that small sections, such as high-traffic areas, can be replaced as needed. Recycled materials made up 20 percent of the materials costs for the LEED-CS project, and 25 percent for the LEED-CI project. Regionally manufactured materials (10 percent extracted) made up 42 percent of total materials costs for the LEED-CS project, and 24 percent for the LEED-CI project. All wood used in the project was certified by the Forest Stewardship Council.

FINANCING

The Christman Building is a public/private partnership between the Christman Company and the city of Lansing which, through its Brownfield Authority, has a development agreement with the project. This enables the recapture of Michigan Single Business Tax Credits for eligible costs associated with the project. The city also provided key economic information that supported requests for the New Market Tax Credits. The city of Lansing, knowing that a healthy downtown leads to healthy communities, was eager to assist in the development.

The financing for the project utilized a number of economic incentives, including federal programs such as New Market Tax Credits and Historic Tax Credits, which help urban projects move forward when traditional financing is not adequate. New Market Tax Credits

provide federal tax credits over a seven-year period to qualified commercial investment properties. In order to qualify, the project must be within a Qualified Census Tract as defined by the U.S. Treasury. The competitiveness of the application process often requires projects to show extra characteristics of how the project is helping the community; in the case of the Mutual Building rehabilitation project, it was the fact that the structure was also designated a brownfield site by the city of Lansing.

The project was also facilitated by real property tax relief through the Federal Obsolete Property Rehabilitation Act (OPRA), a program which freezes the pre-rehabilitated taxable value on a building for 12 years. This enables builders and developers to invest more money into rehabilitations and renovations and pass the savings along to tenants in the form of lower operating costs. To qualify, a company must be working on a commercial property or building that is blighted or deemed functionally obsolete, and submit an OPRA request to the city—in this case, the city of Lansing—who grants the application.

The economic incentives that supported the redevelopment of the Christman Building included the following:

▸▸ $672,500 in Michigan Brownfield Single Business Tax Credits;

▸▸ $2 million in federal historic tax credits;

▸▸ $500,000 in state historic tax credits;

▸▸ Allocation of $8.5 million in federal New Market Qualified Investment; and

▸▸ $1.2 million ($100,000 per year for 12 years) in property tax relief through the establishment of a Federal Obsolete Property Rehabilitation Act (OPRA) District.

While the renovation of the Christman Building attracted significant public support for its urban redevelopment and historic components, green features were not a material factor in project costs and no financial incentives were received specifically for the LEED-related costs. For the LEED-CS project, the costs associated with achieving green goals represented 1.3 percent of the total budget. Two-thirds of those costs were related to the LEED certification process. For the LEED-CI project, the costs associated with achieving LEED certification represented 0.7 percent of the total budget. Of those green costs, 95 percent were related to LEED certification. The minimization of additional proj-

ect costs was a direct result of using a fully integrated design and construction process and using the LEED process to measure how the project performed on a sustainable scale, as opposed to designing specifically to the LEED checklists.

MARKETING AND MANAGEMENT

The Christman Building has proved to be a marketing tool for the Christman Company, and occupant satisfaction with the project's green features is high. Ongoing management of the property has also been influenced by sustainable objectives, as demonstrated by the introduction of a green housekeeping program.

▸▸ **MARKETING BENEFITS**. The Christman Building serves as a high-profile, living example of what an environmentally oriented construction firm can accomplish. As such, the building itself serves as an outstanding marketing tool for the company. Public interest in this green historic preservation project continues to be high. Visitors to the facility learn about sustainable design and construction through permanent signage and guided tours by Christman staff. Media exposure has run the gamut, from trade magazines to websites to television and radio news features. Dozens of local, statewide, and national media covered the story, as did a green news outlet in the United Kingdom.

▸▸ **OCCUPANT SATISFACTION**. Christman volunteered to be a case study subject for a Michigan State University research project that is evaluating the health benefits of working in a LEED building, and the building's staff will be surveyed approximately every three months for the first two years of occupancy. The initial two surveys found that occupants' responses to the green features were overwhelmingly positive.

▸▸ **GREEN HOUSEKEEPING**. The Christman Company developed detailed specifications for a green housekeeping program. The program stipulates the use of environmentally responsible and low-emission cleaning products, and utilizes 100 percent recycled paper products in restrooms. All janitorial and chemical storage rooms are separated and exhausted directly to the outside, and entrance mats catch outdoor debris before it enters the building. The building also has a comprehensive recycling program in which 14 different types of materials are recycled.

EXPERIENCES GAINED

The Christman Building renovation offers the following lessons for teams engaged in sustainable historic preservation or renovation projects:

▸▸ **HISTORIC PRESERVATION** and sustainable renovation can be complementary. The original design of the Christman Building, which incorporated tall windows and an open floor plate, facilitated daylighting—an energy saving feature—and the provision of outside views to occupants. Energy modeling projections for the Christman Building show that it will exceed minimum energy efficiency requirements by 34 percent. The project reused 92 percent of existing walls, roofs and flooring and recycled 77 percent of demolition waste. Water savings are estimated at 40 percent.

▸▸ **HIGH-LEVEL SUSTAINABLE DESIGN** and construction does not need to cost significantly more than conventional practices provided that an integrated design and construction process is used. For the LEED-CS project, the costs associated with achieving green goals represented 1.3 percent of the total budget. Two-thirds of those costs were related to the LEED certification process. For the LEED-CI project, the costs associated with achieving LEED certification represented 0.7 percent of the total budget. Of those green costs, 95 percent were related to LEED certification.

▸▸ **FINANCING INCENTIVES** from a variety of federal and state programs were assembled to support the Christman Building renovation. Developers can frequently couple public and private financing to make green and historic renovations more affordable. It is worthwhile to investigate public as well as private financing sources when embarking on a green or historic renovation.

▸▸ **EARLY PLANNING** is crucial when using the integrated design and construction process. Commitment to the LEED approach and collaboration among the owner, project team and subcontractors are essential to success.

▸▸ **BEGIN TO GATHER REQUIRED LEED DOCUMENTATION** very early in the project, as it is difficult to get the subcontractors to supply the data required at the end of the project. To that end, Christman has developed a broad range of tools to facilitate receiving and documenting the information required for LEED certification.

▸▸ **ONGOING EVALUATION OF ENERGY USE** efficiency measures and perpetual tracking of consumption information are crucial to ensure that a project of this nature attains the projected energy savings.

▸▸ **INTEREST IN SUSTAINABLE CONSTRUCTION** and historic preservation is not limited to architecture, design, and construction circles. The Christman Building renovation has attracted substantial media attention and served as an excellent marketing tool for the Christman Company. The experience suggests that innovative projects that combine historic preservation and sustainability are likely to attract significant positive attention.

Bonney Mayers is a Michigan-based writer specializing in construction and design. James M. Cash is president and chief operating officer, Christman Capital Development Company; Ronald D. Staley, FAPT, is senior vice president and director, National Preservation, the Christman Company; and Gavin L. Gardi, LEED AP, CFD, is Sustainable Programs manager for the Christman Company.

Development Team

OWNER/DEVELOPER:
Christman Capital Development Group, LLC

ARCHITECT:
SmithGroup, Inc.

GENERAL CONTRACTOR:
The Christman Company

MECHANICAL/ELECTRICAL
Engineers:SmithGroup, Inc.

LIGHTING DESIGNER:
SmithGroup, Inc.

SUSTAINABILITY CONSULTANT:
Gavin Gardi, Sustainable Programs Manager, The Christman Company

INTERIOR DESIGNER:
SmithGroup, Inc.

COMMISSIONING AGENT:
The Christman Company

CASE STUDY · HOK

HOK Office

HONG KONG, CHINA

HOK's renovation of its Hong Kong office was part of an effort to design or remodel HOK's Asian offices to LEED standards in accordance with a global corporate mandate. The effort began in 2006 with the opening of HOK's Singapore office, followed by expansions and renovations of its Beijing, Shanghai, and Hong Kong offices in 2007. At that time, the regional green building rating systems—Singapore's

Green Mark, China's Green Building Evaluation Standard, and Hong Kong's Building Environmental Assessment Method (BEAM)—addressed only whole buildings, not building interiors. While applying the LEED process was not the best fit in terms of

the region's climate, environmental and resource issues, and local regulations and industry standards, it was still very relevant as a means to quantify and validate sustainable targets that were set.

HOK's retrofit of its leased office space in Hong Kong was achievable with conventional, industry-available equipment and materials, with a local consultant and contractor, within a medium-to-low-range fit-out budget, and using good design fundamentals.

CONTEXT

The HOK Hong Kong office is located in Central Hong Kong, which is a vibrant, extremely dense, mixed-use urban area containing commercial and residential properties. There is a contrasting mix of modern, upscale, high-rise towers at 30 or more stories and older two- to five-story Chinese walkups intermixed with historic cultural buildings and wet markets.

Market Characteristics

In much of Asia, considering climate change and implementing sustainable growth mechanisms are recognized as imperatives and, if left unaddressed, potential threats to economic stability. In China and Hong Kong, sustainability is therefore increasing in national priority but is still not the highest concern. Recent decades were spent focusing on economic growth; toward the end of 2008 and in early 2009, economic recovery, stability, and stimulus became the primary agendas. In the building industry media, in the plethora of green building forums and conferences, sustainability and "greening" are addressed not as imperatives but as questions: Can sustainability prevail in these times? What will be the impact of the global financial crisis on green building?

Where sustainability is a mainstream topic in Hong Kong is in the area of air quality, because the negative effects of pollution are tangible. The implications of overbuilding, excessive urban density, and wall-like tower structures contributing to stagnant and polluted urban environments are well understood by the average citizen. The contributing effects of building energy use on pollution are just becoming common knowledge and are an emerging topic of public concern.

With respect to accomplishments, Hong Kong's voluntary assessment tool, BEAM, has recognized over 170 office and residential developments for improved building performance. These projects account for more than 25 percent of commercial space, and approximately 10 percent of dwellings, of which 70 percent are private sector buildings and 30 percent public sector buildings.

As of this writing, there is no statute requiring minimum building energy efficiency in Hong Kong. It was only from December 2007 to March 2008 that the government launched a public consultation on a proposal to introduce mandatory implementation of building energy codes. This public consultation began after a decade of operating a voluntary building energy efficiency scheme that was not successfully adopted in the Hong Kong market. More recently, in July 2008, the government launched a voluntary carbon audit campaign; it is expected to implement minimum building energy performance standards later in 2009.

In Asia, construction projects are often very large, include multiple uses in a single development, and occur at an extremely fast pace. Pilings and foundations are often constructed before the design is complete. Early commitment, the perceived risk due to unconventional design and construction methods, the widespread perception that green building costs more, the lack of a regional building energy and performance database, and the absence of disclosure requirements are some of the main barriers to faster market transformation.

Green office interior retrofits take place on a more modest scale that is much more tenable than whole buildings; the potential for significant and quantifiable impact is high—with a significantly lesser degree of financial investment owing to more limited scope and more predictable outcomes. The green office interior retrofit is extremely applicable to Hong Kong: it is a city that is constantly under construction and is built on short-term leases that require tenants to wastefully "restore premises to original." This no doubt contributes to the fact that construction waste represents a disproportionate amount of Hong Kong's landfill waste. The green office interior retrofit is applicable to most of those who have a business, not just to the building industry, and represents the first step by which many businesses might test their commitment to sustainability. In Hong Kong, multinational corporations are taking the lead, probably because of overseas mandates and an international client base.

The HOK Hong Kong office was the first project to pursue LEED certification in Hong Kong. Two projects are currently LEED certified, including this one; both are LEED Gold and both are commercial interiors projects. A handful of additional projects are registered for LEED certification, including the office of a Hong Kong government entity.

Why Owners Deemed Green Renovation Desirable

All of HOK's new or renovated offices must be LEED certified as part of a firm-wide commitment to reduce emissions from office operations. It is a demonstration of the commitment to "walk the talk." As owners and end users, HOK benefits directly from the efficiencies designed into the projects and the practical experience gained from successful implementation in the local Asia market.

HOK's LEED certifications in Asia are not about emphasizing LEED; however, as a global firm, a LEED rating allows for the perception of comparability in the international market. In the very near future, both BEAM and Green Mark will launch systems specifically addressing building interiors, after which HOK will seek to certify the Asia offices under the respective regional rating systems.

DEVELOPMENT PROCESS

The project intent was to accomplish the LEED-CI certification with local HOK employees, engineers, and contractors on a standard budget and a demanding schedule.

How the Team Was Assembled

The HOK Hong Kong office project was carried out entirely by in-house and local team members. HOK Hong Kong's interior designers, architects, and project managers teamed with a local mechanical, electrical, and plumbing (MEP) engineer and a local contractor. The MEP engineer had been proactively engaging the team in discussion about building commissioning, which is not a common practice in this region. All sustainable design, construction, and LEED certification requirements were submitted with the tender documents, after which the team conducted interviews to assess related experience and general attitudes toward green building, and to see what questions, if any, the contractors had regarding performing extremely unconventional tasks.

The contractor selected had never done a green fit-out (buildout) before. However, it was a fairly new company, seemed likely to make a good effort to follow through and be accountable, and was open and frank about processes that were not usually performed in Hong Kong.

How Key Approaches for the Project Were Developed

The primary goal for this project was to create an attractive, healthy, collaborative, naturally daylit workspace for HOK employees while adhering to a firm construction budget—without a special budget allowance for sustainable design aspects—and a tight work schedule. As well, the ongoing work of HOK's Hong Kong office would not be interrupted so construction would take place concurrently. HOK wanted to demonstrate that, if planned from the outset, a green office fit-out can be achieved within a normal budget and a tight schedule. To prove this, the team worked through the LEED certification process as an in-house exercise to gain firsthand experience implementing LEED in Hong Kong.

A secondary goal was to minimize and reduce waste. In Hong Kong, lease terms are extremely short. The effects of the typical two-year lease combined with the typical clause "reinstate premises to original" result in an enormous amount of unnecessary construction waste.

GREEN BUILDING DESIGN AND CONSTRUCTION

The HOK interior was designed to minimize demolition, construction waste, and energy use, while enhancing collegiality and creativity.

Key Design and Construction Considerations

The HOK Hong Kong office is a space designed to facilitate the collaborative process, professional interaction, creativity, easy communication, and flexibility for expansion in a daylit atmosphere with visual connections to the Hong Kong urban setting. The main strategy was to provide an open-plan layout with minimum enclosed spaces and glass partitions to share light and views. Circulation and service areas are concentrated toward the core, so as to dedicate the periphery to users. This strategy was also the primary method to reduce energy use: by maximizing daylight access and minimizing internal walls, the use of electric lighting could be reduced.

Minimizing demolition and construction waste was also a key consideration. The project team, independent of building management, negotiated with the departing tenant to retain a good portion of the expansion space. This, in combination with reuse of a significant amount of existing walls in the original space not only helped to reduce demolition but also minimized quantities of new material and new construction, which in turn reduced costs and helped the project meet its budget.

Phasing was critical to complete the construction quickly. Four phases were needed in order to keep the four departments operating during construction.

By maximizing access to daylight and minimizing internal walls, the building reduces use of electric lighting.

Green Features

Green features of the HOK Hong Kong office include sustainable siting and the use of strategies to realize energy and water savings, construction waste reduction, and superior indoor environmental quality:

▸▸ **SITE**. The HOK Hong Kong office is located conveniently near public transportation and has uncountable amenities within walking distance. Parking is removed from the lease.

▸▸ **ENERGY**. Energy-saving strategies included the reuse of existing light fixtures retrofitted with high-efficiency T5 lamps and ballasts. The lighting retrofit both reduced energy use and avoided the disposal of old fixtures and the cost of new ones. Occupancy and daylight sensors are installed throughout the space as well. The designed lighting power exceeds American Society of Heating, Refrigerating, and Air-Conditioning Engineers standards by 37 percent. Submeters monitor lighting and plug loads separately, to enable monitoring of energy fluctuations and to track the effectiveness of any future energy reduction strategies related to user behavior. The lease requires that utilities be billed separately from base rent; this keeps the lease holder accountable for utilities consumed. Of the office equipment and appliances incorporated, 94 percent are Energy Star rated.

▸▸ **WATER**. Fixtures in the base building's washroom lavatories are timed, conceivably to reduce water use. However, through manual measurement, it was discovered that they are not as efficient as hoped. An extremely efficient auto-sensor faucet has been installed in the office pantry but unfortunately cannot make up for the inefficiency of the lavatories.

▸▸ **MATERIALS**. In addition to reducing demolition and construction by retaining 50 percent of existing non-structural components and reusing 45 percent (by value) of existing furnishings, a construction waste management plan was implemented whereby all waste was sorted and quantified and diverted from disposal where possible. This strategy resulted in the diversion of 80 percent of construction, demolition, debris packaging debris and waste by means of donation, recycling, reusing, and returning materials to manufacterers. An office waste recycling system has been established to recycle paper, cardboard, metal, and plastics.

▸ **INDOOR ENVIRONMENTAL QUALITY.** There was an emphasis on products with low and no volatile organic compounds (VOCs), which include the carpet, paint, sealant, window shades, and task chairs. The carpet is GREENGUARD certified and has recycled content. The ergonomic task chairs are also GREENGUARD certified, with high recycled content, and are certified as a Cradle to Cradle™ Gold product by MBDC (McDonough Braungart Design Chemistry, LLC). The pin boards (bulletin boards) are recyclable and are designed to go back into the product stream after their use. An air purifier with zeolite technology is also installed. Zoned thermostats are installed to increase thermal comfort control by individuals or groups. Ninety-five percent of regularly occupied spaces have access to views.

Challenges and Successes

HOK was able to demonstrate that a green interior retrofit is achievable using good design fundamentals, with conventional, industry-available equipment and materials, with a local consultant and local contractor, and within a mid- to low-range budget. Project success did not occur without effort, early planning, research, and teamwork, but it was entirely achievable and worth the benefits in energy savings and improved interior working environment.

Because monitoring and accountability are long-standing goals, a year's worth of utility bills from the original space was compared against bills for a year of occupancy of the new space. Although the total area is greater due to the expansion, the energy intensity per square foot has been reduced by 32 percent. With an assessment tool, performance is often quantified as a percentage exceeding a benchmark or accepted standard; while this may be useful to compare against percentages achieved in other projects, it is not as tangible as direct measurement and comparison of operational energy use from utility bills.

Some of the challenges encountered involved construction practices of others interfering with HOK's efforts to conduct good air-quality practices: because the neighboring construction site (a few floors below) was using toxic materials and the fumes had come into the space through the elevator shaft, the air quality was compromised and the air test scheduled to occur before occupancy had to be canceled. A lengthy flushout was conducted instead.

In contrast to the Chinese mainland, in Hong Kong there is a lack of proper infrastructure for diverting waste: despite recovering glass and wood during demolition, it was not possible to divert these materials from the waste stream because of the lack of a recycling market for materials other than metal.

Although the building management is part of an international entity, it was not set up to easily address issues related to materials, equipment, systems records, and specifications. The promise of leasing a green office space is not currently a powerful enough incentive for building management to develop such abilities.

Documentation for compliance validation is not easy to acquire in Asia. The manufacturing industry is not yet prepared to address green building as it is in the United States. Even if a manufacturer overseas has compliance documentation, the same manufacturer in Asia may not. This is changing slowly. As of this writing, however, it is more difficult to acquire green compliance information in Asia than in the United States and western Europe.

EXPERIENCE GAINED

Key experiences gained from the retrofit of HOK's Hong Kong headquarters are the following:

▸ **MEASUREMENT ALLOWS FOR IMPROVEMENT.** Committing to a green building rating system or any accounting system is critical to ensure that initial targets and thresholds are not discarded later in the process; by adhering to a system that requires measurement of quantities and performance, goals can actually be met.

▸ **BASE BUILDING CONDITIONS** in leased premises can limit sustainable alternatives. HOK was already occupying this building. Despite all efforts to provide ample daylight access with ample windows and an optimum open layout, the base building's curtain wall is composed of tinted glass with an extremely low visible light transmittance value. The result is a space that offers the sense of daylight but does not actually meet the minimum daylight factor requirements of LEED and offers little savings in electric costs for lighting.

▶ **EFFORTS TO MINIMIZE INITIAL RENOVATION COSTS** may lead to less efficient solutions. For lighting and HVAC zoning, to reduce initial costs, the team did not extensively redesign the existing ductwork. The current supply register zones align with workstation groupings, but a more efficient design would have been to zone the perimeter and interior zones separately, to provide better thermal comfort for more occupants.

▶ **OCCUPANTS NEED TO BE INFORMED** about retrofit processes, goals, requirements, intents, and any effects the project will have on their daily routine. This, in combination with the calibration of systems, is important so that occupants do not get upset if, for instance, the occupant sensors are timed incorrectly and turn off the lights while they are trying to work.

▶ **IT IS IMPORTANT AND HELPFUL** if the building management already has in place building-wide management plans that target reduced energy, water, waste, and clean air quality.

▶ **PLAN FOR SPECIAL, LOCAL CONDITIONS**. Low-VOC, water-based paint application took six times as long to dry as conventional emulsion paint in Hong Kong's humid climate and thus required a virtually dust-free environment. The paint subcontractor said that in the future he would charge a 30 percent premium for work with low-VOC paint because of these issues. However, on the job, a contractor is reported to remark that this was the best project because there was "no smell" and the working environment was very comfortable. To avoid these issues, designers can plan for off-site painting, prefabricated items, or materials and solutions that do not require paint.

▶ **CONTRACTORS IN SOME MARKETS** may be resistant to going green. In a postconstruction interview, the contractor remarked that many of the processes employed in this project were not very common in Hong Kong. The compliance documentation, record keeping, and information chasing is absolutely not something that the contractor's staff is used to doing—nor did they enjoy doing this work. As of this writing, Hong Kong's contracting industry is not ready to provide the level of information required by green certification. One of the main challenges the contractor faced was changing the mind-set of his staff; during this learning process, one staff member is reported to have said "If you want green, don't do fit-out work."

HOK provides planning, design, and delivery solutions for the built environment throughout its 23 offices around the world.

Development Team

ARCHITECT:
HOK

ENGINEER:
Daniel Chan & Associates

CONTRACTOR:
Tingle Co.

CASE STUDY • NATHAN TAFT
Joseph Vance Building

SEATTLE, WASHINGTON

The Rose Smart Growth Investment Fund I acquired the historic Joseph Vance Building in 2006 with the express purpose of transforming it into a leading green building in the Seattle marketplace. Constructed in 1929 by lumber magnate Joseph Vance, the 14-story art deco property was of substantial historic interest but needed substantial renovation in order to fulfill its commercial potential. In the ensuing two years, the Fund made a significant investment in the building and attracted a

A new tenant fit-out on the ninth floor.

dynamic mix of tenants, many of them drawn by the building's green features. The completed project received a Gold rating from the U.S. Green Building Council, under the Leadership in Energy and Environmental Design for Existing Buildings (LEED-EB) protocol.

The Vance Building presented an opportunity to contribute to the mission of the Fund—to create a national portfolio of real

estate transformed with green improvements and within walking distance of convenient forms of mass transit. The Rose Smart Growth Investment Fund I is focused exclusively on assets in "smart growth" locations that have amenities within walking distance, offer access to mass transit, and are most likely to reduce vehicle miles traveled. Because real estate accounts for roughly 43 percent of U.S. greenhouse gas emissions, and new construction accounts for only 1 percent of the U.S. building stock annually, the Fund offers strategies for greening existing commercial stock and provides a model to demonstrate how strides in green real estate can help alleviate global energy and climate challenges.

Following study and analysis, relatively simple and low-cost green improvements that offer appropriate investment paybacks are often possible. In the case of the Vance Building, many of the original attributes—such as high ceilings, terrazzo floors, operable windows, and floor-plan layouts designed to maximize natural light—have intrinsic environmentally sensitive qualities. Therefore, the Fund's capital investment strategy sought to uncover, restore, and leverage these attributes not only in the pursuit of green efficiency, but also in an overall enhancement of aesthetics and tenant experience.

CONTEXT AND OWNERSHIP OBJECTIVES

The Vance Building was something of an overlooked gem, two blocks west of what is traditionally known as the city's best retail along 5th Avenue and two blocks east of Pike Place Market. Nestled in Seattle's downtown retail core at the intersection of Third Avenue and Union Street, the building boasted views of the Puget Sound and ample light and air because of lower-lying historic structures to the south and west.

At the time the Fund first considered acquiring the asset, trends of growth and investment were bringing businesses, culture, amenities, and even housing closer to the Vance Building. Benaroya Hall, arguably Seattle's Carnegie Hall, had relocated to the opposite corner of Third and Union streets several years earlier and provided an important anchor. By 2006, the Vance Building had front-row seats in an emerging and dynamic mixed-use community with premier cultural attractions like Benaroya and the Seattle Art Museum; one of the city's chic fusion restaurants and other busy lunch and dinner spots; a jazz club; the site of a five-star hotel set to break ground one block to the west; and other residential and retail developments by regional and national firms.

From a transit perspective, the Vance Building was an ideal match with the Fund's investment criteria. Six bus lines are available just steps away from the building on Third Avenue, and a light-rail stop (complete in 2009) is one block away. Tenant surveys conducted by the Fund indicate that because the occupants of the building are surrounded by mass transit and rich amenities, they drive less: approximately 85 percent of tenants walk, bike, ride mass transit, or carpool, thereby reducing vehicle miles traveled.

Mindful of its green vision, the Fund concluded that the building's bones, location, and context merited further investment. At the time, no other building linked the historic fabric of the "Emerald City" to modern green values. Thus in a subtle irony, the building constructed in 1929 by the Vance Timber Company was destined to become the cornerstone of the green movement in Seattle. It is critical to note that the Fund's concept of greening the building could not be separated from its comprehensive strategy for repositioning the building. Indeed, although there was some early indication of tenant demand for green space from leasing activity at the time the acquisition closed, it was not certain that the

The Joseph Vance Building is a 14-story art deco property constructed in 1929 in downtown Seattle. From acquisition due diligence through redevelopment, an interdisciplinary team worked to evaluate the building and its systems, and to envision and implement its transformation.

Fund's vision would be supported by a groundswell of like-minded tenants. Greening alone did not take the project from 68 percent to 96 percent leased, but marrying a green vision with an assiduous attention to real estate investment, development, and operating fundamentals has attracted a dynamic tenant mix, increasing top-line revenues, net operating income, and value.

DEVELOPMENT PROCESS: HISTORIC GREEN RENOVATION

From acquisition due diligence through redevelopment, the Fund worked with an interdisciplinary team to evaluate the building and its systems, and to envision and implement its transformation. The Fund drew upon Jonathan Rose Companies' longstanding commitment to managing an integrated design process and benefited from the wisdom and expertise of a broad range of professionals. The team included these members:

▸▸ **ROSE SMART GROWTH INVESTMENT FUND** (owner): The Fund provided team selection and project management, and drove the redevelopment process. Fund managers set the dual goals of greening the building and repositioning the asset in relation to its competitive set in the marketplace.

▸▸ **TURNER CONSTRUCTION** (general contractor): Rose brought Turner on early to assist with preconstruction services during the Fund's acquisition due diligence process, and later as general contractor.

▸▸ **ZIMMER GUNSUL FRASCA (ZGF)** Partnership (architect): ZGF provided schematic design, construction documents, and construction administration services for the project. The architects also took a primary role in coordinating LEED-EB documentation.

▸▸ **ARUP** (MEP engineers): Arup surveyed the building's mechanical, electrical, and plumbing systems; provided recommendations for system replacement and retro-commissioning; and constructed energy models and analysis as a basis for the Fund's decision making.

▸▸ **MAGNUSSON KLEMENCIC ASSOCIATES (MKA)** (structural engineers): MKA provided structural evaluation services, from assessing seismic risks to determining load-bearing capacities for a green roof.

▸▸ **GVA KIDDER MATHEWS** (property manager): As the Fund's third-party property manager, GVA participated in the due diligence process, and later in construction meetings, in order to implement the Fund's green goals related to operations and to coordinate with tenants, because the building was occupied during the redevelopment.

Budget constraints, driven by the Fund's investment return parameters, dictated a rigorous approach to scope definition, based on research and modeling, field testing, mock-ups, and costing exercises. At times, as in many redevelopment projects, the road to completion was winding, and building idiosyncrasies or unforeseen conditions dictated that the scope of work evolve to meet the Fund's objectives.

The Fund's initial building surveys revealed the following conditions:

▸▸ **THE VANCE BUILDING** was constructed of steel-reinforced concrete with terra-cotta cladding on the public-facing southern and western facades. A section of the western facade and parapet had been removed for repair and never restored.

▸▸ **L-SHAPED FLOOR PLATES** on levels 3 to 14 were placed on a two-story rectangular podium, with double-loaded corridors.

▸▸ **TENANT SPACES** had an inconsistent appearance, often with a mixture of current and past tenant improvements.

▸▸ **ORIGINAL TERRAZZO FLOORS** in corridors and tenant suites had been covered over with carpet that was now old and worn.

▸▸ **HIGH CEILINGS IN CORRIDORS** and tenant spaces were covered with drop ceilings, which often concealed a tangled web of mechanical, electrical, and plumbing elements.

▸▸ **THE ORIGINAL SINGLE-PANE**, double-hung wood windows had deteriorated significantly. Many had broken counterweights, requiring that top sashes be nailed shut. Water damage to plaster around the window casements was common.

▸▸ **HEATING WAS PROVIDED** by the original two-pipe steam heating system with cast-iron radiators; localized radiator shutoff values were not consistently functional, and there was no record of trap replacement or maintenance.

▸▸ **LESS THAN 40 PERCENT OF THE BUILDING**, including ground-floor retail space, was mechanically cooled, and rooftop heating, ventilating, and air-conditioning (HVAC) units of diverse vintage were in use.

The results of these building surveys, compiled in a report in August 2006, provided the framework for the Fund's redevelopment strategy. Further energy modeling and scope development was completed in the fall, after the first phase of construction began. The original use (office over ground-floor retail) remained unchanged when the renovation was completed 15 months later.

GREEN BUILDING DESIGN AND CONSTRUCTION

The greening and redevelopment plan that emerged addressed initial capital investments, tenant improvements, management processes, and ongoing investment in building systems and operations. The Fund made numerous investments, as the result of its combined goals of enhancing the tenant experience, preserving the property's historic character, and greening the building for enhanced efficiency. The greening of the Vance Building was received warmly by Seattle officials, who were seeking to reconcile current energy codes with codes for the rehabilitation of historic buildings.

The Fund's investment strategy sought to leverage the environmentally beneficial elements of the building's original design, including high ceilings, terrazzo floors, operable windows, and floor-plan layouts designed to maximize natural light. Key aspects of the renovation, discussed in detail below, included the following:

▸ Building envelope,

▸ New building entrance system,

▸ Green tenant improvements,

▸ Interior amenities and upgrades,

▸ Energy and water efficiency, and

▸ HVAC systems.

Building Envelope

The building envelope was renovated to meet two key objectives: energy efficiency and historic restoration.

ROOF REPLACEMENT

The original, flat, membrane roof was over 15 years old and at the end of its useful life. Leaks were developing, and it was suspected that the insulation might be compromised in certain areas. The Fund installed an Energy Star–rated and LEED-approved, light-colored, reflective, chlorine-free roof system to improve weather resistance and to avoid excess heat gain, and to thereby reduce the need for cooling.

As part of the preparation and planning for roof replacement, an infrared study was conducted to determine the extent to which water had infiltrated the insulation; select core cuts were also made to confirm results. Roof drains, which were observed to clog during heavy rains, were replaced to avoid standing water, and scuppers were cut in the parapet to alert the property management team to drain backups.

WINDOW RESTORATION

The building's 80-year-old windows had deteriorated. Sills were rotted and splintered, especially on the southern and western sides, which had suffered the most direct effects of sun and rain. Degraded caulking between the windows and exterior terra-cotta skin meant that water damage occurred inside the building at the window casements. Loosely sealed sashes were drafty and allowed penetration by driving rain and cold. Many windows had sashes that were not functional.

Each window was cataloged and surveyed for damage in order to get a nuanced view of the magnitude of the problem and to uncover the full range of existing conditions. The Fund worked with Arup to model three different glazing scenarios, including full replacement, retrofitting a sandwich of double-pane glass in the existing wood sashes, and restoring the operability of existing windows. Ultimately, the modeling supported the Fund's decision to restore the existing windows, focusing on operability of top and bottom sashes, and to add weather stripping.

The window restoration proved to be one of the most challenging aspects of the project from a tenant coordination standpoint, because office space was in use at the time. A complex assembly line emerged in a temporary basement workshop, where sashes pulled from a vacant suite were refurbished and then used to replace windows taken from an occupied suite. Sashes were removed, counterweights repaired, and operability restored. Sills were replaced or restored, and joints with the building and exterior terra-cotta were caulked and sealed. When there were not enough refurbished windows to install in an occupied suite, plywood and plexiglass "dummies" were used for temporary protection and for access to light and air. Restoration work in occupied tenant suites typically took place in the early morning hours.

Restoring the windows was key to one of the Fund's primary renovation principles, which was the implementation of a natural ventilation strategy. Operable windows, together with ceiling fans and mechanical shades and light shelves, helped to afford tenants more control over light and temperatures, and enabled them to enjoy Seattle's temperate climate, mitigate solar heat gain, and daylight their spaces to reduce electricity use.

RESTORATION AND REPAIR OF TERRA-COTTA FACADE

The Fund rebuilt the historic terra-cotta parapet and facade sections (which had been removed by a previous owner for repair but never restored), and repointed the mortar. These efforts not only enhanced the building's historic aesthetic, but also improved the facade's weather resistance and functionality.

Under heavy storm conditions, water had been getting behind the terra-cotta at the top of the building and sheeting down to the expansive, double-wide windows on the second floor. This rush of water would cascade through the window headers and inflict damage to plaster and nearby tenant equipment. It was also theorized that this volume of water could compromise the ties and brackets that held the terra-cotta in place, and that upper sections of terra-cotta with degraded connections could exert undue pressure on the tile sections below, creating a hazard of cracking or falling material.

Previous owners had used a helical bolt system to affix select pieces of terra-cotta to the concrete face of the building, but not all pieces had been shored. Initial estimates of the work needed ranged from $400,000 to $500,000, exceeding the budget. After select investigative drops, a targeted repointing program was undertaken for a fixed-price contract of $100,000. To the subcontractor's and the Fund's surprise, the repointing work went faster than expected and the entire terra-cotta facade was repointed for a fifth of the initial estimate.

New Building Entrance System

The Fund installed a new, grander entrance to the building on Third Avenue, the main entrance. Previously, a storefront with a metal-clad sign and transom system had blocked light and left the building entrance feeling small and low, out of keeping with a building of this size. The new system, with clean lines and more open glass, preserves natural light and accentuates the historic detail in the lobby. The storefront system also provides a walk-off mat to reduce the particulate matter tracked into the building and to preserve the air quality of the indoor environment.

Green Tenant Improvements

Through successive leasing and re-leasing, the tenant spaces in the Vance Building had acquired a worn and tired look, with a dissonant admixture of uncomfortably coexisting design aesthetics. Old carpets covered the original terrazzo floors; drop ceilings masked the loftier height of the floor slabs above, blocking exposure to the building's thermal mass (the exposure of which was necessary for the natural ventilation strategy), and obscuring access to natural light; low voltage and electrical wiring, and even plumbing, were installed inconsistently; radiators were covered with wood boxes that blocked ready access to windows. In sum, the tenant spaces were being leased as is and were dilapidated and inefficient with respect to tenant needs and green principles.

One of the Fund's key initiatives involved the creation of a green tenant improvement specification. This specification was incorporated in the tenant improvement manual, which served as a guideline for new tenants. The well-located Class B office building attracted a range of tenants with varying levels of sophistication. Some could handle their own space planning, but the typical business or nonprofit welcomed a more ready-to-lease approach, with decisions pared down to picking paint and carpet colors.

With all new tenants, the Fund used its guidelines not only to encourage green improvements but also to focus on open, flexible floor plans that adapted easily to tenant needs, allowed for growth, and reduced demolition and construction waste upon expansion or re-leasing. The new tenant improvement specifications moved away from half-height fixed partitions to favor systems with high recycled content. The tenant improvement manual served as a great marketing and communications piece, and also helped ensure that the Fund's green investment was protected and that new buildouts would continue to conform to the green specifications. As discussed later, the manual also served to reinforce tenant use of green operating practices that comport with the building's green goals.

Interior Amenities and Upgrades

Interior amenities incorporated into the Joseph Vance Building renovation were developed to support sustainability objectives:

▸▸ **BIKE ROOM, SHOWER, AND BATHROOMS**. The Fund built a new bike room for the convenient and safe storage of tenant bicycles. Located on the lower level, the bike room was created from an abandoned, vacant workshop space. New shower and changing facilities, compliant with the requirements of the Americans with Disabilities Act, were designed and built to support "carbon free" commutes by bicycle, as encouraged by LEED.

The green-friendly shower and changing facility was placed in an abandoned portion of the sixth floor. This usable floor area, once part of a grand men's lounge, had been stripped of its fixtures and finishes and used to collect construction detritus, spare parts, and janitorial equipment. In addition, the original 1920s plumbing design had called for an elevated floor, and sand and soil fill had been packed below the elevated area. Ultimately, the men's bathroom was restored, and a ramp was cut in the terrazzo to provide access to the existing men's room and the new shower facilities.

The Fund also renovated existing men's and women's bathrooms, using efficient light and plumbing fixtures, paints with low volatile organic compounds (VOCs), and countertops made from marble that had been reclaimed from the building. Finishing touches included the use of environmentally sound hand soap and paper towels made with recycled content.

▸▸ **GREEN CONFERENCE ROOMS AND TENANT LOUNGE**. The Fund redesigned conference rooms on the fifth and sixth floors for shared, common use by tenants. The redesign included new exposed ceilings and fans for ventilation; energy-efficient lighting; low-VOC paints; recycled carpet tile; reclaimed conference tables; ergonomic chairs with high recycled content; and wireless Internet access. Because the building has numerous smaller tenants, the green conference rooms serve as a critical amenity.

▸▸ **ELEVATOR LOBBIES AND CORRIDORS**. In the lobbies and corridors, original terrazzo floors and high ceilings were exposed by removing old carpets and drop ceilings. This not only improved aesthetics but also reduced the energy and chemicals needed to clean the floors and the materials needed to maintain the building (drop ceiling tiles had required periodic replacement).

Energy and Water Efficiency

Substantial energy and water efficiencies were realized as a result of the retrofit:

▸▸ **LIGHTING RETROFIT AND BALLAST RECYCLING**. The Fund and GVA Kidder Mathews conducted a full survey of all fixtures in the building, revealing that old T12 fixtures were the norm. This survey provided the basis not only for a retrofit program but also for receiving incentives from the local utility. Old fixtures and ballasts (a component that contains toxic PCBs, or polychlorinated biphenyls) were removed and recycled in common corridors and in tenant spaces upon rollover, and were replaced with high-efficiency T8 fixtures utilizing low-mercury bulbs.

The Fund repaired the existing electrical panel system for increased efficiency and better service for tenants. The electrical system consists of a main electrical supply (2,000 amps) for the building and a separate supply and panel for the building elevators. An emergency generator (run on the maximum allowable biodiesel mixture) provides backup power for emergency systems. Overall, while occupancy increased 28 percent, electrical usage in the building decreased more than 8 percent.

An infrared test of the main supply panels and the subpanels was conducted in order to determine whether there were any loose, inefficient connections. Power to the building was temporarily shut down, and all loose connections were corrected and all grounds were verified. Preventive maintenance will consist of an infrared test conducted every five years. The emergency generator is serviced semiannually, which involves checking all connections, monitoring the amps, checking all fluid levels, and changing the filters as needed.

▸▸ **PLUMBING RETROFIT FOR IMPROVED WATER EFFICIENCY**. In a similar fashion, all plumbing fixtures—toilets, sinks, and showers for office and retail tenants—were surveyed and flow rates were noted. All existing fixtures in common bathrooms were replaced with low-flow, high-efficiency toilets, faucets, and motion sensors, for a 30 percent overall increase in efficiency.

HVAC Systems

Based on the Fund's analysis of cost and net carbon impact, it opted to retain and commission the existing steam system for heating and introduce natural ventilation in tenant spaces as leases expired.

STEAM SYSTEM COMMISSIONING AND REPAIR

The Fund increased the system's efficiency by replacing steam traps throughout the building and implementing an ongoing monitoring and maintenance plan. In addition, Danfoss temperature control valves were installed at each radiator, increasing efficiency by enabling tenants to better control their own environments. The steam provided is by Seattle City Steam. The owners and Arup evaluated the merits of decommissioning the system as a whole, but on a net carbon basis, the continued use of Seattle Steam made sense.

A comprehensive survey and testing of the steam system revealed a number of issues:

➤ **STEAM PRESSURE** from Seattle City Steam was not being properly reduced when it entered the building.

➤ **STEAM TRAPS** at individual radiators had failed completely or were leaking.

➤ **CONDENSATE VACUUM PUMPS** in the basement, which improve efficiency, were no longer operational.

➤ **THE STEAM LINES** to the original decommissioned boiler had not been properly capped and were leaking. Additionally, other steam lines in the building had been cut during previous renovations, but not capped.

➤ **CONTROL VALVES** at individual radiators were in various states of disrepair and often of limited functionality.

A pressure-reducing valve was installed to bring the system pressure in line with intended specifications (from 15 to 20 psi to five to eight psi). The previous owner reported that traps had not been repaired or replaced for more than ten years. As a result, testing of individual traps was abandoned for full trap replacement (and select rebuilding) throughout the building. Every radiator was tagged with a serial number indicating date of replacement, and the information was entered into a preventive maintenance repair log. Steam lines at the original boilers, which were never properly closed off, were capped, and other lines suspected of leaking were also traced and capped. These comprehensive measures have reduced annual steam usage in the building by 47 percent.

AIR CONDITIONING

Building-wide, the Fund focused on the implementation of a natural ventilation strategy, as discussed earlier. As tenant leases expire, cooling units in the building that are nearing the end of their useful life are decommissioned and recycled.

According to a review by Arup, cooling equipment is primarily single-zone, small (less than five tons) split-system air-conditioning units, with a few exceptions. Arup and GVA completed a survey of the air-conditioning equipment at the building and cataloged key data on each unit, screened them for harmful refrigerants, and decommissioned and recycled all inefficient units. Preventive maintenance is provided by contract.

CORRIDOR VENTILATION ENHANCEMENTS

In order to comply with the minimum indoor air quality standard required for certification under the LEED-EB protocol, a mechanical ventilation system was introduced to common corridors on tenant floors and in the basement. The ventilation system was needed to enhance indoor air quality and meet American Society of Heating, Refrigerating, and Air-Conditioning Engineers Standard 62.1-2004.

The Fund focused on finding creative solutions to developing and completing the ventilation system, at times pushing design to trusted subcontractors who could work with outline specifications and cycle back to the design team and engineers for final approval. The final system implemented was relatively simple, consisting of mechanical ventilation being introduced through 300-cubic-feet-per-minute fan units mounted on the ceiling of the inside of

One of two shared conference rooms available to all tenants.

the east end of each corridor from the second to the fourteenth floors. Outside air intakes were fashioned with ducting from the fan units to six-inch core-drills through the building's exterior wall at the end of each corridor. In order to avoid introducing structural steel into the concrete (because detailed as-built plans were not available), ground-penetrating radar equipment was used to site the location of the core-drills properly.[1]

Another challenge emerged on the sixth floor, where the ventilation system needed to exhaust the corridor, as well as the men's and women's bathrooms. Here, fan strength of 600 cubic feet per minute was required. At this volume, a steam coil unit was utilized to temper the outside air. This new system was commissioned and is monitored and tested as part of the preventive maintenance contract. Inspections and maintenance are conducted quarterly.

FINANCING

The acquisition and repositioning of the Vance Building was financed with equity from the Rose Smart Growth Investment Fund I, L.P., and with securitized debt through Citigroup Global Markets Realty Corporation. The debt financing was provided on the basis of in-place income, with holdbacks for capital work and attainment of debt-service coverage targets, which the project has met. Including acquisition, capital, and tenant improvements, the debt represents approximately 67 percent of cost.

Equity infusions from the Fund were used at closing and as needed to finance capital improvements through the redevelopment stages. Local utility incentives were used to help defray the costs of particular investments.

MARKETING AND MANAGEMENT

The Fund has successfully marketed the Vance Building as the leading green historic asset in Seattle. The building was taken from 68 percent to 96 percent leased to more than 60 tenants, and more than 60 percent of the tenant spaces have been retrofitted with green tenant improvements, as of this writing. This change is the direct result of the focused efforts of asset management staff in house and a successful working partnership with the dedicated team of the third-party manager.

The leasing strategy hinged on selling the characteristics that are fundamentally attractive about the building—access to transit, amenities and culture, light, air and views—and also on selling the improved aesthetics and operating benefits of green building space. In furtherance of the marketing strategy, the Fund built out a management office for its local staff, to showcase green features for prospective tenants. In addition, the Fund focused on making the vacant suites market ready, with select office suites built out on a speculative basis to facilitate rapid leasing. The leasing process was streamlined by offering space planning, tenant consultations, and a select set of "building-standard finishes" from which tenants could choose. As discussed earlier, these concepts were also codified in a tenant improvement manual and reinforced by the leasing team and on-site property manager on walk-throughs with prospective tenants.

The Fund and its on-site manager sought to renew as many existing tenants as possible, fostering growth or expansion by offering new tenant improvement packages, though some churn occurred because the redevelopment resulted in rent increases. The Fund relaunched the Vance Building with broker events and established a new profile for the property in the marketplace. Ownership focused on achieving a critical mass of new leases through deals with high-profile green organizations, which in turn served as "bell cows" for other, smaller users who sought to benefit from clustering with similar organizations. Eventually, the tenancy itself was generating its own marketing buzz, and the building continues to attract like-minded tenants.

Leasing at the Joseph Vance Building also has been facilitated by favorable publicity generated by the property's green and historic designations. In addition to the project's Gold rating from the U.S. Green Building Council, the National Trust for Historic Preservation chose the Vance building as a model of green, historic renovation and as the location to launch the Preservation Green Lab, an initiative focused on preserving older, historic buildings sustainably. The Vance Building was also selected as a 2009 winner of a 'What Makes It Green?' Regional Top Ten Award from the American Institute of Architects (AIA), Seattle chapter, Committee on the Environment (COTE).

GREEN BUILDING OPERATIONS

Green building operations have also become a significant feature for prospective tenants. Green operating practices include the following:

▸ **RENEWABLE ENERGY CREDITS (RECS).** The Vance Building invests in RECs in order to meet 100 percent of its energy demands. The credits are a Green-e–certified clean source of energy and commensurate with the building's annual historical baseline kilowatt-hour usage. The credits are locked in with a two-year contract, after which, the credits will be resized to a new usage baseline, given the building's increased energy efficiency. The purchase of renewable certificates supports renewable electricity generation.

▸▸ **GREEN BUILDING AND CONSTRUCTION PRACTICES**. Throughout the building, the Fund has focused on green building techniques to provide tenants with a healthier environment, including—for any new project—indoor air quality management plans that address HVAC and absorptive material protection, source control, and pressure differentials to avoid the spread of dust and contaminants during construction.

▸▸ **GREEN CLEANING**. The Fund has instituted a comprehensive green cleaning program, including the use of green cleaning supplies and recycled paper products, and the introduction of higher-efficiency janitorial tools and equipment. These practices improve indoor air quality and increase the use of recycled materials.

▸▸ **ENVIRONMENTALLY SOUND PEST MANAGEMENT**. A green, organic, integrated approach to pest management that relies on more natural, less toxic approaches has also been implemented. This program focuses on removal of pest habitat, food sources and breeding areas; prevention of access; and management of environmental factors. Pests are primarily controlled through mechanical or physical controls or lures and repellents using synthetic or nonsynthetic substances consistent with the National Organic List.

▸▸ **WASTE AUDITING, RECYCLING, AND COMPOSTING**. Waste produced at the Vance Building is audited, and management and ownership have focused on ways to improve recycling rates over the baseline. Because studies indicate that up to 70 percent of office waste is compostable, building-wide composting efforts have been instituted. The Vance Building was an early adopter of CleanScapes' "dumpsterless waste management" and convinced the management of neighboring buildings to do the same. Subsequently, the city of Seattle implemented the program broadly as part of its Clear Alleys Program. Removing dumpsters provides cleaner and safer business districts, and increased alley access for pedestrians and deliveries. Instead, waste, recyclables, and compostables are sorted, bagged, and placed in the alley for collection.

▸▸ **MANAGEMENT OFFICE SUPPLIES AND PURCHASING**. The Fund and GVA Kidder Mathews purchase office supplies and furniture with high recycled content. The conference table at the property is made from recycled wood.

▸▸ **BIODIESEL FOR BACKUP GENERATOR**. Biodiesel fuel, an environmentally sensitive fuel alternative, is used for the backup generator at the Vance Building. This practice represents a rather modest improvement, but the Fund believes that cost-effectively improving the building's overall environmental impact requires careful focus, even on small items.

EXPERIENCE GAINED

The Fund's thesis and experience is that the inclusion of environmental and social solutions in real estate development can reduce ownership risks and enhance risk-adjusted returns. In this more comprehensive investment approach, economic value is in fact improved through a concurrent focus on environmental and on social goals, the second and third components of the "triple bottom line."

Lessons learned by the Rose Smart Growth Investment Fund I in its redevelopment of the Joseph Vance Building are the following:

▸▸ **SET FORTH A CLEAR INVESTMENT THESIS** for each project, and communicate this message to the entire team. In redeveloping the Vance Building, the Fund called for the "transformation of the asset into the leading green and historic asset in the Seattle marketplace," and put a premium on creativity, cooperation, and problem solving

▸▸ **ESTABLISH A COMPREHENSIVE CAPITAL BUDGET**, with contingencies. The redevelopment of the Vance Building confirmed that with older office buildings, there is always more to do than expected.

▸▸ **SELECT AN ARCHITECT AND CONTRACTOR** with green experience, and bring them on early as the building blocks of the team.

▸▸ **USE AN INTEGRATED DESIGN PROCESS** to add value. Because redevelopment projects are multidisciplinary, it is helpful to have all concerned parties at the table when needed. Integrated design ultimately saves time and money.

A refurbished elevator in the main lobby.

▸▸ **ACHIEVE CRITICAL MASS** in project leasing by targeting high-profile green organizations, which encourages similarly minded smaller firms to lease space. Project leasing was facilitated because the building's message, principles, and value proposition were magnified by the marketing and public relations efforts of tenants, as well as by favorable word of mouth.

▸▸ **SMALLER, CLASS B TENANTS** respond to a streamlined leasing process that simplifies lease negotiations, space planning, and tenant buildouts.

▸▸ **DUMPSTERLESS GARBAGE AND RECYCLING PROGRAMS** can work for downtown office and mixed-use properties, and serve to reduce loitering.

▸▸ **INTEGRATED PEST MANAGEMENT** can work for urban, mixed-use properties, even with restaurant and food uses.

Nathan Taft is director of Acquisitions for the national real estate portfolio of the Rose Smart Investment Growth Investment Fund I, L.P.

NOTE

1 Ground-penetrating radar equipment is used in a variety of construction applications, including geotechnical work, heavy construction, and building renovation. In building renovation applications, the technology is used to inspect concrete, measure slab thickness, identify metallic and other objects embedded in concrete, and locate and mark targets, such as appropriate drilling locations. Handheld scanners are frequently used in renovation work.

▸▸ **REACH OUT TO CITY OFFICIALS** and agencies early in the process; communicate as much as possible. Early contact with local agencies helps to resolve ambiguities in the building code, if any, concerning green renovations.

▸▸ **TO MAXIMIZE EVERY DOLLAR INVESTED**, even in the face of big problems, consider setting high expectations with trusted subcontractors, but with flexible scopes that enable them to do more if conditions are favorable. In the Vance Building, estimates for repointing the facade approached $500,000, but an enterprising contractor completed the work for just over $100,000 when the work went faster than expected.

▸▸ **DO NOT OVERPAY** on building acquisition. The Vance Building transaction came back to the Fund at the desired price, which in turn enabled ownership to invest substantially in the building.

▸▸ **RECYCLE AND REUSE** creatively. Conference room tables were found abandoned in a former tenant's space, and after refinishing work well as a building amenity. Old, large pieces of marble harvested from abandoned spaces in the building were reused as a sink countertop in a remodeled bathroom.

▸▸ **REMEASURE OLD BUILDINGS** to help to identify more leasable square footage and add to top-line revenues as turnover and re-leasing occurs.

▸▸ **MAKE VACANT SPACES "MARKET READY"** to help tenants envision what the space might be like when green improvements are completed.

Development Team

OWNER AND DEVELOPMENT MANAGER:
Rose Smart Growth Investment Fund I

GENERAL CONTRACTOR:
Turner Construction

ARCHITECT:
Zimmer Gunsul Frasca Partnership

MEP ENGINEERS:
Arup

STRUCTURAL ENGINEERS:
Magnusson Klemencic Associates

PROPERTY MANAGER:
GVA Kidder Mathews

CASE STUDY • **DAVE PETERSEN, DONNA PARA, AND HELEE HILLMAN**

McDonald's Campus Office Building
OAKBROOK, ILLINOIS

McDonald's Corporation's Campus Office Building (COB) is a 704,119-gross-square-foot building located in Oak Brook, Illinois, a suburb of Chicago. The COB, which serves as the world headquarters for the corporation, is one of several buildings on a well-preserved wooded campus of 80 acres, commonly referred to as McDonald's Home Office.

Construction of the COB was completed in 1988. The building was designed with a then-pioneering emphasis on environmental sustainability and energy efficiency. Consistent with its eco-friendly origins, the COB recently achieved certification at the Platinum level under the Leadership in Energy and Environmental Design for Existing Buildings (LEED-EB) 2.0 program. The certification process was launched with a LEED-EB gap analysis in the fourth quarter of 2007, and final certification was awarded in the first quarter of 2009.

McDonald's Corporation's Campus Office Building was completed in 1988 with a then-pioneering emphasis on sustainability and energy efficiency. The goal of the recent retrofit was additional green improvements and operating programs.

OVERVIEW

McDonald's undertook numerous green improvements and initiated new operating programs to achieve the Platinum LEED-EB certification:

▶ **A PURCHASING POLICY** specifying low mercury content and high energy efficiency for interior lighting was implemented.

▶ **ADDITIONAL METERS WERE INSTALLED** to monitor building systems' efficiency closely.

▶ **EMPLOYEES CAN NOW TAKE ADVANTAGE** of carpool and vanpool commuting options.

▶ **THERE IS PREFERRED PARKING** for alternative fuel vehicles.

▶ **THE BUILDING HEATING, VENTILATING, AND AIR-CONDITIONING** (HVAC) equipment uses ozone-protecting refrigerants that do not contain chlorofluorocarbons.

▶ **THERE IS OPTIMAL USE** of environmentally friendly paints and cleaning products that reduce levels of volatile organic compounds (VOCs).

▶ **STANDARD BUILDING MAINTENANCE PRACTICES** incorporate the use of environmentally sound cleaning and pest management materials.

▶ **ALL IRRIGATION ON THE CAMPUS** is performed with reclaimed stormwater.

▶ **SEVENTY-FIVE PERCENT OF THE COB GROUNDS** are landscaped with native or adaptive vegetation.

▶ **BIKE RACKS AND LOCKER AND SHOWER FACILITIES** have been installed to support nonvehicle commuting options.

▶ **FORTY-FIVE PERCENT OF THE COB'S ENERGY** is procured from off-site solar and wind sources.

▶ **THE COB HAS BEEN ENERGY STAR CERTIFIED** for two years and has earned an Energy Star score of 93 out of a possible 100 points.

McDonald's adopted numerous best practices to support the COB green retrofit:

▶ **A SHUTTLE IS POWERED** by 100 percent biodiesel fuel made from recycled fry oil from on-site labs and test kitchens. The resulting glycerin byproduct is also used to make shower gel.

▶ **OVER 90 PERCENT OF ALL OFFICE PAPER**, office equipment, furnishings, furniture, and building materials comply with sustainable purchasing requirements.

▶ **MCDONALD'S PROCURES** Energy Star–rated IT equipment including computers, printers, and scanners.

▶ **EMPLOYEES CAN TAKE ADVANTAGE** of an Alternative Work Arrangement (AWA) program, which utilizes telecommuting to reduce vehicle miles traveled and increase work/life balance. To support AWA, employees are given access to an internal tracking tool that highlights the environmental benefits achieved by implementing various commuting options.

▶ **MCDONALD'S HAS ENROLLED** the campus in the Illinois Clean Air Counts Program, committing to track and report reductions of greenhouse gas (GHG) emissions.

▶ **ENVIRONMENTAL EDUCATION** and awareness are kept top of mind through hosted events like Green Week and regular "lunch and learn" meetings.

▶ **LEED ACCREDITED PROFESSIONALS**, drawn from McDonald's staff and the teams of vendor partners, help drive ongoing sustainability efforts.

To date, McDonald's has realized the following outcomes through the green retrofit and operation of the COB:

▶ **DURING 2008**, there was an 8 percent (465,000-kWh) reduction in electrical consumption. Lower energy use is attributed to positive occupant behaviors, building recommissioning, and sound operating practices.

▶ **SIGNIFICANT RESULTS WERE ACHIEVED** through the commingled recycling program and additional programs to reduce the landfill waste associated with paper, scrap metal, building materials, food, and electronics.

- Approximately 130 tons of commingled occupant waste is recycled annually at the COB.
- Between January and June 2008, the COB achieved an occupant waste recycling rate of 58 percent.
- Over 41 tons of scrap metal was recycled during 2008.
- Over 128 tons of paper was recycled through a shredding program.
- Over 16 tons of electronic equipment was diverted from landfills.
- Under a pilot project to design and construct new green workspaces, 91 percent of all waste—over 21 tons—was recycled or diverted from landfills.

CONTEXT AND OWNERSHIP OBJECTIVES

The experience of McDonald's in attaining Platinum certification under LEED-EB indicates that the process can be successfully negotiated without significant operational changes and capital expenditures.

Building Information

The four-story COB, with more than 700,000 square feet of space, averages 1,000 building occupants during a standard work day. The building houses primarily office space and includes two levels of underground parking.

The McDonald's Corporation owns and occupies the building, and no space is leased to third-party tenants. Because the COB is owner occupied, the process for implementing and enforcing operation policies is streamlined, and the collection of data for LEED certification was significantly easier than in multitenant buildings. McDonald's can readily ensure compliance with operation and maintenance policies because the company solely governs purchasing, cleaning, waste management, contract management, and facility management within the building.

Ownership Objectives

McDonald's is a member of the U.S. Green Building Council. Pursuing LEED-EB certification for its headquarters was a natural way to demonstrate corporate commitment to making a positive environmental impact, while providing a comfortable and value-driven workplace for employees and guests.

The LEED-EB application process for the COB building, which was then nearly 20 years old, was initiated in December 2007. Based on a preliminary building assessment completed by the Jones Lang LaSalle Strategic Consulting Group, McDonald's targeted LEED Gold certification. As the process continued, the project team determined that with some additional effort and focus, LEED Platinum certification could be achieved.

The project team submitted final LEED-EB documentation in July 2008. The U.S. Green Building Council completed the initial review of the McDonald's certification application in late August; clarifying comments were submitted by the project team in October. The COB initially received Gold certification in November 2008. Only two points away from Platinum certification, the project team developed an appeal strategy. Completed appeal documentation was submitted in December 2008. The appealed credits were accepted, and the project was certified at the Platinum level for the LEED-EB 2.0 program in February 2009.

The LEED-EB certification effort for the COB did not require significant operational changes or capital expenditures. McDonald's wanted to demonstrate that maintaining a green building could be cost-effective and would not require significant operational changes. Emphasis was placed on completing documentation, standardizing reporting, and educating building staff, outside vendors, and employees about existing policies and procedures.

DEVELOPMENT PROCESS

The McDonald's LEED-EB certification process drew significant participation from throughout the company, with additional support from Jones Lang LaSalle and other third-party experts.

LEED-EB Certification Team and Responsibilities

McDonald's assembled its LEED-EB certification team in September 2007. Jones Lang LaSalle was retained to conduct gap assessments and feasibility studies for four buildings located on the Home Office campus. Upon completion of a thorough analysis, McDonald's determined that pursuing LEED-EB certification for the COB would be the initial priority. The project was launched immediately; building recommissioning and policy review began in December 2007.

Members of McDonald's Facilities and Systems department led the internal LEED-EB effort for the COB. Facilities and Systems acted as executive champion of the LEED certification process, secured project funding, and played an integral role in generating internal support and active participation from other staff. Employees were kept well informed of the certification process and were eager to support and participate in the process. Representatives from numerous departments and vendor partners also participated in the certification effort.

Jones Lang LaSalle was retained to provide LEED consulting, project and budget management, and LEED online project administration services for the project. Three LEED Accredited Professionals and a team of on-site building management professionals from Jones Lang LaSalle were active participants on the project team.

The project manager from Jones Lang LaSalle, a LEED Accredited Professional, had oversight for the project schedule, budget, and the online document submittal process. The on-site facility manager from Jones Lang LaSalle, who was designated as a LEED Accredited Professional during the project, coordinated systems testing and documentation, oversaw the completion of the recommissioning effort, and directed data collection for all mechanical systems. Jones Lang LaSalle's third LEED Accredited Professional provided consulting for energy and certification process questions and for other LEED-related matters that arose during the retrofit.

To complete the necessary documentation, subject matter experts were assigned oversight for the completion of all required LEED documentation in their area of responsibility. Subject matter experts included a combination of consultants, contractors, McDonald's employees, and vendors. They implemented the necessary policies, tracked purchasing activity, and gathered all documentation required for the LEED submittal.

LEED Implementation Process

During the LEED implementation process, emphasis was placed not only on what was required for LEED certification but also on a holistic organizational approach to sustainability and the implementation of green practices throughout the COB. The building's performance period lasted for six months. The project team felt that a six-month performance period would be more beneficial than the standard observation period (three months), providing more comprehensive data for submittal. The performance period ended on June 30, 2008, and the official submittal was made electronically on July 9, 2008. Approximately 450 documents were submitted in support of the LEED-EB application effort.

Additionally, the project team began brainstorming Innovation in Operations and Maintenance credits midway through the performance period. The COB is unique in its sustainable design and building practices, which made it difficult to determine which four ideas to focus on to win the LEED Innovation credits.

Green Operations Tracking

LEED-EB certification required that green operations practices be instituted and tracked. Having appropriate green practices in place before the performance period began in January 2008 was critical to ensure that the implemented sustainable practices could be supported by accurate and complete measurements throughout the performance period. The following policies, procedures, and programs were initiated before the performance period (some were strengthened to comply with LEED-EB requirements):

▸▸ **GREEN SITE AND BUILDING** exterior management plan. The green site and exterior management plan included environmentally friendly landscaping and irrigation practices. The responsibility for monitoring compliance with the building exterior management plan is shared by the facility manager and the grounds manager. The facility manager and grounds manager also provide service contractors with information regarding required practices and document compliance.

▸▸ **ALTERNATIVE TRANSPORTATION**. A comprehensive alternative transportation plan was in effect before the certification efforts.

▸▸ **OCCUPANT RECYCLING**. Although a recycling program for a commingled waste stream had been in place for several years at the COB, improvements were made to the program. These improvements included adding recycling bins under each desk and in the common areas, reducing the contamination of the recyclable waste stream, and most importantly, raising occupants' awareness of how to utilize the recycling infrastructure.

▸▸ **SUSTAINABLE PURCHASING**. Guidelines for the procurement of sustainable office supplies, carpeting, furniture, and ceiling tiles were already in place at the COB.

▸▸ **PROHIBITION OF SMOKING**. The building was smoke free before the certification efforts.

▸▸ **BUILDING MATERIALS**. A building materials recycling program for scrap metal, lightbulbs, and electric wire was in place before the start of the certification process.

▸▸ **CONSTRUCTION INDOOR AIR QUALITY (IAQ)** management plan. The construction IAQ management plan, required to ensure that healthful air quality would be maintained during interior construction or renovation, was implemented by Jones Lang LaSalle as part of the building operations processes, before the start of the LEED certification process.

▸ **CONSTRUCTION DEMOLITION** and renovation waste management. The existing construction waste management program was improved at the onset of the certification process, and additional reporting processes were added to it to meet tracking requirements for LEED-EB certification.

▸ **INTEGRATED PEST MANAGEMENT**. A new contract with an environmentally sensitive pest management vendor was implemented before the start of the certification performance period.

▸ **LOW-ENVIRONMENTAL IMPACT CLEANING**. New cleaning equipment that satisfied LEED criteria was purchased by the site maintenance and cleaning vendor. The COB was already utilizing low-impact cleaning products.

▸ **CLEANING CHEMICAL STORAGE**. A chemical storage plan that met LEED requirements was in place at the COB before the start of the certification process.

All policies were posted on AccessMcD, McDonald's internal communications vehicle, and end user communication and education is ongoing. To ensure that policies and procedures are adhered to, Jones Lang LaSalle and McDonald's personnel will continue to be involved in the management of the building. Reporting will continue on a regular basis, and the results will be used to support other workplace sustainability efforts.

LEED-EB POINTS ATTEMPTED

The project submitted documentation for 67 credits out of a possible 85. Key credits included the following:

▸ **SUSTAINABLE SITES 4.1 AND 4.2** (Protect or restore open space). Two LEED points were attempted for covering at least 75 percent of the site area with natural plantings (one point is awarded for 50 percent or more;

two points are awarded for 75 percent or more). As part of the LEED certification, a civil engineering firm was hired to do the site area calculations and create an erosion and sedimentation control plan for the COB and its surrounding landscape.

▸ **SUSTAINABLE SITES 3.1** (Proximity to public transportation). Building occupants are provided with a convenience shuttle that provides transportation between the buildings and access to nearby connection points for public transportation. Building occupants have access to two or more public and campus bus lines within one-quarter of a mile (see figure 1).

▸ **SUSTAINABLE SITES 3.2** (Bicycle storage, showers, and changing rooms on site). The LEED-required number of bicycle parking spots are available in the COB garage; showers and changing rooms are in close proximity.

▸ **SUSTAINABLE SITES 3.3** (Preferred parking for hybrid or alternative fuel vehicles). Twenty-seven of the 897 parking spaces were designated and reserved for alternative fuel vehicle parking, constituting 3.01 percent of total parking capacity. Stickers were issued to vehicles that meet requirements for an alternative fuel vehicle, and a system of surveillance enforcement was established with security.

▸ **SUSTAINABLE SITES 3.4** (Telecommuting). Of the 853 employees at the COB, over 20 percent reported commute savings by taking advantage of McDonald's AWA program. By reporting their commute activity in an internal Web-based calculator, employees can immediately see the impact their commuting behaviors have on the environment; they can view their reductions for gas, barrels of oil, water, and CO_2. Employees can also view the time they saved in commute offsets, supporting McDonald's emphasis on work/life balance.

GREEN BUILDING DESIGN AND CONSTRUCTION

Though completed in the 1980s, the COB and its surrounding site were forward thinking with regard to sustainability and energy efficiency, and offer many environmentally friendly and innovative building features. In addition, the property management team had already implemented sustainable maintenance practices before the start of the certification effort. Key building features and operations include the following:

Figure 1

Public and Campus Transportation Options

Public or Campus Bus Line Stops	Distance (Miles)
Campus Bus Shuttle Pickup at COB Lobby and Dropoff at McDonald's Plaza Building	0.001
Pace Bus 747, Pace Bus 332 (Walk from McDonald's Plaza Building)	0.15
Pace Bus 888 (Walk from McDonald's Plaza Building)	0.17
Pace Bus 877 (Walk from McDonald's Plaza Building)	0.1
Pace Bus 322 (Walk from McDonald's Plaza Building)	0.15

▸ **DAYLIGHTING STRATEGIES**. Skylights and an open office plan bring daylight into the workspaces, lowering the need for interior lighting and promoting employee well-being and a connection to the natural surroundings.

▸ **SHADING STRATEGIES**: To reduce summer cooling requirements, the building utilizes exterior window shading. Trees shade the building walls and roof to further reduce the summer cooling load. In addition, the skylights are tinted to reduce summer heat gains and windows are low-E for improved energy efficiency.

▸ **NATURAL MATERIALS**. Natural stone and brick pavers require minimal maintenance and are power-washed periodically with water and nontoxic soap.

▸ **INDOOR PARKING**. With the exception of a small visitor's parking lot, all parking is underneath the building, reducing the overall heat island effect and stormwater runoff.

▸ **SOUND ENVIRONMENTAL CONSTRUCTION PRACTICES**. All contractors must adhere to documented environmental policies for on-site construction. For each job, they must complete a waste management form outlining the percentage of waste diverted from landfills. They must also adhere to the indoor air quality management plan.

▸ **TREE INVENTORY**. An on-site horticulturist oversees a strategic forestry plan and manages a tree inventory for all trees on site. All trees have a brass tag and are catalogued individually. Trees are monitored for disease and insect infestation, enabling the team to take preventive measures to protect them. The grounds team, along with community and vendor partners, has been using this integrated program to protect these special assets for over 20 years.

▸ **IRRIGATION**. All stormwater is used for on-site irrigation. The campus site was originally designed and constructed to use lake water for irrigation and a well-water system for backup during severe droughts. No potable municipal water is used for irrigation.

Green Retrofit Results

The project team documented the positive environmental and cost effects associated with operating the COB as a green building under the LEED-EB protocol. Highlights included the following:

▸ **ENERGY REDUCTION**. Owing to the use of energy efficient lighting, equipment upgrades, and operational efficiencies, energy consumption in 2008 was 8 percent lower than in 2007. The COB was designated an Energy Star building in 2007 and 2008 with ratings of 92 and 93, respectively.

▸ **ENVIRONMENTAL IMPACT REDUCTIONS**. During the six-month performance period, more than 250,000 pounds of CO_2 were eliminated through the use of alternative work arrangements. A voluntary, Web-based commute tracking tool was implemented to show employees the positive impact that their alternative work and commute arrangements had on various elements of the environment, including their gas, oil, water, and CO_2 reductions. These metrics supported the LEED submission and will be used for local reporting with programs like Illinois-based Clean Air Counts.

▸ **WASTE REDUCTION**. During the performance period, 58 percent of COB waste targeted for the landfill was diverted through increased recycling efforts. This effort keeps materials out of landfills and controls waste disposal costs.

▸ **SUSTAINABLE LANDSCAPE DESIGN**. Seventy-five percent of the plants on the COB grounds are native or adaptive vegetation, and reclaimed stormwater is used exclusively for irrigation.

As a result of the green initiatives, the building used 8 percent less electricity in 2008 than the year before, attributed to occupant behavior, building recommissioning, and sound operating practices.

Figure 2

Innovation in Upgrades, Operation, and Maintenance

Credit Number	Innovation
Credit 1.1	Biodiesel fuel process and glycerin byproduct utilization and community impact
Credit 1.2	Sustainability education and awareness quarterly events, Green Week, McDonald's recycling Web site and employee awareness communication
Credit 1.3	Clean Air Counts reporting and recognition
Credit 1.4	Site and building best practices

Figure 3

Treatment of Denied Innovation Credits: Innovations in Upgrades, Operation, and Maintenance

Credit Number	Innovation
Credit 1.1	Sustainable purchasing—exemplary performance credit awarded
Credit 1.3	Reduced mercury in light bulbs—exemplary performance credit awarded
Credit 1.4	Site and building best practices-- not appealed

Parallel to the certification effort, the Facilities and Systems department launched a new workplace design concept called "R Place." The "R Place" initiative optimizes the use of available space and promotes energy efficiency through increased daylighting and direct outdoor views for a larger percentage of employees. The "R Place" design included updated furniture and fixtures, and it replaced an obsolete furniture system that was beyond its useful life. The capital expenditures associated with the project, which positively affected procurement, daylight views, and energy efficiency, were included in the certification documentation.

LEED-EB Innovation Credits

As part of the LEED-EB submission, the team selected four original innovation credits for submission (see figure 2). The team felt that the COB was able to show quantifiable positive environmental impacts supported by data for each credit. The U.S. Green Building Council awarded credit 1.2 but initially denied credits 1.1, 1.3, and 1.4, stating that the results associated with those efforts were already captured in other LEED credits awarded for this particular project. After reviewing previous rulings, the team decided to appeal two of the three denied cred-

its with new credit intents focused on exemplary performance (figure 3). The appealed credits 1.1 and 1.3 were approved for the final certification.

FINANCING

The project budget included costs for registration and review fees for the U.S. Green Building Council, LEED consulting and project management fees from Jones Lang LaSalle, and third-party consulting fees required for testing and documentation. The third-party fees included the following services:

▸ Civil engineering,

▸ Electrical contracting,

▸ Waste management (waste stream audit),

▸ Indoor air quality testing,

▸ Airflow measurements, and

▸ Daylight consulting.

The total certification cost for new LEED-EB initiatives was $0.19 per square foot, or approximately $135,000 for 704,119 square feet.

The following cost items were not included in the project budget, because they had already been incorporated in the COB's operating budget:

▸ **BUILDING SYSTEM COMMISSIONING.** As a way to reduce energy costs, the facility management team had incorporated building recommissioning into the 2008 operating budget.

▸ **RENEWABLE ENERGY CREDITS.** As part of the LEED implementation effort, McDonald's chose to purchase RECs equal to about 45 percent of the COB's estimated energy use.

▸ **BIODIESEL FUEL PROGRAM.** With the exception of the purchase of storage barrels and an electric pump, no additional costs were incurred to implement the biodiesel fuel program for the shuttle. The per gallon cost for biodiesel fuel mirrors the cost of commercially available diesel fuel, and fuel is a standard operating cost for the vehicle.

▸ **SITE AND POLICY DOCUMENTATION.** The documentation of building policies, procedures, and plans was already part of the building management's best practices. Although some new reporting was required to meet LEED-EB requirements, existing employees and data sources were used to produce the required reporting.

▸ IN-HOUSE MEASUREMENT AND REPORTING. Data tracking was done utilizing existing tracking tools. No additional costs were incurred to complete required measurement and reporting processes.

Because of the COB's sustainable design and existing workplace management practices, the costs associated with pursuing LEED-EB certification were minimal. With the exception of the "R Place" furniture system, which was already being implemented to support the transition to a new workplace design, no major capital purchases, replacements, or equipment upgrades were required to support this certification effort.

PROJECT MARKETING

Although the COB is owned and operated by the McDonald's Corporation, the LEED certification process required internal champions in order to secure organizational buy-in for the initiative. The sponsoring Facilities and Systems department as well as all building and campus occupants had to understand the positive impact that the LEED certification effort would have on the McDonald's brand.

To secure this buy-in, the team solidified the alignment between LEED-EB certification and McDonald's key business goals. McDonald's business goals are centered on the core values of being a good citizen in the community, growing the business profitably, and striving for continuous improvement. The project team utilized every opportunity available to demonstrate how the LEED certification effort would reinforce these core values while supporting other elements of McDonald's Plan to Win business model. The alignment was clear to employees, and their buy-in made the certification effort a reality.

McDonald's utilized diverse communication methods to get the LEED message out to employees. For example, an overview of the U.S. Green Building Council and the LEED process was highlighted during a "green" lunch–and-learn session in early 2008. Open to all employees, the session also highlighted other opportunities for employees to help green the workplace.

A "green" section was added to the Facilities and Systems Web site. This section featured details about the LEED process, providing application updates for staff.

The LEED initiative was part of a broader workplace sustainability effort at McDonald's. The Facilities and Systems team worked closely with the McDonald's Communications team to show employees how the LEED effort was part of that effort. Team members met with other departments, vendors, and external colleagues to discuss the project and its status. The workplace team also took opportunities to partner with coworkers from the McDonald's restaurant design team so that employees were aware of what was being done to green the company's restaurants as well. Once the project documents were officially submitted, the project sponsors from Facilities and Systems shared personal thank-you notes with each person involved in the project.

Since receiving LEED-EB Platinum certification, the McDonald's communications team has been defining additional opportunities to share the news both internally and externally. In addition, the Facilities and Systems department, with the help of Jones Lang LaSalle, is exploring the feasibility of pursuing LEED certification for other buildings on the Home Office campus.

EXPERIENCE GAINED

The COB LEED team reports the following lessons learned from its certification effort:

▸ A LEED PRE-ASSESSMENT REVIEW is key to project success. For McDonald's, this effort helped the project team prioritize the buildings on the Home Office campus and provided key information regarding each building's overall potential for each LEED point category. This enabled the team to begin the certification effort with a solid base of information.

▸ DOCUMENT ALL BUILDING POLICIES and procedures. Before obtaining LEED certification, McDonald's had implemented a number of sustainable building operations but had not fully documented all of the policies and procedures. Updated documentation and ongoing performance measurements are required as part of the LEED submission. Achieving LEED certification for the COB meant documenting existing operational practices, not necessarily implementing new ones.

▸ TAP THE KNOWLEDGE of building operations staff. The intellectual property associated with building operations resources was critical to the success of the project. The project team initially underestimated the level of involvement required from the building operations staff, but the team got creative in balancing the daily responsibilities of building management with the additional effort required to obtain and document the information required for certification.

▸ PURSUE INNOVATION CREDITS. The team had a long list of items that they originally thought would clearly be considered for an innovation credit. In a campus environment, however, many of the policies and best practices apply to all buildings—they are not unique to the building being certified. After reviewing the comments from the U.S. Green Building Council on the denied credits and reviewing the information available on the Council's Web site from other project submittals, the team refocused its efforts on documenting exemplary performance as innovation credit submittals. This was a successful effort which directly affected the certification level that was ultimately awarded.

▸ ENGAGE EMPLOYEES, BUILDING OCCUPANTS, AND VENDORS. The certification process is an opportunity to educate building occupants, employees and vendors about sustainability, and their specific roles in the process. When undertaking a green retrofit in a large organization such as McDonald's, the project team needs to engage these individuals: occupants, employees, and vendors. All must see the value of specific policies and procedures, and buy in to any changes. The project team should be open to feedback and ideas from these parties and address their questions and concerns.

▸ SEEK INTEGRATED COMMUNICATIONS OPPORTUNITIES to tell the sustainability story in a way that positively affects building occupants and the brand. Both internal and external communications vehicles are necessary. McDonald's has a section on its Web site dedicated to the LEED certification effort. When making external presentations, McDonald's employees used the LEED certification project as a visible demonstration of the company's environmental focus. What provided support for the LEED effort were practices McDonald's had in place all along. In many cases the practices were just never widely publicized to building occupants, fully documented, or validated by a third party.

▸ INTEGRATE GREEN CERTIFICATION EFFORTS with overall corporate sustainability objectives. McDonald's tied the certification efforts to other corporate sustainability goals, focusing on the positive environmental impacts that were being achieved and not on the certification label alone. Information on LEED was included in the company's "Green Week" product fair, along with information on using renewable energy, reducing waste, reducing employees' personal carbon footprint, and greening the restaurants. Employees understood that LEED certification was just one of the things McDonald's was doing to be a good environmental steward.

Dave Petersen, LEED AP, is a vice president at Jones Lang LaSalle in Oak Brook, Illinois. He is the client relationship manager for McDonald's, responsible for the delivery of client-focused business solutions for integrated facilities management, project management, and transaction management for McDonald's corporate headquarters facilities.

Donna Para is the senior director for McDonald's Workplace Solutions Team. She is responsible for the development, implementation, and management of workplace facilities, services, and programs. She also acts as the champion for McDonald's workplace sustainability initiatives in the United States.

Helee Hillman, LEED AP, is a project manager for Jones Lang LaSalle in Chicago, Illinois. She works in the Project Development Services Division and is a member of the firm's Energy and Sustainability Services Global Board.

Development Team

INTERNAL LEED-EB EFFORT:
McDonald's Facilities and Systems Department

LEED CONSULTANT, PROJECT AND BUDGET MANAGER, AND LEED ONLINE PROJECT ADMINISTRATION SERVICES:
Jones Lang LaSalle

CASE STUDY • LARA CONAWAY AND SUSAN LOGAN

Morgan Lovell Headquarters

LONDON, UNITED KINGDOM

When Morgan Lovell decided to refurbish its headquarters, a 526-square-meter (5,725-square-foot) space in a multitenanted building at 16 Noel Street in the Soho neighborhood of London, the office design and interior buildout company decided to practice what it preaches and deliver a showcase sustainable office of the future. Situated on two floors of a 1960s office block, the seven-floor structure

Morgan Lovell, whose headquarters was in an inefficient, multitenant building dating from the 1960s, wanted to demonstrate that companies can create a sustainable office interior even if they cannot alter the main structure of the building, and that it can be financially feasible. Pictured here is the reception area.

would normally be considered an environmental write-off. Morgan Lovell pooled its in-house experts to transform the old office into a model of sustainability and also set an ambitious challenge—to achieve the highest rating under the Building Research Establishment's Environmental Assessment Method (BREEAM).

As a testbed project, the scheme needed to demonstrate that companies can create a sustainable office interior even if they cannot alter the main structure of a building. Most businesses occupy a building with other tenants and think they have no control or financial incentive to deliver a sustainable workplace. Morgan Lovell wanted to show that sustainability could be financially feasible in such buildings.

Success was achieved in March 2008, when the project was granted a BREEAM score of 76 percent, the highest score achieved to that

date by an existing office building in the United Kingdom. The key objectives of the sustainable fit-out (buildout) were to

▸▸ Deliver a fit-out that pushes the envelope for innovative design and utility;

▸▸ Achieve a BREEAM excellent rating, the highest possible score;[1]

▸▸ Create a recognized blueprint for the future of sustainable office design;

▸▸ Deliver a motivational and inspirational workspace, while remediating poor lighting conditions and an inadequate air-conditioning system;

▸▸ Increase communication and connectivity among staff members; and

▸▸ Complete the retrofit in a financially feasible manner.

DEVELOPMENT PROCESS

Team assembly, cost-benefit assessment, and project planning all emphasized sustainability objectives.

Project Team

Morgan Lovell drew on its in-house expertise for interior design and sustainability management. Retrofit subcontractors were managed by in-house project managers.

A consultant from Ecoteric (then operating as Diligentia) was appointed as the BREEAM adviser and assessor. Ecoteric was responsible for all energy modeling for the office retrofit and worked with SDS Energy, a partner company, to conduct a comprehensive review of the opportunity for renewable energy systems in the retrofit.

The sustainable fit-out was carried out by Morgan Lovell's in-house team, which controlled contract terms and payment mechanisms. Performance centered on Morgan Lovell's well-established quality system—Perfect Delivery—which ensures that predetermined benchmark criteria for quality are at the forefront of project requirements.

Cost-Benefit Analysis and Project Planning

During the planning phase, a cost-benefit analysis was undertaken for the fit-out, to determine the financial feasibility of specific energy-saving measures. The benefit analysis demonstrated that the sustainable fit-out had the potential to reduce energy consumption by 30 percent through four approaches:

▸▸ **THE INSTALLATION** of a new, energy-efficient heating, ventilating, and air-conditioning (HVAC) system, which includes a variable refrigerant flow (VRF) system and an auxiliary air-source heat pump. A VRF system can simultaneously heat and cool different building spaces by using a piped refrigerant to efficiently exchange heat between spaces that need to be cooled (like server rooms) and spaces that need to be heated. The air-source heat pump, which measures the difference between outdoor and indoor air temperatures to deliver heating and cooling for interior spaces, is used as a supplemental heating or cooling source for the VRF system.

▸▸ **INNOVATIVE USE** of a zoned heating and ventilation system that provides customized temperature control throughout the office.

▸▸ **STRATEGIES TO MAXIMIZE DAYLIGHTING** for the office interiors, including daylight sensors to reduce the use of electric lighting. Motion sensors and timers are used to further reduce electric lighting usage wherever appropriate.

▸▸ **COMPREHENSIVE SUBMETERING AND ACCOUNTING** of actual energy use, including the submetering of lighting, plug load, and HVAC energy use. These metering systems are connected to a real-time intelligent performance monitoring system.

Even though Morgan Lovell had only six years remaining on its current lease (a comparatively short period in the United Kingdom, where lease terms typically extend to ten or 15 years), the current building systems were inefficient and an energy-efficient retrofit was economically justified. Therefore, the decision was made to install cutting-edge heat recovery units for air conditioning, and to install both movement and light sensors for the lighting system. A proposal to upgrade or replace windows was shelved, as it was not considered to provide a reasonable return for the cost over the remaining lease period.

Ecoteric, the BREEAM adviser, created energy consumption and CO_2 emissions models for the project. Modeling relied on SBEM (Simplified Building Energy Model), a computer program developed by the BRE, the organization that manages BREEAM. The SBEM models estimated that the post-fit-out offices of Morgan Lovell would produce carbon emissions of just over 21 tonnes (23.15 tons) of CO_2 annually. This is significantly less than the equivalent standard for new construction (23.4 tonnes, or 25.8 tons) and substantially less than the carbon emissions expected of a building equivalent in age and construction to 16 Noel Street.

As part of the cost-benefit analysis, a comprehensive review of the opportunities to introduce renewable energy systems was carried out by SDS Energy. The only economically viable renewable technology was found to be an air-source heat pump, which was implemented as part of the heating and cooling system.[2]

Along with the economic benefits, Morgan Lovell also considered the environmental and social benefits of the retrofit. Social benefits included the ability to create a more inspirational office for employees, which enabled new work styles and processes to be introduced. The environmental benefits enhanced and projected Morgan Lovell's own ethical and environmentally responsible identity and image. Although they are not easy to quantify, these benefits were very important to Morgan Lovell.

The BREEAM Certification Process

When Morgan Lovell began the fit-out, a BREEAM fit-out protocol had not been fully developed. The project was therefore assessed using the Bespoke BREEAM methodology. Building types can be assessed under a number of standard BREEAM schemes, including those for offices, schools, retail, and court buildings. When a building does not fit into one of these standard schemes, it can be assessed under the Bespoke BREEAM scheme. The building at 16 Noel Street served as a pilot program in the development of BREEAM fit-out standards, which have since been incorporated into the BREEAM Offices scheme.

With a Bespoke BREEAM assessment, the BRE develops criteria specific to the building and its use. Information to develop the criteria is typically collected through a questionnaire completed by the design team; for technically complex buildings, a team kickoff meeting is held to develop appropriate information. Using the collected information, BRE produces a set of draft assessment criteria which are issued to the assessor and design team for comment or discussion. Once the design team's comments have been received, BRE produces the final criteria and issues them to the appointed assessor. As with a standard BREEAM certification scheme, the assessment is then completed and submitted to BRE for quality checks and certification.

Fit-outs are assessed using a system of credits, grouped in the following categories:

▶▶ **MANAGEMENT**. This category assesses issues such as building commissioning, creating and maintaining sustainable operating manuals, and the use of an operation environmental management system, which is a set of processes and practices for an organization that reduces its environmental impact and improves the efficiency of its operations.

▶▶ **ENERGY**. This category assesses energy use, energy use metering, and CO_2 emissions.

▶▶ **TRANSPORT**. This category assesses access to public transportation and local amenities, the presence of on-site or nearby cyclist facilities, and the implementation of a travel plan for occupants.

▶▶ **HEALTH AND WELL-BEING**. This category covers all aspects of the building interior environment that affect occupant health and productivity and can be controlled by occupants, such as heating, lighting, air quality, and noise.

▶▶ **WATER**. This category assesses the efficient use of water within the space.

▶▶ **MATERIALS AND WASTE**. This category assesses the use of environmentally responsible materials and reuse and recycling during project construction and operation.

▶▶ **POLLUTION**. This category assesses the reduction of gaseous, noise, and light emissions; the use of substances with minimal global warming potential; and the avoidance of pollution to waterways from the fit-out space.

The assessment process results in a project report containing a formal certification and rating. At of the time of the Morgan Lovell project, possible BREEAM ratings were Pass, Good, Very Good, or Excellent. In order to calculate the final BREEAM rating, a weighting is applied to the results achieved under each category.

Decision Making and Credit Documentation

The BREEAM process at 16 Noel Street began with a series of workshops at which the costs and benefits of a green fit-out were discussed and the need for a more analytical approach was highlighted. BREEAM rewards projects in which energy, thermal, and daylighting modeling has been undertaken. When modeling and feasibility studies were completed, specific decisions for the retrofit were made on the basis of their contribution to the whole-life cost-benefit of the project.

A full audit trail of supporting documents (including drawings, specifications, letters, delivery notes, calculations, and reports) is required to document each credit sought under BREEAM. An independent BREEAM assessor reviews the documents against the credit criteria and determines whether credit requirement have been met. If requirements are met and validated, the credit is awarded. If requirements are not met or are insufficiently validated, further information must be submitted. This process culminates in a total score and rating. In the case of 16 Noel Street, there were difficulties in obtaining information, particularly from subcontractors, but most difficulties were eventually overcome to enable the achievement of a high score.

Once the BREEAM process was underway, changes to construction site management and operational practices were put in place to ensure the sorting and recycling of construction waste and the minimization of air and water pollution to surrounding areas. Additionally, the on-site activities of suppliers and subcontractors were monitored to ensure compliance with sustainable construction and material practices. An ongoing quality assurance process ensured consistency and technical accuracy and the effective and efficient execution of retrofit plans.

GREEN BUILDING DESIGN AND CONSTRUCTION

The facade of Morgan Lovell's building in the West End blends in with Soho's street scene, but behind the door lies a new interior that embraces the latest thinking in sustainable office design. The interior of the office appears conventional, which was part of Morgan Lovell's design objective: to create an environmentally efficient office without significant cost implications or undue impact on occupant comfort. Every aspect of the design and refurbishment was carefully considered to minimize impact on the environment.

Health and Well-Being

To create an optimal work environment for office staff and ensure health and well-being, Morgan Lovell included the following components in the fit-out:

▸▸ **DIRECT OUTDOOR VIEWS** for office occupants, providing daylighting and allowing them to refocus their eyes when working with computer equipment.[3] Following the refurbishment, a survey showed that employees reported a 95 percent satisfaction level with exterior views.

▸▸ **HIGH-QUALITY VENTILATION**, providing at least 12 liters (0.42 cubic feet) per second per person of fresh air. In the United Kingdom, minimum standards are 5 to 8 liters (0.18 to 0.28 cubic feet) per second per person.

▸▸ **A HIGH-QUALITY ACOUSTICAL ENVIRONMENT**, with sound levels consistent with the recommended levels from the British Council for Offices. To achieve this outcome, Morgan Lovell appointed an acoustic consultant, who determined the existing internal sound levels and specified low-noise indoor units for cooling and heating.

▸▸ **CAREFUL DESIGN OF WATER SERVICES** to prevent the growth of legionella and other harmful bacteria. Holding-water temperatures were regulated to ensure that bacteria would not thrive, and water service lines were cleaned and disinfected.

▸▸ **LOCALIZED CONTROLS FOR HEATING AND COOLING**, so that occupants can adjust the temperature to their liking.

▸▸ **MORE COMFORTABLE, CONTROLLABLE LIGHTING.** The work environment is illuminated with a combination of indirect lighting (which illuminates a space by directing the light toward the ceiling to produce soft lighting for the entire area), direct lighting (which emits light in the general direction of the surface to be illuminated), and task lighting (which lights work surfaces for visually intensive activities). The lighting scheme allows task lighting to be individually controlled, improves light conditions for occupants, and reduces overlighting in corridors and other locations where intensive lighting is not required.

Energy

Energy efficiency measures were incorporated throughout the Morgan Lovell offices.

ADVANCED, ENERGY-EFFICIENT HVAC

The highly advanced HVAC system combines a VRF system and an air-source heat pump to efficiently heat and cool building interiors. The zoned, ductless HVAC system provides superior thermal comfort to occupants, using a refrigerant to exchange heat between interior spaces to efficiently heat and cool the space. The VRF system can simultaneously heat and cool by moderating refrigerant flows between areas that need to be cooled and areas that need to be heated. The system permits simultaneous heating and cooling in zones where heating and cooling needs differ. Fan coil units installed in each zone to transmit air flow can be turned off if they are not in use, further reducing energy consumption.

An air-source heat pump supplements the VRF system for backup heating and cooling by extracting heat energy from outside air to warm the building interior. If additional cooling is needed, the pump extracts heat from the building interior. Heating and cooling requirements for the space were assessed using thermal modeling software. The software demonstrated that the HVAC system was adequately sized to maintain thermal comfort conditions, in accordance with guidelines set by the Chartered Institution of Building Services Engineers (CIBSE).

REDUCED ELECTRICAL DEMAND

In addition to the efficient HVAC system, a number of additional measures were undertaken as part of the build-out to reduce electrical demand for office functions:

▸▸ **INFRARED MOVEMENT SENSORS** were installed to turn off lighting in zones where people are not working.

▸▸ **DIMMING UNITS** automatically adjust with natural lighting conditions, so that less artificial light is used on sunny days. The dimming system reduced energy usage dramatically.

▸▸ **EACH FLOOR IS METERED SEPARATELY** to monitor energy usage closely, as is the HVAC system.

▸▸ **ELECTRONICS**, such as audiovisual equipment in meeting rooms, operate in "power save" modes where possible, and timers turn them off automatically at the end of the day. It was not practical to have a central "power off" command for computers because of computer-aided design work undertaken in the office (which occasionally requires machines to be left on overnight and at weekends). However, all staff members are aware of their individual responsibility to turn off their computers at the end of the day. Building maintenance and cleaning staff have been instructed to turn off lights that are not on motion sensors.

These measures have resulted in a 30 percent reduction in electricity use, while improving previously inadequate interior lighting conditions and addressing previous concerns about insufficient air-conditioning capacity.

To further reduce Morgan Lovell's carbon footprint, 100 percent of the electricity used in the 16 Noel Street office space comes from renewable energy sources, including wind, wave, and solar. Electricity is purchased through Green Energy UK and has a cost premium of roughly £0.01 ($0.015) per kWh.

Water

Common water closets (WCs or bathrooms) and incoming water services at 16 Noel Street are maintained by the landlord. Owing to the floor configuration and the inclusion of bathroom facilities within the footprint of Morgan Lovell's offices, however, it was possible for the company to fund and implement water-saving measures to assist in achieving a high BREEAM rating, although there was no ongoing cost advantage in so doing. The financial benefits of reduced water consumption accrue to the landlord, who is responsible for the building's water bill.

The following water-saving measures were implemented:

▸▸ **DUAL-FLUSH TOILETS** with full-flush capacity of 6 liters (1.6 gallons) per flush, and user-selected reduced-flush capacity of 4 liters (1.06 gallons) per flush.

▸▸ **LOW-FLOW** faucets and showers.

▸▸ **A LEAK DETECTION ALARM SYSTEM** to highlight abnormal water use.

▸▸ **A PULSED-OUTPUT WATER METER**. The meter monitors water consumption within the office space, so that significant deviations in consumption can be identified and remedial action taken.

▸▸ **WC OCCUPANCY SENSORS**. Occupancy sensors automatically shut off water to the WCs when they are vacated, thereby reducing water use.

Materials

Sustainable use of materials and sustainable and environmentally friendly materials were integral to the fit-out:

▸▸ **REUSED, RECYCLED, AND LOCAL MATERIALS**. Careful attention was paid to materials use, including flooring, ceiling, lighting, wall paints, joinery (cabinetry and woodwork), fabrics, blinds, and furniture. Morgan Lovell's policy was to reuse existing products, to use products sourced as locally as possible, and to use products with a high recycled content and the capacity to be recycled in the future.

▸▸ **SUSTAINABLE WOOD**. The BREEAM process requires a high standard of auditable proof that timber used in the fit-out is from a sustainable source. The hardwood used for fixtures was tracked from the source, through the supply and manufacturing process, to the site, with a full audit trail.

▸▸ **INNOVATIVE, ENVIRONMENTALLY FRIENDLY PRODUCTS**. As part of the fit-out, several new environmentally friendly products are being tested for their performance and long-term durability. Innovative and experimental products and installations featured in the fit-out include utilizing recycled plastic bottles for kitchen surfaces, using recycled car tires for entrance mats, and using low-emission, light-colored reflective paint to reduce the use of lighting, thereby cutting energy bills. With the exception of experimental test products, all products utilized in the fit-out satisfy the durability requirements for contract-grade finishes.

▸▸ **GREEN INSULANTS** (insulation). In addition to reducing greenhouse gases (GHG) emissions through lower energy use, building insulants were chosen which avoided the use of ozone and potential global warming gases in their manufacture.

Other Green Strategies

Ongoing operations were also addressed as part of the overall retrofit:

▶ **ON-SITE RECYCLING**. All rubbish bins have been removed from under desks, and central recycling units were built where employees can sort their waste. Further facilities are in place for recycling lightbulbs, cardboard, glass, electrical items, batteries, wood, and plastics. Recycling rates now stand at 82 percent of all waste.

▶ **GREEN PRINTING POLICY**. Individual desk printers have been removed and centralized printers provided. Default settings are for double-sided printing—saving resources and encouraging staff members to get up from their desks and stretch their legs.

▶ **ALTERNATIVE TRANSPORTATION**. A comprehensive travel plan has been developed and facilities made available for cyclists. No subsidized parking is allocated to the office, and car parking spaces have been given up in place of secure bike racks. Three parking spaces are available for the use of tradespeople working within the building.

▶ **BUILDING SYSTEM ACCESS AND OPERATION**. Careful consideration was given to maintenance and management of key services, including the innovative, new HVAC system. Access to the HVAC plant—which is fully demountable and can be easily removed down a staircase at the end of its life—is easy, requiring no special equipment.

FINANCING

The fit-out cost roughly £65 ($106) per square foot (£699 [$1,137] per square meter), excluding furniture costs. It was accomplished at a cost premium; specifically, the advanced HVAC system cost 30 percent more than a standard system, increasing project expenditures by 10 per-

cent. However, annual electricity savings from the advanced heating, cooling, and lighting systems are estimated at approximately £6,000 ($9,760), leading to a payback period of four to five years.

Consulting and energy and lighting modeling fees were roughly £10,000 ($16,270); the fee for the customized BREEAM assessment was roughly £2,000 ($3,254), plus £740 ($1,204) for certification costs.[5] In total, consulting, modeling, and BREEAM assessment cost roughly £2.25 ($3.66) per square foot (£24.20 [$39.37] per square meter).

MARKETING AND MANAGEMENT

Morgan Lovell's new office has received considerable interest in the industry. The office has been used for a fact-finding visit by members of the British Institute of Facilities Management (BIFM), who are examining issues surrounding sustainable refurbishment. The office has hosted a number of sustainable office seminars. Press coverage has been extensive, enabling best practices to be shared with clients and the wider public.

The fit-out has been recognized for excellence in numerous design competitions, including selection for finalist status in the City of London Corporation's Sustainable City Awards in 2008; the short list in the Sustainable Building category by the Building Research Establishment and the Worshipful Company of Chartered Surveyors; and the Green Apple Award.

LESSONS LEARNED

The fit-out of Morgan Lovell's London offices offers the following lessons:

▶ **DETERMINE THE TARGETED CERTIFICATION** during the planning and design phase. The later that certification is considered, the lower the score and more expensive it will be to implement.

▶ **UNDERSTAND THE COSTS** associated with a sustainable scheme versus a conventional fit-out. As market demand grows and sustainability is incorporated into the design and planning of each project, the "green premium" is decreasing. Morgan Lovell's clients are benefiting from the experience gained during the fit-out of 16

Even though Morgan Lovell had only six years remaining on its current lease—a relatively short period in the U.K., where lease terms typically extend to ten or 15 years—the current building systems were inefficient, helping make an energy-efficient retrofit economically justifiable. Pictured here is the organization of the open-floor plan and the use of various types of lighting.

MORGAN LOVELL

Noel Street; the company is able to advise them on cost-effective sustainability measures and green certification for their projects.

▶▶ **MAKE SURE THE PRODUCTS** used are truly green. A number of building products marketed as green are not actually environmentally friendly, or they do not meet standard performance expectations for contract-grade materials and finishes. To reduce the risk of specifying unsustainable or inferior products, work with experienced consultants and contractors who have previously gone through the "trial and error" of specifying green building materials and products.

▶▶ **FLEXIBLE-ZONE HVAC SYSTEMS** can maximize thermal comfort and energy efficiency in office buildings. Utilizing a VRF system with fan coil units in zones makes it possible to turn units on or off, or adjust them based on occupant usage. For example, air-conditioning systems in meeting spaces can be turned off when they are unoccupied, reducing the square footage that must be cooled.

▶▶ **CONSIDER IN-HOUSE RECYCLING PROGRAMS** and other environmental initiatives during the early stages of project planning. Morgan Lovell designed its recycling program during the initial phases of the 16 Noel Street fit-out, strategically integrating the recycling stations into the workplace and accounting for how occupants will use the space. Morgan Lovell uses their program as a model for their client work.

▶▶ **PRIORITIZE RETROFIT INVESTMENTS** through gap and cost-benefit analysis, when pursuing green certification. Project planning should include a gap assessment, which evaluates the probability and cost of securing the specific points of a green certification system.[5] The project team should use the gap assessment to prioritize the components of the retrofit, balancing costs versus points secured. Cost-benefit assessment can evaluate the longer-term costs and benefits of undertaking specific sustainability strategies, enabling building owners and project management to make sounder choices.

▶▶ **KEEP OCCUPANTS INFORMED AND INVOLVED** in the sustainable fit-out and building operation process. A key strategy to ensuring the success of green operating practices is to keep everyone involved and informed, not only of the design process and how their suggestions have been incorporated, but also with information on how to best use the space once the retrofit is complete.

Lara Conaway, sustainability manager for Morgan Lovell and a BREEAM trained assessor, works with leading organizations in the United Kingdom to make their offices sustainable and energy-efficient. Her work has led Morgan Lovell to rank as one the nation's top 20 greenest companies according to the Sunday Times of London. A frequent commentator, author, and speaker, Ms. Conaway has presented at conferences across the country.

Susan Logan is a chartered building services engineer with 20 years of experience in building services design. Before founding Ecoteric Ltd., she worked for the BRE and trained as a BREEAM assessor. Ms. Logan specializes in low-carbon design and is an accredited Carbon Trust consultant and CIBSE Low-Carbon consultant. Ecoteric is a sustainability and low-carbon consultancy offering BREEAM and LEED assessments.

NOTES

1 In August 2008, the BRE added the Outstanding score, which replaces Excellent as the highest possible score.

2 At the time the BREEAM assessment was undertaken for 16 Noel Street, air-source heat pumps were an allowable technology for renewable energy credits. The assessment criteria now require additional measures for air-source heat pumps to be considered as renewable energy systems.

3 The provision of outside views is important for visual comfort and the avoidance of eyestrain and productivity loss. Daylight increases the sense of well-being and productivity; see, for example, the California Energy Commission's 2003 study, "Windows and Offices: A Study of Office Worker Performance and the Indoor Environment."

4 BREEAM now requires a compulsory postconstruction review and report, which requires an additional certification fee of £380 ($618).

5 For more information on gap assessment for green certification, see chapter 2.

Development Team

DEVELOPER:
Morgan Lovell

ARCHITECT:
Morgan Lovell

GENERAL CONTRACTOR:
Morgan Lovell

MEP ENGINEERS:
Advent

MEP CONTRACTORS:
Advent

SUSTAINABILITY CONSULTANTS:
Susan Logan and Lara Conaway

INTERIOR DESIGNER:
Elaine Duke

PROPERTY MANAGEMENT FIRM:
NB Real Estate

CASE STUDY • PHILIP BOCCALATTE WITH LEANNE TOBIAS

One Beacon Street

BOSTON, MASSACHUSETTS

One Beacon Street is a 1,016,139-square-foot (94,402-square-meter) office tower located in the business district adjoining Boston's famed Beacon Hill. The property, constructed between 1970 and 1973 by Turner Construction, was renovated as a green building by Beacon Capital Partners and a team led by CB Richard Ellis (CBRE) between 2006 and 2008. The project was certified at the Silver level under the

Leadership in Energy and Environmental Design for Existing Buildings (LEED-EB) protocol in April 2008, the first Boston-area multitenant office project to achieve such certification.

Green improvements and operating programs utilized to achieve the certification include the following:

▸▸ **IMPLEMENTATION** of engineering improvements to reduce energy usage, including the installation of variable-frequency drive (VFD) equipment and building controls;

Outreach programs have kept tenants at One Beacon Street abreast of the building's green initiatives. One tenant responded with an energy audit of its leased space that determined certain lighting retrofits would achieve payback in two and a half years.

▸ **COMPLETION** of a lighting retrofit program throughout common areas;

▸ **INSTITUTION** of a construction waste recycling program for base building construction and tenant buildouts; and

▸ **CREATION AND IMPLEMENTATION** of green cleaning, green exterior management, and tenant education programs.

As a substantial Class A project in downtown Boston, One Beacon Street serves a demanding corporate clientele. Tenants are attracted to the building for its central location, 360-degree views, headquarters-style infrastructure, and rich amenity package, which includes Sovereign Bank, Rebecca's Café, Fitcorp, a sundry shop, and the most popular shoeshine stand in Boston. The leasing environment is competitive, with over 410,000 square feet leased from 2006 to 2008. Tenants signing leases at One Beacon Street over this period included top-tier finance and business services firms such as JP Morgan, Deutsche Bank, Boston Consulting Group, and Skadden Arps Slate Meagher & Flom.

OWNERSHIP OBJECTIVES

An affiliate of Beacon Capital Partners (BCP) purchased One Beacon Street in September 2006. Immediately thereafter, CBRE and BCP created a comprehensive ownership plan to address both operational and capital requirements. The capital plan included improvements to the lobby and elevator cabs because the existing finishes were dated and in need of upgrading. Operational improvements focused on two areas: enhancing the property's energy performance through use of the Energy Star system, and obtaining certification under the LEED-EB protocol. In focusing on Energy Star and LEED-EB enhancements, BCP was motivated by two desires: to reduce project operating costs and to maintain market leadership. As well, BCP's investors were expressing increasing interest in green and energy-efficient real estate investments, and BCP recognized that the greening of One Beacon Street was consistent with its fiduciary responsibilities to investors and building occupants.

The Energy Star and LEED targets for One Beacon Street were achieved by April 2008 through operational changes and comparatively modest energy-saving projects. Tenants are key beneficiaries of the energy savings realized, because most leases at One Beacon Street are written net of all expenses save for real estate taxes. As a result, energy savings are realized directly by tenants. At the same time, the building owner realizes savings when space is unoccupied between tenant leases and, in a period of significant energy price inflation, can cite building energy efficiency and green features as a competitive differentiator and tenant benefit. BCP and CBRE therefore believe that the LEED-EB certification and improvement in building energy efficiency have been economically valuable, as well as the environmentally responsible course of action.

ENERGY STAR CERTIFICATION

The Energy Star label of the Environmental Protection Agency (EPA) is conferred on U.S. buildings in the top quartile of energy efficiency. To be certified under LEED-EB, buildings must first be Energy Star certified. Consequently, the owner and manager of One Beacon Street opted to green the property in two phases: first, to achieve the Energy Star label and, second, to become LEED certified.

Figure 1

Flowchart and Table of Organizational Roles

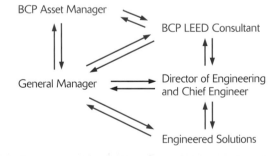

Team Member	Role
General Manager, One Beacon Street, CBRE	Oversee financial aspects and execution. Provide liaison with owner's asset manager.
Owner's LEED Consultant	Provide substantial knowledge of sustainable buildings to guide team.
Director of Engineering, CBRE	Oversight of outside engineering contractor and third-party contractors engaged to execute energy efficiency projects.
Chief Engineer, One Beacon Street, CBRE	Integrate plans into existing building systems and provide day-to-day liaison to outside engineering consultant and contractors.
Outside engineering consultant, Engineered Solutions	Provide high-level guidance and create plans to retrofit existing building systems for energy efficiency.

Team and Responsibilities

A multifunctional Energy Star team assembled and directed by CBRE included CBRE's general manager, chief engineer, and property management staff for One Beacon Street; an energy consultant engaged by BCP; and Engineered Solutions, a Boston engineering firm that specializes in heating, ventilating, and air-conditioning (HVAC) retrofits. The team reported to the asset manager representing BCP, the building owner. Figure 1 depicts the general chain of command on this project and how information was communicated, as well as the roles assumed by each key member of the project team.

Energy Star Benchmarking

The initial step in achieving Energy Star designation, benchmarking the property's energy efficiency, was achieved by documenting trends in utility usage at the EPA's Energy Star Web site. The Web site offers tools to measure a property's electrical, steam, gas, and water usage on an annual basis and to compare usage with other buildings of equivalent size, type of occupancy, and operating schedule. The tools take into account the property's region so that weather conditions can be eliminated when making comparisons. To receive an Energy Star rating, the user must first enter all utility consumption information for 12 consecutive months, including electricity, steam, gas and water usage data. Entering monetary data (fuel costs) is optional, but makes the results more meaningful.

On the basis of the Energy Star benchmarking, the team determined that One Beacon Street had an Energy Star rating of 62. To be awarded Energy Star designation, One Beacon Street needed to achieve a rating of 75 or higher. The next step was to develop and evaluate strategies that would cost-effectively reduce energy usage at One Beacon Street.

Energy Star Operational Changes

The team's initial task was to identify ways to save energy without significant expense. The following operating initiatives were identified:

▸▸ **REDUCTIONS IN GARAGE STEAM USAGE.** The team studied garage usage patterns and determined that approximately $80,000 could be saved annually by reducing the steam used to heat the garage.

▸▸ **COOLING TOWER OPERATIONS.** Annual savings of approximately $50,000 were realized by draining the cooling tower during the winter. On sunny winter days, temperatures at One Beacon Street are now controlled with direct outside air, rather than with live steam. The optimal mix of heated indoor air and direct outside air is determined by the building control system. The previous practice, in which the cooling tower operated with water during the winter, required about $50,000 in live steam to heat the water and prevent it from freezing.

▸▸ **HVAC USAGE REDUCTIONS.** The team checked the operating schedule of the HVAC fans and compared fan usage with actual tenant occupancy schedules. Electricity and steam usage was reduced by shutting down unnecessary equipment early.

▸▸ **REDUCTION IN CHILLED WATER TEMPERATURES.** Another small change that produced energy savings at no cost was to modify the temperatures for the chilled water used to cool One Beacon Street. Engineering records from the building control system were reviewed to establish optimal chilled water temperatures for outside weather conditions. The study found that chilled water could be circulated at slightly higher temperatures under certain weather conditions than previously believed, thereby reducing energy costs associated with chilling. The operating principle is simple: why cool chilled water to 44°F (6.7°C), if the building can be cooled sufficiently with water at 48°F (8.9°C)?

Energy Star Capital Improvements

The One Beacon Street team tasked its engineering consultant, Engineered Solutions, to identify additional cost-effective approaches to save energy. The following capital improvement programs were carried out:

▸▸ **PERIMETER FAN RETROFITS.** Perimeter fans used for the circulation of outside air through One Beacon Street were retrofitted to run on variable-frequency drives (VFDs). The use of a VFD allows the fans to be run at lower speed when appropriate. The VFD retrofit enables fans to supply the optimal amount of air to cool or heat window zones while reducing energy usage and meeting national guidelines for the supply of outside air.

▸▸ **SECONDARY WATER PUMP RETROFITS.** VFDs were also installed on secondary water pumps serving window air-conditioning units at One Beacon Street, to permit the pumps to operate at lower speed when indoor temperatures permit. The installation of VFDs on secondary water pumps reduced energy consumption at One Beacon Street.

▸▸ **INSTALLATION OF CO₂ CONTROLS**. Building controls at One Beacon Street were modified to permit the increased use of return air (air already in circulation in the building) for heating and cooling, which reduces energy costs. The increased use of return air relative to outside air required the installation of CO_2 controls that monitor air quality and signal the air handling system to take in additional outside air when needed, to maintain appropriate indoor air quality.

These capital improvement programs were approved and bids evaluated in 2007. Construction began in the early fall of 2007 and was substantially completed by January 1, 2008.

Energy and Cost Savings Realized

Because of operational improvements at the property undertaken in connection with the Energy Star initiative, One Beacon Street began to realize dramatic energy savings before the capital improvements were fully implemented. By the end of September 2007, the building's Energy Star score had increased to 74. In October 2007, Energy Star changed the methods used to measure a property's Energy Star rating. The methodological change was anticipated, and the project team knew the new results could go either way. The scoring revisions changed One Beacon Street's Energy Star rating from 74 to 77. The final step, undertaken following the completion of both capital and operating programs for energy efficiency, was to have a licensed professional engineer verify building data and submit it to Energy Star for formal approval.

Energy Star enhancements at One Beacon Street cost approximately $450,000 and reduced energy consumption by approximately 9 percent. First year savings—approximately $200,000 in steam cost savings and $400,000 in electricity cost savings—significantly exceeded capital expenditures, producing a project payback in less than one year. In June 2008, Trigen, the central steam plant supplying One Beacon Street, called to complain about low steam usage during May, thinking that the property had installed an alternative chiller system. Although the building's chiller system still relied on steam heat, One Beacon Street had reduced its steam usage by 1 million pounds, saving 1 million Btus in energy through its Energy Star initiatives.

LEED-EB CERTIFICATION

Concurrent with obtaining Energy Star certification, Beacon Capital Partners, CBRE, and project consultants began to pursue certification under the LEED-EB program. LEED-EB goals for One Beacon Street were set in February 2007. It was determined that the building could realistically aim to be certified at the Silver level, and team members were assigned to develop the programs needed to fulfill LEED certification prerequisites and win the required LEED points.

Team and Implementation Process

As had been the case with Energy Star project, One Beacon Street's LEED-EB certification effort utilized a multidisciplinary team:

▸▸ **THE PROJECT WAS OVERSEEN** by the asset manager for BCP, the building's owner, in consultation with the CBRE team.

▸▸ **A LEED CONSULTANT** with specialized expertise in LEED-EB and green cleaning programs was added to the project team to propose changes in property operations and to process documentation developed by the team.

▸▸ **CBRE'S GENERAL MANAGER** for One Beacon Street was assigned tasks related to occupancy and financial data.

▸▸ **CBRE'S OPERATIONS MANAGER** for One Beacon Street worked with the tenant coordinator to collect data related to a new green cleaning program, the ongoing recycling program, and enforcement of policies related to maintaining a smoke-free environment.

▸▸ **CBRE'S CHIEF ENGINEER** for One Beacon Street worked with the CBRE engineering crew to catalog the energy and environmental history for the project, to collect baseline data for tracking the effectiveness of green improvements.

To simplify the LEED process, the team used four phases to track progress:

▸▸ **INFORMATION GATHERING** and knowledge development on property performance, LEED-EB requirements and gaps;

▸▸ **FEASIBILITY ASSESSMENT** of potential improvements;

▸▸ **IMPLEMENTATION** of green improvements; and

▸▸ **REVIEW AND DOCUMENTATION** of program results.

Generally, meetings were held biweekly during the first two phases. During phase three, meetings were held monthly. Less frequent periodic meetings were held during the postimplementation review period, in order to assess program effectiveness. The team found that the two most important facets of the process were the transition from phase 1 (information gathering and knowledge development) to phase 2 (feasibility assessment) and exceptionally strong team execution during the phase 2 feasibility reviews to ensure the development of cost-effective, long-term solutions. The team came to believe that understanding the LEED process thoroughly and, more importantly, understanding existing and desired building performance in the context of the LEED protocol, are crucial in attaining certification.

Low-Cost LEED Points

Certain LEED credits are location-specific and can be implemented for nothing more than documentation costs. Under the LEED-EB guidelines in use through August 2008, One Beacon Street was awarded LEED credit points for its location in a high-density location and its accessibility to public transportation.

Because all parking at One Beacon Street is located in an underground garage, the property was awarded a LEED credit point for the reduction of the heat islands associated with impermeable surface parking. Other comparatively inexpensive LEED credit points were earned by restriping the parking garage to give preference to alternative-fuel vehicles and ensuring adequate bicycle storage and showering facilities for tenants.

LEED-EB Initiatives

The attainment of LEED-EB certification required modifications that spanned numerous aspects of property operations and capital development. Key aspects of the green property operations program include the following:

▸▸ **REVISION OF BUILDING REGULATIONS** to require green practices. Building regulations at One Beacon Street were revised to add battery recycling to the property's already strong recycling program. Tenant buildout requirements were revised to mandate recycling of construction waste; environmental containment and isolation of construction debris, including dust; and the imposition of sound reduction requirements, so that the construction of improvements would not inconvenience

Capital programs undertaken at One Beacon Street to increase energy efficiency cost $0.55 per net rentable square foot, and the payback period was less than one year.

tenants in adjacent spaces. The property's no-smoking regulations were adjusted to comply with LEED guidelines, to forbid smoking within 25 feet of the building.

▸▸ **GREEN CLEANING PROGRAM**. A number of the points associated with LEED-EB certification can be attained by instituting a green cleaning program. In the spring of 2007, CBRE rebid the cleaning contract at One Beacon Street and awarded the contract to a well-established green cleaning provider, UGL Unicco. The cost of the program was competitive with conventional cleaning programs. The Unicco GreenClean program adopted by One Beacon Street incorporates green cleaning products and chemicals certified by the nonprofit Green Seal program; relies on equipment that maximizes reduction of building contaminants; and uses microfiber cloths and floor mops that effectively improve the removal of dust and bacteria from surfaces. The program also uses Green Seal–certified restroom products, provides a LEED-approved system for cleaning entryways and grates, recycles waste generated in cleaning operations, and trains staff on green cleaning procedures. The introduction of the GreenClean program enabled One Beacon Street to win LEED points for entryway and grate cleaning, the use of environmentally friendly cleaning products, the use of environmentally friendly cleaning equipment, and staff training on green operating practices.

▸▸ **GREEN EXTERIOR MANAGEMENT POLICY**. One Beacon Street adopted a green exterior management policy to reduce water usage at the property—a strategy that earned several points toward LEED-EB certification. Cityscapes, the landscaping contractor at One Beacon Street, worked with CBRE to install water-efficient landscaping and an irrigation system that uses fan heads which reduce water flow and associated costs by approximately 50 percent. The green exterior management initiative also selects and rotates low-maintenance plantings on a seasonal basis. Drought and disease-resistant summer plantings are rotated with winter plantings that are resistant to the salt injury associated with municipal snow mitigation. The green exterior management policy also requires the use of organic fertilizers, soil, compost, and weed killers.

▸▸ **THERMAL SCAN AND PERIMETER REPAIRS**. One Beacon Street earned a LEED innovation point by conducting an infrared scan of the property to pinpoint heat loss and identify potential energy improvements. One

Beacon Street opted to perform the scan with the hope of correcting comfort problems in tenant spaces on the eleventh floor. Interior and exterior scans were performed over a five-hour period, with the exterior scan completed under the required clear and cold weather conditions. The $5,000 scan identified major insulation and air infiltration problems at the ceiling level of the eleventh floor. Cost-effective perimeter repairs were identified and implemented, with a significant improvement in tenant comfort and satisfaction.

One Beacon Street was certified at the Silver level under the LEED-EB program on April 1, 2008, the first multi-tenant office property in the Boston area to win such designation.

ONGOING GREEN INITIATIVES

The cost-effectiveness of the Energy Star and LEED-EB improvements at One Beacon Street has led BCP and CBRE to undertake additional green initiatives:

▸▸ **LIGHTING RETROFIT PROGRAM**. After obtaining LEED-EB certification, BCP and CBRE launched a $120,000 lighting retrofit program that surveyed the efficiency of all fixtures at One Beacon Street and replaced lamps and ballasts throughout the common areas. The results of the lighting efficiency survey have motivated several tenants to install more energy-efficient lighting in their suites. BCP and CBRE are also evaluating the installation of highly efficient light-emitting diode (LED) lights, which save electricity and can last five to seven years or 100,000 hours, versus 20,000 hours for the typical fluorescent light.

▸▸ **TENANT EDUCATION**. Tenants at One Beacon Street have been kept abreast of the building's green initiatives through visits from the property management staff, the building Web site, and the electronic screens in the elevator cabs. These practices were initiated to promote green practices and build occupant awareness. Subjects covered in the tenant education initiative have included recycling, indoor air quality, and energy use. One tenant motivated by the outreach program undertook an energy audit which determined that a lighting retrofit and the installation of motion-activated lighting in key areas would achieve payback in 2.5 years.

▸▸ BUILDING STAFF EDUCATION. The green certification efforts at One Beacon Street led several members of the CBRE property management staff at One Beacon Street to become LEED Accredited Professionals. CBRE has also begun to encourage its national management team to pursue LEED professional accreditation.

▸▸ THIRD-PARTY CONTRACTORS. Staff education on green practices also extends to third-party contractors engaged at One Beacon Street. The security staff has been trained to enforce the no-smoking policy, and contractors engaged in hauling and waste management have modified their operations to comply with recycling and construction waste management initiatives required under LEED-EB. CBRE also notes that the expansion of green practices in the building services market enabled the management of One Beacon Street to find competitive vendors for LEED-compliant green cleaning and exterior management programs.

▸▸ ADDITIONAL PROJECTS UNDER CONSIDERATION. The team is evaluating the use of waterless urinals and wind and solar rooftop technologies, including the possible lease of roof space to a solar power provider, to realize additional water and energy savings. Projects will be evaluated on the basis of efficiency and cost-effectiveness.

PROJECT MARKETING

The Boston office market is one of the greenest markets in the country. Municipal buildings must be constructed to the LEED Silver level, and new office developments are required to utilize the LEED New Construction checklist as a planning tool. As a result, building owners, architects, and public officials are well informed on sustainable strategies, and green criteria are beginning to influence tenant leasing choices.

In consequence, the brokerage team at One Beacon Street has actively promoted the recent green initiatives at the property. A key discussion point incorporated into building tours for prospective tenants is One Beacon Street's Energy Star label, which means that tenant utility costs are reduced. The building's LEED certification is an important feature for corporate tenants whose sustainability efforts encourage the use of energy-efficient space and sustainable practices such as recycling.

The LEED-EB certification also appeals to tenants interested in obtaining LEED for Commercial Interiors (LEED-CI) designation for their suites. Base building certification under LEED-EB can help supply points to tenants pursuing the LEED-CI designation through building-wide programs relating to construction waste recycling, the control of construction debris, and the maintenance of thermal comfort. Deutsche Bank has undertaken the LEED-CI renovation of a 60,000-square-foot space at One Beacon Street. The certification of One Beacon Street and the presence of LEED-compliant programs in the building will make certification of the Deutsche Bank space more easily attainable.

Similarly, the Gensler architectural firm has completed a LEED-CI Gold space on the third floor of One Beacon Street. The ability to work closely with an ownership and management team well-versed in the LEED system helped to ensure a smooth buildout process for Gensler. CBRE worked closely with Gensler's LEED team and attended weekly construction meetings to facilitate project completion and the production of necessary documentation. Gensler's Boston offices are a working demonstration of the company's commitment to green building, and both Gensler and CBRE consider One Beacon Street a working example of what can be achieved using the LEED standards.

The greening of One Beacon Street has also brought favorable publicity. In a 2008 press conference held by the city of Boston, One Beacon Street was recognized as one of Boston's 13 greenest buildings.

FINANCIAL IMPACT

BCP dedicated $561,295 in capital budget ($0.55 per net rentable square foot) to green and energy efficiency improvements at One Beacon Street. Utility rebates from NSTAR, the local utility, reduced costs by $70,711, for a net expenditure of $490,584 ($0.48 per net rentable square foot). Annual energy savings associated with these expenditures are estimated at $682,453, producing a payback period of approximately 8.7 months. Initial project operating costs were paid by BCP with available cash flow and billed back to tenants in 2007 and 2008, consistent with the rapid realization of operating savings (figure 2). Financial rewards associated with green and energy efficiency improvements at One Beacon Street will be reaped by tenants in the form of lower utility bills. Management will realize savings on common area and vacant spaces.

Figure 2

Energy Savings Projects: Costs, Savings, and Payback

Project Name	Cost ($)	Utility Rebates ($)	Net Cost ($)	Annual Savings ($)	Payback (Years)
Decommission General Exhaust Fans	0	0	0	2,241	0.00
Decommission Cooling Towers for Winter Season	0	0	0	18,226	0.00
Temperature Control in Garage	0	0	0	19,500	0.00
Reset Chilled-Water Supply Temperature Setpoint	6,500	0	6,500	44,590	0.15
Reset Secondary Hot-Water Supply Temperature for Night Setback	7,286		7,286	51,454	0.14
Energy Star Project (Perimeter Fans, VFD, and CO_2 Controls)	414,827	−56,201	358,626	497,153	0.72
Common Area Lighting Retrofit	132,682	−14,510	118,172	49,289	2.40
Total	561,295	−70,711	490,584	682,453	0.72

EXPERIENCE GAINED

The One Beacon Street team reports the following lessons from its green and energy efficiency programs:

▸▸ PLANNING AND EVALUATION are key to project success. The evaluation of existing building systems and feasibility assessments of planned improvements were a key team focus. The emphasis on planning and evaluation was needed to identify problem areas and the most efficient and cost-effective remediation strategies.

▸▸ GREEN AND ENERGY EFFICIENCY PROGRAMS affect all aspects of building operations, making multidisciplinary staffing a necessity. The attainment of Energy Star and LEED-EB certifications at One Beacon Street affected capital planning, engineering, operations, and project marketing. As a result, the LEED and Energy Star project teams required members versed in finance, energy efficiency, engineering, property management, and tenant relations, as well as LEED specialists. The involvement of multiple disciplines increased the range of options considered by the team and led to smoother property-wide implementation efforts.

▸▸ THE BUILDING SERVICES MARKET is evolving to provide cost-effective green alternatives. The numbers and experience of green service providers are expanding. The introduction of green cleaning and exterior management programs at One Beacon Street was facilitated by the presence of well-trained and competitively priced service providers in the Boston market.

▸▸ ENERGY-EFFICIENT IMPROVEMENTS can be cost-effective. The capital programs undertaken at One Beacon Street cost $0.55 per net rentable square foot and realized payback in less than a year. The rapid payback of project costs allowed building ownership to pass costs through to tenants in 2007 and 2008.

▸▸ GREEN AND ENERGY-EFFICIENT RENOVATIONS can serve as a project marketing tool. One Beacon Street has attracted favorable publicity for its energy efficiency and sustainability programs. While tenant interest in sustainability varies across companies, the One Beacon Street team has found that a growing number of corporate leaders are undertaking social responsibility initiatives that favor the leasing of green space. Tenant reaction to the green and energy efficiency programs at One Beacon Street has been positive, and these efforts have been viewed favorably by tenants seeking green certification for their premises. Gensler and Deutsche Bank have undertaken green buildout programs, and other tenants are evaluating energy efficiency initiatives as a result of the One Beacon Street program.

Philip Boccalatte is general manager with the Boston, Massachusetts, office of CB Richard Ellis and is responsible for the property management and operations of One Beacon Street. Leanne Tobias is the founder and managing principal of Malachite LLC.

Development Team

ORIGINAL ARCHITECT:
Skidmore Owings & Merrill LLP

HEAD ENGINEER:
Fred O'Grady, CB Richard Ellis

SUSTAINABILITY CONSULTANT:
Ken Stack, UGL-Unicco

ENERGY CONSULTANT:
Gus Medeiros

PROPERTY MANAGEMENT FIRM:
CB Richard Ellis

PROPERTY MANAGER:
Philip Boccalatte, CB Richard Ellis

ASSET MANAGER:
Bill Musto, Beacon Capital Partners (building owner)

CASE STUDY · VINCENT CHENG
Shui On Land Headquarters
SHANGHAI, CHINA

China has the largest construction volume in the world, and the environmental awareness of the Chinese government has been rising rapidly in recent years. As a result, a growing number of sustainable and environmentally friendly projects are being completed. Awareness of green building reached a milestone in 2004, when the U.S. Green Building Council presented leadership awards to ten Chinese

real estate developers and government leaders for their "pioneering work in transforming the world's largest building industry." This event demonstrated China's acceptance of green building standards in general, and the Leadership in Energy and Environmental Design (LEED) rating system in particular. In 2006, the Ministry of Construction unveiled the Evaluation Standard for Green Building, which is similar to LEED in its structure and rating process. Today, LEED and the Ministry of Construction's green building evaluation standard have come into increasing use in the Chinese property market.

OWNERSHIP OBJECTIVES

Shui On Land Limited, established in 2004 and headquartered in Shanghai, is the flagship property company of the Shui On Group in mainland China. Shui On Land's projects feature unique commercial, residential, and mixed-use developments that foster quality living, working, and leisure experiences. The company focuses on three key business segments: 1) large-scale, mixed-use, and multiphase developments in urban areas, incorporating residential, office, retail, and entertainment space; 2) multiuse projects with a focus on information technology and technology-based

Shui On Land's headquarters office is on the top floors of Shui On Plaza, a 26-story grade A office building completed in 1997.

industries; and 3) integrated development projects that feature tourism and complementary uses.

As an experienced and responsible property developer, Shui On Land considers sustainability as the key to its long-term development. The company was one of the first Chinese developers to realize the importance of sustainable development and to make it a corporate policy. Since 2006, Shui On Land has incorporated sustainable design, construction, and operational features into every project it has undertaken. Sustainable practices are utilized in all phases of the company's developments from master planning, architectural design, materials procurement, and construction management to property management. Every project aims for the highest possible LEED rating or China-based rating, whichever is deemed more appropriate for the project. Shui On Land's most recent accomplishment has been to earn a LEED-CI Silver rating in 2008 for its renovation of the company's headquarters office in central Shanghai.

DEVELOPMENT INFORMATION

Shui On Land's headquarters office is located on the top floors of Shui On Plaza, a 26-story Grade A office and commercial development completed in early 1997. Sitting directly above a subway station, the building is strategically located in the heart of downtown Puxi, an area of Shanghai that offers optimal connectivity to surrounding neighborhoods, services, and amenities. Puxi is the urban center of Shanghai and houses about 90 percent of Shanghai's population.

The project totals approximately 5,200 square meters (55,970 square feet) in area, including an executive suite, open and private office spaces, meeting rooms, a training room, a gym, a library, and other supporting facilities. The objectives for the renovation project were to upgrade the existing office to one that reflects Shui On's policy on sustainability, and to provide the company's employees with optimum working conditions and maximum comfort to induce productivity.

The need to renovate the space on the 25th and 26th floors became apparent in 2007. The preceding renovations of the two office floors had been completed over the previous five to ten years. With Shui On Land's continuous growth, the old office design was no longer capable of effectively serving the company's programmatic and physical needs. Combined with the commitment to provide employees with a better working environment and

The retrofit of Shui On Land's headquarters resulted in savings on electricity use of 15 percent for appliances and 33 percent for lighting.

improved indoor air quality, functional requirements became the driving force for an office facelift and upgrade.

The project became the perfect opportunity to build an environmentally responsible office that demonstrates and upholds Shui On Land's corporate philosophy and mission and that provides a platform that nurtures a green corporate culture. The LEED for Commercial Interiors (LEED-CI) rating system was selected as the most appropriate to meet and measure the company's sustainable development goals.

PROJECT TEAM

Shui On Land's experience with other LEED projects has demonstrated that active collaboration at the early stages in a project is the optimal way to learn and apply LEED processes, and to ensure greater control on buildability. In keeping with this experience, an integrated design approach was employed in the redevelopment of Shui On Land's headquarters.

The design team consisted of Gensler as the lead interior architect; Daniel Chan and Associates Ltd. as the mechanical, electrical, and plumbing, audiovisual, and acoustics engineer; Bi Hope as the lighting designer; and Arup as the sustainability and LEED consultant. Shanghai Meida Construction and Decoration Company undertook the role of general contractor. Synergis Shui On Property Management was actively involved from the onset of the project.

One of the bigger challenges in delivering the sustainable design was to appoint a suitable contractor to take on this project. Very few contractors in China have knowledge of LEED, and it is certainly not part of their standard business practices. Among the tendering companies, Shanghai Meida Construction and Decoration Company demonstrated a strong commitment to educate its team to become an integral part of the LEED process. Recognizing the challenging learning curve for the general contractor, the project team involved Meida early in the project to aid in the understanding of the LEED point system. This knowledge helped Meida to manage LEED-related resources and paperwork, to make valuable contributions to the process, and to resolve challenges inherent in implementation.

GREEN BUILDING DESIGN AND CONSTRUCTION

Green building design and construction approaches for the Shui On headquarters centered on energy and water efficiency, indoor air quality, and waste reduction. The project's siting in an exceptionally dense urban setting was also helpful in qualifying the retrofit under LEED.

Approach and Implementation

Arup was the sustainable design and LEED consultant for this project. To acquire LEED-CI certification at the Silver level, sufficient points must be awarded in six categories—sustainable sites, water efficiency, energy and atmosphere, materials and resources, indoor environment quality, and innovation in design:

▸▸ **SUSTAINABLE SITES**. Because Shui On Plaza is located in the central area of Shanghai near the South Huangpi Road Metro station, the building is able to offer convenient connectivity to communal facilities and public transportation. Additionally, the site offers all parking spaces as preferred parking for car pools and van pools to encourage use of public transportation and reduce carbon emissions. Thus, the location of the project and its provision of preferred parking for vehicle pools earned credits for LEED certification with no added expense. Because of the exceptional community connectivity in the area surrounding the offices of Shui On Land, the project was also able to claim an exemplary performance credit under the LEED-CI certification scheme without any added expense. The project is located at the heart of the Shanghai Commercial District Center and enjoys exceptionally rich public transportation services, a feature that reduces vehicle usage and emissions, and therefore is environmentally beneficial. Eight bus lines and a subway line within a quarter mile of Shui On Plaza provide more than double the daily transit rides required for exemplary performance under LEED-CI.

▸▸ **WATER EFFICIENCY**. Several design methods were adopted to reduce water use. Water-efficient fixtures were installed in all pantry areas and lavatories, including low-flush urinals and toilets and faucets with sensor controls. These devices have helped to sharply reduce unnecessary water usage throughout Shui On's offices. The installation of water-efficient faucets, urinals, and toilets reduced water use at the Shui On offices by 41 percent.

▸▸ **ENERGY AND ATMOSPHERE**. Shui On Land and the design team set a very high energy efficiency target from the outset of the project. The design strategies sought to optimize the fundamental energy system performance, in compliance with LEED requirements. Energy efficiency and employee comfort were enhanced by the extensive use of occupant temperature controls. The HVAC system was designed to achieve enhanced operating economies. Temperature control mechanisms modulate airflow based on occupancy and interior temperature, rather than limiting HVAC operation to on and off settings. The HVAC plan allows temperature and outdoor airflow to be regulated according to interior building conditions, minimizing energy usage while maintaining occupant comfort and healthful indoor air quality. In addition, 90 percent of the equipment and appliances are Energy Star rated.

▸▸ **LIGHTING EFFICIENCY PLAYED A KEY ROLE** in the renovation of the Shui On Land offices. Efficient lighting was designed to allow lower lighting power density (the wattage used per square meter or square foot of space) when appropriate, and programmable zoned lighting controllers are available for these light sources. In each private office located in the perimeter zone, daylight and occupancy sensors were installed to minimize energy use by artificial lighting and to maximize the use of natural daylight.

▸▸ **THROUGHOUT THE PROJECT**, daylight sensors were installed within 15 feet of windows to keep interior desktop illumination at a fixed level of 350 lux. Task lights were supplied to each staff member. The smart lighting system in combination with the extensive use of natural light provide a state-of-the-art working environment that optimizes occupant comfort and energy savings simultaneously. Together these strategies helped the Shui On Land offices to achieve lighting efficiency superior to that mandated under LEED.

▸▸ MATERIALS AND RESOURCES. Construction waste recycling and the selection of regionally produced materials were additional steps undertaken to obtain LEED-CI certification for the Shui On Land headquarters. Ninety-five percent of the waste (by weight) produced from this project was recycled instead of being sent to a landfill. Through a careful procurement process, 78 percent of total building materials, by cost, were purchased regionally, thus reducing transportation activities and associated pollution. Regionally sourced materials utilized in the project included marble, carpeting, furniture, and wood.

▸▸ INDOOR ENVIRONMENTAL QUALITY. To achieve the LEED-CI Silver rating, maintenance of indoor air quality is a crucial factor. During the construction stage, several measures were adopted to control indoor air quality, including setting up dedicated space for painting, air duct protection, dust control practices, dedicated ventilation of the project space, materials protection, and site enclosure for safety and cleanliness. These measures during the construction stage minimize the construction residues that may endanger the health of the construction team or damage the indoor air quality later on.

For ongoing observation of indoor air quality, CO_2 sensors are provided in all densely occupied spaces, such as the conference room, lounge, and training areas, to monitor CO_2 concentration levels while controlling the ventilation airflow rate without compromising the tenant comfort. Additionally, thermal comfort surveys are carried out periodically, and building operations are subject to adjustment when warranted by survey results. This strategy makes efficient use of energy while maintaining the well-being of employees. All interior materials—including adhesives, sealants, paints, and coatings—were selected for their low chemical emissions, to improve the indoor air quality.

Achievements

The renovated headquarters of Shui On Land demonstrate significant energy savings: 41 percent reduction in water usage through high-efficiency fixtures in toilets and pantries, 15 percent savings in electricity usage from office appliances, and 33 percent savings in electricity usage from lighting. The indoor CO_2 level has been reduced by 21 percent. The distinctive design features provide employees with a progressive, exciting, and comfortable working environment.

Figure 1

Approximate Payback Calculations for Key Features

Green Feature	Added Cost Per Square Meter (RMB)	Savings Per Square Meter Per Year (RMB)	Payback Period (Years)
High-Performance Lighting (Task Lights, Daylight Sensors, Occupancy Sensors)	44	10.1	4
CO_2 Sensors	9.6	1.92	5
Water-Saving Sanitary Fixtures	2	0.6	3.3
Total	55.6	12.62	4.4

FINANCING

The total construction cost for the 5,200 square meter (55,970 square foot) office renovation was RMB 26.66 million ($3.9 million). Green features added approximately RMB 289,100 ($42,300) to the project, increasing costs by roughly 1.1 percent. The LEED-related additional costs, approximate operating savings, and calculated payback periods are detailed in figure 1.

BUILDING OPERATION, COMPANY MANAGEMENT, AND EMPLOYEE FEEDBACK

The newly renovated office spaces on the 25th and 26th floors have been very well received by the staff of Shui On Land. The renovated spaces tangibly communicate the company's commitment to sustainable development with designs that effectively reduce the consumption of energy and water. The staff responded most positively to the extensive daylighting, improved air quality, controllability of lighting and thermal systems, and other strategies that helped to transform and enhance the working environment.

To further increase employees' understanding of the renovation project, Arup has helped to formulate an education pamphlet for Shui On staff members on the LEED-CI process and features. The pamphlet is made available online for staff to become familiar with the process and sustainability strategies adopted.

Shui On Land has also established a sustainable development committee to formulate and promote action plans for resource management and sustainability in the company. As well, Shui On Land has initiated a formal green office project that encourages employees to create a safer and more energy-efficient living and working environment through energy conservation in their daily life and work.

EXPERIENCE GAINED

The Shui On Land headquarters renovation was one of the first LEED-CI projects undertaken in China. Key lessons experienced by the team were the following:

▶▶ **INTEGRATED DESIGN** is important. Shui On Land has found that active collaboration at the early stages in a project is the optimal way to learn and apply LEED processes and to ensure greater control of buildability. All key project disciplines, including design, construction, and property management, were engaged in the development and implementation of the renovation. The integrated design approach also proved instrumental on earlier LEED projects developed by Shui On Land.

▶▶ **CONTRACTOR INVOLVEMENT AND TRAINING** is key. One of the bigger challenges was to appoint a suitable contractor. In order to successfully complete the project, it was necessary to recognize the learning curve faced by the general contractor and to involve the contractor early in the project to facilitate its understanding of the LEED system. Early involvement and education provided by the project team helped the general contractor to manage LEED-related resources and paperwork, to make valuable contributions to the process, and to resolve challenges inherent in implementation.

▶▶ **PROJECT SITING** can facilitate LEED compliance. Shui On Plaza is located in an extremely dense section of Shanghai and enjoys exceptionally rich transportation connections. These locational features won LEED certification points at no cost to Shui On, including an innovation credit for community connectivity. Projects which, like the Shui On Land headquarters, are located in dense urban settings are especially well-positioned to earn green certification.

▶▶ **HIGH-PERFORMANCE LIGHTING** greatly contributed to energy savings. The interior lighting design integrated task lights, occupancy sensors and daylight sensors. These approaches reduced lighting usage to 25 percent below levels allowed by the American Society of Heating, Refrigerating, and Air-Conditioning Engineers under Standard 90.1-2004, the lighting efficiency level required by LEED. Together, lighting strategies have yielded a 33 percent savings relative to conventional lighting and could save almost half of prerenovation lighting energy consumption. The design has not increased lighting fixture costs; added costs derived from the design and installation of daylight and occupancy sensors, which are not normally used in an office environment. It is anticipated that additional design and installation costs for green lighting could be paid back within four years because of the substantial associated energy savings.

▶▶ **MANY GREEN FEATURES** did not add costs, and all added costs are expected to be paid back from operating savings in less than five years. By emphasizing sustainable and green concepts, most green features were integrated seamlessly into the design and construction protocols, material choices, and purchases. Most of these efforts did not increase cost but reflected the use of a consistent strategy in choosing how to make the project more sustainable. Major added costs came from the use of high-tech devices, including daylight, occupancy, and CO_2 sensors, and task-lighting and water-saving fixtures. These features contribute to energy savings and staff working efficiency, and generate significant operating cost savings. As a result, the added costs are expected to be recovered within a reasonable period from operating savings.

Vincent Cheng, LEED AP, is an associate director of Ove Arup & Partners HK Ltd and the leader of the Building Sustainability Group of Arup Hong Kong. He is responsible for all LEED and sustainable building projects in Arup's East Asia Region. Cheng has been practicing as a consultant of sustainable building with Arup since 1997, specializing in building environmental design and evaluation.

Development Team

DEVELOPER:
Shui On Land

ARCHITECT:
Gensler

LIGHTING DESIGNER:
Bi Hope

MEP ENGINEERS:
Daniel Chan & Associates Ltd

SUSTAINABILITY AND LEED CONSULTANT:
Arup

GENERAL CONTRACTOR:
Shanghai Meida Construction and Decoration Company

PROPERTY MANAGEMENT:
Synergis Shui On Property Management Company, Ltd.

Transwestern's Southeast regional headquarters occupies 18,000 square feet of space on the ninth floor of Tower Place 200 in Atlanta.

CASE STUDY • TRANSWESTERN

Transwestern Regional Headquarters
ATLANTA, GEORGIA

Transwestern manages and leases over 135 million square feet (12.5 million square meters) of commercial real estate throughout the United States. The company's portfolio is broad and represents an opportunity to create significant financial savings through sound real estate management. Because the real estate industry has an enormous impact on the environment, from energy consumed and greenhouse gases emitted, to the amount of waste generated during construction and the daily operation of facilities, Transwestern believes that it is uniquely positioned to develop the business case for sustainability and to create, renovate, and operate cost-effective and functional green properties. The breadth of the company's portfolio allows Transwestern to deliver significant economies in energy consumption, environmental efficiency, and real estate operations to its clients.

In late 2007, Transwestern relocated its Southeast regional headquarters to a 17,838-square-foot (1,657-square-meter) suite on the ninth floor of Atlanta's Tower Place 200. Constructed in 1998 at 3348 Peachtree Road NE, Tower Place 200 is a 14-story building measuring 260,000 gross square feet (24,155 square meters). The project is leased and managed by Transwestern and owned by Transwestern Investment Company.

In 2008 the Atlanta team, with the backing and support of Transwestern's national sustainability services team, began work on a sustainable renovation project for its corporate office. In keeping with Transwestern's philosophy on energy efficiency and the environment, the Tower Place 200 renovation launched a new policy that all new Transwestern corporate office space would achieve certification under the Leadership in Energy and Environmental Design for Commercial Interiors (LEED-CI) protocol. The reasoning behind the policy was simple. Because the firm was already pursuing LEED certification on more than 13 million square feet of new and existing commercial space for its clients, it was only fitting that its own space be LEED certified. Transwestern also wanted to demonstrate that it was possible to achieve LEED certification on a strict budget, because financial discipline is important to many of the company's clients and because many office occupants incorrectly believe that green certification is too expensive to be attained by most firms. The Atlanta regional office renovation was therefore designed explicitly to be a cost-effective green office retrofit.

Transwestern assigned a seasoned in-house sustainability team to the property and began assessing the office space in the context of the six LEED categories: Sustainable Sites, Water Efficiency, Energy and Atmosphere, Materials and Resources, Indoor Environmental Quality, and Innovation in Design. Transwestern served as the project lead. Architectural firm Veendendaal|Cave and Malone Construction Company were retained to assist in the project. The project was managed by Transwestern's national sustainability services team, coupled with the local engineering, management and marketing teams. Transwestern maintained a detailed credit-by-credit analysis as the project moved through the LEED-CI documentation process. As this case study was being written, the certification application was being completed.

SUSTAINABLE SITES

Transwestern looked into the physical conditions of Tower Place 200 to make improvements intended to achieve the goal of attaining two credits under this category. Tower Place 200 is one of the most highly regarded properties in the Buckhead submarket because of the building's excellent accessibility to MARTA, Atlanta's light-rail system, and BUC, the Buckhead business bus line, both of which have stops within walking distance of the building. The proximity to mass transit allowed Transwestern to claim a LEED-CI credit for alternative transportation access. The project is also located within a densely developed urban area; is within walking distance of Lenox Square Mall, Phipps Plaza, other area attractions, and shopping; and houses several Class A amenities, such as a café, a sundries shop, and a conference center. Density and proximity to community amenities earned another LEED-CI credit for community connectivity.

WATER EFFICIENCY

Transwestern analyzed existing fixtures to determine water efficiency. Initial calculations indicated that water usage was 20 percent in excess of the LEED-required baseline, leaving many opportunities for improvement. The original toilets were designed for 4 gallons per flush; a new diaphragm retrofit reduced water consumption to 2.4 gallons per flush.

With additional state-of-the art plumbing fixtures installed—0.5-gallon-per-flush urinals and 0.5-gallon-per-minute aerators on all bathroom and break room faucets—two credits were achieved. Overall, this renovation reduced water flow by 2 gallons per minute. Based on LEED calculations, this indicated water efficiency is at least 35 percent below the LEED baseline, which will provide savings estimated at approximately $200 per month.

ENERGY EFFICIENCY

Georgia code requires 1 watt per square foot for all office space. Previous lighting in Tower Place 200 was 1.5 times higher than the required amount. To achieve better results, Transwestern had to first analyze the life expectancy of current light fixtures. In keeping with cost-effective and sustainable renovations, Transwestern chose to keep its three-tube fixtures and eliminate the middle fluorescent tubes throughout the building to decrease the wattage being emitted. This measure, while cost-effective, did not receive a LEED point because it did not comply with LEED requirements, which called for a replacement of the entire fixture. Nonetheless, the company was able to reduce its electric load for lighting by one-third, as well as improve workspace lighting levels for employees.

A new office policy was instated to purchase Energy Star–rated equipment in all eligible areas. Most existing computers and monitors already met this specification. The areas targeted included new kitchen equipment such as refrigerators and microwaves, as well as office equipment such as computers and printers. These appliances will use approximately 35 percent less electricity than standard appliances. All future purchases will also comply with the Energy Star policy in order to continue the reduction of the office plug load and optimize energy performance. The decision to utilize Energy Star equipment in all eligible areas reduced utility bills and met LEED-CI requirements for energy optimization.

MATERIALS AND RESOURCES

Waste recycling and resource reuse initiatives were developed to support application for several LEED-CI certification credits.

▸▸ **WASTE STREAM RECYCLING**. In order to reduce its amount of landfill waste, Transwestern began by rebidding its waste hauling services for the building. Waste Management was selected from three service providers for its ability to offer a single-stream recycling plan. Tower Place 200 was able to recycle 75 percent of its waste stream with little effort on the part of tenants and at a lower cost than with the previous hauler. Single-stream waste recycling provides off-site separation of all paper, bottles, aluminum, batteries, cardboard, and other trash.

▸▸ **CONSTRUCTION WASTE RECYCLING**. Working with Malone Construction Company, Transwestern was also successful in recycling more than 50 percent of its construction waste. Interface, an Atlanta-based carpet company with a strong national sustainability program, provided free recycling of all carpets removed prior to the buildout, and all scrap metal and paper from the project were removed by a local recycler.

▸▸ **MATERIALS REUSE**. Transwestern expects to achieve two credits related to the reuse of resources. More than 40 percent of interior nonstructural components from the previous tenant were reused. For example, the ceilings, interior wall partitions, interior windows, and all office doors were kept in place from the original design. The majority of office furniture and electrical equipment was transported from Transwestern's previous office

space to the new space; this achieved an additional reuse credit while cost-effectively furnishing the office.

INDOOR ENVIRONMENTAL QUALITY

Tower Place 200's office space is expected to achieve eight credits overall for its efforts to improve indoor environmental quality. Low-emitting materials, thermal comfort, lighting, and air quality are all considered crucial factors in attaining LEED-CI status.

▸▸ **LOW-EMITTING MATERIALS**. Products with low emissions of volatile organic compounds (VOCs), such as paints, coatings, and sealants, were purchased to reduce the odor of the buildout and ensure higher air quality for Transwestern's employees. In addition, low-VOC carpet was utilized to match the tenant's pattern selection for a minimal additional cost. Cubicle walls and furnishings were all chosen to meet the low-emitting requirements of LEED and, in conjunction with the other low-VOC materials, have produced a productive workspace.

▸▸ **THERMAL COMFORT AND MONITORING**. To further ensure an efficient and comfortable workspace, a thermal comfort survey was conducted after Transwestern moved in. The purpose of the survey was to determine compliance with American Society of Heating, Refrigerating, and Air-Conditioning Engineers (ASHRAE) Standard 55-2004, as well as to establish the level of comfort valued by employees. The survey indicated a majority of Transwestern employees were comfortable with temperature conditions in the office. The space continues to be monitored by several sensors connected to the building's digital controls system and alerts property management staff if conditions change drastically from the appropriate temperature range. Individual tenant complaints are also promptly checked to ensure proper functioning of the mechanical system throughout the space.

▸▸ **LIGHTING SYSTEMS CONTROLLABILITY**. In an additional effort to improve the working environment, Transwestern utilized occupant-controlled lighting as a critical element in the design of the office space. Every office was allocated at least one light switch to control overhead lighting. Several offices have added task lighting for supplemental luminescence. The interior of the space is composed of cubicles with overhead lighting, with a light switch for every 1,500-square-foot section of the office, as well as adjustable task lighting at each desk.

The design was originally intended to achieve at least one point for natural light. All offices have floor-to-ceiling windows, as well as glass doors to ensure that daylight also reaches cubicle workspaces. However, daylighting calculations indicated that the property's window tinting was too dark to transmit the minimal levels of natural light that LEED required. It was decided that changing out the windows to achieve this credit would not be cost-effective and the credit therefore was not pursued.

Another credit not pursued related to views from seated spaces. While outer offices offer pleasant views of the Buckhead and Atlanta skyline, the interior cubicles utilize high panels, obstructing views for those who work in cubicles as well as those who work in interior offices. These high panels were selected based on personnel's desire for sound reduction and privacy to be taken into greatest consideration in the new office space. If the company had gone against employee recommendations and chosen a lower panel, daylight factors would have been improved and the view credit might have been attainable. In this case, however, employee preferences concerning acoustics and privacy were considered of paramount importance.

▸▸ **INNOVATION IN DESIGN**. Transwestern has implemented comprehensive educational programs for employees and visitors to teach others about its LEED-CI renovation. Signage is displayed to indicate water and energy savings where appropriate, brochures are available at the reception desk, and a presentation

on the sustainable design and implementation of the space is run on a flat-screen television display. This effort is eligible for a LEED Innovation in Design credit. The use of LEED Accredited Professionals in principal project roles also is expected to qualify for a LEED Innovation in Design credit.

PROJECT OUTCOMES

The Transwestern project has applied for LEED-CI certification at the Certified level. Based on studies by the U.S. Green Building Council and Transwestern, Transwestern's national sustainability team and the Atlanta office LEED-CI team were confident that upon completing the certification process, the firm would experience less team member absenteeism, a generally happier workforce, and significantly higher team member satisfaction with the new work environment. Employee comfort and satisfaction levels have indeed increased since the completion of the retrofit. Tenants have also shown interest in the company's sustainability goals for the space and the building.

Demonstrating that green retrofits can be achieved cost-effectively was a key goal of the Tower 200 renovation. The renovation of Transwestern's offices was accomplished at the same cost as a conventional retrofit performed at the same time in the Buckhead submarket. Transwestern's original project budget did not contemplate green features, but careful budgeting and the respecification of fixtures and materials to use environmentally friendly products allowed the project to achieve LEED-CI objectives for no added cost.

EXPERIENCE GAINED

The sustainability and design teams retained during the process came away with several valuable lessons that can be passed along to clients as well as Transwestern additional regional corporate offices as they begin the LEED-CI process:

▸▸ **GREEN SPECIFICATIONS** should be developed prior to project design. Ideally, user specifications for LEED improvements should be developed prior to the design phase of any LEED-CI building, through the use of a LEED charrette. A LEED charrette allows the design and contracting team to meet, communicate a clear vision and

Transwestern recycled over 50 percent of its construction waste, and reused over 40 percent of interior nonstructural components from the previous tenant.

model for the certification process, and brainstorm ways to meet the owner's goals. For this particular renovation, the LEED certification process began near the completion of the design phase. The late start created early obstacles for the team, including missed credit opportunities, and the lack of a fully coordinated team structure that could have been produced through a LEED charrette.

As a result, the early stages of the Tower 200 renovation were marked by inefficiencies and challenges. The LEED consultants, in conjunction with the architects, had to reissue the construction documents prior to buildout to include updated specifications for the contactor. The architect resubmitted additional drawings with detailed notes to ensure the final design was as sustainable as possible, including the reasoning behind each credit and renovation. Earlier incorporation of LEED requirements into the project design would have produced a more efficient flow of work, minimized the need to revise construction drawings, and prevented the resulting delays in procurement and construction.

▸▸ **IN-HOUSE EXPERTISE AND STRONG ORGANIZATION** are critical. Despite the late start of the process, Transwestern was able overcome its early obstacles in pursuing LEED certification. With proficient leadership, clear channels of communication, and cohesive teamwork, Transwestern was able to complete its renovation plans and implement its greening program without additional complications. Having in-house team members experienced in the LEED-CI process was critical to the successful completion of the renovation. The three LEED Accredited Professionals on the team offered in-depth familiarity with the LEED certification process that helped ease numerous challenges along the way. Experience with Tower Place 200 confirmed Transwestern's belief that the LEED-CI process requires proper planning and that the team in charge must have a solid understanding of the LEED requirements before and during the development of a design plan. It is also imperative that efforts be meticulously coordinated between the sustainability team and the design and construction teams.

▸▸ **COST-BENEFIT ASSESSMENT** is critical at the outset. During this learning process, Transwestern's team analyzed every possible credit from a cost-benefit standpoint; it was important that every credit was assessed on the basis of initial costs and on a life-cycle assessment for energy and water savings, and then finalized and submitted using the completed cost-benefit analysis. As noted above, Transwestern chose not to fully pursue credits for lighting, daylighting, and views because the cost-benefit tradeoffs did not meet company needs.

▸▸ **DETAILED RECORD KEEPING** is a key element of green certification. Tower Place 200 had to request documentation stating the amount of recycled material and trash it provided to companies like Waste Management and Interface throughout the project. Material Safety Data sheets were also used by the LEED consultants to track the VOC levels of all products to ensure the purchase and use of environmentally friendly products for the building. The team learned that early and consistent record keeping is the key to making the certification process run as smoothly and successfully as possible.

▸▸ **LEED DOCUMENTATION** and a certification application can be assembled for no added cost. Transwestern did not incur any additional cost over the original budget. That budget did not take into consideration any LEED-CI costs, but the sustainability team was able to revamp the budget using existing figures to make recommendations and modifications to the original plan that would allow the achievement of green certification goals. These changes did not add expense to the base budget amount but instead required the respecification of items to include more environmentally friendly products. In the end, LEED-CI implementation at Tower Place 200 had a net-zero cost. The use of rigorous budgeting and cost-benefit analysis early in the project cycle was integral in maintaining budget discipline.

Development Team

ARCHITECT:
Veenendaal|Cave

GENERAL CONTRACTOR:
Malone Construction

COMMISSIONING AGENT:
Transwestern

LEED CONSULTANT:
Transwestern's in-house sustainability team

CASE STUDY · KEVIN MILLER AND HOWARD PENDER
Trevor Pearcey House

CANBERRA, AUSTRALIA

Trevor Pearcey House is a 19-year-old, two-story commercial building in Fern Hill Technology Park, Bruce ACT (Australian Capital Territory), a northwest suburb of Canberra, Australia's capital. The 1,100-square-meter (11,840-square-foot) building is the new head office for Australian Ethical Investment (AEI), a financial services company specializing in environmental and socially responsible investment.

In 2007, the refurbishment received a 6-star Green Star rating from the Green Building Council of Australia, the highest rating obtainable. It represents a level of sustainability indicating world leadership in environmental design. Trevor Pearcey House is the first building in the ACT and the third in Australia to achieve a 6-star Green Star rating.

Equally important, Trevor Pearcey House combined cost control with green practices. The project was the first privately funded project to receive the top Green Star rating. Fully funded by AEI, the green refurbishment was achieved using conventional low-technology design principles on a conventional budget. Initially, AEI was aiming for a 5-star Green Star rating; it was not thought that a 6-star rating

Among the goals incorporated into the retrofit of the Trevor Pearcey House was the 75 percent reduction in energy use compared with prerenovation use. Energy-saving strategies included solar load reduction features, building envelope changes, use of a natural ventilation system, and efficient lighting.

was achievable because of the anticipated cost. To control cost, AEI wanted a simple environmentally sustainable building and was not interested in buying Green Star points through technology.

Trevor Pearcey House was typical of many low-rise commercial buildings produced throughout Australia in recent decades, which frequently represent the poorest level of environmental design. Without mandatory requirements for environmental performance until 2007, most of Australia's low-rise commercial buildings are little more than sheds or uninsulated boxes. Because the aesthetics of these buildings do not lend themselves to refurbishment, they are not valued and frequently face demolition.

Part of the philosophy of AEI is to promote environmental awareness in business projects, and the finished Trevor Pearcey refurbishment was intended to become part of AEI's investment portfolio. AEI's objective was to create a comfortable, healthy, and productive work environment for its staff. The refurbished Trevor Pearcey House serves as a teaching tool, engaging and educating staff and visitors about how environmental buildings work and function, even in an undistinguished, low-rise commercial setting.

DEVELOPMENT PROCESS

The design team worked with AEI and specialized consultants to prioritize environmental objectives in the extensive refurbishment of Trevor Pearcey House. The design team developed the project goals and engaged in a collaborative process with AEI, specialized consultants, and construction team members to meet the required benchmarks. Key aspects of the design and planning process included managing building material recycling and reuse, and setting the refurbishment budget.

Managing Building Material Recycling and Reuse

Because there was an ongoing emphasis on reusing site materials and on specifying recycled content for building materials, careful collaboration between the management, design and engineering, and construction teams was required throughout the project. A charrette-type process formed, wherein frequent meetings between AEI, the construction team, and the design team helped to solve problems that arose during the refurbishment and to identify previously unseen opportunities.

Reusing materials requires accurate measuring, quantifying, and scheduling before reuse. The labor-intensive nature of reusing site materials required a higher than standard labor component for both documentation and construction.

The extent of the proposed recycling and reuse went beyond the previous experience of the project team. Initially, no one was sure how much could be reused, how difficult the process would be, or what the cost implications of significant recycling and reuse would be. In the end, over 80 percent (by weight) of the removed building materials were reused on site or recycled; a significantly higher figure than initially anticipated.

Setting the Refurbishment Budget

AEI's environmental commitment put green obligations on equal footing with standard budget and program constraints. Although the project had a fixed budget, it had a flexible way of achieving the refurbishment requirements. Therefore savings achieved in one area, such as reduced material supply cost, offset areas of increased cost, such as increased labor costs incurred in disassembling or recycling existing materials.

GREEN BUILDING DESIGN AND CONSTRUCTION

The refurbished Trevor Pearcey House was developed to minimize energy usage through improving the building fabric, employing natural ventilation, and using natural lighting. Energy savings in these categories were achieved by the application of low-technology measures:

▸▸ Insulating the outside of the facade;

▸▸ Insulating the roof;

▸▸ Reorganizing and modifying sun shading;

▸▸ Replacing fixed windows with double-glazed, operable windows;

▸▸ Exposing thermal mass on the building interior;

▸▸ Improving daylight penetration; and

▸▸ Reusing materials.

A range of additional environmental initiatives covered additional areas of building design and operation, including management, waste disposal, transport, water use, and indoor environmental quality.

Reducing Energy Use

The refurbished Trevor Pearcey House was designed to achieve energy usage 47 percent below the 5-star Australian Building Greenhouse Rating (ABGR), and approximately 75 percent below prerenovation usage (figure 1). Energy-saving strategies included solar load reduction features, building envelope changes, the use of a natural ventilation system, and efficient lighting.

REDUCING SOLAR LOAD

The Trevor Pearcey House is located in the southeastern quadrant of Australia. For commercial buildings in this climate zone, it is important to prevent direct solar access, to reduce the heat load on the building. The existing shading on Trevor Pearcey House was inefficient. Solar shading was improved by changing the material used on the solar shades, relocating existing shading panels, and adding additional panels. In addition, adjustable blinds were installed for all windows, and all workstations in open areas were moved 4 feet (1.22 meters) away from exterior windows to avoid extremes of temperature and glare.

INSULATING THE BUILDING ENVELOPE

The existing structure had inadequate insulation that provided minimal internal protection against fluctuating external temperatures. All windows were single-glazed with fixed panes, making them a key source of energy loss. Most of the existing structure had an R value of 1 or less.

To improve the building's energy performance, insulation was installed on the outside of the exterior walls and on the inside of the roof. For the exterior walls, the R value was improved to 3.7 and for the roof it was improved to 6. The windows were then replaced with operable, double-opening, double-glazed windows.

EXPOSING INTERIOR THERMAL MASS

To further aid in the moderation of interior temperatures, the suspended ceilings around the perimeter of the ground floor were removed, exposing the thermal mass of the underside of the first-floor concrete slab. The resulting thermally efficient surface—the exposed concrete heats and cools slowly, protecting the building interior from temperature swings—meant that water-filled radiators added to the perimeter of the floor plate on both levels could easily provide sufficient heat without any supplementary heating. During winter the lowest recorded internal temperature was 16°C (61°F).

UTILIZING NATURAL VENTILATION SYSTEMS

The refurbishment at Trevor Pearcey House was designed to be naturally ventilated, allowing for individual control of comfort settings by occupants. The ventilation strategy includes the use of high and low window openings, cross-ventilation, and stack ventilation—the use of interior ductwork, stairwells, and chimneys and similar structures to regulate airflow and temperature—with fan assistance to draw out hot air when necessary. The quantity of natural ventilation is adequate to ensure that appropriate levels of fresh air are maintained within the building, without the need for recirculation.

Additionally, the building utilizes a nighttime purge ventilation system to cool temperatures in the building by drawing out warm air at night. The system uses computer-controlled automatic windows and vents (located at the top of the ventilation stacks) that are connected to a roof-mounted weather station; this system uses a seasonal control to turn off heating in summer and prevent night purging in winter. Additionally, the ventilation stacks have exhaust fans to aid in drawing out warm air if internal temperatures do not fall quickly enough during the nighttime purge ventilation.

The use of a natural ventilation system, in addition to thermal mass heating and cooling, limits the need to use

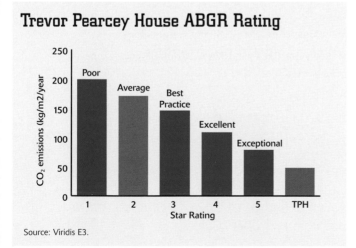

Figure 1

Trevor Pearcey House ABGR Rating

Source: Viridis E3.

"active" mechanical ventilation systems. Initially, mechanical components (radiant panel cooling and heat recovery systems) were designed to be used as a backup and enhancement of the passive systems. However, these systems were not pursued due to their cost and because thermal modeling showed that the building worked well without the additional systems.

Some refrigerated air-conditioning capacity is retained within the building for specific internal rooms that do not function adequately under the natural ventilation system. On the first floor, there is a ducted air-conditioning system for backup cooling. This system is locked in the off position and may be switched on only when there is a consensus of staff on that floor. The print and copy rooms have their own separately ducted exhaust system, to remove airborne contaminants.

UTILIZING EFFICIENT LIGHTING STRATEGIES

The layout of Trevor Pearcey House is conducive to daylighting. The atrium on the first floor provides natural light deep into the open-plan office. In many parts of the building, daylight can enter from two sides of the structure, with additional daylighting from the combined light columns and ventilation stacks that run from the ground floor to the roof. Appropriate shading has been applied to each elevation, in order to reduce direct solar gain while still obtaining indirect natural light.

As a base lighting system, office areas have been provided with high-efficiency, low-brightness light fixtures with T5 fluorescent lamps. This lighting system uses about 40 percent of the energy of a system based on a T8 lamp and an even smaller percentage of the energy used by a T12 lamp–based system. To minimize energy consumption, the base-level lighting is low; it can be supplemented with task lighting in individual work areas.

Lighting in the building is manually switched, and an automated override control turns off lights after hours. This control has calendar function programming, which can reduce energy use during weekends and on holidays. Use of lights outside normal business hours is limited to two-hour periods. Lighting is zoned within the building: perimeter lights next to windows and adjacent to the atrium run on separate switches to save energy when adequate daylight is available.

PURCHASING GREEN POWER

Since occupying the building, AEI has purchased 100 percent of its electricity from renewable sources. In fiscal year 2006–2007 (which represented only a partial year of occupancy because AEI moved into the new office in March), AEI paid roughly A$5,000 ($4,195) premium for electricity from renewable sources on 76,248 kWh of electricity. In subsequent years, AEI estimates that it will use less electricity overall, which will reduce or eliminate the premium. To further reduce the company's environmental footprint, AEI purchases carbon offsets for all of its corporate transport, recently offsetting 108 tons of CO_2 emissions.

Reducing Water Use

Water saving in the building was the simplest to accomplish of the green initiatives. Existing 3.2 gallons per flush (12 liters per flush) single-flush toilet cisterns were replaced with 2.4/1.2 gallons per flush (9/4.5 liters per flush) dual-flush cisterns, achieving a 56 percent reduction in water use for the toilets. Because of piping limitations in the building, a greater reduction in flush rate was not possible. To reduce potable water use, two 790-gallon (3,000-liter) graywater tanks were installed for use with the toilets.

The piping limitations in the building precluded the use of waterless urinals. Instead, semi-waterless systems, which combine a waterless urinal cartridge with an automated low-volume flush system, were utilized. All tap and shower fixtures were replaced with low-flow fittings. To provide ongoing monitoring of water use, AEI is using a simple, low-cost, Web-based leak detection system that is monitored by staff.

Figure 2

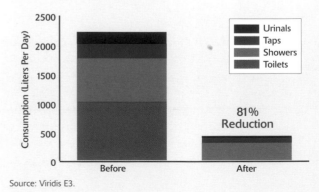

Water Consumption Before and After Renovation

81% Reduction

Source: Viridis E3.

The reduction in potable water use has been projected to be more than 80 percent through these initiatives. Current figures show that water use in the building is less than expected (figure 2). The building's total water use over the past year was roughly 28,800 gallons (109 kiloliters), which equates to 2.43 gallons per square foot annually (0.1 kilo-liter per square meter). This is a 90 percent reduction over the Canberra average, and 68 percent better than the National Australian Built Environment Rating System (NABERS) 5-star benchmark for Canberra.

Interior Design Innovations

The useful life of a typical contemporary fit-out in the Canberra metropolitan area is two to five years. After that, design elements and layouts may be changed significantly. AEI wanted to limit changes to interior design elements; therefore the designers avoided unnecessary additions to the interior finishes and internal structure of the building, and worked primarily with reused material from the existing interiors. The Trevor Pearcey House refurbishment made significant use of recycled and repurposed products and materials from within the building, as well as products and materials recycled from other locations. The architects also incorporated low-emitting materials in the design to enhance indoor air quality.

MATERIAL REUSE AND RECYCLING

The refurbishment demonstrated significant environmental innovation in the reuse of materials beyond that recognized by the Green Star protocol. The building contained a substantial fit-out (buildout) that was carefully assessed for reuse potential. In the demolition phase reusable items were carefully deconstructed and removed for reuse within the new fit-out. This high level of reuse reduced the quantity of waste sent to landfills. Materials that could not be reused, including existing windows, carpeting, floor tiles, and light fittings, were recycled for use elsewhere.

REUSED MATERIALS

Reused items included glass blocks used for walls; partition framing; plasterboard; doors, door frames, and door hardware; insulation; ductwork; electrical cabling; outlet and light switch plates; joinery (cabinetry and woodwork); sinks; and the hot-water tank, which was fitted into a more efficient, evacuated-tube solar hot-water system. Eight computer workstations and 20 conference chairs left by the previous tenant were utilized in the fit-out. All existing carpet tiles were lifted and combined with additional recycled carpet tiles.

REPURPOSED MATERIALS

Additional on-site items were repurposed in the refurbishment:

▶▶ **RETURN-AIR GRILLES** from the old heating, ventilating, and air-conditioning system were reused as air relief grilles in the internal ground-floor offices and meeting rooms.

▶▶ **LIGHT DIFFUSERS** from the existing light fittings were reused for skylights under the ventilation stacks, to provide light to ground-floor offices.

▶▶ **THE BICYCLE ENCLOSURE** was fabricated from recycled metal removed from the building, including shading panels, structural steel support frames, and steel mesh.

▶▶ **RAISED COMPUTER FLOOR TILES** were reused as artwork and incorporated into a backsplash for a cooktop.

▶▶ **METAL-BACKED COMPUTER FLOOR TILES** were recovered and used to create a number of artworks that are located around the building. The artworks show a time series of environmental degradation worldwide, such as coral bleaching of the Great Barrier Reef and deforestation of the Amazon—events that AEI was created to help redress.

MATERIALS RECYCLED FROM OFF SITE

Many materials used in the refurbishment were salvaged off site:

▶▶ **ENTRY MATS** were made from old car tires.

▶▶ **CARPET TILES** were made from reconditioned tiles that had been removed from other buildings, steam cleaned, shaved, and then overprinted with a new pattern. This process extends the useful life of carpet tiles that otherwise would have gone to a landfill.

▶▶ **RECYCLED TIMBER** was used for flooring, cladding, and the reception-area countertop.

▸ **DISCARDED PALLETS** and timber cable reels were used to construct the wall behind the reception desk and a feature wall in the ground-floor corridor. The pallets were of low quality and odd sizes and would have been likely to end up in a landfill. A representation of AEI's corporate symbol (three interconnected circles) was formed from the cable reel ends.

▸ **DESKS WERE BROUGHT** from AEI's existing offices, and additional furniture was sourced from government used-furniture supplies.

As the project progressed, the recycling and reuse process became quite competitive. It became a challenge for the project team to see what and how much could be recycled. This produced surprising and unanticipated results, such as the reuse of electrical cabling and the innovative use of the old computer floor tiles as "canvases" for artworks. During this phase the design team formed a close bond with the construction team as they worked in the building to produce the artwork amid the subcontractors.

LOW-EMITTING MATERIALS

The project architects focused heavily on human health issues, with a concerted effort to minimize pollutants in the new environment by selective use and choice of finishes, paints, sealants, and adhesives. Only products that had very low or no volatile organic compounds were used where new materials were required.

MEASURABLE ENVIRONMENTAL BENEFITS

The refurbishment of Trevor Pearcey House has resulted in numerous, measurable environmental benefits:

▸ **AN ENERGY USE REDUCTION** of 75 percent and a water use reduction of 90 percent, compared with a similar size, conventional structure.

In many parts of the building, daylight can enter from two sides of the structure, with additional daylighting provided by the combined light columns/ventilation stacks that run from the ground floor to the roof.

ENERGY USE FOR THE BUILDING is 30 percent less than a standard 5-star ABGR structure.

OVER 80 PERCENT (by weight) of the removed building materials were either reused as part of the retrofit or were recycled. This significantly reduced the amount of waste material going to the landfill and saved energy that would be required to manufacture and transport new building materials.

REDUCTION OF STAFF SICK DAYS and increased productivity because of increased user comfort. Following project completion, AEI's staff was surveyed through the internationally recognized BUS (Building Use Studies) protocol; the results rank AEI in the top 11 percent of Australian buildings assessed. The feedback from occupants regarding all aspects of the refurbishment has been generally positive, with staff members feeling that it is a great place to work.

FINANCE

Through a cooperative design approach, the refurbishment and fit-out of Trevor Pearcey House created an efficient and sustainable building at a conventional construction cost of A$1,700 per square meter ($107 per square foot). The budget for both the refurbishment and the fit-out were equivalent to the budget for comparable conventional projects undertaken in Canberra. A key aspect of completing the project on budget was maintaining a flexible and creative approach to meeting the refurbishment requirements in the context of the fixed budget. To meet budget objectives, the team was frequently required to identify offsetting savings. For example, savings achieved in one area, such as reduced material supply cost, offset areas of increased cost, such as increased labor costs incurred in recycling or disassembling materials for reuse.

MANAGEMENT

In addition to realizing environmental and financial benefits through the refurbishment, AEI wanted to improve the comfort of the internal environment for employees. Conventional office buildings in Australia typically allow for a temperature comfort band of 20°C to 24°C (68°F to 74°F), which allows occupants to wear suits year-round. Because of the natural heating and cooling systems for Trevor Pearcey House, the target temperature comfort band was expanded to be 19°C to 26°C (66°F to 79°F).

The expanded range substantially reduces energy usage, because each extra 5°C (10°F) in cooling uses nearly 50 percent more energy.

The expanded definition of the acceptable comfort range at Trevor Pearcey House has had staff management and educational implications for AEI. To accommodate wider temperature fluctuations within the building, AEI has adopted a relaxed workplace clothing policy which permits occupants to dress appropriately for weather conditions. Building occupants were educated about the building's features, including how they should dress to cope better with a broader band of comfortable temperatures. Staff members have been trained to manually adjust windows, blinds, and ceiling fans to maximize thermal comfort. As well, staff members have been required to be generally forgiving of idiosyncrasies when systems do not work according to plan. A detailed environmental user's guide has been developed to show when to open windows, when to shut the building, and how to maximize the effectiveness of night purges. These measures have provided the staff with the instruction needed to allow them to maximize their comfort in the new space. Employee surveys after project completion show high satisfaction levels and a 20 percent increase in self-assessed productivity.

EXPERIENCES GAINED

Key experiences gained from the Trevor Pearcey House refurbishment include the following:

HIGHLY SUSTAINABLE RESULTS can be achieved using low-technology design principles and a conventional budget. AEI wanted a simple environmental building and was not interested in buying Green Star points through technology. Accordingly, the design team developed a low-technology refurbishment strategy that could be executed on a conventional budget. The project design emphasized natural ventilation, daylighting, solar shading, good insulation, the regulation of interior temperatures through the exposure of thermal mass, and the reuse and recycling of materials.

▸ **ENSURE THAT OCCUPANTS** are on board. A green retrofit strategy will succeed only if building occupants are committed to environmental responsibility. In the case of AEI, whose business model is based on sustainability, this was not a difficult challenge. Education is necessary to help occupants who need more knowledge of the retrofit process and the value of green before they commit.

▸ **DO NOT FORCE** unconventional sustainability systems on unprepared occupants. Natural heating and cooling systems are very different systems from mechanical heating and cooling systems. If building occupants are not willing to be flexible and work with a different system, the team should not force it upon them. In the short term, such occupants will find a way to override the system, reducing its efficiency. In the long term, such occupants will likely move out. Highly motivated occupants, such as AEI, are likely to be successful in learning to operate natural heating and cooling systems, in developing employee dress policies consistent with these systems, and in developing occupant education materials and programs to support the use of a natural heating and cooling system.

▸ **PAY ATTENTION** to sound transfer. A main source of postoccupancy complaint from occupants of Trevor Pearcey House has been internal and external noise. Internally, the areas of hard surfaces exposed for their thermal mass, combined with an open plan to allow for better passive ventilation, has meant that noise carries between areas. The design and engineering team is investigating using baffles to reduce the sound transfer.

▸ **MATERIAL REUSE AND RECYCLING** is not as difficult as the design team had anticipated, but requires innovative approaches. Collaboration, creativity, and careful attention enabled the team to conserve and reuse materials throughout the building, including partition framing, plasterboard, insulation, ductwork, electrical cabling, outlet and light switchplates, joinery, sinks, computer workstations, furniture, and artwork, as well as carpet tiles, wood flooring, and walls and doors, door frames, and door hardware. The labor-intensive nature of reusing site materials required a higher labor component than

would be standard for both the documentation and construction. Reusing materials requires accurate measuring, quantifying, and scheduling before reuse. A charrette-type process formed through which AEI, the construction team, and the design team met frequently to solve problems that arose during the refurbishment and identify previously unseen opportunities. The recycling and reuse of materials exceeded expectations, owing to a cooperative, team-like approach between all parties.

▸ **BE FLEXIBLE** in the retrofit strategy. Although the Trevor Pearcey House project had a fixed budget, it had a flexible way of achieving the refurbishment requirements. Team members were encouraged to be creative in meeting energy reduction and environmental objectives while remaining within budget parameters. In most instances, savings achieved in one area offset areas of increased cost.

Kevin Miller is a director of Collard Clarke Jackson Canberra Pty Ltd, in Canberra, Australia. He was the project and design director for the Trevor Pearcey House refurbishment.

Howard Pender is the director of Australian Ethical Investment, Ltd. and Australian Ethical Super, located in Canberra, Australia.

Development Team

ARCHITECTURE, INTERIORS, AND ENVIRONMENTAL DESIGN:
Collard Clarke Jackson, Canberra

CONSTRUCTION MANAGER:
Cobul Constructions

STRUCTURAL AND HYDRAULIC:
Hughes Trueman

GREEN STAR CONSULTANT:
Viridis E3

THERMAL MODELING:
Energetics

MECHANICAL, ELECTRICAL, AND FIRE:
Bassett

LANDSCAPE:
Red Box Design Group

ACOUSTICS:
Heggies

COMMISSIONING AGENT:
Sustainable FX

CASE STUDY · RICHARD W. BARTHOLOMEW

WRT Offices

PHILADELPHIA, PENNSYLVANIA

The main office of Wallace Roberts & Todd, LLC (WRT), a firm of architects, landscape architects, urban designers, and planners, is located in downtown Philadelphia, Pennsylvania. In early 2003 WRT started searching for new office space to accommodate its growing national and international practice. The firm's recently adopted 2003 strategic plan emphasized the continuing importance of sustainability in WRT's

work, building upon the pioneering work led by one of its founders, Ian McHarg, author of *Design with Nature*. In order to demonstrate WRT's continuing commitment to sustainable design it was decided to develop the firm's new office space as a pilot project under the U.S. Green Building Council's Leadership in Energy and Environmental Design program for Commercial Interiors (LEED-CI).

It took WRT approximately nine months to find an appropriate space, sign a lease, and

begin the process of design. The firm's existing office was located on the southern edge of downtown Philadelphia, with good transit access and a central location relative to Center City's residential neighborhoods, which provide housing for about 90,000 people within a downtown area of two square miles. When WRT began the search for new space, it surveyed the existing staff and found that 22 percent of the office walked to work, and another 56 percent took transit. There was, not surprisingly, a strong desire to find a new location

Conference rooms range in size from the main conference room, which can accommodate more than 20 people, to a room next to the lobby that is large enough for two.

downtown in order to take advantage of convenient access for the firm's employees as well as easy access to business and professional services.

Working with the Studley real estate firm, WRT selected a vacant 30,609-square-foot floor in the downtown office core. The selected building was constructed in 1969 as a local bank headquarters, and the selected floor was the 28th in a 32-story structure. In order to make the space more readily marketable, the building owner had removed all existing interior partitions and ceilings so that all that remained were the ducts, sprinkler system, and some mechanical equipment. In effect, the existing space was like an industrial loft, with an exposed, poured-in-place, concrete waffle-slab ceiling and large windows set in exterior precast concrete panels. The fenestration was covered in film that reduced heat gain but also reduced daylight and acted at night like a mirror, severely reducing views to the outside. Nevertheless, the raw nature of the space was appealing and provided maximum design flexibility, which was a real advantage in developing a sustainable renovation.

DEVELOPMENT PROCESS

Planning for the new office began before the search for new space. A detailed space program was prepared in early 2003. Based on WRT's current and anticipated needs, a space of about 27,000 square feet was targeted. It was also determined that, ideally, the space should be on one floor to foster collaboration among the firm's four disciplines. The program was constantly updated and refined as the design process unfolded. During the search for new space, competing building owners used the preliminary space program to prepare test layouts for WRT, as the firm went about the process of evaluating alternative locations. After considering about 25 spaces, the firm signed a lease on December 24, 2003, and shortly thereafter assembled the design team. Construction was initiated in May 2004, and move-in took place on September 24, 2004.

Initially WRT leased 28,035 square feet of rentable space to accommodate a total staff of 116. This left 2,574 rentable square feet in the northwest corner of the floor for future expansion. In fact, within a year of move-in the firm rented the remainder of the floor and renovated the additional space to accommodate more growth. Today WRT's 30,609 rentable square feet can accommodate 160 persons.

The space program included several concepts that were new to the WRT office but have proven to be very useful. The program included conference rooms of various sizes, ranging from the main conference room (which accommodates more than 20 persons and is the showcase space for outside clients) to several smaller rooms that accommodate up to six persons, to a small enclosed room next to the lobby seating area that is large enough for two people to hold a conference call with a set of drawings. There was also a multipurpose room: two conference rooms seating 12 persons, separated by a folding wall that could be opened to form a larger space. Furnished with 15 two-foot by five-foot tables and a number of stacking chairs, the room can accommodate a variety of seating options and table configurations. Thirty people can be seated at the tables classroom style, and about 60 can be seated auditorium style in the multipurpose room. The room is used almost daily for in-house continuing education and training sessions, staff meetings, and other activities, such as social events.

After the lease was signed, WRT's managing principal appointed a four-person in-house design committee to develop the plans and to review the work as it progressed. The committee included an in-house sustainability coordinator with extensive experience with the U.S. Green Building Council and LEED experience, who kept track of all of the documentation needed for LEED certification.

The architectural design team for the project was a combination of WRT's design committee and an outside firm that served as the project's executive architect. Although about half of WRT's Philadelphia office is focused on the practice of architecture, it was decided to engage the Philadelphia firm Partridge Architects Inc, to work with WRT on the renovation and fit-out plans. This was done for three reasons. First, although they had never prepared a design for a LEED-certified project, the Partridge firm had extensive experience in the design of office renovations in downtown Philadelphia. Second, WRT's architectural staff was very busy at the time, and there was no space in the existing office to expand the staff. Third, it was felt that having an outside firm serving as the executive architect would help facilitate the involvement of WRT's many design professionals.

The design team included Bruce E. Brooks & Associates, a mechanical, electrical, and plumbing (MEP) consultant; Clanton & Associates of Boulder, Colorado, which provided daylighting and lighting services; and Concord Facility

Services, Inc. for commissioning. The team also worked closely with representatives of Corporate Facilities, Inc. (CFI), a Philadelphia-based office furniture company that represents Knoll, which provided the majority of the open-office workstations and other furniture. Construction was carried out by W.S. Cumby, Inc., which had recently developed its own offices as a LEED-certified project. All these team members were experienced in and committed to green design and construction.

To initiate the space planning process, the design committee prepared three alternative conceptual layouts. These were presented to and discussed by the entire staff on the site of the future office. Comments and suggestions were elicited, systematically recorded, and taken into account in the design. One of the concerns expressed by a number of people was whether the design of the new space would feel "too rigidly corporate." This concern was related to the fact that the new office was located in the heart of the downtown corporate office core, compared with the firm's existing location in an older building on South Broad Street (Philadelphia's "Avenue of the Arts"). By contrast, the design team was concerned that the offices not look particularly green but appear simply as good design.

Discussions within the firm led to the establishment of a few simple goals for the new office:

▸▸ **PROVIDE** a healthy and stimulating work environment, with access to natural light and outdoor views for everyone;

▸▸ **MAXIMIZE OPPORTUNITIES** for collaboration and cross-disciplinary communication; and

▸▸ **SERVE AS AN EXAMPLE** of the firm's commitment to sustainability and design excellence.

Early on, the design team decided that in order to take advantage of the loft-like nature of the space, enclosed spaces such as conference rooms and principals' offices should be located adjacent to the building core, and large studio spaces along the building perimeter would be used for open workstations for the professional staff.

Enclosed spaces hug the building core, leaving most of the perimeter open to maximize access to daylight.

This concept takes maximum advantage of the daylight from the building's large windows, and provides a feeling of spaciousness. In addition, suspended ceilings were limited to enclosed spaces, mostly around the core, so that the existing concrete waffle slab would serve as the predominant ceiling. This also added to the sense of spaciousness. Lighting, ductwork, and fire sprinklers were suspended from the waffle slab.

The first step in the LEED design process was a day-long charrette held in the new space on January 16, 2004. It was attended by the entire design team, the contractor, and representatives of the building's owner. The first half of the day was spent visiting the space and discussing the critical design issues of lighting and daylighting. The afternoon was spent reviewing each item in the LEED-CI list of criteria and deciding how many points were certain to be achieved, possible to achieve, or unlikely (or impossible) to achieve. It was determined at this juncture that a Silver rating was certain and that a Gold rating was a desirable possibility.

Some key early decisions and design strategies resulted from the team charrette:

▸▸ **REPLACING THE EXISTING WINDOW FILM** with film that would transmit approximately 60 percent of the daylight (compared with the existing film, which transmitted only about 30 percent). The new film would also reduce heat gain and eliminate the mirror effect that occurred at night. Ultimately the film was replaced by the building owner and removed entirely from the north-facing windows. Interestingly, on winter evenings when it is dark and each office floor is lit, the windows with the new film stand out, appearing like a halo of light around the building at the 28th floor.

▸▸ **ADDING AN INTERIOR LIGHT SHELF** on the south-facing windows to increase the penetration of natural daylight into the interior of the building.

▸▸ **PROVIDING VIEWS** and natural light to as many of the offices and workstations as possible.

▸▸ **PROVIDING GOOD INDOOR AIR QUALITY** through proper ventilation and selection of healthy building materials.

▸▸ **USING GREEN MATERIALS** such as recycled-content or locally manufactured products.

▸▸ **RECYCLING** construction waste from the job site.

▸▸ **PROVIDING** high-quality and low-energy electric lighting.

Following the charrette, the design team prepared a preliminary layout of the space and presented the proposed plan to the entire WRT staff on February 10. At this point the basic concept was settled and work proceeded to develop the design. The final floor plan for WRT's offices included the following features:

▸▸ **ENCLOSED SPACES** hugged the building core, leaving most of the perimeter open, to maximize the use of daylight. Spaces adjacent to the core included a number of private offices for principals, conference rooms, and support spaces for functions such as plotting, copying, and storage. Typically these areas had suspended ceilings.

▸▸ **A LARGE, CONTIGUOUS, OPEN STUDIO SPACE** was located along the southern, eastern, and northern sides of the floor. Corner spaces were built out as informal meeting areas that staff could use for conferences, group work, or lunch. Several principals elected to sit in the open studio area.

▸▸ **THE WEST SIDE OF THE FLOOR** was designed to accommodate the main conference room (the only conference room with outside windows) and the firm's administrative and support functions.

▸▸ **THE INTERIOR DESIGN** combines contemporary system furnishings, translucent glass and transparent glass walls, and modern lighting to give the office a contemporary aesthetic. The color palette is neutral (grays, silver, and some black) for carpet, fabrics, wood, and system furniture, with color accents through the use of blue, green, and orange paint applied to a selected number of walls. The large, open studios with exposed concrete ceilings, suspending lighting, sprinklers and ductwork, give the space the feeling of a contemporary artist's "loft in the sky."

GREEN BUILDING DESIGN AND CONSTRUCTION

Under the LEED-CI program, the WRT offices achieved a Gold certification level. Key aspects of the certification are discussed here.

Location

Sustainable criteria were important in selecting a location for WRT's offices. The offices are less than one block from Suburban Station, with access to all 16 of Philadelphia's commuter rail lines, one of which serves the Philadelphia International Airport. The office is within three blocks of both of the city's two major subway lines, two blocks from two light-rail stations, and five blocks from an underground station that serves southern New Jersey commuters. Most of these lines offer a direct transit connection to Philadelphia's 30th Street Station, which serves Amtrak's Northeast Corridor routes. Although WRT's building includes a 735-space parking garage, WRT's lease does not include any free parking. Strong mass transit access and WRT's choice to neither lease nor accept free on-site parking were readily achievable ways to earn certification credits under LEED-CI. The locational attributes of the property helped WRT earn sufficient points for LEED certification, although the base building was not LEED certified. (Base building certification under LEED earns three certification credits under LEED-CI.)

In 2006, the firm surveyed the office and found that only 3 percent of WRT's staff members travel to work by car. Sixty-nine percent of the staff commutes by public transportation, 26 percent walk to work, and 2 percent ride bicycles. The 97 percent who take transit, walk, or bike to work represent a sizable increase from the 78 percent logged at the firm's previous location on the edge of downtown. These statistics are attributable to several factors: the high daily cost of parking in the vicinity of the office building, the nearby availability of an extensive regional transit network, and a location that is central to downtown Philadelphia's residential neighborhoods. For local business trips by auto, the firm typically uses PhillyCarShare, which has cars (mostly hybrid) located within walking distance, as does Zipcar, a similar service. This all adds up to an enormous reduction in vehicle miles traveled, one of the most important sustainability metrics, especially with regard to CO_2 emissions.

All needed business services are within easy walking distance of the building. In fact, the lower two levels of the building include a bank, three eateries, a dry cleaner, a daycare center, a travel agent, a florist, a pharmacy, and other services. Easy access to these services is not only convenient but also increases the efficiency of the office, and earned WRT a LEED-CI certification credit.

Energy Efficiency

The encouragement of energy efficiency is a key aspect of LEED-CI. Energy savings resulting from the WRT office renovation were estimated to save 32,500 kWh a year, not including savings from the use of green power. Additionally it was estimated that 92 tons of carbon emissions per year were avoided as a result of the building energy efficiency measures employed. Strategies to reduce electricity use from lighting and equipment were an important part of the design. Energy-efficient features of the WRT space included the following:

▸▸ **HIGH-PERFORMANCE FILM** on windows to reduce heat gain but let in light.

▸▸ **HIGH-EFFICIENCY T5 FLUORESCENT LAMPS**, which are 25 percent more efficient than standard T12 lamps.

▸▸ **ADVANCED LIGHTING CONTROLS** that permit optimal light levels and low power use. Photo sensors turn off lights when daylight is sufficient. Motion sensors turn lights on and off in private offices and conference rooms. Most lighting is programmed to go off automatically at night. These strategies also have indoor environmental quality benefits described below.

▸▸ **LIGHT SHELVES** on the southern wall that shade the bottom part of the windows and bounce natural light off the ceiling (which was painted with a highly reflective white), deep into the studio space.

▸▸ **EFFICIENT SUPPLEMENTAL** heating, ventilating, and air conditioning (HVAC). Three existing ceiling air-conditioning units were retrofitted to provide supplemental cooling for conference spaces and for cooling when the building's system is shut down.

▸▸ **GREEN POWER PURCHASE**. Half of WRT's electrical power (135,000 kWh annually) is purchased from wind-powered generators in central Pennsylvania. It is estimated that this purchase is the equivalent of planting more than 10,000 trees or not driving over 128,000 miles per year.

▸▸ **ENERGY-EFFICIENT COMPUTER MONITORS**. WRT replaced all computer monitors with LCD screens that use half as much electricity and produce half as much heat as do standard CRT monitors.

Indoor Environmental Quality

The following measures were taken to help ensure good indoor air quality and access to daylight and views; achievements in both areas are scored under the LEED-CI certification system:

▶ **PAINTS, GLUES, AND SEALANTS** with low levels of volatile organic compounds (VOCs) were used to help maintain good air quality;

▶ **COPY AND PLOTTER ROOMS** are exhausted separately to keep toner and other equipment fumes out of work areas;

▶ **THE OFFICE LAYOUT PERMITS** all employees access to both outdoor view and natural light; and

▶ **PARTICLEBOARD PRODUCTS** for furniture and doors were specified without added urea-formaldehyde.

RESOURCE CONSERVATION AND MATERIALS

The use of green materials and furnishings—defined as products sourced regionally and made of renewable, recycled, or environmentally sensitive materials—is credited under LEED-CI. Products used in the WRT space were selected using a variety of environmental performance criteria:

▶ **KNOLL GREENGUARD FURNITURE** was selected for its high recycled content and nearby regional manufacturing facility (reducing transport impacts).

▶ **CARPET TILES** have 40 percent recycled content and use an innovative backing containing fly ash (waste from steel manufacturing).

▶ **MECHOSHADE'S "ECOVEIL,"** which is produced entirely without polyvinylchlorides (PVCs), was selected for the window covering.

▶ **DESKTOPS** are made from rapidly renewable wood-stalk board (agricultural waste).

▶ **OVER 75 PERCENT** of construction waste was recycled.

▶ **OVER 40 PERCENT** of the products and materials used in the renovation were manufactured in the region (again reducing transport impacts).

▶ **ALTHOUGH MOST FURNISHINGS WERE NEW**, some were reused from the previous office. Unused furniture was donated to the local Charter High School for Architecture and Design, which was founded by AIA Philadelphia in 1999 as a Legacy Project for the 2000 National AIA convention.

Daylighting and Lighting

Efficient, comfortable lighting and the maximum use of daylight were key design considerations for WRT in attaining LEED-CI certification. Lighting efficiency and the use of natural light increase occupant comfort and can reduce energy costs.

The team's lighting consultant prepared the lighting plan, including controls, and made recommendations regarding window treatments to take advantage of daylight as well as to control glare and heat gain. Computer models of the interior space were used to develop recommendations for window treatments and lighting.

The following principles were applied to the lighting design:

▶ **TAKE ADVANTAGE OF DAYLIGHT**. Bring it into the spaces as close to ceiling level as possible. Avoid direct sunlight on work surfaces.

WRT's offices have windows with a relatively high head height. Eliminating a dropped ceiling in most of the space and using a light shelf on the south-facing windows takes advantage of daylight. The light shelf is actually a hollow core door, painted white and set approximately seven feet high, that both blocks direct sun from perimeter spaces and bounces light off the ceiling and deeper into the space. The angle of the light shelf was designed to optimize the depth of daylight penetration.

▶ **LIGHT SURFACES, NOT VOLUMES**. Avoid using downlights because they light only the floor. Shine light on the ceiling, walls, and other surfaces. Bright surfaces can help maintain the light in the space and reduce eye strain. Dark surfaces can require ten times the amount of lighting as light surfaces.

WRT's raw space has a relatively high ceiling (about ten feet, eight inches). The main lighting strategy uses pendant-hung fluorescent lights that throw most of their light upward, onto the ceiling. This effectively uses the ceiling as the light source. The paint color selected for the exposed concrete ceiling had a high light reflectance value of 83 percent.

▶ **DESIGN LAYERED LIGHTING** that incorporates ambient, task, and accent lighting that work together to save energy and appropriately define the space.

The ambient light in the new WRT space is generated by the reflected light from the ceiling. Task lights are provided for each desk as part of the furniture system. Accent lighting is located on the structural columns that run throughout the space, as well as in special spaces such as the lobby and display areas.

▸▸ PROVIDE AN INTEGRATED LIGHTING SYSTEM using controls, including occupancy sensors, daylight sensors, dimming, and manual-on and auto-off controls.

The daylight harvesting strategy designed for WRT includes daylight sensors that measure the light levels from the windows and adjust the artificial lighting accord-

Corner spaces are built out as informal meeting areas that staff members can use for conferences, group work, or lunch.

ingly. In addition, all enclosed spaces (conference rooms, workrooms, private offices, etc.) have occupancy sensors that turn the lights off when no one is in the office. There is also a timer that will shut off most of the lights at night.

Green Operations Plan

WRT's commitment to sustainability did not end with the design of its new office space. The firm also developed a green operations framework to give direction to a host of issues related to the day-to-day operation of the office. The framework is organized around eight broad areas: office products, new construction and renovation, indoor air quality, water, energy, transportation, community, and service providers. The framework identifies an overall goal, target areas, assessment tasks, and initiatives for each area of concern. Some goals relate directly to the design of the space; others relate to the daily operation of the facility; and still others relate to broader goals, such as fostering sustainable lifestyles.

The general issue of reducing waste and recycling turned out to be more complex than expected. This

resulted in both some new waste receptacles and some in-house education. In general, the disposal and recycling of waste within the building requires separating waste that goes to a landfill and waste that can be recycled. All the recycled waste is commingled when it is collected and then sorted at the off-site recycling facility. However, in order to reduce the number of plastic bags produced by the office, it was decided that the waste receptacle at each workstation would have no plastic liner and would be used for paper waste only. Employees must take other trash to one of several locations on the floor and deposit in the appropriate receptacle. This approach has eliminated approximately 15,000 plastic bags unnecessarily going to the landfill each year.

There was considerable discussion about what type of waste receptacle should be located at the individual workstation, in order to discourage its use for general waste (recyclable or not) and to reserve it for paper only. A creative solution was found using old carpet tiles. Over 700,000 carpet samples are shipped annually to architects and interior designers, and their reuse is obviously a desirable green strategy. One of the members of the "green ops" committee designed a handsome waste receptacle using old carpet tile samples. The tulip-shaped design that now occupies all of WRT's workstations and was entered into the 2008 "Ample Sample" competition for creative reuse of carpet tiles.

The green operations plan influenced company operations in additional ways. The firm tries to avoid the use of unrecyclable paper or plastic plates, cups, and flatware; instead, it uses ceramic plates, glasses, mugs, and stainless steel flatware for catered in-house lunch meetings. This effort, aimed at reducing waste streams from kitchens, resulted in the addition of a dishwasher to the small kitchen outside the main conference room, to complement the existing dishwasher in the main kitchen area. It has also resulted in a guideline for green products and services procurement that WRT now uses when selecting outside vendors of all kinds. The green operations committee continues to meet regularly to assess WRT's operational environmental footprint and work continually to reduce it, using the green operations plan as the framework.

Education and Outreach

As the first LEED-CI certified project in the city of Philadelphia, WRT's office space has been showcased locally as an early example of green design. Four months after move-in, the first of many tours and educational sessions was held in the space. The initial seminar was organized by the Delaware Valley Green Building Council and was attended by 120 persons who heard a presentation of the green design features of the new office. As part of this meeting, WRT developed a self-guided tour of the office, with a key plan annotated with notes about green design features. A series of descriptive text "bubbles" were hung in the space to assist in the tour. These proved so popular that they remain in place nearly four years later, reminding staff and visitors of the office's green features.

The firm has hosted other meetings relating to sustainability, including training sessions for the LEED Accredited Professional exam, visits by groups of university students, and others. When the national convention of the American Planning Association (APA) was held in Philadelphia in 2007, WRT hosted an all-day seminar for the APA in China program and held a reception in the office for friends and clients of the firm, using a sustainable caterer, who served locally produced food and drink. Such events not only spread the word about sustainable design but also raise the profile of the firm within the design community and before the public.

FINANCING

Project financing, including the cost of green furnishings, was obtained through a combination of the tenant improvement allowance negotiated by WRT with its landlord ($30 per square foot) and a bank loan taken by WRT (approximately $20 per square foot). WRT opted to apply the savings from free rent negotiated in its lease toward tenant improvements. The tenant improvement allowance and negotiated landlord concessions covered 85 percent of the costs to retrofit the base building with green features. Lease terms reflected market norms at the time of lease execution. WRT considered the lease terms favorable, because office rental rates in the Philadelphia central business district had declined during its search for space.

EXPERIENCE GAINED

Lessons learned from the retrofit of WRT's offices include the following:

▶▶ **THOUGHTFUL SITING** can reduce the project's carbon footprint and assist in green certification. The siting of WRT's new offices played a key role in reducing the company's carbon footprint and was helpful in green certification. Excellent mass transit access, a central location,

and WRT's choice to forgo free parking as a lease feature increased the percentage of staff who take transit, walk, or bike to 97 percent, up significantly from the 78 percent logged at the firm's previous location on the edge of downtown. These locational features also generated certification credits under the LEED-CI protocol.

▶▶ **TENANTS CAN LEVERAGE CYCLICAL MARKET DOWNTURNS** to rent centrally located space and turn it green. WRT took advantage of a downturn in the Philadelphia office market to do so. Market-rate tenant improvements and lease concessions financed 85 percent of the LEED Gold retrofit.

▶▶ **GREEN SPACE** can enhance occupant recruitment and branding. The relocation of the firm's offices into renovated LEED Gold space has been a success. It has made for a welcoming, high-quality work environment that has helped the firm recruit new staff and has represented the firm well to its clients.

▶▶ **OCCUPANT SATISFACTION** can be enhanced by green space, but challenges may remain postoccupancy. Within eight months (May 2005) of move-in, WRT conducted an extensive occupant satisfaction survey of the new space, using an online survey from the Center for the Built Environment of the University of California. Of 120 persons surveyed, 95 responded, for a response rate of 79 percent. Satisfaction was rated on a seven-point scale ranging from "very satisfied" to "very dissatisfied." Nearly all of the aspects surveyed—general satisfaction with the building, the workspace, office layout, office furnishings, thermal comfort, air quality, lighting, and cleanliness and maintenance—yielded positive responses. Only one category of response was slightly negative: acoustic quality. This is obviously related to the open nature of the office; only 6 percent of occupants have enclosed private offices. Acoustics are often among the lowest rated characteristics of green buildings, because most green offices have open-floor plans to increase the overall penetration of daylight into the space.

▶▶ **DAYLIGHT AND OPENNESS** can be positive features. In addition to the numerical ratings, respondents submitted their feelings about the space. A number of them commented positively on the feeling of openness and daylight.

▶▶ **ACOUSTICS CAN REMAIN A CHALLENGE** with an open plan design. The open office negatively affected acoustics, causing distraction for occupants.

GREEN FEATURES produced good air quality, but temperature controls required upgrades. Only 14 percent of respondents felt "dissatisfied" with air quality; 59 percent felt that it enhances their ability to get work done. By contrast, thermal comfort was an area of concern, although the majority of the heating and cooling system is controlled by the overall building system. WRT reused existing air-handling units to provide supplemental cooling for the main conference room that faces west and for the multipurpose room. Many of the complaints regarding air temperature were related to these rooms, which were felt to be too cool. More sophisticated controls were placed in the multipurpose room to alleviate this problem.

FOLLOW-UP OCCUPANT SURVEYS can help to track green performance over time. In September 2007, the nonprofit Green Building Association of Central Pennsylvania, a regional affiliate of the U.S. Green Building Council, conducted a postoccupancy evaluation (POE) of WRT's offices, three years after initial occupancy. The purpose of the evaluation was to provide a general overview of the project's indoor environment, to determine how the space performs in the real world. As part of this evaluation, a second occupant satisfaction survey of the space was conducted using the Center for the Built Environment survey. This allowed the POE to compare the results from 2005 and 2007.

The September 2007 survey had a 48 percent response rate compared to the 79 percent response rate of the 2005 survey. This could be attributed to the fact that many WRT staff who had responded previously did not feel obliged to duplicate their initial responses. Results of the two surveys were similar but not always consistent. According to the 2007 survey, thermal comfort decreased from 2005 and also fell below the average for LEED certified buildings, although results for air quality were deemed "very good."

INDOOR AIR QUALITY remained high. An indoor air quality test was performed on-site using a test kit from Air Quality Sciences, Inc. Each test kit was capable of testing for VOCs, formaldehyde, and mold spores. The tests demonstrated good air quality for the two locations tested. VOC levels were below the comparable standards, and the formaldehyde levels were acceptable. Mold spores were found in all dust samples, but the lab report stated that these are typical.

Readings were taken outdoors and throughout the floor for temperature, relative humidity, and CO_2. Measurements inside the building were somewhat better than those outside. Survey results showed that most people were dissatisfied with the temperature but mostly satisfied with the air quality in general. This finding was consistent with the findings of the occupant surveys. For an office building with no operable windows, the POE found that the results for air quality were very good.

GREEN DAYLIGHTING was helpful, but additional solar shades were needed to prevent glare from surrounding buildings. The POE found that overall lighting levels were good but there seemed to be some glare on certain facades, due in some cases to reflection from surrounding buildings, a typical situation in an urban high-rise environment. Solar shades, initially installed on the east-, south-, and west-facing windows, were later installed on all windows in response to this problem. The POE found that daylight penetration in WRT's space was better than the rule of thumb, which is that penetration occurs at a distance of 1.5 times the window height. The window height in the space is nine feet, six inches and illuminance levels are still reasonable at the 20-feet depth, even with the coffered ceiling, which adversely affects daylight penetration.

Richard A. Bartholomew, FAIA, AICP, is a principal at Wallace Roberts & Todd, LLC. An urban designer, architect, and planner, he has directed many of WRT's major projects during his 30-year career.

Development Team

ARCHITECTS:
Wallace Roberts & Todd, LLC
Partridge Architects Inc, Executive Architect

GENERAL CONTRACTOR:
W.S. Cumby, Inc.

MEP ENGINEERS:
Bruce E. Brooks & Associates

SUSTAINABILITY CONSULTANT:
Wallace Roberts & Todd, LLC

LIGHTING CONSULTANT:
Clanton & Associates, Inc.

COMMISSIONING:
Concord Engineering Group

FURNISHING SYSTEMS:
Corporate Facilities, Inc.

Selected Resources

Chapter 1

Epstein, Paul R., and Evan Mills, eds. "Climate Change Futures: Health, Ecological and Economic Dimensions." Center for Health and the Global Environment, Harvard Medical School, October 2006. http://chge.med.harvard.edu/programs/ccf/documents/ccf_report_oct_06.pdf.

Fisk, William. "Review of Health and Productivity Gains from Better IEQ." *Proceedings of Healthy Buildings* 2000 (4): 23–34.

"Green Buildings and Climate Change 2008." *Building Design and Construction*. November 2008. www.bdcnetwork.com/contents/pdfs/WP2008.pdf.

International Emissions Trading Association. *Finance and Investment to Address Climate Change.* www.hm-treasury.gov.uk/sternreview_index.htm.

Kats, Greg, et al. "The Costs and Financial Benefits of Green Building: A Report to California's Sustainable Building Task Force." 2003. www.cap-e.com/ewebeditpro/items/.

McAllister, I., and C. Sweett. "Transforming Existing Buildings: The Green Challenge." March 2007. www.rics.org/NR/rdonlyres/381CCB81-EF08-45B9-B42C-54735E0ABF20/0/TransformingExistingBuildingsTheGreenChallenge.pdf.

Moran, Michael, et al. "The Growing Interest in Environmental Issues Is Important to Both Socially Responsible and Fundamental Investors." Goldman Sachs. August 2005. www2.goldmansachs.com/ideas/environment-and-energy/goldman-sachs/port-strat-growing-interest-pdf.pdf.

Pachauri, R.K., and A. Reisinger, eds. *IPCC Fourth Assessment Report: Climate Change 2007.* Intergovernmental Panel on Climate Change (IPCC). 2007. http://www.ipcc.ch/ipccreports/ar4-syr.htm.

Stern, Sir Nicholas, et al. *Stern Review: The Economics of Climate Change.* HM-Treasury, United Kingdom. October 2006. www.hm-treasury.gov.uk/sternreview_index.htm.

World Business Council for Sustainable Development. *Energy Efficiency in Buildings: Business Realities and Opportunities.* September 2008. www.wbcsd.org/includes/getTarget.asp?type=d&id=MzE0Njk.

———. *Energy Efficiency in Buildings: Transforming the Market.* March 2009. www.wbcsd.org/Plugins/DocSearch/details.asp?DocTypeId=33&ObjectId=MzQyMDY.

Chapter 2

American Society of Heating, Refrigerating, and Air-Conditioning Engineers. www.ashrae.org.

Building Research Establishment (BRE). "BREEAM, the Environmental Assessment Method for Buildings Around the World." www.breeam.org.

Building Owners and Managers Association (BOMA), Canada. BOMA BESt. www.bomabest.com.

CASBEE (Comprehensive Assessment System for Built Environment Efficiency). "An Overview of CASBEE." www.ibec.or.jp/CASBEE/english/overviewE.htm.

German Sustainable Building Council (DGNB). www.dgnb.de/en.

Green Building Council of Australia. "Green Star." www.gbca.org.au/green-star.

National Institute of Building Sciences, Whole Building Design Guide. "Life-Cycle Cost Analysis (LCCA)." www.wbdg.org/resources/lcca.php.

The Green Building Initiative. "Green Globes." www.greenglobes.com.

U.S. Green Building Council. "LEED." www.usgbc.org.

World Green Building Council. www.worldgbc.org.

Singapore Building and Construction Authority (BCA). "BCA Green Mark Scheme." www.bca.gov.sg/GreenMark/green_mark_buildings.html.

State of California. "Life-Cycle Cost Assessment Model." www.green.ca.gov/LCCA/default.htm.

Chapter 3

British Fenestration Rating Council. www.bfrc.org.

Build It Solar. "Passive (and Active) Cooling." www.builditsolar.com/Projects/Cooling/passive_cooling.htm.

California Energy Commission. "California Distributed Energy Resources Guide." www.energy.ca.gov/distgen/index.html.

Carpet and Rug Institute. "Green Label, Green Label Plus." www.carpet-rug.org/commercial-customers/green-building-and-the-environment/green-label-plus.

Direct Digital Control Online. www.ddc-online.org.

Esource Companies. "Managing Energy Costs in Office Buildings." *Commercial Energy Advisor*, 2006. www.esource.com/BEA/demo/PDF/CEA_offices.pdf.

Green Roofs for Healthy Cities. www.greenroofs.org.

Greenguard Environmental Institute. www.greenguard.org.

Illumination Engineering Society (IESNA). www.iesna.org.

International Ground Source Heat Pumps Assocation (IGSHPA). www.igshpa.okstate.edu.

Lawrence Berkeley National Laboratory. "Heat Island Projects." http://eetd.lbl.gov/heatIsland/PROJECTS.

Lawrence Berkeley National Laboratory, Windows and Daylighting Group, http://windows.lbl.gov.

National Fenestration Rating Council. www.nfrc.org/contact.aspx.

National Institute of Building Sciences, Whole Building Design Guide. "Sun Control and Sun Shading Devices." www.wbdg.org/resources/suncontrol.php.

National Trust for Historic Preservation. Sustainable Preservation. www.preservationnation.org/issues/sustainability.

Sustainable Sites Initiative. www.sustainablesites.org.

U.S. Department of Energy, Energy Efficiency and Renewable Energy, Geothermal Technologies Program. "Geothermal Heat Pumps." www1.eere.energy.gov/geothermal/heatpumps.html.

U.S. Department of Energy, Energy Star Program. "Green Buildings and Energy Efficiency," www.energystar.gov/index.cfm?c=green_buildings.green_buildings_index.

U.S. Environmental Protection Agency (EPA). "Combined Heat and Power Partnership." www.epa.gov/chp.

———. "Heat Island Effect." www.epa.gov/hiri.

———. "Water Conservation: Typical Laboratory and Office Water Use." www.epa.gov/oaintrnt/water/background.htm.

Whole Building Design Guide. "Protect and Conserve Water." www.wbdg.org/design/conserve_water.php.

Chapter 4

Building Research Establishment (BRE). "BREEAM Assessment Organizations." www.greenbooklive.com/search/search.jsp?partid=10001.

U.S. Green Building Council. "LEED Professional Directory." www.greenbooklive.com/search/search.jsp?partid=10001.

Yudelson, Jerry. *Green Building through Integrated Design.* Green Source Books, 2008.

Chapter 5

Bertoldi, Paolo. "Energy Service Companies (ESCOs) in Europe." European Commission, Directorate Generale, Joint Research Commission, December 16, 2005. www.fire-italia.it/convegni/milanostelline2005/stel_05_conti.pdf.

Capoor, Karan, and Philippe Ambrosi. "State and Trends of the Carbon Market 2008." World Bank and World Bank Institute, 2008. http://siteresources.worldbank.org/NEWS/Resources/State&Trendsformatted06May10pm.pdf.

Eichholtz, Piet, Nils Kok, and John M. Quigley. *Doing Well by Doing Good? An Analysis of the Financial Performance of Green Office Buildings in the USA.* RICS Research, Royal Institution of Chartered Surveyors, March 2009.

Freshfields Bruckhaus Deringer. "A Legal Framework for the Integration of Environmental, Social, and Governance Issues into Institutional Investment." United Nations Environment Programme Finance Initiative, October 2005.

Fuerst, Franz, and Patrick McAllister. "Green Noise or Green Value? Measuring the Price Effects of Environmental Certification in Commercial Buildings." University of Reading, Henley Business School, April 2008. Published as MPRA Paper 1146, University of Munich, November 7, 2008. http://mpra.ub.uni-muenchen.de/11446.

Green Building Finance Consortium. www.greenbuildingfc.com.

Jones Lang LaSalle, CoreNet Global. "Global Trends in Sustainable Real Estate: An Occupiers Perspective." February 2008.

Moran, Michael A., and Abby Joseph Cohen. "U.S. Portfolio Strategy." Goldman Sachs, August 26, 2005.

National Association of Energy Service Companies. www.naesco.org.

Nelson, Andrew J. "The Greening of U.S. Investment Real Estate—Market Fundamentals, Prospects and Opportunities," RREEF Research, Number 57, November 2007.

———. "Globalization and Global Trends in Green Real Estate Investment." RREEF Research, Number 64, September 2008.

———. "How Green a Recession? Sustainability Prospects in the U.S. Real Estate Industry." RREEF Research, Number 70, January 2009.

Renewable Energy and Energy Efficiency Partnership. www.reeep.org/31/home.htm.

Schettler-Köhler, Horst-P, Federal Office for Building and Regional Planning, Germany. "Implementation of the EPBD in Germany: Status and Future Planning, March 2008." European Union, Environmental Performance of Buildings Directive, Country Review P 73, April 18, 2008.

United Nations Environment Programme. "Boosting the 'Green House' Effect—CDM Reform Key to Climate-Friendly Building and Construction Sector." December 6, 2008. www.unep.org/Documents.Multilingual/Default.asp?DocumentID=553&ArticleID=6012&l=en.

Chapter 6

International Facilities Management Association (IFMA) Foundation. *The Business of Green Cleaning,* 2008.

Teitelbaum, Steve. "BOMA Green Lease Guide." Building Owners and Managers Association (BOMA), 2008.

Woodroof, Eric A. *Green Facilities Handbook: Simple and Profitable Strategies for Managers.* Fairmount Press, March 2009.

Chapter 7

British Columbia Climate Exchange, Community Action on Energy and Emissions Initiative. *Energy Efficiency and Buildings,* 2009. www.bcclimateexchange.ca/pdfs/EnergyEfficiencyOnlineGuide2009.pdf.

Chhabara, Rajesh. "The Future of Green Building in China." Climate Change Corp., March 17, 2009. www.climatechangecorp.com/content.asp?ContentID=6023.

Commission for Environmental Cooperation. "Green Building in North America." www.cec.org/green_building.

Communities and Local Governments, UK. "Energy Performance of Buildings." www.communities.gov.uk/planningandbuilding/theenvironment/energyperformance.

Crook, Steven. "Green Buildings Paint Bright Future." *Taiwan Journal,* June 15, 2007. http://taiwanjournal.nat.gov.tw/site/Tj/ct.asp?xItem=24335&ctNode=122.

———. "Taipei's Gre Libraries: Eco-friendly Architecture Making Headway." *Taiwan Culture,* August 28, 2007. www.culture.tw/index.php?option=com_content&task=view&id=242&Itemid=157en.

Database of State Incentives for Renewable Energy. www.dsireusa.org.

District of Columbia. Clean and Affordable Energy Act of 2008. www.imt.org/Capital/DC_EnergyBill.pdf.

European Commission, Directorate Generale for Energy and Transport. "European Performance of Buildings Directive." http://www.buildingsplatform.org/cms.

Harrington, Lloyd. "Energy Labeling and Standards Programs Throughout the World." The National Appliance and Equipment Energy Efficiency Committee, Australia, July 2004.

Republic of South Africa. "Energy Efficiency Strategy." www.dme.gov.za/pdfs/energy/efficiency/ee_strategy_05.

Republic of South Africa, Department of Minerals. "Renewable Energy Summit, 2009." www.dme.gov.za/energy/Renewable_Energy_Summit_2009.stm

Sajjakulnukit, Boonrod. "Thailand's Experience with Its Energy Conservation Fund and EE Revolving Fund." Thailand Ministry of Energy, Department of Alternative Energy Development and Efficiency. June 2008.

Singapore Building and Construction Authority (BCA). "BCA Green Mark Scheme." www.bca.gov.sg/GreenMark/green_mark_buildings.html.

Temas Actuales LLC. "Brazil Proposes Energy Labels for Buildings." March 24, 2009. www.temasactuales.com/temasblog/environmental-protection/energy-the-environment/energy-efficiency/brazil-proposes-energy-labels-for-buildings.

Thailand Ministry of Energy, Department of Alternative Energy Development and Efficiency. "Energy Efficiency and Conservation Promotion in Thailand." December 17, 2007. www.aseanenergy.org/download/projects/promeec/2007-2008/industry/th/TH_Energy%20Efficiency%20and%20Conservation%20Promotion.pdf.

Tobias, Leanne. "Toward Sustainable Financing and Strong Markets for Green Building, U.S. Green Building Finance Review," Background paper 2B, Green Building in North America, Commission for Environmental Cooperation, March 13, 2008. www.cec.org/green_building.

"Toronto Green Building Standard." www.toronto.ca/planning/greendevelopment.htm.

U.S. American Recovery and Reinvestment Act, Public Law 111-5. www.recovery.gov.

U.S. Department of Energy, Energy Efficiency and Renewable Energy, State Energy Program. "The Greening of State Facilities: State Policies to Encourage Green Building Principles in the Public Sector." November–December, 2008. http://apps1.eere.energy.gov/state_energy_program/feature_detail_info.cfm/fid=86/start=3?print.

U.S. Energy Independence and Security Act of 2007, Public Law 110-140.

U.S. Energy Policy Act of 2005, Public Law 109-58.

U.S. Green Building Council. "LEED Initiatives in Government and Schools." www.usgbc.org/DisplayPage.aspx?CMSPageID=1852#state.

Witron, Fernando Mayagoitia. "Green Residential Building in North America: Working Toward Affordable, Sustainable Housing in Mexico." Commission for Environmental Cooperation, Paper 4a, March 2008. www.cec.org/green_building.

Chapter 8

Automated Buildings. www.automatedbuildings.com.

Biomimicry Institute. www.biomimicryinstitute.org.

California Energy Commission (CEC), Lawrence Berkeley National Laboratory. "Advancement of Electrochromic Windows." April 2006. http://windows.lbl.gov/comm_perf/Electrochromic/refs/CEC-500-2006-052_FinalReport.pdf.

Cascadia Region Green Building Council. The Living Building Challenge, Version 1.3. August 2008. www.cascadiagbc.org/lbc/lbc-v1.3.pdf.

McGraw-Hill. "Building Information Modeling (BIM) Smart Report." www.buildingsmartalliance.org/pdfs/mhc_bim_smartmarket.pdf.

Smart Energy Alliance. www.smart-energy-alliance.com

U.S. Department of Energy, Energy Efficiency and Renewable Energy. "Solid-State Lighting." www1.eere.energy.gov/buildings/ssl.

U.S. Zero Energy Commercial Building Initiative. www.zeroenergycbi.org.

Zero Energy Building Database. http://zeb.buildinggreen.com